Causal Learning

Causal Learning

Psychology, Philosophy, and Computation

Edited by

Alison Gopnik
Laura Schulz

OXFORD
UNIVERSITY PRESS

2007

OXFORD
UNIVERSITY PRESS

Oxford University Press, Inc., publishes works that further
Oxford University's objective of excellence
in research, scholarship, and education.

Oxford   New York
Auckland   Cape Town   Dar es Salaam   Hong Kong   Karachi
Kuala Lumpur   Madrid   Melbourne   Mexico City   Nairobi
New Delhi   Shanghai   Taipei   Toronto

With offices in
Argentina   Austria   Brazil   Chile   Czech Republic   France   Greece
Guatemala   Hungary   Italy   Japan   Poland   Portugal   Singapore
South Korea   Switzerland   Thailand   Turkey   Ukraine   Vietnam

Published by Oxford University Press, Inc.
198 Madison Avenue, New York, New York 10016

www.oup.com

Oxford is a registered trademark of Oxford University Press

Library of Congress Cataloging-in-Publication Data
Causal learning : psychology, philosophy, and computation / edited by
Alison Gopnik and Laura Schulz.
     p. cm.
   Includes bibliographical references and index.
   ISBN 978-0-19-517680-3
 1. Learning, Psychology of.   2. Causation.   I. Gopnik, Alison.   II. Schulz, Laura.
   BF318.C38 2007
   153.1'5—dc22   2006018902

9 8 7 6 5 4 3 2 1

Printed in the United States of America
on acid-free paper

Preface

This volume originated in a causal learning "group" (Gopnik, Richardson, and Campbell) and a series of workshops between September 2003 and June 2004 at the Center for Advanced Studies in the Behavioral Sciences at Stanford University, Stanford, California. It is well known that the center is, almost unique among human experiences, even better than you think it is going to be, and we are extremely grateful to everyone at that magnificent institution, particularly Douglas Adams and Mark Turner, the then-directors, and the staff who made organizing the workshops such a pleasure. We are also grateful to the Hewlett Foundation, which supported A. G.'s fellowship at the center. A. G. was also supported in the preparation of this volume by a grant from the National Science Foundation (DLS0132480), and L. S. was supported by a National Science Foundation graduate fellowship and an American Association of University Women Fellowship.

The principal founder of this feast, however, is the McDonnell Foundation. In addition to funding the workshops themselves, the workshops led to the McDonnell Causal Learning Collaborative, linking developmental and philosophical and computational research and involving many of the authors in this volume. We are grateful to the foundation, particularly its president, John Bruer, who saw the potential of this unusual interdisciplinary enterprise.

Finally, we thank Oxford University Press, especially our editor there, Catharine Carlin, for all her support on this project.

Contents

PART III: CAUSATION, THEORIES, AND MECHANISMS

Contributors

Woo-kyoung Ahn
Department of Psychology
Yale University
New Haven, CT 06520

John Campbell
Department of Philosophy
University of California at
  Berkeley
Berkeley, CA 94720-2390

David Danks
Department of Philosophy
Carnegie Mellon University
Pittsburgh, PA 15213

Clark Glymour
Department of Philosophy
Carnegie Mellon University
Pittsburgh, PA 15213

Alison Gopnik
Department of Psychology
University of California at Berkeley
Berkeley, California 94720

Tom Griffiths
Department of Psychology
University of California at Berkeley
Berkeley, California 94720

York Hagmeyer
Department of Psychology
University of Göttingen
37077 Göttingen
Germany

Christopher Hitchcock
Division of the Humanities and Social Sciences
California Institute of Technology
Pasadena, CA 91125

David A. Lagnado
Department of Psychology
University College London
Gower Street
London WC1E 6BT, UK

Andrew N. Meltzoff
Institute for Learning and Brain Sciences
University of Washington
Seattle, WA 98195

Bob Rehder
Department of Psychology
New York University
New York, NY 10003

Thomas Richardson
Department of Statistics
University of Washington
Seattle, WA 98195

Richard Scheines
Department of Philosophy, CALD,
  and HCII
Carnegie Mellon University
Pittsburgh, PA 15213

Laura Schulz
Department of Brain and Cognitive Sciences
Massachussetts Institute of Technology
Cambridge, MA 02139

David Sobel
Causality and Mind Lab
Brown University
Providence, RI 02912

Jessica Sommerville
Department of Psychology and Institute for
  Learning & Brain Sciences
University of Washington
Seattle, WA 98195

Michael Strevens
Department of Philosophy
New York University
New York, NY 10003

Joshua Tenenbaum
Department of Brain and Cognitive Sciences
Massachussetts Institute of Technology
Cambridge, MA 02139

Henry Wellman
Department of Psychology
Center for Human Growth and Development
University of Michigan
Ann Arbor, MI 48103

Jim Woodward
Division of the Humanities and Social
  Sciences
California Institute of Technology
Pasadena, CA 91125

Causal Learning

Introduction

Alison Gopnik & Laura Schulz

From: mherskovits@psych.ucarcadia.arcadia.edu
To: brook_russell@turing.carnegietech.edu

Hi Brook,

We haven't met, but I'm writing about this series of workshops on causal learning that my advisor and yours have cooked up for this year at the center in Stanford. My advisor has gone completely crazy over this causal Bayes nets stuff and is insisting that I go to this conference (on the pittance that supports graduate researchers) and that I learn everything there is to know about the philosophy and computation of causal learning. But, every time I look at one of the papers, all I see are unintelligible sentences like this: For any variable R in the directed graph, the graph represents the proposition that for any set S of variables in the graph (not containing any descendants of R) R is jointly independent of the variables in S conditional on any set of values of the variables that are parents of R!

Let me give you a brief sense of where I'm coming from, as we say in mellow Arcadia (though I'm a New Yorker myself). I went to

Public School 164 and did my undergraduate degree in cognitive science at the City University of Brooklyn, and I've always thought that the problem of how we learn about the world was the most central and interesting question cognitive science could ask. That's why I became a developmental psychologist. But, I'm suspicious about whether philosophy and computation have much to offer. The history of cognitive development, and the study of learning more generally, has been a history of theoretical answers that didn't really fit the phenomena and empirical phenomena that didn't really fit the theories. What we empirical psychologists see is that learners infer abstract, structured hierarchical representations of the world. And those representations are true—they really do get us to a better picture of the world. But, the data that actually reach us from the world are incomplete, fragmented, probabilistic, and concrete. So, the baffling thing for psychologists has been how we could get from that kind of data to those kinds of representations.

The philosophers and computationalists keep telling us that the kind of learning we developmentalists see every day is nothing but an illusion! The Platonic (read Cartesian, read Chomskyan, read Spelkean) view has been that, although we seem to infer structure from data, actually the structure was there all along. Insofar as our representations are accurate, it is because of a long phylogenetic evolutionary history, not a brief ontogenetic inferential one. And, there is no real learning involved in development but only triggering or enrichment.

The Aristotelian (Lockean, behaviorist, connectionist) view has been that, although it looks as if we are building abstract veridical representations, really all we are doing is summarizing and associating bits of data. Accuracy is beside the point; associationistic processes just let us muddle through with the right responses to the right stimuli. There aren't really any abstract representations, just distributed collections of particular input-output links.

So, all that the philosophers and computationalists seem to be doing, on either side, is to tell us empirical developmental psychologists not to believe our eyes. Actually, I think Gopnik puts it quite well in her book about theory formation (Gopnik & Meltzoff, 1997) (she does tend to let her conclusions outstrip her data, but she sure has an ear for a slogan):

Far too often in the past psychologists have been willing to abandon their own autonomous theorizing because of some infatuation with the current account of computation and neurology. We wake up one morning and discover that the account that looked so promising and scientific, S-R connections, Gestaltian field theory, Hebbian cell-assemblies, has vanished and we have spent another couple of decades trying to accommodate our psychological theories to it. We think we should summon up our self-esteem and be more stand-offish in the future. Any implementations of psychological theories, either computational or neurological, will first depend on properly psychological accounts of psychological phenomena (Gopnik & Meltzoff 1997, p. 220).

But anyway, although I've argued and argued, my advisor is still insisting that I go to this thing. And, it sounds like you're in the same boat. So, I'm writing to you with a deal:

How about a tutorial swap? I mean, I'll tell you all about causal learning in psychology if you'll explain those directed acyclic graphs in plain English words? So, how about it?

All best, Morgan Herskovits

From: brook_russell@turing.carnegietech.edu
To: mherskovits@psych.ucarcadia.arcadia.edu

My dear Morgan,

Thank you for your letter of the 21st. I can't say that we seem to have much else in common, but apparently your advisor matches mine in dotty obstinacy. Mine is insisting that I read all this barbaric and incomprehensible stuff about subjects and methods. Worse, it appears that quite a few of the subjects appear to be between 30.1 and 40.8 months old—sprogs in short! But, what on earth methods for sprogs are supposed to have to do with discovering normatively reliable methods for causal inference I can't imagine. He is also insisting that I attend these workshops.

I can't say I caught all your references. Plato certainly, but Spelke? Gopnik? (And what ghastly names.) However, I completely agree with you about the lack of connection between our two enterprises. The philosopher of science Clark Glymour (Glymour 1992) put it very well, I think, in his critique of cognitive theories of science, appropriately called "Invasion of the Mind Snatchers": The idea that theories are something you would find in somebody's head, rather than being abstract mathematical objects, is an idea fit only for Ichabod Crane.

My own work began in my undergraduate days at Oxford, as an attempt at a conceptual analysis of causation. (I also am a public school product by the way, though I find the idea of numbered public schools rather puzzling. Would Eton or Harrow get a lower number on your American scheme?) The conceptual in philosophy, of course, is not like the conceptual in psychology. In philosophy, we want to know what causation *is* in all conceivable circumstances, not what a few mere mortals (let alone sprogs!) think that it is. There is a long history in philosophy of trying to develop an analytic definition of causation through the method of examples and counterexamples; philosophers give examples of cases in which everyone agrees that X causes Y and then try to find some generalization that will capture those examples. Then, other philosophers find examples that fit the definitions but don't seem to be causal or vice versa.

I was working on counterexamples of quadruple countervailing causal prevention (you know the sort of thing where one assassin tries to stop another assassin, but first poison is slipped in the antidote, and then a brick hits a wooden board before the king can brake for the stop sign). I was beginning to find it all rather discouraging when finally my math tutor put me on to the theory of causal graphical models, and it came to me as a revelation.

You see, causal graphical models are to causation as geometry is to space. Rather than providing a reductive definition of causation they instead provide a formal mathematical framework that captures important regularities in causal facts, just as the mathematical structure of geometry captures important spatial regularities. Causal graphical models capture just the right kind of asymmetries in causal relations, allow one to generate the appropriate predictions about conditional probabilities and interventions, and perhaps most significantly discriminate between conditional probabilities and interventions and counterfactuals. So, I decided to move to Carnegie Tech for graduate school and work on some of the many unsolved problems the formalism poses.

Imagine my shock, then, when my advisor, a philosopher of science notorious for the austerity and rigor of his views on just about everything, began insisting that I read psychology and, worse, child psychology! Because, of course, it is obvious that even sophisticated adults are unable to handle even the simplest problems involving causality or probability. The undergraduate students at Carnegie Tech, for example, who, although admittedly handicapped by an American secondary school education, are among the brightest and best but are quite hopeless at these computations. Anyone who has, for their sins, had to teach introductory statistics is aware of that. So, how could mere sprogs of 3 or 4

years be expected to use anything like Bayes net learning algorithms? They are, I understand, inept at even quite elementary differential integration problems and have, at best, only the most primitive understanding of basic linear algebra.

However, one of the benefits of an Oxford education is the training it provides in possessing a deep and thorough knowledge of the most recondite subjects based on a brief weekly perusal of the *Times Literary Supplement*. So, I will, in fact, be grateful for a (preferably equally brief) summary of this work. In return, I will do my best to give you an extremely simple introduction to causal Bayes nets (see attached).

Yours very truly,

Brook Russell

Attachment 1: Causal Bayes Nets for Dummies

Causal Bayes Nets

Causal-directed graphical models, or causal Bayes nets, were developed in the philosophy of science and statistical literature (Glymour, 2001; Pearl, 1988, 2000; Spirtes, Glymour, & Scheines, 1993). Scientists seem to infer theories about the causal structure of the world from patterns of evidence. But, philosophers of science found it difficult to explain how these inferences are possible. Although classical logic could provide a formal account of deductive inferences, it was much more difficult to provide an inductive logic—an account of how evidence could confirm theories. One reason is that deductive logic deals in certainties, but inductive inference is always a matter of probabilities—acquiring more evidence for a hypothesis makes the hypothesis more likely, but there is always the possibility that it will be overturned.

An even more difficult question was what philosophers of science called "the logic of discovery." Again, the conventional wisdom, going back to Karl Popper, was that particular hypotheses could be proposed and could be falsified (definitely) or confirmed (tentatively). The origins of those hypotheses were mysterious; there was no way of explaining how the evidence itself could generate a hypothesis.

Causal Bayes nets provide a kind of logic of inductive inference and discovery. They do so, at least, for one type of inference that is particularly important in scientific theory formation. Many scientific hypotheses involve the causal structure of the world. Scientists infer causal structure by observing the patterns of conditional probability among events (as in statistical analysis), by examining the consequences of interventions (as in experiments), or usually, by combining the two types of evidence. Causal Bayes nets formalize these kinds of inferences.

In causal Bayes nets, causal hypotheses are represented by directed acyclic graphs like that of Figure I-1. The graphs consist of variables, representing types of events or states of the world and directed edges (arrows) representing the direct causal relations between those variables. The variables can be discrete (like school grade) or continuous (like weight); they can be binary (like "having eyes" or "not having eyes") or take a range of values (like color). Similarly, the direct causal relations can have many forms; they can be deterministic or probabilistic, generative or inhibitory, linear or nonlinear. The exact specification of the nature of these relations is called the *parameterization* of the graph. In most applications of the formalism, we assume that the graphs are acyclic—an arrow cannot feed back on itself. However, there are some generalizations of the formalism to cyclic cases.

Causal Structure and Conditional Probabilities

The Bayes net formalism makes systematic connections between the causal hypotheses that are represented by the graphs and particular patterns of evidence. The

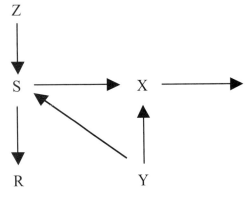

FIGURE I-1 A causal Bayes net.

structure of a causal graph constrains the conditional probabilities among the variables in that graph, no matter what the variables are or what the parameterization of the graph is. In particular, it constrains the conditional independencies among those variables. Given a particular causal structure, only some patterns of conditional independence will occur among the variables.

Conditional and unconditional dependence and independence can be defined mathematically. Two discrete variables X and Y are unconditionally independent in probability if and only if for every value x of X and y of Y the probability of x and y occurring together equals the unconditional probability of x multiplied by the unconditional probability of y. That is $p(x \& y) = p(x) * p(y)$. Two variables are independent in probability conditional on some third variable Z if and only if $p(x, y \mid z) = p(x \mid z) * p(y \mid z)$. That is, for every value x, y, and z of X, Y, and Z the probability of x and y given z equals the probability of x given z multiplied by the probability of y given z. This definition can be extended to continuous variables. When we say three variables x, y, and z are correlated, we mean that they are dependent in probability. When we say that x and y are correlated but that that correlation disappears when z is partialed out, we mean that x and y are independent in probability conditional on z.

The structure of the causal graph puts constraints on these patterns of probability among the variables. These constraints can be captured by a single formal assumption, the causal Markov assumption.

The Causal Markov Assumption   For any variable X in an acyclic causal graph, X is independent of all other variables in the graph (except for its own direct and indirect effects) conditional on its own direct causes.

If we make further assumptions about the parameterization of the graph, that is, about the particular nature of the causal relations among the variables, then we can constrain the kinds of inferences we make still further. For example, if we assume that each cause independently has a certain power to bring about an effect and that this power leads to a certain likelihood of the effect given the cause, then we can further constrain the patterns of conditional probability among causes and effects. This is a common assumption in studies of human causal learning. The causal Markov assumption, however, applies to all parameterizations.

To illustrate, consider a simple causal problem that is far too common for academics who attend many learned conferences. Suppose that I notice that I often cannot sleep when I have been to a party and drunk lots of wine. Partying P and insomnia I covary and so do wine W and insomnia I. There are at least two possibilities about the relations among these variables, which I can represent by two simple causal graphs: Graph 1 is a chain $P \rightarrow W \rightarrow I$; Graph 2 is a common cause structure $I \leftarrow P \rightarrow W$. Maybe parties lead me to drink, and wine keeps me up; maybe parties both keep me up and lead me to drink. The covariation among the variables by itself is consistent with both these structures.

You can discriminate between these two graphs by looking at the patterns of conditional probability among the three variables. Suppose you keep track of all the times you drink and party and examine the effects on your insomnia. If Graph 1 is correct, then you should observe that you are more likely to have insomnia when you drink wine, whether or not you party. If instead Graph 2 is correct, then you will observe that, regardless of how much or how little wine you drink, you are only more likely to have insomnia when you go to a party.

More formally, if Graph 1 is right, and there is a causal chain that goes from parties to wine to insomnia, then $I \perp P \mid W$; the probability of insomnia occurring is independent (in probability) of the probability of party going occurring conditional on the occurrence of wine drinking. If Graph 2 is right and parties are a common cause of wine and insomnia, then $I \perp W \mid P$; the probability of wine-drinking occurring is independent (in probability) of the probability of insomnia occurring conditional on the occurrence of party going.

The philosopher of science Hans Reichenbach (1971) long ago pointed out these consistent relations between conditional independence and causal structure and talked about them in terms of "screening off." When there is a chain going from partying to wine to insomnia, the wine screens off insomnia from the influence of partying; when partying directly causes both wine and insomnia, wine does not screen off insomnia from partying—partying leads to insomnia directly. But, partying does screen off insomnia from the effects of wine. The causal Markov assumption generalizes this screening-off principle to all acyclic causal graphs.

Thus, if we know the structure of the graph and know the values of some of the variables in the graph, we can make consistent predictions about the conditional probability of other variables. In fact, the first applications of Bayes nets involved predicting conditional probabilities (Pearl, 1988). Many real-life inferences involve complex combinations of conditional probabilities among variables—consider a medical expert, for example, trying to predict one set of symptoms from another set. Trying to predict all the combinations of conditional probabilities rapidly becomes an exponentially complicated problem. Computer scientists were trying to find a tractable way to calculate these conditional probabilities and discovered that representing the variables in a directed graph allowed them to do this. The graph allowed computer scientists to "read off" quite complicated patterns of conditional dependence among variables. The first applications of Bayes nets treated the graphs as calculation devices—summaries of the conditional probabilities among events.

Bayes Nets and Interventions

Why think of these graphs as representations of *causal* relations among variables, rather than simply thinking of them as a convenient way to represent the probabilities of variables? The earlier Bayes net iterations were confined to techniques for predicting some probabilities from others. However, the development of causal Bayes net algorithms also allows us to determine what will happen when we intervene from outside to change the value of a particular variable. When two variables are genuinely related in a causal way, holding other variables constant, then intervening to change one variable should change the other. Indeed, philosophers have argued that this is just what it means for two variables to be causally related (J. Woodward, 2003).

Predictions about probabilities may be quite different from predictions about interventions. For example, in a common cause structure like Graph 2, we will indeed be able to predict something about the value of insomnia from the value of wine. If that structure is the correct one, then knowing that someone drank wine will indeed make you more likely to predict that they will have insomnia (because drinking wine is correlated with partying, which leads to insomnia). But, intervening on their wine drinking, forbidding them from drinking, for example, will have no effect on their insomnia. Only intervening on partying will do that.

The Bayes net formalism captures these relations between causation, intervention, and conditional probability through a second assumption, an assumption about how interventions should be represented in the graph.

The Intervention Assumption   A variable I is an intervention on a variable X in a causal graph if and only if (a) I is exogenous (that is, it is not caused by any other variables in the graph), (b) directly fixes the value of X to x, and (c) does not affect the values of any other variables in the graph except through its influence on X.

Given this assumption, we can accurately predict the effects of interventions on particular variables in a graph on other variables. (We can also sometimes make accurate predictions about the effects of interventions that do not meet all these conditions). In causal Bayes nets, interventions systematically alter the nature of the graph they intervene on, and these systematic alterations follow directly from the formalism itself. In particular, when an external intervention fixes the value of a variable, it also eliminates the causal influence of other variables on that variable. If I simply decide to stop drinking wine, then my intervention alone will determine the value of wine drinking; partying will no longer have any effect. This can be represented by replacing the original graph with an altered graph in which arrows directed into the intervened on variable are eliminated (Judea Pearl in 2000 vividly referred to this process as *graph surgery*). The conditional dependencies among the variables after the intervention can be read from this altered graph.

Suppose, for example, I want to know what I can do to prevent my insomnia. Should I sit in my room alone but continue to drink when I want to or go to parties just the same but stick to Perrier? I can calculate the effects of such interventions on each of the causal structures using graph surgery and predict the results. I will obtain different results from these interventions depending on the true causal structure (solitary drinking will lead to insomnia, and sober partying will not for Graph 1; sober partying will lead to insomnia, and solitary drinking will not for Graph 2).

Exactly the same inferential apparatus can be used to generate counterfactual predictions. Suppose I want to ask what would have happened had things been otherwise. If I had refrained from wine at all those conferences, then would my life, or at least my insomnia, have been better? Graph surgery will also answer this question. Just as in an intervention, a counterfactual "fixes" the value of certain variables and allows you to infer the consequences.

A central aspect of causal Bayes nets, indeed the thing that makes them causal, is that they allow us to go back and forth freely from evidence about observed probabilities to inferences about interventions and vice versa.

These two assumptions, then, allow us to take a particular causal structure and accurately predict the conditional probabilities of events, and the consequences of interventions on those events, from that structure.

Bayes Nets and Learning

We just saw that knowing the causal structure lets us make the right predictions about interventions and probabilities. We can also use this fact to learn causal structure from the evidence of interventions and probabilities.

Let us go back to the wine-insomnia example. You could distinguish between these graphs by either intervention or observation. You could, for instance, hold partying constant (always partying or never partying) and vary whether you drink wine, or you could hold drinking constant (always drinking or never drinking) and vary whether you party. In either case, you could observe the effect on your sleep. If drinking affects your sleep when partying is held constant, but partying has no effect on your sleep when drinking is held constant, then you could conclude that Graph 1 is correct. Such reasoning underlies the logic of experimental design in science.

You could also, however, simply observe the relative frequencies of the three events. If you notice that you are more likely to have insomnia when you drink wine, whether or not you party, then you can infer that Graph 1 is correct. If you observe that, regardless of how much or how little wine you drink, you are only more likely to have insomnia when you go to a party, then you will opt instead for Graph 2. These inferences reflect the logic of correlational statistics in science. In effect, what you did was to "partial out" the effects of partying on the wine-insomnia correlation and draw a causal conclusion as a result.

This type of learning, however, requires an additional assumption. The assumption is that the patterns of dependence and independence we see among the variables really are the result of the causal relations among them. Suppose that wine actually makes you sleepy instead of keeping you awake. But, it just happens to be the case that this influence of wine on insomnia is perfectly canceled out by the countervailing exciting influence of parties. We will incorrectly conclude that there are no causal relations between the three variables. We need to assume that these sinister coincidences will not occur. Formally, this is called the faithfulness assumption.

The Faithfulness Assumption   In the joint distribution on the variables in the graph, all conditional independencies are consequences of the Markov assumption applied to the graph.

Given the faithfulness assumption, it is possible to infer complex causal structure from patterns of conditional probability and intervention (Glymour & Cooper, 1999; Spirtes et al., 1993). Computationally tractable learning algorithms have been designed to accomplish this task and have been extensively applied in a range of disciplines (e.g., Ramsey, Roush, Gazis, & Glymour, 2002; Shipley, 2000). In some cases, it is also possible to accurately infer the existence of new unobserved variables that are common causes of the observed variables (Richardson & Spirtes, 2003; Silva, Scheines, Glymour, & Spirtes, 2003).

Causal Bayes net representations and learning algorithms allow learners to predict patterns of evidence accurately from causal structure and to learn causal structure accurately from patterns of evidence. They constitute a kind of inductive causal logic, and a logic of causal discovery. It is possible to prove that only certain patterns of evidence will follow from particular causal structures, given the Markov, intervention, and faithfulness assumptions, just as only certain conclusions follow from particular logical premises given the axioms of logic.

From: mherskovits@psych.ucarcadia.arcadia.edu
To: brook_russell@turing.carnegietech.edu

3:15 a.m., August 5, 2003

Righto Brook.

Well, quadruple countervailing causal prevention sounds just fascinating. I'm so glad I'm going to this conference now.

But, thanks for the attachment. Actually, I think I might be getting the hang of these Bayes net things, even with all the formal stuff. (Though there's one thing about the math I still don't get: Why do you Brits insist on making it plural?) They sound like something we know a lot about in Arcadia: vision. Not of course the political kind or the hallucination kind (although we know a lot about those, too),

but the kind we study in psychophysics and perceptual psychology.

The world out there is full of real three-dimensional objects, but our perceptual system just gets some distorted two-dimensional retinal input. Still, the merest "sprog," as you would say, has the computational power to turn that input back into a three-dimensional representation of a table or a lamp without even thinking about it. And (ignoring the occasional illusion), those representations are accurate: They capture the truth about the spatial world.

In vision science, we have "ideal observer" theories about how that happens—how any system, animal, human or robotic, sprog, or Ph.D. could infer the structure of a three-dimensional world from two-dimensional data. Vision science tells us that the visual system implicitly assumes that there is a world of three-dimensional moving objects and then makes assumptions about how those objects lead to particular patterns on the retina. By making the further assumption that the retinal patterns were, in fact, produced by the objects in this way, the system can work backward and infer the structure of objects from those patterns (see, e.g., Palmer, 1999).

Your causal Bayes net inferences sound sort of like that. The visual system assumes that the patterns at the retina were produced by three-dimensional objects in a particular way and then uses those assumptions to infer the objects from the retinal patterns. Your causal Bayes nets assume that causal structure produced patterns of evidence and uses those assumptions to learn the structure from the evidence (your causal Markov, intervention, and faithfulness assumptions). You guys seem to think that you're going to do the same thing for causality that the psychophysicists have done for vision: You're going to tell us how we could transform information about probabilities and interventions into accurate representations of the causal structure of the world.

So, I guess if you're right (and I'm not committing myself yet there), causal Bayes nets *could* give us a way of formally specifying accurate inductive causal inferences—just like ideal observer theories in vision provide a way of formally specifying accurate visual inferences and like logic provides a way of formally specifying accurate deductive inferences.

But if that's right, then I have to say, Brook, the rest of your letter doesn't make a whole lot of sense :) You seem to be under the bizarre impression that any knowledge you can't find in the *Times Literary Supplement* isn't really "knowledge." So, I guess you think my sprogs can't see because they can't write an article on Fourier transforms.

But, of course, my sprogs see just as well as you and I do. And, of course, sprogs can use vision to learn all sorts of new things about objects. In fact, they engage in perfectly sophisticated "maths" all the time—and if they can perform complex, implicit computations to support vision, then they could, in principle, perform complex, implicit computational procedures to support causal inference.

Your computers may or may not be able to solve this causal learning problem, but it's certain that my sprogs can do it. In fact, they might be the most powerful causal learning devices in the universe. Thirty years of work on the "theory theory" shows that children have abstract, coherent representations of the causal structure of the world. Those representations allow children to make predictions, perform interventions, and even generate counterfactuals. As soon as they can talk, they even offer explanations of the world around them. And, they seem to learn those causal structures from patterns of evidence.

Plus, even the very smallest sprogs can combine information from observation and intervention. Little babies who learn a new skill—like reaching for objects—understand other people's actions on objects better than babies who don't have the skill. Jessica Sommerville will show you next week how giving babies "sticky mittens" and changing their own ability to act on the world changes the babies' ability to understand the actions of others. Andrew Meltzoff will show you something like the reverse: how babies take information they only observe and turn it into actions of their own. Sprogs do all sorts of other things: make good interventions, discriminate confounded and unconfounded interventions, reason about unobserved causes, learn complex causal structure. . . . Laura Schulz, Tamar Kushnir, and that Gopnik woman whose name

you like so much will also show you all that on Saturday. When it comes to grown-ups, York Hagmayer, Steve Sloman, Dave Lagnado, and Michael Waldmann will show you that even those stats class undergraduates can make remarkably sophisticated inferences about both predictions and interventions.

Best of all, sprogs never do absolutely useless things like reason about quadruple causal prevention.

Anyway, I'm doing my part and attaching some fairly primitive stuff about the psychology of causal learning. As you'll see, even the best theoretical accounts we have don't really even start to capture the richness of what people, even very small people, can actually do.

All the best,

Morgan

Attachment 2: The Psychology of Causal Learning for Nerds

The Piagetian Account of Causal Reasoning

Research on children's causal reasoning, like research on cognitive development in general, was initiated by the work of Jean Piaget (1929, 1930). Piaget believed that causal reasoning developed very gradually. Indeed, Piaget proposed no less than 17 distinct stages of causal learning.

In particular, however, Piaget believed that children's reasoning from early to middle childhood was "precausal." It was characterized by a confusion between psychological activity and physical mechanism (Piaget 1930). This conclusion was based chiefly on his investigation of children's explanations of natural phenomena. Piaget found that children's early explanations of physical events were artificialistic (meaning events were attributed to human intervention: clouds move because we walk, the river flows because of boats) and animistic (meaning that physical events were attributed to psychological intention: the string turns because it wants to unwind itself) (1929). According to Piaget's account, not until quite late in development are children able to provide a complete, functional account of a chain of causal events and reason accurately about intervening causal mechanisms.

Nativist and Modular Views of Causal Reasoning

Over the past several decades, however—and with the development of new methods for assessing the cognitive abilities of infants and young children—considerable research has suggested that Piaget underestimated the causal reasoning abilities of young children. Both infants and adults seem to perceive causality when objects (like billiard balls) collide and launch one another (Leslie & Keeble, 1987; Michotte, 1962; Oakes & Cohen, 1990). Infants also seem to expect causal constraints on object motion, assuming that objects respect principles of support, containment, cohesion, continuity, and contact (Baillargeon, Kotovsky, & Needham, 1995; Spelke, Breinlinger, Macomber, & Jacobson, 1992; Spelke, Katz, Purcell, Ehrlich, & Breinlinger, 1994).

Moreover, contra Piaget, considerable evidence suggests that even babies appropriately distinguish psychological and physical causality. Specifically, infants seem to interpret human, but not mechanical, action as goal directed and self-initiated (Meltzoff, 1995; A. L. Woodward, 1998; A. L. Woodward, Phillips, & Spelke, 1993). Thus, for instance, babies expect physical objects to move through contact (Leslie & Keeble, 1987; Oakes & Cohen, 1990) but do not expect the same of human agents (A. L. Woodward et al., 1993); expect that an object will be entrained when grasped by a human hand but not by an inanimate object (Leslie, 1982, 1984); and treat the reach of a human hand, but not the trajectory of a metal claw, as goal directed (A. L. Woodward, 1998). Furthermore, almost as soon as children can speak they offer causal explanations (at least of familiar, everyday events) that respect domain boundaries (Hickling & Wellman, 2001). Finally, preschoolers' predictions, causal judgments, and counterfactual inferences are remarkably accurate across a wide range of tasks and content areas (e.g., Flavell, Green, & Flavell, 1995; Gelman & Wellman, 1991; Gopnik & Wellman, 1994; Kalish, 1996; Sobel, 2004).

To account for the early emergence of structured, coherent, causal knowledge, some psychologists have suggested that children's early causal representations might be largely innate rather than learned. Following Kant's conception of a priori causal knowledge (1787/1899), some researchers have proposed that children's early causal understanding might originate in domain-specific modules (Leslie & Keeble, 1987) or from innate concepts in core domains (Carey &

Spelke, 1994; Keil, 1995; Spelke et al., 1994). These researchers have suggested that children's causal knowledge might be accurate not because of general learning mechanisms designed to infer structure from evidence but because of specialized mechanisms dedicated to relatively constrained information-processing tasks (Leslie, 1994).

It may be that infants' object concepts, their ability to distinguish objects from agents, and their perception of Michottean causality do indeed have an innate basis. However, there seems less reason to believe that children's abilities to reason broadly about the causes of human behavior, physical events, and biological transformations are an outgrowth of domain-specific modules. In particular, modular, domain-specific accounts of causal reasoning do not seem to explain how we identify particular causal relations within a domain, how we make causal inferences that transcend domain boundaries (i.e., that physical causes can be responsible for psychological effects and vice versa), and why causal reasoning is sensitive to patterns of evidence. Nonetheless, the majority of post-Piagetian research on preschool children's causal reasoning has emphasized the centrality of substantive, domain-appropriate principles.

Domain-Specific Causal Knowledge, Causal Mechanisms, and the "Generative Transmission" Account

In particular, researchers have focused on the role that substantive concepts, like force and spatial contact, might play in constraining young children's inferences about physical causal events (e.g., Bullock, Gelman, & Baillargeon, 1982; Leslie, 1984; Shultz, Pardo, & Altmann, 1982; Shultz, 1982). In an influential monograph on children's causal reasoning, the psychologist Thomas Shultz distinguished between a statistical view of causal relations, in which the causal connection between events is determined by the covariation of cause and effect, and a causal mechanism view of causality, in which causation is understood "primarily in terms of generative transmission" of force and energy (1982, p. 46). In a series of experiments, Shultz demonstrated that, in their causal judgments, preschoolers privilege evidence for spatially continuous processes compatible with the transmission of energy over evidence for covariation. Preschoolers inferred, for instance, that a tuning fork with vibrations that were not obstructed was more likely to produce a sound than a tuning fork with vibrations that were blocked, even when the effect immediately followed an intervention on the latter and followed the former only after a delay.

Similarly, Bullock, Gelman, and Baillargeon concluded that the idea that "causes bring about their effects by transfer of causal impetus" is "central to the psychological definition of cause-effect relations" (1982). Consistent with this view, psychologists have shown that even adults prefer information about plausible, domain-specific mechanisms of causal transmission to statistical and covariation information in making causal judgments (Ahn, Kalish, Medin, & Gelman, 1995).

Covariation Accounts

However, the generative transmission view of causation in particular and domain-specific knowledge in general have played a rather limited role in accounts of adult causal learning. Indeed, in the adult cognitive science literature, researchers have largely focused on the role of contingency and covariation in causal learning, as opposed to principles about mechanisms. Two accounts of causal learning have been particularly influential: associative learning or connectionist accounts and Patricia Cheng's causal power theory (1997).

Associative Learning and Connectionist Accounts of Causal Learning

Although not all contingencies are causal, all causal relationships involve contingencies. There is a vast body of literature on contingency learning in both human and nonhuman animals, and some researchers have proposed that mechanisms similar to those underlying contingency learning in operant and classical conditioning can account for human causal reasoning (Dickinson, Shanks, & Evendon, 1984; Shanks & Dickinson, 1987; Shanks, Holyoak, & Medin, 1996; Wasserman, Elek, Chatlosh, & Baker, 1993).

Instrumental and Imitative Learning

Thorndike found that cats could learn to escape from cages by trial and error, and that with practice, the cats became faster at escaping. He described this as the *law of effect*: Actions with positive consequences are likely to be repeated and actions with negative consequences avoided (1911/2000). A large body of research on learning subsequently elaborated the ways in which behavior could be shaped by reinforcing or punishing outcomes. Operant learning has been demonstrated in nonhuman animals ranging from pigeons to primates; unsurprisingly, it has been demonstrated in human babies as well. Thus, infants who learn, for instance, that kicking makes a mobile spin, will both repeat the behavior and remember it after significant delays (Rovee-Collier, 1980; Watson & Ramey, 1972). Instrumental learning—the ability to learn from the immediate consequence of one's own actions—seems to be an early development, both phylogenetically and ontogenetically.

Importantly, human beings (if not uniquely among animals, then at least characteristically; see Tomasello & Call, 1997) are able to learn not only from the consequence of their own actions but also from the consequences of others' actions. Thus, for instance, 9-month-old babies who see an experimenter light up a toy by touching it with his head will spontaneously touch their own heads to the toy (Meltzoff, 1988). By 18 months, infants will even recognize the goal of another's intervention and produce the completed action when they have seen only a failed attempt (Meltzoff, 1995). Such research suggests that young children can learn the causal relation between human actions and the events that follow them. However, it does not explain how children learn causal relations when human action is not the causal variable (e.g., the causal relationship between two parts of a toy, the causal relationship between growth and food, and the causal relationship between mental states and behavior). Instrumental learning and learning from the direct outcome of others' interventions do not seem to explain our ability to engage in nonegocentric causal reasoning about distal events.

Classical Learning and the Rescorla-Wagner Theory

Shortly after Thorndike formulated the law of effect, Pavlov famously discovered that an animal regularly exposed to a temporal contiguity between a conditioned stimulus (like a tone) and an unconditioned stimulus (like food) would learn to associate the two stimuli. When presented only with the conditioned stimulus, the animal would produce a response (e.g., salivating) normally elicited by the unconditioned stimulus (1953). This finding has also been replicated across species and ages; like instrumental learning, classical conditioning is an ontogenetically, phylogenetically, early, robust development.

Rescorla modified Pavlov's theory to suggest that contingency, not just contiguity, was critical for learning Rescorla & Wagner (1972). That is, for learning to occur, cues have to be predictive: The probability of the effect given the cue must be greater than the probability of the effect in the absence of the cue. The Rescorla-Wagner theory (R-W theory; 1972) specified that learning occurred on a trial-by-trial basis and predicted that early trials would be more important to learning than later trials.

In its simplest form, the R-W equation for associative learning is $\Delta V = K(\lambda - \Sigma V)$, where ΔV is the change in the perceived strength of the association (e.g., the amount of learning that occurs on any given trial), K is a parameter between 0 and 1 that reflects the salience of the cue multiplied by the salience of the effect, λ is the association between cue and stimulus at asymptote, and ΣV is the sum of the associative strength on previous trials.

Thus, the R-W theory predicts that the change in associative strength on any trial is proportional to the difference between the maximum possible associative strength between a cue and an outcome and the previous estimate of the strength of association. Thus, the stronger the prior association is, the less learning there will be on any given trial.

The model can be applied to human causal learning by substituting causes for the conditioned stimulus and effects for the unconditioned stimulus. The associative strength between the two variables is then taken as indicating the causal connection between them. This equation successfully predicts findings in the animal learning literature such as blocking, overshadowing, and conditioned inhibition and many findings in the human contingency learning literature (Baker, Mercier, Valee-Tourangeau, Frank, & Maria, 1989; Dickinson et al., 1984; Shanks et al., 1996; Wasserman et al., 1993). The R-W rule, or generalizations of the rule, have often been implemented in connectionist networks aimed at explaining human causal learning (see, e.g., Gluck & Bower, 1988; Rogers & McLelland, 2004; Shanks, 1990).

However, there is substantial agreement that the R-W equation by itself does not adequately account for the psychology of human causal learning (see, e.g., Cheng, 1997; Glymour, 2001; Gopnik et al., 2004; Waldmann, 1996, 2000; Waldmann & Holyoak, 1992). In fact, it may not even explain

animal learning. The R-W account predicts neither learned irrelevancy (the fact that an animal first exposed to a cue without any reward or punishment has difficulty on later conditioning trials learning to associate the cue with an outcome) nor failures of extinction (the fact that an animal that has learned through operant conditioning to avoid a cue once associated with a punishment retains the behavior in the presence of the cue long after the association has disappeared).

In the human case, Patricia Cheng demonstrated, for instance, that the R-W approach fails to account for boundary conditions on causal inference (1997). When an effect always occurs (i.e., whether the candidate cause is present or not), the R-W equation predicts that we should conclude that the candidate generative cause is ineffective. In contrast, human reasoners believe that if the effect occurs at ceiling, then there is no way to determine the efficacy of a candidate cause. Similarly, if an effect never occurs, then the R-W equation predicts that we should believe a candidate inhibitory cause is ineffective, whereas people believe that if the effect never occurs, then it is impossible to determine the strength of an inhibitory cause. Similarly, Waldmann (1996, 2000; Waldmann & Holyoak, 1992) showed asymmetries in the predictive and diagnostic uses of causal information that were difficult to explain in associationist terms.

The R-W account also fails to explain a phenomenon known as *backward blocking* (Sobel, Tenenbaum, & Gopnik, 2004). If two candidate causes A and B together produce an effect and it is also the case that A by itself is sufficient to produce the effect, then human reasoners (including young children) are less likely to believe that B is a cause of the effect. However, since observing A by itself provides no new evidence about the association between B and the effect, the R-W rule predicts that our estimate of the causal strength of B should not change (although some researchers, e.g., Wasserman & Berglan, 1998, have suggested modifications to the R-W rule that do allow for this prediction).

In addition to those aspects of human causal reasoning that seem to contradict the predictions of the R-W model, there are many aspects of human causal learning that would require ad hoc modification of the R-W rule. The R-W model, for instance, calculates the strength of every candidate cause separately; thus, to judge the interaction of two causes, it must treat the interaction as a "third" candidate cause (see Gopnik et al., 2004). Similarly, the R-W equation assumes that all the variables have already been categorized as causes or effects and then calculates the associative strength between each cause and each effect. However, the model cannot determine whether variables *are* causes or effects (i.e., it cannot decide whether A causes B, B causes A, or neither). One might run the equation multiple times, sometimes with one variable as a cause and sometimes with the other, and then compare the relative strength of each pairing, but this is an ad hoc modification of the theory.

The Power Theory of Probabilistic Contrast

Patricia Cheng (1997) proposes an account of human causal learning that resolves some of the difficulties with the R-W account. Cheng proposes that people innately treat covariation as an index of causal power (an unobservable entity) and suggests that people reason about causes with respect to particular *focal sets*, a contextually determined set of events over which people compute contrasts in covariation.

Cheng uses probabilistic contrast (ΔP) as an index of covariation. ΔP is simply the difference between the probability of an effect given a candidate cause and in the absence of the candidate cause; formally, $\Delta P = P(e \mid c) - P(e \mid \sim c)$. However, in distinction from purely covariational accounts of causal reasoning, Cheng introduces the idea of causal power. Although we cannot know the real causal power of any variable (because causal power is a theoretical entity), we can estimate causal power by distinguishing between the probability of the effect in the presence of a candidate cause and the probability of the effect in the presence of all causes (known and unknown) alternative to the candidate cause. Cheng assumes (a) that candidate causes and alternative causes influence the effect independently; (b) that there are no unobserved common causes of the candidate cause and the effect (although the account can be generalized to relax this assumption; Glymour, 2001); and (c) that candidate causes are noninteractive (although Novick and Cheng, 2004, have since modified the account to explain inferences about interactive causes).

The causal power of a candidate cause is not equivalent to either $P(e \mid c)$ or ΔP because even when the candidate cause is present and the effect occurs, the effect could be caused by alternative causes. However, if you assume that alternative causes occur

independently of the candidate cause, then the probability of the effect when the candidate cause is present and all alternative causes are absent can be estimated as $1 - P(e \mid \sim c)$. Thus, generative causal power pc can be estimated as $pc = \Delta P/(1 - P(e \mid \sim c))$.

As this equation illustrates, when alternative causes are absent, ΔP will reflect the causal power of c. However, as $P(e \mid \sim c)$ increases, ΔP becomes an increasingly conservative estimate of causal power. The limiting case, of course, is when the effect always occurs (whether c is present or not). In that case, the reasoner can no longer use covariation as an index of causation, and the causal power of c is undefined. This explains both why ceiling effects are a boundary condition on causal inference and why covariation is not, in general, equivalent to causation. A parallel account explains inferences about candidate inhibitory causes.

Although compelling as a psychological account of human causal learning, one weakness of Cheng's account is that, like the R-W account, it assumes that variables in the world are already identified as causes or effects. The account does not explain how, in the absence of prior knowledge or temporal cues, people could use data to distinguish causes and effects (i.e., to infer whether A causes B or B causes A).

Put another way, both the R-W account and the Cheng account are explanations of how people judge the strength of different causal variables. These theories do not explain how people make judgments about causal structure. In addition, neither the R-W nor the power PC theory provides a unified account of how people might go from judgments about causes to inferences about the effects of interventions. Finally, both of these accounts assume that the candidate causes and effects are observed. Neither account explains how people might use observational data to infer the existence of unobserved causes.

From: brook_russell@turing.carnegietech.edu
To: mherskovits@psych.ucarcadia.arcadia.edu

My dear Morgan,

Thank you for your letter and the attachment. Well, perhaps you are right that there is more similarity between our problems than one might at first think. Your description of the different positions in the psychology of causal learning is indeed reminiscent of the classical positions in the philosophical literature –partly, I suppose, because historically speaking this is where the psychological positions ultimately come from. In philosophy, accounts of causation have been similarly divided. Some accounts, like those of Dowe (2000) or Salmon (1998), stress "mechanism" and "transmission." Much like your Shultz they argue that causation involves the spatiotemporal transmission of some sort of "mark" or "impetus" from cause to effect. Since Hume, the alternative account, usually phrased in skeptical terms, has been that causation just amounts to covariation–sounding rather like your associationists two centuries later. As, Bertrand Russell put it: "The law of causality, I believe, like much that passes muster among philosophers, is a relic of a bygone age, surviving, like the monarchy, only because it is erroneously supposed to do no harm."

But, you see recently, and in tandem with all the new maths I told you about in that attachment, there's been a new way of thinking about causation in philosophy. Philosophers increasingly think about causation in relation to intervention: In terms that would suit your sprogs—if X causes Y, then if you wiggled X, Y would also wiggle. Jim Woodward will tell you all about it on Saturday, and Chris Hitchcock will show you how it helps explain even those cases of quadruple countervailing prevention you find so amusing. And, John Campbell will tell you how it applies to even the kind of causation your particular brand of scientist deals in—the psychological kind.

Here is the really important and, I must confess, somewhat against my will, even intriguing thing about your letter. The unsolved problems you describe in the psychology of causal learning—the things you say your sprogs are so good at doing and the theories are so bad at explaining—well, they're just the sort of things that the interventionist/causal Bayes net account seems, well, destined for.

My learning algorithms, like your sprogs, can infer causal structure rather than just strength; they can appropriately combine information from interventions and observations and distinguish appropriately

between them, and they can even infer unobserved variables from evidence. So, if the two actually were conjoined, . . .

As ever,

Brook

P.S. Oh and, by the way, there seems to be a defect in your word-processing program. In several places where a full stop is clearly intended, it seems to transmit a colon or semicolon followed by a right parenthesis instead; quite mysterious.

References

Ahn, W. K., Kalish, C. W., Medin, D. L., Gelman, S. A. The role of covariation versus mechanism information in causal attribution. *Cognition*, *54*, 299–352.

Baillargeon, R., Kotovsky, L., & Needham, A. (1995). The acquisition of physical knowledge in infancy. In D. Sperber & D. Premack (Eds.), *Causal cognition: A multidisciplinary debate. Symposia of the Fyssen Foundation; Fyssen Symposium, 6th January 1993, Pavillon Henri IV, St-Germain-en-Laye, France* (pp. 79–115). New York: Clarendon Press/Oxford University Press.

Baker, A., Mercier, P., Valee-Tourangeau, F., Frank, R., & Maria, P. (1993). Selective associations and causality judgments: Presence of a strong causal factor may reduce judgments of a weaker one. *Journal of Experimental Psychology: Learning, Memory, and Cognition*, *19*, 414–432.

Bullock, M., Gelman, R., & Baillargeon, R. (1982). The development of causal reasoning. In W. J. Friedman (Ed.), *The developmental psychology of time* (pp. 209–254). New York: Academic Press.

Carey, S., & Spelke, E. S. (1994). Domain-specific knowledge and conceptual change. In L. A. Hirschfeld & S. A. Gelman (Eds.), *Mapping the mind: Domain specificity in cognition and culture; based on a conference entitled "Cultural Knowledge and Domain Specificity," held in Ann Arbor, Michigan, October 13–16* (pp. 169–200). New York: Cambridge University Press.

Cheng, P. W. (1997). From covariation to causation: A causal power theory. *Psychological Review*, *104*, 367–405.

Dickinson, A., Shanks, D. R., & Evendon, J. (1984). Judgment of act-outcome contingency: The role of selective attribution. *Quarterly Journal of Experimental Psychology, 36,* 29–50.

Dowe, P. (2000). *Physical causation.* Cambridge: Cambridge University Press.

Flavell, J. H., Green, F. L., & Flavell, E. R. (1995). Young children's knowledge about thinking. *Monographs of the Society for Research in Child Development, 60,* pp. v–96.

Gelman, S. A., & Wellman, H. M. (1991). Insides and essence: Early understandings of the non-obvious. *Cognition, 38,* 213–244.

Gluck, M., & Bower, G. H. (1988). Evaluating an adaptive network model of human learning. *Journal of Memory and Language, 27,* 166–195.

Glymour, C. Invasion of the mind snatchers. In Giere, R. (1992) (ed.) *Cognitive models of science.* Minneapolis, University of Minnesota Press, pp. 419–501.

Glymour, C. (2001). *The mind's arrows: Bayes nets and causal graphical models in psychology.* Cambridge, MA. MIT Press.

Glymour, C., & Cooper, G. F. (1999). *Computation, causation, and discovery.* Cambridge, MA: MIT/AAAI Press.

Gopnik, A., Glymour, C., Sobel, D. M., Schulz, L., Kushnir, T., & Danks, D. (2004). A theory of causal learning in children: Causal maps and Bayes nets. *Psychological Review, 111,* 1–31.

Gopnik, A., & Wellman, H. M. (1994). The theory theory. In S. A. Gelman & L. A. Hirschfeld (Eds.), *Mapping the mind: Domain specificity in cognition and culture; based on a conference entitled "Cultural Knowledge and Domain Specificity," held in Ann Arbor, Michigan, October 13–16, 1990* (pp. 257–293). New York: Cambridge University Press.

Hickling, A. K., & Wellman, H. M. (2001). The emergence of children's causal explanations and theories: Evidence from everyday conversation. *Developmental Psychology, 37,* 668–684.

Kalish, C. (1996). Causes and symptoms in preschoolers' conceptions of illness. *Child Development, 67,* 1647–1670.

Kant, I. (1899). *Critique of Pure Reason* (J. Meiklejohn, Trans.). New York: Colonial Press. (Original work published 1787)

Keil, F. C. (1995). The growth of causal understandings of natural kinds. In D. Sperber & D. Premack (Eds.), *Causal cognition: A multidisciplinary debate. Symposia of the Fyssen Foundation; Fyssen Symposium, 6th January 1993, Pavillon Henri IV, St-Germain-en-Laye, France* (pp. 234–267). New York: Clarendon Press/Oxford University Press.

Leslie, A. M. (1982). The perception of causality in infants. *Perception, 11,* 173–186.

Leslie, A. M. (1984). Infant perception of a manual pick-up event. *British Journal of Developmental Psychology, 2,* 19–32.

Leslie, A. M. (1994). ToMM, ToBy, and agency: Core architecture and domain specificity. In L. A. Hirschfeld & S. A. Gelman (Eds.), *Mapping the mind: Domain specificity in cognition and culture; based on a conference entitled "Cultural Knowledge and Domain Specificity," held in Ann Arbor, Michigan, October 13–16, 1990* (pp. 119–148). New York: Cambridge University Press.

Leslie, A. M., & Keeble, S. (1987). Do six-month-old infants perceive causality? *Cognition, 25,* 265–288.

Meltzoff, A. N. (1988). Infant imitation after a 1-week delay: Long term memory for novel acts and multiple stimuli. *Developmental Psychology, 24,* 470–476.

Meltzoff, A. N. (1995). Understanding the intentions of others: Re-enactment of intended acts by 18-month-old children. *Developmental Psychology, 31,* 838–850.

Michotte, A. E. (1962). *Causalite, permanence et realite phenomenales; etudes de psychologie experimentale.* Louvain, France: Publications universitaires.

Novick, L. R., & Cheng, P. W. (2004). Assessing interactive causal influence. *Psychological Review, 111,* 455–485.

Oakes, L. M., & Cohen, L. B. (1990). Infant perception of a causal event. *Cognitive Development, 5,* 193–207.

Palmer, S. (1999). *Vision science: From photons to phenomenology.* Cambridge, MA: MIT Press.

Pavlov, I. P. (1953). *Collected works.* Oxford, England: Akademie Verlag.

Pearl, J. (1988). *Probabilistic reasoning in intelligent systems.* San Mateo, CA: Morgan Kaufmann.

Pearl, J. (2000). *Causality.* New York: Oxford University Press.

Piaget, J. (1929). *The child's conception of the world.* New York: Harcourt, Brace.

Piaget, J. (1930). *The child's conception of physical causality.* London: Kegan Paul.

Ramsey, J., Roush, T., Gazis, P., & Glymour, C. (2002). Automated remote sensing with near-infra-red reflectance spectra: Carbonate recognition. *Data Mining and Knowledge Discovery, 6,* 277–293.

Reichenbach, H. (1971). *The direction of time.* Berkeley: University of California Press.

Rescorla, R. A., & Wagner, A. R. (1972). A theory of Pavlovian conditioning: Variations in the effectiveness of reinforcement and nonreinforcement. In A. H. Black & W. F. Prokasy (Eds.), *Classical conditioning II: Current theory and research* (pp. 64–99). New York: Appleton-Century-Crofts.

Richardson, T., & Spirtes, P. (2003). Causal inference via ancestral graph models. In P. Green, N. Hjort, & S. Richardson (Eds.), *Highly structured stochastic systems.* Oxford, England: Oxford University Press pp. 1–12.

Rogers, T., & McLelland, J. (2004). *Semantic cognition: A parallel distributed approach.* Cambridge, MA: MIT Press.

Rovee-Collier, C. (1980). Reactivation of infant memory. *Science 208,* 1159–1161.

Salmon, W. C. (1998). *Causality and explanation.* New York, Oxford University Press.

Shultz, T. (1982). Rules of causal attribution. *Monographs of the Society for Research in Child Development,* 194, 47, 1.

Shultz, T. R., Pardo, S., & Altmann, E. (1982). Young children's use of transitive inference in causal chains. *British Journal of Psychology,* 72, 235–241.

Shanks, D. R. (1990). Connectionism and the learning of probabilistic concepts. *Quarterly Journal of Experimental Psychology: Human Experimental Psychology,* 42, 209–237.

Shanks, D. R., & Dickinson, A. (1987). Associative accounts of causality judgment. In G. H. Bower (Ed.), *The psychology of learning and motivation: Advances in research and theory* (Vol. 21, pp. 229–261). San Diego, CA: Academic Press.

Shanks, D. R., Holyoak, K., & Medin, D. L. (1996). *Causal learning.* San Diego, CA: Academic Press.

Shipley, B. (2000). *Cause and correlation in biology.* Oxford, England: Oxford University Press.

Silva, R., Scheines, R., Glymour, C., & Spirtes, P. (2003). Learning measurement models for unobserved variables. *Proceedings of the 18th Conference on Uncertainty in Artificial Intelligence.* AAAI Press. pp. 191–246.

Sobel, D. M. (2004). Exploring the coherence of young children's explanatory abilities: Evidence from generating counterfactuals. *British Journal of Developmental Psychology,* 22, 37–58.

Sobel, D. M., Tenenbaum, J., & Gopnik, A. (2004). Children's causal inferences from indirect evidence: Backwards blocking and Bayesian reasoning in preschoolers. *Cognitive Science,* 28(3), pp. 305–333.

Spelke, E. S., Breinlinger, K., Macomber, J., & Jacobson, K. (1992). Origins of knowledge. *Psychological Review,* 99, 605–632.

Spelke, E. S., Katz, G., Purcell, S. E., Ehrlich, S. M., & Breinlinger, K. (1994). Early knowledge of object motion: Continuity and inertia. *Cognition,* 51, 131–176.

Spirtes, P., Glymour, C., & Scheines, R. (1993). *Causation, prediction, and search* (Springer Lecture Notes in Statistics). New York: Springer-Verlag.

Thorndike, E. L. (2000). *Animal intelligence: Experimental studies.* New Brunswick, NJ: Transaction. (Original work published 1911)

Tomasello, M., & Call, J. (1997). *Primate cognition.* London: Oxford University Press.

Waldmann, M. R. (1996). Knowledge-based causal induction. In D. R. Shanks, K. Holyoak, & D. L. Medin (Eds.), *Causal learning* (pp. 47–88). San Diego, CA: Academic Press.

Waldmann, M. R. (2000). Competition among causes but not effects in predictive and diagnostic learning. *Journal of Experimental Psychology: Learning, Memory, and Cognition,* 26, 53–76.

Waldmann, M. R., & Holyoak, K. J. (1992). Predictive and diagnostic learning within causal models: Asymmetries in cue competition. *Journal of Experimental Psychology: General,* 121, 222–236.

Wasserman, E. A., & Berglan, L. R. (1998). Backward blocking and recovery from overshadowing in human causal judgment: The role of within compound associations. *Quarterly Journal of Experimental Psychology: Comparative and Physiological Psychology,* 51, 121–138.

Wasserman, E. A., Elek, S. M., Chatlosh, D. L., & Baker, A. G. (1993). Rating causal relations: Role of probability in judgments of response-outcome contingency. *Journal of Experimental Psychology: Learning, Memory, and Cognition,* 19, 174–188.

Watson, J. S., & Ramey, C. T. (1972). Reactions to response-contingent stimulation in early infancy. *Merrill-Palmer Quarterly,* 18, 219–227.

Woodward, A. L. (1998). Infants selectively encode the goal object of an actor's reach. *Cognition,* 69, 1–34.

Woodward, A. L., Phillips, A. T., & Spelke, E. S. (1993). *Infants' expectations about the motion of animate versus inanimate objects.* Paper presented at the 15th annual meeting of the Cognitive Science Society, Chicago, August.

Woodward, J. (2003). *Making things happen: A theory of causal explanation.* New York: Oxford University Press.

Part I

_____

CAUSATION AND INTERVENTION

1

Interventionist Theories of Causation in Psychological Perspective

Jim Woodward

Introduction

Broadly speaking, recent philosophical accounts of causation may be grouped into two main approaches: difference-making and causal process theories. The former rely on the guiding idea that causes must make a difference to their effects, in comparison with some appropriately chosen alternative. Difference making can be explicated in a variety of ways. *Probabilistic theories* attempt to do this in terms of inequalities among conditional probabilities: A cause must raise or at least change the probability of its effect, conditional on some suitable set of background conditions. When probabilistic theories attempt to define causation in terms of conditional probabilities, they have obvious affinities with associative theories of causal learning and with the use of contingency information (conditional Δp) as a measure of causal strength (Dickinson & Shanks, 1995). *Counterfactual* theories explicate difference making in terms of counterfactuals: A simple version might hold that C causes E if and only if it is true both that (a) if C were to occur, then E would

occur, and (b) if C were not to occur, then E would not occur. Following David Lewis, counterfactuals are often understood in the philosophical literature in terms of relationships among possible worlds: Roughly, a counterfactual like (a) is true if and only if there is a possible world in which C and E hold that is "closer" or "more similar" to the actual world than any possible world in which C holds and E does not hold. A set of criteria is then specified for assessing similarity among possible worlds (cf. Lewis, 1979, p.47).

The interventionist theory described in the next section is a version of a counterfactual theory; the counterfactuals in question describe what would happen to E under interventions (idealized manipulations of) on C. The interventionist theory does not require (although it permits) thinking of counterfactuals in terms of possible worlds and, as noted below, the specification of what sorts of changes count as interventions plays the same role as the similarity metric in Lewis's theory. When causal information is represented by directed graphs as in Bayes net representations, these may be given an interventionist interpretation (Gopnik & Shulz, 2004; Woodward, 2003).

It is usual in the philosophical literature to contrast so-called type causal claims that relate one type of event or factor to another ("Aspirin causes headache relief") with token or singular causal claims that relate particular events ("Jones's taking aspirin on a particular occasion caused his headache to subside"). There are versions of difference-making accounts for both types of claim, although it is arguable that such accounts apply most straightforwardly to type causal claims. In contrast, causal process accounts apply primarily to singular causal claims. The key idea is that some particular event c causes some other event e if and only if there is a connecting causal process from c to e (Salmon, 1994). Processes in which one billiard ball collides with another and causes it to move are paradigmatic.

There are a number of different accounts of what constitutes a causal process, but it is perhaps fair to say that the generic idea is that of a spatiotemporally continuous process that transmits a conserved quantity such as energy and momentum or, as it sometimes is described in the psychological literature, "force." Theorists in this tradition often deny that there is any intimate connection between causation and difference making; they claim that whether c causes e depends only on whether there is a causal process connecting c and e, something that (it is claimed) does not depend in any way on a comparison with what happens or would happen in some other, contrasting situation (Bogen, 2004; Salmon, 1994). In contrast, such comparisons are at the heart of difference-making accounts.

Although most philosophical versions of causal process accounts are not committed to claims about the possibility of perceiving causal connections, an obvious analogue in the psychological literature are approaches that focus on launching or Michotte-type phenomena. Psychological theories that attempt to understand causation in terms of mechanisms or generative transmission (where these notions are not understood along difference-making lines) are also in broadly the same tradition.

Interventionism

Interventionist accounts take as their point of departure the idea that causes are potentially a means for manipulating their effects: If it is possible to manipulate a cause in the right way, then there would be an associated change in its effect. Conversely, if under some appropriately characterized manipulation of one factor, there is an associated change in another, then the first causes the second.

This idea has a number of attractive features. First, it provides a natural account of the difference between causal and merely correlational claims. The claim that X is correlated with Y does not imply that manipulating X is a way of changing Y, while the claim that X causes Y does have this implication. And, given the strong interest that humans and other animals have in finding ways to manipulate the world around them, there is no mystery about why they should care about the difference between causal and correlational relationships. Second, a manipulationist account of causation fits naturally with the way such claims are understood and tested in many areas of biology and the social and behavioral sciences and with a substantial methodological tradition in statistics, econometrics, and experimental design, which connects causal claims to claims about the outcomes of hypothetical experiments.

Although it is possible to provide a treatment of token causation within a manipulability framework,[1] I focus on the general notion of one type of factor being causally relevant (either positively or negatively) to another. There are two more specific causal concepts that may be seen as precifications of this more general notion: total causation and direct causation. X is a *total cause* of Y if and only if it has a nonnull total effect on Y—that is, if and only if there is some intervention on X alone (and no other variables) such that for some values of other variables besides X, there will be a change in the value of Y under this intervention. Woodward (2003) argues that this notion is captured by the conjunction of two principles (**TC**):

(**SC**) If (a) there are possible interventions (ideal manipulations) that change the value of X such that (b) if such an intervention (and no others) were to occur X and Y would be correlated, then X causes Y.

(**NC**) If X causes Y, then (a) there are possible interventions that change the value of X such that (b) if such interventions (and no other interventions) were to occur, X and Y would be correlated.

Before turning to the notion of direct causation, several clarificatory comments are in order. First, note that if **TC** is to be even prima facie plausible, then we need to impose restrictions on the sorts of changes in X that count as interventions or ideal manipulations. Consider a system in which A = atmospheric pressure is a common cause of the reading B of a barometer and a variable S corresponding to the occurrence/nonoccurrence of a storm but in which B does not cause S or vice versa. If we manipulate the value of B by manipulating the value of A, then the value of S will change even though, in contradiction to (**SC**), B does not cause S. Intuitively, an experiment in which B is manipulated in this way is a badly designed experiment for the purposes of determining whether B causes S. We need to formulate conditions that restrict the allowable ways of changing B so as to rule out possibilities of this sort.

There are a number of slightly different characterizations of the notion of an intervention in the literature; including those by Spirtes, Glymour, and Scheines (2000); Pearl (2000); and Woodward (2003). Because the difference between these formulations will not be important for what follows, I focus on the core idea. This is that an intervention I on X with respect to Y causes a change in X that is of such a character that any change in Y (should it occur) can only come about through the change in X and not in some other way. In other words, we want to rule out the possibility that the intervention on X (or anything that causes the intervention) affects Y via a causal route that does not go through X, as happens, for example, when B in the example above is manipulated by changing the common cause A of B and S. I also assume in what follows that the effect of an intervention on X is that X comes entirely under the control of the intervention variable and that other variables that previously were causally relevant to X no longer influence it, that, as it is commonly put, an intervention on X, "breaks" the causal arrows previously directed into X. In the case of the ABS system, an intervention having these features might be operationally realized by, for example, employing a randomizing device that is causally independent of A and B and then, depending on the output of this device, experimentally imposing (or "setting") B to some particular value. Under any such intervention, the value of S will no longer be correlated with the value of B, and (**NC**) will judge, correctly, that B does not cause S. Note that, in this case, merely observing the values of B and S that are generated by the ABS structure without any intervention is a different matter from intervening on B in this structure. In the former case, but *not* in the latter, the values of B and S will be correlated. It is what

happens in the latter case that is diagnostic for whether B causes S.

The difference between observation and intervention thus roughly corresponds to the difference between so-called backtracking and non-backtracking counterfactuals in the philosophical literature. The mark of a backtracking counterfactual is that it involves reasoning or tracking back from an outcome to causally prior events and then perhaps forward again, as when one reasons that if the barometer reading were low (high), then this would mean that the atmospheric pressure would be low (high), which in turn would mean that the storm would (would not) occur. Evaluated in this backtracking way, the counterfactual "If the barometer reading were low (high), then the storm would (would not) occur" is true. By contrast, when the antecedent of a counterfactual is understood as made true by intervention, backtracking is excluded because, as emphasized above, an intervention breaks any previous existing relationship between the variable intervened on and its causes. Thus, when the barometer reading is set to some value by means of an intervention, one cannot infer back from this value to the value that the atmospheric pressure must have had. For this reason, the counterfactual "If the barometer reading were low (high), then the storm would (would not) occur" is false when its antecedent is regarded as made true by an intervention.

Lewis holds that non-backtracking rather than backtracking counterfactuals are appropriate for understanding causation, and the interventionist theory yields a similar conclusion. This illustrates how, as claimed, interventions play roughly the same role as the similarity metric in Lewis's theory and how they lead, as in Lewis's theory, to non-backtracking counterfactuals, with arrow breaking having some of the features of Lewisian miracles.[2]

What is the connection between this characterization of interventions and manipulations that are performed by human beings? I explore this issue below, but several comments are helpful at this point. Note first that the characterization makes no explicit reference to human beings or their activities; instead, the characterization is given entirely in nonanthropocentric causal language. A naturally occurring process (a "natural experiment") that does not involve human action at any point may thus qualify as an intervention if it has the right causal characteristics. Conversely, a manipulation carried out by a human being will fail to qualify as an intervention if it lacks the right causal characteristics, as in the example in which the common cause A of B and S is manipulated. Nonetheless, I think that it is plausible (see the Interventions and Voluntary Actions section) that, as a matter of contingent, empirical fact, many voluntary human actions as well as many behaviors carried out by animals do satisfy the conditions for an intervention. Moreover, I also think that it is a plausible empirical conjecture that humans and some other animals have a default tendency to treat their voluntary actions as though they satisfy the conditions for an intervention and to behave, learn, and (in the case of humans) make causal judgments as if their learning, behavior, and judgments are guided by principles like **TC**. The connection between interventions and human (and animal) manipulation is thus important to the empirical psychology of causal judgment and learning, even though the notion of an intervention is not defined by reference to human action.

Second, note that both **SC** and **NC** involve counterfactual claims about what would happen if certain "possible" interventions "were" to be performed. I take it to be uncontroversial that the human concept of causation is one according to which causal relationships may hold in circumstances in which it may never be within the power of human beings actually to carry out the interventions referred to in **SC** and **NC**. (In this respect, the human concept may be different from whatever underlies nonhuman causal cognition; see section on primate causal cognition.) Both conditions should be understood in a way that accommodates these points: What matters to whether the relationship between X and Y is causal is not whether an intervention is actually performed on X but rather what would happen to Y if (perhaps contrary to actual fact) such interventions *were* to be performed.

SC and **NC** connect the content of causal claims to certain counterfactuals and, as such, are not claims about how causal relationships are learned. However, if **SC** and **NC** are correct, it would be natural to expect that human beings often successfully learn causal relationships by performing interventions; in fact, this is what we find. But this is not to say (and **SC** and **NC** do not claim) that this is the *only* way in which we can learn about causal relationships. Obviously, there are many other ways in which humans may learn about causal relationships; these include passive observation of statistical relationships, instruction, and the combination of these with background knowledge. What **SC** and **NC** imply is

that if, for example, one concludes on the basis of purely observational evidence that smoking causes lung cancer, this commits one to certain claims about what would happen if certain experimental manipulations of smoking were to be performed.

Finally, a brief remark about an issue that will probably be of much more concern to philosophers than to psychologists: the worry that **TC** is "circular." Because the notion of intervention is characterized in causal terms, it follows immediately that **TC** does not provide a reductive definition of causation in terms of concepts that are noncausal. I argue elsewhere (Woodward, 2003) that it does not follow from this observation that **TC** is uninformative or viciously circular. Rather than repeating those arguments here, let me just observe that **TC** is inconsistent with many other claims made about causation, for example, claims that causal relationships require a spatiotemporally connecting causal process. So, regardless of what one makes of the circularity of **TC**, it is certainly not vacuous or empty.

Let me now turn to the notion of direct causation. Consider a causal structure in which taking birth control pills B causally affects the incidence of thrombosis T via two different routes (Figure 1-1). B directly boosts the probability of thrombosis and indirectly lowers it by lowering the probability of an intermediate variable pregnancy P, which is a positive cause of T (cf. Hesslow, 1976). Suppose further that the direct causal influence of B on T is exactly canceled by the indirect influence of B on T that is mediated through P, so that there is no overall effect of B on T. In this case, B is not a total cause of T because there are no interventions on B alone that will change T. Nonetheless, it seems clear that there is a sense in which B is a cause, indeed a direct cause, of T.

The notion of direct causation can be captured in an interventionist framework as follows:

(**DC**) A necessary and sufficient condition for X to be a direct cause of Y with respect to some variable set **V** is that there be a possible intervention on X that will change Y (or the probability distribution of Y) when all other variables in **V** besides X and Y are held fixed at some value by other independent interventions.

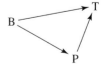

FIGURE 1-1

In the example under discussion, B counts as a direct cause of T because, if we intervene to fix the value of P and then, independent of this, intervene to change the value of B, then the value of T will change. The notion of X as a direct cause of Y is thus characterized in terms of the response of Y to a combination of interventions, including both interventions on X and interventions on other variables Z. This contrasts with the notion of a total cause, which is characterized just in terms of the response of the effect variable to a single intervention on the cause variable. The notion of direct causation turns out to be normatively important because it is required to capture ideas about distinctness of causal mechanisms and to formulate a plausible relationship between causation and probabilities (for details, see Woodward, 2003, chapter 2). Of course, it is a separate question whether the notion corresponds to anything that is psychologically real in people's causal judgments and inferences. I suggest that it does: It is involved in or connected to our ability to separate out means and ends in causal reasoning. It is also centrally involved in the whole idea of an intervention, which turns on existence of a contrast between doing something that affects Y directly and doing something that affects Y only indirectly, through X. We will see that even young children are able to reason causally about the consequences of combinations of interventions.

Finally, let me note that both **TC** and **DC** address a specific question: Is the relationship between X and Y causal rather than merely correlational? However, if we are interested in manipulation and control, then we typically want to know much more than this: We want to know which interventions on X will change Y, how they will change Y, and which background circumstances will cause the change—that is, we want to know a whole family of more specific and fine-grained interventionist counterfactuals connecting X to Y. We may view this more detailed information, which may be captured by such devices as specific functional relationships linking X and Y, as the natural way of spelling out the detailed content of causal claims within an interventionist framework. Such information about detailed manipulability or dependency relationships is often required for tasks involving fine-grained control such as tool use.

Additional Features of Interventionism

I said that interventionist accounts are just one type of approach in the more general family of theories that conceive of causes as difference makers. To bring out further what is distinctive about interventionism, consider the following causal structures:

$$X \leftarrow Y \rightarrow Z \qquad (1\text{-}1)$$

$$X \rightarrow Y \rightarrow Z \qquad (1\text{-}2)$$

Let us make the standard Bayes net assumption connecting causation and probabilities: the causal Markov condition **CM**, according to which, conditional on its direct causes, every variable is independent of every other variable, singly or in combination, except for its effects. Given this assumption, both structures 1-1 and 1-2 imply exactly the same conditional and unconditional independence relationships: In both, X, Y and Z are dependent and X and Z are independent conditional on Y. The difference between the structures 1-1 and 1-2 shows up when we interpret the directed edges in them as carrying implications about what would happen if various hypothetical interventions were to be performed in accordance with **DC**. In particular, if structure 1-1 is the correct structure, then under some possible intervention on Y, X and Z will change; if structure 1-2 is the correct structure, then Z but not X will change under an intervention on Y. Similarly, structure 1-2 implies that, under some intervention on X, both Y and Z will change; while structure 1-1 implies that neither Y nor Z will change. In general, if two causal structures differ at all, then they will make different predictions about what will happen under some hypothetical interventions, although, as structures 1-1 and 1-2 illustrate, they may agree fully about the actual patterns of correlations that will be observed in the absence of these interventions.

Although an interventionist account does not attempt to reduce causal claims to information about conditional probabilities, it readily agrees that such information can be highly relevant as evidence for discriminating between competing causal structures. Indeed, as I explain (Woodward, 2003, p. 339ff.), we may think of **CM** as a condition that connects claims about what happens under interventions to claims about conditional probabilities involving observed outcomes, thus allowing us to move back and forth between the two kinds of claims. Arguably (see the section on primate causal cognition), the ability to move smoothly from claims about causal structure that follow from information about the results of interventions to claims about causal structure that are supported by observations and vice versa is one of the distinctive features of human causal cognition. In this connection, there is considerable evidence that, at least in simple cases, humans can learn causal Bayes nets from passive observations, interventions, and combinations of the two. Indeed, for at least some tasks the assumption that subjects are Bayes net learners does a better job of accounting for performance than alternative learning theories.

I suggested above that an interventionist account will lead to different causal judgments about particular cases than causal process accounts. Consider cases of double prevention, in which A prevents the occurrence of B, which had it occurred, would have prevented the occurrence of a third event C, with the result that C occurs (cf. Schaffer, 2000). Cases of this sort occur in ordinary life and are common in biological contexts. For example, the presence A of lactose in the environment of *Escherichia coli* results in the production C of a protein that initiates transcription of the enzyme that digests lactose by interfering with the operation B of an agent that (in the absence of lactose) prevents transcription. There is dependence of the sort associated with interventionist counterfactuals between whether lactose is present and the synthesis (or lack of synthesis) of the enzyme that digests it—manipulating whether lactose is present changes whether the enzyme is synthesized—but no spatiotemporally continuous process or transfer of energy, momentum, or force between lactose and the enzyme.[3] Interventi-onist accounts along the lines of **TC** will judge such relationships as causal; causal process theories will not. Biological practice seems to follow the interventionist assessment, but it would be useful to have a more systematic experimental investigation of whether ordinary subjects regard double prevention relationships as causal, how they assess causal efficacy or strength in such cases, and the ease with which such relationships can be learned.

Double prevention cases suggest that energy transmission is not necessary for causal relatedness. Is it sufficient? Arguably, energy transmission between two events is sufficient for there to be some causal process connecting the two. However, the information that such a process is present is not tantamount to the detailed information about dependency relationships provided by interventionist counterfactuals. This is suggested by the following example (Hitchcock, 1995).

A cue stick strikes a cue ball, which in turn strikes the eight ball, causing it to drop into a pocket. The stick has been coated with blue chalk dust, some of which is transmitted to the cue ball and then to the eight ball as a result of the collision. In this case, energy, momentum, and force are all transmitted from the stick to the cue ball. These quantities are also transmitted through the patches of blue chalk that eventually end up on the eight ball. The sequence leading from the impact of the cue stick to the dropping of the eight ball is a causal process, as is the transmission of the blue chalk, and a connecting mechanism is present throughout this sequence. The problem is that there is nothing in all this information that singles out the details of the way in which the cue stick strikes the cue ball (and the linear and angular momentum that are so communicated) rather than, say, the sheer fact that the cue stick has struck the cue ball in some way or other or the fact that there has been transmission of blue chalk dust as causally relevant to whether the eight ball drops. Someone might both fully understand the abstract notion of a causal process and be able to recognize that the process connecting cue stick, cue ball, and eight ball is a causal process that transmits energy and yet not understand how variations in the way the cue strikes the cue ball make a difference to the subsequent motion of the eight ball and that the transmission of the chalk dust is irrelevant. Yet, this information, which is captured by interventionist counterfactuals of the sort described in **TC**, is crucial for manipulating whether the eight ball drops in the pocket.[4] As discussed below this observation has implications for primate causal understanding.

In general, then, an interventionist account predicts that, when information about spatiotemporal connectedness is pitted against information about dependency relations of the sort captured by interventionist counterfactuals, the latter rather than the former will guide causal judgment. For example, if the relationship between C and E satisfies the conditions in **TC**, people will judge that C causes E even if there appears to be a spatiotemporal gap between C and E. Moreover, even if there is a connecting spatiotemporally continuous process from C to E, they will judge that C does not cause E if the dependence conditions in **TC** are not satisfied. Similarly, for the information that something has been transmitted from C to E; although chalk dust is transmitted to the eight ball, subjects will not judge that its presence causes the ball to go into the pocket because the conditions in **TC** are not satisfied.

Despite these observations, adherents of an interventionist account can readily acknowledge that information about causal mechanisms, properly understood, plays an important role in human causal learning and understanding. However, rather than trying to explicate the notion of a causal mechanism in terms of notions like force, energy, or generative transmission, interventionists will instead appeal to interventionist counterfactuals. Simplifying greatly, information about a mechanism connecting C to E will typically be information about a set of dependency relationships, specified by interventionist counterfactuals, connecting C and E to intermediate variables and the intermediate variables to one another, perhaps structured in a characteristic spatiotemporal pattern (cf. Woodward, 2002). Among other things, such counterfactuals will specify how interventions on intermediate variables will modify or interfere with the overall pattern of dependence between C and E.

As an illustration, consider Shultz's classic 1982 monograph in which he argues that children rely heavily on mechanism information in causal attribution. This mechanism information can be readily reinterpreted as information about interventionist counterfactuals. For example, in Experiment 2, subjects must decide which of two different lamps is responsible for the light projected on a wall. Here, the relevant interventionist counterfactuals will describe the relationship between turning on the lamp and the appearance of a spot on the wall, the orientation of the lamp and the position of the spot, the effect of inserting a mirror in the path of transmission, and so on. Similarly, in the cue ball example, the relevant mechanism will be specified in terms of the dependence of the trajectories of the cue and eight ball on variations in the momentum communicated by the stick, the effect of intervening independently on the eight ball (e.g., gluing it to the table), and so on.

On this construal, detailed information about the operation of mechanisms is not, as is often supposed, something different in kind from information about dependency or manipulability relationships, understood in terms of interventionist counterfactuals, but rather simply more of the same: more detailed fine-grained information about dependency relationships involving intermediate variables.[5] An additional advantage of this way of looking at things is that it provides a natural account of how it is possible, as it clearly is, for people to learn that there is a causal relationship between C and E without knowing anything about a connecting mechanism. This is much harder to

understand if, as some mechanism-based approaches claim, the existence of a causal relationship between C and E just consists of the obtaining of a connecting mechanism between C and E and the information that C causes E consists of or implies information to the effect that there is such a mechanism. By contrast, according to **TC**, people will judge that C causes E if they are presented with evidence (e.g., from repeated experimental manipulations) that the relevant interventionist counterfactuals hold between C and E even if they have no information about an intervening mechanism.

Philosophy and Psychology

The interconnections between philosophical and psychological treatments of causation are complex and intricate. Many, although by no means all, philosophical accounts are (at least officially) intended as accounts about the world rather than accounts of anyone's psychology, that is, as accounts of what causation is or (less ambitiously) of constraints that hold between causal relationships, as they exist in the world, and other worldly relationships (having to do, e.g., with the obtaining of regularities). Nonetheless, it is common for philosophers to move back and forth between such worldly claims and claims that do sound more psychological: claims about what people mean (or ought to mean) when they make causal claims, the evidence on which such claims are or should be based, and so on. Even when no such accompanying psychological story is explicitly described, it is often implicit in or at least naturally suggested by the ostensibly worldly account. For example, it is natural to suppose that philosophers who claim that causation can be reduced to facts about conditional probabilities will also think that human causal beliefs and representations encode facts about conditional probabilities, and that causal learning consists of learning facts about conditional probabilities. Similarly, if a theorist claims, as some adherents of causal process/mechanistic approaches do, that whether C causes E has nothing to do with what does or would happen to E in the absence of C, one would not expect (at least on the face of things) human causal judgment to represent or to be sensitive to such information.[6]

Matters are further complicated, though, by the fact that insofar as philosophical accounts of causation have psychological implications, they are often presented primarily as normative rather than straight-forwardly descriptive accounts; that is, they are presented as accounts of the causal judgments people ought to make in various situations, how they ought to use evidence in reaching such judgments, and so on. I assume, however, that it is always in order to ask how these accounts fare when taken as descriptive theories: We may construe them as descriptive claims regardless of the intentions of their authors. Moreover, quite apart from its great intrinsic interest, there is an obvious motivation for proceeding in this way. Humans and other animals engage in a remarkable amount of successful causal learning and form many true or correct causal representations of the world. There must be some unified story about this that is both an accurate description of what they do and that enables us to understand how what they do leads, often enough, to normatively correct outcomes.[7] Asking about the descriptive adequacy of various normative theories is an obvious route to this sort of understanding.

In addition, there are many other interconnections between normative and descriptive theories. It is common for philosophers to appeal both to claims about the causal judgments that ordinary people or experts will make in particular cases and to claims about the types of considerations on which those judgments are based to motivate the particular theories they favor. It is also common for philosophers to make claims about how people's causal judgments connect with or fail to connect with various other concepts and patterns of reasoning, such as the use of counterfactuals, to motivate particular approaches. Claims of this sort are of course descriptive claims about the empirical psychology of causal inference and judgment and should be evaluated accordingly. In addition, although adherents of a normative theory always have the option, in any particular case, of responding to evidence that subjects do not in fact reason and judge in the way that theory says they should, by saying that such subjects are subject to processing limitations, or are confused, extensive and fundamental divergence between normative prescriptions and actual behavior is often plausibly regarded as at least a prima facie problem for a normative theory—a problem that the normative theory needs to address rather than ignore. In the spirit of these remarks, I explore, in the remainder of this chapter, some issues concerning the empirical plausibility of interventionist accounts and their philosophical rivals as descriptions of human and nonhuman causal inference and judgment.

Instrumental Learning

A useful point of departure is the difference between classical or Pavlovian conditioning and instrumental or operant conditioning. In *classical conditioning*, a subject learns an association between two events that are outside its control (e.g., an association between the ringing of a bell and the provision of food). The subject is thus in the position of learning through passive observation rather than active intervention, and what is learned is that one stimulus predicts another, where this predictive relationship may or may not reflect the fact that the first stimulus causes the second. By way of contrast, in *instrumental conditioning* what is learned is an association between some behavior produced by the subject and an outcome, as when rats learn an association between pressing a lever and the provision of a food pellet.

From an interventionist perspective, instrumental learning has a "causelike" flavor. An organism that was incapable of acting on the world and could only passively observe associations outside its control would have no need for a notion of causation or causelike representations, conceived along interventionist lines. Such an organism might still find it useful to predict what will happen, but sensitivity to correlations and to temporal relationships, rather than to anything distinctively causal, would suffice for this purpose. Given a correlation between two variables X and Y, it would not matter how the correlation arises—whether because (a) X causes Y or because (b) X and Y have a common cause—as long as the correlation is stable and projectable. The difference between (a) and (b) begins to matter when the animal is interested in whether changing X is a way of changing Y.

It is thus of considerable interest that there are striking, if incomplete, parallels between instrumental conditioning in nonhuman animals and causal learning and judgment in humans, a theme that has been systematically explored by Dickinson, Shanks, and others in a series of papers (Dickinson & Balleine, 2000; Dickinson & Shanks, 1995). Both instrumental learning by rats and human judgments of causal strength (as expressed in verbal reports) in instrumental learning tasks exhibit a similar sensitivity to temporal delay between action and outcome. Both rat behavior and human causal judgment are (independently of temporal relations) highly sensitive to the contingency Δp between action A and outcome

O, that is, to $P(O/A) - P(O/-A)$. Although there are important qualifications, both human judgments of causal strength and the rate of lever pressing for rats tend to decline as Δp approaches zero. In addition, in both humans and rats, learning of instrumental contingencies has a number of other features that give it a causal flavor; for example, both exhibit backward blocking, and both rat behavior and human causal judgment are subject to a discounting or signaling effect in which the usual reaction of nonresponse to a noncontingent reward schedule does not occur when rewards that are not paired with the instrumental action are preceded by a brief visual signal. As Dickinson and Balleine remark, "the intuitive explanation [of this effect] is that the signal marks the presence of a potential cause of the unpaired outcomes, thereby discounting these outcomes in the evaluation of control exerted by the instrumental action" (2000, p. 192).

These results suggest that both instrumental learning in rats and human judgments of causal strength (as well as actions based on this) behave as though they track the perceived degree of control or manipulative efficacy of the instrumental action over the outcome, which is what one would expect on an interventionist account on causation. In addition, phenomena such as sensitivity to contingency, backward blocking, and causal discounting show that at least some causal representation and judgment are sensitive not only to information about the rates of occurrence of cause and effect and the processes that connect them but also to information about what would or does happen in the absence of the cause and under the occurrence of potential alternative causes of the effect.[8] This is contrary to what some (psychologized) versions of causal process/mechanism theories seem to imply.

Causal Judgment and Interventionist Counterfactuals

I noted that interventionist theories are just one species of the more general category of difference-making theories. The sensitivity of causal judgment to contingency information is consistent both with various versions of probabilistic theories of causation and with theories that appeal to interventionist counterfactuals. Is there evidence that specifically favors interventionism as a descriptive account of causal judgment, at least in humans?

Let me begin with the issue of the relationship between causal and counterfactual judgments. Although, as noted, there are influential philosophical theories such as those of Lewis (1973) that connect causal claims to counterfactuals, many philosophers continue to regard counterfactuals in general (and *a fortiori*, their use in a theory of causation) with great skepticism. It is contended that counterfactuals are unclear, untestable, unscientific, and in various ways unnatural and artificial in the sense that they are philosophical inventions that correspond to nothing in the way ordinary people actually think and reason.

In fact, there is considerable evidence that people employ counterfactuals extensively in various forms of ordinary reasoning, and that they connect causal claims and counterfactuals in something like the way that interventionist and counterfactual theories suggest.[9] Since the relevant literature is vast, I focus, for illustrative purposes, on a charming set of experiments involving young children described by Harris (2000). Harris presented children aged 3–4 years with a number of scenarios that probed the way in which they connected causal and counterfactual judgments. He found, for example, that when children were presented with a causal sequence (Carol walks across the floor in her muddy shoes and makes the floor dirty) and then asked counterfactual questions about what would have happened under different possible antecedents (what would have happened if Carol had taken her shoes off?), a large majority gave correct answers (that is, answers that respect the intuitive connection between causal and counterfactual claims). They were also able to discriminate correctly between counterfactual alterations in the scenario that would have led to the same and to different outcomes, that is, which alterations in behavior would have avoided mud on the floor and which would not.

Children not only connect causal and counterfactual claims when explicitly prompted to do so by a question about what would happen under a counterfactual possibility, but also when asked why an outcome occurred or how it might have been prevented. For example, in a scenario in which Sally has a choice between drawing with a pen and drawing with a pencil, chooses the pen, and gets ink on her fingers, children who are asked why Sally's fingers got inky motivate the causal role of the pen by appealing to what would have happened if she had instead used the pencil. Indeed, children spontaneously invoke what would have happened under alternative possibilities in arriving at causal judgments even when those alternatives are not explicitly mentioned in or prompted by the scenarios. Harris's (2000) conclusion is that "counterfactual thinking comes readily to very young children and is deployed in their causal analysis of an outcome" (p. 136).

This conclusion may seem surprising if one is accustomed, as many philosophers are, to thinking of counterfactuals as primarily having to do with Lewis-style similarity relationships on possible worlds and similar metaphysical arcana. Clearly, small children (and for that matter most adults) do not have anything remotely like Lewis's framework explicitly in mind when they use counterfactual reasoning. But, whatever one's assessment of Lewis's theory, it is important to bear in mind that one of the main everyday uses of counterfactual and causal thinking, by both children and adults, is in planning and in anticipating what the consequences of various possible courses of action would be (without necessarily performing the actions in question). This is a perfectly ordinary, natural, practically useful activity and (relevantly, to our story) one that even small children appear to be much better at than nonhuman primates. Children engage in such planning involving counterfactuals and causal claims on an everyday basis when they reason, for example, that if they want to avoid getting their fingers inky they should use a pencil rather than a pen, that using a pen with blue ink rather than black ink will not avoid the outcome, and so on. If we think of counterfactuals of this sort, used for this purpose (notice, by the way, that the above counterfactuals are all interventionist counterfactuals), then we should be able to see that there is nothing particularly problematic or obscure about them.

Turning now specifically to the notion of an intervention, a natural worry is that this notion is too complex and cognitively sophisticated to be psychologically realistic. In assessing this worry, we need to distinguish two issues:

1. Do most people consciously or explicitly represent to themselves the full technical definition of a normatively appropriate notion of intervention when they engage in causal reasoning?
2. Do people learn and reason in accord with the normative requirements of the interventionist account?

I assume that the answer to Question 1 is almost certainly no for most people without special training. On the other hand, there is considerable evidence that the answer to Question 2 is yes, for many people at least some of the time.

To begin, there is evidence that, in a substantial range of situations, adults learn causal relationships more reliably and quickly when they are able to perform interventions than when they must rely entirely on passive observations (Lagnado & Sloman, 2004; Sobel & Kushnir, 2006).[10] This true for infants as well; Jessica Sommerville (chapter 3, this volume) reports a series of experiments that show that infants who actively intervene, for example, to obtain a toy by pulling a cloth on which it rests learn to distinguish relevant causal relationships between the cloth and toy (presence of spatiotemporal contact, etc.) more readily than those who rely on passive looking. Moreover, in at least some situations a significant number of subjects (although by no means all) intervene optimally when given a choice among which interventions to perform, choosing those interventions that are maximally informative. For example, when presented with a scenario in which there are several possible candidates for the correct causal structure, one of which is a chain structure in which X causes Y which causes Z, people choose to intervene on the more diagnostic intermediate variable Y rather than on X or Z (Steyvers, Tenenbaum, Wagenmakers, & Blum, 2003). This suggests some appreciation of the connection between intervention and causal structure.

A similar conclusion is suggested by a series of experiments by Lagnado and Sloman (2005). They report the following:

1. Subjects are told that billiard ball 1 causes ball 2 to move, which causes ball 3 to move. Almost all judge that if ball 2 were unable to move, then ball 1 would still have moved, and that billiard ball 3 would not have. On other hand, when presented with a parallel scenario involving conditionals that lack an obvious causal interpretation and are of the form if p then q, if q then r, subjects' responses are far more variable, with a considerable number willing to infer not p from the information than not q. In another words, most subjects endorse the non-backtracking counterfactuals associated with interventionist accounts in the causal scenario but respond differently to noncausal conditionals, for which a considerable number

do endorse a backtracking, noninterventionist interpretation.

2. Subjects are presented with a chain structure in which they are told that A causes B, which causes C. They are then told either (a) someone intervened directly on B, preventing it from happening or (b) we observe that B did not happen. Again, consistent with the interventionist account, subjects treat the intervention condition (a) differently from the observation condition (b). For example, they judge that the probability of A is higher in the intervention condition than in the observation condition; that is, they do not backtrack in the former and are more likely to in the latter.

These and other experiments involving more complex causal structures suggest that subjects do indeed distinguish between observing and intervening in the way that the interventionist account says they should, that in at least some situations they interpret an intervention in an arrow-breaking way, and that they associate interventionist non-backtracking counterfactuals with causal claims and employ them in contexts in which a causal interpretation is natural or a reasonable default, while being at least somewhat more inclined to use non-backtracking counterfactuals in contexts that are obviously noncausal. These results seem inconsistent with claims (e.g., Bennett, 1984) in the philosophical literature that people either do not distinguish at all between backtracking and non-backtracking counterfactuals or do not preferentially employ the latter in contexts involving causal reasoning. In addition, the experiments provide additional evidence (if any is needed) that subjects are indeed able to engage in sophisticated normatively appropriate counterfactual reasoning regarding causal situations.

Interventions and Voluntary Actions

I noted that in many situations people make more reliable causal inferences when they are able to intervene. From a design viewpoint, one thus might expect that subjects will have more confidence in causal inferences and judgments that are directly associated with their interventions and perhaps that some of these inferences will be fairly automatic. This suggests the following hypothesis: Human beings (and perhaps some animals) have (a) a default tendency to behave or reason as though they take their own voluntary actions to have the characteristics of interventions and (b) associated with this a strong tendency to take changes that temporally follow those interventions (presumably with a relatively short delay) as caused by them.[11] *Voluntary* here means nothing metaphysically fancy, just the commonsense distinction between deliberately pouring the milk in one's coffee and spilling it accidentally.

I noted that it is not psychologically realistic to suppose that most people operate with an explicit representation of the full technical definition of the notion of an intervention. Taken together, (a) and (b) suggest one way in which it is nonetheless possible for such subjects to use their interventions (note: not their explicit concepts of intervention) to reach fairly reliable causal conclusions in a way that respects principles like (**TC**). For an account along these lines to work, several things must be true. First, subjects must have some way of determining (some signal that tells them) when they have performed a voluntary action, and this signal must be somewhat reliable, at least in ordinary circumstances. Second, voluntary actions (again in ordinary, ecologically realistic circumstances) must—not always, but often enough—have the characteristics of an intervention.

I suggest that both claims are true. First, human subjects do have a characteristic phenomenology associated with voluntary action; they typically have a sense of agency or ownership of their behavior that is not present when they act involuntarily.[12] This is not surprising: Presumably, it is important for humans and other animals to have some way of distinguishing those cases in which a change occurs in their environments or in their bodies that results from their voluntary actions from those cases in which the change comes about in some other way—not as a result of a movement of their bodies at all or as a result of a movement that is nonvoluntary. It is plausible that one role for the feeling of ownership of one's action is to provide information that helps organisms to monitor this distinction. Once this feeling is available, it may be used for many purposes, including causal inference.

Turning now to the status of (b), it is clear that the correlation between voluntariness and satisfaction of the conditions for an intervention is imperfect. In a badly designed clinical trial, an experimenter might be subconsciously influenced, in decisions to give a drug to some patients and withhold it from others, by the health of the patients; his decisions are voluntary and yet correlated with an independent cause of recovery in a way that means that the conditions for an intervention are not satisfied. Nonetheless, it seems plausible that many voluntary actions do, as a matter of empirical fact, satisfy the conditions for an intervention. If I come on a wall switch in an unfamiliar house and find that there is a regular association between my flipping the position of the switch and whether a certain overhead light is on or off, then often enough flippings will satisfy the conditions for an intervention on the position of the switch with respect to the state of the light. Similarly for a baby whose leg is attached by a string to a mobile and who observes a correlation between leg movements and the motion of the mobile. In both cases, subjects who are guided by (a) and (b) will make fairly reliable causal inferences. The existence of causal illusions in which we experience or "perceive" salient changes that follow our voluntary actions as caused by them similarly suggests that such a heuristic is at work.[13] Going further, it might be conjectured that involuntary behavior is less likely to meet the conditions for an intervention.[14] If this is so, then one might expect that the impression of causal efficacy for outcomes following such behavior should be attenuated. Premack and Premack (2003) report that this is the case, although more systematic experimental investigation would be desirable.

Primate Causal Cognition

Despite the abilities of nonhuman animals in instrumental learning tasks and the similarities between animal instrumental and human causal learning described, it is a striking fact that nonhuman animals, including primates, are greatly inferior to humans, including small children, at many tasks involving causal learning, especially those involving tool use, object manipulation, and an understanding of "folk physics." This is so despite the fact that nonhuman primates and many other mammals have capacities on object permanence and trajectory completion tasks (capacities that are often taken to demonstrate the possession of "causal" concepts in the psychological literature) that that are apparently not so very different from those possessed by human children and adults. This suggests that although these various abilities may well be necessary for the acquisition of the causal learning abilities and understanding possessed by

human beings, they are not sufficient. Can an interventionist perspective cast light on what more is involved?

In approaching this question, let me begin by briefly describing some representative experimental results involving nonhuman primates. In experiments conducted by Kohler and subsequently repeated by others, apes (including chimps, orangutans, and gorillas) were presented with problems that required stacking several boxes on top of each other to reach a food reward. In comparison with humans, including children, the apes had great difficulty. They behaved as though they had no understanding of the physical principles underlying the balancing of the boxes and the achievement of structures capable of providing stable support; as Kohler put it, they had "practically no statics" (Kohler, 1927, p. 149, quoted in Povinelli, 2000, p. 79). The structures they succeeded in building, after considerable trial and error, were highly unstable, and completely neglected center of gravity considerations, with boxes at an upper level extending in a haphazard way far over the edges of lower-level boxes. Subjects even on occasion removed lower-level boxes from beneath boxes they supported. Errors of this sort were made repeatedly, suggesting what from a human perspective would be described as complete lack of insight into the principles governing the construction of stable structures. When stable structures were achieved, this appeared to be the result of trial-and-error learning. There was little evidence that the apes were able to reason hypothetically about what would happen if they were to create this or that structure, without actually creating the structures in question, and then use this reasoning to guide their actions in the way that, for example, the children in Harris's experiments were able to reason.

In another series of experiments, conducted by Visalberghi and Trinca (1989), a desirable food item was placed in a transparent hollow tube, and the animals were given various tools that might be used to push it out. Both apes and monkeys were able to solve some variants of this problem. For example, when given a bundle of sticks that was too thick to fit into the tube, they unbundled the sticks and used appropriate size sticks to dislodge the food item. On the other hand, they also frequently behaved as though they lacked a real understanding of the causal structure of the task. For example, they inserted sticks that were too short to reach the reward when a stick of appropriate length was available. They attempted to use sticks with cross pieces that blocked insertion into the tube. They also inserted nonrigid objects like tape that were incapable of displacing the food. In still other experiments, the animals failed to choose implements with a hook at the end, which would have been effective in retrieving desired objects, instead of straight sticks, which were not.

Povinelli's summary is that the animals "appear to understand very little about why their successful actions are effective" (2000, p. 104). In particular, they appeared not to understand the significance of the mechanical properties of the systems they were dealing with—properties such as weight, rigidity, shape, center of mass, and so on. Instead, as both Povinelli (2000) and Call and Tomasello (1997) remark, they often acted as though (any) spatiotemporal contact between the target object they wished to manipulate and the means employed was sufficient to achieve the desired manipulation.

Both Povinelli (2000) and Call and Tomasello (1997) go on to suggest a more general characterization of the deficits exhibited in the experiments: They claim that these stem from the animals' lack of various abstract concepts having to do with "unobservables" (Povinelli, 2000, p. 300, mentions gravity, force, shape, and mass, among others) that humans think of as mediating causal relationships. In contrast to humans, apes operate entirely within a framework of properties that can be readily perceived, and this underlies their lack of causal understanding.

Philosophers of science are likely to find this invocation of unobservables puzzling. If we think of a property as observable for a subject as long as the subject can reliably discriminate whether it is present (or among different values if the property is quantitative) by perceptual means, then it seems implausible that properties like weight and shape are literally unobservable by apes—presumably, apes can be trained to discriminate reliably between objects of different shapes or weights. There is, however, an alternative way of understanding this claim that makes it seem far more plausible.[15]

Suppose that when an ape learns to discriminate among objects according to (what we would call) weight, the discrimination is made on the basis of sensory feedback and bodily sensations associated with differential effort in lifting. If apes' "concept" of weight is closely linked to these bodily sensations, then it becomes more understandable why they are apparently unable to make use of information about

weight in other sorts of contexts requiring causal reasoning—why, for example, they are unable to recognize the relevance of weight to support relationships. To recognize the relevance of weight to these contexts requires possession of a more abstract way of thinking about weight that is not so closely tied to sensory and motor experience. Similarly for properties like rigidity.

In this way of thinking about the matter, the apes (in comparison with humans) operate with the wrong variables to enable them to engage in the kind of sophisticated causal learning required for the tasks described above; their variables are too closely linked to egocentric sensory experience. From the perspective of the interventionist account, we might describe this as a situation in which certain interventionist counterfactuals cannot be learned by the apes because the variables in terms of which those counterfactuals are framed are unavailable to the apes. For example, apes are unable to learn the appropriate interventionist counterfactuals involving the human concept of weight because they lack that concept. Whether this analysis is accepted, it seems clear, as a more general point, that whatever the apes' grasp of notions like weight and rigidity, they do not understand their causal relevance to the tasks with which they are dealing and cannot integrate these notions into causal representations that successfully guide action in connection with those tasks.

As I see it, this sort of limitation in the apes' understanding is not just a matter of their failure to grasp the abstract notion of a causal process (as a process that transmits force, energy, etc.) or an inability to recognize particular instances of such a process in the system of interest. As noted in the section entitled Additional Features of Interventionism, grasp notion of a causal process is *not* sufficient for the sort of detailed knowledge of dependency relationships that is required for successful manipulation in tasks like balancing boxes or extracting food from a tube. What needs to be explained is the apes' lack of this latter sort of knowledge.

Whenever a primate moves a food source with a stick—whether the food is pushed in an appropriate or inappropriate direction or with an appropriate instrument—there will be transmission of force and energy, the presence of a mechanism, and so on. A creature that possessed the concept of force and "generative transmission" (and could recognize when force was transmitted) and whose heuristic was: "to cause a desired outcome, transmit force to the outcome (or the object associated with the outcome) or set in operation a generative mechanism connected to the outcome" would not get useful guidance from this heuristic about exactly what it should do to balance boxes in the stacking task or to expel food from the tube.[16] To accomplish this, far more specific information about how the outcome that the agent wishes to affect depends on variation in other factors (perhaps including factors that are not linked too closely to egocentric sensory experience) that the agent is able to control is required, where these include factors not linked too closely to egocentric sensory experience. Thus, in the tube experiment the subject must recognize the relevance of the dimensions and rigidity of the implement chosen and so on. This looks far more like information of the sort represented by TC and DC than information about force transmission.

The idea that the apes lack the right variables (and hence cannot grasp counterfactual dependency relationships based on those variables) gives us one way of explaining at least some of their deficits in causal understanding. An alternative line of argument, which I see as complimentary to and not in competition with the "wrong variables" analysis and which also fits naturally into an interventionist framework, focuses on Tomasello and Call's notion of a tertiary relationship (1997, especially pp. 367–400). A relationship qualifies as tertiary for a subject if the relationship is understood or recognized as holding between objects and individuals that are independent of the subject. This contrasts with relationships that are (or are conceived as) more directly egocentric in the sense of holding between the subject and some other object or individual. Clearly, the ability to recognize and reason in terms of tertiary relations is closely related to the ability to think in an abstract or context-independent way. Tomasello and Call suggest that all primates (or at least all simians) have the ability to form and understand concepts of tertiary relationships in both social and physical domains. For example, primates seem to possess concepts of tertiary social relationships between conspecifics, such as the concept of one animal outranking another in a dominance hierarchy (as opposed to the notion of the nontertiary relationship of this animal outranking me).

This suggests the following question: Do primates understand (or at least behave in accordance with a conception of) causation as a tertiary relationship? As argued in the section on interventionism, the human concept of causation is clearly a concept of a tertiary relationship. Although people think of causal relationships as relationships that they may be able to exploit for purposes of manipulation and control, they also conceive of causal relationships as relationships that can exist in nature independently of their (or, indeed, any agent's) manipulative activities. Thinking along these lines suggests the usefulness of distinguishing among the following possibilities or "levels" of causal/instrumental understanding:

1. An agent whose instrumental behavior and learning is purely *egocentric*. That is, the agent grasps (or behaves as if it grasps) that there are regular, stable relationships between its manipulations and various downstream effects but stops at this point, not recognizing (or behaving as though it recognizes) that the same relationship can be present even when it does not act, but other agents act similarly or when a similar relationship occurs in nature without the involvement of any agents at all.
2. An agent with an *agent causal* viewpoint: The agent grasps that the same relationship that it exploits in intervening also can be present when other agents act.
3. An agent with a *fully causal* viewpoint: The agent grasps that the same relationship that the agent exploits in intervening also can be present both when other agents intervene and in nature even when no other agents are involved. This involves thinking of causation as a tertiary relationship.

Tomasello and Call (1997) suggest that nonhuman primates do not operate with this tertiary, Stage 3 conception of causation but rather with something closer to what I take to be the egocentric conception described in Stage 1 (cf. Figure 1-2):

We are not convinced that apes need to be using a concept of causality in the experimental tasks purporting to illustrate its use, at least not in the humanlike sense of one independent event forcing another to occur. More convincing would be a situation in which an individual observes a contiguity of two events, infers a cause as intermediary, and then finds a novel way to manipulate that cause. For example, suppose that an individual ape, who has never before observed such an

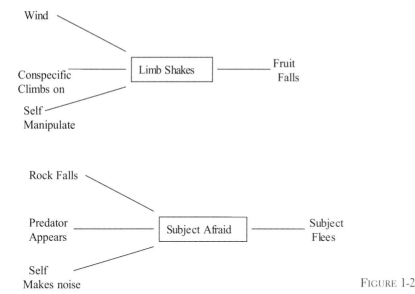

Wind

Conspecific
Climbs on   Limb Shakes ——— Fruit
                                      Falls
Self
Manipulate

Rock Falls

Predator —————— Subject Afraid ——— Subject
Appears   Flees

Self
Makes noise   FIGURE 1-2

event, for the first time observes the wind blowing a tree such that the fruit falls to the ground. If it understands the causal relations involved, that the movement of the limb is what caused the fruit to fall, it should be able to devise other ways to make the limb move and so make the fruit fall. . . . We believe that most primatologists would be astounded to see the ape, *just on the bases of having observed the wind make fruit fall*, proceed to shake a limb, or pull an attached vine, to create the same movement of the limb. Again, the problem is that the wind is completely independent of the observing individual and so causal analysis would have to proceed without references to the organism's own behavior and the feedback it might receive from that (thus, it might be able to learn to shake the limb if its own movements had previously led to a limb shaking and the fruit falling as a result). Moreover, performing some novel behavior to make the fruit fall would involve an even deeper causal analysis of the web of possible ways that the cause could be repeated so as to reinstate the desired effect. (p. 389)

Although some commentators (e.g., Povinelli, 2000) are skeptical, I think that these remarks help to capture some important features of the limitations exhibited in the primate experiments described above.[17] In what follows I want to develop some of the implications of this line of thought in more detail.

First, note that the transitions from Level 1 to Level 3 are important in part because they correspond to progressively stronger forms of instrumental/causal learning.

For example, if I am a creature who thinks only in terms of instrumental relationships that connect my own actions to outcomes (Level 1) and not in terms of Levels 2 and 3, then the relevance of observations concerning what happens under the interventions of others will be unclear to me. Suppose that I do X and observe that Y ensues, and that I have the ability to learn, from repeated experiences of this sort, that (usually or often) when I do X, Y regularly ensues. Clearly, it is logically possible that I might have this ability and yet not be able to learn or recognize that when another actor does X, Y ensues, then this is evidence that if I were to do X, then Y would ensue. Similarly, I may have the Level 1 learning ability just described and not be able to recognize that there are relationships that occur in nature in the absence of human or animal intervention that are such that I could make use of those very relationships for purposes of manipulation. Associated with this, I may not be able to learn from observing naturally occurring events that these instantiate relationships that I might make use of for purposes of manipulation. In short, in Level 1, the only way I learn about a manipulative relationship is if I perform the relevant manipulation. I take Call Tomasello (1997) to be suggesting that this is not only a logical possibility but also that something like this is true for nonhuman primates.

This line of thought suggests that susceptibility to instrumental conditioning shows only that an animal is capable of learning instrumental relationships in the sense of Level 1; it does not in itself show that the animal is capable of understanding or appreciating causal relationships in Sense 3 or the forms of learning associated with it. What would go some way toward establishing the latter would be evidence of transference between operant and classical conditioning.

Suppose that C is some outcome that an animal knows how to produce, and that the animal learns that C is associated with E just via passive observation or classical conditioning, where E is an outcome the animal wants. Will the animal spontaneously produce C (without extensive trial-and-error learning) to get E once it is given the opportunity to intervene? If the animal learns in an instrumental conditioning task that producing C is followed by E, then will the animal expect (or quickly learn to expect) E when it merely observes but does not produce C? Although there is some controversy surrounding this issue, the consensus seems to be that there is relatively little transfer back and forth between instrumental and classical conditioning.[18] This is consistent with the claims of Call and Tomasello (1997) about the inability of nonhuman primates to learn instrumental relationships from passive observation of causal relationships occurring in nature. If correct, then such claims do indeed suggest that the representations and abilities that underlie nonhuman instrumental learning are not fully causal in the human, Level 3 sense, even though, as indicated, they have many features in common with human causal learning and representation.

There is another aspect of the contrast between Stage 1 and Stage 3 that is worth underscoring. An animal that possesses only Stage 1 information is in effect in the position of possessing fused action-outcome representations and behavior patterns: representations that its behaving in a certain way produces such and such a desired outcome or goal. This need not involve any appreciation of causal relationships among variables that are intermediate between the behavior and achievement of the goal. It thus falls well short of what might be thought of as full-fledged means-ends understanding of how the goal might be achieved. This last does involve the postulation of intermediate causal links or what I take to be the same thing, some appreciation of the contrast between direct and more indirect causal relationships.

In particular, means-ends understanding seems to involve a decomposition of a task into an intermediate outcome O that can be produced fairly directly by the subject's action A and a further outcome O' that is more directly caused by O and less directly by A and

where the link between O and O' is a tertiary link between events rather than an action-event link. In Call and Tomasello's diagram (Figure 1-2), this intermediate outcome is described by the variable limb shakes, and this in turn causes the outcome described by fruit falls. Note that this causal relationship holds between events that are not manipulations by the animal.

As Call and Tomasello (1997) suggest, and is apparent from their diagram, it is the introduction of the intermediate variable that makes possible (or corresponds to) the recognition that there are different ways (involving both actions and events occurring in nature) in which the same goal (fruit falls) might be brought about, all of which have in common the fact that they operate through the intermediate variable limb shaking.[19] In general, the postulation of the intermediate link (and with it an appreciation that causal relationships can be more or less direct) goes hand in hand with a decoupling of sought-after final outcomes and the means used to achieve them and a focus on the latter as a separate entity.

As Call and Tomasello (1997) and Tomasello (1999) argue, this decoupling is closely linked to learning through imitation, that is, through observing the interventions of others. The issue of whether nonhuman primates ever learn through genuine imitation, as opposed to such other possibilities as emulation learning, is a complex and controversial one involving, among other things, disputes over how to best characterize imitation and issues about the theory of mind skills required for this activity. However, it seems uncontroversial that, in comparison with humans, including young children, nonhuman animals, including primates, are much inferior at learning means-ends relationships and appropriate tool use by observing the manipulations of other conspecifics. It also seems uncontroversial that, whatever else is required for successful imitation, the ability to perform the kind of means-ends (goal) decomposition described by Call and Tomasello is essential.

One reason for thinking this is that if imitation is to be successful, then it will often not involve the exact copying of another animal's behavior, if only because the copier (particularly if a juvenile) may differ from the target in size, strength, and other relevant characteristics. The successful imitator must be able, as Call and Tomasello (1997) say, to separate the overall goal of the imitation from the particular means employed, viewing the latter as an independent step, and be able to copy the means at something more like a functional level—that is, in a way that reproduces those of its causal characteristics that are essential to produce the goal—while at the same time varying other features to accommodate differences between the targets and imitators situation and abilities. This suggests (here, I take myself to be following Call and Tomasello) that we should expect to find the following abilities occurring together: ability to imitate activities that have a means-ends structure, ability to learn about complex causal structures through combinations of interventions that reveal direct versus indirect causal relationships, ability to learn about causal relationships by observing the interventions of others, a conception of causation according to which it is a tertiary relationship, and associated with this an ability to use information learned about causal relationships through passive observation to guide interventions and vice versa. To a substantial extent, these abilities seem to be unique to humans, with nonhuman animals having abilities (a capacity for instrumental conditioning, ability to learn action outcome sequences, etc.) that have more of a Stage 1 feel to them.

Because a number of the experiments that most clearly show that even small children have these abilities have been performed by Gopnik, Schulz, and others (Gopnik & Schulz, 2004; Gopnik et al., 2004) and are described elsewhere in this volume, I confine the discussion to a brief overview, emphasizing general connections with the interventionist approach. First, young children learn not only the causal consequences of their single interventions but also, more interestingly, other causal relationships from combinations of interventions performed by others. They learn in conformity with a conditional intervention principle that is essentially just the definition of direct cause (**DC**). Moreover, they do this in contexts in which information about generative mechanisms, the transmission of force, and spatiotemporal clues cannot be used to identify the correct causal structure. For example, when confronted with a device with two interlocked gears A and B that move together, which may also be influenced by the position of a switch and which is such that the gears are removable only when the switch is off, the children are able to infer correctly that the motion of A causes B to move (when the switch is on), and that the motion of B does not cause A to move, not on the basis of intervening on A and observing the motion of B, but rather on the basis of information about what happens to A (B) when the switch is first turned off, B (A) is

removed, and then the switch is turned on. In effect, this operation shows that the switch does not directly influence B without going through A, while the switch influences A even with B fixed at the value "removed." Moreover, children can also acquire knowledge of causal structure from information about conditional probabilities and then use this information to predict the outcomes of new interventions or to produce new interventions that are appropriate for desired goals. That is, they can transfer or move back and forth between observational and intervention-based causal learning in a way that nonhuman animals apparently cannot.

The important role that learning from the interventions of others appears to play in the development of human causal understanding suggests that two abilities often regarded as rather different—the social cognition abilities involved in imitation and causal understanding of the nonsocial world—may be closely intertwined.[20] There is also independent evidence that young children are motivated to pay particular attention to the actions of other humans, and that they have primitive imitative or simulative abilities for parsing and copying the actions of other humans. One might speculate that these attentional biases and abilities (which seem to be specific to humans in some respects) are combined with instrumental learning abilities that are shared with nonhuman animals to enable the much stronger forms of causal learning exhibited by humans.[21]

References

Bennett, J. (1984). Counterfactuals and temporal direction. *Philosophical Review, 93,* 57–91.

Bogen, J. (2004). Analysing causality: The opposite of counterfactual is factual. *International Studies in the Philosophy of Science, 18,* 3–26.

Call, J., & Tomasello, M. (1997). *Primate cognition.* New York: Oxford University Press.

Dickinson, A., & Balleine, B. (2000). Causal cognition and goal directed action. In C. Heyes & L. Huber (Eds.), *The evolution of cognition.* Cambridge, MA: MIT Press, 185–204.

Dickinson, A., & Shanks, D. (1995). Instrumental action and causal representation. In D. Sperber, D. Premack, & A. Premack (Eds.), *Causal cognition.* Oxford, England: Oxford University Press.

Glymour, C. (1998). Learning causes: Psychological explanations of causal explanation. *Minds and Machines, 8,* 39–60.

Glymour, C. (2004). We believe in freedom of the will so we can learn. *Behavioral and Brain Sciences, 27,* 661–662.

Gopnik, A., Glymour, C., Sobel, D., Schulz, L., Kushir, T., & Danks, D. (2004). A theory of causal learning in children: Causal maps and Bayes' nets. *Psychological Review, 111,* 3–32.

Gopnik, A., & Schulz, L. (2004). Mechanisms of theory formation in young children. *Trends in Cognitive Science, 8,* 371–377.

Hall, N. (2004). Two concepts of causation. In J. Collins, N. Hall, and L. Paul (Eds.), *Causation and counterfactuals.* Cambridge, MA: MIT Press, 225–276.

Harris, P. (2000). *The work of the imagination.* Oxford, England: Blackwell.

Hesslow, G. (1976). Two notes on the probablistic approach to causality. *Philosophy of Science, 43,* 290–292.

Hitchcock, C. (1995). Discussion: Salmon on explanatory relevance. *Philosophy of Science, 62,* 304 320.

Hitchcock, C. (2001). The intransitivity of causation revealed in equations and graphs. *Journal of Philosophy, 98,* 273–299.

Kohler, W. (1927). *The mentality of apes* (2nd ed.). New York: Vintage Books.

Lagnado, D., & Sloman, S. (2004). The advantage of timely intervention. *Journal of Experimental Psychology: Learning, Memory and Cognition, 30,* 856–876.

Lewis, D. (1973). Causation. *Journal of Philosophy, 70,* 556–567.

Lewis, D. (1979). Counterfactual dependence and time's arrow. *Nous, 13,* 455–476.

Pearl, J. (2000). *Causality: Models, reasoning and inference.* Cambridge, England: Cambridge University Press.

Povinelli, D. (2000). *Folk physics for apes.* Oxford, England: Oxford University Press.

Premack, D., & Premack, A. (2002). *Original intelligence.* New York: McGraw-Hill.

Salmon, W. (1994). Causality without counterfactuals. *Philosophy of Science, 61,* 297–312.

Schaffer, J. (2000). Causation by disconnection. *Philosophy of Science, 67,* 285–300.

Schottmann, A., & Shanks, D. (1992). Evidence for a distinction between judged and perceived causality. *Quarterly Journal of Experimental Psychology, 44A,* 321–342.

Schultz, T. (1982). Rules of causal attribution. *Monographs of the Society for Research in Child Development, 47(1),* 1–51.

Sloman, S., & Lagnado, D. (2005). Do we "do"? *Cognitive Science, 29,* 5–39.

Sobel, D. and Kushnir, T. (2006). The Importance of Decision-Making in Causal Learning from Interventions. *Memory and Cognition, 34,* 411–419.

Spirtes, P., Glymour, C., & Scheines, R. (2000). *Causation, prediction and search* (2nd ed.). Cambridge, MA: MIT Press.

Steyvers, M., Tenenbaum, J., Wagenmakers, E., & Blum, B. (2003). Inferring causal networks from observations and interventions. *Cognitive Science, 27,* 453–489.

Tomasello, M. (1999). *The cultural origins of human cognition.* Cambridge, MA: Harvard University Press.

Visalberghi, E., & Trinca, L. (1989). Tool use in capuchin monkeys: Distinguishing between performance and understanding. *Primates, 30,* 511–521.

Wegner, D. (2002). *The illusion of conscious will.* Cambridge, MA: MIT Press.

Woodward, J. (2002). What is a mechanism? A counterfactual account. In Jeffrey A. Barrett & J. McKenzie Alexander (Eds.), PSA 00, part II. *Philosophy of Science, 69* (3, Supplement), S366–S377.

Woodward, J. (2003). *Making things happen: A theory of causal explanation.* Oxford, England: Oxford University Press.

2

Infants' Causal Learning

Intervention, Observation, Imitation

Andrew N. Meltzoff

Infants' Understanding of Interventions by Self and Other

Causal learning by children combines both observation and action. These two sources of information have not been well integrated in developmental theory. Following Michotte (1963), some developmental scientists argue that young infants are exquisitely tuned observers, and that their perceptual understanding of causality far outstrips their ability to use this information to manipulate the world. Following Piaget (1954), others argue that young infants learn little by pure observation—self-produced motor action is critical; cognitive development generally, and causal reasoning in particular, is charted as a progressive combination of action schemes.

Bayes net approaches provide a way of using both observation and action (in the form of "interventions"), combining them to generate veridical representations of the causal structure in the world. In fact, on some interpretations (Woodward, 2003), the link to intervention is crucial for observed patterns of covariation to be understood as fully causal. The concept of an intervention may help us move beyond a debate about the primacy of perception (Michotte) versus action (Piaget) to theories that map observations and actions to the same abstract causal representations.

For developmental scientists, one striking feature of the philosophical notion of an intervention is that it is abstract—an intervention can be performed by the self or by another person (or even by a "natural experiment" not involving an agent). We can learn not only through our own interventions on the world, but also by watching the interventions of others. This intriguing idea is incompatible with many classical views of infancy, which explicitly deny the equivalence between observing others and acting oneself. In classical developmental views, we observe others from the outside as a series of movements in space, but we feel ourselves from the inside as yearnings, intentions, and freely willed plans. The way we represent self versus other is fundamentally different. This results in a disconnect between learning by doing (self-action) and learning by watching (other's action). A prime developmental achievement is to bring these two modes of learning into line.

There are many ways of testing the psychological linkage between observed and executed interventions. I have used infant imitation, which has several virtues. First, imitation is natural to humans, even babies. Second, in imitating novel acts, infants fashion their interventions based on observing interventions performed by others. Third, it is widely acknowledged that humans are far more proficient imitators than other primates (Meltzoff, 1996; Povinelli, 2000; Tomasello & Call, 1997), and therefore we may be getting at distinctively human cognition by examining human imitation and its development. Fourth, computational models including Bayesian approaches have been applied successfully to both human and robotic imitation (e.g., Demiris & Meltzoff, in press; Meltzoff & Moore, 1983; Rao, Shon, & Meltzoff, 2007).

Historically, there are two principal theories of how infants come to imitate the acts of others: Skinnerian and Piagetian theory. I argue that neither of these can encompass the modern empirical work on infant imitation. The new data are more compatible with the view that there is a fundamental equivalence between the perception and performance of goal-directed acts—an abstract mapping connecting acts seen and acts done—that was not envisioned in the classical frameworks.

Skinner (1953) proposed that young infants cannot imitate the acts of others without specific training. When a young infant sees a mother perform an act such as shaking a rattle to make a sound, the infant does not know what movements to recruit to copy this act. Rather, the mother needs to shape the child's response through operant conditioning. Mom shakes the rattle, and then the infant responds with random motor acts. Mom selectively reinforces those acts that are similar to shaking the rattle. Over time, the mother's shaking comes to serve as a discriminitive cue (a bell or a light would do as well) that elicits the reinforced act (the baby's rattle shaking). To the outside observer, the infant is imitating, but this is *not* because the baby is able to translate the acts seen into acts done. The parent essentially teaches the infant what to do and when to do it through operant conditioning.

This is not an entirely hypothetical example. In fact, Skinner (1953) has shown that pigeons can be conditioned to peck a key when they see other pigeons peck: If Pigeon 1 (P-1) pecks at a key to obtain food and an observer Pigeon 2 (P-2) is reinforced for pecking on seeing this event, then P-2 will eventually be shaped to peck when seeing P-1 pecking. But, P-2 did not learn this intervention on the basis of observing the other animal. All that has happened is that the behavior of P-1 has become a cue for eliciting a conditioned response in P-2. It follows that the observer pigeon could be conditioned to perform a nonimitative act just as easily. Skinner (1953) endorses this implication: "The similarity of stimulus and response in imitation has no special function. We could easily establish behavior in which the 'imitator' does exactly the opposite of the 'imitatee'" (p. 121).

It is known that human infants as young as 3 to 6 months old can be operantly conditioned quite readily (e.g., Rovee-Collier, 1990). This means that they can learn the contingency between their own actions and results in the world. But, the capacity for operant conditioning does not mean that the infant can learn these action-outcome relations from observing the acts of others. In other words, the fact that infants can learn an intervention through their *own* trial and error (learning by doing) does not mean that they can learn to perform the intervention on the basis of observing the interventions of others (learning by watching). The latter would be imitation. The former is just a special case of operant conditioning in which a friendly demon (a clever mother or experimenter) has arranged it so the discriminative cue matches the reinforced response. The moral is that if we want to know whether infants can learn an intervention through observation, then we need to know the infant's reinforcement history or, failing that, use a novel act for which prior shaping is unlikely.

Piagetian theory (1962) came to similar conclusions as Skinner, albeit for entirely different reasons. Piaget also thought that young infants could not imitate spontaneously. In Piaget's case, it was not that infants needed to be conditioned to learn to imitate, but rather that they needed to reach a certain stage of cognitive sophistication. Piaget realized that translating a seen intervention into one executed by the self was nontrivial, and he claimed it was beyond the capacity of infants in the first half year of life. He hypothesized that infants were "egocentric," even "solipsistic." The youngest infants could not learn novel acts from observing others (whether these acts were complex means-ends relationships or simple body acts) because learning at first occurred through self-action independently of other people (what Piaget called *practical intelligence*).

The Piagetian concept of infantile egocentrism was most famously illustrated in his predictions about facial imitation. Infants can see you make a facial movement, but they cannot see their own faces. If the infant is young enough, he or she will never have seen his or her face in a mirror. How could the infant link the observed facial acts of others with personal unseen bodily acts? According to Piaget, this "invisible imitation" was impossible because self and other were known in such different terms; there was no abstract framework for connecting observation and performance. Piaget (1962) put it this way: "The intellectual mechanism of the child will not allow him to imitate movements he sees made by others when the corresponding movements of his own body are known to him only tactually or kinesthetically (as, for instance, putting out his tongue) . . . since the child cannot see his own face, there will be no imitation of movements of the face [before approximately 1 year old]" (p. 19).

Thus, Piaget shared Skinner's view that actions could be observed and performed, but that the *observation* of an act did not engender the *production* of a matching act without a long path of prior learning. Neither Skinner nor Piaget thought that imitation was a mechanism for early learning; rather, imitation itself needed to be learned, and a good deal of theoretical effort was put into explaining how babies could eventually associate the observation of others' actions with manipulations performed by the self.

Newborn Imitation: Innate Mapping Between Observation and Execution

In part because of Skinner's and Piaget's theories about a gulf between the observation and the execution of human acts, I designed a series of tests of facial imitation in young infants. Contrary to classical theories, the results show that newborns imitate facial gestures. The work suggests an abstract notion of goal-directed action that cuts across the observed acts of others and one's own freely willed actions.

In an early study, Meltzoff and Moore (1977) tested facial imitation in 2- to 3-week-old infants. The results showed that they could imitate four different adult gestures: lip protrusion, mouth opening, tongue protrusion, and finger movement. The mapping between observation and execution was quite specific: Infants confused neither actions nor body parts. They differentially responded to tongue protrusion with tongue and not lip protrusion, revealing an innate

body scheme that maps from observed body parts to their own body, despite never having seen their own face. Similarly, they responded accurately to lip protrusion versus lip opening, showing that different patterns of action can be extracted and imitated when the specific body part is controlled.

As my psychology colleagues quickly pointed out, these infants may not have been young enough to answer the objections of Skinner and Piaget. In their 2 weeks of life, they might have learned the relevant associations. Perhaps mothers conditioned their children to stick out their tongues whenever they saw this gesture. The definitive test involved newborns who averaged 32 hours old at the time of the test. The oldest infant was 72 hours old, and the youngest was just 42 minutes old. The newborns accurately imitated (Meltzoff & Moore, 1983, 1989). Apparently, facial imitation is innate. This suggests a fundamental equivalence between the perception and production of acts that is built into the mind of the human baby.

Goal-Directedness in Early Imitation

Does facial imitation involve a "goal-directed" act? In this chapter, I discuss goal-directed acts that cause something to happen in the world. These simple bodily acts do not do that. Nonetheless, I think that early imitation is goal directed.

A characteristic of goal-directed action is that it converges toward the endpoint along flexible routes. This has been demonstrated in early imitation. Accurate imitation does not pop out fully formed. Infants have to work on it. They make errors and gradually correct their motor attempts to achieve a more accurate match to the observed target (Meltzoff & Moore, 1994). This error correction occurs even though the adult gives no feedback to the child (no smiles or encouragement) and, most important, even though the child observes the others' act but not their own.

The goal directedness of the response is also illustrated in the "creative errors" infants make. One study showed infants the novel gesture of poking out the tongue at 45° off midline (from the side of the mouth) (Meltzoff & Moore, 1994). The predominant pattern was to poke the tongue into the inside of their check and then gradually adjust. However, some infants adopted a novel approach. They poked out their tongues and simultaneously turned their heads to the side, thus creating a new version of "tongue to the side" (Meltzoff & Moore, 1997). This head movement was not something the adult demonstrated but was the infants' construction of how to combine a tongue protrusion and an off-midline direction. Although the literal muscle movements were very different, the end-state orientation of the tongue was similar, and in this sense it can be seen as an act organized by a goal.

The Innate Representation of Human Action

One way of accounting for these results is to hypothesize that infants innately represent the perception and performance of elementary human acts using the same mental code. There is thus something like an act space or primitive body scheme that allows the infant to unify the visual and motor information into one common "supramodal" framework (Meltzoff & Moore, 1997).

The nature of the supramodal framework can be further dissected. Three pieces of data suggest that the supramodal system is not simply a Gibsonian resonance device that directly turns observations into like movements—a perception-production transducer. First, the voluntary nature of the response indicates that the infant need not produce what is given to perception. The observations of others' acts can be stored and accessed after a delay. At minimum, there is an intermediary representation and not simply an automatic transduction. Second, as we have seen, infants correct their imitative efforts (and make creative errors). Information about one's acts has to be available for comparison to the representation of the adult's act, but the representation of the observed act is not confused with or modified by one's own multiple motor attempts. Third, infants show special interest in being imitated themselves; they recognize when their behavior is being copied (Meltzoff, 2007). Such recognition implies that there is a representation of their bodily acts.

This takes us beyond the simple transducer story. The data suggest a differentiation in the supramodal system. The representation of the observations are tagged to keep them differentiable from the representation of one's own motor acts. The cognitive act is to compare these two representations—in one case to match one's own acts to the other (imitative correction) and in the other case to detect being matched oneself (recognizing being imitated). The mental code may be abstract enough to unite perception and production, but the representations deriving from observation and self-action are not confused. They retain some source information (e.g., tongue-beyond-lips [observed] and tongue-beyond-lips [produced]).

I would argue that this fundamental equivalence (with differentiation) between self and other is a starting point for social cognition, not an endpoint reached after months of postnatal learning à la Piaget. The chief goal for the remainder of the chapter is to flesh out the thesis that these innately registered equivalences between observed and self-generated actions provide a substrate for infants' learning causal relations from others' interventions.

Learning Interventions From Observation: Making Things Happen

Adults manipulate objects to cause other things to happen in the world. Infants carefully observe adult's causally directed acts and begin reproducing what they see as soon as they become capable of handling objects.

One study tested whether 14-month-olds could learn an intervention purely from observation. To ensure that a new causal relation was being learned, a novel act was used (Meltzoff, 1988). The adult put a flat box on the table, looked down at it, and then bent from the waist, touching it with his head, which caused the top panel to light up. (This was an early blicket detector that was activated by human heads.) Later, when infants were given the box themselves, 67% of them leaned forward from the waist and touched the panel with their own foreheads. Many kept their eyes open, staring at the top of the box, and smiled when the light came on. Control infants showed that the baseline probability of infants touching the panel with their foreheads was literally 0%. Not a single infant did so in the absence of seeing the intervention. In a recent study, I changed the head-touch apparatus to incorporate a remote effect. When the adult touched the box with his forehead, this caused a remote box to light up. The remote box was 2 feet away. When the infants were given their turn, they touched the adult's box with their foreheads and immediately turned to stare at the remote box, waiting for it to activate (Meltzoff & Blumenthal, 2006). Carpenter, Nagell, & Tomasello (1998) reported related effects. Taken together, the experiments show that infants can learn novel interventions based purely on observation.

A Privileged Role for Manipulations Performed by Self

These head-touch studies show that infants can learn an intervention by watching others. Is anything added if infants perform the intervention themselves (Kushnir & Gopnik, 2005; Meltzoff, 2006)?

I conducted a relevant study with 14-month-olds (Meltzoff, 2006). Infants were randomly assigned to two groups. Infants in Group 1 watched the adult perform manipulations of two novel objects. The experimenter shook one object to cause it to make a sound; he held another one from a string and bounced it up and down on the tabletop. Infants observed these acts and then were sent home without manipulating the objects themselves. Infants in Group 2 were treated similarly but were immediately given the objects before being sent home. Virtually all of them imitated the actions they saw and thus had manipulatory experience as well as observational information.

The critical test came the next day when both groups returned to the laboratory, and the objects were put before them. The adult gave no hint what to do. Infants who had been given the opportunity for immediate imitation performed significantly more of the target acts on Day 2. Something appears to be gained if infants perform the action themselves directly after observing it. Infant performance is boosted if they quickly convert an observed manipulation into a self-produced manipulation. In line with the work on facial imitation, it appears that the actions of self and other are coded in commensurable terms, but that the self-produced acts are tagged distinctively from acts that were merely observed; converting observation into a self-action makes it memorable.

I hasten to add that infants can remember causal events without taking concurrent action. We know this because the first group of children, who only observed on the first day (by experimental design), imitated from memory on the next day. Evidently, the observed intervention can be stored and used to generate one's own manipulations after a delay. But, it is equally interesting that memory for the causal act is stronger if the act is first performed by the self before the delay.

Inferring an Intervention Based on Unsuccessful Action Patterns

Learning Actions Versus Learning Outcomes

We have seen that infants who see an adult use unusual means to accomplish an intervention do not simply reproduce the result (making the light come on) using any motor acts at their disposal (e.g., their hands), but instead faithfully copy the whole behavioral envelope. Based on this research, one might wonder whether means and ends are differentiable aspects of an intervention, or whether infants achieve causal results by reenacting the precise actions used by the adults.

This makes a difference to theories because it could be that (a) infants faithfully copy the adult's actions, and sharing body types and the laws of physics, the causal results naturally follow; or (b) infants represent the causal results and strive to achieve them by their own invented means. This is a tricky distinction to test empirically because if infants copy our actions, then they are likely to achieve our causal results "for free."

The way I investigated this question was to have infants observe an unsuccessful intervention. I wanted to test whether infants can read through our failed attempts and infer the intervention we intended to achieve. Because the adult's actions were unsuccessful, infants could not copy the adult's actions and achieve the desired result.

Inferred Interventions

I showed 18-month-olds unsuccessful interventions (Meltzoff, 1995). For example, the adult used a stick tool in an attempt to push a button to make a sound but "accidentally" under- or overshot the target. Or, the adult grasped the ends of a dumbbell-shaped object and attempted to yank it in two, but his hands slid off as he yanked, and thus the goal was not achieved. To an adult, it was easy to decode the actor's intended intervention. The measure of how infants interpreted the event was what they chose to reenact. In this case the "correct answer" was not to imitate the manipulation that was seen (the unsuccessful attempt), but to perform the intervention the adult "meant to do."

The study compared infants' tendency to perform the target act in several situations: (a) after they saw the successful intervention demonstrated, (b) after they saw the unsuccessful attempt to perform the intervention, and (c) after the intervention was neither shown nor attempted (control). The results showed that 18-month-olds can infer interventions from adult attempts to perform them. Infants who saw the unsuccessful attempts and infants who saw the successful interventions both performed the goal acts at a significantly higher rate than the controls. Evidently, infants can understand our goals even if we use means that are insufficient to fulfill them.

In further work, 18-month-olds were shown similar displays but were handed a trick toy that prevented them from performing the intervention (Meltzoff, 2006). For example, the dumbbell-shaped object was surreptitiously glued shut. If infants attempted to pull it apart, then their hands slipped off the ends, duplicating the adult's behavior. The question was whether this satisfied infants. It did not. They did not terminate their behavior. They varied the way they yanked on the dumbbell, systematically changing their interventions to find one that worked. They also appealed to their mothers and the adult for help. About 90% of the infants looked up at an adult within 2 seconds after failing to pull apart the trick toy, and many vocalized while staring at the adult's face. Why were they appealing for help? They had matched the adult's surface behavior, but evidently they were striving toward something else—the adult's intended intervention.

Inventing New Means to Achieve an Inferred Intervention

If infants are inferring the adult's goal, then they should also be able to achieve it using a variety of means. I tested this. As before, an adult grasped the ends of a gigantic dumbbell and attempted to yank it apart, but his hands slid off. The dumbbell was then presented to the infants. Infants did not even try to copy the adult's exact movements. Rather, they put their tiny hands on the inside faces of the cubes and pushed outward, or stood upright and used both hands to pull upward, and so on. They used different means than the experimenter, but these acts were directed toward the same causal result. This fits with the hypothesis that the infants had inferred the goal of the intervention, differentiating it from the surface behavior that was observed.

Work by Want and Harris (2001) goes further and shows that older children, 3-year-olds, benefit from observing others using multiple means to achieve a goal. They benefit more from watching an adult modify a failed attempt into a successful act than from watching the demonstration of successes alone. Other work also underscores the importance of goals in imitation (e.g., Gattis, Bekkering, & Wohlschläger, 2002; Gleissner, Meltzoff, & Bekkering, 2000; Williamson & Markman, 2005).

Agents and Goals: Infants Infer Interventions for Agents

In the adult commonsense framework, the acts of people can be goal directed and intentional, but the motions of inanimate devices are not; they are governed by physics, not psychology. Do infants interpret the world in this way? Meltzoff (1995) designed an inanimate device made of plastic and wood. The device had short poles for arms and mechanical pincers for hands. It did not look human, but it traced the same spatiotemporal path the human actor traced and manipulated objects much as the human actor did. When the pincers slipped off the ends of a dumbbell, infants did not infer the intervention as they did with the human agent. The infants were no more (or less) likely to pull the toy apart after seeing the unsuccessful attempt of the inanimate device than infants in the baseline condition. However, if the inanimate device successfully completed this act, then infants did perform the successful intervention.

Evidently, infants can understand and duplicate a successful intervention displayed by the inanimate device but do not read meaning into the device's unsuccessful "attempts." This makes sense because successes lead to a visible change in the object. Failures leave the object intact and therefore must be interpreted at a deeper level, in terms of the intended interventions of the agent. Perhaps infants do not interpret inanimate devices as psychological agents with goals and intentions; thus, no intervention is inferred.

In summary, the research shows that infants distinguish between what the adult meant to do and what he actually did. They ascribe goals to human acts; indeed, they can infer an intended intervention from a pattern of behavior (multiple unsuccessful attempts) even when the intervention was not performed. The acts of persons—but not the motions of mechanical devices—are understood within an agentive framework involving goals and intentions.

A Natural Experiment: The Primacy of People in Infants' Notion of Interventions

The Involvement of People Causes Infants to Interpret the Same Scene Differently

As we have seen, infants interpret the acts of people in special ways. This suggests a way of testing Woodward's idea of a natural experiment in which a causal event occurs without an agent as the source of the change. I showed 18-month-old infants an intervention and varied whether a person was involved in producing the result.

Infants saw the dumbbell-shaped object in three successive states. The three views were separated from each other by raising a black screen, so that the infants saw three snapshot views of an event that unfolded over time. What varied is the causal story of how it got to be that way. After infants saw the three displays, they were given the dumbbell. The question was whether they produced the target behavior, which was to pull the object apart.

Group 1 was a baseline control condition to assess infants' spontaneous tendency to manipulate the object. For this control group, infants simply saw three identical states—the assembled object sitting in place with no person present. As expected, infants did not pull the object apart spontaneously: They mouthed it, banged it, and slid it across the table, but they did not spontaneously discover pulling it apart in the absence of seeing this intervention. For Group 2, the three snapshots revealed the affordances of the object but did not specify the involvement of a person. The views were the following: (a) object assembled, no person present; (b) object disassembled, no person present; (c) object assembled again, no person present. For Group 3, the snapshots revealed an agent as a potential cause. The views were the following: (a) object assembled, in person's hands; (b) object disassembled, in person's hands; (c) object assembled, in person's hands.

Infants in Group 2 did not pull apart the toy; in fact, they did not differ from the baseline controls. In contrast, infants in Group 3 pulled the object apart significantly more often than those in Group 1 or Group 2. Thus, the involvement of a person as a potential cause led infants to interpret the same scene differently. In the case of the natural experiment in which the object was seen in its pre- and posttransformed state (Group 2), infants observed but did not try to re-create the event. However, if a person held the object, although sitting stony-faced and displaying no effort at acting, infants did so.

These results are especially interesting when combined with the Meltzoff (1995) intention-reading study. In that study, the dumbbell remains untransformed, and the person is trying to perform an intervention. In the current study, the person is present and shows no intent, but the results of the object transformation are shown (three static states: assembled, apart, reassembled). In the former case, there is human effort and no object transform, and this suffices for infants to infer the intervention. In the latter case, there is an outcome state and no effort, but if the

person is present, this can be interpreted as a potential cause for what happened. In both cases, it provides enough for infants to interpret the observations as relevant to their own actions and for them to fill in the blanks and produce a manipulation that was never directly observed but only inferred.

Agentless Transformations: Magic

In a further study, the dumbbell object was magically pulled apart and reassembled in front of the child's eyes but appeared to do so autonomously. This provides object transformation data in full view.

The object was placed on a black box, and inside the box there were magnets. The magnets were moved, and thus the dumbbell came apart and was reassembled without this being caused by a human agent. The results were that 15-month-olds did not pull the toy apart at any higher than baseline levels. Interestingly, half of the infants picked up the object and placed it back on the box several times, as if situating the object on the magic spot would cause the result. Infants saw the intervention and wanted it to repeat but, in the absence of a human cause, drew no implication for their own causal actions. Evidently, they thought the object transformation would happen *to* the object if it was spatially positioned, rather than thinking *they* could cause the transform through their own manipulation.

Learning to Use a Tool

In the developmental and animal psychology literatures, one of the most celebrated examples of causal reasoning is the case of tool use. We know a lot about the ability of chimpanzees to use tools—starting from Köhler's (1927) observations of Sultan moving crates below an overhead banana to reach it and extending to Jane Goodall's (1968) reports of termite fishing on the Gombe Stream Reserve. Although it was once argued that tool use was uniquely human, it is now widely acknowledged that other animals are successful tool users, including the gold standard of using a stick to obtain an out-of-reach target. The debate concerns whether animals use tools based on trial and error or based on insight about the causal relations involved (Povinelli, 2000; Tomasello & Call, 1997).

For the purposes of this chapter, I am interested in exploring tool use from a different perspective. Instead of asking whether animals and infants use tools when left on their own to "figure it out," I wish to examine learning through observation—in particular, seeing an expert use a stick to obtain an out-of-reach goal. The extant data are mixed. Tomasello and Call (1997) suggest that wild chimpanzees do not readily learn how to use a tool from observation, but that some enculturated chimps may; Povinelli (2000) remains skeptical of the latter.

The literature concerning human infants is similar. There is good evidence that infants can eventually learn to use sticks as tools when left to their own devices (Bates, Carlson-Luden, & Bretherton, 1980; Brown, 1990; Piaget, 1954) but much sparser evidence concerning learning from the interventions of others. Of course, it is well known that adults and older children learn how to use a wide variety of tools and complex machinery by watching experts; the debate concerns younger ages.

To test for observational learning of tool use, one needs a few conceptual distinctions. To begin, one needs to distinguish imitation from stimulus enhancement. The latter refers to the fact that the infants' attention may simply be drawn to a tool by virtue of the adult handling it. With their attention drawn to the stick, infants may increase their random play with the object, thereby increasing the probability that they will learn through trial and error that it can be used as a tool. The child is not learning a new causal relation based on what they see the other do. Rather, the child is learning that the stick is interesting—stimulus enhancement—and thereby is more likely to pick it up, with the rest following by chance or trial and error.

In the developmental literature, there have been surprisingly few well-controlled tests of learning to use complex tools through observation. Nagell, Olguin, and Tomasello (1993) performed a relevant experiment comparing chimps and human infants. They reported that the 18-month-old children failed to learn how to use a rake (to obtain a distant object) from observation, but that 24-month-olds could do so.

I tested younger infants. The sample consisted of 120 infants evenly distributed at 16, 18, 20, and 22 months of age (Meltzoff, 2006). Within each age group, infants were randomly assigned to one of three test conditions: (a) learning by observation, in which the adult modeled the correct use of the rake to obtain the out-of-reach goal; (b) Control 1 (baseline), in which infants saw no modeling and were simply given the rake; and (c) Control 2 (stimulus enhancement), in which infants saw the adult use the rake to touch the

goal, thereby drawing attention to the rake and to the fact that it could make spatial contact with the goal (correct use of the rake was not shown).

The tool was a 17-inch long rake. It was placed horizontally in front of the infant, with approximately a 2-foot spatial gap between it and the goal object. The goal was a highly desirable rubber giraffe. Infants had 1 minute to solve the problem. Preliminary studies in our lab suggested that infants performed better when they observed the model from a first-person perspective—when the adult and infant were side by side, rather than facing each other across the table. This may be important because previous studies have not modeled tool use from this perspective (e.g., in the Nagell et al. 1993 study the adult faced the infant, so the modeling entailed using the tool to pull the object away from the infant and toward the adult). Viewing the goal-directed act of the model from the same perspective as one's own may facilitate learning from observation.

Infants showed great enthusiasm for obtaining the goal (stretching out their arms, vocalizing, looking at the adult, etc.). In the two control groups, there was no significant difference in the successful use of the rake as a function of age. Across all 120 subjects, only 7.5% (6 of 80) of the infants solved the problem spontaneously; in contrast, fully 50% (20 of 40) of the infants succeeded after they saw the adult show them how to use the tool, $p < .001$. The older infants (20- and 22-month-olds) profited far more from observation (70% succeeded) than did the younger infants (30% succeeded), $p < .05$.

Infants learn from observation but not automatically. There appears to be an interaction between the infants' initial cognitive level and what they gain from observing others. The young infants learn, but they do not exceed spontaneous rates by the same degree that the older infants do. I would predict that still younger infants would not learn how to use the rake from observation. I say this because of the nature of the failures. After watching the expert adult, the younger infants pounce on the rake and wield it with great confidence. However, once they move the rake to the quarry, they are not be able to "think through" the causal relations—that the business end of the rake has to be behind the goal-object and the tines pointed downward before the rake could be pulled in. (Their reaction reminds me of undergraduates who get halfway through a difficult conceptual distinction and then, face fallen, find themselves lost, unable to bring things to conclusion. The "uh-oh, what-do-I-do-next" expression seems to be invariant across age.) One possibility that arises from this work is that infants have to be "on the cusp" of solving the problem themselves to get the boost from seeing how someone else solves it (see Gopnik & Meltzoff, 1986, 1997, for related findings). The older infants would be more intelligent consumers of the observed interventions. I am exploring this possibility through further research.

Conclusions

The work described in this chapter has implications for both psychology and philosophy.

Psychology

The power of imitation has always been underestimated in psychology. Skinner underestimated imitation because he thought it was simply a variant of operant conditioning in which the infants' response had been shaped up. Just as infants could be trained to perform Behavior X when they saw a red light, so they could be trained to perform Behavior X in response to Behavior X. There was nothing special about the match between self and other. Skinner thought that the opposite behavior would do just as well as a cue. I doubt it. I think you would be in for a long series of training sessions if you tried to teach a baby to open his or her hand every time the baby saw you close yours. The intrinsic connection would interfere with learning the arbitrary association.

Chomsky underestimated imitation because it was a learning mechanism. To say children learn through imitation means that they are sculpted by experience. Chomsky relegated experience to "parameter setting" or the "triggering" of innately structured systems. It is difficult to see how these concepts can explain the imitation of novel acts like head-touch. Infants duplicate this act, but it is unlikely to be biologically specified and simply triggered. Chomsky may (or may not) be correct about the domain of grammar, but in the domain of action, observing others' novel acts has a powerful effect of sculpting infants' own actions. Parents do not need to slavishly condition their child for the child to begin to act like those around the dinner table. The babies are observing and learning. Moreover, research suggests that "auditory observation" may be more powerful in language acquisition than traditionally assumed, particularly for the acquisition of culturally specific phonology. Kuhl (2004) reports that infant phonology, as indexed by both brain measures

and perceptual measures, is influenced by the sounds infants hear in their culture; furthermore, studies show that young infants reproduce speech sounds they hear through imitation (Kuhl & Meltzoff, 1996).

Piaget underestimated imitation because he thought that infants were born with "heterogeneous spaces"—a "visual space" that was initially independent of their "motor space." A major task of the first 2 years of life was to unify these spaces so infants could learn from watching, not just from doing. Piaget predicted that facial imitation was impossible until about 1 year of age and deferred imitation (imitation from the memory of observed, now absent, events) impossible before about 18 months of age. My research shows facial imitation at birth and deferred imitation soon thereafter.

These theorists missed the idea that there is a fundamental equivalence between observing and performing goal-directed motor acts. It is not that seeing and doing need to be linked by associative learning or conditioning. Imitation is innate. Infants can even imitate facial gestures they have never seen themselves perform. Infants have an abstract mental code, we call it a supramodal code, that unites acts seen and acts done within the same framework.

The innate equivalence between elementary acts of self and other has implications for learning about cause-effect relations. Instead of relying exclusively on the contingencies between your acts and the consequences in the world, you can learn through observing the actions of others—actions that you immediately recognize as "like my own." If acts performed by another make something happen, perhaps they will make the same thing happen when I do them. Such learning could not get off the ground if the observed acts were not recognized to be the same as my own acts. That much is nature's share.

Philosophy

Woodward (chapter 1, this volume) describes three levels of causal understanding:

1. A *purely egocentric* causal view: The subject understands the relationships between personal actions and the resulting effects but is unable to grasp that the same relationships can occur when the self is not the cause.
2. An *agent causal* view: The subject understands that the causal relationships that exist between personal actions and effects also apply to the actions of other people.

3. A *fully causal* view: The subject understands that the same causal relationships that the subject exploits in intervening can also be used by other agents and can exist in nature even when no other agents are involved.

The egocentric infant described by Piaget's theory (1952, 1954) closely resembles what Woodward called the *egocentric causal view.* This egocentric organism is capable of being conditioned because he or she can grasp the relation between bodily movements and effects in the world but cannot learn from watching the causal actions of others. The modern empirical results suggest that the egocentric infant is a fiction. Laboratory rats and other animals may conform to this description, but the human infant does not.

There is evidence, however, that up to about 18 months of age, the human infant is not fully causal in Woodward's sense. Several experiments suggest that the human infants learn interventions differently from a person than from an inanimate device (inferred intervention studies) and draw only limited inferences when no agent is present (natural experiment studies). Based on the current research, it may be that Woodward's (chapter 1, this volume) characterization of an "agentive view" is a reasonable description of the prelinguistic toddler. How and when an infant develops into a fully causal agent is a central question for developmental cognitive science (Gopnik et al., 2004; Meltzoff, 2006).

Summary

The perception of others' actions and production of self-action are mapped onto commensurate representations starting from birth. This allows infants not only to learn interventions through their own manipulations but also to multiply greatly their learning opportunities by observing the manipulations of others and profiting from them. For example, in the novel head-touch case, infants immediately knew how to activate the object 24 hours after seeing the adult do so, without ever having handled the object themselves. Importantly, infants do not seem to confuse acts of self and other. On the one hand, they correct their behavior (showing a retention of the observed target that is differentiable from the self's motor efforts). On the other hand, they treat their own acts in a privileged manner that suggests some sort of mental tagging that helps track whether an act was of external or internal origins.

Infants imitate but do not blindly copy everything they see. First, they make creative errors. Second, they skip over the literal behavior they see and choose to duplicate inferred interventions—what the adult meant to do, not what the adult did do. Third, when causal relations are difficult, as in the rake case for younger infants, observation alone does not seem to guarantee success; older infants glean more from the modeling than do younger ones.

Starting at birth, there seems to be a delicate interplay between learning by observation and learning by doing. The two are not quarantined from each other as Michotte (with an emphasis on observation over motor experience) or Piaget (with an emphasis on motor experience over pure perception) might have supposed. Instead, there seems to be a reciprocal exchange between these two modes of learning. What infants observe influences what they do (novel head-touch imitation), and what they can do changes their attention to the model and how they interpret it (tool use from observation).

ACKNOWLEDGMENTS   This work was supported by the National Institutes of Health (HD-22514), the James S. McDonnell Foundation, and the Tamaki Foundation. I thank Alison Gopnik for her causal powers as editor, colleague, and friend. I also acknowledge helpful conversations with Jim Woodward, Laura Schulz, and other members of the McDonnell Foundation Causal Inference Workshop at the Stanford Center for Advanced Study in 2003. Thanks also to Craig Harris and Calle Fisher for help on the final stages of chapter preparation.

References

Bates, E., Carlson-Luden, V., & Bretherton, I. (1980). Perceptual aspects of tool using in infancy. *Infant Behavior & Development, 3,* 127–140.

Brown, A. L. (1990). Domain-specific principles affect learning and transfer in children. *Cognitive Science, 14,* 107–133.

Carpenter, M., Nagell, K., & Tomasello, M. (1998). Social cognition, joint attention, and communicative competence from 9 to 15 months of age. *Monographs of the Society for Research in Child Development, 63*(4, Serial No. 255).

Demiris, Y., & Meltzoff, A. N. (In press). The robot in the crib: A developmental analysis of imitation skills in infants and robots. *Infant and Child Development.*

Gattis, M., Bekkering, H., & Wolschläger, A. (2002). Goal-directed imitation. In A. N. Meltzoff & W. Prinz (Eds.), *The imitative mind: Development, evolution, and brain bases* (pp. 183–205). Cambridge, England: Cambridge University Press.

Gleissner, B., Meltzoff, A. N., & Bekkering, H. (2000). Children's coding of human action: Cognitive factors influencing imitation in 3-year-olds. *Developmental Science, 3,* 405–414.

Goodall, J. (1968). The behavior of free-living chimpanzees in the Gombe Stream Reserve. *Animal Behavior Monographs, 1,* 3.

Gopnik, A., Glymour, C., Sobel, D. M., Schulz, L. E., Kushnir, T., & Danks, D. (2004). A theory of causal learning in children: Causal maps and Bayes nets. *Psychological Review, 111,* 3–32.

Gopnik, A., & Meltzoff, A. N. (1986). Relations between semantic and cognitive development in the one-word stage: The specificity hypothesis. *Child Development, 57,* 1040–1053.

Gopnik, A., & Meltzoff, A. N. (1997). *Words, thoughts, and theories.* Cambridge, MA: MIT Press.

Köhler, W. (1927). *The mentality of apes* (E. Winter, Trans.) (2nd ed.). London: Routledge & Kegan Paul.

Kuhl, P. K. (2004). Early language acquisition: Cracking the speech code. *Nature Reviews Neuroscience, 5,* 831–843.

Kuhl, P. K., & Meltzoff, A. N. (1996). Infant vocalizations in response to speech: Vocal imitation and developmental change. *Journal of the Acoustical Society of America, 100,* 2425–2438.

Kushnir, T., & Gopnik, A. (2005). Young children infer causal strength from probabilities and interventions. *Psychological Science, 16,* 678–683.

Meltzoff, A. N. (1988). Infant imitation after a 1-week delay: Long-term memory for novel acts and multiple stimuli. *Developmental Psychology, 24,* 470–476.

Meltzoff, A. N. (1995). Understanding the intentions of others: Re-enactment of intended acts by 18-month-old children. *Developmental Psychology, 31,* 838–850.

Meltzoff, A. N. (1996). The human infant as imitative generalist: A 20-year progress report on infant imitation with implications for comparative psychology. In C. M. Heyes & B. G. Galef (Eds.), *Social learning in animals: The roots of culture* (pp. 347–370). New York: Academic Press.

Meltzoff, A. N. (2006). The "Like Me" framework for recognizing and becoming an intentional agent. *Acta Psychologica,* doi:10.1016/j.actpsy.2006.09.005.

Meltzoff, A. N. (2007). "Like Me": A foundation for social cognition. *Developmental Science, 10,* 126–134.

Meltzoff, A. N., & Blumenthal, E. J. (2006, April). Causal monitoring. Paper given at the meeting of the McDonnell Foundation Causal Learning Workshop. Pasadena, CA.

Meltzoff, A. N., & Moore, M. K. (1977). Imitation of facial and manual gestures by human neonates. *Science, 198,* 75–78.

Meltzoff, A. N., & Moore, M. K. (1983). Newborn infants imitate adult facial gestures. *Child Development, 54,* 702–709.

Meltzoff, A. N., & Moore, M. K. (1989). Imitation in newborn infants: Exploring the range of gestures imitated and the underlying mechanisms. *Developmental Psychology, 25,* 954–962.

Meltzoff, A. N., & Moore, M. K. (1994). Imitation, memory, and the representation of persons. *Infant Behavior & Development, 17,* 83–99.

Meltzoff, A. N., & Moore, M. K. (1997). Explaining facial imitation: A theoretical model. *Early Development and Parenting, 6,* 179–192.

Michotte, A. (1963). *The perception of causality* (T. R. Miles & E. Miles, Trans.). London: Methuen & Co. Ltd.

Nagell, K., Olguin, R. S., & Tomasello, M. (1993). Processes of social learning in the tool use of chimpanzees (*Pan troglodytes*) and human children (*Homo sapiens*). *Journal of Comparative Psychology, 107,* 174–186.

Piaget, J. (1952). *The origins of intelligence in children* (M. Cook, Trans.). New York: International Universities Press.

Piaget, J. (1954). *The construction of reality in the child* (M. Cook, Trans.). New York: Basic Books.

Piaget, J. (1962). *Play, dreams and imitation in childhood* (C. Attegno & F. M. Hodgson, Trans.). New York: Norton.

Povinelli, D. J. (2000). *Folk physics for apes: The chimpanzee's theory of how the world works.* New York: Oxford University Press.

Rao, R. P., Shon, A. P., & Meltzoff, A. N. (2007). A Bayesian model of imitation in infants and robots. In K. Dautenhahn & C. L. Nehaniv (Eds.), *Imitation and Social Learning in Robots, Humans and Animals: Behavioural, Social and Communicative Dimensions.* Cambridge, UK: Cambridge University Press.

Rovee-Collier, C. K. (1990). The "memory system" of prelinguistic infants. In A. Diamond (Ed.), *The development and neural bases of higher cognitive functions* (Vol. 608, pp. 517–542). New York: New York Academy of Sciences.

Skinner, B. F. (1953). *Science and human behavior.* New York: Macmillan.

Tomasello, M., & Call, J. (1997). *Primate cognition.* New York: Oxford University Press.

Want, S. C., & Harris, P. L. (2001). Learning from other people's mistakes: Causal understanding in learning to use a tool. *Child Development, 72,* 431–443.

Williamson, R. A., & Markman, E. M. (2006). Precision of imitation as a function of preschoolers' understanding of the goal of the demonstration. *Developmental Psychology, 42,* 723–731.

Woodward, J. (2003). *Making things happen: A theory of causal explanation.* New York: Oxford University Press.

3

Detecting Causal Structure

The Role of Interventions in Infants' Understanding of Psychological and Physical Causal Relations

Jessica A. Sommerville

Introduction

Humans are causal animals. We see events not merely as occurring, but as caused. Integral to mature causal reasoning is the ability to understand particular causal relations in our environment. Indeed, adults readily detect both psychological and physical causal relations across a range of human action and object motion events. Imagine watching a dinner companion hungrily devouring his dessert. You might assume that the actor's grasp of the dessert fork is caused by his goal of obtaining the brownie, and that the movement of the dessert item on his plate is caused by the contact between fork and brownie. Thus, at a basic level, identifying causal relations involves at least two components. First, one must segment ongoing human action and object motion into psychological and physical causal episodes. In the example, one must recognize that the fork-grasping, brownie-moving, and brownie-eating actions cohere to form causal units. Second, one must identify variables relevant to causal outcomes. A desire or predisposition to eat

sweets and a particular type of contact between the fork and brownie are relevant to identifying the respective psychological and physical causal relations involved in our dessert scenario.

An integral question then is how an understanding of these rudimentary aspects of causal understanding is achieved. In this chapter, I argue that infants' experience of their own actions and the consequences that these actions have on the world play an important role in their developing understanding of causal relations. Recent philosophical theories of causation take an interventionist perspective on causality: If manipulations on one factor (interventions) are associated with a change in a second factor, then the first causes the second (e.g., Woodward, chapter 1, this volume). In addition, empirical evidence suggests that both adults and young children readily learn causal structure from enacting and observing interventions (see Gopnik & Schulz, 2004, for a review). In this chapter, I present evidence that infants' developing ability to act on the world is intimately linked to their causal understanding. Infants' interventions may enable them to evaluate causal hypotheses and detect the causal structure of various events in the world.

Infants' Understanding of Physical and Psychological Causation

A variety of research reveals that children have a rich understanding of the causal structure of the physical and psychological world (e.g., Gopnik & Meltzoff, 1997). By the end of the preschool period, children appreciate human action as psychologically caused: They describe, predict, and explain their own and others' behavior with reference to mental states (Bartsch & Wellman, 1995; Gopnik & Astington, 1988; Wellman, Cross, & Watson, 2001). These developments are paralleled in children's understanding of physical causation.

The sophistication of young children's causal reasoning has led researchers to focus on the origins of causal understanding. Work suggests that toddlers possess at least one key aspect of understanding behavior as psychologically caused: They understand human action as guided by goals. Eighteen-month-old infants readily imitate the inferred goals of others (Meltzoff, 1995), selectively reproduce goal-directed acts (vs. accidental acts; Carpenter, Akhtar, & Tomasello, 1998), and can distinguish between their own goals and those of another person (Repacholi & Gopnik, 1997).

Studies have assessed the roots of preverbal infants' ability to view human action as goal directed. This work reveals that even young infants construe simple actions of others as goal or object directed. After watching an actor reach for and grasp an object, 6-month-old infants attend more to changes in an actor's goal than they do to other, more superficial aspects of the reach and grasp, such as the reach trajectory or location (Woodward, 1998). Over the next 6 months of life, infants' ability to construe action as goal directed becomes increasingly elaborate: 12-month-olds also perceive attentional (e.g., eye gaze; Woodward, 2003), instrumental (e.g., point gesture; Woodward & Guajardo, 2002), and novel actions (e.g., pushing with the back of hand; Jovanovic et al., 2006; Kiraly, Jovanovic, Prinz, Aschersleben, & Gergely, 2003) as object directed. Infants can also move beyond construing action as goal directed to parse the ongoing stream of behavior into goal-relevant units (Baldwin, Baird, Saylor, & Clark, 2001) and are able to use previous action and attentional cues to predict future action (Phillips, Wellman, & Spelke, 2002; Sodian & Thoermer, 2004). These findings suggest that a key element of understanding psychological causal relations begins in infancy and is elaborated over the first year of life.

A nascent sensitivity to physical causal relations is also present in infancy. Traditionally, infants' understanding of physical causal relations has been examined from the vantage point of problem solving or tool use. Piaget (1953) suggests that causal understanding emerges toward the end of the first year of life; this was based on observing that his own infants developed the ability to use an intermediary object to achieve a target object (e.g., pulling a support to obtain an out-of-reach toy, pulling a string to get a toy) by this age. Additional empirical works bear out and extend Piaget's observations. Numerous studies demonstrate that, by the end of the first year of life, infants can solve a variety of simple tool use tasks (Bates, Carlson-Luden, & Bretherton, 1980; Uzgiris & Hunt, 1975; Willatts, 1984, 1999). Shortly thereafter, infants can generalize tool use solutions across problems based on their underlying causal structure, as opposed to strictly on the basis of shared perceptual features (Chen, Sanchez, & Campbell, 1997). Moreover, older infants not only can transfer causal solutions across problems, but also can pick tools to solve a problem based on their causal efficacy. After learning to solve a tool use problem, toddlers select novel tools based on their utility in goal attainment as opposed to their perceptual similarity to previous tools (Brown, 1990; Chen & Siegler, 2000).

Subsequent work has revealed that preverbal infants detect causal relations in certain types of object motion events. By 6 months of age, infants recognize the causal status of Michottian-type launching sequences and distinguish this causal event from other events that share spatiotemporal properties but are not causal (e.g., delayed launching and no collision events; Leslie, 1982; Leslie & Keeble, 1987). Over the next several months, infants' causal perception becomes more sophisticated. By 10 months of age, infants respond to the causal status of the launching events that feature real objects (Oakes & Cohen, 1990) and perceive the causality of launching events in which objects move along dissimilar paths (Oakes, 1994). It is also by this age that infants become increasingly sensitive to causal roles within a causal event (Cohen & Oakes, 1993). Several months later, infants differentiate the primary cause of a causal chain versus a temporal chain (Cohen, Rundell, Spellman, & Cashon, 1999). Thus, over the first year of life infants recognize physical causal relations in a variety of different object motion events.

Taken together, these findings suggest that the roots of causal understanding are present in infancy. Infants recognize psychological and physical causal episodes and can identify some of the variables affecting these relations. Controversy exists, however, over the means by which this understanding is achieved.

Mechanisms Underlying the Development of Causal Understanding

Some investigators have argued that infants are innately endowed with an ability to understand certain psychological and physical causal relations. For example, it has been suggested that infants possess an abstract system for construing action as goal directed, and that such a system is automatically activated by a set of perceptual cues (such as self-propelled motion, contingent action, etc.; e.g., Baron-Cohen, 1995; Gergeley, Nasady, Csibra, & Biro, 1995; Premack, 1990). Similarly, Leslie argues that infants' sensitivity to causality in launching events is guided by an innate perceptual module (e.g., Leslie, 1994).

However, innate knowledge cannot be the whole story. Prior to 6 months of age, infants respond to launching events on the basis of simpler perceptual features (e.g., spatial-temporal features) but not causality (Cohen & Amsel, 1998), and they do not spontaneously encode the goal of a human actor's reach and grasp (Sommerville, Woodward, & Needham, 2005). In addition, there is general agreement that sensitivity to both psychological and physical causal relations becomes increasingly elaborate over the course of infancy (e.g., Cohen, Chaput, & Cashon, 2002; Csibra, Biro, Koos, & Gergely, 2003; Gopnik & Meltzoff, 1997; Woodward, Sommerville, & Guajardo, 2001).

Other authors suggest that various domain-general developments may underlie infants' causal understanding. Cohen and colleagues (e.g., Cohen et al., 2002) argue that information-processing developments throughout infancy enable infants to integrate increasingly higher-order elements, including causal relations, of object motion displays. Studies have documented that infants are adept at detecting statistical regularities across a range of stimuli, and that infants' ability to do so forms the basis of learning (e.g., Aslin,

Saffran, & Newport, 1998; Kirkham, Slemmer, & Johnson, 2002; Saffran, Aslin, & Newport, 1996; Saffran, Johnson, Aslin, & Newport, 1999). For example, infants segment words from fluent speech based on statistical relationships between adjacent speech sounds (Saffran et al., 1996) and appear to do so based on transitional probabilities of successive speech sounds (e.g., Aslin, Saffran, & Newport, 1998). Baldwin and colleagues (Baird & Baldwin, 2001; Baldwin et al., 2001) have argued that infants may capitalize on such statistical learning skills to identify behavioral cues associated with goal attainment when observing ongoing human action. By extension, infants could also use statistical covariation detection to identify aspects of physical causal structure.

The Role of Interventions in Infants' Developing Sensitivity to Causal Relations

All of the aforementioned abilities likely contribute to infants' capacity to appreciate physical and psychological causal relations. In addition, infants' developing experience as actors may play a powerful role in their causal understanding. Indeed, Piaget suggests that infants' causal understanding emerges through their sensorimotor actions on their environment (e.g., Piaget, 1953). Other scholars argue that understanding human behavior as psychologically caused relies on our ability to map from our own experience to those of others (e.g., Goldman, 1989; Gordon, 1986; Harris, 1989; Heal, 1989), and that this may be particularly true in early development (Meltzoff, 2002; Meltzoff & Brooks, 2001; Tomasello, 1999; Woodward et al., 2001).

Previous work suggests that adults and children readily detect causal structure by intervening on their environment (Gopnik & Schulz, 2004; Gopnik et al., 2004; Kushnir & Gopnik, in press; Lagnado & Sloman, 2004; Sobel & Kushnir, 2003; Steyvers, Tenenbaum, Wagenmakers, & Blum, 2003). Inter-ventions are particularly crucial when one must disambiguate multiple causes or identify variables relevant to causal outcomes. Critically, interventions enable learners to test causal hypotheses and compare the outcomes of their interventions to expected outcomes (e.g., Sobel & Kushnir, 2003). In keeping with this suggestion, evidence suggests that, at least in some circumstances, self-generated interventions may result in more accurate and thorough causal learning than watching the interventions of others (e.g., Kushnir & Gopnik, in press; Sobel, 2003).

Dramatic changes occur over the first 2 years of life in infants' ability to act effectively on their world. Infants' changing action capacities may provide them with the opportunity to intervene on their environment, that is, to manipulate one factor intentionally and observe the results of their manipulations on another factor. Infants' own interventions may be a particularly rich source of information for causal learning as they allow them to investigate directly the causal hypothesis that infants hold in the moment and to observe the effects of their interventions. Such a perspective predicts that infants should (a) be able to learn from their own causal interventions and (b) be able to relate their interventions to those of others.

Existing studies provide preliminary evidence for both of these proposals. Infants' ability to solve a box-opening problem improves as a result of their own dynamic engagement with this problem-solving task (Bojcyzk & Corbetta, 2004). Put another way, infants readily and spontaneously learn from their own interventions. In addition, even very young infants relate their own interventions to those of others. Three-month-old infants who participated in a task that facilitated their ability to intervene on objects subsequently appreciated similar interventions performed by another person as goal directed (Sommerville et al., 2005).

Thus, infants possess prerequisites that may enable them to use information from their own interventions as a means to understanding psychological and physical causal relations.

In the studies discussed in this chapter, Woodward and I (Sommerville & Woodward, 2005a, 2005b) investigated the extent to which infants' ability to intervene on a particular problem was related to their sensitivity to causal relations in a similar problem when watching another person act. To do so, we presented infants with a simple tool use scenario: Infants saw an actor pull a support supporting an out-of-reach toy and grasp the toy. An observer watching this sequence must understand that the actor acts on the support with the intention of getting the toy (psychological causal relation), and that the movement of the support causes the toy to move (physical causal relation). Moreover, observers must understand variables influencing the causal relations in this sequence, namely, the presence of the

actor's desire to get the toy and the need for contact between the support and toy so that the first can cause the second to move.

Across both studies (Sommerville & Woodward, 2005a, 2005b), infants received an intervention task in which they were given the opportunity to act on the support to obtain the out-of-reach toy. To assess whether infants understand the psychological causal relations of this sequence, one group of infants subsequently took part in a paradigm that assessed whether infants recognized that an actor acting on a similar support did so with the intention of getting the toy. To assess whether infants were sensitive to the physical causal structure of the sequence, another group of infants subsequently took part in a paradigm that assessed their ability to recognize the need for contact between the toy and support for movement of the support to cause the toy to be displaced. Our questions were whether (a) infants were sensitive to the respective psychological and physical causal relations and (b) whether this sensitivity was linked to their own intervention experience.

The Role of Interventions in Infants' Understanding of Psychological Causal Relations

Adults shown the support-pulling sequence understand that the actor's goal in this situation (getting the toy) guides the actor's actions on the support. Previous work suggests that the support-pulling problem is readily solved by 1 year of age (e.g., Piaget, 1953; Willatts, 1999). Moreover, a study provided evidence that by this same age infants recognize the psychological causal relations of the support-pulling sequence. After watching an actor pull a support that supported a toy, infants construed the actor's subsequent actions on the support as directed toward the toy rather than the support itself (Sommerville & Woodward, 2005a). The present study assessed whether younger infants could also appreciate the psychological causal relations involved in the support-pulling sequence and whether their ability to do so is related to their developing experience intervening on a similar problem.

Ten-month-old infants took part in two paradigms. During the support-pulling intervention task, infants were given multiple opportunities to pull a support that supported an out-of-reach toy, bringing the toy within reach so that it could be grasped.

We assessed infants' ability to solve this problem in a spontaneous manner without prior instruction. Specifically, we assessed how frequently infants solved the task in a way that appeared clearly directed at obtaining a toy.

Infants also took part in a habituation paradigm (see Figure 3-1 psychological structure paradigm). This paradigm capitalizes on infants' visual attention as a way to gauge their event representations. While sitting in a high chair or on a caregiver's lap, infants watch live events presented by a human actor on a puppet stage. An experimenter who is unaware of the events that infants are watching observes infants' eye gaze using a computer program that times infants' looking to the outcomes of the events. Infants are separated from the stage by a screen that can be lowered to reveal the event and raised when a trial is terminated. During the initial phase of the study, infants repeatedly watch a single event until their attention wanes (habituation). Infants then see two test events in alteration that each differ along a single dimension from the habituation event. The features that infants weight most heavily in their event representations are gauged by examining infants' novelty preference (e.g., which event they look longer at) to the test events. Some test events are perceptually similar to the habituation event but feature a change in the actor's overarching goal. Other test events preserve the actor's overarching goal but feature changes in the way in which this goal is achieved in comparison to the habituation event. Infants' sensitivity to the psychological causal relation of the sequence is inferred from the

Habituation event

New support event

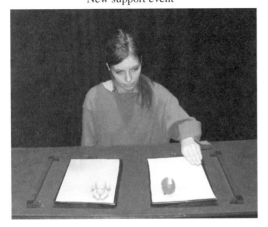

New toy event

Figure 3-1

extent to which they prefer (e.g., look longer at) events that vary the actor's goal over those that vary the way in which the actor's original goal is achieved.

During the habituation trials, infants saw an actor sitting behind a stage that contained two different colored supports, each of which sat under a different toy. The screen was lowered, and the actor said "Hi. Look." while subsequently reaching toward and grasping one of the supports. She next pulled the support toward her and grasped the toy that it supported. Infants' looking was timed to the static outcome of this event (the actor grasping the toy).

Once infants' looking time had decreased to half of its initial level (habituation), the locations of the toys were switched. This enabled us to show infants two new test events that tapped their sensitivity to the goal of the sequence. On new support events, infants saw the actor turn in a new direction and grasp a different support than she had during habituation trials (which now supported the same toy that she had acted toward during habituation). On new toy events, infants saw the actor turn in the same direction and grasp the same support that she had during habituation trials (which now supported a different toy than she had acted on during habituation trials). In both cases, infants' looking was timed to the static outcome of the event (the actor grasping the support). Longer looking to the new support events would suggest that infants construed the actor's initial actions on the support as directed toward the support itself rather than as directed toward the toy. Longer looking on the new toy events would suggest that infants inferred that the actor's actions on the support were directed toward the toy and thus showed a novelty preference for events featuring a change in this dimension of the action sequence.

To address our question of interest, we sought to assess the extent to which infants' ability to intervene on the support-pulling problem was related to their habituation performance. To do so, we categorized infants into two groups based on their intervention task performance. Infants in the top 25% in terms of action task performance were dubbed planful infants. Planful infants produced clearly goal-directed strategies to solve the action task on 83%–100% of trials. Infants in the bottom 25% in terms of action task performance were dubbed nonplanful infants. Nonplanful infants produced clearly goal-directed strategies to solve the action task on 0%–20% of trials.

To assess whether planful and nonplanful infants construed the habituation events differently, we compared looking times to the new toy and new support events for both groups. Planful infants looked significantly longer to the new toy than new support events. Nonplanful infants showed the opposite pattern of looking: They preferred the new support over the new toy event. These findings suggest that infants who were good at organizing their actions toward the goal of the sequence (the toy) likewise perceived the actions of another person in a similar context as directed toward the overarching goal of the sequence. Infants who were poor at organizing their actions toward the goal of the sequence, in contrast, may have misperceived the actor's actions on the support as directed toward the support itself.

These findings suggest that infants begin to abstract the goal of action sequences toward the end of the first year of life, and that this ability is tightly linked to infants' own tendency to intervene on the support in a goal-directed manner. In another study Woodward and I (Sommerville & Woodward, 2005b) assessed whether infants' experience intervening on the support-pulling problem was related to their ability to detect physical causal relations.

The Role of Interventions in Infants' Understanding of Physical Causal Relations

The ability to understand the support-pulling sequence entails not only an appreciation of the causal relations between actor and toy in this situation, but also an appreciation of the causal relation between the toy and support. This entails the ability to recognize the need for contact between the toy and the support: If the toy were sitting adjacent to, rather than on top of, the support, then the toy would not move when the support was pulled. Previous work suggests that infants begin to take into account the need for contact between the toy and the support by about 12 months of age, both in their own actions (e.g., Piaget, 1953; Schlesinger & Langer, 1999) and the actions of others (Schlesinger & Langer, 1999; Sommerville & Woodward, 2005b). In this study (Sommerville & Woodward, 2005b), Woodward and I sought to assess whether younger infants are also sensitive to this physical causal relation and whether their ability to appreciate the need for contact between the toy and the support was related to their own intervention experience in a similar situation.

A different group of 10-month-old infants from those in the aforementioned study took part in a support-pulling intervention task and a habituation paradigm. The intervention task was similar to that described; however, in this task infants were given multiple opportunities to pull the support both when the toy sat on the support and when it sat adjacent to the support. We assessed infants' ability to solve the problem in a goal-directed manner as a function of the location of the toy.

The habituation paradigm differed slightly from that of Woodward and I in 2005. Infants again watched live events presented by a human actor on a puppet stage, and their looking was timed to the static outcome of these events. In this study, however, after seeing a simple support-pulling event, infants saw events that were perceptually similar to the initial event but causally implausible along with those that were perceptually dissimilar to the initial event but causally plausible. The prediction was that sensitivity to the physical causal structure of this event would be evident in longer looking at the causally implausible event.

During habituation trials, infants saw an actor sitting behind a stage that contained a single support that supported a toy. The screen was lowered, and the actor said, "Hi. Look." She subsequently pulled the support toward her, entraining motion on the part of the toy. Unlike in the previous study, the actor did not grasp the toy. Infants' looking was timed to the static outcome of the event (the actor grasping the support). Infants watched this event on repeated trials until looking had declined to half of its initial level (habituation criteria).

While the stage was hidden from view, we next removed the toy from the support and placed it on an invisible black platform that sat roughly 3.5 inches adjacent to the support. On test trials, infants saw two types of test events. On consistent test events, once the screen was lowered the actor said "Hi. Look." and subsequently pulled the support toward her while the toy remained in place. On inconsistent test events, once the screen was lowered, the actor said "Hi. Look." and subsequently pulled the support toward her while the toy moved alongside the support. The actor accomplished this by surreptitiously pulling the toy on the platform along a track from underneath the display. To an adult observer, the inconsistent event represents a causal violation: The toy appears to be moving "magically" along with the support.

Our prediction was that the extent to which infants varied their own interventions as a function of the location of the toy would be related to their ability to

recognize causal violations to the support sequence in the actions of another person. To test this prediction, we subdivided infants into two groups based on their performance on the intervention task. Infants dubbed discriminators pulled the support as a means to get the toy more frequently when the toy sat on, rather than adjacent to, the support. Infants dubbed nondiscriminators did not vary their support-pulling behavior as a function of the toy location. The results of this study met with our predictions. Discriminators looked longer at the inconsistent than consistent test events, suggesting that they recognized that a causal violation had occurred when support movement appeared to cause the toy to move in the absence of contact between the toy and the support. Nondiscriminating infants looked equally to both test events, suggesting that they were not sensitive to this causal violation. Thus, the way in which infants intervened on the support problem predicted whether they would be sensitive to the physical causal violation of the support sequence.

Subsequent analyses revealed interesting and important differences among nondiscriminating infants with respect to their intervention task and habituation performance. Some nondiscriminating infants pulled the support as a means to get the toy at high frequencies regardless of the location of the toy. Other nondiscriminating infants pulled the support to get the toy infrequently regardless of the location of the toy. Thus, high-frequency pullers had multiple opportunities to observe the effects of their interventions under two different setting conditions: when the toy sat on and when the toy sat off the support. Low-frequency pullers had far fewer opportunities. In subsequent analyses, we took into account that frequently infants pulled the support across both contact and noncontact trials during the intervention task. High-frequency pullers subsequently recognized the causal violation featured in the habituation paradigm. Specifically, they looked longer at the inconsistent than the consistent test event. These findings suggest that infants may use their interventions to evaluate causal hypotheses, and that they can rapidly detect causal structure in the actions of others based on this experience.

Taken together, the results indicate that infants begin to appreciate causal relations in the support sequence toward the end of the first year of life, and that their ability to do so is intimately linked to their own intervention experience and expertise. Infants' ability to planfully solve the support sequence was related to their ability to recognize that another person's actions on the support were directed at the toy (psychological causal relation). Infants' ability to guide their interventions according to the degree of contact between the support and the toy was related to how readily they attended to the need for contact between the support and the toy for the first to cause the second to move (physical causal relation). Importantly, the way in which infants enacted interventions in this latter case predicted their ability to learn which variables were important for producing a successful causal outcome. Thus, like young children (e.g., Gopnik et al., 2004; Kushnir & Gopnik, in press), infants may also utilize their own interventions as a means to detecting causal structure.

Conclusion

Research using a range of methodologies suggests that causal understanding has its roots in infancy and is instantiated in infants' sensitivity to a number of psychological and physical causal relations. In addition, evidence suggests that infants may possess or encounter a range of learning mechanisms and abilities that support early causal learning. Chief among these factors is infants' own active experience. Formal and descriptive accounts of causation stress the role of interventions, actions that bring about or prevent a certain event from occurring, in detecting causal structure (e.g., Gopnik & Schulz, 2004; Woodward, chapter 1, this volume). Indeed, causal learning in both adults and children is informed by an opportunity to enact interventions (Gopnik et al., 2004; Kushnir & Gopnik, in press; Lagnado & Sloman, 2004; Sobel, 2003; Steyvers et al., 2003). The evidence discussed in this chapter suggests that infants' developing action abilities, their action experience, and the extent to which they capitalize on opportunities to act on their environment and observe the consequences of their actions may play on important role in causal learning. Through acting on the world, infants can bring about interventions that may enable them to test causal hypotheses and observe the effect that these interventions have on the causal structure of the world.

ACKNOWLEDGMENTS   I would like to thank Alison Gopnik, Laura Schulz, and David Sobel for comments on this chapter. I would also like to thank the parents and infants who participated in the research presented in this chapter. A significant portion of this chapter was completed at the University of Washington's Whiteley Center. I am grateful to the Whiteley Center for their resources and support.

References

Aslin, R. N., Saffran, J. R., & Newport, E. L. (1998). Computation of conditional probability statistics by 8 month-old infants. *Psychological Science, 9,* 321–324.

Baird, J., & Baldwin, D. A. (2001). Making sense of human behavior: Action parsing and intentional inference. In B. F. Malle, L. J. Moses, & D. A. Baldwin (Eds.), *Intentions and intentionality: Foundations of social cognition.* Cambridge, MA: MIT Press.

Baldwin, D. A., Baird, J. A., Saylor, M. M., & Clark, M. A. (2001). Infants parse dynamic action. *Child Development, 72,* 708–717.

Baron-Cohen, S. (1995). *Mindblindness: An essay on autism and theory of mind.* Cambridge, MA: MIT Press.

Bartsch, K., & Wellman, H. M. (1995). *Children talk about the mind.* London: Oxford University Press.

Bates, E., Carlson-Luden, V., & Bretherton, I. (1980). Perceptual aspects of tool using in infancy. *Infant Behavior & Development, 3,* 127–140.

Bojczyk, K. E., & Corbetta, D. (2004). Object retrieval in the first year of life: Learning effects of task exposure and box transparency. *Developmental Psychology, 40,* 54–66.

Brown, A. L. (1990). Domain-specific principles affect learning and transfer in children. *Cognitive Science, 14,* 107–133.

Carpenter, M., Akhtar, N., & Tomasello, M. (1998). Fourteen- through 18-month-old infants differentially imitate intentional and accidental actions. *Infant Behavior & Development, 21,* 315–330.

Chen, Z., Sanchez, R. P., & Campbell, T. (1997). From beyond to within their grasp: The rudiments of problem-solving in 10- and 13-month-olds. *Developmental Psychology, 33,* 790–801.

Chen, Z., & Siegler, R. S. (2000). Across the great divide: Bridging the gap between understanding of toddlers' and older children's thinking. *Monographs of the Society for Research in Child Development, 65,* 1–108.

Cohen, L. B., & Amsel, G. (1998). Precursors to infants' perception of the causality of a simple event. *Infant Behavior & Development, 21,* 713–731.

Cohen, L. B., Chaput, H. H., & Cashon, C. H. (2002). A constructivist model of infant cognition. *Cognitive Development, 17,* 1323–1343.

Cohen, L. B., & Oakes, L. M. (1993). How infants perceive a simple causal event. *Developmental Psychology, 29,* 421–433.

Cohen, L. B., Rundell, L. J., Spellman, B. A., & Cashon, C. H. (1999). Infants' perception of causal chains. *Psychological Science, 10,* 412–418.

Csibra, G., Biro, S., Koos, O., & Gergely, G. (2003). One-year-old infants use teleological representations of actions productively. *Cognitive Science, 27,* 111–133.

Gergely, G., Nasady, Z., Csibra, G., & Biro, S. (1995). Taking the intentional stance at 12 months of age. *Cognition, 56,* 165–193.

Goldman, A. (1989). Interpretation psychologized. *Mind and Language, 4,* 161–185.

Gopnik, A., & Astington, J. W. (1988). Children's understanding of representational change and its relation to the understanding of false belief and the appearance-reality distinction. *Child Development, 59,* 26–37.

Gopnik, A., Glymour, C., Sobel, D. M., Schulz, L. E., Kushnir, T., & Danks, D. (2004). A theory of causal learning in children: Causal maps and Bayes' Nets. *Psychological review, 11,* 3–22.

Gopnik, A., & Meltzoff, A. N. (1997). *Words, thoughts and theories.* Cambridge, MA: MIT Press.

Gopnik, A., & Schulz, L. (2004). Mechanism of theory formation in young children. *Trends in Cognitive Science, 8,* 371–377.

Gordon, R. M. (1986). Folk psychology as simulation. *Mind and Language, 1,* 158–171.

Harris, P. (1989). *Children and emotion.* Oxford, England: Blackwell.

Heal, J. (1998). Co-cognition and off-line simulation: Two ways of understanding the simulation approach. *Mind and Language, 13,* 477–498.

Jovanovic, B., Kiraly, I., Elsner, B., Gergely, G., Prinz, W., & Aschersleben, G. (2006). *The role of effects for infants' perception of action goals.* Manuscript submitted for publication.

Kiraly, I., Jovanovic, B., Prinz, W., Aschersleben, G., & Gergely, G. (in press). The early origins of goal attribution in infancy. *Consciousness and Cognition, 12,* 752–769.

Kirkham, N. Z., Slemmer, J. A., & Johnson, S. P. (2002). Visual statistical learning in infancy: Evidence for a domain general learning mechanism. *Cognition, 83,* B35–B42.

Kushnir, T., & Gopnik, A. (2005). Young children infer causal strength from probabilities and interventions. *Psychological Science, 16,* 678–683.

Lagnado, D. A., & Sloman, S. (2004). The advantage of timely intervention. *Journal of Experimental Psychology: Learning, Memory and Cognition, 30,* 856–876.

Leslie, A. M. (1982). The perception of causality in infants. *Perception, 11,* 173–186.

Leslie, A. M. (1994). ToMM, ToBy, and Agency: Core architecture and domain specificity. In L. A. Hirschfeld, & S. A. Gelman (Eds). *Mapping the mind: Domain specificity in cognition and cultrue* (pp. 119–148). New York, NY: Cambridge University Press.

Leslie, A. M., & Keeble, S. (1987). Do 6-month-old infants perceive causality? *Cognition, 25,* 265–288.

Meltzoff, A. N. (1995). Understanding the intentions of others: Re-enactment of intended acts by 18-month-old children. *Developmental Psychology, 31,* 838–850.

Meltzoff, A. N. (2002). Imitation as a mechanism of social cognition: Origins of empathy, theory of mind, and the representation of action. In U. Goswami (Ed.), *Blackwell handbook of childhood cognitive development. Blackwell handbooks of developmental psychology* (pp. 6–25). Malden, MA: Blackwell.

Meltzoff, A. N., & Brooks, R. (2001). "Like me" as a building block for understanding other minds: Bodily acts, attention and intention. In B. F. Malle, L. J. Moses, & D. A. Baldwin (Eds.), *Intentions and intentionality: Foundations of social cognition* (pp. 125–148). Cambridge, MA: MIT Press.

Oakes, L. M. (1994). Development of infants' use of continuity cues in their perception of causality. *Developmental Psychology, 30,* 869–879.

Oakes, L. M., & Cohen, L. B. (1990). Infant perception of a causal event. *Cognitive Development, 5,* 193–207.

Piaget, J. (1953). *The origins of intelligence in the child.* London: Routledge & Kegan Paul.

Phillips, A. T., Wellman, H. M., & Spelke, E. S. (2002). Infants' ability to connect gaze and emotional expression to intentional action. *Cognition, 85,* 53–78.

Premack, D. (1990). The infants' theory of self-propelled objects. In D. Frye & C. Moore (Eds.), *Children's theories of mind: Mental states and social understanding* (pp. 303–325). Hillsdale, NJ: Erlbaum.

Repacholi, B. M., & Gopnik, A. (1997). Early reasoning about desires: Evidence from 14- and 18-month-olds. *Developmental Psychology, 33,* 12–21.

Saffran, J. R., Aslin, R. N., & Newport, E. L. (1996). Statistical learning by 8-month-old infants. *Science, 274,* 1926–1928.

Saffran, J. R., Johnson, E. K., Aslin, R. N., & Newport, E. L. (1999). Statistical learning of tone sequences by human infants and adults. *Cognition, 70,* 27–52.

Schlesigner, M., & Langer, J. (1999). Infants' developing expectations of possible and impossible tool-use events between ages 8 and 12 months. *Developmental Science, 2,* 195–205.

Sobel, D. M., & Kushnir, T. (2003). *Interventions do not solely benefit causal learning: Being told what to do results in worse learning than doing it yourself.* Poster presented at the 25th annual meeting of the Cognitive Science Society, Boston, MA.

Sodian, B., & Thoermer, C. (2004). Infants' understanding of looking, pointing, and reaching as cues to goal-directed action. *Journal of Cognition & Development, 5,* 289–316.

Sommerville, J. A., & Woodward, A. L. (2005a). Pulling out the intentional structure of action: The relation between action processing and action production in infancy. *Cognition, 95,* 1–30.

Sommerville, J. A., & Woodward, A. L. (2005b). Infants' sensitivity to the causal features of means-end support sequences in action and perception. *Infancy, 8,* 119–145.

Sommerville, J. A., Woodward, A. L., & Needham, A. (2005). Action experience alters 3-month-old infants' perception of others' actions. *Cognition, 96,* B1–B11.

Steyvers, M., Tenenbaum, J., Wagenmakers, E., & Blum, B. (2003). Inferring causal networks from observation and interventions. *Cognitive Science, 27,* 453–489.

Tomasello, M. (1999). Having intentions, understanding intentions and understanding communicative intentions. In P. D. Zelazo, J. W. Astington, & D. R. Olson (Eds.), *Developing theories of intention: Social understanding and self-control* (pp. 63–75). Mahwah, NJ: Erlbaum.

Uzgiris, I. C., & Hunt, J. M. (1975). *Assessment in infancy: Ordinal scales of psychological development.* Chicago: University of Illinois Press.

Wellman, H. M., Cross, D., & Watson, J. (2001). Meta-analysis of theory-of-mind development: The truth about false belief. *Child Development, 72,* 655–684.

Willatts, P. (1984). The stage IV infants' solution of problems requiring the use of supports. *Infant Behavior & Development, 7,* 125–134.

Willatts, P. (1999). Development of means-end behavior in young infants: Pulling a support to retrieve a distant object. *Developmental Psychology, 35,* 651–667.

Woodward, A. L. (1998). Infants selectively encode the goal object of an actor's reach. *Cognition, 69,* 1–34.

Woodward, A. L. (2003). Infants' developing understanding of the link between looker and object. *Developmental Science, 6,* 297–311.

Woodward, A. L., & Guajardo, J. J. (2002). Infants' understanding of the point gesture as an object-directed action. *Cognitive Development, 17,* 1061–1084.

Woodward, A. L., Sommerville, J. A., & Guajardo, J. J. (2001). How infants make sense of intentional action. In B. F. Malle, L. J. Moses, & D. A. Baldwin (Eds.), *Intentions and intentionality: Foundations of social cognition* (pp. 149–169). Cambridge, MA: MIT Press.

4

An Interventionist Approach to Causation in Psychology

John Campbell

This chapter extends the interventionist analysis of causation to give an account of causation in psychology. Many aspects of empirical investigation into psychological causation fit straightforwardly into the interventionist framework. I address three problems. First is the problem of explaining what it is for a causal relation to be properly psychological rather than merely biological. Second is the problem of rational causation: how it is that reasons can be causes. Finally, I look at the implications of an interventionist analysis for the idea that an inquiry into psychological causes must be an inquiry into causal mechanisms. I begin by setting out the main ideas of the interventionist approach.

Interventionism

Interventionism is the view that for X to be a cause of Y is for intervening on X to be a way of intervening on Y (cf. Pearl 2000; Spirtes, Glymour, & Scheines, 1993; Woodward, 2003; Woodward & Hitchcock, 2003; see also Woodward, chapter 1, this volume). The interventionist approach can be vividly

expressed by means of causal graphs, which use arrows to depict causal relations between variables. These arrows may represent positive or inhibiting causal relations. Suppose we consider a causal relation between variables X and Y. Suppose, for example, that X represents the level of a drug in someone's blood, and that Y represents whether and how well the subject recovers from an illness. Suppose further that the body endogenously produces the drug in varying quantities in different people. There will be some biological factor responsible for the level of endogenous production of the drug in someone's body; suppose we express this by variable R. And, suppose that the drug is also spontaneously ingested by people as part of their ordinary diet, in varying amounts by different people; suppose we summarize the factors responsible for spontaneous ingestion of the drug in ordinary diet by variable S. Then, we can represent the hypothesis that the level of the drug is a cause of degree of recovery from the illness as in Figure 4-1.

The arrows in Figure 4-1 show variables R and S causally affecting X and X causally affecting Y.

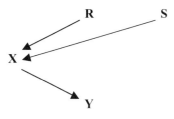

FIGURE 4-1

The objective of an interventionist analysis is to explain what it is for X to be causally affecting Y. The intuitive idea is that for X to cause Y is for intervening on X to be a way of intervening on Y (intervening on the level of drug will be a way of intervening on degree of recovery from the illness).

Following Woodward and Hitchcock (2003), we can exhibit an intervention on X in terms of a variable I that acts on X. (For instance, we might think of an external agent giving people various amounts of the drug and observers keeping track of the subsequent degrees of recovery of people from the illness.) The idea then is that there are at any rate some circumstances in which, if there were an intervention on X, then there would be a difference in the value of Y (Figure 4-2).

There is a possibility that R and S might be common causes of both X and Y. In that case, variations in X will be correlated with variations in Y, but that may not be because X causes Y. (So, for example, we have to keep in mind the possibility that the factors that cause endogenous production of the drug, or lead a person to ingest a lot of it, might each be a common cause of both the level of drug in a person's body and the degree of recovery from the illness. In that case, we will find that there is indeed a correlation between degree of recovery and level of drug in the body but that will not constitute a causal relation between the level of drug and the degree of recovery. So, we should want an intervention on X to suspend the influence of

these other factors on the level of drug in the blood.) In general, then, the intervention variable I should take over control of the value of X, removing it from the influence of R and S. To use Pearl's term, the intervention should be surgical, breaking the arrows from R and S to X. Given that condition on the intervention variable I, then we can say that for X to cause Y is for it to be the case that there is a correlation between X and Y under potential interventions on X.

There are further conditions to be met. We have to exclude the possibility that the intervention I on X also affects Y directly. (For example, administering the drug should not have a placebo effect.) So, we should stipulate that an intervention variable for X with respect to Y must not affect Y otherwise than by affecting X. We should require that there is no bias in which interventions are carried out; that is, that there should be no correlation between intervention and recovery (i.e., we should not be administering the drug only to those who are going to recover anyway). Finally, we should have a requirement of causal sufficiency on the variables we have explicitly represented; in particular, there should be no unrepresented variables that are common causes of pairs of variables we do have explicitly represented, so that spurious correlations can be generated.

With these stipulations in place, though, we can define what it is for X to cause Y by saying that if there were an intervention on X, then there would in some cases be a difference in the value of Y. Or, equivalently, we can say that for X to cause Y is for X and Y to be correlated under potential interventions on X. This is not a reductive definition of causation. On the contrary, it makes free use of causal notions in defining the idea of an intervention and in explaining what it is for a set of variables to be causally sufficient. Nonetheless, the definition I have just given does not appeal to the idea of a causal relation specifically between X and Y. It has therefore some claim to provide a nonreductive illumination of the notion by locating it in a broader framework of causal notions.

In my remarks in this section, I follow closely the approach to causation developed by Woodward and Hitchcock, building on the earlier work of Pearl (2000) and Spirtes, Glymour and Scheines (1993); any originality so far is accidental. Notice that the approach presupposes a certain modularity in the system of variables in question. It presupposes that interventions on the system can in principle leave undisturbed the causal relations among particular variables.

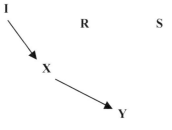

FIGURE 4-2

That is, an intervention can selectively disturb certain causal relations—those involving the usual causes of the target variable X—while leaving others intact, particularly the causal relation between the target variable X and the outcome variable Y (cf. Hausman, and Woodward 1999).

Control Variables

I want now to ask whether this approach can be used to illuminate causation in psychology. On the face of it, there should be no special problem here. Consider any psychological variable M1 and the hypothesis that M1 is a cause of some other psychological variable M2. So, for example, consider the hypothesis that worry is a cause of insomnia (Harvey (2005)). For worry to be a cause of insomnia is, on this approach, for it to be the case that if there were an intervention on worry, then there would be a difference in the level of insomnia. The trouble with this, though, is that any intervention on worry is also going to be an intervention on some underlying set of biological variables. You cannot affect worry without affecting the underlying biology. So, how do we describe the situation? Is it that the worry is causing the insomnia—that intervening on the worry is correlated with a difference in the insomnia? Or, is it that there is a biological variable underlying the worry, and it is causally related to a biological variable underlying the insomnia? In that case, the situation is better described by saying that intervention on the first biological variable is correlated with the second biological variables. The psychological variables, in that case, are epiphenomenal on the underlying biological causation.

Think how you would characterize the relation between the positions of the controls on a radio and the output of the radio, such as the volume of the sound or the radio station heard. All that goes on here does indeed supervene on a microphysical reality. But, we would ordinarily have no hesitation in saying that someone turning the controls is making a difference to the output. Why does it seem so evident here that the position of the dials is causing the output, and that we are not here dealing merely with epiphenomena?

I think we can get at this by recalling a famous set of criteria proposed in 1965 by the epidemiologist Austin Bradford Hill to determine whether particular environmental hazards were causes of particular diseases or merely correlated with them. Central among

Hill's criteria are three things. The first is the existence of a dose-response effect. Most simply, this demands that there be an identifiable relationship between the value of the input variable and the correlated output variable. To demonstrate that smoking is a cause of cancer, for example, one critical piece is the datum that the amount one smokes is correlated with the probability of contracting cancer. Second, it enhances the case for saying that smoking causes cancer if there is a large effect of smoking on cancer. Finally, it enhances the case for saying that smoking is a cause of cancer if smoking is correlated specifically with cancer rather than any other outcome. I can sum this up by saying that the case for saying that smoking causes cancer is a case for saying that smoking is a *control variable* for cancer. Here, I am using *control* in the sense in which the buttons on a radio are controls. There is a large, specific, and systematic correlation between the volume coming out of the radio and the degree to which you turn the volume dial. Just so, under interventions on the level of smoking, there are large, specific, and systematic effects on cancer.

I am proposing that we should use this notion of a control variable to identify the level at which we find the causally significant variables in a complex system. I think there is no question but that, in the case of the radio, the positions of the various buttons and knobs are control variables in this sense, and that this is why it seems so evident that making a difference to the controls of the radio is making a difference to the upshot; we are not dealing here with epiphenomena. For the case of smoking, consider how you would react to a spokesperson for the tobacco industry who argued that smoking is not a cause of cancer, that smoking and cancer are both merely epiphenomenal on an underlying microphysical reality at which the true causal relations are to be found. The natural point to make in reply is that smoking is a control variable for cancer; interventions on smoking have large, specific, and systematic correlations with cancer. That is the case for saying that the causal relations between smoking and cancer are to be found at the macrophysical level.

The example of the controls on a radio is in some ways special. The relationship between control variable and output need not always be analog. This will be particularly important when we consider how we can affect one another through the use of language. You can tell me how things are or make requests of me, and the control system here, assuming I am compliant, is not analog.

But, you may nonetheless have large, specific, and systematic effects on my states.

Of course, it will be a matter of degree whether one variable functions as a control variable for another, and there will be a certain relativity to context. But, that is how it is with causal ascription generally. Hill (1965) did not explicitly formulate his criteria as criteria for choice of variables to use in characterizing the data, and what I have said here by no means exhausts his points. But, the force of the idea, that we find the right level at which to characterize causal relations by looking for the level of control variables, seems undeniable.

One way to see the force of that idea is to look again at the background picture of an interventionist approach to causation. An interventionist approach sees the interest or point of our notion of cause as having to do with our manipulations of our environment. It is not that the notion of cause is explained in terms of agency; it is, rather, that to characterize causal relations is to characterize the aspects of the world that we exploit when we manipulate it. If you think of causation in this way, then it seems evident that control variables will be of great importance in describing causation. For, in manipulating the world, we want, as much as possible, to be intervening on variables that are correlated with large, specific, and systematic upshots. We want to be intervening on control variables in our actions. In these terms, then, the case for saying that worry is a cause of insomnia is that worry is a control variable for insomnia. What is it to say that worry causes insomnia, and that the two are not merely epiphenomena? It is to say that interventions on worry are correlated with large, specific, and systematic variations in insomnia.

Causation by Reasons

Some difficult issues concern the application of the interventionist picture to what we might call *rational causation*, cases in which the causal explanation appeals to the subject's possession of reasons. Suppose we consider, for instance, the hypothesis that the intention to do X causes doing X. Can we think of this in terms of whether there would be differences in whether X was performed if there were interventions on the intention to do X?

The really difficult thing here is to find the right characterization of a psychological intervention.

What is it to intervene on whether someone has the intention to do X? We would naturally think of this in terms of providing someone with reasons to do X or reasons not to do X. "You think doing X will make you happy, but it won't," you might say as an opening move. And, you might present further considerations in favor of your remark. You would be appealing to the rationality of the subject. The trouble with this is that it leaves intact the factors that are the usual causes of the someone's forming, or not forming, the intention to do something.

For example, suppose that one of the usual causes of a person's intending to do X is that they think doing X will make them happy. If your intervention takes the form of arguing about whether doing X will in fact make that person happy, then you have left in place one variable that is a usual cause of whether the person forms the intention to do X. This means that the intervention is not, in Pearl's term, surgical. To use again the example of a drug trial, suppose you are asking whether the level of drug in someone's body causes recovery from illness. If you manipulate the level of drug in that person's body by acting on the mechanism involved in the body's endogenous production of the drug, then this does not constitute an intervention in the sense I explained in the last section. Similarly, if an endogenous cause of whether someone forms the intention to do X is whether the person believes that doing X will make them happy, then a manipulation of whether the person forms the intention that proceeds by manipulating whether the person believes that doing X will make them happy does not constitute an intervention in the sense I explained.

The reason for insisting on a surgical intervention in the case of the drug trial was the problem of common causes: that the endogenous cause of the level of drug in the blood might also be directly causing recovery from illness, so that the level of drug in the blood actually played no role in causing recovery from illness despite being correlated with recovery. It is to rule out this scenario that we have to consider interventions that seize control from outside the level of drug in the blood. Similarly, suppose we leave intact the endogenous causes of formation of the intention to do X, such as the belief that doing X will make one happy. Then, it is possible that the belief that doing X will make one happy causes both formation of the intention to do X and directly causes performance of the action itself. In that case, the intention to do X will be correlated with doing X even though the intention plays no role in causing the action. It is to rule out this scenario that we have to consider only surgical interventions on the intention to do X, according to the interventionist picture as I have so far set it out.

What would it be to have a surgical intervention on someone's possession of an intention to do X? The intervention would have to come from outside and seize control of whether the subject had the intention, suspending the influence of the subject's usual reasons for forming an intention, such as whether the subject had reasons for forming the intention to do X. We can diagram the situation by means of a causal graph (Figure 4-3).

This is evidently quite an unusual situation. It does not happen very often, if it happens at all, that a person's rational autonomy is suspended and some alien force seizes control over whether that person has a particular intention. Still, even though it does not happen very often, it could still be that an interest in psychological causation is an interest in what would happen in such an unusual case. Similarly, you might say that an interest in causation in physics often deals with what would happen in various idealized conditions—in a complete vacuum or on a frictionless plane, for example—even though such situations do not arise often.

The real problem for the interventionist picture here is that it is not credible that our interest in psychological causation is an interest in what would happen under such idealized conditions of alien control. There are two aspects of our ordinary conception of the psychological life that have been removed in this scenario, and without them our psychological life would not be recognizable.

Notice first that ordinarily we have our intentions under continuous review. If you hit an obstacle in trying to execute your plan, then you may review whether to sustain the intention in the light of all your background beliefs and objectives—just how important is

this anyhow?—and how far you stick with an intention often depends on continuous review in the light of your other psychological states, your priorities, and your beliefs regarding the likelihood of success. If you could not do this kind of continuous monitoring, then you would be said to be "not responsible for your actions." It is exactly this situation that we are envisaging, though, when we think in terms of surgical intervention on possession of an intention.

Second, this scenario is one that would undermine our ordinary conception of the ownership of an intention. One element in our ordinary notion of the ownership of an intention is the idea that the long-standing objectives, interests, preferences, and so on of that person were causally responsible for the formation of that particular intention. It is a reasonable description of the situation envisaged as surgical intervention here to say that someone else's intention has been thrust into the mind of the subject. Someone who seemed to find him- or herself in that situation—someone who encountered in introspection an intention that seemed to have been the direct result of someone else's long-standing objectives, interests, preferences, and so on—would experience this as *thought insertion*, the feeling that someone else's token thought has been pushed into your mind, one of the symptoms of schizophrenia.

There are many systems for which an approach in terms of surgical interventions seems appropriate. Suppose, for example, that our descendants come upon an archive of electrical machines, present-day radios, perhaps. And, they want to find out just how the circuitry works. They are not concerned with the function of these devices. They just want to understand the electrical engineering involved. In this case, an approach in terms of surgical interventions seems entirely apt. Even if it turns out not to be in practice possible to tear the systems apart into their modular constituents, still the objective is to find out what would happen in each constituent module were we to have a surgical intervention that ripped out this piece of wiring from its context and tampered with the input end to see what would happen at the output. We have understood the causal structure of the circuitry when we have answered all such questions. In the case of rational causation, in contrast, we have no such interest in ripping out individual pieces of circuitry from their context to see how they would behave in isolation. The attempt to do this would result in a system so different from the original that

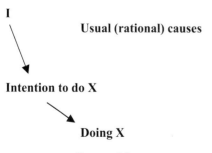

I

Usual (rational) causes

Intention to do X

Doing X

Figure 4-3

what happened in that context could not be said to have any significant implications for the functioning of the original intact system. This is a fundamental point about rational causation in psychology, which underpins some of the hesitation philosophers have felt in talking about mental causation at all.

Two Types of Intervention

I think that we can resolve this problem within a broadly interventionist framework, but to do so we have to rethink our conception of an intervention; we have to move away from the focus on surgical interventions. We want to consider interventions that keep intact the rational autonomy of the subject, which means leaving in place the usual causes of the subject's psychological states and actions. Then, what kind of thing are we looking for, to be a psychological intervention? Let me first give a couple of examples, then provide a more abstract statement of the general notion of intervention being presupposed.

Suppose that I am the passenger and you are driving as we come to a pool of water in the middle of the road. You stop to weigh the situation. Should you drive on, or should you back off? As you pause, I say, "Go for it!" and you put your foot on the accelerator. One possibility is that you have such admiration for my judgment and such concern to act as I would like that the mere fact of my making my remark gives you a reason to form the intention to press on. However, that is not the most obvious or the natural analysis of the situation I have described. Perhaps you know that my judgment is in general questionable; perhaps you and I have just quarreled so that far from giving you a reason to form the intention to proceed, had you paused to reflect on the matter for a moment you would have found that my remark gives you good reason to swing around and go the other way. As it is, though, it is undeniable that my remark had the effect of making you form the intention to drive on, and that consequently you did drive on. In this case, my intervention affects the formation of your intention, but it does not do so by providing you with reasons for or against forming the intention. Rather, it directly affects the formation of your intention. I did manage to reach into your mind and affect the formation of your thought, otherwise than by giving reasons.

It is not, though, as if you had given over the reins of your mind to me. You remained an autonomous rational

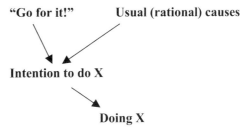

FIGURE 4-4

agent throughout. You could have resisted my remark; you may later regret that you did not do so. Had you mustered reasons that struck you as compelling, one way or another, it could have been that my remark would have had little effect. The structure of the example can be given by the causal graph of Figure 4-4.

The problem we encountered with this kind of situation was as follows. We are attempting to explain the existence of a causal relation between the intention to act and the action as a matter of the intention and the action being correlated under interventions on the intention. But, we have not yet excluded the possibility that the usual causes of the intention may also be direct causes of performance of the action. So, even if the intention and the action are correlated under this kind of intervention on the intention, it may be that this correlation is only a residue of the role of the usual causes of the intention in operating as common causes of both the intention and the action.

There is, though, another way in which we could think of interventions. Suppose we go back to the example of drug level and recovery from illness. Suppose we consider a range of actual or possible external administrations of the drug to individuals across a population. And, suppose that when the drug is administered to an individual it is administered without the level of endogenous or spontaneous ingestion of the drug being taken into account; these factors are allowed to operate as usual. So, this is not a surgical intervention. Nonetheless, we can look at the level of drug that is endogenously produced by the individual and at the level of drug that is spontaneously ingested by the individual. For each combination of a particular level of endogenous production and a particular level of spontaneous ingestion, we can consider what would be the outcome of administering a particular level of the drug.

We can say the following: Suppose that there is some combination of a particular level of endogenous production of the drug and some level of spontaneous ingestion of the drug such that, were the external administration of the drug to be varied while those levels remained the same, there would be a difference in whether the subject recovered from illness. In that case, the level of drug in the blood is a cause of recovery from illness. In fact, in the way I propose of developing the interventionist account, this is what it is for the level of drug in the blood to be a cause of recovery from illness. (For formal development of a related notion of *soft intervention*, see Markowetz, Grossman, & Spang, 2005.)

The difference between this formulation of interventionism and the analysis I reported in the section on control variables emerges vividly when we consider cases, such as that of rational causation, for which modularity assumptions are not correct. We are not any longer considering whether the value of Y is independent of the value of X, when the value of X is set by surgical intervention. We are, rather, considering whether Y is independent of the intervention variable *I* given the usual causes of X. And, the conditions that have to be met by the intervention variable *I* are just as before, except that we are no longer requiring that the influence of the usual causes of X should be suspended, and that *I* should be the sole determinant of the value of X.

We can apply this picture to rational causation in psychology. We do not need to consider a scenario in which the rational autonomy of the agent is suspended and some external factor seizes control of the agent's intentions. We can, rather, consider cases in which the usual causes of the agent's formation of intentions operate as usual and look at whether external interventions that make a difference to whether the agent forms an intention, for some set of values for the agent's other psychological states, would be correlated with differences in whether the agent performs the action. Is intention a cause of action? My proposal is that this is the question is whether interventions on intention are correlated with action given the agent's other psychological states.

Psychological Causation Without Psychological Mechanisms

One of the most striking features of an interventionist approach to causation in psychology is that it makes no appeal to the idea of mechanism. All that we are asking, when we ask whether X causes Y, is whether X is correlated with Y under interventions on X. Whether there is a mechanism linking X and Y is a further question.

Indeed, you could maintain an interventionist approach to causation while being skeptical about the very idea of a mechanism. What does it mean to ask whether there is a mechanism linking X and Y? All that it comes to, you might say, is that we are asking whether we can find any causally significant variables mediating X and Y. Or, perhaps in some cases, we are asking merely that the link between X and Y should be explained in terms of one or another familiar pattern of explanation, for example, biological explanation. But, the very idea of a causal link does not demand that there should be intervening variables, or that assimilation to a favored paradigm should be available.

To see why this perspective matters, consider some findings in psychiatry. It has long been known that stressful life events such as bereavement or unemployment are good predictors of chronic depression. In a study of several thousand subjects, Kendler, Hettema, Butera, Gardner, and Prescott (2003) tried to determine which aspects of stressful life events might be playing a causal role here. They found that the strongest correlations with later chronic depression were with humiliation rather than with loss; that other-initiated separation was a stronger predictor of chronic depression than bereavement, for example. To interpret the study as showing something about the causes of depression is to read it as having implications for what the upshot would be of clinical interventions: The implication is that, under interventions to ameliorate the sense of humiliation, there would be differences in the degree of chronic depression. In the sense I explained, humiliation is a control variable, in the kind of nonsurgical intervention I just described, for later depression.

Stressful life events, however, are not the only predictors of later depression; there are also biological factors that seem to be relevant. Kendler, Kuhn, Vittum, Prescott, and Riley (in press) found that genetically acquired deficiencies in the serotonin transport system are correlated with later depression. Now, given the complexity of the phenomena, all such findings have to be regarded as provisional. In this chapter, I want finally to suggest a simple reading of them, on which they provide a simple, illlustrative example of a quite general pattern emerging from current empirical work in psychology and psychiatry.

Although stressful life events predict depression, not everyone who is humiliated ends up with depression. People vary in how resilient they are. One reading of the serotonin data is that they reveal serotonin deficiencies to be the basis of a lack of resilience.

On this reading, then, we have found two causal variables underlying later chronic depression: humiliation and serotonin deficiency. These are control variables for depression, let us suppose. And, the relevant notion of intervention, let us suppose, is of the kind I indicated, for which we consider psychological factors that affect the level of humiliation directly rather than by acting on the usual causes of humiliation. So, we have two variables, one psychological and one biological, that are joint causes of later depression.

In this situation, it is natural to ask, What is the mechanism by which these variables jointly cause later depression? The radical suggestion I want to consider is that there may be no mechanism. Explanation by means of mechanisms must bottom out somewhere, and then we are left with the bare facts about what would happen under interventions. At the moment, the empirical data show only that both psychological and biological variables are in general relevant to psychological outcomes. There is no empirical support for the idea that all causation that involves both psychological and biological variables bringing about a psychological outcome must be sustained by biological mechanisms. In particular, there is no reason to suppose that a comprehensive set of control variables for depression will ever be found at the biological level. It may be that the control variables for depression will always include psychological as well as biological variables.

For anyone familiar with vision science, the ubiquity of something like Marr's three levels of computation, algorithm, and implementation may seem to provide a pattern that has been so successful that its application ought to be pursued across the board. Scientists working on vision move back and forth between the cognitive level and the level of biological mechanism so seamlessly that, in vision science, doing without the level of biological mechanism is almost unimaginable. Although that is certainly so for vision science, it depends on quite special features of the area that do not hold for psychological causation in general.

To explain what these special features are, I want to introduce the notion of the "robustness" of a variable. The idea here is that if a variable does play a self-standing role in some causal process, then it ought also to play a role in endlessly many other causal processes. For example, consider the so-called hot chocolate effect: As you stir a cup of hot chocolate and the spoon sounds against the base of the cup, each successive "ting" rises in pitch. Why is that? The usual explanation is in terms of the aeration of the liquid. As you stir, trapped air bubbles are released from the liquid, and it becomes stiffer. The more rigid a substance, the faster sound travels through it. Hence, the pitch of the sound goes up (Crawford, 1982). This explanation appeals to a variable, aeration. Now, this variable does not figure only as the explanation of the hot chocolate effect. There are endlessly many ways in which you can get at the air bubbles trapped in a liquid. They are affected by the temperature of the liquid being poured into the contained and the speed at which it is poured, and they show up in as simple a way as the visible clouding of the liquid. This is what I mean by the robustness of the variable: It shows up in endlessly many different causal processes and so can be investigated in endlessly many different ways.

Now, consider the kinds of variables appealed to in information-processing accounts of vision. Vision is generally thought to be modular, in something like the sense of Fodor (1983; cf. Coltheart, 1999). So, the variables appealed to in explaining, for instance, the finer points of motion perception or color perception are being used to explain processing going on within a module. Now, the cognitive variables—wavelength pattern X at place p, for instance—that are used in this kind of explanation really are internal to the characterization of the processing in a single module. What gives the brain states the contents they have is their role in the processing within a particular modular system. It makes no sense to ask, What is the representational content of that cell-firing? outside the context of inquiry into the processing going on in some particular module.

For that reason, the cognitive variables appealed to in an account of some aspect of visual information processing cannot be allowed to take on a life of their own. As purely cognitive variables, it would make no sense to suppose that the very cognitive variable that is playing a causal role in the processing going on in one module could also be playing a role in the processing going on in some other module; the determination of the content of a cognitive state here is always internal to the working of one particular module or other. The whole situation is in sharp contrast to the appeal to aeration in explaining the hot chocolate effect, for which one and the same variable can evidently figure in a whole sequence of quite different processes. In that sense, then, the cognitive variables appealed to in the psychology of vision are not robust.

That is why we have the seamless moving back and forth between these variables and biological mechanisms. The physiological variables are, of course, robust and can be investigated through their roles in endlessly many different processes. In contrast, we give a cognitive characterization of the physiology only when we are considering the working of some one modular system.

I think that this point about robustness explains why we cannot, in vision science generally, make sense of the idea of cognitive explanation without biological mechanisms. The point evidently does not generalize to every psychological variable. Humiliation, for example, is evidently robust. The degree to which you have been humiliated shows up in many different causal processes. So, too, do the variables of rational psychology. A particular desire may figure in causal process after causal process, leading from endlessly many different inputs to endlessly many different outputs. Your attentive awareness of an object before you may be caused by anything from it suddenly lighting up to it having been the target of years of search, and it may play a role in processes as diverse as the starting of a train of thought and the fading of a smile. So, these personal-level variables are, in general, robust. We can therefore appeal to them in causal explanation without having to look for the robust biological variables that might underlie them.

There may be such variables. It may be that, in the end, it will turn out that the most effective control variables for psychological outcomes in human beings are one and all biological. At the moment, we have no evidence to support such a conclusion. What we find are more and more biological variables working together with ever-better understood psychological variables to yield psychological outcomes. One great merit of an interventionist approach to causation in psychology, it seems to me, is that it acknowledges the possibility that this may be the right picture. We are not obliged to force the empirical findings to yield biological mechanisms where there may be none.

ACKNOWLEDGMENTS   This chapter was begun while I was on leave at Stanford's Center for Advanced Study in the Behavioral Sciences, and I am deeply indebted to Alison Gopnik and Thomas Richardson for many discussions of these problems. I also had many helpful discussions with Ken Kendler. This chapter was presented to a Center for Advanced Study in the Behavioral Sciences workshop on causal reasoning and benefited from many helpful comments there. I also thank the Institute of Cognitive and Brain Sciences in Berkeley.

References

Coltheart, M. (1999). Modularity and Cognition. *Trends in Cognitive Sciences*, 3, 115–120.

Crawford, F. S. (1982). The   hot chocolate effect. *American Journal of Physics*, 50, 398–404.

Fodor, J. (1983). *The Modularity of Mind*. Cambridge, Mass.: MIT Press.

Harvey, A. G. (2005). Unwanted intrusive thought in insomnia. In D. A. Clark (Ed.), *Intrusive thoughts in clinical disorders: research, theory and treatment*. New York: Guilford Press.

Hausman, D., & Woodward, J. (1999). Independence, invariance, and the causal Markov condition. *British Journal for the Philosophy of Science*, 50, 521–583.

Hill, A. B. (1965). The environment and disease: association or causation? *Proceedings of the Royal Society of Medicine*, 58, 295–300.

Kendler, K. S., Hettema, J. M., Butera, F., Gardner, C. O., & Prescott, C. A. (2003). Life event dimensions of loss, humiliation, entrapment, and danger in the prediction of onsets of major depression and generalized anxiety. *Archives of General Psychiatry*, 60, 789–796.

Kendler, K. S., Kuhn, J. W., Vittum, J., Prescott, C. A., & Riley, B. (2005). The interaction of stressful life events and a serotonin transporter polymorphism in the prediction of episodes of major depression: A replication. *Archives of General Psychiatry*, 529–535.

Markowetz, F., Grossman, S., & Spang, R. (2005). Probabilistic soft interventions in conditional Gaussian networks. In R. Cowell & Z. Ghahramani (Eds.), *Proceedings of the tenth international workshop on artificial intelligence and statistics*, Barbados: Society for Artificial Intelligence and Statistics.

Marr, D. (1982). *Vision*. San Francisco: W.H. Freeman.

Pearl, J. (2000). *Causation*. Cambridge, England: Cambridge University Press.

Spirtes, P., Glymour, C., & Scheines, R. (1993). *Causation, prediction and search*. New York: Springer-Verlag.

Woodward, J. (2003). *Making things happen: A theory of causal explanation*. Oxford, England: Oxford University Press.

Woodward, J., & Hitchcock, C. (2003). Explanatory generalizations, part 1: A counterfactual account. *Nous*, 37, 1–24.

5

Learning From Doing

Intervention and Causal Inference

Laura Schulz, Tamar Kushnir, & Alison Gopnik

> There is something fascinating about science. One gets such wholesale returns of conjecture out of such a trifling investment of fact.
>
> *Mark Twain*, 1883

Twain meant his comment as a witticism, of course, but there *is* something fascinating about science. From a few bones, scientists infer the existence of dinosaurs; from a few spectral lines, the composition of nebulae; and from a few fruit flies, the mechanisms of heredity. From a similarly trifling investment, some of us presume to conjecture even about the mechanisms of conjecture itself.

Why does science, at least some of the time, succeed? Why does it generate accurate predictions and effective interventions? With due respect for our accomplished colleagues, we believe it may be because getting wholesale returns out of minimal data is a commonplace feature of human cognition. Indeed, we believe the most fascinating thing about science may be its connection to human learning in general and in particular to the rapid, dramatic learning that takes place in early childhood. This view, the *theory theory*, suggests that starting in infancy, continuing through the life span, and canalized in scientific inquiry, many aspects of human learning can

be best explained in terms of theory formation and theory change.

Theories have been described with respect to their structural, functional, and dynamic properties (Gopnik & Meltzoff, 1997). Thanks to several decades of work in developmental psychology, we now know a great deal about the structural and functional aspects of children's theories. That is, in many domains, we know that children have abstract, coherent, causal representations of events, we know something about the content of those representations, and we know what types of inferences they support.

We know, for instance, that 6-month-olds' naïve physics includes principles of cohesion, continuity, and contact but not the details of support relations (Baillargeon, Kotovsky, & Needham, 1995; Spelke, Breinlinger, Macomber, & Jacobson, 1992; Spelke, Katz, Purcell, Ehrlich, & Breinlinger, 1994). We know that 4-year-olds' naïve biology supports inferences about growth, inheritance, and illness but not the adult concept of living thing or alive (Carey, 1985;

Gelman & Wellman, 1991; Inagaki & Hatano, 1993; Kalish, 1996). We know that 2-year-olds' naïve psychology includes the concepts of intention and desire but not the concept of belief (Flavell, Green, & Flavell, 1995; Gopnik & Wellman, 1994; Perner, 1991). Moreover, we know that, across domains, children's naïve theories support coherent predictions, explanations, and even counterfactual claims (Harris, German, & Mills, 1996; Sobel, 2004; Wellman, Hickling, & Schult, 1997).

However, the theory theory is not just a theory about what children know or what children can do. It is, centrally, a claim about how children learn. In this respect, it is the dynamic rather than the structural and functional aspect of theories that is critical. If children's reasoning is like scientific theory formation, then children's naïve theories should be subject to confirmation, revision, and refutation, and children should be able to make inferences based on evidence from observation, experimentation, and combinations of the two.

Until recently, this dynamic feature of theories has been difficult to explain. If children's knowledge about the world takes the form of naïve theories—and if conceptual development in childhood is analogous to theory change in science—then we would expect the causal reasoning of even very young children to be very sophisticated. A causal "theory" (as distinct from, for instance, a causal module or a causal script) must support novel predictions and interventions, account for a wide range of data, enable inferences about the existence of unobserved and even unobservable causes, and change flexibly with evidence (Gopnik & Meltzoff, 1997). Moreover, theories have a complex relationship with evidence; they must be defeasible in the face of counterevidence, but they cannot be too defeasible. Because evidence is sometimes misleading and sometimes fails to be representative, the process of theory formation must be at once conservative and flexible.

In recent work, we have focused on causal learning as a fundamental dynamic mechanism underlying theory formation. In thinking about what causal knowledge is, we have been influenced by philosophical and computational work proposing an "interventionist" view of causation (see Woodward, Hitchcock, & Campbell, chapters 1, 7, 4, this volume). This view stands in contrast to many traditional ideas about causation in both adult and developmental psychology. However, we believe that an interventionist account of causation not only helps to elucidate tricky metaphysical questions in philosophy but also provides a particularly promising way to think about children's causal knowledge.

As noted, much developmental research on causal reasoning has looked at children's understanding of domain-specific causal mechanisms (Bullock, Gelman, & Baillargeon, 1982; Leslie & Keeble, 1987; Meltzoff, 1995; Shultz, 1982; Spelke et al., 1992; Wellman et al., 1997; A. L. Woodward, 1998; A. L. Woodward, Phillips, & Spelke, 1993). Although this research tradition has successfully overturned Piaget's idea that young children are "precausal" (1930), it has followed Piaget's lead in treating knowledge of distinct physical and psychological mechanisms of causal transmission as the hallmark of causal understanding.

Specifically, developmental researchers have largely accepted the idea that causal knowledge involves knowing that causes produce effects by transfer of information or energy through appropriate intervening mechanisms. In an influential monograph on children's causal reasoning, the psychologist Thomas Shultz wrote that children understand causation "primarily in terms of generative transmission" (1982, p. 48). Similarly, Schlottman writes that "mechanism is part of the very definition of a cause" (2001, p. 112), and Bullock et al. (1982, p. 211) conclude that the idea that "causes bring about their effects by transfer of causal impetus" is "central to the psychological definition of cause-effect relations."

Consistent with this causal mechanism or "generative transmission" approach, psychologists have suggested that even adults prefer information about plausible, domain-specific mechanisms of causal transmission to statistical and covariation information in making causal judgments (Ahn, Kalish, Medin, & Gelman, 1995). Some philosophers have also adopted a transmission perspective, arguing that causal interactions are characterized by spatiotemporally continuous processes involving the exchange of energy and momentum or the ability to transmit "a mark" (Dowe, 2000; Salmon, 1984, 1998).

However, although the generative transmission model of causation is arguably the dominant view of causal knowledge in the developmental literature, there are several respects in which this model critically fails to account for our causal intuitions. Many events that we believe are causally connected (e.g., losing track of time and being late for class; taxing cigarettes and reducing smoking) are not, at least in any obvious way, characterized by mechanisms of transmission. Second, as the philosopher Jim Woodward observes, there is no obvious reason why it should be of value to us to distinguish those events that transmit energy or information from those that do not (2003); those aspects of causality that make it of central importance to human cognition (prediction and control) do not seem to be captured by the concern with spatial and energy relations that characterize the transmission view. Furthermore, nothing in the generative transmission model distinguishes causally relevant from causally irrelevant features of transmission. Generative transmission models fail to explain why, for instance, the momentum transferred from a cue stick to a cue ball is causally relevant to the ball's movement, while the blue chalk mark, transmitted at the same time and in the same manner, is not (Hitchcock, 1995, and chapter 7, this volume).

Critically, the tendency to equate causal understanding with an understanding of mechanisms of causal transmission may pose a particular problem for the theory theory. Research suggests that adults cannot generate a plausible account of causal mechanisms, even in domains in which they consider themselves highly knowledgeable (Rozenblit & Keil, 2002). Keil has suggested that we suffer from an "illusion of explanatory depth," and that our causal knowledge may amount to little more than "one or two connected causal beliefs" (2003). He has argued that "calling this causal knowledge folk 'science' seems almost a misnomer," and that "the rise of appeals to intuitive theories in many areas of cognitive science must cope with a powerful fact. People understand the workings of the world around them in far less detail than they think."

If having a theory is coextensive with having an account of causal mechanisms, then Keil's suggestion is troubling, particularly because an impoverished understanding of causal mechanisms is presumably even more characteristic of young children than adults. Perhaps children's causal reasoning is not particularly sophisticated after all.

However, the interventionist account explicit in recent philosophical work and implicit in computational models such as causal Bayes nets provides a quite different account of what it might mean to have causal knowledge. In the context of a causal model, the proposition that X causes Y (X → Y) means, all else being equal, that an intervention to change the value or probability distribution of X will change the value or probability distribution of Y. That is, the causal arrows in the graphical models are defined, not with respect to their relevance to a domain, their spatiotemporal features, or their ability to transmit energy or force, but (mirroring the way causality is understood in science) in terms of possible interventions. These interventions need not actually be realized or even feasible, but they must be conceivable (see J. Woodward, 2003, for details). A causal relation then is defined not in terms of its physical instantiation but in terms of the real and counterfactual interventions it supports. A theory, in this view, represents a coherent and organized set of such relations rather than necessarily involving a set of beliefs about physical processes or mechanisms.

Both statisticians and philosophers have argued that this interventionist account captures precisely what it means for a variable to be a cause (see, e.g., Pearl, 2000, and J. Woodward, 2003). Learning algorithms based on these models support novel predictions, interventions, inferences about a range of causal structures, and inferences about unobserved causes. Arguably, then, knowledge of causal mechanisms and processes of transmission may not be of central importance for at least some of what we need theories to do.

Note, moreover, that an interventionist account of causal learning is consistent with and indeed predicts many of the findings that have been associated with the generative transmission model. In looking, for instance, at children's inferences about force relationships, Shultz (1982) first taught the children what types of interventions were relevant to outcomes (e.g., that striking a tuning fork in front of an open box created a sound). Shultz then struck two tuning forks; the first failed to covary temporally with the sound (because it was positioned to the side of the box); the second did covary with the effect (because the experimenter struck the second fork and simultaneously turned the box to face the first). Children chose the first tuning fork (with the appropriate transmission relationship) as a cause and rejected the tuning fork that merely covaried with the effect.

However, the relevant covariation information for children might not be merely the temporal covariation of the tuning fork with the effect but the covariation of interventions and outcomes; that is, children could have learned that turning the box was as critical to the effect as striking the fork. Indeed, in novel cases like this, arguably the only information that children have about processes of causal transmission is the evidence of effective patterns of intervention. Given that any causal relationship (e.g., flipping a switch and a light turning on) can be instantiated by a vast number of causal mechanisms (many types of wires, bulbs, circuits, etc.), it may make sense that children's naïve theories should focus on the connection between interventions and outcomes rather than on the myriad mechanisms that might realize it. Indeed, one of the virtues of theories may be that they enable us to make powerful predictions *despite* our often-substantial ignorance about underlying processes and mechanisms (our "trifling investment in fact").

Note that scientific theories, as well as naïve ones, often remain agnostic about processes of transmission while committing to hypothetical interventions. Newton developed his theory of gravitation without knowing any mechanism that might enable masses to attract one another; Darwin developed his theory of evolution without knowing any mechanism that might make variation in the species heritable. Thus, although we might say informally that Darwin posited natural and sexual selection as "mechanisms" for evolution, we do not mean that Darwin discovered spatiotemporally continuous processes by which energy or information is transferred. Rather, Darwin inferred that traits that enhance an organism's reproductive success will be more prevalent in the population; that is, changes to one set of variables will affect the outcome of other variables. Thus, scientific theories, like naïve ones, are not necessarily derived from, or committed to, particular causal mechanisms. Rather, in identifying the causal structure—the real and hypothetical interventions the variables support—theories help narrow the search space for the relevant physical processes.

Critically, we do not mean to suggest that substantive assumptions about spatiotemporal relations and domain-specific knowledge do not play a fundamental role in children's causal understanding. Indeed, one of the important challenges for cognitive science is to understand how knowledge about particular physical relations in the world is integrated with evidence about interventions and patterns of covariation. In what follows, we discuss some important interactions between children's substantive causal knowledge and formal learning mechanisms. Even more critically, we do not mean that children only learn causal relations from interventions. Children may infer causal

relations in myriad ways, including from spatial relations, temporal relations, patterns of covariation, and simply by being told. The claim rather is that certain patterns of interventions and outcomes indicate causal relationships, and when children infer that a relationship is causal, they commit to the idea that certain patterns of interventions and outcomes will hold.

One of the exciting features of the interventionist account of causation is that, together with theory theory, it generates an array of interesting and testable predictions about children's early learning. At a minimum, if children's causal knowledge takes the form of naïve theories and if causal knowledge is knowledge that supports interventions, then children should be able to (a) use patterns of evidence to create novel interventions; (b) do this for any of a variety of possible causal structures; (c) use evidence from interventions to infer the existence of unobserved causes; (d) distinguish evidence from observation and intervention in their inferences about causal structure; (e) effectively weigh new evidence from interventions against prior beliefs; and (f) distinguish good interventions from confounded ones.

In what follows, we walk through this alphabet of inferences. We discuss respects in which the causal Bayes net formalism provides a normative account of these components of theory formation, and we review evidence from our lab suggesting that young children are capable of this type of learning.[1]

Making Novel Interventions

In the absence of theories, you could safely navigate a lot of causal territory. Classical conditioning, trial-and-error learning, and hardwired causally significant representations (of the sort that make nestlings cower when hawks fly overhead, and arguably of the sort that is triggered by seeing one object strike and displace another; e.g., Michotte, 1962) are effective ways of tapping into real causal relations in the world. Each of these abilities lets us track regularities in the environment and predict some events from the occurrence of others. Some of these abilities even support effective interventions.

Like other animals, human beings seem to have innate, domain-specific causal knowledge (Spelke et al., 1992), the ability to detect statistical contingencies (Saffran, Aslin, & Newport, 1996), and the ability to learn from the immediate consequences of our own actions (Rovee-Collier, 1980; Watson & Ramey, 1987). Unlike other animals, however, we routinely use the contingencies and interventions we observe to design novel interventions. We routinely meet regularities with innovation.

Some of this inferential power may come from the way that human beings represent causal knowledge. Elsewhere (see Gopnik et al., 2004), we have suggested that causal Bayes net representations provide a causal map of events in the world. The analogy to a spatial map is helpful because it explains both some of the advantages of the causal Bayes net representation and some of the disadvantages of alternative ways of storing causal knowledge.

Some animals, like ants, seem to represent spatial relations egocentrically. Ants know where their nest is in relation to their own body movements, but if they are scooped up and displaced even slightly, they lose their way, even in familiar terrain (Sommer & Wehner, 2004). Other animals, like mice, construct spatial maps. Once mice have explored a territory, they can always take the shortest route to a goal, no matter where they are placed initially (Tolman, 1932). Such cognitive spatial maps reveal the underlying stability of geometric relations.

Causal relations can also be represented egocentrically in terms of the immediate outcome of one's own actions (e.g., as in operant learning). However, like an egocentric spatial representation, operant learning fails to represent the relationship of variables to one another. Operant learning restricts you to learning the immediate outcome of your own actions, and even these can only be learned by trial and error. However, if you represent causal events as they relate to one another, then—even if you are not part of the causal structure, or even if you own relationship to the event changes—the stability of the underlying causal structure is preserved. From such stability may come the ability to negotiate novelty.

Causal Bayes nets provide just such a coherent, nonegocentric representation of the causal relationship among events. In a literature rife with stories about cigarette smoking, stained fingers, and lung cancer; birth control pills, thrombosis, and strokes; and prisoners, sergeants, and firing squads, almost any concept can be illustrated with a macabre example. We work with preschoolers, however, so we make use of a more benign, indeed suburban, illustration (adapted from Pearl, 2000): Suppose you walk outside and see that the grass in your front yard is wet. You might guess that it has rained. Because you believe the weather is a common cause of the state of your front yard and your backyard, you will be able to infer that the grass in your backyard is most likely wet as well. You could represent this causal structure as the causal Bayes net in Figure 5-1, in which each node is a binary variable taking either the value wet or dry.

In this causal structure, the state of the front yard and the state of the backyard are dependent in probability. Knowing something about the front yard will tell you (in probability) something about the state of the backyard. That is, you can use knowledge of the causal graph and the known value of some variables in the system to predict the (otherwise unknown) value of other variables.

However, the critical thing about causal Bayes nets, indeed the thing that makes them causal, is that they can also support inferences about the effects of interventions. We discuss interventions in more detail in the following section, but roughly speaking, the arrow in the graph between the weather and the front yard encodes the proposition that, all else being equal, changing the state of the weather will change the state of the front yard. Importantly, the arrow retains this meaning even though (in the real world) we cannot actually intervene on the weather (short of global climate change, anyway). Knowing the causal graph lets you predict the outcome of interventions—whether or not you have ever seen them performed and indeed whether or not you could ever perform them. Thus, unlike hardwired representations or trial-by-error learning, causal graphs support genuinely novel inferences.

However, the absence of the arrow between the front yard and the backyard is also informative. Although the states of the yards are dependent in probability, there is no direct causal link between them; all else being equal, changing the one will not change the other. Causal graphs thus represent the

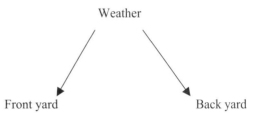

FIGURE 5-1 A causal Bayes net.

FIGURE 5-2 Evidence about three flowers.

distinction between predictions from observation (if the front yard is dry, then the backyard is probably dry as well) and predictions from intervention (wetting the front yard will not wet the backyard).

In a series of experiments, we looked at whether, consistent with the formalism, young children could use patterns of dependence and independence to make novel predictions and interventions (Gopnik, Sobel, Schulz, & Glymour, 2001; Schulz & Gopnik, 2004). We showed preschoolers, for instance, that three flowers were associated with a monkey puppet sneezing (see Figure 5-2). One flower (A) always made the monkey sneeze; the other flowers (B and C) only made the monkey sneeze when Flower A was also present.

Formally, A and the effect were unconditionally dependent; B, C, and the effect were independent conditional on A. Applied to this case (and assuming no unobserved common causes), a Bayes nets learning algorithm will construct the graph in Figure 5-3\ The graph in Figure 5-3 says that A causes the effect, and B and C do not. (It also says that there is an undetermined causal link between A, B, and C, represented by the circles and the ends of the edge connecting those variables. In fact, there is such a link, namely, the experimenter, who put all three flowers in the vase together.) This structure in turn generates predictions about interventions. In particular, it implies that an intervention on A will change the value of C, but an intervention on B or C will not have this effect.

Children were asked, "Can you make it so that Monkey won't sneeze?" Consistent with the prediction of the formalism, children screened-off flowers B and C and removed only flower A from the vase. Control experiments established that the inference was caused by the pattern of conditional dependence and independence, not frequency information.

One might argue, however, that children have only a limited ability to make novel and appropriate inferences. Children might, for instance, be able to

use patterns of dependence to differentiate equally plausible causal candidates within a domain (i.e., the causal power of one flower vs. another). However, innate or domain-specific knowledge might restrict the range of evidence children are willing to consider in the first place. Formal inference procedures might not be able to override or change children's prior beliefs.

However, if, consistent with the theory theory, children develop their causal understanding *from* patterns of evidence, then domain-specific judgments ought to be defeasible. Given appropriate evidence, children ought to be able to override prior knowledge and reason about truly novel events, including events that cross the boundaries of domains, and design truly novel interventions accordingly. To look at the extent to which children could flexibly use evidence and formal inferential procedures to make genuinely novel causal inferences, we pitted children's domain-specific knowledge against patterns of evidence.

We showed children, for instance, that three causes were associated with a machine turning on. Two of the causes were domain appropriate (buttons), and one was domain inappropriate (talking to the machine). Talking to the machine and the machine turning on were unconditionally dependent but conditional on talking; the buttons were independent of the effect. Thus, the structure was formally identical to the structure in Figure 5-3. We asked the children if they could turn off the machine. In a baseline condition, we provided children with no evidence and simply asked the children whether

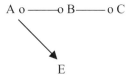

FIGURE 5-3 Graph representing inference that Flower A screens off B and C as a cause of E.

talking or pushing buttons was more likely to turn off the machine.

Consistent with past research showing that children's causal inferences respect domain boundaries, children in the baseline condition chose the domain-appropriate causes (the buttons) at ceiling. However, consistent with the predictions of the formalism, when asked to turn off the machine, 75% of the children ignored the buttons and said, "Machine, please stop." Children were able to use the pattern of conditional dependence and independence to create a new causal map and to generate an appropriate, but novel, causal intervention.

In this experiment, the relations between causes and effect were deterministic. Such definitive evidence might have made it particularly easy for children to override their prior knowledge. However, in another experiment (Kushnir, Gopnik, & Schaefer, 2005), we tested whether children's domain-specific preference for contact in physical causal relations could be overridden in light of probabilistic evidence that physical causes could act at a distance. We showed children a toy with a colored surface and told them, "Sometimes the toy lights up." Without further instruction, we gave children a block and asked them to make the toy light up. Of 16 children, 13 (81%) demonstrated a strong initial assumption of contact causality, touching the block to the surface of the toy (the other 3 did nothing). After their intervention, we showed children four pairs of blocks. In each pair, one block activated the toy one third of the time and always by contact. The other block activated the toy two thirds of the time and always at a distance (i.e., by being held 5–6 inches above the toy). At the end of the experiment, we asked children to make the toy light up again. A significant number of children revised their original intervention and activated the toy at a distance (McNemar's test, $p < .05$). Thus, children seem to be able to revise their domain-specific knowledge and create novel interventions, even when given only stochastic evidence for new causal relations.

If children's causal reasoning were constrained by innate representations or informationally encapsulated modules, then such flexibility and sensitivity to evidence would be surprising. However, it is less surprising from a theory theory perspective. The ability to overturn prior knowledge and learn something genuinely new is one of the chief virtues of scientific inquiry. It may also be one of the hallmarks of childhood.

Learning a Wide Range of Causal Structures

If you were a Martian reading much of the classic literature on human causal reasoning, then you might assume that Earth was a relatively simple place. The stakes are sometimes high (Does camouflage protect tanks from being blown up? Does gender affect college admissions? Does medication cause headaches? Baker et al., 1989; Bickel, Hammel, & O'Connell, 1975; Novick & Cheng, 2004), but the questions, at least, are straightforward: Given a particular set of evidence, is C a cause of E?

Many theories have tried to explain how people answer this question. Accounts ranging from the associative learning accounts we discussed to Patricia Cheng's elegant power theory of probabilistic contrast (Cheng, 1997; Novick & Cheng, 2004) have looked at how people might estimate the relative strength (or, uniquely in Novick & Cheng, 2004, the conjunctive strength) of variables to produce an outcome.

However, both the question and the ways we might answer it assume that variables in the world are already identified as (potential) causes or as effects. A Martian might reasonably wonder whether events on Earth come with labels. The question does not ask, and the theories do not answer, how we might distinguish causes from effects in the first place. Put another way, both associative learning accounts and the power theory account aim to explain how people distinguish the *strength* of different causal variables. They do not explain how people make judgments about causal *structure*.

Sometimes, of course, events in the world *are* essentially "labeled" by the information around them. Spatial cues, combined with prior knowledge about plausible causal mechanisms, may identify some variables as potential causes and others as effects. In other cases (not coincidentally including camouflage and explosions, gender and college admissions, medicine and headaches), temporal priority makes the distinction transparent (Lagnado, Waldmann, Hagmayer, & Sloman, chapter 10, this volume).

However, spatiotemporal cues are not always available in the input. If cause and effect occur at nearly the same time (the dog barks, and the cat runs) or if you walk in on the middle of a scene (brother is sulking, and sister is mad), there may be no way to know "who started it." Moreover, even when temporal cues are present, they may be misleading. A naïve learner who sees Mom search under the bed and then exclaim with joy on finding her car keys might be justified in concluding that searching caused Mom to want her keys rather than that desire motivated the search.

More critically, any theory (naïve or scientific) requires knowing something more than the set of binary relations (does X cause Y?) that obtain between events. A prerequisite to theory formation must be the ability not only to distinguish the strength of causal variables, but also to organize variables within a causal structure. Indeed, part of what differentiates a theory from an empirical generalization is that, within a theory, causal relations are coherent and mutually reinforcing.

The causal Bayes net formalism provides a way to represent and learn complex, coherent causal structures without prior knowledge about whether variables are causes or effects. Although the formalism can incorporate background information from prior knowledge, substantive cues, and temporal order (see the section on weighing new evidence against old beliefs), the direction of causal arrows can also be derived directly from the patterns of conditional dependence and independence in the data. Some structures can be distinguished by observation only; others require a combination of observation and interventions.

Suppose, for instance, that you see three correlated events and are trying to decide whether A and B cause C or whether C causes A and B. If the causal structure is a common effect (A → C ← B), then you are more likely to see A and C co-occur and B and C co-occur than to see A and B co-occur. However, if the structure is a common cause (A ← C → B), then you are likely to see all three variables co-occur. B will be independent of A conditional on C in the common cause case but not the common effects case. These structures can be distinguished just by observation.

The situation is more complex if you are trying to distinguish other structures. For example, suppose you are trying to distinguish the common cause structure (A ← C → B) from the causal chain (A → C → B). In the common cause structure, if C occurs exogenously, then it will activate both A and B, and you will tend to see all three variables together. Similarly, in the chain, if A occurs exogenously, then it will activate C, which will activate B, and again you are likely to see all three variables co-occur. In both cases, B is independent of A conditional on C. Such Markov-equivalent structures are indistinguishable under observation. However, these structures can be distinguished by intervention.

If you intervene to make C happen, then you will increase the probability of seeing A and B if the structure is a common cause (A ← C → B) but will have no impact on the probability of observing A if the structure is a chain (A → C → B) (see Steyvers, Tenenbaum, Wagenmakers, & Blum, 2003, for discussion and evidence that adults are sensitive to these distinctions). Given a combination of evidence from observation and intervention, the causal Bayes net formalism allows for learning the structure even of complex, multivariable systems.

Within the formalism, interventions are treated as variables with special features. Specifically, they must be exogenous (that is, they must not be influenced by any other causal factors in the graph), and they must fix the value or probability distribution of the variables of interest. After an intervention, the value of the intervened-upon variable is entirely determined by the intervention and not by any preexisting causes (see Figure 5-4). Thus, interventions on a causal Bayes net break arrows *into* the variables of interest, performing what Judea Pearl vividly described as *graph surgery* (2000). We can then look at the "postsurgical" graph (after the intervention has taken place) and figure out what has happened to the other variables in the graph.

There are several different ways of formally capturing these relations between interventions, dependencies, and causal arrows (see Pearl, 2000; Spirtes, Glymour, & Scheines, 1993; J. Woodward, 2003). One way to do this is in terms of what we have called the conditional intervention principle. The conditional intervention principle can be formally stated as follows: For a set of variables in a causal graph, A directly causes B (that is, A → B) if and only if (a) there is some intervention that fixes the values of all other variables in the graph, results in B having a particular probability distribution $pr(Y)$ such that (b) there is another intervention that changes the value of A, (c) changes the probability distribution of B from $pr(B)$ to $pr'(B)$ but (c) does not influence B other than through A, and (d) does not undo the fixed value of the other variables in the graph (Gopnik et al., 2004).

X→Y→Z   X I→Y→Z
(a)   (b)

FIGURE 5-4 (a) A causal chain. (b) A causal chain after graph surgery; the intervention on Y breaks the arrow between X and Y.

Although this principle may sound complex, it is simply a formal statement of the sort of intuitions about intervention and causation that underlie experimental design. In an experiment, if you want to find out the causal relationship between two variables, then you intervene to hold all other variables constant, and then you intervene to manipulate the value of the variable of interest. If, for instance, you want to know the causal relationship between A and B (represented by an arrow with a question mark in Figure 5-5a), then you can perform one intervention (I_1 in Figure 5-5a) to hold all other potential causes of B constant and another intervention to change the value of A (I_2 in Figure 5-5a). If the value (or probability distribution) of B changes, then you can conclude that A causes B.

Note also that the conditional intervention principle rules out confounded interventions. Line 4 of the conditional intervention principle eliminates the graph in Figure 5-5b (because the intervention on A cannot influence B except through A), and Line 5 rules out the confounded graph in Figure 5-5c (because interventions cannot change the fixed value of any other variable in the graph).

Motivated by causal Bayes net theory (in this volume, see also Hagmeyer, Sloman, Lagnado, & Waldmann, chapter 6; Lagnado et al., chapter 10; Rehder, chapter 12; Griffiths & Tenenbaum, chapter 20), researchers have shown that adults can make appropriate inferences about a wide range of causal structures beyond simple cause-effect pairings. Importantly, the evidence suggests that causal strength learning (and subsequent inferences) can and does take place in the context of complex causal models.

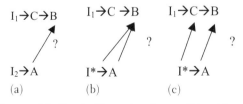

FIGURE 5-5 Graphs illustrating the conditional intervention principle (a) I_1 fixes the value of other causes of B (Clause 1 of the conditional intervention principle). I_2 changes the value of A (Clause 2 of the conditional intervention principle). (b) I^* is ruled out by Clause 4 of the intervention principle because the intervention affects the value of B directly. (c) I^* is ruled out by Clause 5 of the intervention principle because the intervention affects other causes of B.

For example, Waldman (2000, 2001) has shown that adults are sensitive to the direction of causal arrows when learning and reasoning about causal strength relations; that is, they make the distinction between predictive and diagnostic inferences, a fact that cannot be predicted based on associative learning mechanisms alone. Other studies (Lagnado et al., chapter 10, this volume; Sloman & Lagnado, 2005; Waldman & Hagmayer, 2005) have shown that, given causal models, adults can make inferences about the effects of hypothetical interventions as well. Thus, psychologically, causal strength judgments do not take place outside the context of causal structures.

All this should satisfy a Martian that adult humans can make appropriate predictions about observations and interventions in a broader causal context. But, of course, adult humans, particularly the university undergraduates tested in these studies, have extensive experience and often quite explicit tuition in causal inference. Moreover, for the most part these studies have focused on making inferences about evidence given knowledge of a particular structure rather than learning structure from evidence. These studies do not tell us whether this sort of causal learning is part of a more fundamental human learning mechanism and in particular whether it might be responsible for the impressive learning we see in young children. Conversely, the studies of children we have just described all presented them with the classical problem of inferring which cause was responsible for a particular effect—which blicket set off the detector, which flower made the monkey sneeze. In principal, these results might be explained by variations of earlier theories such as associationism or causal power theory. Studies so far have not tested explicitly whether adults or children can use the conditional intervention principle to make inferences about complex causal structures, as the Bayes net formalism would suggest. In the absence of distinguishing spatiotemporal information, can children use evidence from observations and interventions to learn the structure of causal chains, common effects, common causes, and causal conjunctions?

To find out, we introduced preschool children (mean age 4 years 6 months) to a gear toy. Children saw that, when a switch was flipped, two gears, A and B, spun simultaneously. There were four possibilities: (a) The switch activated gear A and A made B go; (b) the switch activated gear B and B made A go;

(c) the switch activated each gear independently; or (d) the switch activated the gears but neither gear would spin without the other. Note that these structures are indistinguishable under observation; no matter which structure obtains, when you flip the switch, both gears will spin together.

The structures, however, are distinguishable under intervention. If, for instance, you remove gear B, flip the switch on, and gear A spins, then you can eliminate structures (b) and (d). If you replace gear B, remove gear A, flip the switch on, and gear B fails to spin, then you can eliminate structure (c) and infer that structure (a) is correct. This type of inference is a direct application of the conditional intervention principle. Controlling for other causes of A (the state of the switch), an intervention on A changes the value of B (when the switch is on and A is present, B spins; when A is absent, B does not), whereas controlling for other causes of B, an intervention on B does not change the value of A. You should conclude that structure (a) is correct, and A → B. Because the patterns of evidence under intervention are unique to each structure, the correct structure can be determined from the data that result from interventions.

Over a series of experiments, we found that, consistent with the formalism, 4.5-year-olds were able to learn the correct causal structure, represented by a simple picture, from the type of evidence described. Children were equally good at learning all four structures (the two chains, the common effect, and the conjunction). In each case, when children were presented with the appropriate evidence, they chose the correct structure significantly more often than any of the other structures. Control experiments suggested that children's judgments were not based on substantive cues or prior knowledge about gears. In addition, consistent with the data reported in the section on making novel interventions, children were able to use their knowledge of the causal structure to make novel predictions. Children who had never seen gears A and B on the toy but were told the structure (e.g., that A spun B) were able to predict the evidence that would result from interventions (e.g., that when the switch was on and A was on the toy by itself, A would spin, but that when B was on by itself, B would not). Again, children were equally good at predicting the outcomes of interventions for all four structures (Schulz, 2003; Schulz, Gopnik, & Glymour, in press).

These experiments are particularly noteworthy because they were explicitly inspired by the Bayes net formalism and are not explicable by any other existing theory of causal learning. The physical and mechanical features of the gears were identical in all cases, and the associations and covariations between the gears were also held constant. The complex pattern of relations between interventions and observations allowed children to learn complex causal structure—in just the way the formalism would suggest.

In their everyday life, children intervene widely on the world and see a wide range of interventions performed by others. At least in simple, generative, deterministic cases, preschool children seem to be able to infer a range of different causal structures from patterns of evidence and to predict patterns of evidence from knowledge of causal structure. Even young children seem to rely on some of the same formal principles of causal inference that underlie scientific discovery. Such mechanisms may help children to develop intuitive theories of the world around them.

Inferring the Existence of Unobserved Causes

One of the critical respects in which science sometimes brings us genuinely new insight is by invoking unobserved causes to explain events. However, unobserved causes are not the exclusive provenance of scientific theories. Children's naïve physics relies on unobservable forces, children's naïve psychology on unobservable mental states, and children's concept of natural kinds on unobservable essences (e.g., Bullock et al., 1982). It is thus perhaps surprising that most psychological accounts of causal reasoning (Cheng, 1997; Shanks & Dickinson, 1987) relegate unobserved causes to a background condition.

We already discussed respects in which the causal Bayes net formalism supports inferences about the unknown value of some variables from the known value of others. However, in some cases the formalism supports inferences about the existence of variables themselves. In particular, if the known values in the graph generate patterns of conditional dependence and independence that appear to violate the causal Markov assumption, then the formalism infers the existence of an unobserved cause.

In a series of experiments, participants (both adults and children) were introduced to a "stickball machine" (see Figure 5-6). The two stickballs could move up and down (either simultaneously or independently) without any visible intervention (because they could be manipulated from behind the machine). The experimenter could also visibly intervene on a stickball by pulling up on the stick. This might cause—or fail to cause—the other stickball to move.

We looked at whether, consistent with the causal Markov assumption, adults and kindergarteners could use interventions and the pattern of outcomes to infer the existence of an unobserved common cause. In these studies, participants saw that the movement of the two stickballs was correlated in probability. They then saw that an intervention on Stickball A (pulling on A) failed to move B, and that an intervention on B failed to move A. On comparison trials, participants were given evidence consistent with A → B (e.g., they saw that pulling on B failed to move A, but they did not see an intervention on A).

If the movements of A and B are probabilistically dependent but intervening to do A fails to increase the probability of B moving and intervening to do B fails to increase the probability of A moving, then the causal Markov assumption can be preserved only by inferring the existence of an unobserved common cause of A and B (i.e., that the true causal structure is A ← U → B). This structure predicts the observed evidence: A and B are unconditionally dependent in probability, but an intervention on either A or B breaks the dependence.

Consistent with the formalism, both adults and children inferred the existence of an unobserved common cause when interventions on either stickball failed to correlate with the movement of the other. Adults drew the appropriate graph (A ← U → B); children inferred that "something else" (besides either of the stickballs) was making the stickballs

move (Kushnir, Gopnik, Schulz, & Danks, 2003; Schaefer & Gopnik, 2003). Importantly, participants only postulated an unobserved common cause when no other graph was consistent with the observed pattern of dependencies. The causal Bayes net formalism thus provides a mechanism by which evidence about observed variables can lead to inferences about the existence of unobserved variables. Processes like these might help explain how both children and scientists bring new theoretical entities into the world.

Distinguishing Evidence From Observations and Interventions

At the core of the theory theory is the idea that children learn causal structure from evidence. There are two ways we can get (firsthand) evidence about an event: We can see the event happen, or we can make the event happen. Importantly, as we have implied in the previous sections, these two ways of getting data—seeing and doing—can lead to radically different conclusions, even when the evidence itself is otherwise identical. What you can learn depends not only on what you already know, but also on how you know it.

In the section on making novel interventions, we discussed a simple causal graph in which the weather was a common cause of the state of the front yard and the backyard (F ← W → B). We noted that, using this graph, you could predict the state of the backyard from the state of the front yard.

Suppose, however, that you buy a sprinkler for your front yard and set it to go off every morning at 6 a.m. Setting the sprinkler cuts the arrow between the weather and the front yard and breaks the dependence between the front yard and the backyard. The altered graph is shown in Figure 5-7.

If the graph is as depicted in Figure 5-7, then when you look outside and see that the grass in your front yard is wet, you will not be able to infer that the grass in your backyard is also wet. Evidence that was informative under observation is uninformative under this intervention.[2]

One of the strengths of the causal Bayes net formalism is that it supports accurate inferences whether the evidence comes from observations, interventions, or combinations of the two. Because the causal graph under intervention is different from the graph under

Child's View

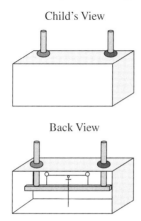

Back View

FIGURE 5-6 The stickball machine.

Sprinkler   Weather

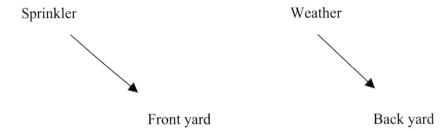

Front yard   Back yard

FIGURE 5-7 A causal Bayes net with a sprinkler.

observation, the same evidence should lead to different inferences.

The theory theory implies that young children should be sophisticated causal reasoners. Are children also sensitive to the distinction between evidence from observations and evidence from interventions, and do they modify their inferences accordingly? Note that such sensitivity is not predicted by all models of causal reasoning. Accounts of causal reasoning that use the strength of the association between two variables as indicative of the probabilistic strength of the causal connection between them (see, e.g., Dickinson, Shanks, & Evenden, 1984; Shanks, 1985; Shanks & Dickinson, 1987; Wasserman, Elek, Chatlosh, & Baker, 1993) are indifferent to whether the association is caused by intervention or observation. Because of this, the predictions made by causal variants of the Rescorla-Wagner equation and the causal Bayes net formalism sometimes differ.

In a series of experiments (designed primarily to look at children's ability to distinguish common cause structures from causal chains), we looked at whether children's conclusions changed depending on whether they observed the relevant evidence with or without an intervention. Children were introduced to the stickball machine described in the section on inferring the existence of unobserved causes. Children were told the following: "Some stickballs are special. Special stickballs almost always make other stickballs move." Children were taught that one stickball might be special, both stickballs might be special, or neither stickball might be special.

In the test condition, children saw the stickballs move up and down simultaneously (without an intervention) three times. The experimenter then visibly intervened by pulling on the top of one stickball; the other stickball failed to move. In the control condition, the experimenter intervened by pulling on one stickball, and both stickballs moved simultaneously three times. The experimenter then pulled on the

stickball a fourth time, and the other stickball failed to move. At the end of the trials, the experimenter pointed to each stickball and asked, "Is this stickball special?"

In the test condition, there is a correlation between seeing stickball Y move and seeing stickball X move. However, intervening to move Y breaks the dependence. From a causal Bayes net perspective, this pattern of evidence is consistent with the graph X → Y but not with the graph Y → X. Children should say that X is special but deny that Y is special. In the control condition, intervening on Y and seeing X move are probabilistically dependent throughout. This is consistent with Y → X but not X → Y; children should say that Y is special, and X is not.

Note, however, that from an associative learning perspective, the strength of association between the stickballs is the same in both conditions. The movement of stickball Y is associated with the movement of stickball X every time but one. If children are reasoning associatively, then in both conditions they should say that Y is special.

The children (4.5-year-olds) distinguished between evidence from observations and interventions and reasoned not as predicted by associative learning models, but as predicted by the causal Bayes net formalism. That is, children were significantly more likely to affirm that X was special and deny that Y was special in the test condition than in the control condition and significantly more likely to affirm that Y was special and deny that X was special in the control condition than in the test (Gopnik et al., 2004; Schulz, 2001).

Similarly, in the unobserved cause studies discussed in the preceeding section, we reported that participants saw that intervening to move stickball X failed to move stickball Y, and intervening to move Y failed to move X. In control conditions, however, participants saw X move by itself and Y move by itself, but this time the stickballs moved without visible intervention—the experimenter simply pointed at X when it moved by itself and then pointed at Y while it moved by itself. Consistent with the predictions of the formalism, participants distinguished between the two conditions and only inferred the existence of an unobserved common cause of X and Y ($X \leftarrow U \rightarrow Y$) in the intervention condition. (In the observation condition, they inferred the existence of two independent unobserved causes: $U1 \rightarrow X$ and $U2 \rightarrow Y$.)

Pearl writes that, "Scientific activity, as we know it, consists of two basic components: Observations and interventions. The combination of the two is what we call a laboratory" (2000). Although making inferences about stickball machines may seem a far cry from scientific inquiry, the ability to distinguish evidence from observations and interventions is fundamental to both. Sensitivity to the different role played by these "basic components" may help support children's ability to learn the causal structure of events in the world.

Weighing New Evidence Against Old Beliefs

We reported that preschoolers ignored a machine's buttons and asked a machine to stop after seeing—once—that talking and the toy activating were unconditionally dependent. We reported this as partial proof of the cleverness of 4-year-olds. This might worry you. This might also worry our institutional review board. Are preschoolers unreasonably impressionable? Surely, it is not that clever to override the whole of naïve physics on the evidence of a single trial. Surely—even in Berkeley—we do not want children going around talking to machines. Learning flexibly from evidence is all very well, but can causal Bayes nets run amok?

Well, no—at least not in this respect. Causal Bayes net representations can be inferred by a variety of different learning algorithms discussed, such as constraint-based and Bayesian learning algorithms (see Gopnik et al., 2004, for discussion). Both of these algorithms can take prior knowledge into account. Constraint-based algorithms test pairs and triads of variables for independence and conditional independence. By adjusting the significance level of the statistical test used to deter-mine independence, constraint-based methods ensure that variables likely to be independent based on prior knowledge (e.g., talking and a machine activating) are subject to less-rigorous

tests of independence than variables that, given prior knowledge, are less likely to be independent.

A somewhat more elegant approach is adopted by Bayesian causal learning methods. Bayesian algorithms assign all the possible causal hypotheses (the causal graphs) a prior probability. This probability is then updated given the actual data (by application of Bayes theorem). The posterior probability of each causal graph is evaluated to see which model best fits the data. Thus, it will take more evidence to support an initially unlikely causal hypothesis than an initially probable one.

Several studies show that, under conditions of uncertainty, people do take current evidence and prior knowledge into account as predicted by Bayesian learning algorithms (Griffiths & Tenenbaum, 2001; Tenenbaum & Griffiths, 2003, Griffiths & Tenenbaum, chapter 20, this volume). In one study, for instance, adults were taught that "superpencils" would activate a "superlead" detector. During a training period, adults were taught that superpencils were either rare (2 of 12 pencils activated the detector) or common (10 of 12 activated the detector). Two (previously untested) pencils were then placed on the detector, and adults saw that both pencils (A and B) together activated the detector, and that A by itself activated the detector. The adults were asked to estimate the likelihood that B by itself would activate the machine.

As predicted by the Bayesian learning algorithms (but not as predicted by associative learning accounts), prior knowledge about the prevalence of superpencils affected people's causal judgments. Despite seeing identical evidence about B in both conditions, participants believed B was much more likely to activate the machine in the common condition than in the rare condition (Tenenbaum & Griffiths, 2003). Other studies showed that 4-year-old children could make similar judgments. Taught either that blickets were rare or common and shown the "backwards blocking" condition described in the previous paragraph, children inferred that B was a blicket when blickets were common and that B was not a blicket when blickets were rare (Sobel & Kirkham, chapter 9, this volume; Sobel, Tenenbaum, & Gopnik, 2004; Griffiths & Tenenbaum, chapter 20, this volume).

So, if preschool children take prior knowledge into account when making causal judgments, why did children in the talking machine experiment violate their knowledge about domain-appropriate causes on the evidence of a single trial? Note that in the cross-domain experiment, children were given deterministic data: Buttons and the machine turning on were *always* independent conditional on talking; talking and the machine turning on were *always* unconditionally dependent. When evidence is deterministic, you do not need statistical tests to determine independence, and whatever the prior probability of the hypothesis, the posterior probability is 100%. Given the deterministic evidence, children's inferences were identical to those that would be made by the formalism.

Importantly, however, in a more ambiguous scenario, children did take prior knowledge into account. We replicated the machine/talking experiment with a new group of children and then tested the children on a "transfer condition" with a novel toy, a novel speech act, and two novel switches. In the transfer condition, children received no evidence about the novel stimuli; we simply asked the children how they would activate the novel toy: by talking to it or by flipping the switches. In the test condition, the children talked to the machine, just as in the previous study. However, in the transfer condition, despite the similarity of the stimuli, the children largely reverted to their prior knowledge: 75% of the children chose the switches (the domain-appropriate cause).

Equally important, however, the prior exposure to the domain-inappropriate evidence did affect children's causal judgments. Children were significantly more likely to choose the domain-inappropriate cause in the transfer condition than in the previous baseline condition (i.e., in which they had no evidence whatsoever about domain-inappropriate causes). The recent exposure to counterintuitive evidence affected how children extended their causal inferences. Similarly, as discussed in the section on making novel interventions, we found that many children would override their preference for contact in physical causal relations in light of probabilistic evidence for action at a distance. Thus, the combination of prior knowledge and formal inference procedures seems to allow for learning that is both conservative and innovative.

This tension between conservativism and innovation is consistent with a theory theory approach to conceptual development and is also a salient feature of adult scientific inquiry. Surprising evidence is often questioned or dismissed before it is taken seriously enough to establish the theories that will, in turn, make the evidence predictable. As William James

(perhaps apocryphally) is said to have quipped: "When a thing is new, people say: 'It is not true.' Later, when its truth becomes obvious, they say: 'It is not important.' Finally, when its importance cannot be denied they say: 'Anyway, it is not new.'"

As scientists, we may complain about the tendency of prior beliefs to squelch innovation; however, as an extension of the inferential procedures used in childhood, the advantages of carefully weighing new evidence against old is clear. If children's learning were too flexible—if it were, for instance, wholly dictated by the most recent evidence observed—then children would be subject to endless error. Children live in a noisy world and might easily be exposed to misleading data. If, on the other hand, innate or prior knowledge acted as a strong constraint on children's causal learning, then errors made early in development would be irreparable. Children would be intransigent in the fact of corrective evidence and helpless in genuinely novel environments.

Although science has a reputation for objectivity, one of the advantages of having a theory (naïve or scientific) is precisely that all evidence is *not* treated equally. By limiting the evidence to which we attend, or that we take seriously, theories explain in part why science can get so much inferential power out of a "trifling investment in fact." Formal inference procedures, able to take into account both prior knowledge and new evidence, may provide just the sort of learning mechanism that allows children's causal theories to be both stable and defeasible.

Distinguishing Good Interventions From Confounded Ones

People who become exercised by the concept of child as scientist frequently point out what is indisputably the case: Children, unlike scientists, do not go around designing controlled experiments to test their theories. Moreover, when children do try to design experiments (i.e., because a teacher or a researcher asks them to), they perform poorly. Children tend to intervene on many variables at once, change interventions between conditions, and then draw all the wrong conclusions. Adults (and often scientists) do little better (Kuhn, 1989; Kuhn, Amsel, & O'Laughlin, 1988; Masnick & Klahr, 2003).

However, designing an experiment requires metacognition. To design an appropriate intervention, you have to know what makes an intervention appropriate. Learning from interventions does not require metacognition. You may have no idea what makes one intervention better than another and still be able to draw correct conclusions from the patterns of evidence that result.

In the previous sections, we provided evidence suggesting that when children are given good evidence, they draw normative causal conclusions. What happens, however, when children are given bad evidence? Are there conditions under which children realize that interventions are confounded? Does confounding change the types of inferences children make?

The conditional intervention principle defined an intervention to rule out instances of confounding: An intervention on X should be exogenous, should break all the arrows into X, and should not influence any other variable in the graph except through X. In the test condition of the gear toy experiment, we showed children evidence consistent with the conditional intervention principle, and children were able to learn the relationship of the gears to one another.

In the control condition, however, we concealed the state of the switch. Thus, just as in the test condition, children saw, for instance, that gear A spun when B was removed, but gear B failed to spin when gear A was removed. However, with the switch hidden, the children could not know whether B failed to spin because gear A was removed or because the experimenter failed to flip on the switch. That is, there was no way to know whether the intervention to remove gear A broke all the arrows into B or not. Although the movement of the gears was the same in both conditions, children in the control conditions responded at chance and—anecdotally—tried to look behind the machine to determine whether the switch was on or off.

In a different set of studies, we looked at children's sensitivity to probabilistic causes and the role played by their own interventions. In an observation condition, children saw an experimenter place a block on a toy three times in a row. The children saw that one block made the toy light up two of three times, and another block made the toy light up only one of three times. Children were told that each block had "special stuff" inside and were asked which block has more special stuff. The children distinguished the 2/3 probability from the 1/3 probability and said that the 2/3 block had more special stuff.

The intervention condition was identical except that children were allowed to intervene on the block on

the third trial. For the 2/3 block, children saw the block light up the toy twice, but when they tried the block, it failed to light up. For the 1/3 block, children saw the block fail to light up the toy twice, but when they tried the block, the toy did light up. In this condition, children said that the 1/3 block had more special stuff. Children seemed to prefer making inferences based on their own interventions.

Critically, however, the children were also tested in a confounding control condition. In the control condition, children saw exactly the same evidence as in the test condition; however, this time when the child intervened, the experimenter simultaneously pushed a button "to make the toy light up." The child's "intervention" was thus no longer a real intervention—it did not break other arrows (like the experimenter pushing the button) into the effect. When the children's own interventions were confounded in this way, they did not express a preference for their own interventions; the children returned to judging the blocks on the basis of the probabilities (Kushnir, 2003; Kushnir & Gopnik, in press).

These findings suggest that, although children may not be able to design controlled experiments, they do, at least in certain cases, recognize instances of confounding. Children seem to be sensitive to some of the fundamental features of experimental design and make different inferences when causal manipulations are consistent with the conditional intervention principle than when they are not.

Still, we might ask how, in the absence of controlled experiments, children are able to learn so much from interventions. We rely on experimental design heavily in science; how can children learn so much in its absence? Why aren't children constantly running into confounded interventions and drawing inaccurate causal conclusions?

One possibility is that the very fact of being a child might serve children well. Children are notorious for being impulsive (they get into a lot of things) and perseverative (they get into the same things over and over again). Cast in a more positive light, children tend to intervene a lot, and they tend to replicate their interventions. Children's very immaturity and, in particular, the protracted development of their prefrontal cortex, which (in adults) seem to inhibit impulsivity (e.g., Casey, Giedd, & Thomas, 2000; Chao & Knight, 1998) and prevent perseveration (e.g., Goel & Grafman, 1995), may support causal learning.

How might immaturity and noise substitute for controlled experimental design? Note that to infer that X causes Y, you do not necessarily have to hold other causes of Y constant. You can also randomize other causes of Y. Children's tendency to intervene in many different contexts and their tendency to replicate their actions might be advantageous. Other causes of Y (whatever Y is) might exist, but children's own actions are unlikely always to coincide with those causes. Certainly, children may occasionally leap to the wrong causal conclusion from bad evidence. Wu and Cheng (1999), for instance, cite a childhood anecdote in which one of the authors dropped a vase at the same time that a power outage occurred and thus blamed herself for the blackout. However, such anecdotes are funny in part because they are rare. In general, children's own actions may be a trustworthy foundation for their causal inferences and naïve theories.

Conclusion

In many respects, the causal Bayes net formalism seems to provide a learning mechanism that captures the dynamic nature of theories—and in many respects, children's learning seems to be commensurate with the predictions made by the formalism. However, the causal Bayes net formalism may not tell the whole story. In particular, the formalism may not entirely satisfy Mark Twain. How we get such "wholesale returns of conjecture out of a trifling investment in fact" remains something of a mystery.

Causal Bayes net algorithms were developed for use in procedures like data mining, for which evidence is plentiful, but the causal relationships are obscure. Constraint-based search methods thus rely on the evidence of many trials or assume the available data are representative of a larger sample. Bayesian learning algorithms rely on either an abundance of data or an abundance of prior knowledge.

In our experiments, by contrast, evidence was scarce. Children made causal inferences from a minimal amount of data, often using only the evidence of a single trial. As Tenenbaum and Griffiths (2003) note, in "many cases . . . causal inference follow(s) from just one or a few observations, where there isn't even enough data to reliably infer correlation!"

Note, however, that the causal Bayes net formalism was also developed to infer causal structure from noisy, probabilistic data in contexts in which interventions were impossible (e.g., in epidemiological studies).

By contrast, in all of our studies, children observed or performed interventions, and in most cases the evidence they saw was deterministic. Such contexts (when interventions are possible and determinism is assumed) may be plentiful in everyday life, and within such contexts, children may not need the full apparatus of the causal Bayes net learning algorithms. Children may be able to represent structure as a causal Bayes net and may use some of the same principles about the relationship between evidence and structure without requiring the full power of the learning algorithms (see Richardson, Schultz, & Gopnik, chapter 13, this volume). Thus, the causal Bayes net formalism may be "too big" for what children need to accomplish.

Alternatively, causal Bayes nets formalism may be "too small." The algorithms may miss a level of abstraction (what Tenenbaum & Niyogi, 2003, and Griffiths & Tenenbaum, chapter 20, this volume, call a *causal grammar*) that encompasses higher-order causal laws that are assumed but never explicitly presented to the children (i.e., that blocks activate detectors, and detectors do not activate blocks). Children may be successful at learning causal relationships from a few observations (in our lab and in the world) because they are already bringing a rich theoretical structure to bear on the inferential tasks. Thus, the causal Bayes net algorithms may allow children to learn structure from minimal data only when they are embedded within higher-order causal theories (see Tenenbaum & Griffiths, 2003; Tenenbaum & Niyogi, 2003; Griffiths & Tenenbaum, chapter 20, this volume).

Critically, however, this account may only move the problem of causal inference back a step. Knowledge of higher-order causal laws might support children's ability to learn particular causal relations. However, somehow children must also learn the higher-order causal laws—and it seems tempting to assume that children infer higher-order causal laws from particular causal relations. One of the challenges for future research is to determine whether such circles can be benign rather than vicious. In principle, children might be able to bootstrap an abstract causal grammar from clear evidence for particular causal relationships and then use the higher-order theory to handle more complex or ambiguous evidence for particular causal relations.

However, even if (as we expect) the causal Bayes net formalism does not end up being "just right," it more than any other current computational account suggests a learning mechanism that does justice to much of the breadth and depth of children's naïve theories. In supporting novel predictions, novel interventions, structure learning, inferences about unobserved causes, distinctions between observations and interventions, and the criteria for a good intervention, the causal Bayes net formalism captures much that is critical about a theory. Our hope is that children's ability to engage in theory formation and theory change might similarly set the standard for future computational accounts of learning.

If you are persuaded by little else by this chapter, we hope we have at least convinced you of the value of interdisciplinary work. Research in computer science, artificial intelligence, and philosophy has suggested some of the fundamental assumptions that might underlie the development of children's naïve theories. Work in developmental psychology has demonstrated that young children are able to learn the causal structure of events with remarkable speed and accuracy. We hope that investigators in all these areas will continue to find causal learning, in both children and science, fascinating for years to come.

References

Ahn, W., Kalish, C. W., Medin, D. L., & Gelman, S. A. (1995). The role of covariation versus mechanism information in causal attribution. *Cognition*, 57, 299–352.

Baillargeon, R., Kotovsky, L., & Needham, A. (1995). The acquisition of physical knowledge in infancy. In D. Sperber & D. Premack (Eds.), *Causal cognition: A multidisciplinary debate. Symposia of the Fyssen Foundation; Fyssen Symposium, 6th January 1993, Pavillon Henri IV, St-Germain-en-Laye, France* (pp. 79–115). New York: Clarendon Press/Oxford University Press.

Baker, A. G., Berbrier, M., & Vallée-Tourangeau, F. (1989). Judgements of a 2 × 2 contingency table: Sequential processing and the learning curve. *Quarterly Journal of Experimental Psychology*, 41B, 65–97.

Bickel, P. J., Hammel, E. A., & O'Connell, J. W. (1975). Sex bias in graduate admissions: Data from Berkeley. *Science*, 187, 389–404.

Bullock, M., Gelman, R., & Baillargeon, R. (1982). The development of causal reasoning. In W. J. Friedman (Ed.), *The developmental psychology of time* (pp. 209–254). New York: Academic Press.

Carey, S. (1985). *Conceptual change in childhood*. Cambridge, MA: MIT Press/Bradford Books.

Casey, B. J., Giedd, J. N., & Thomas, K. M. (2000). Structural and functional brain development and its relation to cognitive development. *Biological Psychology*, 54, 241–257.

Chao, L. L., & Knight, R. T. (1998). Contribution of human prefrontal cortex to delay performance. *Journal of Cognitive Neuroscience*, 10, 167–177.

Cheng, P. W. (1997). From covariation to causation: A causal power theory. *Psychological Review*, 104, 367–405.

Dickinson, A., Shanks, D. R., & Evendon, J. (1984). Judgment of act-outcome contingency: The role of selective attribution. *Quarterly Journal of Experimental Psychology*, 36, 29–50.

Dowe, P. (2000). *Physical causation*. New York: Cambridge University Press.

Flavell, J. H., Green, F. L., & Flavell, E. R. (1995). Young children's knowledge about thinking. *Monographs of the Society for Research in Child Development*, 60, v-96.

Gelman, S. A., & Wellman, H. M. (1991). Insides and essence: Early understandings of the non-obvious. *Cognition*, 38, 213–244.

Goel, V., & Grafman, J. (1995). Are the frontal lobes implicated in "planning" functions? Interpreting data from the Tower of Hanoi. *Neuropsychologia*, 33, 623–642.

Gopnik, A., Glymour, C., Sobel, D. M., Schulz, L., Kushnir, T., & Danks, D. (2004). A theory of causal learning in children: Causal maps and Bayes nets. *Psychological Review*, 111, 1–31.

Gopnik, A., & Meltzoff, A. N. (1997). *Words, thoughts and theories*. Cambridge, MA: MIT Press.

Gopnik, A., Sobel, D. M., Schulz, L. E., & Glymour, C. (2001). Causal learning mechanisms in very young children: 2-, 3-, and 4-year-olds infer causal relations from patterns of variation and covariation. *Developmental Psychology*, 37, 620–629.

Gopnik, A., & Wellman, H. M. (1994). The theory theory. In S. A. Gelman & L. A. Hirschfeld (Eds.), *Mapping the mind: Domain specificity in cognition and culture; based on a conference entitled "Cultural Knowledge and Domain Specificity," held in Ann Arbor, Michigan, October 13–16, 1990* (pp. 257–293). New York: Cambridge University Press.

Griffiths, T. L., & Tenenbaum, J. B. (2001). Randomness and coincidences: Reconciling intuition and probability theory. *Proceedings of the 23rd Annual Conference of the Cognitive Science Society*. Edinburgh: LEA. pp. 370–375.

Harris, P. L., German, T., & Mills, P. (1996). Children's use of counterfactual thinking in causal reasoning. *Cognition, 61,* 233–259.

Inagaki, K., & Hatano, G. (1993). Young children's understanding of the mind body distinction. *Child Development, 64,* 1534–1549.

Kalish, C. (1996). Causes and symptoms in preschoolers' conceptions of illness. *Child Development, 67,* 1647–1670.

Keil, F. C. (2003). Folkscience: Coarse interpretations of a complex reality. *Trends in Cognitive Sciences, 18,* 663–692.

Kuhn, D. (1989). Children and adults as intuitive scientists. *Psychological Review, 96,* 674–689.

Kuhn, D., Amsel, E. & O'Laughlin, M. (1988). *The development of scientific thinking skills.* Orlando, FL: Academic Press.

Kushnir, T. (2003, April). *Seeing versus doing: The effect of direct intervention on preschooler's understanding of probabilistic causes.* Poster presented at the biennial meeting of the Society for Research in Child Development, Tampa, FL.

Kushnir, T., & Gopnik, A. (2005). Children infer causal strength from probabilities and interventions. *Psychological Science, 16(9),* 678–683.

Kushnir, T., Gopnik, A., & Schaefer, C. (2005, April). *Children infer hidden causes from probabilistic evidence.* Paper presented at the biennial meeting of the Society for Research in Child Development, Atlanta, GA.

Kushnir, T., Gopnik, A., Schulz, L., & Danks, D. (2003). Inferring hidden causes. In R. Alterman & D. Kirsh (Eds.), *Proceedings of the 25th Annual Meeting of the Cognitive Science Society.* Boston, pp. 699–703.

Leslie, A. M., & Keeble, S. (1987). Do 6-month-old infants perceive causality? *Cognition, 25,* 265–288.

Masnick, A. M., & Klahr, D. (2003). Error matters: An initial exploration of elementary school children's understanding of experimental error. *Journal of Cognition & Development, 4,* 67–98.

Meltzoff, A. N. (1995). Understanding the intentions of others: Re-enactment of intended acts by 18-month-old children. *Developmental Psychology, 31,* 838–850.

Michotte, A. (1962). *The perception of causality.* New York: Basic Books. (Original work published 1946).

Novick, L. R., & Cheng, P. W. (2004). Assessing interactive causal influence. *Psychological Review, 111,* 455–485.

Pearl, J. (2000). *Causality.* New York: Oxford University Press.

Perner, J. (1991). *Understanding the representational mind.* Cambridge, MA: MIT Press.

Piaget, J. (1930). *The child's conception of physical causality.* London: Kegan Paul.

Rovee-Collier, C. (1980). Reactivation of infant memory. *Science, 208,* 1159–1161.

Rosenblit, L. R., & Keil, F. C. (2002). The misunderstood limits of folk science: an illusion of explanatory depth. *Cognitive Science, 26,* 521–562.

Saffran, J. R., Aslin, R. N., & Newport, E. L. (1996). Statistical learning by 8-month-old infants. *Science, 274,* 1926–1928.

Salmon, W. (1984). *Scientific explanation and the causal structure of the world.* Princeton, NJ: Princeton University Press.

Salmon, W. (1998). *Causality and explanation.* Oxford, England: Oxford University Press.

Schaefer, C., & Gopnik, A. (2003, April). *Causal reasoning in young children: The role of unobserved variables.* Paper presented at the biennial meeting of the Society for Research in Child Development, Tampa, FL.

Schlottman, A. (2001). Perception versus knowledge of cause and effect in children: When seeing is believing. *Current Directions in Psychological Science, 10,* 111–115.

Schulz, L. E., (2001, December). *Spinning wheels and bossy ones: Children, causal structure and the calculus of intervention.* Paper presented at the Causal Inference in Humans and Machines Workshop of the Neural Information Processing Systems annual meeting, Vancouver, BC.

Schulz, L. (2003, April). *The play's the thing: Interventions and causal inference.* Paper presented at the biennial meeting of the Society for Research in Child Development, Tampa, FL.

Schulz, L., & Gopnik, A. (2004). Causal learning across domains. *Developmental Psychology, 40,* 162–176.

Schulz, L., Gopnik, A., & Glymour, C. (in press). Preschool children learn causal structure from conditional interventions. *Developmental Science.*

Shanks, D. R. (1985). Forward and backward blocking in human contingency judgment. *Quarterly Journal of Experimental Psychology: Comparative and Physiological Psychology, 37,* 1–21.

Shanks, D. R., & Dickinson, A. (1987). Associative accounts of causality judgment. In G. H. Bower (Ed.), *The psychology of learning and motivation: Advances in research and theory* (Vol. 21, pp. 229–261). San Diego, CA: Academic Press.

Shultz, T. R. (1982). Rules of causal attribution. *Monographs of the Society for Research in Child Development, 47,* 1–51.

Sloman, S. A., & Lagnado, D. A. (2005). Do we "do"? *Cognitive Science, 29,* 5–39.

Sobel, D. M. (2004). Emploring the coherence of young children's explanatory abilities: Evidence from generating counter factuals. *British Journal of Developmental Psychology, 22,* 37–58.

Sobel, D. M., Tenenbaum, J. B., & Gopnik, A. (2004). Children's causal inferences from indirect evidence: Backwards blocking and Bayesian reasoning in preschoolers. *Cognitive Science, 28,* 303–333.

Sommer, S., & Wehner, R. (2004). The ant's estimation of distance travelled: Experiments with desert ants, *Cataglyphis fortis. Journal of Comparative Physiology A, Neuroethology Sensory Neural Behavioral Physiology, 190,* 1–6.

Spelke, E. S., Breinlinger, K., Macomber, J., & Jacobson, K. (1992). Origins of knowledge. *Psychological Review, 99,* 605–632.

Spelke, E. S., Katz, G., Purcell, S. E., Ehrlich, S. M., & Breinlinger, K. (1994). Early knowledge of object motion: Continuity and inertia. *Cognition, 51,* 131–176.

Spirtes, P., Glymour, C., & Scheines, R. (1993). *Causation, prediction, and search* (Springer Lecture Notes in Statistics). New York: Springer-Verlag.

Strevens, M. (2000). The essentialist aspect of naive theories. *Cognition, 74(2),* 149–175.

Steyvers, M., Tenenbaum, J., Wagenmakers, E. J., & Blum, B. (2003). Inferring causal networks from observations and interventions. *Cognitive Science, 27,* 453–489.

Tenenbaum, J. B., & Griffiths, T. L., (2003). Theory-based causal inference. In S. Becker, S. Thrun, & K. Obemayer (Eds.), *Advances in neural information processing systems 15.* Cambridge, MA: MIT Press (pp. 35–42).

Tolman, E. C. (1932). *Purposive behavior in animals and men.* New York: Century.

Wasserman, E. A., Elek, S. M, Chatlosh, D. L., & Baker, A. G. (1993). Rating causal relations: Role of probability in judgments of response-outcome contingency. *Journal of Experimental Psychology: Learning, Memory, and Cognition, 19,* 174–188.

Watson, J. S., & Ramey, C. T. (1987). Reactions to response-contingent stimulation in early infancy. In J. Oates, & S. Sheldon (Eds.), *Cognitive development in infancy; cognitive development in infancy; portions of this paper were initially reported at the biennial meeting of the Society for Research in Child Development, Santa Monica, CA, 1969* (pp. 77–85). Hillsdale, NJ: Erlbaum.

Wellman, H. M., Hickling, A. K., & Schult, C. A. (1997). Young children's psychological, physical, and biological explanations. In H. M. Wellman & K. Inagaki (Eds.), *The emergence of core domains of thought: Children's reasoning about physical, psychological, and biological phenomena* (New Directions for Child Development, No. 75, pp. 7–25). San Francisco: Jossey-Bass/Pfeiffer.

Tenenbaum, J., & Griffiths, T. L. (2003). Theory-based causal inference. In S. Becker, S. Thrun, & K. Obemayer (Eds.), *Advances in neural information processing systems 15* (pp. 67–74). Cambridge, MA: MIT Press.

Tenenbaum, J., & Niyogi, S. (2003). Learning causal laws. In R. Alterman & D. Kirsh (Eds.), *Proceedings of the 25th Annual Conference of the Cognitive Science Society.* Boston, pp. 1152–1157.

Waldmann, M. R. (2000). Competition among causes but not effects in predictive and diagnostic learning. *Journal of Experimental Psychology: Learning, Memory, and Cognition, 26,* 53–76.

Waldmann, M. R. (2001). Predictive versus diagnostic causal learning: Evidence from an overshadowing paradigm. *Psychonomic Bulletin and Review, 8,* 600–608.

Waldmann, M. R., & Hagmayer, Y. (2005). Seeing versus doing: Two modes of accessing causal knowledge. *Journal of Experimental Psychology: Learning, Memory, and Cognition, 31,* 216–227.

Wellman, H. M., Hickling, A. K., & Schult, C. A. (1997). Young children's psychological, physical, and biological explanations. *New Directions for Child Development, 75,* 7–25.

Woodward, A. L. (1998). Infants selectively encode the goal object of an actor's reach. *Cognition, 69,* 1–34.

Woodward, A. L., Phillips, A. T., & Spelke, E. S. (1993). Infants' expectations about the motion of animate versus inanimate objects. In *Proceedings of the 15th annual meeting of the Cognitive Science Society* (pp. 1087–1091). Hillsdale, NJ: Erlbaum.

Woodward, J. (2003). *Making things happen: A theory of causal explanation.* New York: Oxford University Press.

Wu, M., & Cheng, P. W. (1999). Why causation need not follow from statistical association: Boundary conditions for the evaluation of generative and preventive causal powers. *Psychological Science, 10,* 92–97.

6

Causal Reasoning Through Intervention

York Hagmayer, Steven Sloman, David Lagnado, & Michael R. Waldmann

Introduction

Causal knowledge enables us to predict future events, to choose the right actions to achieve our goals, and to envision what would have happened if things had been different. Thus, it allows us to reason about observations, interventions, and counterfactual possibilities. Philosophers and computer scientists have begun to unravel the relations among these three kinds of reasoning and their common basis in causality (e.g., Pearl, 2000; Spirtes, Glymour, & Scheines, 1993; Woodward, 2003).

Observations can provide some information about the statistical relations among events. According to the principle of common cause (Reichenbach, 1956), there are three possible causal explanations for a reliable statistical relation between two events A and B: A causes B, B causes A, or both events are generated by a third event or set of events, their common cause. For example, dieting and obesity are statistically related because obesity causes people to go on a diet, because dieting disturbs regulatory physiological processes that

eventually lead to obesity (many obese people went on a diet before they became extremely overweight), or because obesity and dieting may be causal consequences of our modern eating habits. In this last case, we can say that the correlation between obesity and dieting is spurious. Regardless of the underlying causal structure, an observation of one of these events allows us to infer that other events within the underlying causal model will be present or absent as well. Thus, when we have passively observed an event, we can reason backward diagnostically to infer the causes of this event, or we can reason forward and predict future effects. Moreover, we can infer the presence of spuriously related events.

Interventions often enable us to differentiate among the different causal structures that are compatible with an observation. If we manipulate an event A and nothing happens, then A cannot be the cause of event B, but if a manipulation of event B leads to a change in A, then we know that B is a cause of A, although there might be other causes of A as well. Forcing some people to go on a diet can tell us whether the diet increases or decreases the risk of obesity. Alternatively, changing people's weight by making them exercise would show whether body mass is causally responsible for dieting.

In contrast to observations, however, interventions do not provide positive or negative diagnostic evidence about the causes of the event on which we intervened. Whereas observations of events allow us to reason diagnostically about their causes, interventions make the occurrence of events independent of their typical causes. Thus, because of the statistical independence created by interventions, these events will occur with their usual base rate independent of the outcome of an intervention. For example, forcing somebody to eat 50 (and only 50) grams of fat per day fixes fat intake independent of the presence or absence of other factors normally affecting diet.

Counterfactual reasoning tells us what would have happened if events other than the ones we are currently observing had happened. If we are currently observing that both A and B are present, then we can ask ourselves if B would still be present if we had intervened on A and caused its absence. If we know that B is the cause of A, then we should infer that the absence of A makes no difference to the presence of B because effects do not necessarily affect their causes. But, if our intervention had prevented B from occurring, then we should infer that A also would not occur. For example, Morgan Spurlock (director and guinea pig of the movie *Supersize Me*, released in 2004) ate fast food for 4 weeks and gained more than 20 pounds. What would have happened if he had not eaten burgers and fries all the time? Assuming that his heavy consumption of fast food was causally responsible for his increase in weight rather than the increased weight being the cause of eating, we can conclude that he would have stayed in better shape without all the carbohydrates and fats.

The example indicates that counterfactual reasoning combines observational and interventional reasoning. First, we observe Morgan eating fast food and gaining weight. Second, we assume that one of the events had been different. We imagine him not eating such a diet, while all other observed or inferred factors (e.g., his genetic makeup, amount of physical exercise, etc.) are assumed to stay at the observed level. Thus, instantiating a counterfactual event is causally equivalent to an imaginary intervention on a causal model in which all variables that are not affected by the intervention are assumed to stay at currently observed levels.

Finally, causal consequences of the intervention are inferred on the basis of the given causal model. We infer that Morgan would not have gained as much weight as he did (see next section; Pearl, 2000; and Sloman & Lagnado, 2005, for a more detailed discussion of counterfactuals).

There are important differences among observation, intervention, and counterfactuals. Nevertheless, they can be given a unified treatment within the causal model framework. Whereas probabilistic and associative accounts of causal knowledge fail to capture these three interrelated functions of causal knowledge, causal Bayes nets do (Glymour, 2001; Pearl, 2000; Spirtes et al., 1993). The next section summarizes these accounts. Although causal Bayes nets provide successful formal tools for expert systems, few experiments have tested whether causal Bayes nets also capture everyday reasoning with causal models by people who are not formally trained. The remainder of the chapter presents experimental evidence from the areas of logical reasoning, learning, and decision making demonstrating the plausibility of causal Bayes nets as psychological theories.

Modeling

We do not give a detailed description of causal Bayes nets here (see Pearl, 2000, or Spirtes et al., 1993, for detailed introductions). Research on causal Bayes nets focuses not only on causal representation and inference but also on other questions, such as those regarding learning (see Lagnado, Waldmann, Hagmayer, & Sloman, chapter 10, this volume). Here, we show how to derive predictions from causal Bayes nets based on observations, interventions, and counterfactual assumptions. Although causal Bayes nets provide tools for reasoning with complex models, experimental studies typically present problems that are within the grasp of naïve participants. We therefore concentrate our brief introduction on inferences using the three basic causal models involving most research: common-cause, common-effect, and causal chain models. More complex models can be generated by combining these three models (see Sloman & Lagnado, 2005, and Waldmann & Hagmayer, 2005, for research on more complex models).

Figure 6-1 shows the graphs for the three models, with the nodes representing event variables and the arrows signifying direction of causal influence: (a) a

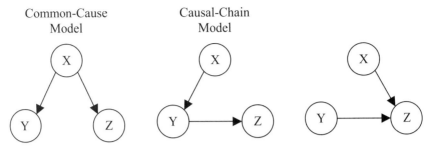

FIGURE 6-1 Three basic causal models.

common-cause model in which a single cause X influences two effects Y and Z, (b) a causal chain model in which an initial cause X affects an intermediate event Y influencing a final effect Z, and (c) a common-effect model in which two causes X and Y independently influence a joint effect Z.

The graphs encode assumptions about dependence and independence, simplifying the representation of the causal domain. One important assumption underlying Bayes nets is the Markov assumption, which states (informally) that each event in a causal graph is independent of all events other than its descendants (i.e., its direct and indirect effects) once the values of its parent nodes (i.e., its direct causes) are known.

The graph of the common-cause model expresses the spurious correlation between effects Y and Z (because of their common cause) and their independence once the state of cause X is known. This is a consequence of the Markov condition. Once we know that X is present, the probability of Y is the same regardless of whether Z is present. Similarly, the causal chain implies that the initial cause X and the final effect Z are dependent but become independent when the intermediate event Y is held constant. Once we know that Y, the direct cause of Z, is present, the probability of Z stays constant regardless of whether X has occurred. Finally, the common-effect model implies independence of the alternative causes X and Y and their dependence once the common effect is held fixed. This is an example of explaining away. X and Y should occur independently, but once we know that X and its effect Z are present, it is less likely that Y is also present.

Independence is advantageous in a probabilistic model not only because it simplifies the graph by allowing omission of a link between variables but also because it simplifies computation. Conceived as a computational entity, a Bayes nets is merely a

representation of a joint probability distribution— $P(X,Y,Z)$ in Figure 6-1—that provides a more complete model of how the world might be by specifying the probability of each possible state. Each event is represented as a variable. Causal relations are assumed to generate the conditional probabilities relating causes to their effects, and arrows in a causal graph represent those causal relations. The factorizations of the three models at issue are

Common cause: $P(X, Y, Z) = P(Y \mid X) \, P(Z \mid X) \, P(X)$

Causal chain: $P(X, Y, Z) = P(Z \mid Y) \, P(Y \mid X) \, P(X)$

Common effect: $P(X, Y, Z) = P(Z \mid Y, X) \, P(Y) \, P(X)$

The equations specify the probability distribution of the events within the model in terms of the strength of the causal links and the base rates of the exogenous causes that have no parents (e.g., X in the common-cause model). Implicit in the specification of the parameters of a Bayes net are rules specifying how multiple causes of a common effect combine to produce the effect or (in the case of continuous variables) functional relations between variables. A parameterized causal model allows it to make specific predictions of the probabilities of individual events or patterns of events within the causal model.

Modeling Observations

Observations not only tell us whether a particular event is present or absent but also inform us about other events that are directly or indirectly causally related to the observed event. Therefore, the structure of the causal model is crucial for inference. Observing an event increases the probability of its causes and its effects. For example, if someone has a high level of cholesterol, then you can make the diagnostic inference that the person has probably had an unhealthy diet (cause) and you can predict that the person's risk of contracting heart problems is relatively high (effect). These inferences can be justified on the basis of the structure of the causal model. No specific information about the strength of the causal relations or the base rates of the events is necessary to make these qualitative predictions. More specific predictions of the probabilities of events can be made when the model is parameterized.

Formally, observations are modeled by setting the event variables to the values that have been observed. Based on our equations and probability calculus, the probabilities of other events conditional on the observed variable can be calculated. The structure of the causal model is crucial for these calculations. Imagine that an effect Y of a common cause X that also generates Z is observed. The resulting increase in probability of the cause X can be computed using Bayes' rule:

$$P(X = 1 \mid Y = 1)$$
$$= P(Y = 1 \mid X = 1) \, P(X = 1) / \left[P(Y = 1 \mid X = 1) \right.$$
$$P(X = 1) + P(Y = 1 \mid X = 0) \, P(X = 0) \left. \right]$$

For example, if the base rate of following an unhealthy diet is $P(X=1)=.5$, the probability that an unhealthy diet will cause being overweight is $P(Y = 1 \mid X = 1) = .9$, and the probability of being overweight despite eating healthy food is $P(Y = 1 \mid X = 0) = .1$, then being overweight indicates a probability of $P(X = 1 \mid Y = 1) = .9$ that the diet was unhealthy. The probability of the other effect Z has to be computed by using the updated probability of the common cause and the conditional probability $P(Z \mid X)$ referring to the causal relation connecting the common cause and the second effect. For example, if the probability of having high levels of cholesterol given an unhealthy diet is $P = .4$ and $P = .1$ otherwise, then the observation of a person's being overweight implies that the probability of having a high level of cholesterol is .37. Note that this calculation rests on the assumptions that the events are connected by a common-cause model. The same conditional probabilities have different implications given other causal structures.

Modeling Interventions

There are different types of intervention (see Woodward, 2003). Interventions can interact with the other causes of events. For example, when we increase fat in our diet, then the resulting cholesterol level in our blood depends on our metabolism, prior level of cholesterol, and many other factors. The causal Bayes net literature has focused on a specific type of intervention that completely determines the value of the variable the intervention targets (see Pearl, 2000; Spirtes et al., 1993; Woodward, 2003). For example, if we set the temperature of a room to 20°C, our intervention fixes room temperature while disconnecting it from all its causes. In this chapter, we focus on this strong type of intervention.

How can interventions be formally modeled? The most important assumption can be traced to Fisher's (1951) analysis of experimental methods. Randomly assigning participants to experimental and control groups creates independence between the independent variable and possible confounds. Thus, if we, as external agents, set cholesterol levels to a specific value, then the level of cholesterol is independent of other factors normally determining its level. To qualify as an intervention of this strong kind, the manipulation has to force a value on the intervened variable (e.g., cholesterol), thus removing all other causal influences (e.g., diet). Moreover, the intervention must be statistically independent of any variable that directly or indirectly causes the predicted event (e.g., all causes of cholesterol), and it should not have any causal relation to the predicted event except through the intervened-on variable (see Pearl, 2000; Spirtes et al., 1993; Woodward, 2003).

As with observation, predictions of the outcomes of hypothetical interventions are based on specific values of event variables, but whereas observations leave the surrounding causal network intact, interventions alter the structure of the causal model by rendering the manipulated variable independent of its causes. Thus, predictions on the basis of interventions need to be based on the altered causal model, not the original model. For example, the passive observation of low cholesterol level indicates a healthy diet because of the causal link between diet and cholesterol, but medically inducing a specific cholesterol level does not provide evidence about a person's eating habits. Manipulating cholesterol independent of the prior value and other factors creates independence between cholesterol level and diet. Thus, predictions about eating habits can only be based on assumptions about base rates, not on evidence about cholesterol level.

The changes in a causal model caused by interventions (of the strong type) can be modeled by procedures that Pearl (2000) vividly calls *graph surgery*. These procedures result in a "manipulated graph" (Spirtes et al., 1993). The key idea is that interventions introduce an external independent cause that fixes the value of the manipulated event. As a consequence, all other causal arrows pointing toward this event need to be removed because these causal influences are not operative during the intervention. Thus, both types of predictions are grounded in a representation of the underlying causal model. However, whereas observational predictions are based on the original causal graph, interventional predictions are based on the manipulated graph. Figure 6-2 illustrates for the three causal models from Figure 6-1 how observing differs from intervening. In general, the manipulated graphs are generated by removing the incoming causal links that point to the manipulated variable.

Traditional Bayes nets (e.g., Pearl, 1988) and other probabilistic theories are incapable of distinguishing between observations and interventions because they lack the expressive power to distinguish observational and interventional conditional probabilities. Both types are subsumed under the general concept of conditional probability. To distinguish observations from interventions, Pearl (2000), following previous work by Spirtes

et al. (1993), introduces a do-operator. The do-operator represents an intervention on an event that renders the manipulated event independent of all its causes (i.e., it is the formal equivalent of graph surgery).

For example, $do(Y = 1)$ represents the event that Y was fixed to the value of 1 by means of an intervention. Thus, it implies the removal of all previous causal influences in Y. Applying the do-operator allows it to make specific interventional predictions about events within the causal model. For example, the equations for the factorization of the joint distribution of the causal chain model (Figure 6-2) in which the intermediate event is observed to be present $(Y = 1)$ or manipulated $[do(Y = 1)]$, respectively, are

Observation of Y:
$$P(X, Y = 1, Z) = P(Z \mid Y = 1)\ P(Y = 1 \mid X)\ P(X)$$
Intervention on Y:
$$P(X, do(Y = 1), Z) = P(Z \mid Y = 1)\ P(X)$$

If the parameters of the causal model are known, we can calculate the probabilistic consequences of interventions. The hypothetical intervention on Y (i.e., Y is fixed to the value of 1 and therefore known to be present) in the causal chain implies that Z occurs with the observational probability conditional on the presence of Y $(P(Z \mid Y=1)$, and that X occurs with a probability

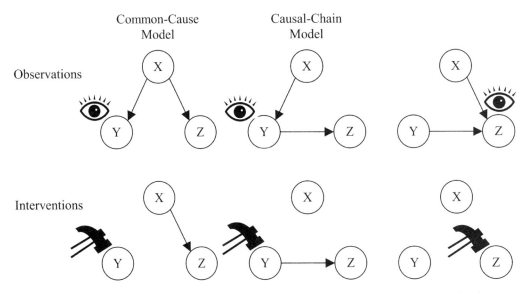

FIGURE 6-2 Examples of observations of (symbolized as eyes) and interventions on (symbolized as hammers) the three basic causal models.

corresponding to its base rate ($P(X)$). Notice that the interventional probability requires fewer parameters because graph surgery involves simplification by inducing independence between a variable and its causes.

As a second example, consider the common-cause model in Figure 6-1. Whereas observing Y allows us to reason diagnostically back to its cause X and then reason forward predictively to its spurious correlate Z, predictions for hypothetical interventions in effect Y need to be based on the manipulated graph in Figure 6-2 in which the link between X and Y is removed. Formally, this can be expressed by the equation[1]

$$P(X, do(Y = 1), Z) = P(Z \mid X) \, P(X)$$

Thus, fixing Y at the value 1 removes the link to this variable from the causal model. However, predictions are still possible on the basis of the manipulated graph. The common cause X should occur with a probability corresponding to its base rate, and Z is determined by the base rate of its cause X and the strength of the probabilistic relation between X and Z.

Modeling Counterfactuals

Counterfactuals combine observations and interventions. The current state of the world is modeled as an observation, and then the counterfactual is set by an imaginary intervention altering the state of the variables assumed to be different. For example, we may currently tend to eat unhealthy fast food. For a counterfactual analysis, we would first model this fact as if it were an observation by inferring the consequences for other unobserved events within the causal model. We may infer that we have an increased probability of contracting diabetes. Next, we want to know what would happen if we had eaten healthy food instead. We model this counterfactual by means of a hypothetical intervention that fixes the value of the diet variable. Note that counterfactuals differ from interventions because counterfactual interventions alter causal models, which have been updated before on the basis of the given facts.

As in the case of observations and interventions, graphical causal models are sufficient to draw qualitative inferences from counterfactuals. For example, consider a causal chain model connecting diet, weight, and diabetes. To model the statement, "If she were not obese, she would not have developed diabetes," we first assume that we observe diabetes and obesity in a woman. Based on these observations, we can infer that the woman probably tends to eat an unhealthy diet. Next, we hypothetically eliminate obesity by means of an intervention that influences this variable by means of a factor external to the chain model. This hypothetical intervention would cut the causal link between diet and weight, but the link between weight and diabetes would stay intact. Therefore, the counterfactual implies that the person in this alternative world would be spared diabetes, while her eating habits would stay the same.

Formal modeling of counterfactuals requires updating of the model twice. First, the probabilities of all events are calculated conditional on the facts stated in the counterfactual treating facts as observations. Second, the counterfactual event is set by the do-operator, which entails a reanalysis of the probabilities of the events in the manipulated graph. Thus, assuming the validity of the causal model and the attached parameters, causal Bayes nets allow us to generate precise predictions for counterfactuals.

Summary

Causal Bayes nets capture the structure of causal models. They allow us to generate qualitative predictions for observations, interventions, and counterfactuals. Moreover, parameterized causal models enable us to make precise predictions about the probabilities of events within the causal model. Whereas observational predictions are within the grasp of traditional associative or probabilistic (including Bayesian) theories, modeling interventions and counterfactuals transcends the conceptual power of these models. To model hypothetical interventions and counterfactuals correctly, a preliminary stage has to be assumed in which the structure of the causal model generating the predictions is modified. Based on this modified causal model, precise predictions can be made for situations that may never before have been observed.

The distinction between observation and intervention is crucial for the theory of causal Bayes nets. Although observations allow drawing inferences about causes and effects of the observed event, interventions cut the event off from its causes by deleting the causal links pointing toward the event. Sloman and Lagnado (2005) coined the term *undoing* for this process.

If causal Bayes nets are veridical models of intuitive human causal reasoning, then participants have to be sensitive to undoing. Thus, a key issue will be whether human participants are capable of predicting outcomes of hypothetical interventions and of reasoning about causal counterfactuals. This competency would imply that people have access to reasoning processes that modify causal representations prior to deriving predictions. The next three sections report evidence concerning this question.

Causal Reasoning Versus Logical Reasoning

Causal Bayes nets can be used to represent and model qualitative logical inferences in causal domains. One implication of this account is that causal inference differs from inference in a context in which the standard rules of propositional logic also apply. Although standard logic does not distinguish between the observation of an event and the generation of the same event by an intervention, the distinction is central to causal Bayes nets. Causal models have the ability to represent both action (intervention in the world) and imagination (intervention in the mind). If participants are sensitive to the difference between observation and intervention, then they should infer that the observation of an event is diagnostic of the presence of its causes, but when the same event is physically or mentally manipulated, it no longer is.

Observation Versus Intervention in Counterfactual Scenarios

To verify that people are sensitive to the difference between observation and intervention, Sloman and Lagnado (2005) gave a group of students the following scenario:

> All rocketships have two components, A and B. Movement of Component A causes Component B to move. In other words, if A, then B. Both are moving.

Notice that this scenario describes the simplest possible causal model involving only a single link (see Figure 6-3). Furthermore, the current values of the variables A and B are stated.

After reading the scenario, half the group was then asked the observational counterfactual question concerning what they would expect if they had *observed* components not moving: (a) Suppose Component B were observed to not be moving, would Component A still be moving? The other half was asked the interventional counterfactual question concerning what they would expect if components had been intervened on and thereby prevented from moving: (b) Suppose Component B were prevented from moving, would Component A still be moving?

The difference between observation and intervention should show up in the comparison of (a) and (b). Observing that the effect B is not moving should be diagnostic of A, suggesting that A also is not moving. In contrast, the logic of intervention says that we should represent an intervention on B as $P(A$ moves $\mid do(B$ does not move$))$, which reduces to $P(A$ moves$)$ because B is disconnected from its normal cause A under the *do* operation. As participants were told before that A is moving, they should stick to that belief and answer yes. This is just what happened: 85% of participants answered yes to (b) but only 22% answered yes to (a). B's movement was only treated as diagnostic of A's movement when B was observed not to move, not when its movement was prevented. This shows that people are sensitive to the logic of a counterfactual intervention in a situation with a transparent causal structure.

Causal Reasoning Versus Propositional Logic

The causal model framework predicts that people are sensitive to the logic of intervention when reasoning causally, not necessarily when reasoning in other ways. Sloman and Lagnado (2005) compared reasoning in a situation with causal relations to one with parallel relations that were not causal.

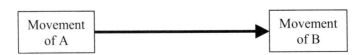

FIGURE 6-3 Simplest possible causal model.

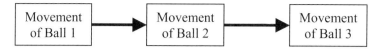

FIGURE 6-4 Causal chain model used by Sloman and Lagnado (2005).

Consider the following causal problem described in terms of conditional (if ... then) statements:

Causal conditional: There are three billiard balls on a table that act in the following way: If Ball 1 moves, then Ball 2 moves. If Ball 2 moves, then Ball 3 moves.

Imagine that Ball 2 could not move. Would Ball 1 still move?

The fact that we are talking about billiard balls—prototypical causal elements—strongly suggests that the conditional statements should be interpreted as describing causal relations. The causal model underlying this scenario is depicted in Figure 6-4. The causal modeling framework represents the two questions using the do-operator because an outside agent is preventing the ball from moving, represented as *do*(Ball 2 does not move):

P(Ball 1 moves | *do*(Ball 2 does not move)).

To evaluate this, we must assume that Ball 2 does not move. We must also simplify the causal model by removing any links into Ball 2 as depicted in Figure 6-5.

It is immediately apparent, parallel to the last example, that the value of Ball 1 is no longer affected by Ball 2, and therefore the causal Bayes model framework predicts that Ball 2's lack of movement is not diagnostic of its normal cause, Ball 1. Of participants, 90% agreed, affirming that Ball 1 could move if Ball 2 could not.

Standard propositional logical systems have no way to represent this argument. They not only do not have a representation of cause, but also have no way of representing an intervention. A conventional logical analysis of this problem might go as follows: The problem tells us that if Ball 1 moves, then Ball 2 moves. We know that Ball 2 does not move. Therefore, Ball 1 does not move by *modus tollens*, a logical schema that dictates that the antecedent of a conditional must be false if its consequent is. This particular argument does not explain people's judgments, which are that Ball 1 can move even if Ball 2 cannot.

In the noncausal realm, *modus tollens* can be a perfectly valid form of argument for deriving definite conclusions. For example, *modus tollens* would be an appropriate inference scheme to use on a problem similar to the causal one just shown but based on logical if-then relations rather than causal ones. Maybe people would make inferences conforming to *modus tollens* with such an argument. To find out, Sloman and Lagnado (2005) gave a group of people the following scenario:

Logical conditional. Someone is showing off her logical abilities. She is moving balls without breaking the following rules: If Ball 1 moves, then Ball 2 moves. If Ball 2 moves, then Ball 3 moves.

Sloman and Lagnado then asked the group the same question as for the causal case:

Imagine that Ball 2 could not move, would Ball 1 still move?

In this case, only 45% of participants said yes. The majority gave the inference consistent with *modus tollens*, no. Clearly, there is less consistency than in the causal case, probably because participants are more confused in a logical than in a causal context.

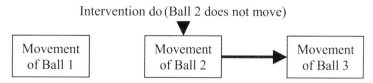

FIGURE 6-5 Causal chain model altered by an intervention on the intermediate event (adapted from Sloman & Lagnado, 2005).

Their answers are more wide ranging, and they tend to express less confidence. People's discomfort with logical problems relative to causal ones arises either because there are different forms of logic and they are not sure which one to pick or because no form of deductive logic comes naturally.

The experiments by Sloman and Lagnado (2005) show that causal reasoning is not adequately modeled by either standard propositional logic formalisms nor traditional probabilistic theories that do not distinguish intervention from observation. Causal Bayes nets are the best currently available account that models this competency.

Reasoning With Parameterized Causal Models

The preceding section showed that people can reason qualitatively with causal models, and that they distinguish between observation and intervention. Waldmann and Hagmayer (2005) have addressed similar questions in the realm of learning. Following the framework of causal model–theory (Waldmann, 1996; Waldmann & Martignon, 1998; see also Lagnado et al., chapter 10, this volume), participants were told about the structure of a causal model generating the learning data before being shown the data. The learning data consisted of individual cases that allowed participants to estimate the parameters of the assumed causal model (e.g., causal strength, base rates). The main questions were whether learners were capable of deriving precise predictions on the basis of the parameterized models and whether their predictions differ depending on whether the predictions are based on hypothetical observations or hypothetical interventions. Again, causal Bayes nets provided the formal tools to analyze this competency.

Associative theories are the dominant approach in the realm of learning. They can differentiate between observing and intervening by postulating separate learning modes: Whereas *classical conditioning* might be viewed as underlying prediction, intervention might be driven by *instrumental conditioning* (Dickinson, 2001; see Domjan, 2003, for an overview). Thus, we might learn in an observational learning paradigm (classical conditioning) that the barometer reading predicts the weather; in an interventional learning paradigm (instrumental learning), we might also learn that fiddling with the barometer does not change the weather. However, although this approach approximates causal knowledge in many contexts, it fails to capture the relations between observation and intervention. The separation between classical and instrumental conditioning predicts that, without a prior instrumental learning phase, we should be incapable of correctly predicting what would happen in case of an intervention in situations in which our knowledge is based on observational learning. Our experiments show that this is wrong. People not only were capable of deriving predictions for hypothetical interventions after a purely observational learning phase, but also their predictions were sensitive to the structure of the underlying causal model and the size of the parameters.

Predicting the Outcomes of Hypothetical Interventions From Observations

Experiment 2 of Waldmann and Hagmayer (2005) provides an example of the learning task. In this experiment, participants were taught either a common-cause or a causal chain model. In a fictitious medical scenario that involved hormone levels of chimpanzees, they were told either that an increased level of the hormone pixin P causes an increase in the level of sonin S and of xanthan X (common-cause model), or that an increase in the level of sonin causes the level of pixin to rise, which in turn increases the amount of xanthan (causal chain model) (see Figure 6-6). Waldmann and Hagmayer compared these two models because the common-cause model implies a dissociation between observational and interventional predictions, whereas the chain model implies identical predictions for both types, allowing us to test whether people correctly differentiate between causal models.

After the initial instructions, participants received descriptions of the hormone levels of a set of 20 individual chimpanzees as observational data. The causal relations were probabilistic (see Figure 6-6). Using the data, learners could estimate the parameters of the causal models. Causal chain and common-cause models have the same structural implications (they are Markov equivalent); therefore, only one set of data was presented that was coherent with both. The models and the implied parameters are shown in Figure 6-6.

A Bayesian analysis of these parameterized models implies for both models that the probability of increased levels of xanthan conditional on sonin being observed to be at an elevated level is $P(X = \uparrow \mid S = \uparrow) = .82$, whereas the corresponding conditional probability is $P(X = \uparrow \mid S = \leftrightarrow) = .18$ when

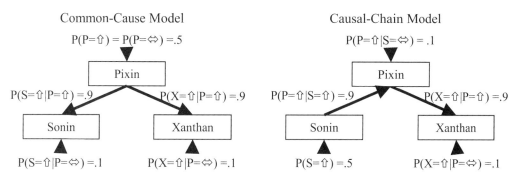

FIGURE 6-6 Conditions and data of Experiment 2 by Waldmann and Hagmayer (2005). Upward arrows symbolize increased hormone levels; sideways arrows indicate normal levels. The parameters represent causal strength (conditional probabilities) and base rates (unconditional probabilities).

the sonin level is normal. The base rate of the exogenous causes in both models (i.e., sonin in the common-cause model, pixin in the chain model) was set to 0.5.

For the causal chain model, the interventional probabilities are identical to the observational probabilities. For example, regardless of whether sonin is observed to be increased or whether an increased level was caused by means of an inoculation, the other two hormones should be affected equally. However, an intervention on sonin in the common-cause model entails the removal of the causal arrow connecting pixin and sonin. Therefore, the probability of xanthan depends only on the base rate of its cause pixin and the causal impact of this hormone on xanthan.

Thus, the interventional probability of xanthan is $P(X = \uparrow \mid do[S = \uparrow]) = P(X = \uparrow \mid do[S = \leftrightarrow]) = .5$, regardless of whether sonin is increased or normal.

To test whether participants' judgments follow these predictions, they were asked to make predictions about hypothetical observations and hypothetical interventions after having studied the learning data. All participants were requested to estimate for a set of 20 new, previously unseen chimpanzees the number of animals showing elevated levels of xanthan based on the hypothetical observation that sonin was at either an increased or normal level in these animals. The corresponding questions about hypothetical interventions asked participants to imagine inoculations that increased or lowered the level of sonin in the 20 animals. The order of the test

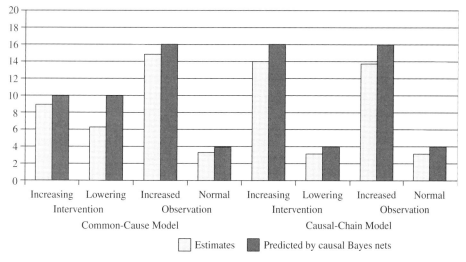

FIGURE 6-7 Results of Experiment 2 of Waldmann and Hagmayer (2005). Mean responses and predicted frequencies to observation and intervention questions.

questions was counterbalanced. The mean response to the test questions and the answers predicted by the causal model framework are shown in Figure 6-7.

The pattern of results shows that participants correctly differentiated between observational and interventional predictions, and that they were sensitive to the different implications of the contrasting causal models. Whereas for the causal chain model learners correctly predicted similar levels of xanthan independent of whether sonin levels were observed or generated, a clear dissociation was observed for the common-cause model. The majority of participants concluded that the probability of xanthan is independent of the type of intervention on sonin. A second finding was that, on average, estimates were as predicted, although in some cases there was a slight tendency to underestimate. The largest deviation between the estimates and the normative values was found for the intervention lowering the level of sonin (second pair of columns in Figure 6-7), which is probably because participants had no data about what would happen if the level of one hormone fell below a normal level.

These results are beyond the grasp of associationist theories. This is most obvious in the common-cause model in which the predictions of the outcomes of the hypothetical interventions turned out close to the predicted value of 50%, even though participants had never observed this value in the learning phase. These predictions clearly support causal models as descriptions of human reasoning. Apparently, reasoners rely not only on the observed associations but also on the underlying causal model to generate predictions.

Sensitivity to Parameters

To examine whether learners used the learned parameters for their predictions, Waldmann and Hagmayer (2005) ran additional studies manipulating parameter values across conditions. Their Experiment 4 provides

an example of this manipulation. In this experiment, participants were instructed that a fictitious bacterial infection in dogs has two causal effects, gastric problems and increased antibodies (i.e., common-cause model). In two conditions, two different data sets were shown to participants in a list format. The two data sets varied the strength of the two causal relations. In one condition ("strong-weak"), the bacterial infection had a strong influence on gastric problems ($\Delta P = .91$) and only a medium influence on the presence of antibodies ($\Delta P = .45$). (ΔP is a measure of contingency that reflects the numeric difference between the probability of the effect, gastric problems, conditional on the presence and absence of the cause [e.g., bacterial infection].) In the other condition, the assigned causal strength was reversed ("weak-strong") (see Figure 6-8). The base rate was the same (0.55) in both conditions.

Participants were requested to estimate the frequency of antibodies in a new set of 20 dogs assuming either that gastritis was observed to be present or absent or that the presence or absence of gastritis was caused by means of an external intervention (inoculation).

Although the structure of the causal model is identical in both conditions, the parameters implied by the two data sets have distinctive implications for the different types of predictions (see Figure 6-8). Because of the underlying common-cause model, an external intervention in gastric problems has no causal influence on the infection rate and the presence of antibodies. This is because of graph surgery, which requires removal of the causal arrow between the common-cause infection and gastritis. The probability of antibodies is solely determined by the base rate of the bacterial infection and its causal impact on the antibodies. Therefore, antibodies are more likely in the condition in which bacterial infection has a strong influence (i.e., weak-strong) than when it has only a weak impact (i.e., strong-weak).

The different parameters in the two conditions imply different predictions not only for the intervention

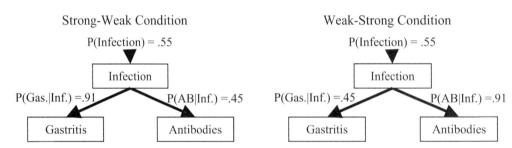

FIGURE 6-8 Conditions and data of Experiment 4 of Waldmann and Hagmayer (2005).

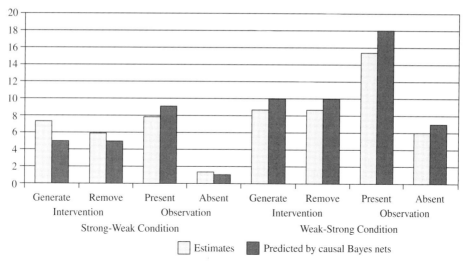

FIGURE 6-9 Results of Experiment 4 of Waldmann and Hagmayer (2005). Mean responses and predicted frequencies for the observation and intervention questions.

questions but also for the observation questions. In general, the implied probabilities are higher if gastritis is observed to be present than if it is absent. In addition, the probability of antibodies is higher in the weak-strong condition than in the strong-weak condition.

In Figure 6-9, the mean responses are compared with the values predicted by the causal model. The results show that participants again differentiated between predictions for hypothetical observations and hypothetical interventions. Moreover, the estimates also demonstrate that participants were sensitive to the parameters of the causal model. On average, participants' estimates were quite accurate, although there were again small deviations that could be due to regression effects. This competency is rather surprising considering the complexity of the task.

Sensitivity to the size of parameters was shown not only for the causal strength parameters but also for the base rate parameters. In another experiment (Waldmann & Hagmayer, 2005, Experiment 3), the base rate of the common cause was manipulated while holding causal strength constant. This should particularly affect the interventional predictions (based on interventions on the first effect) as the probability of the predicted second effect in this case varied in proportion to the base rate of its cause (see Figure 6-2). The results showed that participants incorporated the base rate information in their predictions in a way that was surprisingly close to the predictions of causal Bayes nets.

Causal Decision Making

The distinction between observation and intervention also has practical implications for decision making (Sloman, 2005). For example, if we observe low values on a barometer, then we will probably take our umbrella because the probability of rain is high. But, we also know that setting the barometer by means of an intervention will not affect the weather. The evidential relation between the barometer reading and the weather is spurious and mediated by atmospheric pressure, which acts as a common cause that independently affects the barometer and the weather. Thus, observing a low reading of the barometer because of tampering should not influence our decision to take an umbrella. This example shows that causal models and the distinction between observation and intervention are highly relevant to decision making. Specifically, choice is a form of intervention and should be modeled as such by breaking the edge between the variable with the value that is chosen and its normal causes. However, most theories of decision making, certainly most normative theories, analyze decision making on the basis of evidential relations between variables (e.g., subjective expected utility theory).

In contrast, in line with the analyses of causal Bayes nets and previous work on causal expected utilities (Nozick, 1969, 1995), Sloman and Hagmayer (2006) propose that choice is equivalent to an intervention in a causal network. They claim that in decision making people first consider a causal model of the decision context and then explore the causal consequences of their possible interventions.

Simple Choices

Hagmayer and Sloman (2005) presented participants with simple decision problems, such as the following:

> Recent research has shown that of 100 men who help with the chores, 82 are in good health, whereas only 32 of 100 men who do not help with the chores are. Imagine a friend of yours is married and is concerned about his health. He read about the research and asks for your advice on whether he should start to do chores or not to improve his health. What is your recommendation? Should he start to do the chores or not?

Hagmayer and Sloman also provided participants in different conditions with one of two causal models that might underlie the correlation between chores and health. In one condition, the relation was because of a common cause, the degree of concern, that independently influences the likelihood of doing the chores and of entertaining health-related activities, or in the alternative direct-link model, it was pointed out that chores are an additional exercise directly improving health.

Participants received several different decision problems involving a range of issues, from the relation between high-risk sports and drug abuse to the relation between chess and academic achievement. If participants equate choices with interventions, then they should often recommend not acting in the common-cause condition because intervening on an effect of a common cause does not alter the spuriously correlated collateral effect. Such an intervention would simply render the action independent of the rest of the model, including the desired outcome. In contrast, in the second condition, participants should recommend doing the chores because this variable is directly causally related to health. Participants' judgments turned out to be in accordance with the causal model–theory of choice. Despite learning about an identical evidential relation, only 23% of the participants in the common-cause condition advised their hypothetical friend to act, in contrast to 69% of the participants in the direct-link condition.

Complex Choices and Newcomb's Paradox

The difference between observational and interventional probabilistic relations is crucial in more complex cases as well. Newcomb's paradox is an interesting test case because it involves a conflict between two principles of good decision making: (a) maximizing expected utility and (b) dominance (i.e., choosing the option that always leads to the better outcome) (see Nozick, 1969, 1995). Classical decision theory cannot handle this paradox as it has no principled way to choose between these alternative criteria; however, a causal analysis in some cases can.

Table 6-1 illustrates a variant of Newcomb's paradox that Hagmayer and Sloman (submitted) used in an experiment. In this experiment, students were asked to imagine being the marketing executive of a car manufacturer and having to choose between two advertising campaigns. The manufacturer could promote either their sedan or their minivan. However, according to the instructions, the expected sales depend not only on the executive's decision but also on the marketing decision of the manufacturer's main competitor (see Table 6-1).

As the payoff matrix of Table 6-1 shows, higher sales are expected for the minivan regardless of the competitor's campaign. Therefore, the principle of dominance prescribes promoting the minivan. However, participants were also informed that in the past the two car companies ended up promoting the same type of car in 95% of the cases, with either car promoted equally often. If this additional information is taken into account, then the expected value of promoting the sedan turns out to be higher than that of the minivan (29.250 vs. 21.000). Thus, the principle of maximizing expected value implies the opposite of the principle of dominance.

To investigate the influence of the assumed causal model, participants were also informed about the causal relations underlying the observed evidential relations. In one condition, participants were told that the competitor tends to match the participant's strategy (direct-cause model); in the other condition, they were told that both car companies make their decisions independently based on the market (common-cause model). After considering the information, participants were requested to choose one of the available options.

TABLE 6-1 Payoff Matrix ($)

	Additional Sales	
	Competitor Promotes Sedan	Competitor Promotes Minivan
You promote sedan	30,000	15,000
You promote minivan	40,000	20,000

Source: Hagmayer and Sloman (in preparation).

Under the direct-cause model, the evidential probabilities between the choices of the two competitors indicate a stable causal relation. Therefore, the causal expected utility equals the evidential expected utility, and the sedan should be promoted. In contrast, under a common-cause model, the choice should be viewed as an intervention that is independent of the competitor's choice, with the competitor supposed to choose on the basis of the state of the market. Because a free choice destroys the evidential relation between the choices of the participant and the hypothetical competitor, the assumption that both choices are almost guaranteed to coincide is no longer tenable. Thus, the dominant option is the best choice under a common-cause model.

The results show that decision makers were sensitive to the structure of the underlying causal model, and that they tended to treat choices as interventions. Whereas traditional theories of decision making fail, causal Bayes nets provide a coherent account to model decision making in causal domains.

Final Remarks

Causal Bayes net theories differentiate between predictions based on observations, interventions, and counterfactuals. In this chapter, we reviewed evidence concerning this distinction. Traditional probabilistic and associationist theories are incapable of distinguishing between the different predictions entailed by hypothetical observations and interventions. The results of the experiments show that people are remarkably good at distinguishing between predictions based on observed events on one hand and predictions based on hypothetical interventions on the other. Although observational predictions are based on the structure of a relevant causal model, interventions require mentally modifying the model prior to deriving predictions by "undoing" the link between the intervened-on variable and its causes. People not only are capable of deriving qualitative predictions implied by the structure of a causal model, but also proved capable of incorporating learned quantitative parameters in their predictions (Waldmann & Hagmayer, 2005).

It turns out that children also excel at differentiating interventions from observations (see Schulz, Kushnir, & Gopnik, chapter 5, this volume). They proved capable of deriving predictions for novel interventions from previous observations. For example, in one experiment children were shown different causal structures, such as a switch turning a gear A, which spins a second gear B. Children 4.5 years old were able to predict what would happen if either of the gears was placed on a toy and the switch turned on. Although they expected Gear A to spin, they did not expect Gear B to rotate. This shows that children are able to derive correct predictions, at least for simple, deterministic causal structures (see Schulz, Kushnir, & Gopnik, chapter 5, this volume, for more details and further evidence). Recently Blaisdell and Waldmann (Blaisdell et al., 2006) showed that even rats grasp the difference between interventions and observations.

The distinction between observation, interventions, and counterfactuals is relevant not only for inference within a causal model, but also for the induction of causal models (in this volume, see Schulz, Kushnir, & Gopnik, chapter 5; Lagnado et al., chapter 10; Sobel, chapter 9; Griffith & Tenenbaum, chapters 19 and 20, for theory and evidence). The empirical results indicate that adults as well as children can infer causal models using evidence from observations and interventions together (Gopnik et al., 2004, Steyvers, Tenenbaum, Wagenmakers, & Blum, 2003; Tenenbaum & Griffiths, 2003). However, people seem to have a limited capacity to derive causal models based on observations alone (Hagmayer, 2001; Lagnado & Sloman, 2004).

The evidence reviewed in this chapter strongly suggests that people find it natural and easy to draw different inferences from observations and from interventions when reasoning and when making decisions. The difference between observation and intervention has to do with why an event occurs or how a variable obtains its value (i.e., with the mechanism that produces the event or value).

Hence, the distinction between observation and intervention is grounded in causal knowledge, in an understanding of the mechanisms that produce change. Thus, people's ease of reasoning about observation versus intervention would seem to indicate quite directly competence with causal reasoning, and this would be a direct consequence of a system that is designed for action, for achieving effects through intervention.

References

Blaisdell, A. P., Sawa, K., Leising, K. J., & Waldmann, M. R. (2006). Causal reasoning in rats. *Science, 311,* 1020–1022.

Dickinson, A. (2001). Causal learning: An associative analysis. *Quarterly Journal of Experimental Psychology, 54B,* 3–25.

Domjan, M. (2003). *The principles of learning and behavior* (5th ed.). Belmont, CA: Thomson/Wadsworth.

Fisher, R. (1951). *The design of experiments.* Edinburgh: Oliver and Boyd.

Glymour, C. (2001). *The mind's arrows: Bayes nets and graphical causal models in psychology.* Cambridge, MA: MIT Press.

Gopnik, A., Glymour, C., Sobel, D. M., Schulz, L. E., Kushnir, T., & Danks, D. (2004). A theory of causal learning in children: Causal maps and Bayes nets. *Psychological Review, 111,* 3–32.

Hagmayer, Y. (2001). *Reasoning through causal models versus reasoning about causal models.* Unpublished doctoral thesis, University of Göttingen, Göttingen, Germany.

Hagmayer, Y., & Sloman, S. A. (2005). A causal model theory of choice. In B. G. Bara, L. Barsalou, and M. Bucciarelli (eds.), *Proceedings of the Twenty-Seventh Annual Conference of the Cognitive Science Society.* Mahwah, NJ: Erlbaum.

Hagmayer, Y., & Sloman, S. A. (subm.). Causal considerations in Newcomb's Paradox. Paper submitted for publication.

Lagnado, D. A., & Sloman, S. A. (2004). The advantage of timely intervention. *Journal of Experimental Psychology: Learning, Memory, and Cognition, 30,* 856–876.

Nozick, R. (1969). Newcomb's problem and two principles of choice. In N. Rescher (Ed.), *Essays in honor of Carl G. Hempel* (pp. 107–133). Dordrecht, Netherlands: Reidel.

Nozick, R. (1995). *The nature of rationality.* Princeton, NJ: Princeton University Press.

Pearl, J. (1988). *Probabilistic reasoning in intelligent systems: Networks of plausible inference.* San Francisco, CA: Morgan Kaufmann.

Pearl, J. (2000). *Causality.* Cambridge, England: Cambridge University Press.

Reichenbach, H. (1956). *The direction of time.* Berkeley, CA: University of California Press.

Sloman, S. A. (2005). *Causal models: How we think about the world and its alternatives.* Cambridge, MA: Oxford University Press.

Sloman, S. A., & Hagmayer, Y. (2006). The causal logic of choice. *Trends in Cognitive Science, 10,* 407–412.

Sloman, S. A., & Lagnado, D. (2005). Do we "do"? *Cognitive Science, 29,* 5–39.

Spirtes, P., Glymour, C., & Scheines, R. (1993). *Causation, prediction, and search.* New York: Springer.

Steyvers, M., Tenenbaum, J. B., Wagenmakers, E.-J., & Blum, B. (2003). Inferring causal networks from observations and interventions. *Cognitive Science, 27,* 453–489.

Tenenbaum, J. B., & Griffiths, T. L. (2003). Theory-based causal induction. In S. Becker, S. Thun, and F. Obermayer (eds.), *Advances in neural information processing systems, 15,* 35–42. Cambridge: MIT Press.

Waldmann, M. R. (1996). Knowledge-based causal induction. In D. R. Shanks, K. J. Holyoak, & D. L. Medin (Eds.), *The psychology of learning and motivation: Vol. 34. Causal learning* (pp. 47–88). San Diego, CA: Academic Press.

Waldmann, M. R., & Martignon, L. (1998). A Bayesian network model of causal learning. In M. A. Gernsbacher & S. J. Derry, *Proceedings of the 20th Annual Conference of the Cognitive Science Society* (pp. 1102–1107). Mahwah, NJ: Erlbaum.

Waldmann, M. R., & Hagmayer, Y. (2005). Seeing versus doing: Two modes of accessing causal knowledge. *Journal of Experimental Psychology: Learning, Motivation, and Cognition, 31,* 216–227.

Woodward, J. (2003). *Making things happen. A theory of causal explanation.* Oxford, England: Oxford University Press.

7

On the Importance of Causal Taxonomy

Christopher Hitchcock

Introduction

Karl Popper (1962) characterized science as a process of "conjectures and refutations." Scientists formulate hypotheses or conjectures that yield falsifiable predictions. They then set about testing those predictions. If the predictions are not borne out, then the hypothesis is refuted, and a new conjecture must be found. For better or for worse, analytic philosophy has largely proceeded according to a parallel method, a method of analyses and counterexamples. Philosophers formulate an analysis of some important concept, which is then compared with a variety of test cases (often hypothetical). I offer a standard illustration involving the concept of causation, which may be useful for readers without a philosophical background.

My main concern, however, is to use this example to illustrate the variety of causal concepts that we deploy. When we ask whether one thing causes another, we may be asking many different things. For instance, we may be asking whether the relationship between them is

genuinely causal, as opposed to accidental or spurious. Or, we may be asking about the direction of the relationship between them: Does the one cause or prevent the other? Or, we may be asking about the strength of the relationship between them: Does the one have enough of an impact on the other to count as causing it? Treatments of causation in philosophy and psychology typically run these questions together, but there is no reason to expect all of these questions to have a uniform answer. I argue that when we carefully distinguish these sorts of questions, the different combinations of answers that may be provided form the basis of a taxonomy of causal relationships. Such a taxonomy is better able to illuminate the nature of causal reasoning than is any theory that aims only to define causation simpler.

An Analysis and a Counterexample

Let us begin by formulating a probabilistic theory of causation, which I call the R-S theory because it is based on (although not quite identical to) definitions offered by Reichenbach (1956) and Suppes (1970). According to this theory, causes and effects are represented by events in a probability space and are indexed according to the time when they occur. C_t is a cause of $E_{t'}$ just in case the following conditions hold:

(i) $t < t'$
(ii) $P(E_{t'} \mid C_t) > P(E_{t'})$
(iii) There is no time $t'' < t$ and no event $B_{t''}$ such that

$$P(E_{t'} \mid C_t B_{t''}) = P(E_{t'} \mid B_{t''})$$

The time at which C occurs must be earlier than the time at which E occurs; the occurrence of C at time t must render the occurrence of E at t'' more probable, and there must be no earlier event B that "screens off" C from E, that renders C probabilistically irrelevant to E. Although I treat R–S as illustrative of the sorts of attempts philosophers have made to define causation, I am not concerned here to evaluate the specific proposals put forward by either Reichenbach or Suppes.[1]

Hesslow (1976) has offered a counterexample to this analysis of causation involving the effect of birth control pills on thrombosis (the formation of blood clots in the arteries). Let us make some background assumptions: We have a population of healthy women, all of whom are married, under the age of 35, nonsmokers, and capable of conceiving children. Such women are among the most likely consumers of birth control pills. Thrombosis is considered to be one of the most dangerous side effects of birth control pills. This means, presumably, that the consumption of oral contraceptives is a cause of thrombosis. Pregnancy is also an important risk factor for thrombosis. This is hardly a coincidence: Birth control pills prevent pregnancy by mimicking the hormonal effects of pregnancy, so birth control pills have many of the same side effects as pregnancy itself. It turns out that pregnancy is a much stronger risk factor for thrombosis than birth control pills. Thus, by using birth control pills, a woman in our hypothetical population would actually lower her overall probability of thrombosis because birth control pill use is such an effective preventive measure against pregnancy.

We represent this case schematically in Figure 7-1. Intuitively, the thickness of the arrow corresponds to the strength of the causal influence in question; the sign attached to each arrow indicates whether one factor causes or prevents the other.

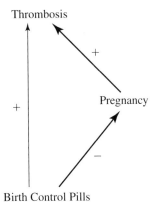

FIGURE 7-1 Hesslow's counterexample.

The probabilities of the various outcomes (using obvious abbreviations and suppressing temporal subscripts) are as presented in Table 7-1. In the table,

1. The probability of thrombosis is lower, conditional on birth control pill use, than it is overall.
2. Conditional on becoming pregnant, the probability of thrombosis is higher conditional on birth control pill use.
3. Conditional on avoiding pregnancy, the probability of thrombosis is higher conditional on birth control pill use.

We have, then, an apparent counterexample to the R-S analysis of causation: The consumption of birth control pills is a cause of thrombosis, even though Clause (ii) of the analysis is not satisfied (it is contradicted by inequality 1 in Table 7-1). Some authors, such as Salmon (1984) and Dowe (2000), use related examples to reject probabilistic analyses of causation generally and to recommend in their place accounts of causation that focus on the physical process that connect causes with their effects. (But, see Hitchcock, 1995a, and Schaffer, 2000, for criticisms of these proposals.)

Many Questions

When we ask about a particular causal relationship, such as the relationship between thrombosis and the

TABLE 7-1 The probabilities in Hesslow's counterexample

1. P(Throm|Pills) < P(Throm)

2. P(Throm|Pills & Preg) > P(Throm|Preg)

3. P(Throm|Pills & No Preg) > P(Throm|No Preg)

consumption of birth control pills, there are a number of different questions that might be posed. Let us start by drawing a distinction between two main questions:

1. Is the relationship between birth control pills and thrombosis causal at all?
2. Given that the relationship is causal in some broad sense, what specifically is the nature of the relationship?

We can elaborate further on the second question by introducing a number of subquestions:

2a. What is the direction of causal influence? Do birth control pills promote or encourage thrombosis? Or, do they rather prevent or inhibit thrombosis?
2b. What is the strength of the relationship? How efficacious are birth control pills in bringing about thrombosis? Are they stronger causes of thrombosis than pregnancy is?
2c. How does birth control pill use compare with various alternatives? What are the consequences of birth control pill use for thrombosis in contrast with other birth control methods or in contrast with the failure to employ contraception at all?
2d. To what extent is the relationship between birth control pills and thrombosis stable across different background conditions? How do birth control pills interact with other causes of thrombosis? Is the effect of birth control pill use on thrombosis different for different kinds of women, and if so, how?
2e. Via what causal pathways do birth control pills affect thrombosis? How does the influence of birth control pills differ along these various paths? How do these pathways combine to yield an overall effect?

Let us now examine each of these questions in greater detail.

Question 1: Causal Relationships

I do not attempt to offer any precise account of what a *relationship* is. The sorts of things I have in mind are: (a) regularities or predictable patterns of co-instantiation among types of events; (b) probabilistic correlations of the sort described in Table 7-1; and (c) mathematical functions connecting the values of quantitative variables. The first key question, then, is

whether a specific relationship between events, event types, or variables reflects a causal influence of one on the other.

Let us suppose that we have observed the population of women described in Hesslow's (1976) example, and that we have kept careful statistics regarding which have taken birth control pills, which have become pregnant, and which have suffered from thrombosis. Let us suppose, moreover, that these statistics are in accord with the probabilities presented in Table 7-1. These probabilities describe certain statistical relationships that hold between birth control pill use and thrombosis. What does it mean to ask whether these relationships are causal?

We may start by saying what we mean to exclude. There are at least two different ways in which these relationships might fail to be causal. First, our sample might not be representative. In this case, although thrombosis rates happen to be lower among pill users in our particular population sample, this would not reflect any kind of underlying connection between them; if we were to continue sampling from an idealized infinite population, then the negative correlation between pill use and thrombosis would (with probability 1) disappear. In language familiar to philosophers, the correlations are *accidental*. This terminology is drawn from philosophical discussions about laws of nature. According to one traditional view, laws of nature are universal generalizations. For example, it is a law of nature that all massive objects travel at a velocity less than that of light. But, not all universal generalizations are laws of nature. It may be that all samples of pure gold that ever have existed or ever will exist have a mass of less than 1,000 kilograms, but this is not a law. It is, rather, an accidental generalization, a contingent feature of the way our world just happens to unfold. (See, for example, Goodman, 1955, for a classic exposition of this issue.) Causal relationships need not be laws—in saying that birth control pills cause (or prevent) thrombosis, we are not claiming that all (or none) of the women who consume birth control pills develop thrombosis. Nonetheless, causal relationships do seem to be distinguishable from accidental relationships in much the same way that laws of nature are often thought to be.

Second, it may be that the relationship between birth control pills and thrombosis, although not merely accidental, is sustained by a common cause or by some more complex causal structure that does not involve any causal influence of birth control pills on thrombosis. It may be, for example, that women who have more limited access to health care are less likely to employ birth control pills and are more susceptible to thrombosis. If this were the case, then the first inequality of Table 7-1 would not reflect any causal influence of birth control pills on thrombosis: Birth control pill use would merely be a symptom of access to medical care, the factor that would really be influencing whether thrombosis occurs. In this case, we would say that the (negative) correlation between birth control pills and thrombosis is *spurious*. The third clause of the R-S analysis is intended to rule out spurious correlations: In the hypothetical case just described, conditioning on access to health care would render oral contraceptive use probabilistically irrelevant to thrombosis.

We should also briefly mention the possibility that thrombosis affects birth control pill use rather than vice versa. This possibility is consistent with the probabilistic information reported in Table 7-1. However, if we have the further information that birth control pill use commences before the onset of thrombosis, then this possibility can be ruled out. Condition (i) of R-S reflects this temporal constraint on causal relationships.

Thus, a causal relationship between birth control pill use and thrombosis is a relationship that is neither accidental nor spurious. But, what are the positive characteristics of these relationships that distinguish them from other, noncausal relationships? It is in response to this particular question that the interventionist approach to causation, developed especially by Woodward (2003, chapter 1, this volume), is particularly promising.

This approach is best motivated by asking why we are so interested in learning about causal relationships.[2] Suppose, first, that we are interested in predicting who will develop thrombosis and who will not. It is easy to see why the probabilistic information presented in Table 7-1 will be especially useful for us: It tells us that women who fall into certain categories are more likely than others to develop thrombosis. If the probabilistic relationships described in Table 7-1 are merely accidental, then, although these relationships are still useful for predicting thrombosis within this particular population of women, we would have no reason to expect that they would provide reliable guides to prediction within other groups of women. So, it is not surprising that we should find nonaccidental relationships to be particularly important.

Why should we be interested in causal rather than spurious relationships? If we were only interested in predicting the outcomes of observed initial conditions, then we would have no reason to prefer causal relationships to spurious ones. The consumption of birth control pills can be a reliable indicator of whether a woman will develop thrombosis regardless of whether it affects thrombosis or is merely symptomatic of some other underlying condition that itself affects thrombosis. It is only when we seek to intervene in the normal course of events that causal relations take primacy of place.

Suppose, for example, that we are contemplating a policy of providing free oral contraceptives to some of the women in our hypothetical population, and we wish to predict the incidence of thrombosis under this protocol. If the correlation between birth control pill use and thrombosis is spurious, then we cannot necessarily rely on the probabilities given in Table 7-1 to predict the outcome. For example, if the correlation arises because access to health care influences both pill use and thrombosis, then we would not expect this correlation to persist under our new protocol. If we provide free access to birth control pills, then we can no longer expect birth control pill use to be symptomatic of access to health care more generally. Causal relationships, by contrast, remain stable under the sorts of interventions that would disrupt spurious relationships. It is for this reason that knowledge of causal relationships is especially valuable to us. According to the interventionist approach to causation developed by Woodward and others, this invariance of a relationship under interventions is a defining feature of a genuinely causal relationship, in the sense of Question 1.

This is only a preliminary sketch of an interventionist approach to causation; see Woodward's chapter 1 in this volume for a more detailed presentation. My intent here is not to defend the interventionist approach in detail, but only to appeal to its broadly practical orientation to help give a sense of what the first question—whether the relationship between birth control pills and thrombosis is causal at all—is asking. The same practical orientation can also be used to motivate the second question, along with its various subquestions. If we want to know what the effect of our contemplated policy intervention will be, then it is not nearly enough to know that there is *some* causal relationship between pill use and thrombosis; we will also need to know something more about the details of this relationship.[3]

Question 2a: Causal Direction

In our interventions in the world, we typically seek to promote those outcomes that we deem desirable and to prevent or inhibit those outcomes that we wish to avoid. Thus, we will typically aim to prevent or inhibit thrombosis, while we may seek to either prevent or promote pregnancy, depending on our desires at a particular stage in our lives. This distinction is fairly intuitive and was marked by the inclusion of + and − signs in Figure 7-1. Unfortunately, our language can be treacherous here, for we often use the word *cause* specifically to mean *promote*. In this usage, cause and prevent (or inhibit) are antonyms. Nonetheless, prevention is a kind of causal relationship. Birth control pills prevent pregnancy; they do not cause pregnancy. But, it would be wrong to conclude from this that the relationship between birth control pills and pregnancy is not causal (i.e., that it is merely accidental or spurious). Thus, when we ask whether one thing is a cause of another, we must take care to specify if we are inquiring whether a causal relationship exists or more specifically whether the causal relationship points in a certain direction—whether the cause promotes the effect rather than inhibiting or preventing it.

How might we characterize the distinction between promoting causes on the one hand and preventing or inhibiting causes on the other? Within the probabilistic framework of R-S, a natural proposal would be that a promoting cause increases the probability of the outcome in question; a preventing cause decreases the probability. This proposal would have the advantage of tying our practical maxim— promote desirable outcomes and prevent undesirable ones—to standard decision theory: An action increases expected utility to the extent that it renders high-utility outcomes more probable and low-utility outcomes less probable.

In examining the probabilities in Table 7-1, we see that conditioning on birth control pill usage can either increase or decrease the probability of thrombosis, depending on what else is being conditioned on. For this reason, it is not possible to characterize pill use unambiguously as either a promoting or a preventing cause of thrombosis. We return to this point in the section on Question 2e regarding causal pathways.

So far, we have been restricting our attention to binary variables; we have supposed that one can take birth control pills or not, develop thrombosis or not, become pregnant or not. (Pregnancy is a proverbial binary variable: There is no such thing as being a "little bit pregnant.") The natural and social sciences are often concerned with quantitative variables, however. For example, a physicist might be interested in the relationship between electrical potential and current, a sociologist in the relationship between education level and income, and a macroeconomist in the relationship between unemployment and inflation. If the relationship between two variables is monotonically increasing or monotonically decreasing, then it might be perfectly natural to import the language of promotion and prevention to describe the direction of a causal relationship. If increasing levels of education correspond with increasing levels of income, then it might be natural to say that education is a promoting cause of income (assuming that the relationship is causal at all, rather than accidental or spurious). If the relationship between unemployment and inflation is monotonically decreasing, then high unemployment levels inhibit inflation. There is no guarantee, however, that a relationship between quantitative variables will be monotonic; it might be U-shaped or sinusoidal. In such a case, it will not be possible to provide a simple characterization of the direction of the causal influence. (See Hitchcock, 1993, for further discussion of this point.)

Question 2b: Causal Strength

Some causal influences are stronger than others. In Hesslow's (1976) example, pregnancy is a stronger cause of thrombosis than is pill use; we marked this in Figure 7-1 by drawing a thick arrow from pregnancy to thrombosis and a thin arrow from pills to thrombosis. Within a probabilistic framework, it is natural to measure the strength of a causal influence in terms of the size of the difference in probability that a causal factor makes. To say that pregnancy is a stronger cause of thrombosis than pill use, for example, would suggest that, if we look at the inequalities 2 and 3 in Table 7-1, then we might expect the difference between the left- and right-hand sides of each inequality to be small compared to the difference between the left-hand sides of 2 and 3 or to the difference between the right-hand sides of 2 and 3.

One of the great virtues of Cheng's (1997) PowerPC model of causation is that it offers a probabilistic measure of causal strength that is in many ways superior to simpler measures that look only at the difference or ratio of probabilities. When quantitative variables stand in linear relationships, it is natural to measure the strength of the relationship between them in terms of correlation coefficients. As with the case of causal direction, however, if the relationship between two variables is sufficiently complex, then there may be no natural way to characterize the strength of the causal influence of one on the other.

In practice, we often ignore weak causal influences. Indeed, by selecting outcomes of interest we effect a kind of course-graining that renders many causal influences irrelevant. For example, the gravitational influence of Alpha Centauri will make a slight difference to the exact location of every molecule in a woman's body. We are, however, particularly interested in which women will develop thrombosis, and it is extraordinarily unlikely that the effects wrought by our stellar neighbor will ever make the difference between developing thrombosis or not.

In connection with this last point, a distinction is sometimes made between causing some outcome and affecting or influencing it.[4] Consider a woman who is already at high risk of developing thrombosis—indeed, she will eventually succumb regardless of whether she takes birth control pills or becomes pregnant. Nonetheless, her use of birth control pills may hasten or delay the onset of thrombosis; it may affect the severity of her thrombosis or otherwise be relevant to the manner in which thrombosis occurs. In such a case, we might say that her taking birth control pills did not cause her thrombosis (since she was going to suffer from it anyway), but that it did affect or influence her thrombosis. We cannot take this distinction too far, however: Socrates was mortal, but his drinking hemlock nonetheless caused his death and did not merely affect or influence it.

Question 2c: Contrasting Alternatives

In most philosophical treatments, and arguably in common sense as well, causes and effects are events or event-types. We ask about the effect of consuming birth control pills on thrombosis or about the effects of a particular woman's consuming birth control pills during a particular time frame on her case of thrombosis. As we have remarked, however, it is common in the sciences to represent causal relationships as relationships among variables. The social scientist, for example, does not ask whether having a high school education causes one to have an income of greater

than $40,000 per year, but asks rather about the causal relationship between education and income more generally. The variable education might have values representing the following education levels: never completed high school; high school diploma; some university education; bachelor's degree; master's degree; doctorate or highest professional degree.

I have argued at length elsewhere (Hitchcock, 1993, 1995b, 1996a, 1996b) that there is something deeply misleading about the ordinary philosophical conception of causation as a relation among events or event-types and something deeply right about the scientific practice of thinking in terms of causal relations among variables. Causal claims are always explicitly or implicitly contrastive: When we represent causal relationships as relations among variables, we are making explicit the range of contrasting alternatives under consideration.

In Hesslow's (1976) example, we are interested in the effect of birth control pill use on thrombosis. But, we must ask: Birth control pills as opposed to what? If we contrast the use of oral contraceptives with the failure to employ contraception, then the probabilities might well be as reported in Hesslow's example. But, suppose instead that we compare birth control pills with other reliable forms of contraception. Then, birth control pill use might make relatively little difference for whether a woman becomes pregnant—women who use oral contraceptives become pregnant at more or less the same rate as women employing other effective means of contraception—while still posing an additional risk of thrombosis. When we make this comparison, then, it may turn out that birth control pills increase the probability of thrombosis relative to other forms of contraception.

Putting the same point in a slightly different way, we may embed the event-type birth control pill use as a value of many different variables. One variable might take as values {birth control pill use, no contraception}; another might take as values {birth control pill use, abstinence, male sterilization, female sterilization, condom use, … }. These two variables need not stand in the same relation to the variable that takes as values {thrombosis, no thrombosis}.

Question 2d: Stability Across Background Conditions

In presenting Hesslow's (1976) counterexample, we made a number of assumptions about the condition of the women in our hypothetical population. Let us now remove those assumptions: Suppose that some of the women are celibate or infertile; some are older, smokers, and otherwise at high risk of thrombosis. Why not throw some men in there as well? The probabilistic profile described in Table 7-1 will no longer characterize all of the members of the population. More specifically, there will now be some background conditions B such that

$$P(\text{Throm} \mid \text{Pills \& } B) < P(\text{Throm} \mid B);$$

and other background conditions B' such that

$$P(\text{Throm} \mid \text{Pills \& } B') > P(\text{Throm} \mid B');$$

and perhaps even B'', such that

$$P(\text{Throm} \mid \text{Pills \& } B'') = P(\text{Throm} \mid B'').$$

The effect of birth control pills on thrombosis will depend on what other relevant factors are present in the background. In such a case, we say that birth control pill use *interacts* with these other factors.

How stable must the effect of birth control pills be across the different background conditions in a heterogeneous population for us to continue talking meaningfully of the effect of birth control pills? One proposal, originally of John Stuart Mill (1843) and given a probabilistic reformulation by Humphreys (1989), is that a cause must raise the probability of its effect in every possible background condition. One upshot of this proposal is that event-types such as birth control pill consumption will rarely count as causes of anything. Rather, a cause will typically be a complicated conjunction of factors. Thus, for example, we would not be able to say that birth control pill consumption causes (or prevents) thrombosis, but only that pill consumption by women who are in such-and-such specific physiological condition does so. A slightly different proposal, that of Eells (1991) is that causal claims are population relative. Thus, we might say that the consumption of birth control pills prevents thrombosis in the subpopulation of women who are fertile and sexually active and satisfy various other physiological conditions; birth control pills cause thrombosis in a different subpopulation of women. In the population as a whole, the best we can do is to say that oral contraceptive use is a "mixed cause" of thrombosis. It is clear, however, that our ordinary usage of words like *cause* and *prevent* is considerably more permissive than either of these proposals would allow.

Question 2e: Causal Pathways

Figure 7-1 shows two causal pathways connecting birth control pill use with thrombosis. Intuitively, birth control pills affect one's chances of developing thrombosis in (at least) two different ways. First, they have a direct effect by introducing hormones into the subject's body; second, they have an indirect effect by preventing pregnancy, which is itself a risk factor for thrombosis. This example is particularly interesting because it turns out to be difficult to distinguish these pathways by any kind of appeal to physical processes or mechanisms. The reason is that the mechanisms underlying the arrows in Figure 7-1 are more or less identical. The chemical agents in birth control pills that cause thrombosis are the same as the ones that prevent pregnancy; pregnancy itself causes thrombosis because it leads to production of essentially the same agents.[5]

How, then, are we to distinguish the two different causal pathways? From within a probabilistic framework, it is the second and third inequalities in Table 7-1 that supply the clue. Pregnancy is a causal intermediary between pill use and thrombosis: Oral contraceptive use influences whether pregnancy occurs, and this in turn affects the occurrence of thrombosis. Yet, when we control for pregnancy by conditioning on whether pregnancy has occurred, there is a residual correlation between birth control pill use and thrombosis. If the only effect of birth control pill use on thrombosis was the one mediated by its effect on pregnancy, then we would expect pregnancy to screen off pill use from thrombosis.

This idea is captured in the Markov condition, a standard condition relating the probability distribution over a set of variables to the structure of a directed graph representing the causal relations among them (see Spirtes, Glymour, & Scheines, 2000). Although the arrow diagram in Figure 7-1 was originally presented as an intuitive representation of the structure of Hesslow's example, it has the structure of a directed graph. (We need to make a few changes to turn it into a proper causal graph: Lose the $+$ and $-$ signs, ignore the differences in the thickness of arrows, and interpret the nodes as binary variables rather than event-types.) When a graph contains an arrow from variable X to variable Y, then X is said to be a *parent* of Y. The Markov condition says that a variable X is independent of all other variables (either singly or in combination) except for descendents of X when we condition on all of the parents of X; the parents of X screen it off from all of its nondescendents. Now, we can see that if we were to remove the arrow from Pill use to Thrombosis in Figure 7-1, then the resulting graph would no longer satisfy the Markov condition. With the arrow removed, Pregnancy becomes the only parent of Thrombosis. Yet, Pregnancy does not screen Pill use off from Thrombosis, even though Pill use is not a descendent of Thrombosis.

As Woodward notes in this book (chapter 1, section on interventionism), an interventionist approach to causation of the sort outlined in the section on Question 1, causal relationships, may also be used to identify the distinct causal pathways. First, we note that by separately intervening on whether birth control pills are used and on whether pregnancy occurs, we can determine that birth control pills prevent pregnancy, and that pregnancy is a cause of thrombosis. (Never mind the ethical problems involved in intervening to cause or prevent pregnancy; thought experiments do not need to pass human subject review boards.) Now, we can further inquire into what happens when we intervene to determine whether a woman uses birth control pills, while simultaneously and independently intervening to determine whether pregnancy occurs. If the probabilistic correlations reported in the second and third lines of Table 7-1 persist under this protocol, then birth control pills have an effect on thrombosis in addition to the influence they have in virtue of their effect on pregnancy.

It is now possible to distinguish a variety of different kinds of causal relation. The arrows in a causal graph (such as the one derived from Figure 7-1) represent what are called *direct effects*. One variable has a direct effect on another if it has an effect that is unmediated by any other variable in some specified variable set. Obviously, the notion of direct effect must be relativized to a choice of variable set. In another work (Hitchcock, 2001b), I provide a generalization of the notion of direct effect that is invariant under the number of variables that are interpolated along a causal pathway.[6] I call this notion the *component effect* of one variable on another along a causal pathway. Pearl (2001) provides an even more powerful generalization, defining the notion of a *path-specific effect* for any causal pathway or complex network of causal pathways. Finally, there is the notion that is variously called *net*, *total*, or *causal effect*. This is the overall effect that one variable has on another along

all of the available causal pathways. This effect is reflected in the overall correlation between the two variables when *no* causal intermediates are controlled for. Thus, the first inequality in Table 7-1 reflects the net effect of birth control pills on thrombosis. Although I favor the term net effect to emphasize the analogy between net and component forces in Newtonian mechanics, net effects cannot simply be computed by adding the various component effects; the various component effects may interact with each other in complicated ways (see Hitchcock, 2001b for discussion).

In Hesslow's (1976) example, birth control pill use has two distinct component effects on thrombosis. Along the direct pathway, the effect of birth control pills is to weakly promote the occurrence of thrombosis. Along the indirect pathway, the effect of birth control pills is to strongly prevent thrombosis. The net effect is to moderately prevent thrombosis. Thus, there is a sense in which it is correct to say both that birth control pills cause thrombosis and that birth control pills prevent thrombosis. The R-S theory captures the second claim; Hesslow's counterexample appeals to the first claim.

Causal Taxonomy

The different ways in which Questions 2a through 2e can be answered correspond to different ways in which one event or event-type can be causally related to another. This is by no means an exhaustive list of the ways in which we can articulate the nature of a causal relationship, but it provides at least a healthy start on a causal taxonomy. Note that these various issues are not independent, but that there are interaction effects between them. For example, we cannot say anything unambiguous about the direction (Question 2a) or the strength (2b) of the relationship between birth control pill use and thrombosis unless we specify whether we are asking about one or another component effect or about the net effect (2e). How many causal pathways there are (2e) will depend on which background conditions we are considering (2d). Among women who are incapable of becoming pregnant (for reasons independent of birth control pill use), there will be no indirect effect of birth control pill use on thrombosis mediated by the possibility of pregnancy. And, if it should turn out that the influence of birth control pills on thrombosis has zero strength (2b) or no direction (2a), then we might reject the initial assumption that they are causally related in the first place (1).

One might try to classify causal relationships along different dimensions. It may turn out, for instance, that causation functions differently in the physical, biological, and social domains. Or, we might try to classify causal concepts according to theoretical approach. I have discussed the R-S theory in some detail and have made passing reference to a number of other philosophical approaches: other probabilistic theories, interventionist theories, counterfactual theories (for those of you paying close attention to the footnotes), and causal process theories. All but the last of these theories share a common idea: the occurrence of a cause *makes a difference* for its effect. The different types of causal relationship that emerge from a consideration of Questions 2a through 2e all correspond to different ways in which a cause might make a difference to its effect; thus, I expect that the sort of taxonomy that I advocate may be adopted from within the framework of any difference-making approach to causation. Causal processes and interactions, the key concepts in process theories of causation such as those of Salmon (1984) and Dowe (2000), are certainly causal concepts that are distinct from those enumerated, but they do not really belong in the taxonomy that I have been developing. Indeed, I am rather skeptical that these concepts really help us to understand better the nature of causal relationships, in part for reasons noted (see also Hitchcock, 1995a, 2004a, 2004b; Schaffer, 2000).

Morals for Philosophy

The holy grail of philosophy, or at least for the project of analyzing causation, has been to provide an adequate account of *the* causal relation, to spell out just what it means to say that C causes E. This analytic project tacitly assumes that there is just one special type of causal relationship called *causing* that is the target of analysis. We can see how this is true of our R-S theory by considering our various questions in turn.

First, the intent behind the R-S theory is that when C causes E, the relationship between them is genuinely causal in the sense of Question 1. Both Reichenbach (1956) and Suppes (1970) advance versions of Condition (iii) for the purpose of ruling out spurious correlations. With hindsight, we now recognize that it is not possible to distinguish causal relationships from spurious ones using purely probabilistic criteria. Cartwright (1979/1983) offers a powerful argument for this conclusion, and Spirtes et al. (2000) provide a variety of "statistical indistinguishability" results that bear on this issue. Despite this shortfall, the screening-off relations originally introduced by Reichenbach (1956) have proven to be helpful for detecting certain kinds of spurious relationship.

When we look closely at R-S, however, it is apparent that it is not simply an attempt to define the notion of a causal relationship in the sense of Question 1. Let us look at how R-S relates to each of Questions 2a through 2e in turn.

Question 2a. According to R-S, a cause must increase the probability of its effect. This suggests that a cause in the sense of R-S must be a promoting cause.

Question 2b. R-S imposes no lower bound on how much difference a cause must make to the probability of its effect. This suggests that something may count as a cause no matter how weak or insignificant its influence.

Question 2c. R-S requires us to compare the probability of E conditional on C with the unconditional probability of E, rather than with the probability of E conditional on any specific alternative to C. In effect, we must compare $P(E \mid C)$ with the weighted average of probabilities of the form $P(E \mid C')$, where C' ranges over C and all possible alternatives to C. So, for R-S, a cause must be a promoting cause *on average*, where the average is taken with respect to alternatives to the cause. This has the rather odd consequence that, whether or not birth control pills cause thrombosis (e.g.) will depend on the probabilities of various other forms of contraception being used. (See Hitchcock, 1993, for elaboration.)

Question 2d. R-S does not require that a cause raise the probability of its effect in every background condition: Conditions (i)–(iii) are all compatible with the existence of a background condition $B_{t''}$ such that $P(E_{t'} \mid C_t B_{t''}) < P(E_{t'} \mid B_{t''})$ [although Condition (iii) is obviously incompatible with a background condition $B_{t''}$ such that $P(E_{t'} \mid C_t B_{t''}) = P(E_{t'} \mid B_{t''})$]. R-S also does not require that a cause raise the probability of its effect in any circumscribed range of background conditions. There is, however, an obvious sense in which Condition (ii) requires that a cause raise the probability of its effect on average, where the average is here taken over background conditions.

Question 2e. Finally, R-S is suitable only for net causes, for it never asks us to consider probabilities conditional on events intermediate between the cause and the effect. It is because of this feature, in particular, that R-S fails to rule that birth control pills cause thrombosis.

In brief, then, a cause in the sense of R-S is a net-promoting-cause-on-average.

The principal moral that I wish to draw from our taxonomy is that we should reject the assumption that there is one specific kind of causal relationship that is the referent of the word *cause*. We use the word *cause* to mark a variety of different distinctions: the distinction between a causal relationship and one that is merely spurious; the distinction between causing an outcome and preventing it; the distinction between causing an outcome and merely affecting it; and so on. When we reflect on the multifaceted nature of Hesslow's (1976) example, it seems clear that there is no univocal answer to the seemingly simple question: Does the consumption of birth control pills cause thrombosis? There is a genuinely causal relationship between birth control pills and thrombosis. The use of birth control pills, when compared with substantially less-effective forms of contraception (or no contraception at all), has a net inhibiting effect on thrombosis among women in certain conditions. In those same background conditions, birth control pills also have a relatively small, direct, promoting effect on thrombosis. Birth control pills also have a small promoting net effect on thrombosis among women who are unable to become pregnant or when contrasted with equally effective forms of contraception. Does this specific causal profile amount to causation or not? We should reject the question. The reason that all attempts to analyze causation have met with failure is that there simply is no one specific relationship of causation to be analyzed. At any rate, there is no one specific relationship that is picked out by our pretheoretic use of the word *cause*. (See Hitchcock, 2003, for further polemics on this issue.)

Nonetheless, we should not simply reject all attempts to analyze causation as bankrupt. What is needed is a little redirection of effort. What we should demand of a theory of causation is that it be able to provide an account of at least some of the causal concepts brought out by our various questions. In my discussion, I offered some suggestions for how a probabilistic approach to causation in the spirit of R-S might be used to illuminate some of the diverse causal concepts we have encountered. I do not attempt to pass judgment on the ultimate success of any of these strategies.

The important point to recognize is that a theory's success or failure in analyzing one of these concepts may be largely independent of its performance in analyzing another. It is one thing to ask whether it is possible to capture the distinction between causal relationships and spurious correlations in purely probabilistic terms; it is quite another to ask whether the intuitive distinction between causing and preventing some outcome corresponds to the difference between raising and lowering the probability of that outcome. Yet, when authors such as Salmon (1984) and Dowe (2000) argue that we should abandon probabilistic theories of causation altogether, based primarily on counterexamples like Hesslow's (1976) in which causes lower the probabilities of their effects, they are conflating just these kinds of questions.

One of the reasons that philosophers have been so interested in the topic of causation is that many other concepts of interest to philosophy appear to have a causal dimension: explanation, rational deliberation, moral responsibility, perception, knowledge, reference, temporal direction, and so on. Indeed, the importance of causation as an analytical ingredient in other philosophical concepts is often cited as a motivation for attempts at understanding causation. How does the dismantling project that I have been recommending affect these further analytical projects? I would argue that the availability of diverse causal concepts can only help to further our understanding of other concepts with a causal dimension.

Let us consider two such concepts: prudential rationality and morality. Prudential rationality would seem to recommend that we aim to cause those outcomes that are (prudentially) desirable and to prevent those outcomes that are (prudentially) undesirable. Morality would seem to recommend that we aim to cause those outcomes that are (morally) desirable and to prevent those outcomes that are (morally) undesirable. Are the two, then, at root the same, differing only in the criteria that we use to evaluate the intrinsic desirability of the outcome? I would argue that they are not, and the difference lies, at least in part, in the different notions of *cause* that are at work in the two cases.

Let us begin with prudential rationality. The importance of causation to prudential rationality is brought out by so-called medical Newcomb problems.[7] Marie is an up-and-coming young economist who is very fond of pickles—as she likes to put it, she derives a great deal of *utility* from eating pickles. Unfortunately, Marie also believes that pregnant women crave—and hence eat—a lot of pickles. Because pregnancy would disrupt her career goals, causing her a great deal of disutility, she decides that it would be wiser to forego the pleasures of pickle-eating. It is easy to see where Marie has gone wrong. Although pickle-eating is correlated with pregnancy (assuming Marie's beliefs in this matter are correct), it is merely a symptom of the underlying condition rather than a cause of pregnancy. Whether pregnant or not, Marie has nothing to lose by enjoying her pickles.

A version of expected utility theory formulated in terms of simple conditional probabilities (such as Jeffrey, 1965) will yield the wrong advice in this sort of case. This has led a number of theorists (such as Gibbard & Harper, 1978; Skyrms, 1980; Lewis, 1981) to formulate versions of causal decision theory. Some of these versions, especially Skyrms (1980), resemble the R-S theory of causation in that they require us to condition on certain background conditions to eliminate spurious correlations. There is a further feature that these theories share with R-S: They do not require us to condition on any events intermediate between the contemplated actions and their possible outcomes. This suggests that decision theory is concerned with the net effects of our actions rather than with the component effects. When it comes to prudential deliberation, we are concerned with how our actions affect the overall probability of good and bad outcomes.

The case of moral deliberation is quite different. Consider the case of an Outback doctor who receives two emergency calls. She can fly to one remote town to save a single life, or she can fly to a remote town in the opposite direction where two people are dying. She cannot do both. It is certainly morally permissible, and perhaps even morally obligatory, for her to save two lives instead of one. The next day, she faces a different dilemma. Three people are dying. This time, fortunately, all three are in the same town. The first patient has a condition that is quite treatable, albeit lethal if left untreated. Unfortunately, the other two are dying from organ failure. The only way to save them would be to find an organ donor, and as it happens, the only suitable match is the first patient. It is certainly morally permissible, and perhaps even morally obligatory, for her to save the first patient, even

if this results in the death of the other two patients: The moral imperative to save two lives rather than one is hardly an absolute. What this example suggests is that moral evaluation is much more sensitive to the nature of the causal pathways involved. It is permissible to save two lives, even if this results in the loss of a third life as an unavoidable side effect, but it is something quite different to save two lives by allowing a third person to die. The so-called doctrine of double effect is an attempt to codify just when it is permissible to perform actions that have both good and bad outcomes. The concepts of direct effect and component effect seem better suited to the articulation of such principles than is the concept of net effect that seems to be central to prudential rationality.

Morals for Psychology

I have argued that there is no single relation that holds between events or event-types that serves as the referent of the verb *cause*. Nonetheless, we frequently do make judgments about what causes what in actual and hypothetical cases, even when the question is not more fully specified along the lines of Questions 2a–2e. There is thus an empirical question of just what people attend to when they make such judgments, and the sort of taxonomic project that I have been encouraging can supply a ready-made set of hypotheses.

There seems to be some evidence, for example, that people tend to focus on direct causes. Consider the experiment reported in Baker, Mercier, Vallée-Tourangeau, Frank, and Pan (1993), which is discussed in detail by Glymour (2001, chapters 4, 5). In this experiment, subjects observe a video screen on which a tank attempts to navigate a minefield safely. The subjects observe a number of trials, on some of which the tank makes it safely across the minefield and on some of which it does not. There is also an airplane that appears on some occasions and not on others. Finally, subjects have the option of moving a joystick, which has the effect of changing the color ("camouflaging") the tank.

Subjects were asked to assign a numerical value to the efficacy of the camouflage in allowing the tank to pass through the minefield safely. In one set of observed trials, camouflaging the tank was positively correlated with the appearance of the plane, and the appearance of the plane was perfectly correlated with safe navigation through the minefield.

On average, subjects ruled that the camouflage had negligible efficacy in guiding the tank to safety. Baker et al. (1993) claimed that this was a mistake because camouflage is positively correlated with safe passage.

Glymour (2001, pp. 63–66) notes that one plausible interpretation of the data is that camouflaging the tank causes the plane to appear, which in turn causes the tank to pass safely through the minefield, with no direct effect of the tank's color on its ability to get through. On this interpretation, the camouflage has a net effect and a component effect on safe passage, but no direct effect.[8] This suggests that the subjects, when asked to assess the efficacy of camouflage, implicitly judged the direct effect of camouflage on safe passage.

Is there a tension here? I have argued that there is no one relationship that holds (or that we take to hold) whenever we judge that one event or event-type is a cause of another. Yet, I have also urged psychologists to look for such a relationship and even suggested that it might be direct causation. What I fully expect that such research will discover, however, is that what kind of relationship we attend to when asked to make causal judgments is a highly context-sensitive affair. It may depend on the nature of the example, it may depend on our interests and our reasons for seeking causal information, and it may even depend on framing effects. For example, in the Baker et al. (1993) experiment, the subjects were told that the mines were "visual mines" that could only destroy a tank "if they could see it" (but the subjects did not know which color the mines could see). In this context, it would hardly be surprising if the subjects interpreted questions about the efficacy of the camouflage as questions about how well the mines could see the color in question, a causal mechanism that bypasses any effect the plane might have on safe passage. In other words, the wording used to describe the hypothetical scenario naturally suggested to subjects that the direct effect of the tank's color on the mines was of particular interest. It is my hope that careful investigation into the ways in which our causal judgments are sensitive to contextual cues such as these will help us to make sense of the cacophony of intuitions that currently underlies philosophical investigation into the nature of causation.

Finally, more careful attention to the different causal concepts evoked by Questions 1 and 2a through 2e can help us to understand better the nature of causal learning and causal induction. We should expect causal learning to be multifaceted: There is learning whether a relationship is causal or not (Question 1); learning the strength and direction of a causal relationship (2a and 2b); learning how a cause compares with a variety of alternatives (2c); learning how stable a causal relationship is (2d); and learning about causal pathways (2e). Causal learning of any one of these sorts will typically take place while making use of background assumptions about other facets of the causal relationships involved.

Many of the successes and failures of psychological investigation into causal learning can be better understood from within this framework. For example, a central shortcoming of the traditional associationist program of predicting and measuring associative weights (see, e.g., Rescorla & Wagner, 1972) is its attempt to answer questions about associative strengths, questions of type 2b, while ignoring the effect of our underlying assumptions about whether the relationship is causal or not (Question 1). (See Waldmann & Holyoak, 1992, and Waldmann, 2000, for detailed critiques.) Contrast this with Patricia Cheng's (1997) PowerPC model of causal inference. This model is intended to capture the way in which we estimate the strength of specific causal relationships—the way in which we attempt to answer questions of type 2b. The model is explicit about the types of assumptions that need to be made about the nature of the underlying relationships. For example, the formalism that is used is different depending on whether we are measuring promoting causes (which Cheng, 1997, calls generative causes) or inhibiting causes and depending on whether other inhibiting causes are present. So, the model requires assumptions about answers to questions of type 2a. The model, at least in its simplest form, also requires assumptions about the absence of interactions between the various causes that are present—assumptions about answers to questions of type 2d. It is, of course, an empirical question whether ordinary reasoners do in fact make just these assumptions when estimating causal strengths; my point is simply that it is highly implausible that we judge causal strengths in a cognitive vacuum, and that the sort of taxonomy I have been encouraging would suggest a variety of hypotheses about the sorts of assumptions we bring to the table.

As a second illustration, consider the blicket detector experiments of Gopnik and her collaborators (see, e.g., Gopnik et al., 2004). In these experiments, children are shown a variety of objects, which are placed on a device—a "blicket-detector"—in various combinations. On some occasions, the machine lights up and makes noises. The children are then asked which objects activate the machine (i.e., which ones are blickets). Gopnik and her collaborators argue that the children are using screening-off relations to make inferences about which objects are causally efficacious in setting off the machine, and more generally, that they represent causal structure using Bayes nets (directed acyclic graphs with a probability distribution satisfying the Markov condition).

Some commentators (see, e.g., Griffiths and Tenenbaum, forthcoming) have remarked on the speed with which the children infer that some objects affect the machine; sometimes, the children make such inferences on the basis of a single observation. Subjects make such inferences on the basis of sample sizes much too small to detect, at a statistically significant level, the conditional independence relations entailed by the Markov condition. A plausible explanation is that the subjects are exploiting background assumptions about the nature of the causal relationships that will be present. First, the number of possible graphs may be restricted in various ways: It is the objects being placed on the machine that cause it to go off, rather than the other way around; the objects are not causing each other to be blickets, and so on. Indeed, the set of possible graphs is restricted to the extent that the only causal relationships under consideration are direct effects of the objects on the machine. Second, the subjects may have a particular model in mind: The machine goes off if and only if one or more blickets are placed on it.

Griffiths and Tenenbaum (forthcoming) present some experimental results suggesting that subjects do indeed work with this sort of background assumption. In this case, the central question is of type 1. Subjects have observed certain correlations between objects being placed on the machine and its going off, and they are trying to determine which objects are causing it to go off. Their implicit model makes a number of assumptions about the nature of the causal relationships involved: There are no objects that act to inhibit the operation of the detector (Question 2a); all of the causal relations are deterministic or of maximal strength (2b); the ability of an object to set off the machine is not affected by the presence or absence of other objects on the machine (2d); and all effects are direct (2e). These assumptions are defeasible—they may be abandoned if they prove to be incompatible

with observation—but while they are in place, causal inferences may be made efficiently and rapidly.

Causal learning is a bootstrapping affair: Inferences about one facet of a causal relationship are facilitated by assumptions about other facets of that relationship. Understanding causal learning therefore requires that we understand the multidimensional nature of causal relationships.

ACKNOWLEDGMENTS   For helpful comments and suggestions, I would like to thank Clark Glymour, Alison Gopnik, Steve Sloman, Jim Woodward, and the participants in the workshop of causal learning and theory formation held at the Center for Advanced Studies in the Behavioral Sciences at Stanford University.

References

Baker, A. G., Mercier, P., Vallée-Tourangeau, F., Frank, R., & Pan, M. (1993). Selective associations and causality judgments: Presence of a strong causal factor may reduce judgments of a weaker one. *Journal of Experimental Psychology: Learning, Memory, and Cognition, 19,* 414–432.

Cartwright, N. (1979). Causal laws and effective strategies. *Noûs, 13,* 419–437. (Reprinted in Cartwright, *How the laws of physics lie,* Oxford: Clarendon Press, 1983, pp. 21–43).

Cheng, P. (1997). From covariation to causation: A causal power theory. *Psychological Review, 104,* 367–405.

Collins, J. (2000). Preemptive prevention. *Journal of Philosophy, 98,* 223–234.

Dowe, P. (2000). *Physical causation.* Cambridge, England: Cambridge University Press.

Dupré, J. (1984). Probabilistic causality emancipated. In P. A. French, T. E. Uehling, Jr., & H. K. Wettstein (Eds.), *Midwest studies in philosophy IX* (pp. 169–75). Minneapolis: University of Minnesota Press.

Eells, E. (1991). *Probabilistic Causality.* Cambridge: Cambridge University Press.

Gibbard, A., & Harper, W. (1978). Counterfactuals and two kinds of expected utility. In C. A. Hooker, J. J. Leach, and E. F. McClennen (Eds.), *Foundations and applications of decision theory* (Vol. 1, pp. 125–162). Dordrecht, The Netherlands: Reidel.

Glymour, C. (2001). *The mind's arrows: Bayes nets and graphical causal models in psychology.* Cambridge, MA: MIT Press.

Goodman, N. (1955). *Fact, fiction, and forecast.* Cambridge, MA: Harvard University Press.

Gopnik, A., Glymour, C., Sobel, D., Schulz, L., Kushnir, T., & Danks, D. (2004). A theory of causal learning in children: Causal maps and Bayes nets. *Psychological Review, 111,* 3–32.

Griffiths, T., & Tenenbaum, J. (forthcoming). Elemental causal induction. *Cognitive Psychology.*

Hesslow, G. (1976). Discussion: Two notes on the probabilistic approach to causality. *Philosophy of Science, 43,* 290–292.

Hitchcock, C. (1993). A generalized probabilistic theory of causal relevance. *Synthese, 97,* 335–364.

Hitchcock, C. (1995a). Discussion: Salmon on explanatory relevance. *Philosophy of Science, 62,* 304–320.

Hitchcock, C. (1995b). The mishap at Reichenbach Fall: Singular versus general causation. *Philosophical Studies, 78,* 257–291.

Hitchcock, C. (1996a). Farewell to binary causation. *Canadian Journal of Philosophy, 26,* 267–282.

Hitchcock, C. (1996b). The role of contrast in causal and explanatory claims. *Synthese, 107,* 395–419.

Hitchcock, C. (2001a) The intransitivity of causation revealed in equations and graphs. *Journal of Philosophy, 98,* 273–299.

Hitchcock, C. (2001b). A tale of two effects. *The Philosophical Review, 110,* 361–396.

Hitchcock, C. (2003). Of Humean bondage. *British Journal for the Philosophy of Science, 54,* 1–25.

Hitchcock, C. (2004a). Causal processes: What are they and what are they good for? *Philosophy of Science,* S71 (Proceedings).

Hitchcock, C. (2004b). Routes, processes, and chance lowering causes. In P. Dowe & P. Noordhof (Eds.), *Cause and chance* (pp. 138–151). London: Routledge.

Humphreys, P. (1989). *The chances of explanation.* Princeton, NJ: Princeton University Press.

Jeffrey, R. (1965). *The logic of decision.* New York: McGraw-Hill.

Lewis, D. (1981). Causal decision theory. *Australasian Journal of Philosophy, 59,* 5–30.

Lewis, D. (2000). Causation as influence. *Journal of Philosophy, 97,* 182–197.

Mellor, D. H. (1995). *The facts of causation.* London: Routledge.

Mill, J. S. (1843). *A system of logic.* London: Parker & Son.

Nozick, R. (1969). Newcomb's problem and two principles of choice. In N. Rescher (Ed.), *Essays in honor of Carl G. Hempel* (pp. 114–146). Dordrecht, The Netherlands: Reidel.

Pearl, J. (2001). Direct and indirect effects. In *Proceedings of UAI-2001* (pp. 411–420). San Mateo, CA: Morgan Kauffman.

Popper, K. (1962). *Conjectures and refutations.* London: Routledge & Kegan Paul.

Reichenbach, H. (1956). *The direction of time.* Berkeley, CA: University of California Press.

Rescorla, R. A., & A. R. Wagner (1972). A theory of Pavlovian conditioning: Variations in the effectiveness of reinforcement and nonreinforcement. In A. H. Black and W. F. Prokasy (Eds.), *Classical conditioning II: Current theory and research* (pp. 64–99). New York: Appleton Century Crofts.

Salmon, W. (1984). *Scientific explanation and the causal structure of the world.* Princeton, NJ: Princeton University Press.

Schaffer, J. (2000). Causation by disconnection. *Philosophy of Science, 67,* 285–300.

Skyrms, B. (1980). *Causal necessity.* New Haven, CT: Yale University Press.

Spirtes, P., Glymour, C., & Scheines, R. (2000). *Causation, prediction, and search* (2nd ed.). Cambridge, MA: MIT Press.

Suppes, P. (1970). *A probabilistic theory of causality.* Amsterdam: North-Holland.

Waldmann, M. R. (2000). Competition among causes but not effects in predictive and diagnostic learning. *Journal of Experimental Psychology: Learning, Memory, and Cognition, 26,* 53–76.

Waldmann, M. R., & Holyoak, K. J. (1992). Predictive and diagnostic learning within causal models: Asymmetries in cue competition. *Journal of Experimental Psychology: General, 121,* 222–236.

Woodward, J. (2003). *Making things happen.* Oxford, England: Oxford University Press.

Part II

CAUSATION AND PROBABILITY

Introduction to Part II:
Causal Learning and Probability

From: brook_russell@turing.carnegietech.edu
To: mherskovits@psych.ucarcadia.arcadia.edu

Dear Morgan,

What an amazing weekend! It has completely changed my mind about the value of your kind of psychology, and I simply cannot wait for the next workshop. My head is buzzing with questions and thoughts about human causal learning, and I'm so longing for the answers the next workshop seems all set to provide.

There is the whole question of probability, for example. I am struck that so many of those brilliant examples of causal learning you and the rest of them described, especially with the sprogs, seem restricted to deterministic contexts, in which causes always follow effects. Of course, causal Bayes nets can be applied to such contexts. But, the canonical application of the systems is to cases involving what may be quite complicated systems of conditional probabilities. And, while Bayes nets can be applied to deterministic systems, such systems raise special problems for learning. Often, they result in violations of faithfulness. I'm sure that Thomas Richardson and Clark Glymour can take care of that if anyone can.

Along the same lines, I do still have that query about whether human beings of any age are really capable of calculating probabilities. Didn't one of your psychologists recently get a Nobel Prize for showing how bad even sophisticated adults were at probabilistic reasoning?

And, I am curious also about the question of classification and categorization. The Bayes net formalism depends on the idea that variables are specified beforehand. That is, we already have some sense of how a particular event fits into a category—how a particular token is a member of a type as we say in philosophy—before we do any causal inference at all. But, it appears that people often categorize objects precisely according to their causal powers. Could the formalism be applied to answer these questions, too?

I'm sure this next workshop will answer all this and more.

All the best,
Brook

From: mherskovits@psych.ucarcadia.arcadia.edu
To: brook_russell@turing.carnegietech.edu

Hi Brook,

Well, I have to say I feel the same way. Remember that quote from Gopnik I sent in that first letter? Well, I guess it's too soon to say for sure, of course, but this does seem awfully like the real thing. For once, a computational set of ideas really does seem to make contact with the things we care about in psychology. And, even better, it gives us psychologists all sorts of new work to do. I already can think of a zillion experiments to do to test the ideas.

And, you know, I think a lot of your questions are going to be answered at the next workshop. It's true that people are just awful at explicitly representing probabilities, but David Sobel and Natasha Kirkham will show you that even tiny babies, as young as 8 months old, already can do some kinds of statistical reasoning; in fact, they already seem to use a kind of "screening off." Dave Lagnado and his colleagues will show you that adults can use probabilities to infer causation when they're combined with the right kinds of other cues; Richard Scheines will show that even those

undergraduate statistics students are, well, a lot smarter than they look.

As for categorization, that's an interesting one because for a long time in psychology people noticed that "causal powers" seemed to play an important role in the way people categorized objects. In fact, one of the first areas of psychology in which people talked about the theory theory was precisely in the domain of categorization. Adults' categories seemed to be based more on their theories of the deeper causal powers of objects—their "essences"—than on more superficial perceptual features. David Danks and Bob Rheder will show how we can use the Bayes net formalism to make quite precise predictions about how ordinary folk will categorize objects.

Best,
Morgan

8

Teaching the Normative Theory of Causal Reasoning

Richard Scheines, Matt Easterday, & David Danks

Introduction

By the early to mid-1990s, a normative theory of causation with qualitative as well as quantitative substance, called causal Bayes nets (CBNs),[1] achieved fairly widespread acceptance among key proponents in computer science (artificial intelligence), philosophy, epidemiology, and statistics. Although the representational component of the normative theory is at some level fairly stable and commonly accepted, how an ideal computational agent should learn about causal structure from data is much less settled and, in 2005, was still a hot area of research.[2] To be clear, the CBN framework arose in a community that had no interest in modeling human learning or representation. They were interested in how a robot, or an ideal computational agent, with obviously far different processing and memory capacities than a human, could best store and reason about the causal structure of the world. Much of the early research in this community focused on efficient algorithms for updating beliefs about a CBN from evidence (Pearl, 1988;

Spiegelhalter & Lauritzen, 1990) or on efficiently learning the qualitative structure of a CBN from data (Pearl, 1988; Spirtes, Glymour, & Scheines, 2000).

In contrast, the psychological community, interested in how humans learn not in how they *should* learn if they had practically unbounded computational resources, studied associative and causal learning for decades. The Rescorla-Wagner theory (1972) was offered, for example, as models of how humans (and animals, in some cases) learned associations and causal hypotheses from data. Only later, in the early 1990s, did CBNs make their way into the psychological community and only then as a model that might describe everyday human reasoning. At the least, a broad range of psychological theories of human causal learning can be substantially unified when cast as different versions of parameter learning within the CBN framework (Danks, 2005), but it is still a matter of vibrant debate whether and to what degree humans represent and learn about causal claims as per the normative theory of CBNs (e.g., Danks, Griffiths, & Tenenbaum, 2003; Glymour, 1998, 2000; Gopnik et al., 2004; Gopnik, Sobel, Schulz, &

Glymour, 2001; Griffiths, Baraff, & Tenenbaum, 2004; Lagnado & Sloman, 2002, 2004; Sloman & Lagnado, 2002; Steyvers, Tenenbaum, Wagenmakers, & Blum, 2003; Tenenbaum & Griffiths, 2001, 2003; Tenenbaum & Niyogi, 2003; Waldmann & Hagmayer, in press; Waldmann & Martignon, 1998).

Nearly all of the psychological research on human causal learning involves naïve participants, that is, individuals who have not been taught the normative theory in any way, shape, or form. Almost all of this research involves single-trial learning: observing how subjects form and update their causal beliefs from the outcome of a series of trials, each either an experiment on a single individual or a single episode of a system's behavior. No work, as far as we are aware, attempts to train people normatively on this and related tasks, and no work we know of compares the performance of naïve participants and those taught the normative theory. The work we describe in this chapter begins just such a project. We are specifically interested in seeing if formal education about normative causal reasoning helps students draw accurate causal inferences.

Although there has been, to our knowledge, no previous research on subjects trained in the normative theory, there has been research on whether naïve subjects approximate normative learning agents. Single-trial learning, for example, can easily be described by the normative theory as a sequential Bayesian updating problem. Some psychologists have considered whether and how people update their beliefs in accord with the Bayesian norm (e.g., Danks et al., 2003; Griffiths et al., 2004; Steyvers et al., 2003; Tenenbaum & Griffiths, 2001, 2003; Tenenbaum & Niyogi, 2003) and have suggested that some people at least approximate a normative Bayesian learner on simple cases. This research does not extend to subjects who have already been taught the appropriate rules of Bayesian updating, either abstractly or concretely.

In the late 1990s, curricular material became available that taught the normative theory of CBNs.[3] Standard introductions to the normative theory in computer science, philosophy, and statistics do not directly address the sorts of tasks that psychologists have investigated, however. First, as opposed to single-trial learning, the focus is on learning from samples drawn from some population. Second, little or no attention is paid to the severe computational (processing time) and representational (storage space) limitations of humans. Instead, abstractions and algorithms

are taught that could not possibly be used by humans on any but the simplest of problems.

In the normative theory, learning about which among many possible causal structures might obtain is typically cast as iterative:

1. Enumerate a space of plausible hypotheses.
2. Design an experiment that will help distinguish among these hypotheses.
3. Collect a sample of data from such an experiment.
4. Analyze these data with the help of sophisticated computing tools like R[4] or TETRAD[5] to update the space of hypotheses to those supported or consistent with these data.
5. Go back to Step 2.

Designing an experiment, insofar as it involves choosing which variable or variables to manipulate, is a natural part of the normative theory and has just recently become a subject of study.[6] The same activity, that is, picking the best among many possible experiments to run, has been studied by Lagnado and Sloman (2004), Sobel and Kushnir (2004), Steyvers et al. (2003), and Waldmann and Hagmayer (in press).

Another point of contact is what a student thinks the data collected in an experiment tell them about the model that might be generating the data. Starting with a set of plausible models, some will be consistent with the data collected, or favored by it, and some will not. We would like to know whether students trained in the normative theory are better, and if so, in what way, at determining what models are consistent with the data.

In a series of four pilot experiments, we examined the performance of subjects partially trained in the normative theory on causal learning tasks that involved choosing experiments and deciding which models were consistent with the data. Although we did not use single-trial learning, we did use tasks similar to those studied recently by psychologists, especially Steyvers et al. (2003). Our students were trained for about a month in a college course on causation and social policy. The students were not trained in the precise skills tested by our experiments. Although our results are not directly comparable to those discussed in the psychological literature, they certainly suggest that students trained on the normative theory act quite differently from naïve participants.

Our chapter is organized as follows: We first briefly describe what we take to be the normative theory of causal reasoning. We then describe the online corpus we have developed for teaching it. Finally, we describe four pilot studies we performed in the fall of 2004 with the Causality Lab, a major part of the online corpus.

The Normative Theory of Causal Reasoning

Although Galileo pioneered the use of fully controlled experiments almost 400 years ago, it was not until Sir Ronald Fisher's (1935) famous work on experimental design that real headway was made on the statistical problem of causal discovery. Fisher's work, like Galileo's, was confined to experimental settings in which treatment could be assigned. In Galileo's case, however, all the variables in a system could be perfectly controlled, and the treatment could thus be isolated and made to be the only quantity varying in a given experiment. In agricultural or biological experiments, however, it is not possible to control all the quantities (e.g., the genetic and environmental history of each person). Fisher's technique of randomization not only solved this problem, but also produced a reference distribution against which experimental results could be compared statistically. His work is still the statistical foundation of most modern medical research.

Representing Causal Systems: Causal Bayes Nets

Sewall Wright pioneered representing causal systems as "path diagrams" in the 1920s and 1930s (Wright, 1934), but until about the middle of the 20th century the entire topic of how causal claims can or cannot be discovered from data collected in nonexperimental studies was largely written off as hopeless. Herbert Simon (1953) and Hubert Blalock (1961) made major inroads but gave no general theory. In the mid-1980s, however, artificial intelligence researchers, philosophers, statisticians, and epidemiologists began to make real headway on a rigorous theory of causal discovery from nonexperimental as well as experimental data.[7]

Like Fisher's statistical work on experiments, CBNs seek to model the relations among a set of random variables, such as an individual's level of education or annual income. Alternative approaches aim to model the causes of individual events, for example,

the causes of the space shuttle Challenger disaster. We confine our attention to relations among variables. If we are instead concerned with a system in which certain types of events cause other types of events, then we represent the occurrence or nonoccurrence of the events by binary variables. For example, if a blue lightbulb going on is followed by a red lightbulb going on, we use the variables red lightbulb [lit, not lit] and blue lightbulb [lit, not lit].

Any approach that models the statistical relations among a set of variables must first confront what we call the *ontological problem*: How do we get from a messy and complicated world to a coherent and meaningful set of variables that might plausibly be related either statistically or causally. For example, it is reasonable to examine the association between the number of years of education and the number of dollars in yearly income for a sample of middle-aged men in western Pennsylvania, but it makes no sense to examine the average level of education for the aggregate of people in a state like Pennsylvania and compare it to the level of income for individual residents of New York. It also does not make sense to posit a "variable" with a range of values that is not exclusive because it includes has blond hair, has curly hair, and so on. After teaching causal reasoning to hundreds of students over almost a decade, the ontological problem seems the most difficult to teach and the most difficult for students to learn. We need to study it much more thoroughly, but for the present investigation, we simply assume it has been solved for a particular learning problem.

Assuming that we are given a set of coherent and meaningful variables, the normative theory involves representing the qualitative causal relations among a set of variables with a directed graph in which there is an edge from X to Y just in case X is a direct cause of Y relative to the system of variables under study. X is a direct cause of Y in such a system if and only if there is a pair of ideal interventions that hold the other variables in the system Z fixed and change only X, such that the probability distribution for Y also changes. We model the quantitative relations among the variables with a set of conditional probability distributions: one for each variable given each possible configuration of values of its direct causes (see Figure 8-1).

The asymmetry of causation is modeled by how the system responds to ideal intervention, both qualitatively and quantitatively. Consider, for example, a two-variable system: room temperature (of a room an

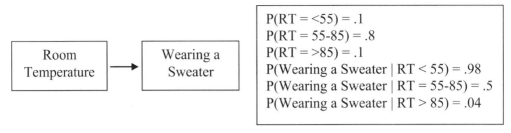

FIGURE 8-1 Causal Bayes net.

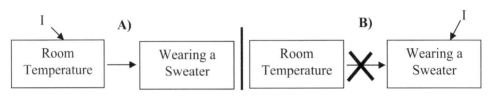

FIGURE 8-2 Manipulated graph.

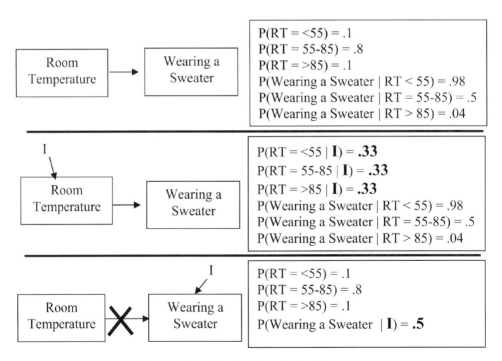

FIGURE 8-3 Original and manipulated systems.

individual is in) <55°, 55°–85°, >85°], and wearing a sweater [yes, no], in which the graph and set of conditional probability tables in Figure 8-1 describe the system.

Ideal interventions are represented by adding an intervention variable that is a direct cause of only the variables it targets. Ideal interventions are assumed to have a simple property: If I is an intervention on variable X, then when I is active, it removes all the other edges into X. That is, the "other" causes of X no longer influence X in the postintervention, or *manipulated*, system. Figure 8-2 captures the change and nonchange in the Figure 8-1 graph in response to interventions on room temperature (A) and on wearing a sweater (B).

Modeling the system's quantitative response to interventions is almost as simple. Generally, we conceive of an ideal intervention as imposing not a value but rather a probability distribution on its target. We thus model the move from the original system to the manipulated system as leaving all conditional distributions intact save those over the manipulated variables, in which case we impose our own distribution. For example, if we assume that the interventions depicted in Figure 8-2 impose a uniform distribution on their targets when active, then Figure 8-3 shows the two manipulated systems that would result from the original system shown in Figure 8-1.[8]

To simplify later discussions, we include the "null" manipulation (i.e., we intervene on no variables) as one possible manipulation. A CBN *and* a manipulation define a joint probability distribution over the set of variables in the system. If we use *experimental setup* to refer to an exact quantitative specification of the manipulation, then when we collect data we are drawing a sample from the probability distribution defined by the original CBN and the experimental setup.

Learning Causal Bayes Nets

There are two distinct types of CBN learning given data: parameter estimation and structure learning. In parameter estimation, one fixes the qualitative (graphical) structure of the model and estimates the conditional probability tables by minimizing some loss function or maximizing the likelihood of the sample data given the model and its parameterization. In contrast, structure learning aims to recover the qualitative structure of graphical edges. The distinction between parameter estimation and structure learning is not perfectly clean because "close-to-zero parameter" and "absence of the

edge" are roughly equivalent. Danks (2005) shows how to understand most non-Bayes net psychological theories of causal learning (e.g., Cheng, 1997; Cheng & Novick, 1992; Perales & Shanks, 2003; Rescorla & Wagner, 1972) as parameter estimation theories for particular graphical structures.

A fundamental challenge for CBN structure learning algorithms is the existence of *Markov equivalence classes* (MECs): sets of CBNs that make identical predictions about the way the world looks in the absence of experiments. For example, $A \rightarrow B$ and $A \leftarrow B$ both predict that variables A and B will be associated. Any data set that can be modeled by $A \rightarrow B$ can be equally well modeled by $A \leftarrow B$, so there is no reason—given only observed data—to prefer one structure over the other. This observation leads to the standard warning in science that "correlation does not equal causation." However, patterns of correlation can enable us to infer something about causal relationships (or, more generally, graphical structure), although perhaps not a unique graph. Thus, structure learning algorithms will frequently not be able to learn the "true" graph from data, but will be able to learn a small set of graphs that are indistinguishable from the "truth."

For learning the structure of the causal graph, the normative theory splits into two approaches: constraint based and scoring. The constraint-based approach (Spirtes et al., 2000) aims to determine the class of CBNs consistent with an inferred (statistical) pattern of independencies and associations, as well as background knowledge. Any particular CBN entails a set of statistical constraints in the population, such as independence and tetrad constraints. Constraint-based algorithms take as input the constraints inferred from a given sample, as well as background assumptions about the class of models to be considered, and output the set of indistinguishable causal structures. That is, the algorithms output the models that (a) entail all and only the inferred constraints and (b) are consistent with background knowledge. The inference task is thus split into two parts: statistical, inference from the sample to the constraints that hold in the population, and causal, inference from the constraints to the CBN or nets that entail such constraints.

Suppose, for example, that we observe a sample of 100 individuals on variables X_1, X_2, and X_3 and after statistical inference conclude that X_1 and X_2 are statistically independent, conditional on X_3 (i.e., $X_1 \perp X_2 \mid X_3$). If we also assume there are no unobserved common causes for any pair of X_1, X_2, and X_3, then the PC

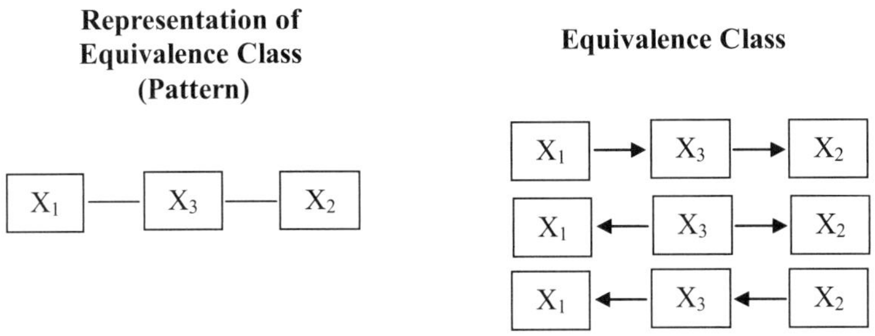

**Representation of
Equivalence Class
(Pattern)**

Equivalence Class

FIGURE 8-4 Equivalence class for $X_1 \perp X_2 \mid X_3$.

algorithm (Spirtes et al., 2000) would output the pattern shown on the left side of Figure 8-4. That pattern is a graphical object that represents the MEC shown on the right side of Figure 8-4; all three graphs predict exactly the same set of unconditional and conditional independencies. In general, two causal graphs entail the same set of independencies if and only if they have the same adjacencies and unshielded colliders, where X and Y are adjacent just in case $X \rightarrow Y$ or $X \leftarrow Y$, and Z is an unshielded collider between X and Y just in case $X \rightarrow Z \leftarrow Y$ and X and Y are not adjacent. Thus, in a pattern, we need only represent the adjacencies and unshielded colliders. Constraint-based searches first compute the set of adjacencies for a set of variables and then try to "orient" these adjacencies, that is, test for colliders among triples in which X and Y are adjacent, Y and Z are adjacent, but X and Z are not: X-Y-Z.

Testing high-order conditional independence relations—relations that involve a large number of variables in the conditioning set—is computationally expensive and statistically unreliable, so the constraint-based approach sequences the tests to minimize the number of higher-order conditional independence facts actually tested. Compared to other methods, constraint-based algorithms are extremely fast and under multivariate normal distributions (linear systems) can handle hundreds of variables. Constraint-based algorithms can also handle models with unobserved common causes. Their drawback is that they are subject to errors if statistical decisions made early in the algorithm are incorrect.

If handed the independence relations true of a population, then people could easily perform by hand the computations required by a constraint-based search, even for many causal structures with dozens of variables. Of course, people could not possibly compute

all of the precise statistical tests of independence relations required, but they could potentially approximate a subset of such (unconditional and conditional) independence tests (see Danks, 2004, for one tentative proposal).

In the score-based approach (Heckerman et al., 1999), we assign a "score" to a CBN that reflects both (a) the closeness of the CBN's "fit" of the data and (b) the plausibility of the CBN prior to seeing any data. We then search (in a variety of ways) among all the models consistent with background knowledge for the set that has the highest score. The most common scoring-based approach is based on Bayesian principles: Calculate a score based on the CBN's *prior*—the probability we assign to the model being true before seeing any data, and the model's likelihood—the probability of the observed data given this particular CBN.[9] Scoring-based searches are accurate but are slow, as calculating each model's score is expensive. Given a flat prior over the models (i.e., equal probabilities on all models), the set of models that have the highest Bayesian score is identical to the MEC of models output by a constraint-based algorithm.

Bayesian approaches are straightforwardly applied to standard psychological tasks. By computing the posterior over the models after each new sample point, we get a learning dynamics for that problem (as in, e.g., Danks et al., 2003; Griffiths et al., 2004; Steyvers et al., 2003; Tenenbaum & Griffiths, 2003). However, even if naïve subjects act like approximately rational Bayesian structure learners in cases involving 2 or 3 variables, they cannot possibly implement the approach precisely or possibly implement the approach for larger numbers of variables, e.g., 5–10. Hence, the Bayesian approach is not necessarily appropriate for teaching the normative theory.

The Causality Lab

Convinced that the qualitative story behind causal discovery should be taught to introductory-level students either prior to or simultaneously with a basic course on statistical methods, a team[10] from Carnegie Mellon and the University of California, San Diego, created enough online material for an entire semester's course in the basics of CBNs. By the spring of 2004, over 2,600 students in more than 70 courses at almost 30 different colleges or universities had taken all or part of our online course, which is available through Carnegie Mellon's Open Learning Initiative at www.cmu.edu/oli/.

Causal and statistical reasoning involves three components: 16 lessons, or concept modules; a virtual laboratory for simulating social science experiments, the Causality Lab;[11] and a bank of over 120 case studies, which are reports of "studies" by social, behavioral, or medical researchers. Each of the concept modules contains approximately the same amount of material as a textbook chapter. The Causality Lab embodies the normative theory by making explicit all the ideas we discussed.

Figure 8-5 shows the navigation panel for the lab. Each of the icons may be clicked to reveal, and in some cases manipulate, the contents of an object for a given exercise. The instructor creates the "true" CBN

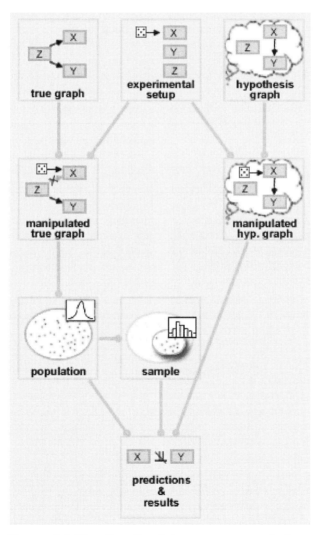

FIGURE 8-5 The Causality Lab navigation panel. hyp., hypothetical.

with an exercise building tool, and this constitutes the "true graph" to be discovered by the student. Of course, just as real scientists are confined to one side of the Humean curtain, so are students of the Causality Lab. In most exercises, they cannot access any of the icons in the left column, all of which represent one aspect of the truth to be discovered. Students cannot simply click and see the truth.

Using the example of room temperature and sweaters, suppose the true graph and conditional probability distributions are as given in Figure 8-1. To fully determine the population from which the student may draw a sample, however, the student must also provide the (possibly null) experimental setup. Once the student specifies one or more experimental setups, that student can "collect data" from any of them.

For example, suppose we clicked on the Experimental Setup icon and then created three distinct experimental setups (Figure 8-6). On the left, both room temperature and sweater will be passively observed. In the middle, the value of room temperature will be randomly assigned (indicated by the icon of a die attached to Room_Temp), and the value of sweater will be passively observed. On the right, the value of sweater will be randomly assigned, and the value of room temperature will be passively observed.

As the navigation panel in Figure 8-5 shows, it is the combination of the experimental setup and the true CBN that defines the manipulated system, which determines the population probability distribution. So, if we click on Collect Data from Exp-Setup 1 (far left side of Figure 8-6), then we will be drawing a sample from the distribution shown at the top of Figure 8-3. If we collect data from Exp-Setup 2, then our sample will be drawn from the distribution shown

in the middle of Figure 8-3, and so on. The fact that the sample population depends on both the experimental setup and the true CBN is a pillar of the normative theory, but this fact is rarely, if ever, taught.

Once a sample is pseudorandomly drawn from the appropriate distribution, we may inspect it in any way we wish. To keep matters as qualitative as possible, however, the focus of the Causality Lab is on independence constraints—the normative theory's primary connection between probability distributions and causal structure. In particular, the Predictions and Results window allows the student to inspect the following for each experimental setup: the independence relations that hold in the population[12] and the independence relations that cannot be rejected at α =.05 by a statistical test applied to any sample drawn from that population

For example, Figure 8-7 shows the results of an experiment in which wearing a sweater is randomly assigned and a sample of 40 individuals was drawn from the resulting population. The Predictions and Results window indicates that, in the population, room temperature and sweater wearing are independent (notated as ⊥⊥). The lab also allows students to inspect histograms or scatterplots of their samples and then enter their own guesses regarding which independence relations hold in a given sample. In this example, a student used the histograms to guess that room temperature and sweater wearing were associated (not independent), although the statistical test applied to the sample of 40 could not reject the hypothesis of independence. Thus, one easy lesson for students is that statistical tests are sometimes better at determining independence relations than students who eyeball sample summaries.

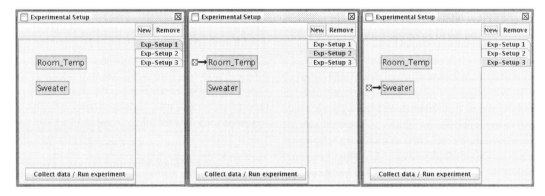

FIGURE 8-6 Three experimental setups.

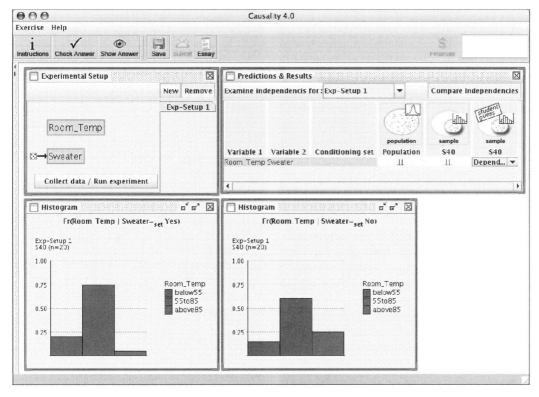

FIGURE 8-7 Independence results.

Students can also create hypotheses and then compare the predictions of their hypotheses to the results of their experiments. For example, we may rebel against common sense and hypothesize that wearing a sweater causes the room temperature. The Causality Lab helps the students learn that their hypothetical graph only makes testable predictions about independence in combination with an experimental setup, which leads to a manipulated hypothetical graph (see Figure 8-5).

Causal Discovery in the Lab

Equipped with the tools of the Causality Lab, we can decompose the causal discovery task into the following steps:

1. Enumerate all the hypotheses that are consistent with background knowledge.
2. Create an experimental setup and collect a sample of data.
3. Make statistical inferences about the independences that hold in the population from the sample.
4. Eliminate or reallocate confidence in hypotheses on the basis of the results from Step 3.
5. If no unique model emerges, then go back to Step 2.

Steps 1 (enumeration) and 3 (statistics) are interesting, although only necessary if one is following a constraint-based approach. The interesting action is in Steps 2 and 4. As operationalized in the Causality Lab and defined in the normative theory, the first part of Step 2 (experimental design) amounts to determining, for each variable under study, whether that variable will be observed passively or have its values assigned randomly.

Depending on the hypotheses still under consideration, experimental setups differ in the informativeness of the experiment's results. For example, suppose the currently active hypotheses include $X \rightarrow Y \rightarrow Z$ and $X \leftarrow Y \rightarrow Z$. An experimental setup (call it ES1) in which X is randomized and Y and Z are passively observed will uniquely determine the correct graph no matter the outcome.[13] A different experiment (call it ES2) in which Z is randomized and X and Y passively observed will tell us nothing, again regardless of the outcome of the experiment. The difference in the

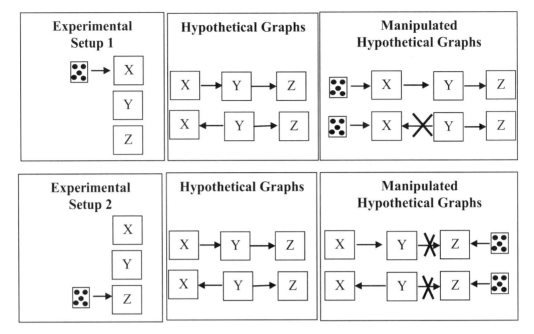

FIGURE 8-8 Informative and uninformative experimental setups.

experiments' informativeness arises because the manipulated graphs are distinguishable in ES1 but not in ES2 (Figure 8-8). In ES1, the two possibilities have different adjacencies ($X \to Y$ in one, and no edges in the other) and thus entail different sets of independencies. In ES2, however, the two manipulated graphs are indistinguishable; they have the same adjacencies.

From this perspective, the causal discovery task involves determining, for each possible experimental setup one might use, the set of manipulated hypothetical graphs and whether they are (partially) distinguishable. This is a challenging task. What are the general principles for experimental design, if any? When the goal is to parameterize the dependence of one effect on several causes, then there is a rich and powerful theory of experimental design from the statistical literature (Berger, 2005; Cochran & Cox, 1957). When the goal is to discover which among many possible causal structures are true, however, the theory of optimal experimental design is much less developed. From a Bayesian perspective, we must first specify a prior distribution over the hypothetical graphs. Given such a distribution, each experimental setup has an expected gain in information (reduction in uncertainty), and one should thus pick the experiment that would most reduce uncertainty (Murphy, 2001; Tong & Koller, 2001). Computing this gain is intractable for all but the simplest of cases, although Steyvers et al. (2003) argue that naïve subjects approximate just this sort of behavior. Regardless of the descriptive question, a theory of so-called active learning provides normative guidance regarding the optimal sequencing of experiments. Taking a constraint-based approach, Eberhardt, Glymour, and Scheines (2005) show that for N variables, $N - 1$ experiments that randomize at most a single variable are always sufficient to identify the correct graph and in the worst case that many are necessary.

Although there is not yet a graphical characterization of the best experiment given a set of active hypotheses, we do have a few powerful heuristics. For example, passive observation is sufficient, under a constraint-based approach, to identify all the adjacencies among a set of variables. Given the adjacencies, an intervention on X will orient all the edges adjacent to X. Suppose X and Z are adjacent. If X and Z are independent after an intervention on X, then the edge is $X \leftarrow Z$; if X and Z are associated, then the edge must be $X \to Z$.

Pilot Studies

An obvious question about teaching the normative theory is as follows: Does learning it improve a student's performance on causal learning tasks? In the fall of

2004, one of us (R. S.) taught an upper-level seminar at Carnegie Mellon on causation and social policy. For about a month in the middle of the seminar, the students went through the causal and statistical reasoning material and learned the rudiments of the representational theory of CBNs. The class covered the idea of causation, causal graphs, manipulations, manipulated models, independence, conditional independence, and d-separation,[14] but included no instruction on model equivalence and no instruction on a procedure for causal discovery. All 15 of the students in the class agreed to participate in a pilot study in which they were given four discovery tasks. The students all worked for a little over an hour in a computer cluster. We were unable to enforce strict silence between students, and thus the results of our pilot study cannot be considered rigorous. They are nevertheless interesting and suggestive.

In all of our experiments, participants were allowed to see the full independence relations that hold in the population defined by an experimental setup of their choice, and so no statistical judgments were required. We recognize that this is different from the standard presentation in psychological experiments, but our intent was to focus on the skills involved in causal discovery from known facts about the population, as opposed to making statistical inferences from samples. To provide familiarity with the Causality Lab interface, all participants were provided a simple training problem. In the training task, the students were instructed to (a) do a passive observation, then (b) eliminate all the models they could, and finally (c) determine the true graph using the fewest number of experiments.

Experiment 1

In Experiment 1, we asked students to determine which model in Figure 8-9 was the true graph in the minimum number of experiments. Students were

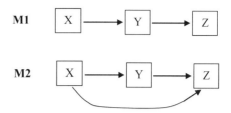

FIGURE 8-9 Choices in Experiment 1.

randomly assigned to a model, and there was no effect of condition. The experiment explored whether students understood the difference between direct and indirect causation. All 15 students learned the correct model in a single experiment.

We were also interested in the students' choices of experimental targets. Table 8-1 shows the independence relations entailed by both models in every possible experimental setup, as well as whether M1 and M2 can be distinguished in that experiment. From a normative point of view, no one should choose to randomize Z because that experiment will not distinguish between these two models. Randomizing Y is optimal because under that intervention the two models make different predictions about both $X \perp\!\!\!\perp Z$ and $X \perp\!\!\!\perp Z \mid Y$.

Steyvers et al. (2003) report a source bias in choosing interventions: People prefer to intervene on variables believed to have no edges into them (i.e., no causes in the system). If this bias holds, then people should prefer to randomize on X when they randomize on any variable at all. Note that the source bias refers only to choices among experiments; no prediction was made about whether people will prefer to experiment or passively observe.

Figure 8-10 shows the frequency with which each experiment was chosen first. All students were normatively correct; no one chose to randomize on Z. Our students preferred the passive observation, which can be explained by its use in the training experiment.

TABLE 8-1 Independencies Implied by M1 and M2

Experimental Setup	$X \perp\!\!\!\perp Y$	$X \perp\!\!\!\perp Z$	$X \perp\!\!\!\perp Z \mid Y$	M1 and M2 Distinguishable?
Passive observation	Neither	Neither	M1, not M2	Yes
Randomize X	Neither	Neither	M1, not M2	Yes
Randomize Y	Both	M1, not M2	M1, not M2	Yes
Randomize Z	Neither	Both		No

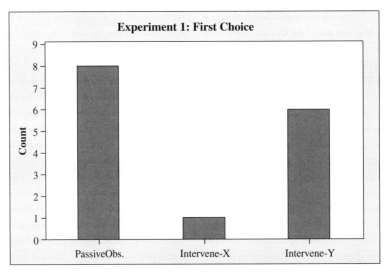

FIGURE 8-10 Choice of experiments in Experiment 1. Obs., observation.

And, in contrast to the results reported in Steyvers et al. (2003), students exhibited no source bias whatsoever: Six of the seven who chose to intervene did so on the mediating variable Y.

Experiment 2

In the second experiment, the students had to choose among four possibilities (Figure 8-11). They were again told to find the true graph in the minimum number of experiments, although they understood that they were not required to do the passive observation experiment first. Since M3 and M4 are essentially the same a priori, we randomized the students to a true graph of M1, M2, or M3.

This experiment aimed to determine whether students could choose an informative intervention; in this problem, the choice of experimental setup matters greatly, as shown in Table 8-2. For example, if we passively observe all variables, then we can tell only whether M1 is the true model or not the true model (i.e., that the true model is one of {M2, M3, M4}). The normatively optimal experiment to perform is the one in which the middle variable C is randomized. That experiment is guaranteed to uniquely identify the correct model regardless of outcome.

Again, students were quite successful in the overall task: 14 of 15 correctly identified the model. The number of experiments it took to arrive at an answer varied considerably: Two experiments were the mode,

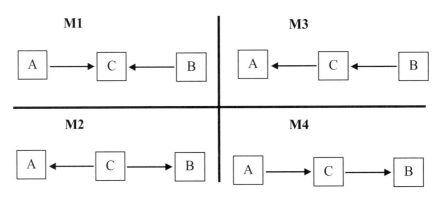

FIGURE 8-11 Possibilities in Experiment 2.

TABLE 8-2 Distinguishable Models by Intervention Choice

Experimental Setup	Distinguishable?
Passive observation	M1 from {M2, M3, M4}
Randomize A	M1 from {M2, M3} from M4
Randomize B	M1 from {M2, M4} from M3
Randomize C	M1 from M2 from M3 from M4

but several students used three or four. Figure 8-12 shows the students' first experimental choice (top graph) and the target of the first intervention they performed regardless of when that first intervention experiment occurred (bottom graph). Clearly, students preferred passive observation as a first choice, but the first choice for an intervention was overwhelmingly the mediator C as opposed to either endpoint variables A or B.

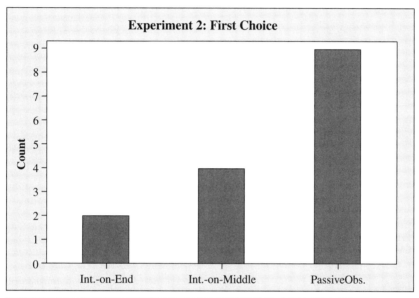

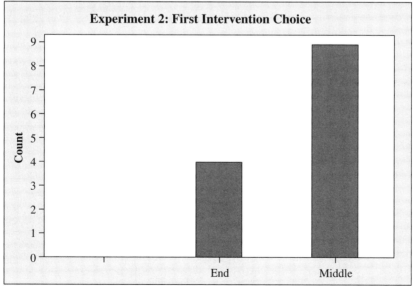

FIGURE 8-12 Results of Experiment 2.

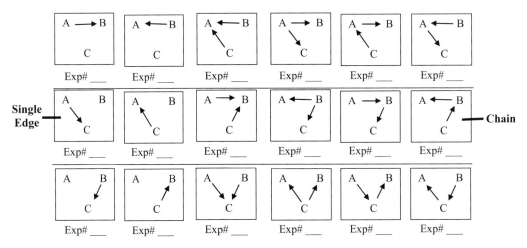

FIGURE 8-13 Possibilities for Experiment 3.

Experiment 3

In the third experiment, students were told that the true model was one of the models in Figure 8-13, and we randomly assigned students to have either the single-edge model or the chain model (both highlighted in Figure 8-13) as the true underlying causal structure. (Students were not told that those were the only two possibilities.) All participants were required to (a) begin with the passive observation experiment, (b) eliminate as many models as possible after each experiment, and (c) find the true model in the minimum number of experiments. Students recorded the experimental design used to eliminate each model except the final one. Students did not use the hypothetical graph window of the Causality Lab and so had no computational aids to calculate the independencies implied by each hypothesis under a given experimental setup.

In our experiment, over two thirds of participants (11 of 15) answered correctly, and success was independent of condition. Including the passive observation, students averaged just under three experiments before reaching a final answer, and the number of experiments was also independent of condition. As one would expect, the 11 students who got the answer right averaged significantly fewer experiments than the 4 who got it wrong. For the remaining analyses, we restrict our attention to the participant responses after only the initial passive observation.

One question behind our experiment was whether students acted as if they understood the concept of MECs: sets of models that are indistinguishable by passive observation because they imply the same set of

independence relations. In Figure 8-14 we show again the 18 possible models, but group them in boxes corresponding to the 9 MECs.

Individuals who (act as if they) understand the idea of MECs should, for every equivalence class, either keep or remove all its members together after the passive observation stage. For equivalence classes D, E, and F, which have only a single member, this necessarily happens, so we exclude those classes. We then define a (weighted) MEC "integrity" score as follows:

MEC integrity

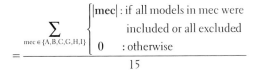

The weighting captures the fact that it is more challenging to have MEC integrity for equivalence classes G, H, and I, which have three members, than it is for equivalence classes A, B, or C, which have two. If a participant always keeps or removes members of an MEC together, then MEC-Integrity equals 1; if members of an MEC are never kept or removed together, then MEC-Integrity equals 0. Figure 8-15 shows that students exhibited an extremely high degree of MEC integrity: 12 of 15 participants were perfect, and only 1 student was massively confused.

Even if someone exhibited perfect MEC integrity, they might still be retaining or excluding the wrong graphs (or the wrong MECs) given the data they received. To measure whether they are including too

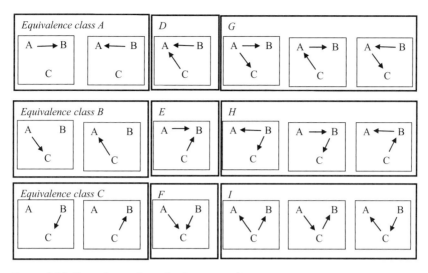

FIGURE 8-14 Equivalence classes for the passive observation experiment in Experiment 3.

many graphs, we computed the percentage of commission errors:

$$\text{Commission Error} = \frac{\text{Number of graphs retained by student, but not in correct MEC}}{\text{Number of graphs not in correct MEC}}$$

Similarly, to measure whether they are excluding graphs equivalent to the truth, we computed the percentage of omission errors:

$$\text{Omission Error} = \frac{\text{Number of graphs in the correct MEC omitted by the student}}{\text{Number of graphs not in correct MEC}}$$

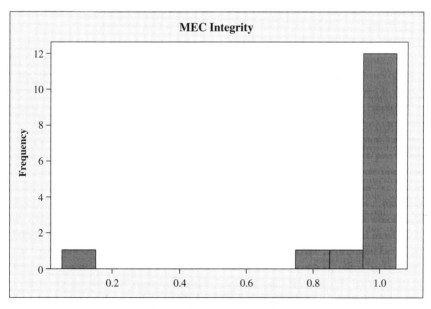

FIGURE 8-15 MEC integrity.

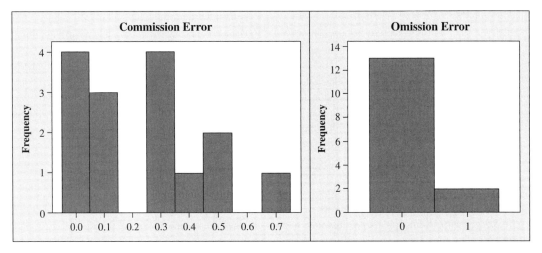

FIGURE 8-16 Commission and omission error.

Not surprisingly, students were not as good on the accuracy of their inferences. Figure 8-16 shows that, although their omission error was quite low (few correct graphs were left out), students often retained more graphs than were consistent with the passive observation.

Interestingly, we think we can explain why. Although we did not include equivalence classes D, E, and F in our computation of MEC-Integrity (because they each have only one graph as a member), we did include those graphs in our calculations of omission and commission error. These graphs each have the same adjacencies as some equivalence class, although they differ from the class in edge orientation. In Figure 8-14, classes D and G share the same adjacencies, as do E and H, and F and I. If, for example, the true graph was $C \rightarrow B \rightarrow A$ (part of equivalence Class H) and I included every graph in Classes E and H, then I would have a perfect score on MEC-Integrity but a nonzero commission error. In general, if I attend only to adjacencies and ignore orientations, I will (provably) always receive a perfect score on MEC-Integrity, even though I might make a number of commission errors.

After looking at the data, we hypothesized that students were quite good at determining the correct adjacencies but not very good at determining the correct orientations. To explore this, we first computed participants' Adjacency-Integrity to determine whether the students included or excluded graphs that share adjacencies as a unit.

Adjacency-Integrity

$$
= \frac{\displaystyle\sum_{\text{adj} \in \{A,B,C,D+G,E+H,F+I\}} \begin{cases} |\textbf{adj}| & : \text{if all models in adj were} \\ & \quad \text{included or all excluded} \\ 0 & : \text{otherwise} \end{cases}}{18}
$$

The histogram in Figure 8-17 shows that students had relatively high Adjacency-Integrity, suggesting that the high MEC-Integrity scores were caused (at least in part) by people keeping/removing graphs with the same adjacencies and not necessarily those that made the identical observational predictions.

This explanation does not completely account for students' performance. Many included graphs that were neither Markov nor adjacency equivalent to the truth. But, not all mistakes are quite the same. Suppose the truth is $A \rightarrow B \rightarrow C$. Including the graph $A \rightarrow B \leftarrow C$ is arguably a less-severe mistake than including the graph $B \rightarrow C \rightarrow A$. In the former case, the adjacencies were correctly learned, although not the orientations. In the latter case, however, a true adjacency (A-B) was excluded, and a false adjacency (C-A) was included. We will say that a graph G is *adjacency consistent* with a graph H if G's adjacencies are a subset of H's or vice versa. The former error in this example is adjacency consistent with the truth; the latter error is not.

To understand better the severity of the students' errors, we computed the proportion of the commission

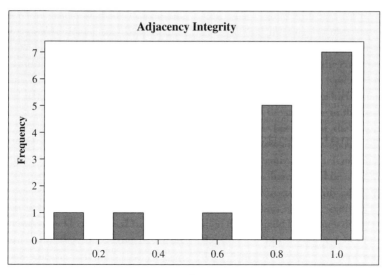

FIGURE 8-17 Adjacency-integrity.

errors that were adjacency consistent with the true MEC.

$$\text{Adjacency Consistent Error}$$
$$= \frac{\begin{array}{c}\text{Number of graphs committed}\\\text{that are adjacency consistent}\end{array}}{\text{Number of graphs committed}}$$

Figure 8-18 shows that students' errors tend to be adjacency consistent; the majority of their mistakes involved keeping a graph that was either a subgraph or supergraph of the truth.

Of course, this high percentage could arise if most graphs are adjacency consistent with the truth (although this is not actually the case in this experiment).

To normalize for the number of errors that *could* be adjacency consistent or inconsistent, we also computed:

$$\text{Adjacency Consistent Inclusion}$$
$$= \frac{\begin{array}{c}\text{Number of committed graphs}\\\text{that are adjacency consistent}\end{array}}{\begin{array}{c}\text{Number of committable graphs}\\\text{that are adjacency consistent}\end{array}}$$

$$\text{Adjacency Inconsistent Inclusion}$$
$$= \frac{\begin{array}{c}\text{Number of committed graphs}\\\text{that are adjacency inconsistent}\end{array}}{\begin{array}{c}\text{Number of committable graphs}\\\text{that are adjacency inconsistent}\end{array}}$$

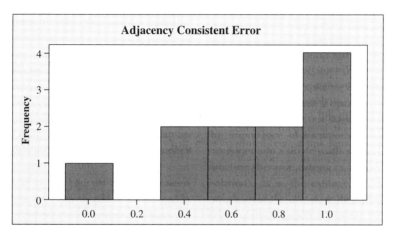

FIGURE 8-18 Adjacency consistent error.

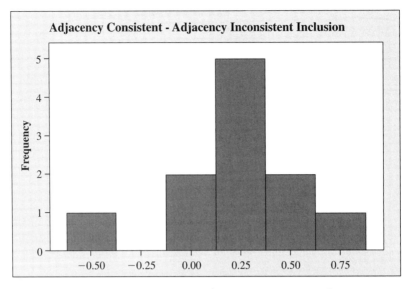

FIGURE 8-19 Adjacency consistent-adjacency inconsistent inclusion.

If students were indifferent between adjacency consistent and adjacency inconsistent errors, then the within-student difference between these two measures should center around 0. As Figure 8-19 shows, it clearly does not.

These results seem to indicate that

1. Students have very high Adjacency-Integrity (Figure 8-17).
2. A large fraction of the graphs committed are adjacency consistent (Figure 8-18).
3. The fraction of the committable adjacency consistent graphs that are actually committed is much higher than the fraction of committable adjacency inconsistent graphs that are actually committed (Figure 8-19).

We interpret these results to mean that, like constraint-based algorithms and consistent with Danks (2004), students are using one cognitive strategy for detecting when two variables are adjacent and another for detecting how the adjacencies are oriented, especially in the case of data collected from passive observation. Detecting whether X and Y are adjacent is as simple as detecting whether X and Y are independent conditional on any set. Detecting whether X-Y-Z is oriented as $X \rightarrow Y \leftarrow Z$ or as one of $\{X \rightarrow Y \rightarrow Z, X \leftarrow Y \rightarrow Z, X \leftarrow Y \leftarrow Z\}$ is much more difficult.

Conclusions

The pilot studies discussed here are suggestive but still preliminary. Subjects had direct access to the independence data true of the population, and in several of our experiments the choices they confronted were limited. Nevertheless, these studies suggest that there is a lot to be learned from comparing naïve subjects to those trained even for a short time on the normative theory of CBNs. For whatever reason, trained subjects can reliably differentiate between direct and indirect causation, and many can do so with an optimal strategy for picking interventions. Indeed, our first experiment suggests that trained students are not subject to source bias in picking interventions, even though they were never trained in this particular skill. We speculate that simple training in the normative theory sensitizes subjects to the connection between conditional independence and indirect causation, and attending to the mediating variable, which is the conditioning variable, leads subjects to intervene on the mediator instead of the source. Our pilot studies also suggest that only minimal training in the normative theory is needed to exhibit sensitivity to model equivalence, a core idea in the normative theory. Finally, they suggest that students pursue a strategy by which they find which pairs of variables are adjacent and then attempt to find in which direction the causal relations obtain.

Strategies for automatically learning causal structures in the normative theory divide into constraint-based and score-based methods.[15] In constraint-based methods, one decides on individual constraints (e.g., independence or conditional independence facts) to decide on local parts of the model (e.g., whether a given pair of variables is adjacent or not). In score-based searches, one computes a score reflecting the goodness of fit of the entire model. Human subjects, both naïve and trained, arguably execute a simple version of a constraint-based search. Our subjects used particular independence relations to decide on questions of adjacency, and were reliable at this, and then used interventions to decide on orientation for local fragments of the model, and were moderately reliable at this. None judged models as a whole and attempted to maximize some global score. As it turns out, constraint-based approaches are much more efficient but less accurate in the face of noisy data. Our conjecture is that human subjects employ a constraint-based approach because it allows a sequence of decisions, each involving a potentially simple computation, like whether two variables are independent or not.

In systems of more than toy complexity, that is, systems involving more than two or three variables, a score-based strategy would become computationally prohibitive for a human cognitive agent, while a constraint-based approach would still be viable. Because a constraint-based approach also lends itself to an anytime approach, that is, using only the simplest constraints first and then stopping "any time" the constraints under test become too complicated to compute or to trust statistically, it is also well suited to systems with severe computational or memory constraints (e.g., human learners).

Nevertheless, we do not claim that evolution has trained humans to execute anything like the theoretically correct version of a constraint-based search for causal structure. Even minimally trained subjects using a constraint-based approach well suited for toy systems but not theoretically correct might quickly be overcome by the complexity of a five-variable system. In informal observation, this is exactly what happens. Even on systems involving four variables, if subjects are given no background knowledge whatsoever about which variables are prior to which others (e.g., which variable is the "outcome" variable), then they become quickly lost in the more than 50 models in their search space. In future experiments, we will investigate the discontinuities in performance for trained subjects as a function of system complexity. We will train subjects to execute a modified version of a constraint-based approach that would handle much larger systems and see if this will help students to become truly more reliable causal learners.

ACKNOWLEDGMENTS   This research was supported by the James S. McDonnell Foundation, the Institute for Education Science, the William and Flora Hewlett Foundation, the National Aeronautics and Space Administration, and the Office of Naval Research (grant to the Institute for Human and Machine Cognition: Human Systems Technology to Address Critical Navy Need of the Present and Future 2004).

We thank Adrian Tang and Greg Price for invaluable programming help with the Causality Lab, Clark Glymour for forcing us to get to the point, and Dave Sobel and Steve Sloman for several helpful discussions.

References

Berger, M. (2005). *Applied optimal designs*. New York: Wiley.

Blalock, H. (1961). *Causal inferences in nonexperimental research*. Chapel Hill: University of North Carolina Press.

Bowden, R., & Turkington, D. (1984). *Instrumental variables*. New York: Cambridge University Press.

Cheng, P. W. (1997). From covariation to causation: A causal power theory. *Psychological Review, 104*, 367–405.

Cheng, P. W., & Novick, L. R. (1992). Covariation in natural causal induction. *Psychological Review, 99*, 365–382.

Cochran, W., & Cox, G. M. (1957). *Experimental designs* (2nd ed.). New York: Wiley.

Danks, D. (2004). Constraint-based human causal learning. In M. Lovett, C. Schunn, C. Lebiere, & P. Munro (Eds.), *Proceedings of the Sixth International Conference on Cognitive Modeling* (ICCM-2004; pp. 342–343). Mahwah, NJ: Erlbaum.

Danks, D. (2005). Causal learning from observations and manipulations. In M. Lovett & P. Shah (Eds.), *Thinking with data*. Mahwah, NJ: Erlbaum.

Danks, D., Griffiths, T. L., & Tenenbaum, J. B. (2003). Dynamical causal learning. In S. Becker, S. Thrun, & K. Obermayer (Eds.), *Advances in neural information processing systems 15* (pp. 67–74). Cambridge, MA: MIT Press.

Eberhardt, F., Glymour, C., & Scheines, R. (2005). $N - 1$ *experiments suffice to determine the causal relations among* N *variables* (Tech. Rep. No. CMU_PHIL-161), Carnegie Mellon University, Department of Philosophy, Pittsburgh, PA.

Glymour, C. (1998). Learning causes: Psychological explanations of causal explanation. *Minds and Machines, 8,* 39–60.

Glymour, C. (2000). Bayes nets as psychological models. In F. C. Keil & R. A. Wilson (Eds.), *Explanation and cognition.* Cambridge, MA: MIT Press.

Glymour, C., & Cooper, G. (1999). *Computation, causation, and discovery.* Cambridge, MA: AAAI Press/MIT Press.

Gopnik, A., Glymour, C., Sobel, D. M., Schulz, L. E., Kushnir, T., & Danks, D. (2004). A theory of causal learning in children: Causal maps and Bayes nets. *Psychological Review, 111,* 3–32.

Gopnik, A., Sobel, D. M., Schulz, L. E., & Glymour, C. (2001). Causal learning mechanisms in very young children: 2-, 3-, and 4-year-olds infer causal relations from patterns of variation and covariation. *Developmental Psychology, 37,* 620–629.

Griffiths, T. L., Baraff, E. R., & Tenenbaum, J. B. (2004). Using physical theories to infer hidden causal structure. *Proceedings of the 26th Annual Conference of the Cognitive Science Society.*

Lagnado, D., & Sloman, S. A. (2002). Learning causal structure. *Proceedings of the 24th Annual Conference of the Cognitive Science Society,* Maryland.

Lagnado, D., & Sloman, S. A. (2004). The advantage of timely intervention. *Journal of Experimental Psychology: Learning, Memory, and Cognition, 30,* 856–876.

Murphy, K. (2001). *Active learning of causal Bayes net structure* (Tech. Rep.), University of California-Berkeley, Computer Science Division, Berkeley, CA.

Pearl, J. (1988). *Probabilistic reasoning in intelligent systems.* San Mateo, CA: Morgan Kaufmann.

Pearl, J. (2000). *Causality: Models, reasoning, and inference.* Cambridge, England: Cambridge University Press.

Perales, J. C., & Shanks, D. R. (2003). Normative and descriptive accounts of the influence of power and contingency on causal judgement. *The Quarterly Journal of Experimental Psychology, 56A,* 977–1007.

Rescorla, R. A., & Wagner, A. R. (1972). A theory of Pavlovian conditioning: Variations in the effectiveness of reinforcement and nonreinforcement. In A. H. Black & W. F. Prokasy (Eds.), *Classical conditioning II: Current research and theory* (pp. 64–99). New York: Appleton-Century-Crofts.

Simon, H. (1953). Causal ordering and identifiability. In Hood & Koopmans (Eds.), *Studies in econometric methods* (pp. 49–74). New York: Wiley.

Sloman, S. A., & Lagnado, D. (2002). Counterfactual undoing in deterministic causal reasoning. *Proceedings of the 24th Annual Conference of the Cognitive Science Society,* Maryland.

Sobel, D. M., & Kushnir, T. (2004). *Do it, or watch it done: The importance of decision demands in causal learning from interventions.* Manuscript submitted for publication, Brown University.

Spiegelhalter, D., & Lauritzen, S. (1990). Sequential updating of conditional probabilities on directed graphical structures. *Networks, 20,* 579–605.

Spirtes, P., Glymour, C., & Scheines R. (2000). *Causation, prediction and search* (2nd ed.), Cambridge, MA: MIT Press.

Steyvers, M., Tenenbaum, J. B., Wagenmakers, E. J., & Blum, B. (2003). Inferring causal networks from observations and interventions. *Cognitive Science, 27,* 453–489.

Tenenbaum, J. B., & Griffiths, T. L. (2001). Structure learning in human causal induction. In T. Leen, T. Deitterich, & V. Tresp (Eds.), *Advances in neural information processing 13* (pp. 59–65). Cambridge, MA: MIT Press.

Tenenbaum, J. B., & Griffiths, T. L. (2003). Theory-based causal inference. In S. Becker, S. Thrun, & K. Obermayer (Eds.), *Advances in neural information processing systems 15* (pp. 35–42). Cambridge, MA: MIT Press.

Tenenbaum, J. B., & Niyogi, S. (2003). Learning causal laws. In *Proceedings of the 25th Annual Conference of the Cognitive Science Society.*

Tong, S., & Koller, D. (2001). Active learning for structure in Bayesian networks. *Proceedings of the International Joint Conference on Artificial Intelligence.*

Waldmann, M. R., & Hagmayer, Y. (in press). Seeing versus doing: Two modes of accessing causal knowledge. *Journal of Experimental Psychology: Learning, Memory, and Cognition.*

Waldmann, M. R., & Martignon, L. (1998). A Bayesian network model of causal learning. In M. A. Gernsbacher & S. J. Derry (Eds.), *Proceedings of the 20th Annual Conference of the Cognitive Science Society.* Mahwah, NJ: Erlbaum.

Wright, S. (1934). The method of path coefficients. *Annals of Mathematics Statistics, 5,* 161–215.

9

Interactions Between Causal and Statistical Learning

David M. Sobel & Natasha Z. Kirkham

Causal knowledge enables children to interpret the current state of the world rationally and to engage in predictive inference and explanation. Traditionally, young children's causal knowledge has been considered "perceptually driven" or "precausal" (e.g., Piaget, 1929). Contemporary research, however, has shown that young children's causal reasoning abilities are actually quite sophisticated. Infants recognize causal properties of objects, including containment, support, and contact (e.g., Hespos & Baillargeon, 2001; Leslie & Keeble, 1987; Needham & Baillargeon, 1993; Spelke, Breinlinger, Macomber, & Jacobson, 1992). Before their second birthday, toddlers recognize various nonobvious causal relations, especially about others' desires and intentions (e.g., Meltzoff, Gopnik, & Repacholi, 1999). By age 5, children understand that biological and psychological events rely on nonobvious, hidden causal relations (e.g., Gelman & Wellman, 1991; Gopnik & Wellman, 1994). More generally, preschoolers recognize the importance of Hume's principles—temporal priority, spatial priority, and contingency—in making judgments about causal relations (Bullock, Gelman, & Baillargeon, 1982; Shultz, 1982). Preschoolers also appear to have sophisticated explanative and counterfactual reasoning abilities (Harris, German, & Mills, 1996; Schult & Wellman, 1997; Sobel, 2004; Wellman & Liu, chapter 16, this volume).

As developmentalists, we wish to describe how children learn causal knowledge and develop their reasoning abilities. How children represent and acquire causal knowledge, however, is an interdisciplinary question, and this volume illustrates how philosophy, computer science, and cognitive psychology can offer different insights into the process. We would like to suggest that other branches of developmental research—specifically research on infants' statistical learning—offer insight into causal learning. Conversely, understanding how children learn and reason about causal relations might provide insight into other areas of development.

In this chapter, we examine the relation between young children's causal learning and inference abilities and their capacity to perceive the statistical associations between salient events. Of course, there are significant differences between recognizing statistical relations and causal knowledge. Knowing what causal relations exist allows learners to generate explanations and reason about counterfactuals, neither of which is supported by pure statistical association. Statistical associations do allow for simple predictions about future events and the chunking of correlated stimuli (for more efficient processing). But, causal knowledge goes much further than that, allowing for a "calculus of intervention" (Pearl, 2000): inferences about the outcome of intentional manipulative actions that change the state of events in the world. Recognizing that two events are associated provides no information about the result of interventions on either event. But, although correlations do not equate to causal relations, they are often a good place to start. Understanding whether and how children acquire statistical information about events in the world should provide a starting point for researchers interested in causal learning. Likewise, children's causal reasoning abilities might provide insight into phenomena discussed in the statistical learning literature.

How Statistical Regularity Can Translate to Causal Knowledge

A system for causal learning has a particular problem: Although some causal relations seem directly perceivable—such as watching a ball launch another ball (Michotte, 1963)—in general, causal knowledge is not directly perceptible. One goal of research in children's causal learning has been to describe how causal knowledge can be recovered from the environment. How children recognize correlations between objects and events seems a good place to start. For example, knowing that a particular causal relation exists suggests that certain data will occur; if event X causes event Y, then the occurrence of X will make the occurrence of Y more likely (all other things being equal). Observing such correlations might offer insight into causal structure. Seeing that Y is more likely in the presence of X than in its absence often leads us to conclude that X is a cause of Y. Indeed, some adult experiments on causal learning suggest that such probabilistic reasoning might be considered a normative model of causal inference (Allan, 1980; Cheng, 1997; Shanks, 1995).

Of course, such correlations do not always equate to genuine causal conclusions. Consider three events related by a simple causal chain $X \rightarrow Y \rightarrow Z$. In this situation, X and Y are correlated, X and Z are correlated, and Y and Z are correlated. Temporal priority (or other forms of prior knowledge) might inform you of the directions of the potential causal relations specified by these correlations, but the correlations themselves potentially overgeneralize the causal structure. Whether X causes Z directly or only indirectly through Y is ambiguous given only this information. What is necessary is a system that recognizes not only the dependencies among these events, but also their conditional independencies as well. Observing that X and Z only co-occur in the presence of Y (and thus are independent in the absence of Y) suggests the causal chain model. If this conditional independence relationship was absent, then a more general model in which X directly causes both Y and Z (and in which Y causes Z) is more likely.

What this suggests is that children must recognize the dependencies among events as well as conditional probability information to learn the causal structure of the world. Researchers in causal learning have examined whether children recognize conditional dependence and independence information when making causal inferences (Gopnik, Sobel, Schulz, & Glymour, 2001; Sobel, Tenenbaum, & Gopnik, 2004). Much of this research introduced children to a *blicket detector*, a machine that lights up and plays music when certain objects are placed on it. The blicket detector presents a novel, nonobvious property of each object: its potential to activate the detector. (The machine is actually controlled through an "enabling" switch. When the switch is on, any object will activate the detector. When it is off, no object will activate the detector.)

Gopnik et al. (2001) trained 3- and 4-year-olds that objects that activated the detector were called *blickets*. Children quickly learned this association. Then, children observed a set of trials in which objects either independently activated the machine or did so only dependent on the presence of another object. Specifically, in the *one-cause* trials, children were shown two objects. Children observed one object A activate the detector by itself. Then, they saw that the other object B did not activate the detector by itself. Finally, they saw objects A and B activate the detector twice together (see Figure 9-1 for a schematic of this procedure). Children were asked whether each object

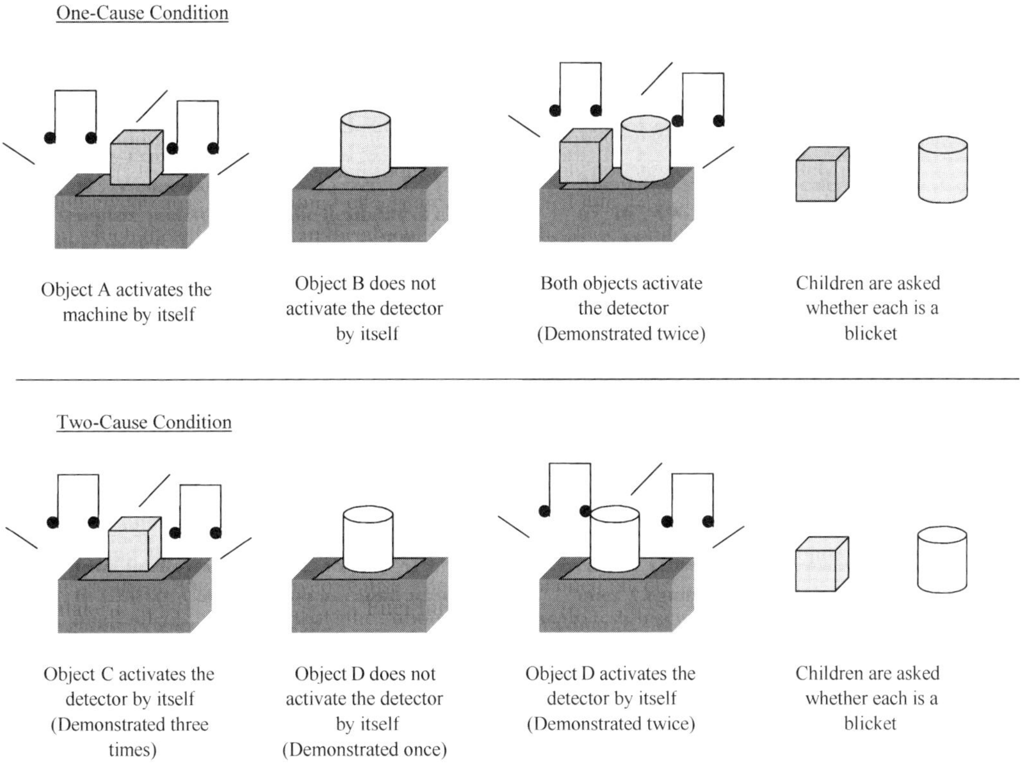

One-Cause Condition

| Object A activates the machine by itself | Object B does not activate the detector by itself | Both objects activate the detector (Demonstrated twice) | Children are asked whether each is a blicket |

Two-Cause Condition

| Object C activates the detector by itself (Demonstrated three times) | Object D does not activate the detector by itself (Demonstrated once) | Object D activates the detector by itself (Demonstrated twice) | Children are asked whether each is a blicket |

FIGURE 9-1 Schematic representation of the procedures used by Gopnik et al. (2001, Experiment 1).

was a blicket. In this condition, 3- and 4-year-olds labeled only object A as a blicket. Object B only activated the detector in the presence of the object A.

Performance on these trials was compared with performance on the *two-cause* trials, in which children were shown two objects that activated the detector with the same frequency as in the one-cause trials. Specifically, children saw two new objects (C and D). Object C was placed on the machine three times and activated it all three times. Object D was placed on the machine three times and activated it two of three times (see Figure 9-1). On these trials, 3- and 4-year-olds categorized both objects as blickets. Both objects independently activated the detector; they just did so with different frequencies.

These data suggest that children can recognize the difference between dependencies and conditional independencies between two events when faced with information about their statistical regularity (what Reichenbach in 1956 called *screening-off* reasoning). This type of reasoning represents a move from recognizing just the co-occurrence among events to recognizing the information necessary to make causal inferences.

This procedure generalizes beyond reasoning about physical events: Schulz and Gopnik (2004) demonstrated that 3- and 4-year-olds make similar screening-off inferences across a variety of domains (see also Schulz et al., chapter 5, this volume). Younger children also appear to make similar inferences. Using slight manipulations to the procedure, Gopnik et al. (2001) demonstrated that 30-month-olds made these inferences. Sobel and Kirkham (in press) demonstrated that children as young as 19 months also reasoned in this manner about objects placed on a blicket detector.

The Associative Challenge

The trouble with the procedure described is that a mechanism for causal reasoning does not exclusively explain children's ability to make screening-off inferences. Screening off is a form of *blocking*, a phenomenon from the animal conditioning literature. In a classic blocking experiment (Kamin, 1969), an animal is shown an association between a conditioned and an unconditioned stimulus (e.g., that a tone predicts the occurrence of food). This association is trained until asymptote, and then the animal is shown a novel conditioned stimulus presented in compound with the established stimulus (e.g., that the same tone paired with a light will predict food). Animals do not learn that the light is predictive. One interpretation of these data is that the animals recognize that light only predicts food in the presence of an established predictor (i.e., the tone). Various models of associative learning (e.g., Rescorla & Wagner, 1972) were designed to explain this phenomenon.

However, inferential models that rely on calculating the associative strength among events can have difficulty when the data involve learners making retrospective inferences. One example, taken from the contingency judgment literature, is the phenomenon of *backward blocking* (Shanks, 1985; Shanks & Dickinson, 1987). In these experiments, adult learners were presented with two stimuli in compound (A and B) that elicited some effect. Learners were then shown that one of those two events alone (A) elicits the effect. Given this information, adults rated that the B stimulus did not have the causal efficacy necessary to produce the effect.

Can children engage in backward blocking about causal events? Sobel et al. (2004) introduced preschoolers to the blicket detector and trained them that

blickets activated the machine. They showed children two objects (A and B) that activated the machine together. Then, they showed children that Object A activated the machine by itself. This procedure is shown in Figure 9-2. The critical question was how children would rate Object B. Its causal status is uncertain. If children engage in backward blocking, then they should determine that it is not a blicket. This was the case: Children rarely labeled Object B as a blicket.

Sobel et al. (2004) also demonstrated that children did not follow a simple algorithm that only recognized associations among events (e.g., Rescorla & Wagner, 1972). In a different type of trial—indirect screening-off trials—children were shown two different objects (C and D) that activated the machine together and then that Object C failed to activate the detector. This procedure is also shown in Figure 9-2. In this circumstance, only Object D should be considered a blicket: Object C fails to activate the detector independently, so the only logical conclusion children could draw is that Object D has the causal efficacy necessary to activate the detector. Indeed, 3- and 4-year-olds generated this response. However, responding on the basis of only associations, one would consider Objects B and D's associative strength with the detector's activation to be the same. In both

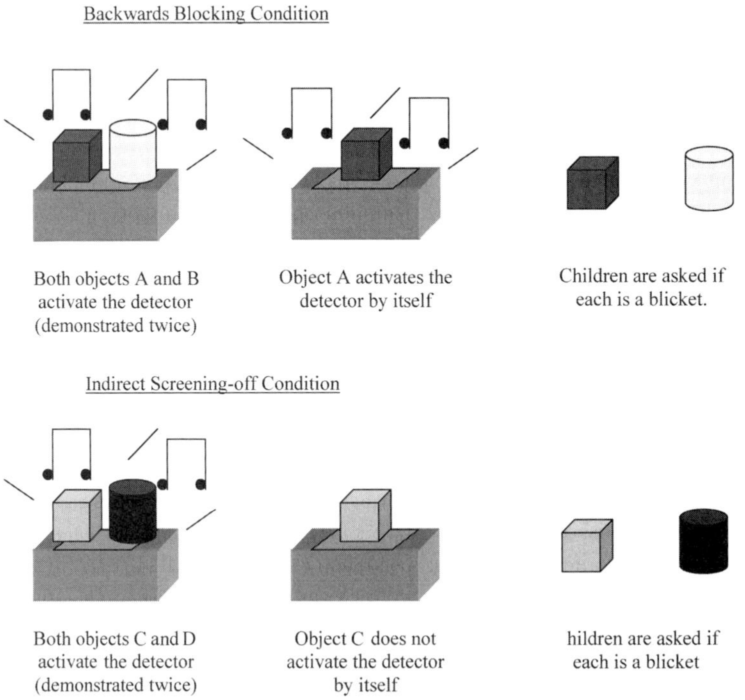

FIGURE 9-2 Schematic representation of the procedures used by Sobel et al. (2004, Experiment 1).

cases, the object activates the detector with another object. The efficacy of that other object alone should have no bearing on its associations with the detector.

Although these data are inconsistent with various associative accounts, there are several different categories of learning algorithms that describe how adults make inferences about contingencies among events, which can explain these findings. Children might recognize causal relations based on a calculation of associative strength among events that relies on more complicated associative mechanisms (Dickinson, 2001; Kruschke & Blair, 2000; Wasserman & Berglan, 1998). These models were designed with the backward blocking phenomenon in mind. Alternatively, children might make causal inferences through estimates of causal strength based on the frequency with which events co-occur. Such models, like the ΔP model (Allan, 1980; Jenkins & Ward, 1965; Shanks, 1995) and the PowerPC model (Cheng, 1997, 2000), calculate an estimate of the strength of a presumed causal relationship given a set of data. The backward blocking data are also consistent with these possibilities.

Sobel et al. (2004) and others (Tenenbaum, Griffiths, & Niyogi, this volume) pointed out that many of these learning mechanisms rely on multiple exposures to data (i.e., large sample sizes). Models that calculate causal structure through associative strength or through parameter estimation, like the ΔP and PowerPC models, must have large sample sizes to function properly. In this view, the backward blocking data are inconsistent with all of these accounts because children make inferences based on relatively small sample sizes. However, Sobel et al. (2004) also wanted to demonstrate that children's causal inferences were well described by a different type of learning algorithm: one that relies on Bayesian inference. In Bayesian inference, learners assign a probability value to a set of potential causal hypotheses and then update the values of those probabilities given the observed data based on the application of Bayes' rule. The resulting posterior probabilities are a rational estimate of the likelihood of each hypothesis being the correct causal model (see Tenenbaum, Griffiths, & Niyogi, this volume, for a more detailed description of this model).

This account relies on the assumption that children assign the initial probabilities of each hypothesis nonrandomly: Those priors are set by the base rate of blickets. If children recognize that there are many blickets out there in the world, then hypotheses that specify that many objects are blickets should have a higher initial probability than hypotheses that specify

few objects are blickets. In this case, the hypothesis in which both Object A and Object B are blickets should have a higher initial probability than the hypothesis that only Object A is a blicket. Both are consistent with the observed data, and thus both will be updated equally by the application of Bayes' rule. Thus, the hypothesis that both objects are blickets will have a higher posterior probability. Thus, Bayesian reasoning predicts that if children know there are many blickets in the world, then they should not demonstrate backward blocking.

To test this hypothesis, Sobel et al. (2004, Experiment 3) showed children a set of identical objects that were placed on the blicket machine. They trained children that blickets were either rare or common: 12 objects were scanned 1 at a time, and either 2 or 10 activated the machine in the rare and common conditions, respectively. Then, they presented children the same backward blocking procedure with two new objects (from the same set). When 4-year-olds were trained that blickets were rare, they demonstrated backward blocking: The uncertain object was not categorized as a blicket. When 4-year-olds were trained that blickets were common, they did not demonstrate backward blocking: The uncertain object was categorized as a blicket. There was not enough counterevidence to exclude the hypothesis that both objects were blickets.

These data were qualitatively consistent with the Bayesian account. The same ambiguous backward blocking data were presented across the conditions, and children relied on the base rates of blickets to make an inference about an object with causal powers that were uncertain. Further research demonstrated that adults also reason about such data in a similar manner (Tenenbaum, Sobel, Griffiths, & Gopnik, submitted). Tenenbaum et al. also introduced a new learning problem in which both children and adults observed only ambiguous data. Adult learners were introduced to a machine like a blicket detector (a detector that responded to a special kind of lead in pencils, dubbed *superlead*, and hence, *superpencils*) and were trained that the occurrence of pencils containing this lead was rare (using the same manipulation as that of Sobel et al. in 2004–by showing them that 2 of 12 pencils chosen at random from a set activated the detector). Then, they were shown 3 pencils taken from the set at random (A, B, and C). Objects A and B activated the machine together, and then Objects A and C activated the machine together. Participants were asked to rate the likelihood that each object was a super pencil after each event.

The Bayesian account predicts four levels of performance given these data. First, ratings of Object A at the end of the trial should be highest, but not at ceiling. This reflects the fact that learners did not unambiguously observe Object A activate the machine, but the majority of hypotheses consistent with the data suggest that Object A is a super pencil. The ratings of A and B after they are placed on the machine together should be slightly lower. This reflects the fact that the data at this point in the trial suggest that at least one of those objects must be a superpencil. The ratings of B and C at the end of the trial should be lower, but still higher than the initial ratings of each object. There are some hypotheses consistent with B and C being superpencils (namely, the hypothesis that B and C are superpencils, and A is not). Tenenbaum et al. (submitted) observed exactly this four-level pattern of responses. This pattern of performance also extends to children. In a subsequent experiment, they found that 4-year-olds made similar responses, consistent with these qualitative predictions of the Bayesian model.

In general, these experiments integrate children's (and adults') use of statistical information from the environment with their causal inferences. In the rare-common backward blocking manipulation, children's retrospective inferences were guided by the base rate of blickets. Because the blicket detector introduced a novel causal relation, children had to rely on that initial exposure to establish the training. Indeed, the original backward blocking experiments can be reanalyzed in terms of the base rate of blickets. In Sobel et al.'s first experiment, the base rate of blickets was exactly 50%. In this case, 4-year-olds rated the B object (the blocked object) as a blicket 13% of the time in the backward blocking condition. In their second experiment, the base rate of blickets was slightly higher (it varied between 60% and 80%, with a mean of 68%). In this case, 4-year-olds categorized this object as a blicket 35% of the time, slightly higher than the previous experiment. Even without explicit training, 4-year-olds seemed to pick up on the base rate of objects that activated the detector and used that information to guide their inferences.

Can Younger Children Make Retrospective Inferences?

Sobel and Kirkham (in press) examined whether toddlers were capable of retrospectively making

screening-off inferences. They introduced 19- and 24-month-olds to the blicket detector and established that both age groups would place causally efficacious objects on the machine. Then, children were shown two objects (A and B) that activated the machine together, and then that object A did not activate the machine by itself. When these objects and the machine were presented to the child with the instruction to "make it go," 24-month-olds placed Object B on the detector by itself significantly more often than all other responses put together. The 19-month-olds, in contrast, responded no differently from chance.

Sobel and Kirkham (in press) also presented these children with a backward blocking inference. Because the children were too young for verbal measures, they could not replicate the Sobel et al. (2004) procedure. Instead, they showed children three objects (A, B, and C). Objects A and B activated the machine together, and then Object A activated the machine by itself. Object A was removed from the display, and Objects B and C and the machine were presented to the child. If children made a backward blocking inference, then they might be more inclined to choose Object C (the novel object) in this condition because they would infer that Object B is ineffective. Both 19- and 24-month-olds chose between Objects B and C at chance.

The importance of this procedure, however, is not in these results, but in the comparison with the indirect screening-off procedure because the associative strength of Object B is the same across the two tasks (at least on many associative models like the Rescorla-Wagner model). The 24-month-olds' use of Object B to activate the detector differed between these two conditions; 19-month-olds chose Object B with the same frequency across the two trials. Importantly, Sobel and Kirkham (in press) did find that these 19-month-olds recognized screening-off inferences that involved no retrospection. The critical question is whether these causal reasoning abilities are developing during the toddler years.

Statistical Learning

A difficulty with testing toddlers' causal inferences is that there are some cases in which 18-month-olds fail to engage in simple, imitative "means-ends" behaviors (e.g., Uzgiris & Hunt, 1975; see also Gopnik & Meltzoff, 1992). Although the children who participated in Sobel and Kirkham's (in press) experiment were slightly older, to count as making a retrospective inference in the indirect screening-off trials, they had to inhibit an event they observed activate the machine (placing both objects on it) in favor of a novel intervention (placing only Object B on it). The demand characteristics of this experiment might have overwhelmed the toddlers from producing these inferences.

There is reason to believe that 18-month-olds, and even younger children, have the ability to detect conditional probabilities among events. Saffran, Aslin, and colleagues found that 8-month-old infants could parse a stream of auditory stimuli based solely on the transitional probabilities within and between syllables (i.e., the likelihood that one syllable would predict the next syllable; Aslin, Saffran, & Newport, 1998; Saffran, Aslin, & Newport, 1996).

For example, Saffran et al. (1996) presented infants with a 2-minute constant speech stream of 12 unique syllables, which could be parsed into four 3-syllable "words." These words were presented through speakers located on either side of the seated infant and were defined only by the transitional probabilities between syllables (i.e., there were no pauses or other cues to word beginnings or endings). Syllables that occurred within words always predicted each other; their transitional probabilities were always equal to 1. In other words, the first syllable in a word always predicted the second syllable, and the second syllable always predicted the third. Syllables that occurred across word boundaries were less predictable. In this particular case, because there were only four words in the speech stream, the transitional probability was equal to .33. The last syllable in a word predicted the first syllable of the three other words with equal likelihood. Infants were conditioned to turn their heads toward the speaker producing the novel strings (using a preferential head-turn paradigm). When they turned away from the speaker, the speech stream would stop. In this way, infants controlled their individual exposure to the auditory stimuli.

After familiarization, infants listened to three syllables that made up words [i.e., three syllables A, B, and C, in which $p(B|A)=1$ and the $p(C|B)=1$], alternating with three syllables that did not make up a word (i.e., three syllables that did not obey these transitional probabilities). The infants showed significantly greater interest in the nonwords than in the words, as measured by the amount of time spent looking at the speakers. Because infants will consistently look longer at novel stimuli, postfamiliarization (Bornstein, 1985),

these results suggest that the infants discriminated between the words and the other stimuli based on learning the transitional probabilities defining word boundaries (see also Aslin et al., 1998, for evidence that the results stem from true computation of input statistics rather than simple frequency counting).

Infants' statistical learning abilities extend beyond learning word boundaries. Infants are capable of recognizing and discriminating between complex grammars relating words together. Using the preferential head-turn paradigm, Gomez and Gerken (1999) exposed 12-month-olds to a subset of novel strings produced by one of two artificial grammars. These grammars differed only in terms of the ordering of word pairs: Individual words in the two sets and the starting and ending words were always the same. The only cues to recognition were contained in the transitional probabilities inherent in the word order. After familiarization to the grammar, infants were exposed to novel words embedded in either the original grammar or a novel grammar. Infants showed significantly increased looking time to the speaker producing novel words in the original grammar, suggesting that they could discriminate between the two grammars even when the words were unfamiliar.

The ability to extract regularities in sequential input does not seem to be a language-specific mechanism, but exists broadly across audition. Infants parse auditory streams based on statistical probabilities even when the stimuli are tones (Saffran, Johnson, Aslin, & Newport, 1999). Further, at least one species of nonhuman primates, cottontop tamarins (which never develop humanlike language skills), can learn statistically structured sounds (Hauser, Newport, & Aslin, 2001). This suggests that the ability to perceive statistical structure is perhaps not language specific.

There is evidence from other paradigms that infants show some sensitivity to visual spatial relations among repetitive events. Young infants learn simple two-location, predictable spatial sequences in a visual expectation paradigm (Haith, 1993). Infants also show sensitivity to spatial contingency in temporal sequences. Wentworth, Haith, and Hood (2002) presented 3-month-old infants with a spatiotemporal sequence in which a stimulus appeared on the left, in the center, or on the right of a computer monitor. Infants viewed either a fixed or a random pattern of locations, and in some cases there was a contingent relation between the identity of the central stimulus and the location of the next peripheral picture. The fixed sequence of three locations resulted in more eye movement anticipations, and there were more anticipatory saccades to the correct location when there was a contingent relation between central and peripheral events.

Infants can also recognize statistical structure in displays of greater complexity than simple two- and three-location events. Kirkham, Slemmer, and Johnson (2002) demonstrated that infants as young as 2 months old could learn temporal sequences of shapes that were defined by transitional probabilities. Kirkham, Slemmer, and Johnson (2004) found that 8-month-olds were capable of extracting these probabilities even when the visual sequence was both temporal and spatial. In addition, Fiser and Aslin (2003) demonstrated that 9-month-olds are capable of picking up on the correlations between individual visual elements in a series of static multielement scenes. After being exposed to a number of these scenes, the infants were shown isolated element pairs that had co-occurred either frequently within the scenes or rarely; infants were capable of discriminating between the two.

Statistical Learning Across Modalities

These data suggest that infants—perhaps as young as 2 months—recognize conditional probabilities among events and respond to sequences based on those transitions. These learning and inferential abilities go beyond observing sequences of events; knowledge about the environment requires correctly correlating events across sensory modalities.

Indeed, infants develop a variety of intersensory capacities that allow them to integrate information across modalities. Newborns bind auditory stimuli to visual stimuli and then expect that the sounds and their associated objects will move together (Morrongiello, Fenwick, & Chance, 1998; Richardson & Kirkham, 2004). By 4 months of age, infants perceive the bimodal nature of objects (Spelke, 1979, 1981), and they can perceive speech bimodally (Kuhl & Meltzoff, 1982). Four-month-olds also match faces with voices based on age, gender, and (at 5 months) affective expression of the speaker (Bahrick, Netto, & Hernandez-Reif, 1998; Walker, 1982). By 5 months, infants also recognize the importance of this sensory integration. Bahrick and Lickliter (2000) demonstrated that infants habituated to a bimodal presentation of an event sequence (e.g., a hammer tapping out a particular rhythm) would dishabituate to the unimodal presentation of that information (e.g., just the visual of the hammer tapping, without the sound).

These capacities indicate that infants not only prefer multimodal cues that present them with statistical redundancies but also recognize their importance in perceiving the world. Infants' sensitivity to cross-modal information stands in contrast to the sparse, unimodal presentations of many laboratory experiments described here (e.g., Fiser & Aslin, 2003; Kirkham et al., 2002; Saffran et al., 1996). If experimental studies do not fully exploit the cross-modal sensitivity of infants, then perhaps they risk underestimating the full capacity of their learning abilities. Bahrick, Lickliter, and colleagues have presented evidence that *intersensory redundancy*, the overlap of information provided by amodal stimuli, drives selective attention (e.g., Bahrick & Lickliter, 2000; Bahrick, Lickliter, & Flom, 2004). Can infants usefully integrate statistical information across different modalities?

One way in which this question can be answered is in considering infants' understanding of objects as enduring across space and time behind an occluder. In experimental settings, typically the demonstration is unimodal (e.g., a silent visual display of a ball traveling across the visual field and passing behind and then remerging from an occluder). Kirkham and Johnson (2006) demonstrated that 4-month-old infants, who are right at the beginning of a transition toward success at perceptual completion in an object constancy paradigm (e.g., correctly perceiving the constant trajectory the ball), benefit greatly from the presence of cross-modal information. They incorporated a continuous moving sound into the ball-and-occluder paradigm such that the sound traveled with the object from one side of the occluder to the other side. When given these multiple, redundant, cross-modal cues, 4-month-old infants could anticipate trajectories as well as 6-month-olds in a unimodal condition.

Multiple redundant cues are useful when one has to learn from probabilistic information. For example, if you test positive for a disease on a blood test that is 90% effective on two separate occasions, then you can be more than 90% sure that you are indeed suffering from the disease. Research modeling language learning has shown that multiple probabilistic cues (e.g., lexical stress, phonemes, and pauses) can be integrated to produce faster learning of word boundaries and syntax, even though each cue individually might be unreliable (Christiansen, Allen, & Seidenberg, 1998; Christiansen & Dale, 2001). Further, models have shown a particularly robust effect of cross-modal information in the service of learning (de Sa & Ballard, 1998).

Kirkham, Slemmer, and Johnson (2006) demonstrated one method in which redundant cue integration benefited infants' statistical learning. When 8-month-olds were presented with a visuospatial pattern (e.g., a red circle that appeared in one of six locations and in a statistically probable pattern), they were unable to learn the statistical relationships within the sequence successfully. However, when redundant color and shape cues were added into the sequence (e.g., each shape in the pattern had a unique color and shape), performance improved significantly. Redundant information supported infants' statistical learning abilities.

How Statistical Learning Informs Our Understanding of Causal Learning

These studies provide compelling evidence that infants are sensitive to statistical regularities across various modalities but leave open the intriguing question of how such abilities could support the complex inferences that exist in causal reasoning. When preschoolers use conditional probability to make judgments about whether objects are blickets, are they relying on the same mechanisms as infants learning word boundaries or structural information about the visual world?

Several different research groups have suggested that children's and adults' causal knowledge and reasoning abilities can be described by a particular computational framework: causal graphical models (Glymour, 2001; Gopnik et al., 2004; Lagnado & Sloman, 2004; Waldmann & Hagmayer, 2001). The data on children's causal inferences are all consistent with this representation of causal knowledge. To make these models causal, they must meet a set of assumptions (see Gopnik et al., 2004), but at heart, causal graphical models represent joint probability distributions—the frequency with which all possible combinations of events occur. This would imply that recognizing statistical regularities among events is critical for causal learning and reasoning, and infants' statistical learning abilities build up to an understanding of causal relations among events.

One implication of this hypothesis is that infants should be able to engage in the kind of retrospective inferences about statistical regularity among events. Our previous investigations suggested that 19-month-olds could not make these kinds of inferences when presented with the blicket detector procedure. However, these difficulties could have resulted from the motor demands of the experiment. Using statistical learning procedures that involve measuring infants' eye gaze eliminated these demands. We have begun investigating this hypothesis by presenting 8-month-old infants with a statistical learning procedure that examines these abilities (Sobel & Kirkham, in press, Experiment 2). Our procedure is shown in Figure 9-3a to 9-3c. In both conditions, 8-month-olds observed a sequence of four events. During the familiarization stage (Figure 9-3a), two of these events (A and B) always occurred together and predicted the occurrence of another event (C) with 100% frequency. The C event equally predicted a fourth event (D) or the AB compound. Likewise, the D event was equally predictive of C or AB. A sound effect (the same one) accompanied the C and D events.

After this familiarization, which lasted until infants observed the AB→C sequence four times, infants observed that one member of that compound (B) predicted either the C or the D event (Figure 9-3b). After observing these data, infants were presented with the other member of the compound (A), followed by a blank screen (Figure 9-3c), and the sound effect that accompanied the C and D events was played. Infants' eye gaze was measured for an 8-second period. When the B event did predict the C event on its own, infants were faced with a similar backward blocking inference concerning the A event; when B did not predict C, the data were similar to the indirect screening-off procedure used with the blicket detector.

We observed a significant interaction between looking time to the C and D locations and experimental condition. When infants were presented with the backward blocking data, they looked more often to the D location than the C location. The data suggest that the infants did not believe that the A event predicted the C event, even though they observed no evidence to the contrary. When infants were presented with the indirect screening-off inference, the pattern of looking times was reversed: Infants looked longer to the C location than the D location. Critically, following the A event, infants' looking times to the C location were different between the two conditions, suggesting that they were not responding on the basis of a simple associative mechanism.

The present data are inconsistent with certain models that might underlie recognizing statistical regularities. In particular, the hypothesis that children's reasoning is based solely on recognizing associations does not seem to provide the proper framework to explain these data. Similarly, models that rely

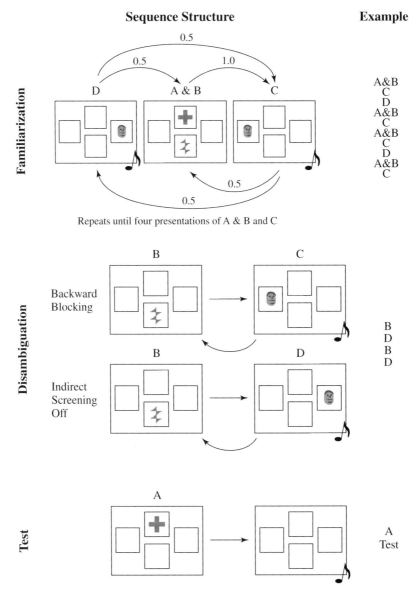

FIGURE 9-3 Schematic representation of the procedure used by Sobel and Kirkham (in press, Experiment 2). During the familiarization phase, infants were shown that Events A and B co-occurred and were always followed by Event C, but that no other event predicted any other. After four occurrences of the AB → C sequence, infants observed that the B event alone was followed by Event C (backward blocking condition) or Event D (indirect screening-off condition). After two of these sequences, infants were shown Event A, and their looking time was measured.

primarily on calculations of associative strength that do not distinguish between forms of retrospective inference, such as the Rescorla-Wagner (1972) equation and others based on it (e.g., Cramer et al., 2002), seem inconsistent with the present data.

These inferential abilities are consistent with the hypothesis that children recognize conditional probability and engage in screening-off inferences at early ages. However, unlike the blicket detector experiments, which showed that preschoolers' causal inferences could not be explained by a variety of alternative models of causal reasoning, the present data are consistent with models of causal learning that rely on causal strength designed with retrospective inferences in mind (e.g., Kruschke & Blair, 2000; Wasserman & Berglan, 1998) as well as various parameter estimation models (e.g., Allan, 1980; Cheng, 1997; Shanks, 1995).

Like the experiments on preschoolers, there is one aspect of these data that is inconsistent with these models: Infants appear capable of making these kinds of inferences based on a small sample of data. Estimates of causal strength and measures of parameter estimation require a relatively large amount of data to make a meaningful estimation. In the present experiment, infants could do so with only four trials with the compound AB event and two trials with one of those events in isolation. However, a stronger argument would be to present infants with inferences that would be inconsistent with the models listed, parallel to the method used in previous research on preschoolers' causal inference (Sobel et al., 2004; Tenenbaum et al., submitted). We are currently attempting to determine whether one of these models best describes infants' abilities to recognize statistical regularities among events.

New Directions for Integrating Causal Learning With Statistical Learning

In addition to attempting to map out how infants recognize co-occurrences among events, we believe there are several other interactions between the causal and statistical learning literature that are worthy of future investigation. This list is not meant to be exclusive or exhaustive. Rather, we wish to articulate particular relations between the statistical learning and causal learning literature and suggest that each can benefit from discussions with the other.

The Problem of Multimodal Integration

The literature on infants' multimodal integration suggests that redundant information supports infants' statistical learning abilities. Are similar effects found in children's causal inferences? Does redundant information benefit children's understanding of causal relations?

This question has been examined indirectly by researchers interested in relation of the role of causal properties to conceptual development. Gopnik and Sobel (2000) examined whether children would extend a novel label to objects that shared the same causal properties. They introduced children to the blicket detector without using that description. They showed children four objects and demonstrated each on the blicket detector. Critically, in "conflict" trials, two identical pairs of objects were used, and one of each activated the detector. The experimenter then labeled one of the objects that activated the detector a blicket and asked the child to show him the other blicket. The 3- and 4-year-olds chose between the perceptually identical and causally identical object with equal frequency.

Nazzi and Gopnik (2000) replicated this experiment, but added a critical piece of redundant information: They pointed out either the causal or the perceptual features of each object. When an object was placed on the detector in the causal condition, the experimenter said, "Look, it activates the detector," and in the perceptual condition, the experimenter said, "Look, this one is red." They found that children in the causal condition made more causal responses on these conflict tasks than children in the perceptual condition or those in a baseline condition.

These data suggest that children's inferences about category membership are influenced by redundant information (the machine's activation and the experimenter's language). However, there is little research investigating what information would be considered redundant and at what ages children are sensitive to this information.

The Problem of Constraining Statistical Learning

A good deal of evidence suggests that infants can recognize correlations among environmental factors and use that information to make inferences. For example, Younger and colleagues (Younger, 1990; Younger & Cohen, 1983, 1986; Younger & Gottlieb, 1988) suggested that, by the age of 10 months, infants recognize correlations among object features. A question that emerges from this discussion is whether infants are capable of detecting *any* correlation or whether constraints must be in place to guide the child.

This question has been investigated across a number of laboratories, and often developmental differences emerge. Younger children appear more capable of detecting any kind of correlation; older children only detect correlations that have some theoretical rationale (see, e.g., Madole & Cohen, 1995; Rakison, 2004). For instance, Madole and Cohen found that both 14- and

18-month-olds detected the co-occurrence between the form and function of an object part. However, 14-month-olds could also detect a correlation between the part of an object and the function of another part of that object. Although there are many objects in the world in which a part's form and function co-occur, the latter co-occurrence has little bearing on reality. Indeed, 18-month-olds did not detect this correlation.

There are a variety of theoretical interpretations of these data, from a top-down, theory-driven approach that suggests features correlate based on a set of explanatory principles (e.g., Murphy & Medin, 1985) to a bottom-up approach to conceptual development motivated by detecting which correlations are critical to category membership (e.g., Smith & Heise, 1992). In a discussion of these data, Madole and Oakes (1999) state that "the child's own experience acting on and observing objects is probably the primary instigator of developmental change" (p. 289). We agree, but how this occurs remains an open question.

The Problem of Setting Priors

Tenenbaum and Griffiths (2003; Tenenbaum et al., this volume; Tenenbaum et al., 2005) presented a Bayesian algorithm that accounts for much of the data on both preschoolers' and adults' causal inferences presented here (Sobel et al., 2004; Tenenbaum et al., sunmitted; see also Griffiths & Tenenbaum, 2005). An important aspect of this account is that children (at least by age 4) might use statistical information to set the probability of particular causal hypotheses. In these experiments, children use the frequency with which particular events occur to set their prior for each hypothesis.

However, other information about the way objects and events causally interact may be detectable from statistical information in the environment. Griffiths (2005) reexamined the original Gopnik et al. (2001) screening-off experiment, in which 3- and 4-year-olds were shown the examples of one-cause and two-cause trials shown in Figure 9-1. Children received two of each trial in a random order. Griffiths suggested that the order in which these trials were presented might have presented different information about the nature of the blicket detector. If children observe a two-cause trial first, in which one object's causal power is probabilistic, then children might interpret the detector as a probabilistic device. When they then observe the one-cause trial, in which Object B does not activate

the detector by itself once, children might interpret Object B as a blicket that simply failed on that trial (because, after all, it was shown to activate the detector with Object A two times subsequently).

Griffiths (2005) found that performance of 4-year-olds demonstrated this particular order effect. Their performance on the first one-cause trial depended on whether it was the first test trial or if they had observed a two-cause trial previously. If children observed a two-cause trial before, then they were more likely not to make a screening-off inference (i.e., to say that Object B was a blicket). Here, 4-year-olds are not recognizing the statistical regularity among events but rather that patterns of data suggest how new data could be interpreted. Younger children did not show this pattern of response. Is this developmental difference robust, or does it reflect something specific about the blicket detector paradigm? Griffiths and Sobel (in preparation) are currently investigating this question systematically. But, an open question remains: How else might the data children observe influence which causal inferences they make?

Concluding Thoughts

What infants know about the statistic of an environment has been a seminal question in language learning for some time (Aslin et al., 1998; Jusczyk & Aslin, 1995; Saffran et al., 1996). Questions about children's knowledge and use of statistical regularities in the environment have also motivated research in conceptual development (e.g., work by Younger and colleagues) as well as what infants know about object concepts (Johnson, Amso, & Slemmer, 2003; Johnson, Bremmer, Slater, et al., 2004; Spelke & Van de Walle, 1993). These questions have also begun to permeate the field of theory of mind, examining what infants know about statistical regularities in detecting intentions (Baldwin, Baird, Saylor, & Clark, 2001; Brand, Baldwin, & Ashburn, 2002) or pretending (Lillard & Witherington, 2004).

What these literature bodies all have in common is that they describe some type of causal knowledge that children develop. There seem to be several places in which children's causal learning and their statistical learning abilities interact and can inform each other. Mapping out those interactions, both generally and in specific domains of knowledge, is critical to a set of exciting new research questions that can be asked.

ACKNOWLEDGMENTS   We would like to thank the parents and children who have made all of the research presented here possible. We would also like to thank Alison Gopnik, Daniel Richardson, Laura Schulz, and Jessica Sommerville for comments on this chapter.

References

Allan, L. G. (1980). A note on measurement of contingency between two binary variables in judgment tasks. *Bulletin of the Psychonomic Society, 15,* 147–149.

Aslin, R. N., Saffran, J. R., & Newport, E. L. (1998). Computation of conditional probability statistics by 8-month-old infants. *Psychological Science, 9,* 321–324.

Bahrick, L. E., & Lickliter, R. (2000). Intersensory redundancy guides attentional selectivity and perceptual learning in infancy. *Developmental Psychology, 36,* 190–201.

Bahrick, L. E., Lickliter, R., & Flom, R. (2004). Intersensory redundancy guides the development of selective attention, perception, and cognition in infancy. *Current Directions in Psychological Science, 13,* 99–102.

Bahrick, L. E., Netto, D., & Hernandez-Reif, M. (1998). Intermodal perception of adult and child faces and voices by infants. *Child Development, 69,* 1263–1275.

Baldwin, D. A., Baird, J. A., Saylor, M. M., & Clark, A. M. (2001). Infants parse dynamic action. *Child Development, 72,* 708–717.

Bornstein, M. H. (1985). Habituation of attention as a measure of visual information processing in human infants: Summary, systematization, and synthesis. In G. Gottlieb & N. A. Krasnegor (Eds.), *Measurement of audition and vision in the first year of postnatal life: A methodological overview* (pp. 253–300). Norwood, NJ: Ablex.

Brand, R. J., Baldwin, D. A., & Ashburn, L. J. (2002). Evidence for "motionese": Modifications in mothers' infant-directed action. *Developmental Science, 5,* 72–83.

Bullock, M., Gelman, R., & Baillargeon, R. (1982). The development of causal reasoning. In W. J. Friedman (Ed.), *The developmental psychology of time* (pp. 209–254). New York: Academic Press.

Cheng, P. W. (1997). From covariation to causation: A causal power theory. *Psychological Review, 104,* 367–405.

Cheng, P. W. (2000). Causality in the mind: Estimating contextual and conjunctive power. In F. Keil & R. A. Wilson (Eds.), *Explanation and cognition* (pp. 227–253). Cambridge, MA: MIT Press.

Christiansen, M. H., Allen, J., & Seidenberg, M. S. (1998). Learning to segment speech using multiple cues: A connectionist model. *Language and Cognitive Processes, 13,* 221–268.

Christiansen, M. H., & Dale, R. A. C. (2001). Integrating distributional, prosodic and phonological information in a connectionist model of language acquisition. In *Proceedings of the 23rd Annual Conference of the Cognitive Science Society.* Mahwah, NJ: Erlbaum.

Cramer, R. E., Weiss, R. F., Williams, R., Reid, S., Nieri, L., & Manning-Ryan, B. (2002). Human agency and associative learning: Pavlovian principles govern social process in causal relationship detection. *Quarterly Journal of Experimental Psychology: Comparative and Physiological Psychology, 55B,* 241–266.

de Sa, V. R., & Ballard, D. H. (1998). Category learning through multimodality sensing. *Neural Computation, 10,* 1097–1117.

Dickinson, A. (2001). Causal learning: Association versus computation. *Current Directions in Psychological Science, 10,* 127–132.

Fiser, J., & Aslin, R. N. (2003). Statistical learning of new visual feature combinations by infants. *Proceedings of the National Academy of Sciences of the United States of America, 99,* 15822–15826.

Gelman, S. A., & Wellman, H. M. (1991). Insides and essence: Early understandings of the non-obvious. *Cognition, 38,* 213–244.

Glymour, C. (2001). *The mind's arrow.* Cambridge, MA: MIT Press.

Gomez, R. L., & Gerken, L. (1999). Artificial grammar learning by 1-year-olds leads to specific and abstract knowledge. *Cognition, 70,* 109–135.

Gopnik, A., Glymour, C., Sobel, D. M., Schulz, L. E., Kushnir, T., & Danks, D. (2004). A theory of causal learning in children: Causal maps and Bayes nets. *Psychological Review, 111,* 1–30.

Gopnik, A., & Meltzoff, A. N. (1992). Categorization and naming: Basic-level sorting in 18-month-olds and its relation to language. *Child Development, 63,* 1091–1103.

Gopnik, A., & Sobel, D. M. (2000). Detecting blickets: How young children use information about causal properties in categorization and induction. *Child Development, 71,* 1205–1222.

Gopnik, A., Sobel, D. M., Schulz, L., & Glymour, C. (2001). Causal learning mechanisms in very young children: 2-, 3-, and 4-year-olds infer causal relations from patterns of variation and co-variation. *Developmental Psychology, 37,* 620–629.

Gopnik, A., & Wellman, H. M. (1994). The theory theory. In L. Hirschfield & S. Gelman (Eds.), *Mapping the mind: Domain specificity in cognition and culture* (pp. 257–293). New York: Cambridge University Press.

Griffiths, T. L., & Sobel, D. M. (in preparation). *Learning about probabilistic and deterministic causal systems.* Brown University.

Griffiths, T. L. (2005). *Causes, coincidences, and theories.* Unpublished doctoral dissertation, Stanford University, Stanford, CA.

Griffiths, T. L., & Tenenbaum, J. B. (2005) Structure and strength in causal induction, *Cognitive Psychology, 51,* 354–384.

Haith, M. M. (1993). Future-oriented processes in infancy: The case of visual expectations. In C. Granrud (Ed.), *Visual perception and cognition in infancy* (pp. 235–264). Hillsdale, NJ: Erlbaum.

Harris, P. L., German, T., & Mills, P. (1996). Children's use of counterfactual thinking in causal reasoning. *Cognition, 61,* 233–259.

Hauser, M. D., Newport, E. L., & Aslin, R. N. (2001). Segmentation of the speech stream in a non-human primate: Statistical learning in cotton-top tamarins. *Cognition, 78,* B53–B64.

Hespos, S. J., & Baillargeon, R. (2001). Infants' knowledge about occlusion and containment events: A surprising discrepancy. *Psychological Science, 12,* 141–147.

Jenkins, H. M., & Ward, W. C. (1965). Judgment of contingency between responses and outcomes. *Psychological Monographs: General and Applied, 79,* 17.

Johnson, S. P., Amso, D., & Slemmer, J. A. (2003). Development of object concepts in infancy: Evidence for early learning in an eye tracking paradigm. *Proceedings of the National Academy of Sciences, 100,* 10568–10573.

Johnson, S. P., Bremner, J. G., Slater, A., Mason, U., Foster, & Cheshire, A. (2003). Infants' perception of object trajectories. *Child Development, 74,* 94–108.

Jusczyk, P. W., & Aslin, R. N. (1995). Infants' detection of sound patterns of words in fluent speech. *Cognitive Psychology, 29,* 1–23.

Kamin, L. J. (1969). Predictability, surprise, attention, and conditioning. In B. A. Campbell, & R. M. Church (Eds.), *Punishment and aversive behavior* (pp. 279–296). New York: Appleton-Century-Crofts.

Kirkham, N. Z., & Johnson, S. P. (2006). *Moving sounds: The role of inter-modal perception in solving the problem of occlusion.* Manuscript submitted for publication.

Kirkham, N. Z., Slemmer, J. A., & Johnson, S. P. (2002). Visual statistical learning in infancy. *Cognition, 83,* B35–B42.

Kirkham, N. Z., Slemmer, J. A., & Johnson, S. P. (2006). *Location, location, location: Development of spatiotemporal sequence learning in infancy.* Manuscript submitted for publication.

Kruschke, J. K., & Blair, N. J. (2000). Blocking and backward blocking involve learned inattention. *Psychonomic Bulletin and Review, 7,* 636–645.

Kuhl, P. K., & Meltzoff, A. N. (1982). The bimodal perception of speech in infancy. *Science, 218,* 1138–1140.

Lagnado, D. A., & Sloman, S. (2004). The advantage of timely intervention. *Journal of Experimental Psychology: Learning, Memory, and Cognition, 30,* 856–876.

Leslie, A. M., & Keeble, S. (1987). Do 6-month-old infants perceive causality? *Cognition, 25,* 265–288.

Lillard, A. S., & Witherington, D. C. (2004). Mothers' behavior modifications during pretense and their possible signal value for toddlers. *Developmental Psychology, 40,* 95–113.

Madole, K. L., & Cohen, L. B. (1995). The role of object parts in infants' attention to form-function correlations. *Developmental Psychology, 31,* 637–648.

Madole, K. L., & Oakes, L. M. (1999). Making sense of infant categorization: Stable processes and changing representations. *Developmental Review, 19,* 263–296.

Meltzoff, A. N., Gopnik, A., & Repacholi, B. M. (1999). Toddlers' understanding of intentions, desires and emotions: Explorations of the dark ages. In P. D. Zelazo, J. W. Astington, & D. R. Olson (Eds.), *Developing theories of intentions* (pp. 17–46). Mahwah, NJ: Erlbaum.

Michotte, A. (1963). *The perception of causality.* Oxford, England: Basic Books.

Morrongiello, B. A., Fenwick, K. D., & Chance, G. (1998). Cross modal learning in newborn infants: Inferences about properties of auditory-visual events. *Infant Behavior and Development, 21,* 543–554.

Murphy, G. L., & Medin, D. L. (1985). The role of theories in conceptual coherence. *Psychological Review, 92,* 289–316.

Nazzi, T., & Gopnik, A. (2000). A shift in children's use of perceptual and causal cues to categorization. *Developmental Science, 3,* 389–396.

Needham, A., & Baillargeon, R. (1993). Intuitions about support in 4.5-month-old infants. *Cognition, 47,* 121–148.

Pearl, J. (2000). *Causality.* New York: Oxford University Press.

Piaget, J. (1929). *The child's conception of the world.* London: Routledge & Kegan Paul.

Rakison, D. H. (2004). Infants' sensitivity to correlations between static and dynamic features in a category context. *Journal of Experimental Child Psychology, 89,* 1–30.

Reichenbach, H. (1956). *The direction of time.* Berkeley, CA: University of California Press.

Rescorla, R. A., & Wagner, A. R. (1972). A theory of Pavlovian conditioning: Variations in the effectiveness of reinforcement and nonreinforcement. In A. H. Black & W. F. Prokasy (Eds.), *Classical conditioning II: Current theory and research* (pp. 64–99). New York: Appleton-Century-Crofts.

Richardson, D. C., & Kirkham, N. Z. (2004). Multimodal events and moving locations: Eye movements of adults and 6-month-olds reveal dynamic spatial indexing. *Journal of Experimental Psychology: General, 133,* 46–62.

Saffran, J. R., Aslin, R. N., & Newport, E. L. (1996). Statistical learning by 8-month-old infants. *Science, 274,* 1926–1928.

Saffran, J. R., Johnson, E. K., Aslin, R. N., & Newport, E. L. (1999). Statistical learning of tone sequences by human infants and adults. *Cognition, 70,* 27–52.

Schult, C. A., & Wellman, H. M. (1997). Explaining human movements and actions: Children's understanding of the limits of psychological explanation. *Cognition, 62,* 291–324.

Schulz, L. E., & Gopnik, A. (2004). Causal learning across domains. *Developmental Psychology, 40,* 162–176.

Shanks, D. R. (1985). Forward and backward blocking in human contingency judgment. *Quarterly Journal of Experimental Psychology, 37b,* 1–21.

Shanks, D. R. (1995). Is human learning rational? *Quarterly Journal of Experimental Psychology: Human Experimental Psychology, 48,* 257–279.

Shanks, D. R., & Dickinson, A. (1987). Associative accounts of causality judgment. In G. H. Bower (Ed.), *The psychology of learning and motivation: Advances in research and theory* (Vol. 21, pp. 229–261). San Diego, CA: Academic Press.

Shultz, T. R. (1982). Rules of causal attribution. *Monographs of the Society for Research in Child Development, 47,* 1–51.

Smith, L. B., & Heise, D. (1992). Perceptual similarity and conceptual structure. In B. Burns (Ed.), *Percepts, Concepts, and Categories: Representation and Processing of Information* (pp. 233–272). Oxford, England: North-Holland.

Sobel, D. M. (2004). Exploring the coherence of young children's explanatory abilities: Evidence from generating counterfactuals. *British Journal of Developmental Psychology, 22,* 37–58.

Sobel, D. M., & Kirkham, N. Z. (in press). Blickets and babies: The development of causal reasoning in toddlers and infants. *Developmental Psychology.*

Sobel, D. M., Tenenbaum, J. B., & Gopnik, A. (2004). Children's causal inferences from indirect evidence: Backwards blocking and Bayesian reasoning in preschoolers. *Cognitive Science, 28,* 303–333.

Spelke, E. S. (1979). Perceiving bimodally specified events in infancy. *Developmental Psychology, 15,* 626–636.

Spelke, E. S. (1981). The infant's acquisition of knowledge of bimodally specified events. *Journal of Experimental Child Psychology, 31,* 279–299.

Spelke, E. S., Breinlinger, K., Macomber, J., & Jacobson, K. (1992). Origins of knowledge. *Psychological Review, 99,* 605–632.

Spelke, E. S., & Van de Walle, G. (1993). Perceiving and reasoning about objects: Insights from infants. In N. Eilan, R. A. McCarthy, & B. Brewer (Eds.), *Spatial representation: Problems in philosophy and psychology* (pp. 132–161). Oxford, England: Blackwell.

Tenenbaum, J. B., & Griffiths, T. L. (2003). Theory-based causal inference. *Proceedings of the 14th Annual Conference on the Advances in Neural Information Processing Systems.* Vancouver, CA.

Tenenbaum, J. B., Sobel, D. M., Griffiths, T. L., & Gopnik, A. (2006). *Bayesian inference in causal learning from ambiguous data: Evidence from adults and children.* Manuscript submitted for publication, Brown University.

Uzgiris, I. C., & Hunt, J. M. V. (1975). *Assessment in infancy: Ordinal scales of psychological development.* Oxford, England: University of Illinois Press.

Waldmann, M. R., & Hagmayer, Y. (2001). Estimating causal strength: The role of structural knowledge and processing effort. *Cognition, 82,* 27–58.

Walker, A. S. (1982). Intermodal perception of expressive behaviors by human infants. *Journal of Experimental Child Psychology, 33,* 514–535.

Wasserman, E. A., & Berglan, L. R. (1998). Backward blocking and recovery from overshadowing in human causal judgment: The role of within-compound associations. *Quarterly Journal of Experimental Psychology: Comparative and Physiological Psychology, 51,* 121–138.

Wentworth, N., Haith, M. M., & Hood, R. (2002). Spatiotemporal regularity and interevent contingencies as information for infants' visual expectations. *Infancy, 3,* 303–321.

Younger, B. A. (1990). Infants' detection of correlations among feature categories. *Child Development, 61,* 614–620.

Younger, B. A., & Cohen, L. B. (1983). Infant perception of correlations among attributes. *Child Development, 54,* 858–869.

Younger, B. A., & Cohen, L. B. (1986). Developmental change in infants' perception of correlations among attributes. *Child Development, 57,* 803–815.

Younger, B. A., & Gottlieb, S. (1988). Development of categorization skills: Changes in the nature or structure of infant form categories? *Developmental Psychology, 24,* 611–619.

10

Beyond Covariation

Cues to Causal Structure

David A. Lagnado, Michael R. Waldmann, York Hagmayer, & Steven A. Sloman

Introduction

Imagine a person with no causal knowledge or concept of cause and effect. That person would be like one of Plato's cave dwellers—destined to watch the shifting shadows of sense experience but knowing nothing about the reality that generates these patterns. Such ignorance would undermine that person's most fundamental cognitive abilities: to predict, control, and explain the world around them. Fortunately, we are not trapped in such a cave; we are able to interact with the world and learn about its generative structure. How is this possible?

The general problem, tackled by philosophers and psychologists alike, is how people infer causality from their rich and multifarious experiences of the world, not only the immediate causality of collisions between objects, but also the less transparent causation of illness by disease, of birth through conception, of kingdoms won through battle. What are the general principles that the mind invokes to identify such causes and effects, and build larger webs of causal links to capture the complexities of physical and social systems?

Structure Versus Strength

When investigating causality, a basic distinction can be made between *structure* and *strength*. The former concerns the qualitative causal relations that hold between variables, for example, whether smoking causes lung cancer or aspirin cures headaches. The latter concerns the quantitative aspects of these relations: To what degree does smoking cause lung cancer or aspirin alleviate headaches? This distinction is captured more formally in the causal Bayes net framework. The structure of a set of variables is represented by the graph of Figure 10-1, with the strength of these links captured in the parameterization of the graph (see introductory chapter).

Conceptually, the question of structure is more basic than that of strength—one needs to know or assume the

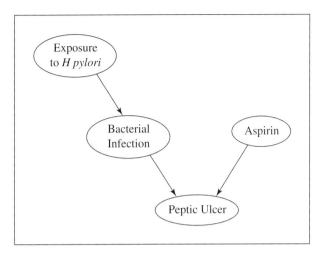

FIGURE 10-1 A simple Bayesian network representing the potential causes of peptic ulcers. H. *pylori, Helicobacter pylori*.

existence of a link before one can estimate its strength. This is reflected in many of the discovery algorithms used in artificial intelligence, for which there is an initial structure learning step prior to estimating the parameters of a graph (see Neapolitan, 2004). A natural conjecture is that this priority of structure over strength is likewise marked in human cognition (Pearl, 1988; Tenenbaum, Griffiths, & Niyogi, 2001, chapter 19, this volume; Waldmann, 1996; Waldmann & Martignon, 1998).

This idea receives intuitive support. We often have knowledge about what causes what but little idea about the strength of these relations. For example, most of us believe that smoking causes cancer, that exercise promotes health, that alcohol inhibits speed of reaction, but we know little about the strengths of these relations. Likewise, in the case of learning, we seek to establish whether causal relations exist before trying to assess how strong they are. For example, in a medical scare in the United Kingdom, research focused on whether the measles-mumps-rubella vaccine causes autism, not on the degree of this relation. Indeed, the lack of evidence in support of the link has preempted studies into how strong this relation might be.

The idea that causal cognition is grounded in qualitative relations has also influenced the development of computational models of causal inference. To motivate his structural account, Pearl (2000) argued that people encode stable aspects of their experiences in terms of qualitative causal relations. This inverts the traditional view that judgments about probabilistic relations are primary, and that causal relations are derived from them. Rather, "if conditional independence judgments are by-products of stored causal relationships then tapping and representing those relationships directly would be a more natural and more reliable way of expressing what we know or believe about the world" (p. 22).

Despite the apparent primacy of structure over strength, most research in causal learning has focused on how people estimate the strength of separate links. In a typical experiment, variables are presorted as potential causes and effects, and participants are asked to estimate the strength of these relations (e.g., Cheng, 1997; Shanks, 2004). This approach has generated a lot of data about how people use contingency information to estimate causal strength and how these judgments are modulated by response format, but the approach does not consider the question of how people learn about causal structure. Thus, it fails to address an important, arguably the most fundamental, part of the learning process.

This neglect has had various repercussions. It has led to an overestimation of the importance of statistical data at the expense of other key cues in causal learning. For example, associative theories focus on learning mechanisms that encode the strength of covariation between cues and outcomes (e.g., Shanks & Dickinson, 1987), but they are insensitive to the important structural distinction between causes and effects. As a consequence, they are incapable of distinguishing between associations that link spurious relations (e.g., barometer and storm) from true causal relations (atmospheric pressure and storm). More generally, these models are incapable of distinguishing between direct and indirect causal relations or covariations that are generated by hidden causal events (Waldmann, 1996; Waldmann & Hagmayer, 2005).

Another shortcoming of this focus on strength is that it restricts attention to a small subset of causal structures (mainly common-effect models). For example, PowerPC theory (Cheng, 1997) focuses on the assessment of causal strength based on covariation information. Although the main focus of the empirical studies lies in how people estimate causal power (see Buehner, Cheng, & Clifford, 2003), the theory clearly states that these power estimates are only valid under the assumption that the causal effect is generated by a common-effect structure with specific characteristics. The question of how people induce these models, which are a prerequisite for the strength calculations, is neglected in this research. Moreover, people routinely deal with other complex structures (e.g., common-cause and chain models). The questions of how people learn such structures and how they combine simple structures into more complex ones are clearly crucial to a proper understanding of causal cognition.

Furthermore, the focus on strength fails to give due weight to the importance of intervention (rather than passive observation) and to the temporal order of experienced events (over and above their temporal contiguity). Both of these factors are primarily cues to structure rather than strength, and there is growing evidence that people readily use them (Gopnik et al., 2004, chapter 9, this volume; Lagnado & Sloman, 2004, 2006; Kirkham, chapter 9, this volume; Steyvers, Tenenbaum, Wagenmakers, & Blum, 2003; Tenenbaum, Griffiths, & Niyogi, chapter 19, this volume; Waldmann, 1996).

Even the traditional studies on strength estimation are open to reevaluation in the light of the structure/strength distinction. Tenenbaum and Griffiths (2001) contend that participants in these studies are actually assessing the degree to which the evidence supports the existence of a causal link rather than the strength of that link. More generally, they propose that people adopt a two-step procedure to learn about elemental causal relations, first inferring structure and then estimating strength. Although decisive experiments have yet to be run, Griffiths and Tenenbaum (2005) support this claim through the reinterpretation of previous data sets and some novel experimental results.

The main moral to be drawn from these considerations is not that strength estimation has no place in causal learning, but that the role of structural inference

has been neglected. By recognizing the central role it plays in both representation and learning, we can attain a clearer perspective on the nature of causal cognition.

Causal Model Theory

Causal model theory was a relatively early, qualitative attempt to capture the distinction between structure and strength (see Hagmayer & Waldmann, 2002; Waldmann, 1996, 2000, 2001; Waldmann & Hagmayer, 2001; Waldmann & Holyoak, 1992; Waldmann, Holyoak, & Fratianne, 1995; Waldmann & Martignon, 1998; see also Rehder, 2003a, 2003b; Tenenbaum, Griffiths, & Niyogi, chapter 19, this volume). According to this proposal, causal induction is guided by top-down assumptions about the structure of causal models. These hypothetical causal models guide the processing of the learning input.

The basic idea behind this approach is that we rarely encounter a causal learning situation in which we do not have some intuitions about basic causal features, such as whether an event is a potential cause or effect. If, for example, the task is to press a button and observe a light (e.g., Wasserman, Chatlosh, & Neunaber, 1983), we may not know whether these events are causally related, but we assume that the button is a potential cause, and the light is a potential effect. Once a hypothetical causal model is in place, we can start estimating causal strength by observing covariation information. The way covariation estimates are computed and interpreted is dependent on the assumed causal model (Hagmayer & Waldmann, 2002; Waldmann & Hagmayer, 2001).

The distinction between causal structure and causal strength raises the question of how assumptions about causal models are generated. Our working hypothesis is that people use a number of nonstatistical cues to generate hypothetical causal models. We do not rule out the possibility that people occasionally induce causal structure on the basis of covariation information alone, but this seems rare in the world in which we live. Whenever people do not have clear assumptions about causal structure, causal reasoning easily falls prey to cognitive biases, such as confusing spurious with causal relations. In contrast, whenever people have hypothetical knowledge about causal structure, they show a remarkable competence to tune this knowledge to the statistical relations in the learning input and use this knowledge for predictions, diagnoses, and for planning actions.

Cues to Causal Structure

People are active agents immersed in a dynamic physical world. Not only do they experience events in a diversity of ways, but also they experience a variety of relations between these events. Perhaps most significant, they can also interact with the world, thereby creating new relations and disrupting old ones. The richness of these experiences of the world affords people a variety of cues to its causal structure. Here is a partial list:

- Statistical relations
- Temporal order
- Intervention
- Prior knowledge

Following Einhorn and Hogarth (1986), we note that these cues are fallible, sometimes redundant (separate cues support the same conclusion), and at other times inconsistent (separate cues suggest opposing conclusions). These cues can be combined to construct and update causal models. For example, typical cases of intervention combine multiple cues—proximity in space and time, temporal order, and covariation. This synergy explains the power of intervention as a route to causal knowledge. Cues are generally strongly correlated in natural environments; causes tend to be nearby, prior to, and correlated with their effects.

Statistical Covariation

Hume's (1748/1975) analysis of causation has set the agenda for most contemporary theories of learning. These theories assume that causation cannot be perceived directly and suppose that people infer it from the statistical patterns in what they can observe. The key idea is that people are exposed to patterns of data, such as the occurrence or nonoccurrence of patterns of events, the presence or absence of features, or more generally, the values of variables. From this body of data, they extract certain statistical relations on which they base their causal judgments. There are various statistical relations that have been implicated in this process (Cheng, 1997; Glymour, 2001; Shanks, 2004). One of the simplest is the covariation between two events. For example, smoking increases the probability of heart disease. The existence of a stable covariation between two events A and B is a good indication that some underlying causal relation exists, but by itself does not reveal whether A causes

B, B causes A, or both are effects of a common cause. This highlights the incompleteness of any model of structure learning based solely on covariation detection.

The advent of Bayesian networks provides a more general framework to represent the statistical relations present in a body of observed data (Pearl, 1988). As well as representing straightforward (unconditional) relations between variables, they also represent conditional relations. In particular, they represent relations of *conditional independence*, which holds whenever an intermediate variable (or set of variables) renders two other variables (or sets of variables) probabilistically independent. For example, the unconditional dependence between intravenous drug usage and acquired immunodeficiency syndrome (AIDS) is rendered independent conditional on human immunodeficiency virus (HIV) status. In other words, the probability that someone develops AIDS, given that they are HIV positive, is not affected by whether they contracted the virus through drug use (assuming that drug usage does not affect the passage from HIV infection to AIDS). Establishing the conditional independencies that hold in a body of data is a critical step in constructing an appropriate Bayesian network.

Work in statistics and artificial intelligence forges a crucial link between statistical data and causal structure (Pearl, 2000; Spirtes, Glymour, & Schienes, 1993). Given certain assumptions (e.g., the causal Markov condition and faithfulness; see introductory chapter, and Woodward, chapter 1, this volume), they detail the patterns of dependencies that are associated with a given causal structure and, conversely, the causal structures that can be inferred from a given pattern of dependencies. Based on this analysis, a range of algorithms have been developed that can infer causal structure from large databases of statistical information. The success of this computational work has prompted some to model human causal learning along similar lines (Glymour, 2001; see the section Computational Models of Learning).

Despite the sophistication of Bayesian networks, it is generally recognized that statistical data alone is insufficient for inferring a unique causal model. Even with the notion of conditional independence, a particular body of correlational data will typically be associated with several possible causal structures (termed *Markov equivalent*) rather than a unique model. For example, if it is known that A, B, and C are all correlated (unconditionally dependent), and that A is conditionally independent of C given B, then there are three possible causal structures compatible with these relations (A → B → C, A ← B → C, A ← B ← C). To narrow these possibilities to just one requires some additional information. For instance, if one also knows that A occurs before B, then A → B → C is the only possible model.

This sets a theoretical limit on what can be inferred through correlation alone. At best, statistical cues can narrow the set of possible models to those that are Markov equivalent. There are also practical limitations. Even with just three variables, there are a large number of correlations and conditional correlations to compute to determine viable causal models. Each of these relations requires a sizable amount of data before their individual reliability is established. Thus, inferring possible causal models in a purely data-driven fashion involves a significant computational load. Although this may be manageable by a powerful computer, it is less likely to be achievable by humans with limited processing and memory resources.

Indeed, current evidence suggests that people are limited in their ability to learn structure from correlations alone, even to Markov equivalence. For example, Lagnado and Sloman (2004) presented subjects with probabilistic data generated by a three-variable chain A → B → C. In the absence of other cues (intervention, time order, etc.), most subjects failed to learn the correct structure or its Markov equivalents. This result holds across several different learning paradigms (Lagnado & Sloman, 2006; Sobel & Kushnir, 2006; Steyvers et al., 2003; Danks & McKenzie, 2006).

What people seem to find most difficult is establishing the appropriate conditional independence relations between sets of variables and using this as a basis for inferences about causal structure. This is tricky because learners must track the concurrent changes in three different variables. They must determine whether the correlation between any pair of these variables is itself dependent on a third variable. For example, in Lagnado and Sloman (2004), participants had to figure out that (a) two different chemicals covaried with a given effect, and (b) one of these chemicals was probabilistically independent of the effect conditional on the presence or absence of the other chemical. It is not surprising that most participants failed to work this out and settled for a simpler (but incorrect) causal model.

The experiments of Steyvers et al. (2003) also demonstrated the difficulty of inducing structure from covariation data. In their experiments, learners observed data about three mind-reading aliens. The task was to find which of the three mind readers can send messages (i.e., is a cause) and which can receive messages (i.e., is an effect). Generally, performance was better than chance but was still poor. For example, in Experiment 3, in which learners could select multiple models compatible with the data, only 20% of the choices were correct. This number may even overstate what people can do with covariation alone. In the experiments, learners were helped by the fact that the possible models were shown to them prior to learning. Thus, their learning was not purely data driven but was possibly aided by top-down constraints on possible models.

Moreover, the parameters of the models were selected to make the statistical differences between the models quite salient. For example, the pattern that all three mind readers had the same thought was very likely when the common-cause model applied but was extremely unlikely under a common-effect model. Similarly, the pattern that only two aliens had the same thought was very likely under the common-effect model hypothesis but unlikely with chains or common-cause models. Under the assumption that people associate these different prototypic patterns (e.g., three mind readers with identical thoughts) with different causal structures (e.g., common-cause model), some participants might have solved the task by noticing the prevalence of one of the prototypic patterns. Additional cues further aided induction. As in Lagnado and Sloman (2004), performance improved when participants were given the opportunity to add an additional cue, interventions (see also Sobel & Kushnir, 2006; and the section Intervention).

In sum, there is little evidence that people can compute the conditional dependencies necessary for inferring causal structure from statistical data alone without any further structural constraints. In contrast, when people have some prior intuitions about the structure of the causal model with which they are dealing, learning data can be used to estimate parameters within the hypothetical model or to select among alternative models (see also Waldmann, 1996; Waldmann & Hagmayer, 2001). Thus, the empirical evidence collected so far suggests that cues other than statistical covariation take precedence in the induction of structure before statistical patterns can meaningfully be processed. In the next section, we show that the temporal order cue can override statistical covariation as a cue to causal structure.

Temporal Order

The temporal order in which events occur provides a fundamental cue to causal structure. Causes occur before (or possibly simultaneously with) their effects, so if one knows that Event A occurs after Event B, one can be sure that A is not a cause of B. However, although the temporal order of events can be used to rule out potential causes, it does not provide a sufficient cue to rule them in. Just because events of Type B reliably follow events of Type A, it does not follow that A causes B. Their regular succession may be explained by a common cause C (e.g., heavy drinking first causes euphoria and only later causes sickness). Thus, the temporal order of events is an imperfect cue to causal structure. This is compounded by the fact that we often do not have direct knowledge of the actual temporal order of events but are restricted to inferring that order from the order in which we experience (receive information about) these events. In many situations, the experienced order will reflect the true temporal order, but this is not guaranteed. Sometimes, one learns about effects prior to learning about their causes. For example, the presence of a disease is typically learned about after experiencing the symptoms that it gives rise to (see the section on prior knowledge for further examples).

Despite its fallibility, temporal order will often yield a good cue to causal structure, especially if it is combined with other cues. Thus, if you know that A and B covary and that they do not have a common cause, then discovering that A occurs before B tells you that A causes B and not vice versa. It is not surprising, therefore, that animals and humans readily use temporal order as a guide to causality. Most previous research, however, has focused on how the temporal delay between events influences judgments of causal strength and paid less attention to how temporal order affects judgments of causal structure. The main findings have been that judged causal strength decreases with increased temporal delays (Shanks, Pearson, & Dickinson, 1989) unless people have a good reason to expect a delay (e.g., through prior instructions or knowledge; see Buehner & May, 2002). This fits with the default assumption that the closer two events are in time, the more likely they are to be causally related.

In the absence of other information, this will be a useful guiding heuristic.

Temporal order versus statistical data

Both temporal order and covariation information are typically available when people learn about a causal system. These sources can combine to give strong evidence in favor of a specific causal relation, and most psychological models of causal learning take these sources as basic inputs to the inference process. However, the two sources can also conflict. For example, consider a causal model in which C is a common cause of both A and B, and where B always occurs after A. The temporal order cue in this case is misleading as it suggests that A is a cause of B. This misattribution will be particularly compelling if the learner is unaware of C. However, consider a learner who also knows about C. With sufficient exposure to the patterns of correlation of A, B, and C, they would have enough information to learn that A is probabilistically independent of B given C. Together with the knowledge that C occurs before both A and B, the learner can infer that there is no causal link from A to B (without such temporal knowledge about C, they can only infer that A is not a direct cause of B because the true model might be a chain A → C → B).

In this situation, the learner has two conflicting sources of evidence about the causal relation between A and B: a temporal order cue that suggests that A causes B and (conditional) correlational information that there is no causal link from A to B. Here, a learner must disregard the temporal order information and base structural inference on the statistical data. However, it is not clear how easy it is for people to suppress the temporal order-based inference, especially when the statistical information is sparse. Indeed, in two psychological studies, Lagnado and Sloman (2004, 2006) show that people let the temporal order cue override contrary statistical data.

To explore the impact of temporal order cues on people's judgments about causal structure, Lagnado and Sloman (2006) constructed an experimental learning environment in which subjects used both temporal and statistical cues to infer causal structure. The underlying design was inspired by the fact that viruses (electronic or otherwise) present a clear example of how the temporal order in which information is received need not reflect the causal order in which events happen.

This is because there can be considerable variability in the time of transmission of a virus from computer to computer, as well as variability in the time it takes for an infection to reveal itself. Indeed, it is possible that a virus is received and transmitted by a computer before it reveals itself on that computer. For example, imagine that your office mate's computer becomes infected with an e-mail virus that crashes his computer. Twenty minutes later, your computer also crashes. A natural reaction is to suppose that his computer transmitted the virus to you, but it is possible that your computer received the virus first and then transmitted it to your office mate. It just so happened that the virus subverted his computer more quickly than yours. In this case, the temporal order in which the virus manifests itself (by crashing the computer) is not a reliable cue to the order in which the computers were infected.

In such situations, then, the order in which information is received about underlying events (e.g., the order in which viruses manifest themselves on computers in a network) does not necessarily mirror the underlying causal order (e.g., the order in which computers are infected). Temporal order is a fallible cue to causal structure. Moreover, there might be statistical information (e.g., the patterns of correlation between the manifestations of the viruses) that does provide a veridical cue to the underlying structure. How do people combine these two sources of information, and what do they do when these sources conflict?

In Lagnado and Sloman's (2006) experiment, participants had to learn about the connections in a simple computer network. To do so, they sent test messages from a master computer to one of four computers in a network and then observed which of the other computers also received the messages. They were able to send 100 test messages before being asked about the structure of the network. Participants completed four tasks, each with a different network of computers. They were instructed that there would sometimes be delays in the time taken for the messages to be transmitted from computer to computer. They were also told that the connections, where they existed, only worked 80% of the time. (In fact, the probabilistic nature of the connections is essential if the structure of the network is to be learnable from correlational information. With a deterministic network, all the connected computers would covary perfectly, so it would be impossible to figure out the relevant conditional independencies.)

Unknown to participants, the networks in each problem had the same underlying structure and only differed in the temporal order in which the computers displayed their messages. The four different temporal orderings are shown in Figure 10-2 along with the links endorsed by the participants in the test phase. When the temporal ordering reflected the underlying network structure, the correct model was generally inferred (see lower right panel in Figure 10-2). When the information was presented simultaneously, learners did less well (adding incorrect links) but still tended to capture the main links. When the temporal ordering conflicted with the underlying structure, participants erroneously added links that fitted with the temporal order but did not correspond to the underlying structure.

In sum, people allowed the temporal ordering to guide their structural inferences, even when this conflicted with the structure implied by the correlational information. However, this did not amount to a total disregard of the correlational information. For example, in the problem with temporal ordering ABDC (top right panel in Figure 10-2), participants erroneously endorsed the link from D to C (as suggested by the temporal order) but also correctly added the link from B to C. We hypothesize that they first used

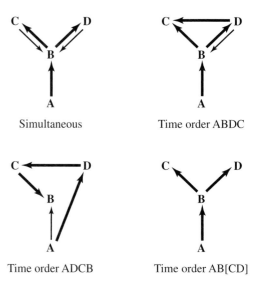

FIGURE 10-2 Model choices for the four temporal conditions in Lagnado and Sloman (2006). The correct model is that chosen in the lower right panel. Note that thick arrows represent links endorsed by 75%–100% of participants, thin arrows by 50–75% of participants.

the temporal ordering to set up an initial model (A → B → D → C). This model would be confirmed by most of the test trials. However, occasionally they saw a test pattern that contradicted this model (A, B, not-D, C). To accommodate this new evidence, they added a link from B to C but did not remove the redundant link from D to C because this still fit with the temporal ordering.

Interpreted within the causal model framework, this study shows that people use both temporal order and correlational cues to infer causal structure. It also suggests that they construct an initial model on the basis of the temporal ordering (when available) and then revise this model in the light of the covariational information. However, because of the persisting influence of the temporal order cue, these revisions may not be optimal.

Although the reported study highlights how people can be misled by an inappropriate temporal ordering, in many contexts the temporal cue will reliably indicate the correct causal structure. As with other mental heuristics, its fallibility does not undermine its effectiveness in most naturalistic learning situations. It also works best when combined with other cues. In the next section, we examine how it combines with interventions.

Intervention

Various philosophers have argued that the core notion of causation involves human intervention (Collingwood, 1940; Hart & Honoré, 1983; von Wright, 1971). It is through our actions and manipulations of the environment around us that we acquire our basic sense of causality. Several important claims stem from this: that causes are potential handles on the world; that they "make a difference"; that they involve some kind of force or power. Indeed, the language and metaphors of causal talk are rooted in this idea of human intervention on a physical world. More contemporary theories of causality dispense with its anthropomorphic connotations but maintain the notion of intervention as a central concept (Glymour, 2001; Pearl, 2000; Spirtes et al., 1993; Woodward, 2003, chapter 1, this volume).

Intervention not only is central to our notion of causation, but also is a fundamental means by which we learn about causal structure. This has been a commonplace insight in scientific method since Bacon (1620) spoke of "twisting the lion's tail" and was refined into axioms of experimental method by Mill (1843/1950).

More recently, it has been formalized by researchers in artificial intelligence and philosophy (Pearl, 2000; Spirtes et al., 1993; see Hagmayer, Sloman, Lagnado, & Waldmann, chapter 6, this volume).

The importance of intervention in causal learning is slowly beginning to permeate through to empirical psychology. Although it has previously been marked in terms of instrumental or operant conditioning (Mackintosh & Dickinson, 1979), the full implications of its role in causal structure learning had not been noted. This is largely because of the focus on strength estimation rather than structural inference. Once the emphasis is shifted to the question of how people infer causal structure, the notion of an intervention becomes critical.

Informally, an intervention involves imposing a change on a variable in a causal system from outside the system. A strong intervention is one that sets the variable in question to a particular value and thus overrides the effects of any other causes of that variable. It does this without directly changing anything else in the system, although of course other variables in the system can change indirectly as a result of changes to the intervened-on variable (a more formal definition is given by Woodward, chapter 1, this volume).

An intervention does not have to be a human action (cf. Mendelian randomization; Davey Smith & Ebrahim, 2003), but freely chosen human actions will often qualify as such. These can range from carefully controlled medical trials to the haphazard actions of a drunk trying to open a door. Somewhere in between lays the vast majority of everyday interventions. What is important for the purposes of causal learning is that an intervention can act as a quasi-experiment, one that eliminates (or reduces) confounds and helps establish the existence of a causal relation between the intervened-on variable and its effects.

A central benefit of an intervention is that it allows one to distinguish between causal structures that are difficult or impossible to discriminate among on the basis of correlational data alone. For example, a high correlation between bacteria and ulcers in the stomach does not tell us whether the ulcers cause the bacteria or vice versa (or, alternatively, if both share a common cause). However, suppose an intervention is made to eradicate the bacteria (and that this intervention does not promote or inhibit the presence of ulcers by some other means). If the ulcers also disappear, then one can infer that the bacteria cause the stomach ulcer.

Intervention aids learning

Can people make use of interventions to learn about causal structure? Several studies have compared learning through intervention with learning through observation, with both adults (Lagnado & Sloman, 2002, 2004; Sobel & Kushnir, 2006; Steyvers et al., 2003) and children (Gopnik et al., 2004, this volume; Sobel & Kirkham, chapter 9, this volume). All these studies have shown a distinct advantage for intervention. When participants are able to intervene freely on a causal system, they learn its structure better than when they are restricted to passive observation of its autonomous behavior.

What are the factors that drive this advantage? In addition to the special type of information afforded by intervention, because of the modification of the system under study, interventions can facilitate learning in several other ways. For instance, an intervener has more control over the type of data they see and thus can engage in more directed hypothesis testing than an observer. Intervention can also focus attention on the intervened-on variables and its effects. Further, the act of intervention introduces an implicit temporal cue into the learning situation because interventions typically precede their effects. Interveners may use any of these factors to enhance their learning.

By using yoked designs, Lagnado and Sloman (2004, 2006) ruled out the ability to hypothesis test as a major contributor in their experiments (although Sobel & Kushnir, 2006, report conflicting results). However, they also showed that the presence of a temporal cue had a substantial effect. When the information about the variables in the causal system was presented in a temporal order that matched the actual causal order (rather than being inconsistent with it), learning was greatly facilitated, irrespective of whether participants were intervening or observing. The authors suggested that in general people might use a temporal order heuristic by which they assume that any changes that occur subsequent to an action are effects of that action. This can be an effective heuristic, especially if these actions are unconfounded with other potential causes of the observed effects. Such a heuristic can also be used in observation but is more likely to lead to spurious inferences (because of unavoidable confounding).

An online learning paradigm

Although all of the studies reported so far demonstrate an advantage of intervention, they also reveal low levels of overall performance. Even when learners were able to intervene, many failed to learn the correct model (in most of the experiments, fewer than 40% chose the correct models). We conjecture that this is because of the impoverished nature of the learning environment presented to participants. All of the studies used a trial-based paradigm, in which participants viewed the results of their interventions in a case-by-case fashion. And, the causal events under study were represented by symbolic descriptions rather than direct experience (cf. Waldmann & Hagmayer, 2001). This is far removed from a naturalistic learning context. Although it facilitates the presentation of the relevant statistical contingencies, it denies the learner many of the cues that accompany real-world interventions, like spatiotemporal information, immediate feedback, and continuous control.

To address this question, Lagnado and Sloman (2003) introduced a learning paradigm that provided some of these cues; participants manipulated on-screen sliders in a real-time environment. Participants had to figure out the causal connections between the sliders by freely changing the settings of each slider and observing the resultant changes in the other sliders. In these studies, the majority of learners (>80%) rapidly learned a range of causal models, including models with four interconnected variables. This contrasted with the performance of observers, who watched the system of sliders move autonomously and seldom uncovered the correct model. Thus, the benefits of intervention seem to be magnified greatly by the dynamic nature of the task. This reinforces our claim that causal cognition operates best when presented with a confluence of cues, and in particular, that intervention works best when combined with spatiotemporal information.

In addition, in a separate condition many learners were able to make use of double interventions to disambiguate between models indistinguishable through single interventions. For example, when restricted to moving one slider at a time, it is impossible to discriminate between a three-variable chain $A \rightarrow B \rightarrow C$ and a similar model with an extra link from A to C. However, with an appropriate double intervention (e.g., fixing the value of B and then seeing whether manipulation of A still leads to a change in C), these models can be discriminated. The fact that many participants were able to do this shows that they can reason using causal representations (cf. Hagmayer et al., chapter 6, this volume). They were able to represent the two possible causal models and work out what combination of interventions would discriminate between them.

Intervention versus temporal order

The trial-based experiments by Lagnado and Sloman (2004) show that temporal order plays a substantial role in causal learning. However, the low levels of performance made it difficult to assess the separate influences of intervention and temporal order cues. A subsequent study by Lagnado and Sloman (2006) used the slider paradigm to investigate this question. Participants completed six problems, ranging from two-variable to four-variable models. Participants were divided into three groups: those who could freely intervene on the causal system, those who observed the system's behavior, and those who observed the results of another person's interventions (yoked to the active interveners). Within each group, participants were presented with information about the slider values in two temporal orders, either consistent with or opposite to the underlying causal structure. The main results are shown in Figure 10-3 (in which the intervention group is denoted as intervention 1). There is a clear advantage of intervention (active or yoked) over observation. There is also a clear influence of temporal

consistency for the observational and yoked groups but not for the active interveners. The authors conjectured that the active interveners overcame the inconsistent temporal order cue by (correctly) learning that the variable information was presented in reverse order. To test this, they ran a second intervention condition in which the temporally inconsistent time order was randomized rather than reversed (with the constraint that it could never produce a consistent order). The results for this follow-up are also shown in Figure 10-3 (the new intervention group is intervention 2). The interveners now showed a similar decline in performance when information was presented in an inconsistent order. Overall, these results confirm that intervention and temporal order provide separate cues to causal structure. They work best, however, in combination, and this may explain the efficacy of interventions made in naturalistic learning environments.

Prior Knowledge

Temporal order is a powerful cue to causality when we experience causal events online. Whenever we directly experience causal events, the sequence of the learning input (i.e., learning order) mirrors the asymmetry of causal order (causes generate effects but not vice versa). The correlation between learning order

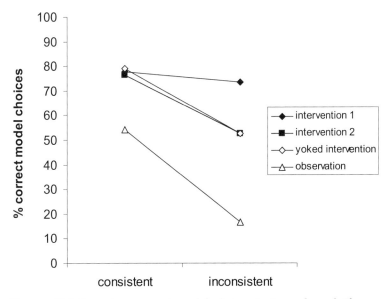

FIGURE 10-3 Percentage correct model choices in Lagnado and Sloman (2006) showing influence of intervention and temporal order. Note that in intervention 2 time-inconsistent orders were randomized rather than reversed.

and causal order is so strong in these situations that some theories (e.g., associative learning models) collapse causal order and learning order by assuming that learning generally involves associations between cues and outcomes, with cues presented temporally prior to their outcomes (see Shanks & Lopez, 1996; Waldmann, 1996, 2000).

However, whereas nonhuman animals indeed typically experience causes prior to their effects, the correlation between learning order and causal order is often broken when learning is based on symbolized representations of causal events. In fact, most experimental studies of human learning are now carried out on a computer in which cues and outcomes are presented verbally. The flexibility of symbolic representations allows it to present effect information prior to cause information so that learning order no longer necessarily corresponds to causal order. For example, many experiments have studied disease classification in which symptoms (i.e., effects of diseases) are presented as cues prior to information about their causes (i.e., diseases; e.g., Gluck & Bower, 1988; Shanks & Lopez, 1996; Waldmann, 2000, 2001).

Learning order and causal order may also mismatch when the causal events are not readily observable but have to be measured or searched with more complicated procedures. For example, a physician may immediately observe symptoms of a new patient prior to searching for possible causes. Or, parents might become aware of school problems of their child prior to finding out about the causes. Thus, although the temporal order of learning events is often a valid cue to causal structure, it is sometimes necessary to override this cue when other cues appear more valid.

Coherence with prior knowledge is a potent cue to causal structure. Regardless of when we observe fever in a patient, our world knowledge tells us that fever is not a cause but rather an effect of an underlying disease. Prior knowledge may be specific when we have already learned about a causal relation, but prior knowledge can also be abstract and hypothetical. We know that switches can turn on devices even when we do not know about the specific function of a switch in a novel device. Similarly, we know that diseases can cause a wide range of symptoms prior to finding out which symptom is caused by which disease. In contrast, rarely do we consider symptoms as possible causes of a disease.

Prior knowledge versus temporal order

The possible mismatch between causal order and learning order raises the question whether people are capable of ignoring the temporal order of learning events when their prior knowledge suggests a different causal order. Following the framework of causal-model theory, Waldmann and Holyoak (1990, 1992) developed an experimental paradigm addressing this question. In general, learners in different conditions receive identical cues and outcomes in identical learning order. However, based on initial instructions, different causal orders are suggested so that in one condition the cues represent causes and the outcomes effects (predictive learning), whereas in the contrasting condition the cues represent effects and the outcomes causes (diagnostic learning).

A study by Waldmann (2001) exemplifies this paradigm. In Waldmann's Experiment 2, participants were told that they were going to learn about new diseases of the blood. In all conditions, learners observed learning trials in which they first received information about the presence of a Substance 1 in a patient followed by feedback about the presence of a disease (e.g., *Midosis*). Other trials showed patients whose blood contained two substances, Substances 2 and 3, which were a sign of a different disease (e.g., *Xeritis*). Associative learning theories are only sensitive to learning order and would therefore generally predict that the associative strength between Substance 1 and *Midosis* should be greater than between the two other substances and *Xeritis* (see Cobos, López, Cano, Almaraz, & Shanks, 2002). This so-called overshadowing effect derives from associative learning theories (e.g., Rescorla & Wagner, 1972), which predict that the two redundant always co-occurring substances compete for predicting *Xeritis*. Once asymptotic performance is achieved, this should lead to either substance contributing only about half of the associative strength needed to predict the disease correctly.

To pit learning order against causal order, Waldmann (2001) created two contrasting conditions: In the predictive learning condition, the substances were described as coming from food items, which gives them the status of potential causes of the diseases (see Figure 10-4). In contrast, in the diagnostic learning condition, the substances were characterized as potentially generated by the diseases, which assigns them the causal status of effects. Although cues, outcomes, and learning order were identical in both conditions, overshadowing interacted with causal status. Overshadowing was stronger in the predictive than in the diagnostic learning condition. Similar interactions have also been shown for the related blocking phenomenon (Waldmann, 2000; Waldmann & Holyoak, 1992; Waldmann & Walker, 2005).

This interaction can be modeled by an account that assumes that people use prior knowledge conveyed to them through the cover stories to form tentative causal models with the structures displayed in Figure 10-4 (see Waldmann & Martignon, 1998, for a Bayesian causal model account; see also Tenenbaum et al., chapter 19, this volume). These models free learners from learning order as a cue to causality and allow them to assign the learning input flexibly to the causal variables in the tentative causal model. Thus, in the predictive learning condition, the cues are mapped to the cause layer and the effects to the outcome layer (Figure 10-4A), whereas in the diagnostic learning condition the cues are mapped to the effect layer and the outcomes to the cause layer (Figure 10-4B). Although prior knowledge generates the structure of the causal models underlying the learning domain, the cover stories made it clear to participants that the causal relations were only hypothetical and needed to be verified by checking the learning data. Thus, in the learning stage the learning input is used to parameterize the model or test whether the hypothesized links are present.

The overshadowing study illustrates this account (Waldmann, 2001). In Experiment 2, learners observed Substance 1 by itself as a deterministic cause (predictive learning) or a deterministic effect (diagnostic learning). However, the situation differed across the two learning conditions for the two redundant substances. In the diagnostic learning condition, the data suggest that each of the two substances is deterministically caused by their common cause, the disease *Xeritis* (see Figure 10-4B). Although there may

be alternative unknown diseases also affecting these symptoms, these alternative causes were not mentioned in the instructions so that their potential impact on learners' assessment should be relatively small. By contrast, in the predictive learning condition, learners were confronted with an ambiguous situation. Here, the two substances represented perfectly confounded alternative potential causes, so it was impossible to determine whether only one of these potential causes was effective or whether both shared responsibility in generating the common effect, *Midosis* (see Figure 10-4A). Thus, learners should have been uncertain about their causal status, which would lead to a lowering of ratings (i.e., overshadowing). This pattern was indeed found in the study.

Temporal order of learning events was also pitted against causal order in other task domains. In a study on category learning, Waldmann et al. (1995) showed that sensitivity to correlations among cues is influenced by the causal status of the cues (see also Rehder, 2003a, 2003b; Rehder & Hastie, 2001). As predicted by Bayesian models, when the cues represent effects within a common-cause model, learners expect cue correlations, whereas statistical independence among cues is expected when they represent multiple causes of a common effect. These expectations influenced how difficult it was for participants to learn about different category structures. Again, these findings support the view that learners formed a structural representation of a causal model on the basis of the initial instructions and then tried to map these models to the learning data (see Waldmann & Martignon, 1998, for the formal details).

Prior knowledge and parameter estimation

Even when causal order and temporal order coincide, temporal order alone is not sufficiently constrained to

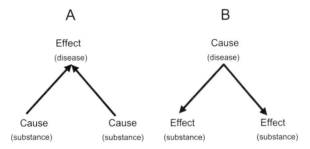

FIGURE 10-4 Predictive learning (A) and diagnostic learning (B) in Waldmann (2001).

determine how learning events should be processed. In a stream of learning events, the relevant events need to be parsed first, and then it is necessary to decide how the events are interrelated. Often, this problem is solved by assuming that events that are spatiotemporally contiguous (see the section on temporal order) are interrelated. But, this is not always true. For example, when eating a fish dish, we would not view the fish as a cause of subsequent nausea that occurred within 0.5 seconds of eating the meal. Based on prior knowledge, we expect a longer latency of the causal mechanism. In contrast, we would not relate a light to a button press if there was a latency of 10 seconds between pressing the button and the light going on.

Hagmayer and Waldmann (2002) have shown that prior expectations about temporal delays between causes and effects indeed mediate how causes and effects are interrelated within a stream of events. This selection consequently affects how causal strength is estimated within the data set. Despite observing identical event streams, different assessments of causal strength resulted based on how the stream was parsed and how the events were interrelated prior to assessing the strength of covariation.

Prior assumptions also affect which statistical indicators are chosen to estimate causal strength parameters. When the task is to estimate causal strength between a cause and effect, it is necessary to compute the covariation between these events while holding constant alternative causes that may confound the relation. For example, the strength of the causal influence of smoking on heart disease should ideally be assessed when alternative causes of heart disease (e.g., junk food) are absent or held constant. In contrast, causally irrelevant events, alternative effects of the target cause (within a common-cause model), or events that lie downstream on a causal chain between the target cause and the target effect must not be held constant (Eells, 1991; Pearl, 2000). Otherwise, erroneous parameter estimates might result.

Waldmann and Hagmayer (2001) have shown that participants are indeed sensitive to these normative constraints. In a set of experiments, learners were given identical learning input with three interrelated events. The participants' task was to assess the strength of the causal relation between a given cause and an effect. The causal status of the third event was manipulated by means of initial instructions. The results showed that learners only tended to hold the third event constant when this event was assumed to be an alternative cause of the target effect. When it was causally irrelevant, an alternative effect of the cause, or an intermediate event on a causal chain between cause and effect, participants ignored the status of the third variable. Again, this is a case in which temporal order is an insufficient cue because the learning events were presented identically to all participants. The correct parameter estimates depended on prior knowledge about the causal status of the learning events.

Use of prior knowledge and processing constraints

Processing learning data on the basis of a prior causal model can be demanding. For example, in a diagnostic learning task the learning order of cues and outcomes conflicts with causal order. Also, holding constant alternative causes can sometimes be difficult when the presence and absence of the alternative cause alternates so that it is hard to store separately in memory the events in which the confound was present and absent. A number of studies have shown that, in situations that tax processing capacity, people may incorrectly process the learning data, although in less complex tasks they do better (De Houwer & Beckers, 2003; Tangen & Allan, 2004; Waldmann & Hagmayer, 2001; Waldmann & Walker, 2005). Waldmann and Walker have also shown that it is crucial that people have a strong belief in the validity of the causal model; otherwise, their learning is dictated by other cues that require less effort to use. These studies show that people have the competence to interrelate causal models and learning data correctly when they strongly believe in their prior assumptions and when the learning task is within the grasp of their information-processing capacity. Otherwise, other cues may dominate.

Integrating Fragments of Causal Models

We rarely acquire knowledge about a complex causal network all at once. Rather, we learn about these models in a piecemeal fashion. Consider, for example, the search for the causes of ulcer by medical science (see Thagard, 1999, for a detailed description of the history of medical theories of ulcer). It was first thought that ulcers were caused by excessive stomach acid, which was caused by stress. Later, scientists found out that excessive acidity is not the cause of many ulcers, but that the majority of ulcers are caused by bacteria (*Helicobacter pyloris*). In addition, it was discovered by other researchers that some acid-based pain relievers, such as aspirin, might also cause ulcers. As a consequence, an initially simple causal chain model (Stress → Excessive acid → Ulcer) was replaced by a more complex causal model (see Figure 10-1). Theory change occurred as a result of many independent empirical studies that focused on individual links. These individual pieces of knowledge were eventually integrated into a coherent, global causal model that incorporated what we now know about ulcers.

Similarly, in everyday life, we may independently learn that peanuts cause an allergy and later discover that strawberries cause the same allergy. Although we may never have eaten peanuts and strawberries together, we could still integrate these two pieces of causal knowledge into a common-effect model. Similarly, we might independently learn about two causal relations in which the same common cause is involved. For example, we may first experience that aspirin relieves headache. Later, a physician might tell us that our ulcer is also caused by aspirin. Again, although we may never have consciously experienced the two effects of the common cause together, we can integrate the two fragments into a coherent common-cause model.

What is the advantage of integrating fragments of causal knowledge into a coherent global causal model? In addition to representing only the direct causal relations within the model (i.e., causes, effects, and causal arrows), causal models allow us to infer the relation between any pair of events within the model, even when they are not directly causally connected. For example, the causal model for aspirin would imply that relief of headache and ulcer should tend to co-occur despite no causal relation to each other. These structural implications are a consequence of the patterns of causal directionality inherent in causal models.

Bayes nets provide formal tools to analyze structural implications of causal models (see Pearl, 1988, 2000; Spirtes et al., 1993). The graph of a common-cause model expresses that the two effects are spuriously related (because of their common cause) but become independent once the state of the common cause is known (see Figure 10-4B). This is a consequence of the Markov condition. For example, once we know that aspirin is present, the probability of

ulcers is fixed regardless of whether headache is present or absent. Similarly, causal chains imply that the initial cause and the final effect are dependent but become independent when the intermediate event is held constant. Finally, a common-effect model (Figure 10-4A) implies independence of the alternative causes, but they become dependent once the common effect is held constant. This is an example of explaining away. Eating peanuts and eating strawberries should normally occur independently. But, once we know that someone has an allergy, finding out that they have eaten peanuts makes it less likely that they have also eaten strawberries.

Hagmayer and Waldmann (2000, 2006) have investigated the question of whether people are capable of integrating fragments into global causal models in a normative fashion (see also Ahn & Dennis, 2000; Perales, Catena, & Maldonado, 2004). In a typical experiment, participants had to learn about the causal relations between the mutation of a fictitious gene and two substances. The two relations were learned on separated trials, so no information about the covariation between the two substances was available. Although the learning input was identical, the underlying causal model differed in different conditions. To manipulate causal models, participants were told either that the mutation of the fictitious gene was the common cause of two substances or they were told that the two substances were different causes of the mutation of the gene. The strength of the causal relations was also manipulated to test whether people are sensitive to the size of the parameters when making predictions.

The main goal of the study was to test the conditions under which people are aware of the different structural implications of the common-cause and the common-effect models. A correlation should be expected between the two substances when they were caused by a common cause, with the size of the correlation dependent on the size of causal strength. By contrast, two causes of a common effect should be independent regardless of the size of the causal relations.

To test sensitivity to structural implications, participants were given two tasks: In the first task, participants were given new cases along with information about whether a mutation had occurred or not. Their task was to predict for each trial whether either of the two substances was present or absent. Thus, in the common-cause conditions people predicted the presence or absence of the two effects based on information about the presence or absence of the common cause; in the common-effect condition, people diagnosed the presence or absence of either cause based on information about the presence or absence of the common effect. This way, participants made predictions for the two substances they had never observed together. Across multiple predictions, participants generated a correlation between the two substances that could be used as an indicator of sensitivity to the implied correlations. The second task asked participants directly to estimate the conditional frequency of the second substance given that the first substance was present or absent.

The two tasks assess sensitivity to structural implications in different ways. Whereas the second task assessed more explicit knowledge of the structural implications of causal knowledge, the first task required participants to use the causal models to predict patterns of events. Thus, this task probes sensitivity to structural implications in a more implicit fashion. For example, in the common-cause condition a possible strategy would be to run a mental simulation of the underlying common-cause model. Whenever the presence of the common cause is stated in the test trial, the two effects could be individually predicted with probabilities that conform to the learned strength of the causal relation. This strategy would yield the normatively implied spurious correlation between the substances, although the predictions focused on the individual links between the common cause and either effect.

Similarly, in the common-effect condition people could simulate diagnoses of the two causes based on information about the presence or absence of the common effect by running the causal model backward from effect to causes (see Figure 10-4A). Simultaneous diagnoses of either cause should make participants aware of the possible competition between the causes. Because either cause suffices to explain the effect, people should be reluctant to predict both causes too often. This would yield correct diagnoses of the patterns of causes without requiring participants to reflect directly on the correlation between alternative causes.

The results of this and other experiments show little sensitivity to the differences between common-cause and common-effect models in the explicit measure. Although some basic explicit knowledge cannot be ruled out (see also Perales et al., 2004), Hagmayer

and Waldmann's (2000, 2006) experiments show that people do not use the strength parameters to predict the implied correlations very well. By contrast, the implicit tasks revealed patterns that corresponded remarkably well to the expected patterns. Whereas a spurious correlation was predicted in the common-cause condition, the predicted correlation stayed close to zero in the common-effect condition. Hagmayer and Waldmann attribute this competency to mental simulations of causal models.

Further experiments by Hagmayer and Waldmann (2006) explored the boundary conditions for these effects. The dissociation between explicit and implicit knowledge disappeared with causal chains in which the individual links were taught separately and in which the task in the test phase was to predict the final effect based on information about the initial cause (see also Ahn & Dennis, 2000). In this task, both explicit and implicit measures were sensitive to the implied correlation between these two events. This result shows that spurious relations (e.g., between two effects of a common cause) need to be psychologically distinguished from indirect causal relations. Whereas people obviously have little explicit knowledge about spurious relations, they may view indirect relations as a subdivided global causal relation. In fact, all direct causal relations can be subdivided into chains that represent the underlying mechanisms. Thus, combining links of causal chains into a global prediction is easier than deriving prediction for spurious relations.

The implicit task also turned out to be sensitive to boundary conditions. Whereas performance for the common-cause model and the chain model showed fairly robust sensitivity to spurious and indirect relations, it turned out that people's implicit estimates in the common-effect condition are only adequate when the task required them to predict patterns of causes, as in the experiment described. In this task, the links of the causal models were simulated in parallel, which apparently proved important for making learners aware of the implied competition among the causes. When the task was first to predict the effect based on one cause and then make inferences about the other cause, people erroneously predicted a spurious correlation between the causes. Probably, participants accessed each link consecutively and tended to forget about the possible competition between the causes.

In sum, people are capable of integrating fragments of causal knowledge in a way that corresponds to the normative analyses of Bayes nets. However, this competency is not as robust as the computer models used to implement Bayes nets. It rather depends on a number of task factors that include the type of relation within a causal model and the specifics of the task.

Computational Models of Learning

Although our main concern has been with how people learn causal structure, the story we have told is linked in important ways to current computational models of inference and learning. For one, the causal Bayesian network formalism (Pearl, 2000; Spirtes et al., 1993) offers a normative framework for causal representation and inference. And, at a qualitative level human inference seems to fit with the broad prescriptions of this theory (see Hagmayer et al., chapter 6, this volume; Sloman & Lagnado, 2004, 2005). The causal Bayesian network framework also suggests various computational procedures for learning causal structure. These are often grouped into two types: Bayesian methods (Heckerman, Meek, & Cooper, 1999) and constraint-based methods (Spirtes et al., 1993). It is instructive to compare and contrast these approaches as models of human learning in the light of the proposals and empirical evidence surveyed in this chapter.

In short, Bayesian methods assume that learners have some prior belief distribution across all possible causal structures and update these beliefs as statistical data are gathered. Bayes rule is used to compute posterior probabilities for each of the possible models given the data, and a best-fitting model is derived from this computation (see Tenenbaum et al., chapter 19, this volume). Constraint-based methods work by computing the independencies and dependencies (both conditional and unconditional) in the data set and then returning the structures that are consistent with these dependencies (for more details, see Danks, 2004, in press).

At present, these computational models have been used as rational rather than psychological models of human learning (Anderson, 1990; Marr, 1982). They aim to specify what the learner is computing rather than how they are actually computing it. Both Bayesian methods (Steyvers et al., 2003; Tenenbaum et al., chapter 19, this volume) and constraint-based methods have been used for this purpose. A question closer to the concerns of the empirical psychologist, however, is whether these models tell us anything about the psychological or process level of causal learning. What are the mechanisms that people actually use to learn about causal structure?

In their current state, these computational approaches seem to both overestimate and underestimate the capabilities of human learners. For instance, they overestimate the computational resources and processing power available to humans to make the appropriate Bayesian or constraint-based computations. Bayesian models require priors across all possible models and Bayesian updating with each new piece of evidence. Constraint-based models require the computation of all the dependencies and independencies in the data and inference of the set of Markov equivalent structures. Both methods appear to place insurmountable demands on a human mind known to be limited in its processing capacities.

There are potential solutions to these shortcomings. Bayesian methods can be heuristic rather than exhaustive, and constraint-based methods can use more psychologically realistic methods for computing dependencies (Danks, 2004). However, both approaches still need to deal with the basic problem, detailed in this chapter, that there is little evidence that people who only observe patterns of covariation between events (without further constraints) can induce causal models. In particular, there is no clear evidence that people can use statistical information from triples of events to infer causal models via conditional dependence relations. And, this ability seems to lie at the heart of both approaches.

In addition, these computational approaches seem to underestimate human capabilities (or, more precisely, the richness of the environment around them and their ability to exploit this information). As we have seen throughout this chapter, people make use of various cues aside from statistical data. These cues are typically used to establish an initial causal model, which is then tested against the incoming statistical data. Bayesian approaches have sought to model this by incorporating prior knowledge and assumptions in the learner's prior belief distribution (Tenenbaum et al., chapter 19, this volume; for a more general approach, see Griffiths & Tenenbaum, chapter 20, this volume) and thus account for inferences made on sparse data. But, it is not clear how they handle cases for which people test just a single model and then abandon it in favor of an alternative. This kind of discontinuity in someone's beliefs does not emerge naturally from the Bayesian approach.

On the face of it, constraint-based methods are largely data driven, so the use of prior knowledge and other assumptions appears problematic, but they also have the resources to address this issue. Along with the constraints that stem from the statistical dependencies in the data, they can include constraints imposed by prior knowledge, temporal order information, and other cues. This approach also seems to fit well with the discontinuous and incremental nature of human learning (Danks, 2004, in press).

However, in both cases further work is needed to develop a comprehensive framework that can integrate the diverse constraints and cues to structure[1] (e.g., from temporal ordering, interventions, etc.) and capture the heuristic methods that humans seem to adopt. In particular, this framework needs to be able to combine and trade off these constraints as new information arrives. For example, although an initial causal model might be based on the assumption that temporal order reflects causal order, a revised model could reject this constraint in the light of statistical data that contradicts it (see the section on temporal order).

Summary

In this chapter, we have argued for several interconnected theses. First, the fundamental way that people represent causal knowledge is qualitative in terms of causal structure. Second, people use a variety of cues to infer structure aside from statistical data (e.g., temporal order, intervention, coherence with prior knowledge). Third, once a structural model is hypothesized, subsequent statistical data are used to confirm or refute the model and (possibly) to parameterize it. The structure of a posited model influences how the statistical data are processed. Fourth, people are limited in the number and complexity of causal models that they can hold in mind to test, but they can separately learn and then integrate simple models and revise models by adding and removing single links. Finally, current computational models of learning need further development before they can be applied to human learning. What is needed is a heuristic-based model that shares the strengths and weaknesses of a human learner and can take advantage of the rich causal information that the natural environment provides.

References

Ahn, W., & Dennis, M. (2000). Induction of causal chains. In L. R. Gleitman & A. K. Joshi (Eds.) , *Proceedings of the 22nd Annual Conference of the Cognitive Science Society* (pp. 19–24). Mahwah, NJ: Erlbaum.

Anderson, J. R. (1990). *The adaptive character of thought.* Hillsdale, NJ: Erlbaum.

Bacon, F. (1620). *Novum organum.* Chicago: Open Court.

Buehner, M. J., Cheng, P. W., & Clifford, D. (2003). From covariation to causation: A test of the assumption of causal power. *Journal of Experimental Psychology: Learning, Memory, and Cognition, 29,* 1119–1140.

Buehner, M. J., & May, J. (2002). Knowledge mediates the timeframe of covariation assessment in human causal induction. *Thinking and Reasoning, 8,* 269–295.

Cheng, P. W. (1997). From covariation to causation: A causal power theory. *Psychological Review, 104,* 367–405.

Cobos, P. L., López, F. J., Cano, A., Almaraz, J., & Shanks, D. R. (2002). Mechanisms of predictive and diagnostic causal induction. *Journal of Experimental Psychology: Animal Behavior Processes, 28,* 331–346.

Collingwood, R. (1940). *An essay on metaphysics.* Oxford, England: Clarendon Press.

Danks, D. (in press). Causal learning from observations and manipulations. In M. Lovett & P. Shah (Eds.), *Thinking with data.* Hillsdale, NJ: Erlbaum.

Danks, D. (2004). Constraint-Based Human Causal Learning. In M. Lovett, C. Schunn, C. Lebiere, & P. Munro (Eds.), *Proceedings of Sixth International Conference on Cognitive Modelling* (pp. 342–343). Mahwah, NJ: Erlbaum.

Danks, D., & McKenzie, C. R. M. (2006). *Learning complex causal structures.* Manuscript in preparation.

Davey Smith, G., & Ebrahim, S. (2003). "Mendelian randomization": Can genetic epidemiology contribute to understanding environmental determinants of disease? *International Journal of Epidemiology, 32,* 1–22.

De Houwer, J., & Beckers, T. (2003). Secondary task difficulty modulates forward blocking in human contingency learning. *Quarterly Journal of Experimental Psychology, 56B,* 345–357.

Eells, E. (1991). *Probabilistic causality.* Cambridge, England: Cambridge University Press.

Einhorn, H. J., & Hogarth, R. M. (1986). Judging probable cause. *Psychological Bulletin, 99,* 3–19.

Gluck, M. A., & Bower, G. H. (1988). From conditioning to category learning: An adaptive network model. *Journal of Experimental Psychology: General, 117,* 227–247.

Glymour, C. (2001). *The mind's arrows*. Cambridge, MA: MIT Press.

Gopnik, A., Glymour, C., Sobel, D. M., Schulz, L. E., Kushnir, T., & Danks, D. (2004). A theory of causal learning in children: Causal maps and Bayes nets. *Psychological Review, 111*, 1–31.

Griffiths, T. L., & Tenenbaum, J. B. (2005). Structure and strength in causal induction. *Cognitive Psychology, 51*, 354–384.

Hagmayer, Y., & Waldmann, M. R. (2000). Simulating causal models: The way to structural sensitivity. In L. Gleitman & A. Joshi (Eds.), *Proceedings of the 22nd Annual Conference of the Cognitive Science Society* (pp. 214–219). Mahwah, NJ: Erlbaum.

Hagmayer, Y., & Waldmann, M. R. (2002). How temporal assumptions influence causal judgments. *Memory & Cognition, 30*, 1128–1137.

Hagmayer, Y., & Waldmann, M. R. (2006). *Integrating fragments of causal models–Implicit versus explicit sensitivity to structural implications*. Manuscript in preparation.

Hart, H. L. A., & Honoré, T. (1983). *Causation in the law* (2nd ed.). Oxford, England: Clarendon.

Heckerman, D., Meek, C., & Cooper, G. (1999). A Bayesian approach to causal discovery. In C. Glymour & G. Cooper (Eds.), *Computation, causation, and discovery* (pp. 143–167). Cambridge, MA: MIT Press.

Hume, D. (1748/1975). *An enquiry concerning human understanding*. Oxford, England: Clarendon.

Lagnado, D. A., & Sloman, S. A. (2002). Learning causal structure. In W. Gray & C. D. Schunn (Eds.), *Proceedings of the 24th Annual Conference of the Cognitive Science Society* (pp. 560–565). Mahwah, NJ: Erlbaum.

Lagnado, D. A., & Sloman, S. A. (2003). Using multiple interventions. Unpublished raw data.

Lagnado, D. A., & Sloman, S. A. (2004). The advantage of timely intervention. *Journal of Experimental Psychology: Learning, Memory, and Cognition, 30*, 856–876.

Lagnado, D. A., & Sloman, S. A. (2006). Time as a guide to cause. *Journal of Experimental Psychology: Learning, Memory, and Cognition, 32*, 451–460.

Mackintosh, N. J., & Dickinson, A. (1979). Instrumental (Type II) conditioning. In A. Dickinson & R. A. Boakes (Eds.), *Mechanisms of learning and motivation* (pp. 143–169). Hillsdale, NJ: Erlbaum.

Marr, D. (1982). *Vision*. San Francisco: Freeman.

Mill, J. S. (1950). *Philosophy of scientific method*. New York: Hafner. (Original work published 1843)

Neapolitan, R. E. (2004). *Learning Bayesian networks*. Upper Saddle River, NJ: Pearson US.

Pearl, J. (1988). *Probabilistic reasoning in intelligent systems: Networks of plausible inference*. San Mateo, CA: Morgan Kaufmann.

Pearl, J. (2000). *Causality*. Cambridge, England: Cambridge University Press.

Perales, J. C., Catena, A., & Maldonado, A. (2004). Inferring non-observed correlations from causal scenarios: The role of causal knowledge. *Learning and Motivation, 35*, 115–135.

Rehder, B. (2003a). Categorization as causal reasoning. *Cognitive Science, 27*, 709–748.

Rehder, B. (2003b). A causal-model theory of conceptual representation and categorization. *Journal of Experimental Psychology: Learning, Memory, and Cognition, 29*, 1141–1159.

Rehder, B., & Hastie, R. (2001). Causal knowledge and categories: The effects of causal beliefs on categorization, induction, and similarity. *Journal of Experimental Psychology: General, 130*, 323–360.

Rescorla, R. A., & Wagner, A. R. (1972). A theory of Pavlovian conditioning: Variations in the effectiveness of reinforcement and nonreinforcement. In A. H. Black & W. F. Prokasy (Eds.), *Classical conditioning II: Current theory and research* (pp. 64–99). New York: Appleton-Century-Crofts.

Shanks, D. R. (2004). Judging covariation and causation. In D. Koehler & N. Harvey (Eds.), *Blackwell handbook of judgment and decision making* (pp. 220–239). Oxford, England: Blackwell.

Shanks, D. R., & Dickinson, A. (1987). Associative accounts of causality judgment. In G. H. Bower (Ed.), *The psychology of learning and motivation: Advances in research and theory* (Vol. 21, pp. 229–261). San Diego, CA: Academic Press.

Shanks, D. R., & López, F. J. (1996). Causal order does not affect cue selection in human associative learning. *Memory and Cognition, 24*, 511–522.

Shanks, D. R., Pearson, S. M., & Dickinson, A. (1989). Temporal contiguity and the judgment of causality by human subjects. *Quarterly Journal of Experimental Psychology, 41B*, 139–159.

Sloman, S. A., & Lagnado, D. A. (2004). Causal invariance in reasoning and learning. In B. Ross (Ed.), *The psychology of learning and motivation* (Vol. 44, pp. 287–325). San Diego, CA: Elsevier Science.

Sloman, S. A., & Lagnado, D. A. (2005). Do we "do"? *Cognitive Science, 29*, 5–39.

Sobel, D. M., & Kushnir, T. (2006). The importance of decision demands in causal learning from interventions. *Memory & Cognition, 34*, 411–419.

Spirtes, P., Glymour, C., & Schienes, R. (1993). *Causation, prediction, and search*. New York: Springer-Verlag.

Steyvers, M., Tenenbaum, J. B., Wagenmakers, E. J., & Blum, B. (2003). Inferring causal networks from observations and interventions. *Cognitive Science, 27*, 453–489.

Tangen, J. M., & Allan, L. G. (2004). Cue-interaction and judgments of causality: Contributions of causal and associative processes. *Memory & Cognition, 32,* 107–124.

Tenenbaum, J. B., & Griffiths, T. L. (2001). Structure learning in human causal induction. In T. K. Leen, T. G. Dietterich, & V. Tresp (Eds.), *Advances in neural information processing systems 13* (pp. 59–65). Cambridge, MA: MIT Press.

Tenenbaum, J. B., & Griffiths, T. L. (2003). Theory-based causal inference. In S. Becker, S. Thrun, & Obermayer (Eds.), *Advances in Neural Information Processing Systems 15* (pp. 35–42). Cambridge, MA: MIT Press.

Thagard, P. (1999). *How scientists explain disease.* Princeton, NJ: Princeton University Press.

von Wright, G. H. (1971). *Explanation and understanding.* Ithaca, NY: Cornell University Press.

Waldmann, M. R. (1996). Knowledge-based causal induction. In D. R. Shanks, K. J. Holyoak, & D. L. Medin (Eds.), *The psychology of learning and motivation* (Vol. 34, pp. 47–88). San Diego, CA: Academic Press.

Waldmann, M. R. (2000). Competition among causes but not effects in predictive and diagnostic learning. *Journal of Experimental Psychology: Learning, Memory, and Cognition, 26,* 53–76.

Waldmann, M. R. (2001). Predictive versus diagnostic causal learning: Evidence from an overshadowing paradigm. *Psychonomic Bulletin and Review, 8,* 600–608.

Waldmann, M. R., & Hagmayer, Y. (2001). Estimating causal strength: The role of structural knowledge and processing effort. *Cognition, 82,* 27–58.

Waldmann, M. R., & Hagmayer, Y. (2005). Seeing versus doing: Two modes of accessing causal knowledge. *Journal of Experimental Psychology: Learning, Memory, and Cognition, 31,* 216–227.

Waldmann, M. R., & Holyoak, K. J. (1990). Can causal induction be reduced to associative learning? In M. Piattelli-Palmarini (Ed.), *Proceedings of the 12th Annual Conference of the Cognitive Science Society* (pp. 190–197). Hillsdale, NJ: Erlbaum.

Waldmann, M. R., & Holyoak, K. J. (1992). Predictive and diagnostic learning within causal models: Asymmetries in cue competition. *Journal of Experimental Psychology: General, 121,* 222–236.

Waldmann, M. R., Holyoak, K. J., & Fratianne, A. (1995). Causal models and the acquisition of category structure. *Journal of Experimental Psychology: General, 124,* 181–206.

Waldmann, M. R., & Martignon, L. (1998). A Bayesian network model of causal learning. In M. A. Gernsbacher & S. J. Derry (Eds.), *Proceedings of the 20th Annual Conference of the Cognitive Science Society* (pp. 1102–1107). Mahwah, NJ: Erlbaum.

Waldmann, M. R., & Walker, J. M. (2005). Competence and performance in causal learning. *Learning & Behavior, 33,* 211–229.

Wasserman, E. A., Chatlosh, D. L., & Neunaber, D. J. (1983). Perception of causal relations in humans: Factors affecting judgments of response-outcome contingencies under free-operant procedures. *Learning and Motivation, 14,* 406–432.

Woodward, J. (2003). *Making things happen: A theory of causal explanation.* Oxford, England: Oxford University Press.

11

Theory Unification and Graphical Models in Human Categorization

David Danks

Introduction

Disparate, mutually incompatible theories of categorization are widespread in cognitive psychology. Although there are various formal results connecting pairs of these theories, the primary research focus has been on particular empirical tests of people's favorite theories. This chapter steps back from the question of which single theory (if any) is "right" and focuses instead on understanding the intertheoretic relationships among these models. Specifically, I use the framework of probabilistic graphical models—a set of closely related computational and mathematical model types—to provide a common *lingua franca* for a significant subset of the extant psychological theories of categorization. This unified theoretical framework thus enables us to better understand the systematic relationships between the theories. In particular, we can gain a clearer picture of the overlaps and differences in the models' empirical predictions and underlying assumptions. Furthermore, expressing

these psychological models in a common framework helps to identify several natural generalizations of currently proposed models as well as currently underexplored alternative theories.

This graphical framework for representing various alternative models of categorization has a further, less-obvious, benefit. Categorization research suggests that at least some categories are defined or described by an underlying causal structure (Ahn, Marsh, Luhmann, & Lee, 2002; Hadjichristidis, Sloman, Stevenson, & Over, 2004; Rehder, 2003a, 2003b, chapter 12, this volume; Rehder & Burnett, in press; Rehder & Hastie, 2004). Lien and Cheng (2000) found that people preferentially attend to one category from a set of possible categories, possibly a large set, based on which category optimizes causal learning and inference. Categorization thus seems to rely (sometimes) on causal reasoning. At the same time, all causal learning theories currently available—whether associationist or computational, normative or descriptive—assume that people are trying to learn causal relationships among a fixed set of well-defined variables; in other words, all current theories of causal learning assume some fixed categorization of the world. We also know that causal learning and prediction can suffer significantly if we do not have the appropriate (in a still unclear sense) categories (e.g., Spirtes & Scheines, 2004).

These results and observations all point toward a deep interdependence between (at least parts of) the cognitive abilities of causal learning, inference, and prediction on the one hand and categorization and category generation/learning on the other hand. As a result, we should aim to find a common representational language for categorization and causation, so that clear questions can be simultaneously asked about both. Given the growing evidence (much of it described elsewhere in this book) that Bayesian networks—one particular type of probabilistic graphical model—underlie parts of causal cognition, this chapter's framing of categorization theories in terms of probabilistic graphical models provides an important early step toward understanding the relationships between causation and categorization.

In the next section, I introduce three different categorization theories, all of which have figured prominently in recent research. I then introduce two different types of probabilistic graphical models— Bayesian networks and Markov random fields—and describe how these categorization theories can be straightforwardly understood in terms of inference in particular instances of these model types. These formal equivalencies have various implications, both theoretical and experimental. Some of the implications are clear and immediate, including simple explanations for various model-fitting results in the experimental literature. Other implications are more suggestive. In particular, the mathematical equivalencies described suggest several substantive categorization theories that are, to my knowledge, novel to the psychological community (though not within machine learning). In the final substantive section, I focus on one particular model and (programmatically) describe how it could account for a range of intriguing phenomena in various domains.

Three Similarity Functions

The general problem of categorization is to classify an object as belonging to a particular group. This classification can then be used for many different purposes, including inference of unobserved properties of this individual based on common properties within the group. For example, when hiking, I frequently (and quickly) classify poorly seen animals in terms of their species. To make this judgment, I must attend to particular features and properties in the world, some of which I consciously attend to, others of which I do not. In addition, my classification will depend (in part) on the other possibilities I consider. The same critter that I classify as a "pika" in Colorado might be classified as a "squirrel" in Pennsylvania (since I know that there are no pikas in Pennsylvania). Once I have classified the animal, I then decide whether to be concerned about the animal based on what I know about that species (e.g., a mountain lion or a squirrel, respectively). This latter task is typically referred to as *feature inference* or *property induction*: determining the likelihood that some novel instance of this category will have a particular property. In this section, I describe three different psychological theories that aim to model the cognitive representations and algorithms underlying this process.

Although there are some exceptions, most psychological models of categorization separate categorization into two stages. For a novel instance X and some set of possible categories, I first determine how representative X is of each potential category. These "similarity ratings" are then integrated in a second step to produce a behavioral response, such as my categorization of this critter as a squirrel. In experimental settings, the relevant possible categories for a particular novel instance are invariably dictated by the cover story; in the real world, the possible categories are selected on some poorly understood bases, such as pragmatics or prior knowledge. Most psychological research has focused on the similarity rating function; relatively little empirical work has been done on the second-stage integration of similarity ratings (though see Wills, Reimers, Stewart, Suret, & McLaren, 2000).

More formally, suppose that we represent individuals in terms of n (binary or continuous[1]) features, denoted by $F_1, \ldots, F_n$. These features are presumably selected by some process outside the categorization theory itself. Throughout this chapter, I make the standard assumption for categorization theories that these features are well defined and well specified. Similarity ratings for a particular category are thus just functions on these n features. The standard second-stage integration rule for the similarity ratings is the Shepard-Luce rule (Shepard, 1957; Luce, 1963): If $S_C(X)$ denotes the similarity of X to category C and Q indexes over all of the potential categories, then $P(\text{Respond "C"} \mid X) = S_C(X) / \Sigma S_Q(X)$. That is, the probability of classifying X as a C is given by X's similarity to C divided by the sum of X's similarity to every possible category (including C). Bias parameters are occasionally used (Logan, 2004), as well as other rules with significant formal connections to the Shepard-Luce rule (Ashby & Maddox, 1993).

In this section, I focus on the similarity functions for standard versions of exemplar (e.g., Kruschke, 1992; Lamberts, 1998, 2000; Nosofsky, 1986; Nosofsky & Palmeri, 1997; Zaki, Nosofsky, Stanton, & Cohen, 2003; Logan, 2004, provides a good overview of recent work), prototype (e.g., Minda & Smith, 2001; J. D. Smith & Minda, 1998), and causal model (e.g., Rehder, 2003a, 2003b) theories of categorization. Substantial empirical support has been found for all three types of model, depending on the particular category, cover story, and task. Although these three similarity functions do not exhaust the space of proposed theories, they underlie the most widely discussed theories. In particular, this analysis includes Nosofsky's (1986) generalized context model (GCM; described in this section), which is the almost universal standard against which new psychological theories are judged. Rule-based categorization theories (including Nosofsky, Palmeri, & McKinley's 1994 RULEX (RULE-plus-eXception) model) are indirectly covered by this section because single-feature rules are equivalent to exemplar/prototype models in which we attend to only one feature. More direct analysis of rule-based models is rarely possible because simulations are almost always required to generate predictions for any realistic situation. Note that dynamic measures of categorization, including category learning dynamics and response time predictions, will not be considered here.[2]

The GCM (Nosofsky, 1986) provides the basis exemplar similarity function for numerous other categorization theories (e.g., Erickson & Kruschke, 1998; Kruschke, 1992; Lamberts, 1998, 2000; Nosofsky & Palmeri, 1997). The core intuition behind the GCM is that the similarity or typicality of some novel instance X for category A is given by the average distance in the "category space" between X and some subset of previously observed category instances (the exemplars). In other words, I represent a category in terms of exemplars (previous instances known to be in the category). A new object is similar just to the extent that it is "close" to the previous observations. For example, my category of bird is defined by remembered previous instances of birds (e.g., a robin, an ostrich, and so on). My category of squirrel is defined by previously observed squirrels.

And, some new critter is classified as a bird rather than a squirrel just when its average distance to the bird exemplars is less than its average distance to the squirrel exemplars (and those are the only two possibilities considered).

Mathematically, we define a GCM (i.e., exemplar-based) category A by a set of exemplars $E_1, \ldots, E_m$, each of which is a full specification of values for the n relevant features. Let $Y(i)$ denote Y's value for the ith feature. The similarity between novel instance X and a particular exemplar E_j is then given by $Sim(X, E_j) = \Pi_{i=1}^{n} \exp[-c \times \alpha_i |X(i) - E_j(i)|]$ where α_i is a salience parameter for the ith feature, and c is a global weighting parameter.[3] That is, the similarity is the product of (the exponential of) the distances between X and E_j on each of the feature dimensions. Note that, if the features are all binary valued, then the similarity is just the product of $\exp[-c \times \alpha_i]$ for each feature F_i on which X and E_j differ. The overall similarity rating of novel instance X for category A in the GCM—that is, the output of the first stage of the categorization model—is the weighted sum of similarities for all category exemplars: $GCM(X, A) = \Sigma_{i=1}^{m} W_j Sim(X, E_j)$. The similarity ratings for each GCM category, for example $GCM(X, A)$, $GCM(X, B)$, and so on, are then combined using the Shepard-Luce rule to generate behavioral responses. In addition, the set of exemplars (i.e., the category definition) can straightforwardly be used for inference about unobserved features of objects placed into the same category, such as, "This is a squirrel, and most of my squirrel exemplars were not aggressive; therefore, this squirrel probably won't be aggressive."

Prototype-based theories offer a different picture of categorization from exemplar-based models. Instead of basing the category on a set of previously remembered instances, categories are defined by prototypes—single objects—that encode a summary or average of people's experiences with the category; these prototypes need not correspond to any actual category instance (and almost never will). A novel instance's similarity to the category then depends on its distance in "category space" to that single prototype. The prototypical bird, for example, is not any bird that has ever been observed, although various actual birds (e.g., robins) are closer to it than others (e.g., ostriches). Mathematically, the prototype model (e.g., Minda & Smith, 2001; J. D. Smith & Minda, 1998; see also versions in Johansen & Palmeri, 2002; Olsson, Wennerholm, & Lyxzèn, 2004) is almost always a GCM model with only one exemplar for the category, but for which the exemplar might not have been observed.[4] However, this standard, simple proto-type model fails to do justice to the intuition behind prototype models. Information about interfeature connections or correlations is an important part of any summary of a series of observations, and this information cannot be expressed in the description of a single instance. The standard prototype similarity function requires some augmentation to capture the underlying intuition.

A simple way to incorporate interfeature correlations is with second-order features: features with a value that is entirely determined by the values of two first-order features. (Second-order features are only one way to capture correlations; a more powerful option is discussed in Applying the Graphical Model Equivalencies.) For example, it might be important that both F_2 and F_{17} occur, perhaps because of an observed correlation. In that case, we could define a second-order feature that "occurs" if and only if F_2 and F_{17} both occur.

Second-order features consisting of logical AND functions are common (e.g., Rehder, 2003a, 2003b) but are certainly not the only kind of second-order feature that could be introduced; Danks (under review) gives a general, mathematical definition of (plausible) second-order features. If we allow second-order features into a category prototype, then we have to adjust the first-order feature prototype similarity function (which was just the GCM similarity function).

For simplicity, I use $d(i, j)$ to denote the distance between (instance) X and (prototype) E along the feature composed of F_i and F_j (if $i = j$, then this is the appropriate first-order feature). Let α_{ii} be the salience of first-order feature F_i and α_{ij} be the salience of the second-order feature composed of F_i and F_j. ($\alpha_{ij} = 0$ implies no second-order feature for F_i and F_j.) Given this notation, the second-order prototype (SOP) category similarity function is $SOP(X, A) = \Pi_{i=1}^{n}\Pi_{j=1}^{n}\exp[-c \times \alpha_{ij}d(i,j)]$. That is, the similarity between some instance X and category A is the product of (the exponentials of) the distances between X and A for each feature, including second-order ones. Once X is categorized into a particular prototype-based category, feature inference is based entirely on the summary statistics encoded in the prototype itself. If the value of flies is 0.95 for the prototypical bird (i.e., 95% of birds summarized in the prototype could fly), then the probability that this bird flies is .95.

The third psychological theory of categorization is causal model theory (CMT; Rehder, 2003a,

2003b, chapter 12, this volume). CMT defines a category in terms of a particular causal structure among the features, including possibly unobserved features (e.g., an animal's "essence"). The underlying intuition about similarity is that a particular instance is more likely to be a member of category A just when its observed features respect the causal relationships among the various features. Thus, the similarity function for a category in CMT is the probability that a particular novel instance would be generated by that category's causal structure (perhaps multiplied by some scaling factor). For example, a particular object is similar to "bird" when the combination of observed features would likely be produced by something with the causal structure underlying the category of "bird".

Obviously, the mathematical details of CMT depend heavily on the particular representation of causal structures. Current versions of the theory model these structures using causal Bayesian networks (or causal Bayes nets). Details about causal Bayes nets are provided in the next section. For now, the relevant feature of a causal Bayes net is that it can be used to determine the probability of any particular combination of feature values given some causal structure; the CMT similarity function is directly proportional to that probability. That is, $CMT(X, A)$ is proportional to $P(X \mid M)$, where M is the causal Bayes net for the category. Given a particular categorization, the causal structure can straightforwardly be used for feature inference (Ahn et al., 2002; Hadjichristidis et al., 2004; Rehder & Burnett, in press; Rehder & Hastie, 2004).

In this section, I have left out several different types of categorization theories; perhaps most notably, I excluded connectionist models (e.g., Gluck & Bower, 1988; McClelland & Rogers, 2003; Rogers & McClelland, 2004). There is reason for their exclusion. Connectionist models have the ability to model or approximate large classes of input-output functions. However, to determine the exact space of similarity ratings that can be modeled by a particular network, we must perform significant simulations, except in specific networks that can model *all* possible input-output relationships. Without analytic results about the input-output relationships that can be modeled by a particular neural network structure, there is no definite target for expression in the framework of probabilistic graphical models. Moreover, it is notoriously difficult to determine which representations are contained in a connectionist model because much depends on the particular connection weights that emerge from a learning history. As a result, process equivalencies that directly map the symbolic operations of the connectionist model onto a graphical model are also not forthcoming.

Probabilistic Graphical Models

The central theoretical claim of this chapter is that the similarity functions from the preceding section can be usefully and interestingly described in the framework of probabilistic graphical models. In this section, I outline two types of graphical models—Bayesian networks and Markov random fields—and then describe how various similarity functions are proportional to calculating $P(X \mid Model)$, where $Model$ is one of these probabilistic graphical models. That is, the various psychological theories make different predictions because they assume different graphical model types: a subclass of Bayesian networks for exemplar-based theories (the GCM), causal Bayesian networks for CMT, and a subclass of Markov random fields for prototype-based theories. Thus, these diverse theories can be viewed (from a mathematical point of view) as different parameterizations of a single unified theory. These mathematical observations raise a range of psychological implications and questions; I take up those issues in the subsequent two sections. Because of space constraints, I have omitted the full proofs and technical details about the various equivalencies; the relevant mathematical specifics can all be found in my previous work (2004, under review).

In general, probabilistic graphical models provide a compact representation of a probability distribution by encoding various facts about independence and association in some type of graph. Strevens (chapter 15, this volume) explores the importance of (usefully) compact representations of probability and statistical facts. Bayes nets are one of the most popular probabilistic graphical models for such purposes; I here provide a brief introduction to the framework. Neapolitan, 2003; Pearl, 2000; Spirtes, Glymour, & Scheines, 1993/2001, and other chapters in this volume all provide more comprehensive introductions to Bayes nets'. It is important to realize that, despite the name, there is nothing intrinsically Bayesian about a Bayes net; the name is derived from the original uses of the framework. One can be, but need not be, a Bayesian about Bayes nets.

A Bayes net is defined relative to a set of variables; in our current setting, these are the observed features. One half of a Bayes net is a directed acyclic graph containing one node per variable/feature (see Figure 11-1). These nodes are (possibly) connected by directed edges (e.g., $F_i \rightarrow F_j$), indicating an asymmetric relationship. In "simple" Bayes nets, the asymmetric relationship is purely probabilistic. In contrast, a *causal* Bayes net (used by CMT as well as multiple psychological theories of causal reasoning) is a Bayes net in which the edges in the graph are provided a causal interpretation. If the causal interpretation is justified by background knowledge, then $X \rightarrow Y$ indicates that X is a direct cause of Y, where no particularly substantive theory of causation is presupposed (see Woodward, 2003, for one possibility). We use family terminology (e.g., parent or child) to describe the graphical relationships. The *acyclicity* property of the graph means that there is no (nontrivial) arrow-following path from a variable back to itself (e.g., there cannot be a path like $F_1 \rightarrow F_3 \rightarrow F_{17} \rightarrow F_1$ in the graph).

The other half of a Bayes net is a joint probability distribution (or density, for continuous variables) that specifies the probability of any particular set of feature values. When the causal interpretation is justified, the joint probability distribution encodes information about the quantitative causal dependencies among the variables. The two Bayes net components—the directed acyclic graph and the joint probability distribution—are connected by a Markov assumption: Every variable is probabilistically independent of its nondescendants conditional on its graphical parents. This assumption implies that the joint probability distribution (density) factors as $P(X) = \Pi_{i=1}^{n} P(F_i \mid pa(F_i))$, where $pa(F_i)$

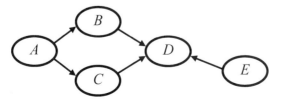

$$P(A, B, C, D, E) = P(A) \times P(B \mid A) \times P(C \mid A) \times P(D \mid B, C, E) \times P(E)$$

Figure 11-1 Example Bayesian network.

denotes the graphical parents of F_i. The components are also connected by the faithfulness assumption: The only probabilistic independencies are those predicted by the Markov assumption. The primary effect of the faithfulness assumption is to exclude the possibility of multiple pathways with effects that *exactly* cancel out (e.g., $X \to Y \to Z$ and $X \to Z$, but X and Z are unconditionally independent). Faithfulness is assumed (either explicitly or implicitly) by essentially every Bayes net learning algorithm. An example of a Bayes net is provided in Figure 11-1.

The causal model similarity function is already expressed using causal Bayes nets: The causal structure defining category A must be a causal Bayes net, and the similarity of X to A is given by the probability of X in the joint probability distribution represented by the causal Bayes net. That is, the similarity rating of X for category A is equal to $P(X)$, where the probability distribution is represented by a causal Bayes net.[5] Thus, this categorization theory can easily be represented in terms of inference for probabilistic graphical models.

Perhaps more surprisingly, Bayes nets can also be used to express the exemplar-based GCM similarity function. In general, the similarity functions used in these two-stage categorization theories are defined for all possible instances. Therefore, the pattern of those ratings for a particular category is proportional to some probability distribution over those same possible instances. So, for example, if we have some exemplar-based (i.e., GCM) category A with its corresponding similarity function $GCM(X, A)$, then there is necessarily some probability distribution $P(X)$ such that $GCM(X, A) \propto P(X)$ for all instances X [i.e., there is some constant K such that $GCM(X, A) = K \times P(X)$ for all X]. Hence, to establish an equivalence between the GCM and some probabilistic graphical model, it suffices to show that, for every probability distribution proportional to a possible set of ratings for a GCM category, there is a perfect map in some class of probabilistic graphical models and vice versa. A graphical model provides a perfect map of a probability distribution if and only if the graph implies (by Markov and faithfulness) all and only the probabilistic independencies that occur in that distribution. In general, the (high-level) strategy for expressing categorization theories in terms of probabilistic graphical models is as follows: Determine the patterns that could possibly be produced by (normalized) similarity functions and then find a set of probabilistic graphical models that perfectly represent exactly those patterns.

In the case of the exemplar-based GCM, consider a Bayes net with the directed acyclic graph in Figure 11-2. E is an unobserved variable with a number of values that depends on the category modeled. By the Markov assumption, the joint probability distribution for this Bayes net factors into $P(E, F_1, \ldots, F_n) = P(E) \times P(F_1 \mid E) \times \ldots \times P(F_n \mid E)$. The structure of this model is similar to the oft-used naïve Bayes models of machine learning classification problems, although the role and interpretation of the (unobserved) common cause is different in this situation.

Regardless of whether the features are binary (e.g., either present or absent) or continuous (e.g., height), every GCM category is proportional to a probability distribution over the F_i's that has a perfect map given by a Bayes net[6] with this graph. That is, for every GCM category, there is a Bayes net with the Figure 11-2 graph and associated probability distribution such that $GCM(X, A) \propto P(X)$ for every possible instance X over features $F_1, \ldots, F_n$. The converse of this claim holds with a slight addition: For every probability distribution over the observed F_i's for a Bayes net with the Figure 11-2 graph *and* a "regularity" constraint on the form of the $P(F_i \mid E)$ terms, there is a GCM category with ratings that are proportional to that distribution. The exact regularity constraint depends on whether the features are binary or continuous, but neither constraint is particularly strong.[7] Because similarity ratings are determined only up to a choice of scale, we can conclude that GCM categories and Bayes nets with a Figure 11-2 graph (plus regularity constraint) describe exactly the same set of similarity ratings; any responses that can be fit to one model can be fit to the other.

In contrast, there is no corresponding equivalence between Bayes nets and prototype-based categorization models with second-order features. These two types of models are fundamentally different in that

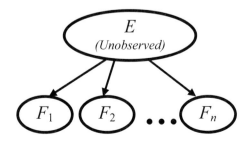

FIGURE 11-2 Bayesian network analogue for the generalized context model.

the intervariable connections in a Bayes net are asymmetric (whether in a probabilistic or causal sense), and the second-order features are symmetric. Hence, we need a probabilistic graphical model with *undirected* edges between the features to indicate symmetric connections. This model type is called a *Markov random field* (see, e.g., Darroch, Lauritzen, & Speed, 1980; Lauritzen, 1996, for more technical introductions).

As with Bayes nets, Markov random fields are defined only relative to a set of variables (features) and are composed of a joint probability distribution (density) and a graph. In contrast with a Bayes net, though, a Markov random field graph contains undirected edges between the nodes (see Figure 11-3). Roughly speaking, two features connected by an edge in the graph implies that there is a probabilistic dependence between those features' values, but no explanation of the correlation is given or presumed (and so there is no asymmetry between the variables).

The graph and probability distribution in the Markov random field are connected by a Markov assumption: The probability of any feature value is dependent only on its graphical neighbors. So, for example, in Figure 11-3, $P(A)$ depends only on B and C; A is probabilistically independent of D and E conditional on B and C. The Markov assumption implies that the joint probability distribution can be factored into the product of functions (called *clique potentials*) over the maximal cliques in the undirected graph. A *graphical clique* is any set of nodes for which every pair is connected by an edge, and a clique is *maximal* if adding any other variable renders it no longer a clique. Thus, the Markov assumption for a Markov random field G implies that, if the maximal cliques in G are denoted by $C_1, \ldots, C_q$, then we can express the probability of some novel instance X as $P(X|G) = \frac{1}{Z} \prod_{i=1}^{n} g_i(X)$, where $g_i(X)$ depends only on the values of variables in C_i (and Z is a normalization constant). Figure 11-3 provides an example of a Markov random field, including both the graph and

the factorization of the joint probability distribution into clique potentials.

As with Bayes nets and exemplar-based models, we can successfully apply the same high-level strategy to connect Markov random fields and prototype-based models. The patterns of ratings produced by prototype-based similarity functions can be understood as probability distributions, and we can represent that space of probability distributions in terms of Markov random fields. More specifically, for a particular (second-order feature) prototype-based category, its Markov random field counterpart contains an edge between two nodes (features) just when there is a second-order feature for those two. Then, for every possible pattern of similarity ratings, there is a corresponding (proportional) probability distribution that has a perfect map given by the category's Markov random field counterpart. And, for every probability distribution with a Markov random field perfect map (with clique potentials that satisfy a further, relatively weak, regularity constraint), there is a corresponding prototype-based category with similarity ratings that are proportional to the distribution. Just as GCM categories are equivalent to (probability distributions with perfect maps given by) Bayes nets with the Figure 11-2 graph, (second-order) prototype-based categories are equivalent to (the probability distributions for) a subset of Markov random fields.

In summary, all three types of similarity functions (GCM, SOP, and causal model) can be expressed (up to a scaling parameter) as computations of $P(X \mid Model)$, where the differential theory predictions arise from different assumptions about the underlying graphical model. The precise psychological model $\leftrightarrow$ graphical model relationships are

GCM rating for $X \leftrightarrow P(X \mid$ Bayes net with Figure 11-2 graph and constraint)

SOP rating for $X \leftrightarrow P(X \mid$ Markov random fields with a constraint)

Causal model rating for $X \leftrightarrow P(X \mid$ Causal Bayes net)

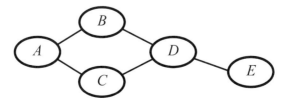

$$P(A, B, C, D, E) = G_1(A, B) \times G_2(A, C) \times G_3(B, D) \times G_4(C, D) \times G_5(D, E)$$

FIGURE 11-3 Example Markov random field.

The representation of category similarity functions as probability distributions has been explored by Myung (1994), Ashby and Alfonso-Reese (1995), and Rosseel (2002). In contrast to that work, the results detailed here use the framework of probabilistic graphical models, which allow us to extend the formal results to a broader class of prototype theories, as well as to include CMT. In related research, Nosofsky (1990) and Ashby and Maddox (1993) pursued a more direct strategy and found conditions in which exemplar models could be directly transformed into prototype models and vice versa without the framework of probability theory or graphical models (see also Barsalou, 1990). Although important for understanding those two theory types, the direct results are not readily extensible to other psychological theories (e.g., CMT) because they do not situate the theories in a more general framework.

With these equivalencies in hand, I now turn to their implications. The next two sections demonstrate several pragmatic uses of the representation of these models as probabilistic graphical models, including better understanding of existing experimental results, suggestions for novel experiments, and more speculatively, the possibility of interesting generalizations of existing psychological theories.

Applying the Graphical Model Equivalencies

The most obvious application of these equivalencies is to facilitate rapid determination of the conditions in which the categorization theories make differential predictions, thus enabling us both to explain previous experimental results and to construct appropriate novel experiments. In particular, if the two probabilistic graphical model types can perfectly represent different probability distributions and people's behavioral responses approximate the observed probability distribution for some category, then we can determine analytically whether some experiment is likely able to discriminate between the SOP (= Markov random field) and causal model (= causal Bayes net) theories. In fact, the expressive potentials of Bayes nets and Markov random fields overlap. That is, there are probability distributions that can be represented perfectly by a Markov random field but not a Bayes net and vice versa. There are also probability distributions (e.g., those equivalent to first-order prototype-based similarity functions) that can be represented perfectly by both Bayes nets and Markov random fields, as well as some that cannot be represented perfectly by models from either framework.

As a concrete example, there is no Bayes net that perfectly represents a probability distribution with the (Markov random field) factorization given in Figure 11-3. Thus, if Figure 11-3 describes the actual underlying category structure (i.e., the probability that any novel instance comes from that category), then a categorizer using causal models would not be able to learn the category structure perfectly. Similarly, there is no Markov random field that perfectly represents a probability distribution with the (Bayes net) factorization in Figure 11-1, so a categorizer using SOP-based categories would not be able to learn that category accurately. Finally, a simple category structure consisting of uncorrelated features can be equally well represented by models from both frameworks, so no experiment based on such categories will be able to distinguish between causal model- and SOP-based categorization (i.e., the psychological theories should have equally good model fits).

We can also apply this analysis to published—not just hypothetical—experiments. Rehder's (2003a) common-cause condition uses a category probability distribution that can be equally well represented by a Bayes net (= causal model) and a Markov random field (= SOP). As predicted, he found no model fit difference between the corresponding psychological theories (see Rehder's Table 5, p. 729). In contrast, Rehder's common-effect condition used a probability distribution that can be represented by Bayes nets but not Markov random fields. Thus, the two psychological theories should be distinguishable by that experiment: SOP categorizers will do poorly, and causal model categorizers should do well. Alternately, if we assume that people can learn a wide range of category structures, then we should expect the SOP theory to have a significantly worse model fit than the CMT. The subsequent data analysis found exactly that significant model-fit difference in favor of CMT, which can represent the underlying probability distribution (see Rehder's Table 5, p. 729). (See also Rehder's Experiment 3 in chapter 12, this volume, for further evidence of an asymmetry between common-cause and common-effect networks.)

Finally, we can use this analysis to design experiments to push the outer boundaries of human category learning. As noted, there are probability distributions, and so categories, that none of the psychological theories can completely model. Correct theoretical predictions of cognitive failures (in this case, failure to represent the category correctly) are typically thought to constitute stronger evidence for a theory than predictions that people will behave close to optimally. Thus, a natural way to separate these three theory types is to present individuals with categories with a structure that cannot be mapped onto any of these representations without loss of information. In particular, we want to find categories for which each theory picks out different aspects of the structure, so they predict different patterns of failure. Chain graphs are probabilistic graphical models that use both directed and undirected edges (further discussed in the next section), and there are perfect map chain graphs for probability distributions with no Markov random field or Bayes net perfect map. One such graph is $F_1 \rightarrow F_2 - F_3 \leftarrow F_4$.[8] All three psychological theories predict that people will make significant, systematic, predictable errors when presented with a category with this structure, and those errors are predictable using the probabilistic graphical model equivalencies described here. The differential error predictions can then be used to determine better which theory best describes an individual's categorization process. To my knowledge, no such experiment appears in the literature (though see Danks, 2006).

In addition to methodological implications, these equivalencies suggest natural generalizations of existing psychological theories. The exemplar-based and SOP-based similarity functions are equivalent with only subclasses of Bayes nets with Figure 11-2 graphs and Markov random fields, respectively. In both cases, the equivalent graphical models have constraints on the probability distribution beyond those implied by the graphical model. From the probabilistic graphical model point of view, these additional constraints seem arbitrary, although they have a natural justification in terms of ensuring computational tractability.

Setting aside computational issues, though, we might naturally consider generalizing the GCM to include patterns of similarity ratings that are proportional to any probability distribution with a perfect map Bayes net with a Figure 11-2 graph. This generalization has a straightforward interpretation within the GCM framework: It corresponds to allowing exemplar-dependent feature saliences in the similarity function. Similarly, we can generalize the SOP model to include any probability distribution with an arbitrary Markov random field perfect map. This generalization would

significantly extend the scope of that theory while retaining the basic intuition of prototype theories that the category representation is a summary of the observed category instances. Importantly, both of these generalizations remain bounded in explanatory power; there are experiments and patterns of similarity ratings, such as Rehder's (2003a) common-effect condition, that can distinguish these generalizations from one another.

Finally, these equivalencies suggest alternate responses to two existing problems for categorization theories: empirical support for (seemingly) inconsistent theories and (apparent) shifts in category structure during learning. The first problem is that there is significant empirical evidence supporting all three of these psychological similarity ratings, depending on the particular domain, presentation format, contrast class, and so on. One response to this fact has been to argue that there are distinct cognitive systems for different categorization strategies (e.g., exemplar vs. rule based), and that contextual factors and background knowledge determine which system is activated. This idea is supported by evidence from reaction time (Allen & Brooks, 1991) and neuroimaging (Grossman et al., 2002; Patalano, Smith, Jonides, & Koeppe, 2001; E. E. Smith, Patalano, & Jonides, 1998) studies (see also Machery, in press). In a similar vein, Ashby and his colleagues have argued that different neural systems underlie implicit and explicit category learning, which are distinguished by whether participants can give a simple, verbal rule to differentiate the categories (Ashby, Alfonso-Reese, Turken, & Waldron, 1998; Ashby & Waldron, 2000; Waldron & Ashby, 2001). These proposals all share the underlying idea that there are multiple processing systems in the brain responsible for the different types of categories.

The equivalencies described here suggest a different response to the range of empirical supports: The differential behaviors (perhaps) arise from differing parameterizations of a common categorization algorithm. That is, these distinct psychological theories might correspond to the same operation applied to three different representations (i.e., types of graphs) rather than distinct cognitive mechanisms. There might be only one process in which similarity ratings are based on $P(X \mid Model)$ but in which the particular category model type depends on factors such as experiential history, context, other background knowledge, and so on. Differential behavior arises from different inputs to the same process rather than fundamentally different processes. If the cognitive representation of the category structure is a Bayes net with a Figure 11-2 graph, the person will exhibit GCM category behavior. If the representation is a suitable Markov random field or causal Bayes net, categorizations will be best understood using SOP or CMT, respectively. Of course, this suggestion is not intended to demonstrate that there cannot possibly be multiple processes; rather, it is intended to defeat the (too quick) inference from "support for multiple theories" to "multiple cognitive processes must exist."

Understanding the different categorization theories in terms of probability calculations using different representations also provides a straightforward solution to the problem of integrating similarity ratings of categories with different structures. Regardless of category structure, all of the similarity ratings are on the same scale and have a clear interpretation, so they can easily be integrated into a single, coherent behavioral response. In contrast, the multiple systems hypothesis must provide some further account (perhaps in terms of probabilities) to explain how similarity judgments from entirely distinct cognitive processes are integrated to produce well-defined categorization judgments.

Finally, the underlying category structure type sometimes seems to change in response to repeated exposure to category examples (Johansen & Palmeri, 2002; J. D. Smith & Minda, 1998). For example, I might initially represent a category using a prototype, but shift to using an exemplar representation (or vice versa). J. D. Smith and Minda (1998) found that exemplar-based (specifically, GCM) structures were predominant throughout learning of small, poorly differentiated categories. During the learning of larger, more clearly delineated categories, however, there seemed to be a shift from prototype-based to exemplar-based category structures (see also Minda & Smith, 2001; Zaki et al., 2003; and the overfitting worries of Olsson et al., 2004). Johansen and Palmeri (2002) found a similar shift toward exemplar models during learning, although rule-based categories rather than prototype-based ones were more prevalent in early stages of their experiments. Rehder (chapter 12, this volume) suggests other trajectories for shifts in underlying category structure type.

The common framework of graphical models enables us to articulate clearly both theoretical and experimental questions about these phenomena. An immediate question that arises in these analyses centers on representational power. The experimental results were analyzed by determining model fits for similarity responses at different times, and so the conclusions about likely shifts in category structure should be qualified by the precise model name. In particular, all of these analyses used only first-order prototype models; that is, they assumed that the category was represented by a single (perhaps unobserved) instance. The representational power of first-order prototype models is easily expressed in graphical model terms: They can only represent probability distributions with perfect maps that are Markov random fields with no edges between features and so no interfeature correlations. The GCM exemplar model, by contrast, can represent interfeature correlations, although (for plausible instances) only of a certain type. As described, the shifts from (apparent) prototype-based to (apparent) exemplar-based structures were more pronounced for categories with correlated features. Thus, given the significantly weaker representational power of first-order prototype models, it is entirely conceivable that these shifts in best-fitting model type are because of this power imbalance rather than actual cognitive changes. Reanalysis with a more sophisticated prototype model, perhaps one based on arbitrary Markov random fields, is warranted.

Some Speculations about Human Categorization

The previous sections focused on the equivalencies between three common similarity functions and computing $P(X \mid Category)$, where the theories differ about the exact form of $Category$. These similarity ratings are the first stage in a two-stage process. The second stage is typically the Shepard-Luce rule: The probability of responding with category C for novel instance X is the similarity rating between C and X divided by the sum of similarity ratings for all other considered categories. Mathematically, if similarity ratings correspond to $P(X \mid Category)$, then use of the Shepard-Luce rule corresponds to computing $P(Category \mid X)$ if every category under consideration is equiprobable.[9] Use of bias parameters in the Shepard-Luce rule (as in Logan, 2004) then corresponds to allowing the possible categories to have different base rates. Thus, the complete (i.e., two-stage) theories solve arguably the central problem for categorization: Given observations of a novel object's features, determine the probability that it falls in one or another category.

Moreover, the two stages of these theories are intended quite seriously: They are supposed to describe cognitively separable steps in categorization. So, for example, some experiments aim to obtain judgments of an item's similarity to a particular category without invoking actual categorization judgments (e.g., Rehder, 2003a, although Barsalou, 1985, argues that many other factors enter into similarity ratings). Alternately, we might suppose that people's conscious access to their categorization judgments is limited to the final output, in particular, $P(Category \mid X)$, where Category can be one of several probabilistic graphical models, including a Bayes net with a Figure 11-2 graph, a Markov random field, or a causal Bayes net.[10] That is, rather than (explicitly) categorizing in two distinct stages, people directly determine the category probability given the instance. The most notable previous example of categorization based directly on $P(Category \mid X)$ is Anderson's (1991) rational analysis model. However, Anderson's model and subsequent extensions are not based on graphical models and so are not considered here.

The central difference between the one- and two-stage views of categorization lies in the requirement of a contrast category to compute anything in the first view; no contrast category is required to compute the similarity ratings of the second view. Any computation of $P(Category \mid X)$—whether by one or two stages—presupposes that there is at least one alternative category, or else the probability is just one (because Category is the only possibility). In contrast, no information about any alternative categories is required to compute $P(X \mid Category)$, which is all that is required for the first stage of the two-stage process. If categorization is really a one-stage process (i.e., the only conscious access is to the probability of the category given the instance, rather than intermediate similarity ratings), then one must explain the source of people's similarity ratings in experimental settings. The most natural explanation is that similarity ratings are actually categorization judgments with some implicitly assumed contrast class. That is, judgments of the typicality of a novel instance X for some category A are not actually similarity ratings but rather are people's judgments of $P(A \mid X)$ relative to an implicit contrast category not-A.

If people's similarity judgments are really categorization judgments, then they should be influenced by variations in the contrast class structure and base rate. One experimental test to distinguish one- from two-

stage views would be to present people with a novel category and instances of that category, all with an explicit contrast class (i.e., instances not in the novel category are definitely in the contrast class). We could then ask for ratings of the typicality of novel instances for the target category, in which we vary between conditions either the structure or the base rate of the contrast category but not of the target category. The central prediction in this proposed experiment is as follows: If categorization is (consciously) a one-stage process, then there should be a statistically significant difference between similarity ratings in the conditions; if categorization is (consciously) a two-stage process, then there should be no such difference. Even though the structure of category A does not change, $P(A \mid X)$ does change between conditions because of changes in the structure/base rate of the contrast class. The precise change will depend on the details of the contrast category structures (or base rates) but can be determined quantitatively. Importantly, note that this proposed experiment tests stability of *representativeness* (or similarity) judgments of some novel instance for a category and not categorization judgments. Both views agree that participants' categorization judgments should vary as the contrast class structure or base rate vary; the disagreement is about whether the contrast class matters for the typicality ratings.

Das-Smaal and De Swart (1986) performed an experiment similar in structure to this proposed one and found limited evidence that representativeness (similarity) ratings for stimuli change depending on the contrast class. Unfortunately, they did not obtain typicality ratings for every possible combination of features, so we cannot use their experiment as even a first step toward development of a formal model. If these results can be suitably replicated and extended, then additional experiments can aim to determine (a) whether people have an implicit contrast class if not given an explicit one and (b) the structure of the implicit contrast class, if it exists.

The reason for exploring categorization as a one-stage process is because it opens a range of mathematical possibilities. The one-stage view draws attention to the importance of incorporating multiple potential categories into a single mathematical/representational structure (because categories are never considered in isolation). As in the existing psychological theories, categories in the one-stage theory can be represented as probabilistic graphical models. We can incorporate multiple probabilistic graphical models into the same

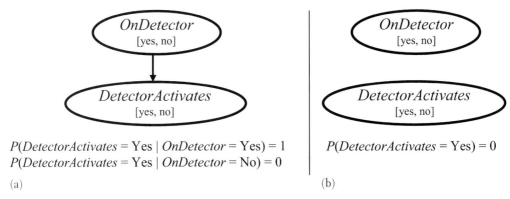

$P(DetectorActivates = \text{Yes} \mid OnDetector = \text{Yes}) = 1$
$P(DetectorActivates = \text{Yes} \mid OnDetector = \text{No}) = 0$

(a)

$P(DetectorActivates = \text{Yes}) = 0$

(b)

FIGURE 11-4 (a) Causal category structure for blickets; (b) causal category structure for not-blickets.

structure by the use of a (qualitatively stated) theorem: There is no mathematical difference between determining which of several probabilistic graphical models is most probable and determining the most probable value of a new variable (*Category*) that ranges over the possible categories and is a graphical parent of the relevant features.

That is, given several probabilistic graphical models, there is a mathematically equivalent structure with a new, unobserved *Category* variable that acts as a switch to produce the appropriate probabilistic graphical model depending on which category is actual. In the Bayes net literature, this unobserved variable is a context variable for a model with context-specific independence (CSI; see Boutilier, Friedman, Goldszmidt, & Koller, 1996; Poole & Zhang, 2003; Zhang & Poole, 1999). Thus, instead of modeling categorization as calculations of $P(\text{Category } A \mid X)$, we can equivalently model it as calculations of $P(CATEG = A \mid X)$ for a context variable $CATEG$ with values that are the various mutually exclusive possible categories. This context variable is similar to the "Being a . . ." variables of Strevens's (2000) minimal essentialism: The context (category) determines the structure (e.g., causal laws)

for an individual, but no claims are made about how the context (category) does so.

As an example of these two ways of thinking about the same (theoretical, mathematical) process, consider the category of blicket studied by Gopnik and her colleagues (e.g., Gopnik et al., 2004). Blickets are objects that cause a particular machine (a blicket detector) to light up and play music. Thus, the category structure for blickets is represented as a causal Bayes net (because it is a causal model) and is given in the left-hand side of Figure 11-4. The (possibly implicit) contrast class of *not*-blickets are all of the things that fail to activate the detector; that category's causal structure is given in the right-hand side of Figure 11-4. The equivalent CSI causal Bayes net is given in Figure 11-5, in which the probability of *DetectorActivates* only depends on the value of *OnDetector* if the context node *Category* has the value blicket. Purely as a visual aid, context variables will be indicated by a dashed circle. The theoretical equivalence here implies that there is no mathematical difference between calculating $P(\text{Left-hand structure} \mid X)$ in Figure 11-4 and $P(\text{Category} = \text{Blicket} \mid X)$ in Figure 11-5.

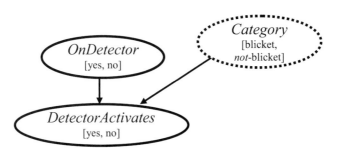

FIGURE 11-5 CSI Bayesian network for the blicket category.

The story gets a bit more complicated when we allow for the possibility that the different categories could have different underlying structures. In the above example, we could represent both category structures as causal Bayes nets. Suppose instead that one category structure is represented by a Markov random field (an SOP-based category) and the other by a Bayes net (perhaps with a Figure 11-2 graph). There is a third type of probabilistic graphical model—chain graphs—that contains both directed and undirected edges (Andersson, Madigan, & Perlman, 1996; Lauritzen & Richardson, 2002; Lauritzen & Wermuth, 1989; Richardson, 1998). The precise interpretation of chain graphs with mixtures of edge types is the subject of current research (Lauritzen & Richardson, 2002), but Markov random fields and Bayes nets emerge as special cases in which either all of the edges are undirected or all are directed. Thus, all of the probabilistic graphical models used in this chapter can themselves be unified in a single framework, and that framework can also exploit the CSI equivalence between multiple structures and a single structure with a context variable.

This picture opens intriguing possibilities for developing integrated hierarchies of multiple category types (when the categories actually are hierarchical; see Malt & Johnson, 1992, and Sloman, 1998, for doubts about this condition).[11] Suppose we have a set of mutually exclusive categories (e.g., dog, cat, mouse, human, etc.) that are complete relative to some supercategory (e.g., mammal), so every instance of the supercategory can be placed into exactly one of the target categories. Then, the context (category) variable for that set corresponds to the supercategory and will be a graphical parent of any feature that is part of one of the category models. Because the GCM, prototype, and causal model categories can all be represented as probabilistic graphical models, a single CSI chain graph model can account for the possibility that these categories do not have the same structure. No special difficulties arise if, for example, dog is a causal model category, cat is an SOP (i.e., Markov random field) category, and human is an exemplar-based GCM (i.e., Bayes net with a Figure 11-2 graph) category. The resulting single graphical structure might look something like Figure 11-6. (Recall that context variables are indicated by a dashed circle for ease of presentation.) Note the undirected edges between features, indicating the association between # of Legs and Vocalization in the categories.

Representing mutually exclusive categories in a single graph provides one picture of how multiple categories could be cognitively represented in a single category structure. Moreover, because this unified model does not require us to choose between the various psychological theories, it inherits their explanatory power (although no account has been given of why a category is represented using a particular structure). The proposal here is thus consistent with previous data supporting these psychological theories. In addition, this unified model provides a plausible mechanism for including one type of prior knowledge about contrast class. Background knowledge about a situation (e.g., I am on land, so all possible animals must be capable of living on land) is equivalent to conditioning on one or more features prior to categorization, which will change the prior distribution of category probabilities. In this example, $P(Category = Whale)$ in Figure 11-6 will be low, even before I observe any features of a particular instance.

Further hierarchies of categories can be straightforwardly modeled in this theory by introducing a node that is a parent (or neighbor) of the Category node. The values of this new variable will range over the superclass encoded in Category, as well as the categories that

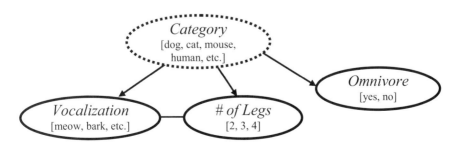

FIGURE 11-6 One-layer category structure.

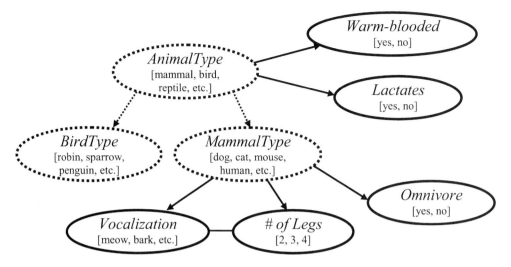

FIGURE 11-7 Multilayer category structure.

are complete and mutually exclusive for the superclass level of the hierarchy. The new variable (e.g., *AnimalType* in Figure 11-7) is the CSI context variable for its children (e.g., *BirdType*, *MammalType*, etc.). Moreover, because the superclass variable (e.g., *AnimalType*) is itself a node, it can have various observed features as its (graphical) children, in addition to other context variables. One plausible resulting model structure is shown in Figure 11-7, in which context variable names have been made more descriptive, and obviously not all relevant variables are included. (Intercontext connections are indicated by dashed edges. As with the dashed circles for context variables, this notation is intended purely as a visual aid.)

By attaching features to the superclass in addition to the subclass, we can arguably explain two contrasting phenomena: some properties (e.g., lactation) are more readily identified with the superclass (mammal) than with any of the subclasses (e.g., dog); while the presence of those features nevertheless increases the likelihood of the subclasses. These two phenomena can only be explained by a framework in which features can be attached (in some sense) directly to the superclass, and there are meaningful connections between the superclass and the subclasses. In this model, *Lactates* is directly associated with *AnimalType* = Mammal rather than any specific mammal, but the *Lactates* = Yes observation increases the probability that *AnimalType* = Mammal, thereby increasing the (unconditional) probability that the individual has each possible *MammalType*. Thus, in this (potential)

unified framework, we have precise, mathematically well specified representations of hierarchies of multiple specific types of category structure in which no particular level of the hierarchy is privileged a priori. Of course, the empirical adequacy of this admittedly quite complicated unified framework remains a substantial open question.

Conclusion

The central theoretical results of this chapter provide a common language for several major psychological theories of categorization: GCMs as Bayesian networks with a particular graphical structure, SOP models as Markov random fields, and causal model categories as causal Bayesian networks. The expression of these theories as probabilistic graphical models opens up a number of methodological and theoretical possibilities. We can readily determine why some experimental designs are unable to distinguish among these theories on the basis of model fits and so design better, more discriminating experiments. In particular, we can construct category structures that cannot be represented perfectly by any of the psychological theories to determine which theory (if any) correctly predicts people's systematic errors. These equivalencies also point toward natural generalizations of the psychological theories, corresponding to elimination of various nongraphical constraints on the probability distributions. These generalizations can easily be tested; for example, we could examine people's performance on categories that can be modeled by an arbitrary Markov random field but not one that corresponds to an SOP model. Moreover, this work suggests a different understanding of the categorization process and not just similarity ratings.

Categorization judgments in these psychological theories all correspond to calculating $P(Category \mid$ Novel instance $X)$ when every considered category is equiprobable via a two-stage process: Calculate the similarity ratings [i.e., $P(X \mid Category)$ for each category] and then use the Shepard-Luce choice rule to get $P(Category \mid X)$. In contrast, we can consider a categorization theory that directly computes $P(Category \mid X)$ without explicitly computing similarity ratings as an intermediate step. Experimental elicitations of similarity ratings are, on this model, just categorization judgments relative to an implicit, unspecified contrast class. There is some preliminary evidence for the idea that all judgments, even typicality ones, are relative to a contrast class. However, significantly more experimental investigation is required. Finally, we can represent all of these probabilistic graphical models as chain graphs and place them into a single graphical model hierarchy by exploiting various context-specific independencies. This process unifies multiple category types into a single, coherent graphical structure.

The results described here matter for more than just categorization research. There is clearly a close interdependence between (at least some) causal cognition and (some) categorization. Causal beliefs and learning shape some of our categorization decisions, including categorizing some novel object and selecting or learning categories for representing the world. In the other direction, our causal learning and decision making depend on both the ways in which we categorize our world and the properties we infer about novel objects based on their category membership. Despite these connections, much of the research in the two fields, whether psychological, philosophical, or computational, has essentially ignored the importance of the other. Frequently, substantial allusions are made to the importance of the other field, but then the other field plays no theoretical or experimental role. Given the scope of these cognitive processes, this has been a reasonable research strategy: At least initially, we should divide and conquer. A range of recent psychological and theoretical research has started to shift this trend, but a common mathematical framework is needed for the two domains. The equivalencies detailed in this chapter thus provide an important early step for the integration of research on categorization and causation: the representation of a major component of categorization theories as probabilistic graphical models, which are the emerging consensus framework for modeling large portions of causal learning and inference.

ACKNOWLEDGMENTS   This chapter has been greatly influenced by conversations with Bob Rehder and Chris Hitchcock. Clark Glymour, Alison Gopnik, Edouard Machery, and Laura Schulz all provided valuable comments on earlier drafts. Thanks also to the audience at the February 2004 CASBS (Center for Advanced Study in the Behavioral Sciences) workshop on causation and categorization for their insightful questions and comments. I was partially supported by grants from the National Aeronautics and Space Administration and the Office of Naval Research.

References

Ahn, W.-K., Marsh, J. K., Luhmann, C. C., & Lee, K. (2002). Effect of theory-based feature correlations on typicality judgments. *Memory & Cognition, 30,* 107–118.

Allen, S. W., & Brooks, L. R. (1991). Specializing the operation of an explicit rule. *Journal of Experimental Psychology: General, 120,* 3–19.

Anderson, J. R. (1991). The adaptive nature of human categorization. *Psychological Review, 98,* 409–429.

Andersson, S. A., Madigan, D., & Perlman, M. D. (1996). An alternative Markov property for chain graphs. In F. V. Jensen & E. Horvitz (Eds.), *Proceedings of the 12th Conference on Uncertainty in Artificial Intelligence* (pp. 40–48). San Francisco: Morgan Kaufmann.

Ashby, F. G., & Alfonso-Reese, L. A. (1995). Categorization as probability density estimation. *Journal of Mathematical Psychology, 39,* 216–233.

Ashby, F. G., Alfonso-Reese, L. A., Turken, A. U., & Waldron, E. M. (1998). A neuropsychological theory of multiple systems in category learning. *Psychological Review, 105,* 442–481.

Ashby, F. G., & Maddox, W. T. (1993). Relations between prototype, exemplar, and decision bound models of categorization. *Journal of Mathematical Psychology, 37,* 372–400.

Ashby, F. G., & Waldron, E. M. (2000). The neuropsychological bases of category learning. *Current Directions in Psychological Science, 9,* 10–14.

Barsalou, L. W. (1985). Ideals, central tendency, and frequency of instantiation as determinants of graded structure in categories. *Journal of Experimental Psychology: Learning, Memory, and Cognition, 11,* 629–654.

Barsalou, L. W. (1990). On the indistinguishability of exemplar memory and abstraction in category representation. In T. K. Srull & R. S. Wyer (Eds.), *Advances in social cognition: Vol. 3: Content and process specificity in the effects of prior experiences* (pp. 61–88). Hillsdale, NJ: Erlbaum.

Boutilier, C., Friedman, N., Goldszmidt, M., & Koller, D. (1996). Context-specific independence in Bayesian networks. In F. V. Jensen & E. Horvitz (Eds.), *Proceedings of the 12th annual Conference on Uncertainty in Artificial Intelligence* (pp. 115–123). San Francisco: Morgan Kaufmann.

Danks, D. (2004). *Psychological theories of categorization as probabilistic models* (Technical Rep. CMU-PHIL-149). Pittsburgh, PA: Carnegie Mellon University, Department of Philosophy.

Danks, D. (2006) (Not) learning a complex (but learnable) category. In R. Sun & N. Miyake (Eds.), *Proceedings of the 28th Annual Meeting of the Cognitive Science Society* (pp. 1186–1191). Mahwah, NJ: Lawrence Erlbaum Associates.

Danks, D. (under review). Psychological theories of categorization as probabilistic graphical models. Manuscript submitted for publication.

Darroch, J. N., Lauritzen, S. L., & Speed, T. P. (1980). Markov fields and log-linear interaction models for contingency tables. *Annals of Statistics, 8,* 522–539.

Das-Smaal, E. A., & De Swart, J. H. (1986). Effects of contrasting category, conjoint frequency and typicality on categorization. *Acta Psychologica, 62,* 15–40.

Erickson, M. A., & Kruschke, J. K. (1998). Rules and exemplars in category learning. *Journal of Experimental Psychology: General, 127,* 107–140.

Gluck, M. A., & Bower, G. H. (1988). From conditioning to category learning: An adaptive network model. *Journal of Experimental Psychology: General, 117,* 227–247.

Gopnik, A., Glymour, C., Sobel, D. M., Schulz, L. E., Kushnir, T., & Danks, D. (2004). A theory of causal learning in children: Causal maps and Bayes nets. *Psychological Review, 111,* 3–32.

Grossman, M., Smith, E. E., Koenig, P., Glosser, G., DeVita, C., Moore, P., et al. (2002). The neural basis for categorization in semantic memory. *NeuroImage, 17,* 1549–1561.

Hadjichristidis, C., Sloman, S., Stevenson, R., & Over, D. (2004). Feature centrality and property induction. *Cognitive Science, 28,* 45–74.

Johansen, M. K., & Palmeri, T. J. (2002). Are there representational shifts during category learning? *Cognitive Psychology, 45,* 482–553.

Kruschke, J. K. (1992). ALCOVE: An exemplar-based connectionist model of category learning. *Psychological Review, 99,* 22–44.

Lamberts, K. (1998). The time course of categorization. *Journal of Experimental Psychology: Learning, Memory, and Cognition, 24,* 695–711.

Lamberts, K. (2000). Information accumulation theory of categorization response times. *Psychological Review, 107,* 227–260.

Lauritzen, S. L. (1996). *Graphical models.* Oxford, England: Oxford University Press.

Lauritzen, S. L., & Richardson, T. S. (2002). Chain graph models and their causal interpretation. *Journal of the Royal Statistical Society, Series B, 64,* 321–361.

Lauritzen, S. L., & Wermuth, N. (1989). Graphical models for association between variables, some of which are qualitative and some quantitative. *Annals of Statistics, 17,* 31–57.

Lien, Y., & Cheng, P. W. (2000). Distinguishing genuine from spurious causes: A coherence hypothesis. *Cognitive Psychology, 40,* 87–137.

Logan, G. D. (2004). Cumulative progress in formal theories of attention. *Annual Review of Psychology, 55,* 207–234.

Love, B. C., Medin, D. L., & Gureckis, T. M. (2004). SUSTAIN: A network model of category learning. *Psychological Review, 111,* 309–332.

Luce, R. D. (1963). Detection and recognition. In R. D. Luce, R. R. Bush, & E. Galanter (Eds.), *Handbook of Mathematical Psychology* (pp. 103–189). New York: Wiley.

Machery, E. (2005). Concepts are not a natural kind. *Philosophy of Science, 72,* 444–467.

Malt, B. C., & Johnson, E. C. (1992). Do artifact concepts have cores? *Journal of Memory and Language, 31,* 195–217.

McClelland, J. L., & Rogers, T. T. (2003). The parallel distributed processing approach to semantic cognition. *Nature Reviews Neuroscience, 4,* 1–13.

Minda, J. P., & Smith, J. D. (2001). Prototypes in category learning: The effects of category size, category structure, and stimulus complexity. *Journal of Experimental Psychology: Learning, Memory, and Cognition, 27,* 775–799.

Myung, I. J. (1994). Maximum entropy interpretation of decision bound and context models of categorization. *Journal of Mathematical Psychology, 38,* 335–365.

Neapolitan, R. E. (2003). *Learning Bayesian networks.* Prentice Hall.

Nosofsky, R. M. (1986). Attention, similarity, and the identification-categorization relationship. *Journal of Experimental Psychology: General, 115,* 39–57.

Nosofsky, R. M. (1990). Relations between exemplar-similarity and likelihood models of classification. *Journal of Mathematical Psychology, 34,* 393–418.

Nosofsky, R. M., & Palmeri, T. J. (1997). An exemplar-based random walk model of speeded classification. *Psychological Review, 104*, 266–300.

Nosofsky, R. M., Palmeri, T. J., & McKinley, S. C. (1994). Rule-plus-exception model of classification learning. *Psychological Review, 101*, 53–79.

Olsson, H., Wennerholm, P., & Lyxzèn, U. (2004). Exemplars, prototypes, and the flexibility of classification models. *Journal of Experimental Psychology: Learning, Memory, and Cognition, 30*, 936–941.

Patalano, A. L., Smith, E. E., Jonides, J., & Koeppe, R. A. (2001). PET evidence for multiple strategies of categorization. *Cognitive, Affective & Behavioral Neuroscience, 1*, 360–370.

Pearl, J. (2000). *Causality: Models, reasoning, and inference*. Cambridge, England: Cambridge University Press.

Poole, D., & Zhang, N. L. (2003). Exploiting contextual independence in probabilistic inference. *Journal of Artificial Intelligence Research, 18*, 263–313.

Rehder, B. (2003a). Categorization as causal reasoning. *Cognitive Science, 27*, 709–748.

Rehder, B. (2003b). A causal-model theory of conceptual representation and categorization. *Journal of Experimental Psychology: Learning, Memory, and Cognition, 29*, 1141–1159.

Rehder, B., & Burnett, R. (2005). Feature inference and the causal structure of categories. *Cognitive Psychology, 50*, 264–314.

Rehder, B., & Hastie, R. (2004). Category coherence and category-based property induction. *Cognition, 91*, 113–153.

Richardson, T. S. (1998). Chain graphs and symmetric associations. In M. I. Jordan (Ed.), *Learning in graphical models* (pp. 231–259). Cambridge, MA: MIT Press.

Rogers, T. T., & McClelland, J. L. (2004). *Semantic cognition: A parallel distributed processing approach*. Cambridge, MA: MIT Press.

Rosseel, Y. (2002). Mixture models of categorization. *Journal of Mathematical Psychology, 46*, 178–210.

Shepard, R. N. (1957). Stimulus and response generalization: A stochastic model relating generalization to distance in psychological space. *Psychometrika, 22*, 325–345.

Sloman, S. A. (1998). Categorical inference is not a tree: The myth of inheritance hierarchies. *Cognitive Psychology, 35*, 1–33.

Smith, E. E., Patalano, A. L., & Jonides, J. (1998). Alternative strategies of categorization. *Cognition, 65*, 167–196.

Smith, J. D., & Minda, J. P. (1998). Prototypes in the mist: The early epochs of category learning. *Journal of Experimental Psychology: Learning, Memory, and Cognition, 24*, 1411–1436.

Spirtes, P., Glymour, C., & Scheines, R. (2001). *Causation, prediction, and search*. 2nd ed. Cambridge, MA: MIT Press. (Original work published 1993)

Spirtes, P., & Scheines, R. (2004). Causal inference of ambiguous manipulations. *Philosophy of Science, 71*, 833–845.

Strevens, M. (2000). The essentialist aspect of naive theories. *Cognition, 74*, 149–175.

Waldron, E. M., & Ashby, F. G. (2001). The effects of concurrent task interference on category learning: Evidence for multiple category learning systems. *Psychonomic Bulletin & Review, 8*, 168–176.

Wills, A. J., Reimers, S., Stewart, N., Suret, M., & McLaren, I. P. L. (2000). Tests of the ratio rule in categorization. *The Quarterly Journal of Experimental Psychology, 53A*, 983–1011.

Woodward, J. (2003). *Making things happen: A theory of causal explanation*. Oxford, England: Oxford University Press.

Zaki, S. R., Nosofsky, R. M., Stanton, R. D., & Cohen, A. L. (2003). Prototype and exemplar accounts of category learning and attentional allocation: A reassessment. *Journal of Experimental Psychology: Learning, Memory, and Cognition, 29*, 1160–1173.

Zhang, N. L., & Poole, D. (1999). On the role of context-specific independence in probabilistic inference. In T. Dean (Ed.), *Proceedings of the 16th International Joint Conference on Artificial Intelligence* (pp. 1288–1293). San Francisco: Morgan Kaufmann.

12

Essentialism as a Generative Theory of Classification

Bob Rehder

It is obvious that we classify the objects we encounter by their appearance, that is, by the particular features, aspects, or characteristics that they display. But, after a moment's reflection, it becomes clear that appearance is sometimes not all there is to it, that there are other factors not available to immediate inspection that might contribute to an object's identity. A study of Rips's (1989) work serves to illustrate. College students were told a story about a bird that had normal birdlike features (wings, ate seeds, lived in a nest in a tree, etc.) and was exposed to hazardous chemicals. As a result, the bird began to take on properties more characteristic of an insect: The wings with feathers were replaced with wings made of a transparent membrane; the nest was abandoned in favor of living on the underside of tree leaves; it developed a brittle iridescent outer shell; and so on. When asked whether the animal was now a bird or an insect, most students judged that it was still a bird. The important point to note is that they made this decision despite the fact that the animal no longer looked like a bird at all;

apparently, there is something more to category membership than just how an object appears. In fact, there is evidence that even children as young as 3 years old believe that the "insides" of objects are relevant in determining its class membership (Gelman & Wellman, 1991; also see Gelman, 2003; Keil, 1989).

The idea that different aspects or characteristics of objects might have different implications for category membership is not (to say the least) new. In philosophy, it dates at least as far back as Aristotle, who distinguished between an entity's *essential properties* (which define what something is) from its *accidental properties* (which determine how it is, that is, which properties just happen to inhere in it). The idea that essential properties might be inaccessible to perception has an equally impressive legacy. Even as central a British empiricist as John Locke distinguished *real essences* (what an object really is, which, according to the Locke, was unknowable in principle) from *nominal essences*, which could be perceived and which formed the basis for everyday categorization.

In psychology, even after the Roschian view that membership in natural categories is probabilistic, or graded, replaced the classical (i.e., defining features) view, the distinction between perceivable-but-only-characteristic and real-but-unobservable properties has persisted in various forms (although, of course, without Locke's pessimism regarding the knowability of the latter). For example, Miller and Johnson-Laird (1976) distinguished between a categories' *core properties* (which could be used during, e.g., reasoning), versus their *identification procedures* which inferred category membership on the basis of perceptual information (also see Armstrong, Gleitman, & Gleitman, 1983; Osherson & Smith, 1981; E. E. Smith, Medin, & Rips, 1984).

But, the separation of perceptual and core properties in this manner would seem to leave us without any elucidation of the relation between the two. One is reminded of Descartes's famous (non)solution to the mind-body problem, which proved unworkable because it failed to specify how the two domains (mind and body) interact. In the absence of any specification of how core and perceptual features interact, we are left, for example, with no principled explanation for why category membership will be decided by observable features in some (i.e., normal) conditions but by core features in others (e.g., those instantiated in Rips's 1989 study).

This chapter presents a solution to the categorization field's own mind-body problem, that is, how core and perceptual features interact. It does so by adopting a move that should be familiar from other fields of cognition. Namely, it will describe a generative theory of categories in which a category's core properties are represented in such a way that they produce or generate the perceptual features that one might observe. But, a unique characteristic of the current approach is that the relations between features will be defined in terms of generative causal relations. As discussed here, once the manner in which perceptual features are causally generated by core properties is specified, one can then "work backward," so to speak, to specify how perceptual information implies the presence of core properties and hence category membership.

To begin, consider in Figure 12-1 the hypothetical causal relations among features of one of the real-world categories used by Rips (1989): birds. The figure includes the observable features of birds, such as having wings, flying, building nests in a tree, singing,

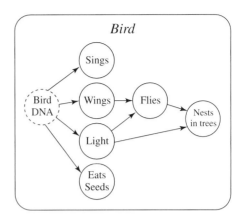

FIGURE 12-1 Causal model of the bird category.

and eating seeds. It also includes what might be considered a core property of birds: bird DNA. Indeed, for many Western-educated adults, bird DNA would seem to approximate a defining feature for birds because an object with bird DNA is virtually certain to be a bird, and one without it is virtually certain to not be. But, the dilemma is that, although flying and eating seeds are features of an animal that are observable, bird DNA is not.

Fortunately, features are not all that we know about birds; we also know how their features are causally related. For example, we know that birds are able to fly because they have wings and have body weight that is low enough to be supported by those wings. We know that birds build nests in trees because they can fly (and they are light enough not to break tree branches when they sit on them). Finally, we (Western-educated adults) all believe that basic morphological and behavior properties like having weight, body size, singing, and eating seeds are (somehow, directly or indirectly) caused by the fact that birds have the right kind of genetic makeup and evolutionary history that lead birds to have bird features.

It is hoped that the claim regarding how core and perceptual properties interact in categorization is now clear. People, of course, usually classify objects on the basis of observable features (what else could they use?), but they use those observable features to infer the presence of more core properties, which are then taken as defining of (or at least more diagnostic of) category membership. In other words, the mental act of categorization can be viewed as a case of causal reasoning in which properties like weight, body size, singing, and eating seeds provide inferential support for properties like bird DNA. This account provides an explanation for not only why people typically use observable features in classification, but also why they can override perceptual information in particular circumstances. When one is told a story about how a particular bird's features are transformed through external intervention into those of an insect's, one recognizes that the underlying core properties remain unchanged and thus so does the animal's category membership.

Accounting for data such as that of Rips is itself no small feat. But, in fact a generative view of classification can gain a large increment in explanatory power (and in its ability to make unique predictions) by making one additional assumption, namely, that the causal relations linking core and observable properties can sometimes be probabilistic rather than deterministic in nature.[1] To illustrate the importance of treating causality as a probabilistic relation, consider a second, somewhat simpler, example of a category and its causal network in Figure 12-2. In Figure 12-2, D represents some disease, S_1 represents a symptom directly caused by that disease, S_2 is a symptom caused by S_1, and S_3 is a symptom caused by S_2. The disease and its three symptoms are assumed to be related by the three *causal mechanisms* depicted as diamonds and labeled M_1, M_2, and M_3 in Figure 12-2. On the one hand, if these causal mechanisms operate deterministically, then whenever the disease D is present, so are the symptoms S_1, S_2, and S_3. In this case, S_1, S_2, and S_3 all provide equally good evidence for the presence of D (all else being equal). But, if the causal mechanisms operate probabilistically instead, then D will produce S_1 with some probability less than 1. Similarly, S_1 will produce S_2 with some probability less than 1, but because S_1 does not always accompany the disease, S_2 will be produced even less often than S_1. The same argument applies to S_3, so the upshot is that $1 > p(S_1|D) > p(S_2|D) > p(S_3|D)$. As a

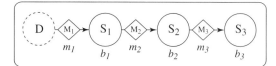

FIGURE 12-2 Causal model of a disease category.

consequence, when causal relations are probabilistic, the generative view predicts that S_1 will serve as better evidence for the presence of D than S_2, which in turn will serve as better evidence for D than S_3 (all else being equal[2]).

This example is important enough that the intuition behind it deserves to be cashed out with some precision. First, note that the representation of causal relations depicted in Figures 12-1 and 12-2 are examples of *Bayesian networks*, which consist of nodes that represent variables and directed edges that can be interpreted as representing direct causal relationships between variables (for details, see Glymour, 1998; Jordan, 1999; Pearl, 1988, 2000). By themselves, Bayesian networks convey no information regarding the details of the causal relationships that link variables (i.e., features) in a network. However, one can assume that the causal relations in such networks take on a specific functional form, and the parameters of those functions can be specified. For example, in Figure 12-2, there are a total of six parameters: m_1, m_2, m_3, b_1, b_2, and b_3. Parameters m_1, m_2, and m_3 represent the probability that the causal mechanisms M_1, M_2, and M_3, respectively, will successfully operate (that is, will bring about effects S_1, S_2, and S_3) when the cause feature is present. Parameters b_1, b_2, and b_3 represent the probability that symptom S_1, S_2, and S_3, respectively, is produced by some unspecified background cause.

Table 12-1 presents the likelihoods that the causal network of Figure 12-2 will generate symptoms S_1, S_2, and S_3. For example, the probability that S_1 is present when D is, $p(S_1|D)$, is the probability that it is caused by the causal mechanism M_1, or brought about by the background cause b_1. Assuming independence, this

TABLE 12-1 Feature Probabilities for the Causal Network of Figure 12-2

Feature	$P(S_i \mid D; M_i, b_i)$	$P(S_i \mid D; m_i = .80, b_i = .20)$
S_1	$m_i + b_1 - m_1 b_1$	.84
S_2	$m_2 P(S_1 \mid D) + b_2 - m_2 b_2 P(S1 \mid D)$	.74
S_3	$m_3 P(S2 \mid D) + b_3 - m_3 b_3 (S2 \mid D)$	.67

probability is $m_1 + b_1 - m_1 b_1$. The probability that S_2 is present $p(S_2 \mid D)$ is the probability that it is caused by the causal mechanism M_2, $m_2 p(S_1 \mid D)$, or brought about by the background cause b_2. This probability is $m_2 p(S_1 \mid D) + b_2 - m_2 b_2 P(S_1 \mid D)$ and so on for $p(S_3 \mid D)$. Table 12-1 also presents the probability that each feature will be generated by disease D when $m_1 = m_2 = m_3 = .80$ and $b_1 = b_2 = b_3 = .20$. These probabilities confirm the intuition that, when causal relations are construed as probabilistic, symptoms that are causally "farther away" from their disease are generated with lower reliability.

In summary, the solution offered to the categorization field's mind-body problem is to assume that core and observable features are interconnected with probabilistic causal relations, and as a result observable features serve as evidence for core properties as a function of the likelihood they are causally generated by those core features. Using a term first introduced by Waldmann, Holyoak, and Fratianne (1995), I refer to this theory as *causal model theory*, although my application of this theory concerns classification rather than category learning (Rehder, 2003a, 2003b). It also differs in the functional form assumed to hold for causal relations. Whereas the representation of causal relations presented here is isomorphic to Cheng's (1997) PowerPC theory of causal induction, Waldmann et al. considered causal relations between continuous variables such that the level of one variable (the effect) changed as a linear function of another (the cause), as in structural equation models. This difference is not fundamental, however, as the generative view can be applied to causal networks that include both continuous variables viewed as being as linearly related and binary (or ordinal) variables connected with the type of discrete causal mechanisms described here. Another extension of the generative view would be to causal mechanisms involving more than two variables. For example, I may not be exactly sure how birds fly, but I believe that the causal mechanism that produces flight somehow involves the lift produced by the wings overcoming the bird's body weight; thus, wing size and body weight (not to mention the wing's flapping motion, the body's aerodynamic shape, and so on) are all factors causally relevant to the production of flight. The generative approach can be applied to cases involving three or more causally related variables as easily as two.

In this chapter, three experiments are presented that provide empirical support for the generative view of classification just described. To assess the kind of causal reasoning that occurs when a category has a defining or essential property, in Experiments 1–3 adult subjects are taught novel categories in which one of the category's features is designated as occurring in 100% of members of the category and in members of no other category. Note that the property will not be DNA or a disease. The purpose of these experiments is not to determine what the defining or essential properties of categories really are, but rather to stipulate such a feature and then show how classification is influenced when it is causally linked to observable properties. Experiments 1–3 differ in terms of the exact network topology by which the defining feature is causally related to those observable properties.

These experiments show classification can be viewed as causal reasoning in which observable features are taken as evidence for features that are unobservable but are defining of category membership. However, although a generative theory of classification subsumes causal reasoning as a special case, its application is in fact not limited to categories with a defining feature. As I argue in the Discussion, the extent to which a category is *essentialized* is a matter of degree, and an advantage of the generative view is that it can also accommodate categories that are essentialized only partially or not at all. To this end, subjects in Experiment 4 are taught the same categories as in Experiments 1–3, with causal relations among observed features but without an unobservable defining feature. This experiment shows that category membership is also influenced by the *coherence* among observed features, that is, whether those feature corroborate the category's causal laws.

Experiment 1: Classification as Diagnosis

The purpose of the first experiment is to conduct a test of the example presented in Figure 12-2. College students were instructed on novel categories in which one feature was described as defining but unobservable; the other features were observable and were related to the defining feature in a causal chain. The generative view predicts (as shown in Table 12-1) that the feature directly caused by the defining feature should provide the strongest evidence for category membership; indirectly caused features should provide weaker evidence.

TABLE 12-2 Features and Causal Relationships for the Lake Victoria Shrimp Experimental Category.

Features	
D	High amounts of ACh neurotransmitter
F1	Long-lasting flight response
F2	Accelerated sleep cycle
F3	High body weight

Causal Relationships	
D → F1	High quantity of the ACh neurotransmitter causes a long-lasting flight response; longer duration of electrical signal to the muscles because of excess amount of neurotransmitter
F1 → F2	Long-lasting flight response causes accelerated sleep cycle, fatigued muscles; muscle fatigue triggers the shrimp's sleep center
F2 → F3	Accelerated sleep cycle causes high body weight; shrimp habitually feed after waking, and shrimp on an accelerated sleep cycle wake three times a day instead of one

Table 12-2 presents an example of features and causal relationships for one of the novel experimental categories, Lake Victoria shrimp. Lake Victoria shrimp were described to participants as possessing four binary features and three causal relationships among those features. One feature (which I continue to refer to in the abstract as D because it is "defining") was described as occurring 100% of the time in category members and never in members of other categories. Features F_1, F_2, and F_3 were described as occurring in most category members. The causal links were arranged in a chain pattern: D → F_1→ F_2 → F_3 (as in Figure 12-2). Each causal relationship consisted of one sentence indicating the cause and effect features (e.g., "A high quantity of ACh neurotransmitter causes a long-lasting flight response.") and then one or two sentences briefly describing the causal mechanism (e.g., "The duration of the electrical signal to the muscles is longer because of the excess amount of neurotransmitter."). The knowledge associated with categories such as Lake Victoria shrimp was intended to be a simplified analogue of real-world category knowledge, such as that bird DNA causes wings, which causes flying, which causes nests in trees, or a disease that causes a chain of symptoms. Participants in a control condition were provided with the identical category information except for the causal relations between features.

Participants learned one of six novel categories: two biological kinds (Kehoe ants, Lake Victoria shrimp); two nonliving natural kinds (myastars, meteoric sodium carbonate); and two artifacts (Romanian rogos, Neptune personal computers). Participants first studied several computer screens of information about their assigned category and were required to pass a multiple-choice test of this knowledge. They then performed a categorization task in which they rated the category membership of one of the three observable features (F_1, F_2, or F_3). For example, participants who learned about Lake Victoria shrimp (Table 12-2) would be presented with a shrimp that was described as possessing a long-lasting flight response and asked, "Is this a Lake Victoria shrimp?" Participants entered their rating by using the left and right arrow keys to move a bar along a response scale to a position that reflected their confidence that the exemplar was a category member. The two ends of the scale were labeled definitely not an X and definitely an X, where X was the name of the category. Responses were recorded as a number in the range 0–100. Thirty-six university undergraduates participated in this experiment and were assigned in equal numbers to the causal and control conditions.

The category membership ratings for features F_1, F_2, and F_3 are presented in Figure 12-3 for both the causal and control conditions. Two things in Figure 12-3 should be noted. First, average ratings were significantly higher in the causal condition (56.7) compared to the control condition (46.5), indicating that features provide stronger evidence for category membership when they are causally linked to the defining feature. This finding was predicted by the generative view because the presence of causal relations allows one to infer the presence of the defining feature on the basis of observable features.

The second important result is that, in the causal condition, feature F_1 received a significantly higher rating (63.3) than feature F_2 (54.6), which received a higher rating than F_3 (52.3). (The difference between F_2 and F_3 did not reach significance.) This result was also as predicted because the generative view assumes that features generated with greater reliability by the underlying defining feature (like F_1) should serve as greater evidence for the presence of that defining features than features generated less reliably (F_2 or F_3). Apparently, when observed features are causally

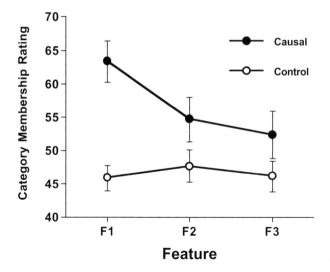

FIGURE 12-3 Results from Experiment 1.

related to defining ones, categorizers can invoke a process of causal inference in which they work backward from observables to defining properties in the same way that one can work backward from a disease's symptoms to the disease itself.

Experiment 2: Boundary Intensification

Experiment 1 instructed participants on one category and asked them to rate the likelihood of whether an object was a member of that category. But classifiers will often have in mind two or more categories an object might belong to. A generative view of classification can easily be applied to such situations by predicting that an object is a member of the category that is most likely to be generated by (also see Danks, chapter 11, this volume). For example, in the context of an experiment in which an object O can belong to one of two categories (A or B), the probability $p(O \mid A)$ that O is an A can be expected to be a function of the relative probability that it was generated by A and B, that is, according to Bayes' law:

$$p(A \mid O) = \frac{p(O \mid A)}{p(O \mid A) + p(O \mid B)} p(A) \quad (12\text{-}1)$$

In Experiment 2, participants are instructed on two categories and are asked to make a binary judgment regarding the category to which an object belongs.

As in Experiment 1, in a causal condition a category's observable features will be causally related to a defining feature. However, in Experiment 2 those features are each directly caused by the defining feature, as shown in Figure 12-4. In Figure 12-4, categories A and B have opposite values on the same stimulus dimensions. For example, some subjects were instructed on both Lake Victoria shrimp, with the defining feature a high quantity of ACh neurotransmitter, and Madagascar River shrimp, with the defining feature a low quantity of ACh neurotransmitter. Similarly, features F_1 and $\sim F_1$ were opposing values on the same dimension (long-lasting flight response vs. short-lasting flight response) and so on for the remaining two stimulus dimensions. Participants in a

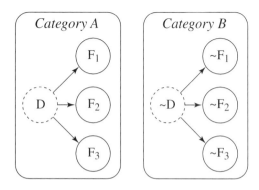

FIGURE 12-4 Causal models for the two categories in Experiment 2.

control condition were provided with identical category information except that the causal relations between features were omitted.

The question addressed in Experiment 2 concerns how the presence of causal relations changes subject's judgments regarding an object's membership in one of two possible categories. Gelman (2003) suggests that essentialized categories should exhibit the phenomenon of *boundary intensification*, in which category boundaries become more extreme, or more dichotomous, than they would otherwise be. This effect is somewhat analogous to the categorical perception of speech sounds. For example, the sounds *d* and *t* differ from one another on a single dimension (voice onset time). But, when voice onset time of those sounds is varied experimentally along a continuum, they are nevertheless perceived "categorically" as either as a *d* or a *t* but rarely a blend of the two (Lisker & Abramson, 1970). Applied to the current experiment, categorical perception would work to make the category boundaries between categories A and B in Figure 12-4 more extreme because the observable features are causally linked to an underlying core property.

Again, it is worthwhile to work out a concrete example. First, suppose that in the absence of causal knowledge category A's three features (F_1, F_2, and F_3) are viewed as each occurring with probability 75% in members of A, but they have no causal relations with defining feature D. Similarly, category B's three features ($\sim F_1$, $\sim F_2$, and $\sim F_3$) occur with probability 75% among members of B and are causally unrelated to $\sim$D. This corresponds to $m = 0$ and $b=.75$ for both causal models of Figure 12-4. If one then observes an object O with features F_1, F_2, and $\sim F_3$, $P(A|O)=(.75)(.75)(.25)=.141$ and $P(B|O)=(.25)(.25)(.75)=.047$. Assuming that the two categories are equally probable beforehand (i.e., $P(A) = .50$), Bayes' law tells us that the probability that O is an A, $P(A|O)$, is .75.

Now consider the case in which the categories' features are thought to be generated by their defining features (D or $\sim$D) via causal mechanisms that operate with 50% reliability, that is, $m = .50$. In this case, each individual feature is now generated with probability $m + b - mb$, that is, .875 (assuming independence again). If one again observes an object O with features F_1, F_2, and $\sim F_3$, then $P(A|O) = (.875)(.875)(.125) = .096$, $P(B|O) = (.125)(.125)(.875) = .014$, and thus the probability that O is an A is now .875. That is, one should be more confident that the object is a category member with causal relations (.875) than without them (.75). The probability that some object O is a member of category A as a function of the number of A features it possesses is presented in Table 12-3 for the case where there are causal relations ($m = .50$) and when there are not ($m = 0$). Table 12-3 demonstrates the phenomenon of boundary intensification: For all objects, one's confidence that it is a member of its most likely category increases when its features are linked to an underlying defining feature.

To test these predictions, the categorization test of Experiment 2 presented objects with values on all three observed dimensions (as opposed to the single features presented in Experiment 1). Participants were asked to choose the two categories to which the object belonged (e.g., Lake Victoria shrimp or Madagascar River shrimp) and then to rate their confidence in that judgment. The eight possible objects that can be formed from three binary dimensions were each presented twice. Thirty-six undergraduates participated in this experiment, and each was instructed on one category pair with causal knowledge and another (control) pair without it (the order of presentation of these two pairs of categories was balanced).

The results are presented in Figure 12-5 for both the causal and control conditions. Figure 12-5 shows the probability that the object was classified as a member of Category A as a function of the number of A features it possessed. Of course, in both conditions

TABLE 12-3 Hypothetical Predictions for Experiment 2

Number of A Features	P (A | O; m = 0, b = .75)	P (A | O; m = .50, b = .75)
0	.047	.003
1	.250	.125
2	.750	.875
3	.964	.997

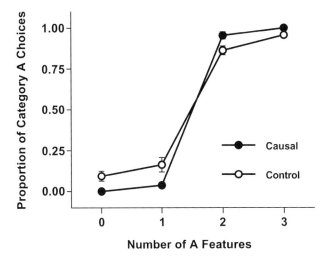

FIGURE 12-5 Results from Experiment 2.

subjects' classifications were sensitive to how many features O possessed that were characteristic of A or B: It was likely to be classified as an A if it possessed mostly A features and as a B if it possessed mostly B features. But, the figure shows that this effect was more pronounced when those features were described as causally related to the underlying defining features D or ~D. This effect manifested itself as a significant interaction between condition (causal vs. control) and number of features. The same pattern of results was reflected in confidence ratings.

These results demonstrate how the boundary between categories can become more extreme when features are causally related to an underlying defining property. According to a generative view of classification, causal relations constrain the generation of features, so that the category becomes more homogeneous and thus less accepting of exemplars that are discrepant with respect to those causal laws. The result is a sharpening of category boundaries in which objects are perceived more "categoricallly."

Experiment 3: Classification as Prospective Versus Diagnostic Reasoning

The first two experiments are examples of how classification can be taken to be a case of causal reasoning in which observable features are diagnostic of core properties. However, classification does not always involve reasoning backward (i.e., diagnostically) but sometimes involves reasoning forward, prospectively, to a core property. Consider the examples in Figure 12-6A,

which shows two causal networks, each involving the human immunodeficiency virus (HIV). In the left panel of Figure 6A, the category being HIV positive (which is itself not directly observable) can be diagnosed in terms of the symptoms it produces, such as lymphoma, sarcoma, and pneumonia. However, the right panel of Figure 6A illustrates how HIV can also be inferred by reasoning forward from its possible causes, such as blood transfusions, intravenous drug use, or participating in unsafe sex. That is, to the extent that an individual has these properties, the likelihood that the person has HIV increases.[3]

Because the generative approach to classification subsumes causal reasoning as a basis for determining category membership, it applies equally well to both diagnostic and prospective reasoning. Moreover, the HIV example is well suited to illustrating how classification can involve specifically causal reasoning because it exemplifies the asymmetries that obtain when reasoning from multiple possible effects to a cause versus from multiple possible causes to an effect. To demonstrate these asymmetries, first consider the (often unrealistic) case that each of the causal relations shown in Figure 12-6A are deterministically sufficient, that is, a cause produces its effects with 100% reliability ($m = 1$). The left panel of Figure 12-7A presents the probability that HIV will generate a given case O as a function of the number of HIV symptoms (lymphoma, sarcoma, or pneumonia) that it has. (I continue to use O to represent an object that displays a set of features, in this case a patient with a set of symptoms.) Analogously, the right panel of Figure 12-7A presents the probability of HIV as a

A

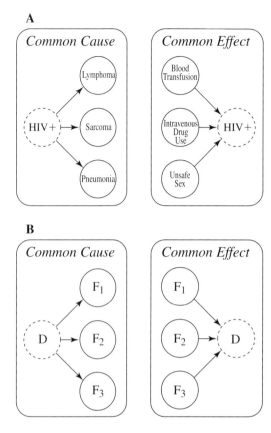

B

FIGURE 12-6 (A) Two hypothetical causal models involving the HIV virus. (B) Causal models for the two categories in Experiment 3.

function of the number of its causes present. Whereas the left panel of Figure 12-7A indicates that, when causal relations are assumed to be deterministic, the probability of HIV is only certain when all of its symptoms are present, the right panel shows that the probability of HIV is certain when one or more of its causes are present. This is the case because each cause can independently result in HIV.

Figure 12-7B presents the more realistic situation in which the causal relations linking HIV with its causes and symptoms are probabilistic ($m < 1$). Figure 12-7B presents the (logarithm) of the probability of HIV as a function of the number of symptoms (left panel) or causes (right panel) present. Because the causal relationships are probabilistic rather than deterministic, the probability of HIV now increases monotonically as the number of symptoms increases. Note that the utility of plotting these probabilities in

log coordinates is that it demonstrates how evidence for HIV increases as a function of the number of symptoms: Because in the generative model evidence consists of individual probabilities that multiply, plotting the overall probability in log coordinates reveals an additive (i.e., linear) relationship (left panel of Figure 12-7B). In contrast, the right panel of Figure 12-7B reveals that the relationship between HIV and its causes is nonlinear, such that adding the first possible cause of HIV produces a larger increase in the probable presence of HIV than adding additional causes. Nevertheless, this cause does not invariably lead to HIV, so the presence of additional causes continues to increase the probability that HIV is present. Note that asymmetries like this between common-cause and common-effect networks have been instrumental in establishing the role of causality in a variety of category-related and inferential tasks, including category learning (Waldmann et al., 1995), categorization (Rehder, 2003a), category-based property induction (Rehder & Hastie, 2004), and prediction (Rehder & Burnett, 2005; Waldmann & Hagmayer, 2005). (Also see Strevens, chapter 15, this volume, for additional discussion about the asymmetries inherent in causal networks.)

To test these predictions, participants in Experiment 3 were instructed on a single category (as in Experiment 1). One group of subjects was presented with the common-cause structure shown in the left side of Figure 12-6B in which one feature (D) was the defining feature and was described as the cause of the three observable features. Another group was instructed on the common-effect structure in the right side of Figure 12-6B in which D was the defining feature and was described as caused by the three observable features. There were also two control groups that were identical to the common-cause and common-effect conditions, respectively, except for the presence of the three causal relationships. All groups then performed a categorization test that presented objects with values on all three observable dimensions. As in Experiment 1, participants were asked to rate how likely the object (e.g., a shrimp with a given set of features) was a member of the category (e.g., Lake Victoria shrimp). The eight possible objects that can be formed from three binary dimensions were each presented twice. Undergraduates (144) were assigned in equal numbers to the four conditions.

The results are presented in Figure 12-7C. To allow comparison with the predictions shown in

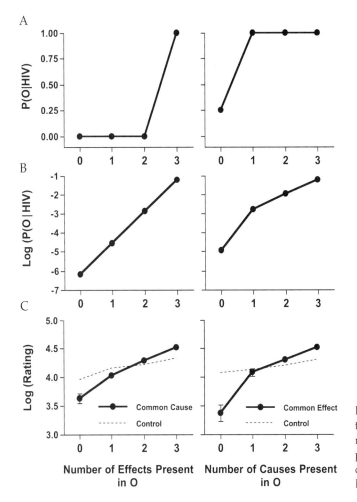

FIGURE 12-7 (A) Theoretical predictions for Experiment 3 assuming deterministic causal relations. (B) Theoretical predictions assuming probabilistic causal relations. (C) Results from Experiment 3.

Figure 12-7B, the logarithm of the categorization ratings have been taken. The left panel of Figure 12-7C indicates that, as predicted, in the common-cause condition the logarithm of the ratings were a linear function of the number of effect features present. In contrast, in the common effect condition those ratings exhibited a nonlinearity in which the presence of one potential cause of D produced a larger increase in the ratings compared to adding a second or third cause (right panel of Figure 12-7C).

Besides being interesting in their own right, these results have important theoretical implications for models of categorization. For example, Rehder (2003a) has shown not only that standard categorization models like prototype and exemplar models cannot account for asymmetries between common-cause and common-effect networks (like those shown

in Figure 7C), but also that those models cannot account for such results even when augmented with certain rudimentary representations of causal relations (e.g., adding to a prototype representation second-order features that encode interfeature causal relations). Of special theoretical importance are the results from the common effect condition that involves higher-order interactions among features—a cause producing a large increase in ratings only when *none* of the other causes are already present. (See Danks, chapter 11, this volume, for an extended discussion of different classes of categorization models and the constraints they place on possible patterns of classification ratings.)

In addition to illustrating the predicted asymmetry between the common-cause and common-effect networks, the results in Figure 12-7C also demonstrate how participants treated the causal relationships as probabilistic because each additional cause (or effect) produced an increase in the probability that the defining feature D was present. In other words, the results correspond to the probabilistic predictions (Figure 12-7B) rather than the deterministic ones (Figure 12-7A). Also note that features in the common-cause and common-effect conditions were more diagnostic of category membership (each additional feature resulted in a larger increment in category membership) compared to the control conditions. That is, as in the first two experiments, categorizers use causal knowledge to infer an underlying defining feature.

Experiment 4: Nonessentialized Categories and Theoretical Coherence

The generative view of categorization presented here borrows much from the view of essentialism described by Medin and Ortony (1989). As here, Medin and Ortony observed that category membership is often based on unobservable properties. And, as here, they proposed that underlying properties not only establish category membership, but also "are best thought of as constraining or even generating properties the might turn out to be useful in identification" (p. 185). By subsuming causal reasoning as a basis for determining category membership, Experiment 3 shows how the generative view can also account for cases in which an observable feature is the cause of, rather than caused by, an underlying property. Moreover, the generative view is not restricted to only essentialized categories. This is important because it is likely that not all categories that humans know are essentialized to the same extent (or at all).

For example, I have used diseases as a paradigm case of essentialized categories. However, the causes of many diseases were unknown at an earlier stage of scientific knowledge, and as a result the categories for diseases were initially organized around their characteristic features (i.e., symptoms) rather than the underlying cause. In addition, although research has shown that biological kinds may be strongly essentialized for adults (as Rips's, 1989, transformed bird illustrates), this may not be true of all individuals—specifically, it may not be true for young children (Keil, 1989). Finally, although underlying causal properties might be important for complex artifacts (e.g., automobiles, computers), simple artifacts like pencils and wastepaper baskets appear to be defined more in terms of their perceptual or functional properties (Malt, 1994; Malt & Johnson, 1992; although see Bloom, 1998; Matan & Carey, 2001; Rips, 1989; for more essentialist-based construals of artifacts).

An advantage of a generative view of classification is that it makes predictions not only for essentialized categories, but also for categories that are essentialized only to a degree (i.e., have underlying properties that provide strong but not defining evidence for category membership) or not all. For example, consider the simple causal network in Figure 12-8, which involves only two category features, C and E, and in which C is the cause of E. Note that the assumption is that neither C nor E is defining of category membership; that is, neither C nor E will appear in all category members.

Nevertheless, it is possible to define the probability with which the network generates particular objects (i.e., particular combinations of C and E). The network has an m parameter that specifies the probability that the causal mechanism generates E when C is present and a b parameter that specifies the probability that E is brought about by some unspecified background cause. The parameter c specifies the probability that C will be present. Table 12-4 presents how these parameters together specify the probability with which a category (A) with this causal network will generate the four combinations of C and E. The probability that C and E will both be absent, $P(\sim C\sim E \mid A)$, is the probability that C is absent $(1-c)$ times the probability that E is not brought about by any background causes $(1-b)$. The probability $P(\sim CE \mid A)$ that C is absent but E is present is $(1-c)$ times the probability that E is brought about by some background cause b. The probability $P(C\sim E \mid A)$ that C is present but E absent is c times the probability that E is not brought about by the causal mechanism and not brought about by the background cause $(1-m)(1-b)$. Finally, the probability $P(CE \mid A)$ that C and E are both present is c times the probability that E is brought about by the causal mechanism or brought about by the background cause $(m+b-mb)$. (Again, in these

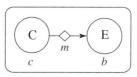

FIGURE 12-8 A two-feature causal model.

TABLE 12-4 Object probabilities for the causal network of Figure 8.

Object (O)	$P(O \mid A; c, m, b)$	$P(O \mid A; c = .67, m = .80, b = .20)$
~C~E	$(1 - c)(1 - b)$	.264
~CE	$(1 - c)(b)$	.066
C~E	$(c)[(1 - m)(1 - b)]$	.107
CE	$(c)(m + b - mb)$	.563

equations I assume that the cause between C and E and E's background cause operate independently.)

Table 12-4 also presents the probabilities that the four cases will be generated when $c = .67$, $m = .80$, and $b = .20$. This example illustrates how a generative theory can be applied to categories without a defining feature because the probability of C [$= P(C\text{~}E) + P(CE) = .67$] and E [$= P(\text{~}CE) + P(CE) = .63$] are both less than 1. It also illustrates how the theory predicts that combinations of features make for better or worse category members. In particular, the two objects in which C and E are both present or both absent are the most probable (.563 and .264, respectively). In contrast, objects in which one is present and the other absent are relatively improbable (.066 for ~CE and .107 for C~E). In fact, these latter objects, which each have one feature present, are both less probable than the one with both features absent. This pattern of probabilities reflects the empirical observations one would expect when a causal law holds between two variables: These variables should be correlated with one another. In other words, a generative view of classification predicts that objects will be good category members to the extent they exhibit *theoretical coherence*, that is, whether they are consistent with or corroborate a category's causal laws (causes and effects either both present or both absent).

To test these predictions, half the participants in Experiment 4 were instructed on one of the six experimental categories with the causal network in Figure 12-9A, in which four features were related by two causal links. The other half learned an identical control category missing the two causal relations (Figure 12-9B). In both conditions, each feature was described as occurring in most category members. A categorization test then followed that presented objects with values on all four dimensions, and participants rated how likely the object was a member of the category. The 16 possible objects that can be formed from four binary dimensions were each presented twice. Thirty-six undergraduates were assigned in equal numbers to the causal and control conditions.

The results are presented in Figure 12-10. For simplicity, only the ratings for objects that are maximally coherent (causes and effect either all present or all absent) or maximally incoherent (both causes present but both effects absent or vice versa) are presented. In the control condition, categorization ratings of course were a monotonic function of the number of features: The object missing all four features received the lowest rating, the one with all four features received the highest rating, and objects possessing two features received an intermediate rating. In contrast, the results in the causal condition showed a strong effect of causal knowledge. For example, incoherent objects received a significantly lower category rating compared to the same items in the control condition. In fact, in the causal condition the incoherent objects (each with two features) received a significantly lower rating than the item

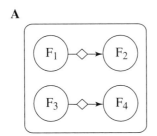 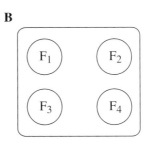

FIGURE 12-9 Causal models for the two categories in Experiment 4.

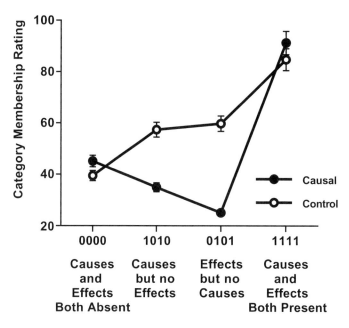

Features in Object O

FIGURE 12-10 Results from Experiment 4.

missing all four features. These results illustrate how the corroboration of causal laws can override the importance of the number of characteristic features that an object displays.

These findings support the claim that subjects judged an object's category membership as a function of the likelihood it was generated by the category's causal laws. Other studies have demonstrated the importance of whether combinations of features exhibit theoretical coherence. Ahn, March, Luhmann, and Lee (2002) have shown that items are viewed as more typical of real-world categories when they manifest correlations between theoretically related pairs of features (e.g., an animal that lives underwater should also have gills) (also see Malt & Smith, 1984). And, I have shown that adults are sensitive to not only whether pairs of features exhibit coherence, but also whether an entire collection of features linked together in more complex networks manifests the higher-order correlations between features that such networks produce (Rehder, 2003a, 2003b). Moreover, effects such as these are not limited to adults: Barrett, Abdi, Murphy, and Gallagher (1993) found that first- and fourth-graders were more likely to classify a bird as a member of a novel category if it manifested an expected correlation (e.g.,

between the bird's memory capacity and brain size) than if it broke that correlation.

Besides illustrating the importance of theoretical coherence, another goal of Experiment 4 was to demonstrate how a generative view of classification can be applied to categories without a defining feature. Note, however, that the importance of coherence is not limited only to nonessentialized categories; even for categories based on an essence, coherence among observable features will contribute to category membership. This fact can be illustrated with the bird category shown in Figure 12-1. If one is presented with an unfamiliar animal (e.g., an ostrich) that should not be able to fly (e.g., because it is too heavy relative to its wingspan), it may be considered likely to be a bird only if it does not fly (despite the fact that flight is usually highly diagnostic of birds). This might be the case because a large, small-winged animal that somehow flies is actually more likely to be some kind of artifact instead (with an invisible propulsion system explaining its otherwise unexplained ability to fly).

Discussion

An enduring problem in the field of categorization has to been to account for both the undisputed fact that everyday categorization is based on observable properties and the fact that categories have an underlying reality that goes beyond that which is perceptually available. By itself, the claim that categories possess both core properties (which define category membership) and observable ones (which serve as the basis for identification) leaves unexplained the conditions under which people will override perceptual information and instead rely on core properties. In this chapter, I have presented a solution to the categorization field's mind-body problem by specifying the interaction between defining and observed features in terms of generative causal relations. On this account, objects' observable features serve as evidence for category membership because they imply the presence of the defining feature. But, people know that such causal inferences are no longer justified when an object's features are transformed through external intervention. As a result, in such cases they will fall back on the object's core properties to establish category membership.

One goal of this work, of course, has been to contrast a generative view of classification with one that merely distinguishes between core and observable properties. It is important to ask how necessary it is that the relation between these two types of properties be conceived of as causal. Indeed, for some categories the relation between core and observable properties is manifestly noncausal. For example, if a late-night TV movie opens on a scene with people doing the hula underneath palm trees, then you might guess that the people are on an island, but this guess is unlikely to be based on your belief that an islands' defining properties (small body of land surrounded by water) causes its observable ones (hula dancing and palm trees). Given examples like this, one might question the presence of causal relations even for biological kinds. For example, Rips's (1989) transformed bird/insect may have still been considered a bird because in the described scenario there was no reason to think that its underlying defining properties had been changed by the transformation. Loosely speaking, they (the defining properties) were there before; there is no reason to believe that they are not there now. So, why should one think that the category membership of the object has changed?

However, this argument leaves unexplained the numerous findings reported in this chapter. First, it leaves unexplained why symptoms might be more diagnostic of a disease when they are causally linked to the disease. This prediction was tested in Experiment 1, which found that in fact observable features provided stronger evidence for category membership when they were stipulated as caused by a defining feature. It also fails to explain the phenomenon of boundary intensification, in which categories become more homogeneous and less tolerant of discrepant category members. This prediction was tested in Experiment 2, which found that in fact judgments of category membership were more extreme when causal knowledge was provided. Finally, it leaves unexplained why there might be asymmetries depending on whether a defining feature causes, or is caused by, the category's observable features. This predicted asymmetry was demonstrated in Experiment 3.

Another important component of the generative view is that causal relations between defining and observable features are typically viewed as probabilistic rather than deterministic. A probabilistic view of causality explains why, in Experiment 1, features more directly caused by the defining feature served as stronger evidence for category membership compared to less directly caused ones. It also explains why, in Experiment 3, an increase in the number of features resulted in a monotonic increase in category membership ratings for both common-cause and common-effect structures. More important, a probabilistic view of causality explains the fundamentally probabilistic nature of real-world categorization. For example, although there are clearly individual features (e.g., flying) that are diagnostic of membership in certain categories (e.g., birds), such features are often not present in all category members (e.g., ostriches). On the present account, flying provides evidence for bird category membership, but because flying is generated by the bird category's causal model (Figure 12-1) with less than certain probability, it admits the possibility of birds that do not fly. This probabilistic view also accounts for the fact that people are often uncertain about objects' category membership (e.g., McCloskey & Glucksberg, 1978, found that subjects were about evenly split over whether a leech is an insect, whether sugar cane is a vegetable, whether an octopus is a fish, etc.). According to the generative view, the uncertainty of whether, say, a leech is an insect arises because the characteristic features of a leech provide only weak inferential support for the essential attributes of insects (as compared to, say, the characteristic features of a mosquito). In other words, cases of fuzziness in category membership arise not necessarily because of the absence of defining features, but rather because of inferential uncertainty, that is, from the fact that sets of observed features vary to the extent they provide evidence of a defining feature.

A third claim of the generative view is that objects will be considered better category members to the extent they make sense, that is, to the extent their observed features are coherent in light of the causal laws the category is thought to possess. In Experiment 4, causal relations between observable features were provided, and in fact objects with a combination of features that were consistent with those causal laws were judged as more likely category members than objects with features that were inconsistent—even when the latter objects possessed more characteristic features. The generative view predicts this result because causal relations will tend to generate coherent objects—cases in which causes and effects are both present (if a bird builds nests in a tree, then it also flies) or both absent (a bird that does not fly does not nest in trees).

Another purpose of Experiment 4 was to demonstrate how the generative view can accommodate categories that are not essentialized. In comparison to the fully essentialized categories used Experiments 1–3 (which each possessed an unobservable defining feature that caused observable ones), the categories used in Experiment 4 had no defining feature. An important advantage of the fact that the generative view can accommodate both essentialized and nonessentialized categories is that it applies to categories for which underlying causal features have not yet been identified—as in earlier scientific epochs in which the causes of many diseases were unknown. It can also accommodate the developmental shift that apparently occurs in which many categories (e.g., biological kinds) increase in the extent to which they are essentialized.

For example, Keil (1989) conducted a transformation experiment similar to Rips's in which children were shown a picture of a raccoon and then told that doctors painted the raccoon black and added a white stripe down its back and a "sac of super smelly yucky stuff." Whereas second- and fourth-graders judged that the animal was still a raccoon (illustrating again that category membership can be based on more than just appearance), kindergartners categorized it as a skunk, that is, perceptually. Although there is evidence that children as young as 4 years old might

be biased to weigh "insides" of objects heavily in categorization (Gelman & Wellman, 1991; also see Diesendruck, 2001; Hirschfeld, 1996), it is frequently assumed that categories are initially organized around perceptual information and are augmented with more conceptual information over time (Keil, 1989, 1994).

This shift in the organization of a category—based either on scientific progress or cognitive development—can be described in terms of an evolving set of causal models, an example of which is shown in Figure 12-11. First, consider what might be a category's initial state in Figure 12-11A. In this early stage, knowledge of the category consists of only its observable features (closed circles) and how those features covary with a category label (depicted as an additional binary variable in Figure 12-11A). As a result, evidence that an object is a member of this category is a simple function of whether it has these features, a relationship depicted in Figure 12-11A by dotted arrows. Note that although the dotted arrows represent a relation between features and the category label that is *inferential* (one infers a category label from features), it is noncausal. Because the category will often possess a family resemblance structure (in which features vary in the extent to which they are correlated with the category label but no one feature covaries perfectly), the function that computes the probability of the category label will usually involve a weighted combination of the number of features present.[4]

In the second stage of the category's development (Figure 12-11B), its representation has been elaborated not only with additional features, but also with an underlying cause that generates several of the observed features. Knowledge of this underlying cause might arise from explicit education (formal or informal). It might also arise because children are causal determinists who postulate the presence of hidden causes to explain what they observe (Gelman, 2003; Gelman, Coley, & Gottfried, 1994). In some instances, the cause might be external to the category itself (often the case with artifacts); in others, knowledge of the cause might be so vague that it functions as a placeholder only (Medin & Ortony, 1989). But, regardless of the source or nature of the cause, at this point it only provides the child with an explanation for what the child observes. Classification itself is still determined by the observable features alone.

In the third stage (Figure 12-11C), the category has begun to undergo an *essential shift* in which

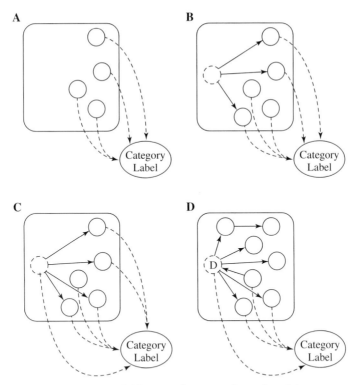

FIGURE 12-11 An evolving set of causal models.

the category label is now directly dependent on the underlying cause. Importantly, however, this shift is not complete because the category label still depends on the observable features as well. At this stage, observable features contribute to category membership in two ways. The first is that they directly imply category membership (as in the first two stages). The second contribution is indirect because from observable features one infers the likely presence of the underlying cause, which then increases the probable presence of the category label yet further. Because of this second inferential path from observable features to the category label, it is at this point that categories begin to become less variable and, as a result, undergo boundary intensification.

The essential shift is completed in Figure 12-11D, which presents a fully essentialized category in which category membership is directly dependent on the underlying cause alone. At this point, observable features still imply the category label but do so indirectly by implying the underlying cause in the same way that one can infer a disease from its symptoms. With increased knowledge, one might also come to learn about more features and more causal links between

features and the underlying cause. In addition, one might learn that some of those feature are causes of the underlying defining feature rather than being caused by it (e.g., one learns that unsafe sex is a potential cause of contracting HIV).

I suggest that it is in this manner that categories shift from primarily perceptually based to having an essentialized underlying causal structure. At each stage, what stays the same is that classification proceeds on the basis of observable features (as it must). What changes is the nature of the inference itself. What starts as a noncausal inference from features to a category label (as assumed by most current theories of categorization) turns into a causal inference from observable to unobservables (and then to the category label).[5]

Of course, not every category necessarily progresses through each of these four stages. For example, the presence of a unique word for a type of object may speed the rate at which the category progresses from the first stage to the third or fourth (Coley, Medin, & Atran, 1997). Conversely, note that for many categories there is good reason to question whether the process of essentialization is ever fully completed, even in adults. For example, Hampton (1995) has demonstrated that even when biological categories' so-called defining properties are unambiguously present (or absent), characteristic features continue to exert an influence on judgments of category membership (also see Braisby, Franks, & Hampton, 1996; Kalish, 1995; Malt, 1994; Malt & Johnson, 1992). Similarly, although most subjects in the Rips's (1989) study thought the transformed bird/insect was still a bird, they were not indifferent to the animal's new, insect-like properties: Average ratings in favor of bird category membership were only about 6.5 on a 1–10 scale (as compared to 9.5 when they were asked the same question of the pretransformed animal). These results are consistent with the causal model in Figure 12-11C in which superficial features continue to exhibit nonzero weight on categorization judgments even when the presence or absence of the so-called defining feature is unambiguous.

But, regardless of whether a category is essentialized in full, in part, or not at all, this chapter has demon-strated how classification can be construed as a process that estimates the likelihood that an object is gener-ated by the category's causal model. For centuries, categorization theorists have wrestled with the problem of the relationship between the observable and the unobservable when discussing human knowledge of categories. No less eminent a philosopher than John Locke distinguished nominal essences (observables that form the basis of classification) from real ones (categories' true underlying nature). If for a moment we treat Locke as a psychologist instead, then we can see that he was on the right track all along:

> Nature, in the production of things, always designs them to partake of certain regulated estab-lished essences, which are to be the models of all things to be produced. (Locke, 1690/1974, pp. 289–290)

References

Ahn, W., March, J. K., Luhmann, C. C., & Lee, K. (2002). Effect of theory based correlations on typicality judgments. *Memory & Cognition, 30,* 107–118.

Armstrong, S. L., Gleitman, L. R., & Gleitman, H. (1983). What some concepts might not be. *Cognition, 13,* 263–308.

Barrett, S. E., Abdi, H., Murphy, G. L., & Gallagher, J. M. (1993). Theory-based correlations and their role in children's concepts. *Child Development, 64,* 1595–1616.

Bloom, P. (1998). Theories of artifact categorization. *Cognition, 66,* 87–93.

Braisby, N., Franks, B., & Hampton, J. (1996). Essentialism, word use, and concepts. *Cognition, 59,* 247–274.

Cheng, P. (1997). From covariation to causation: A causal power theory. *Psychological Review, 104,* 367–405.

Coley, J. D., Medin, D. L., & Atran, S. (1997). Does rank have its privilege? Inductive inference within folkbiological taxonomies. *Cognition, 64,* 73–112.

Diesendruck, G. (2001). Essentialism in Brazilian children's extensions of animal names. *Develop-mental Psychology, 37,* 49–60.

Gelman, S. A. (2003). *The essential child: The origins of essentialism in everyday thought.* New York: Oxford University Press.

Gelman, S. A., Coley, J. D., & Gottfried, G. M. (1994). Essentialist beliefs in children: The acquisition of concepts and theories. In L. A. Hirschfeld & S. A. Gelman (Eds.), *Mapping the mind* (pp. 341–367). Cambridge, England: Cambridge University Press.

Gelman, S. A., & Wellman, H. M. (1991). Insides and essences: Early understandings of the nonobvious. *Cognition, 38,* 213–244.

Glymour, C. (1998). Learning causes: Psychological explanations of causal explanation. *Minds and Machines, 8,* 39–60.

Hampton, J. A. (1995). Testing the prototype theory of concepts. *Journal of Memory and Language, 34,* 686–708.

Hampton, J. A. (1998). Similarity-based categorization and fuzziness of natural categories. *Cognition, 65,* 137–165.

Hirschfeld, L. A. (1996). *Race in the making: Cognition, culture, and the child's construction of human kinds.* London: MIT Press.

Jordan, M. I. (Ed.). (1999). Learning in graphical models. Cambridge, MA: MIT Press.

Kalish, C. W. (1995). Essentialism and graded category membership in animal and artifact categories. *Memory & Cognition, 23,* 335–349.

Keil, F. C. (1989). *Concepts, kinds, and cognitive development.* Cambridge, MA: MIT Press.

Keil, F. C. (1994). The birth and nurture of concepts by domains: The origins of concepts of living things. In L. A. Hirschfeld & S. A. Gelman (Eds.), *Mapping the mind* (pp. 234–254). Cambridge, England: Cambridge University Press.

Lisker, L., & Abramson, A. S. (1970). The voicing dimension & some experiments in comparitive phonetics. In *Proceedings of the 6th International*

Congress of Phonetic Science, pp. 563–567. Academia, Prague.

Locke, J. (1690/1974). *Essay on human understanding.* New York: Meridian.

Malt, B. C. (1994). Water is not H_2O. *Cognitive Psychology, 27,* 41–70.

Malt, B. C., & Johnson, E. C. (1992). Do artifacts have cores? *Journal of Memory and Language, 31,* 195–217.

Malt, B. C., & Smith, E. E. (1984). Correlated properties in natural categories. *Journal of Verbal Learning and Verbal Behavior, 23,* 250–269.

Matan, A., & Carey, S. (2001). Developmental changes within the core of artifact concepts. *Cognition, 78,* 1–26.

McCloskey, M., & Glucksberg, S. (1978). Natural categories: Well-defined or fuzzy sets. *Memory & Cognition, 6,* 462–472.

Medin, D. L., & Ortony, A. (1989). Psychological essentialism. In S. Vosniadou & A. Ortony (Eds.), *Similarity and analogical reasoning.* (pp. 179–196). Cambridge, England: Cambridge University Press.

Miller, G. A., & Johnson-Laird, P. N. (1976). *Language and perception.* Cambridge, MA: Harvard University Press.

Nosofsky, R. M. (1992). Exemplars, prototypes, and similarity rules. In A. F. Healy, S. M. Kosslyn, & R. M. Shiffrin (Eds.), *From learning processes to cognitive processes: Essays in honor of William K. Estes* (pp. 149–167). Hillsdale, NJ: Erlbaum.

Osherson, D. M., & Smith, E. E. (1981). On the adequacy of prototype theory as a theory of concepts. *Cognition, 9,* 35–58.

Pearl, J. (1988). *Probabilistic reasoning in intelligent systems: Networks of plausible inference.* San Mateo, CA: Morgan Kaufman.

Pearl, J. (2000). *Causality: Models, reasoning, and inference.* Cambridge, England: Cambridge University Press.

Rehder, B. (2003a). Categorization as causal reasoning. *Cognitive Science, 27,* 709–748.

Rehder, B. (2003b). A causal-model theory of conceptual representation and categorization. *Journal of Experimental Psychology: Learning, Memory, and Cognition, 29,* 1141–59.

Rehder, B., & Burnett, R. C. (2005). Feature inference and the causal structure of object categories. *Cognitive Psychology, 50,* 264–314.

Rehder, B., & Hastie, R. (2004). Category coherence and category-based property induction. *Cognition, 91,* 113–153.

Rips, L. J. (1989). Similarity, typicality, and categorization. In S. Vosniadou & A. Ortony (Eds.), *Similarity and analogical reasoning* (pp. 21–59). New York: Cambridge University Press.

Smith, E. E., Medin, E. L., & Rips, L. J. (1984). A psychological approach to concepts: Comments on Rey's "Concepts and stereotypes." *Cognition, 17,* 265–274.

Smith, J. D., & Minda, J. P. (2000). Thirty categorization results in search of a model. *Journal of Experimental Psychology: Learning, Memory, and Cognition, 26,* 3–27.

Waldmann, M. R., & Hagmayer, Y. (2005). Seeing versus doing: Two modes of accessing causal knowledge. *Journal of Experimental Psychology: Learning, Memory, and Cognition, 31,* 216–227.

Waldmann, M. R., Holyoak, K. J., & Fratianne, A. (1995). Causal models and the acquisition of category structure. *Journal of Experimental Psychology: General, 124,* 181–206.

13

Data-Mining Probabilists or Experimental Determinists?

A Dialogue on the Principles Underlying Causal Learning in Children

Thomas Richardson, Laura Schulz, & Alison Gopnik

This dialogue is a distillation of a real series of conversations that took place at that most platonic of academies, the Center for Advanced Studies in the Behavioral Sciences, between the first and third authors. The second author had determinist leanings to begin with and acted as an intermediary.

Determinism, Faithfulness, and Causal Inference

Narrator: [*Meno and Laplace stand in the corridor of a daycare, observing toddlers at play through a window.*]

Meno: Do you ever wonder how it is that children manage to learn so many causal relations so successfully, so quickly? They make it all seem effortless. A 16-month-old of my acquaintance got my cordless phone to do things I didn't know it could, and very speedily I might add.

Laplace: Yes . . . not only do they manage to sidestep metaphysical questions, they also seem quite able to make do without randomized controlled experiments and with tiny sample sizes.

Meno: Leaving aside the question of how children learn for a while, can we agree on some basic principles for causal inference by anyone—child, adult, or scientist?

Laplace: I think so. I think we can both generally agree that, subject to various caveats, two variables will not be dependent in probability unless there is some kind of causal connection present.

Meno: Yes—that's what I'd call the weak causal Markov condition. I assume that the kinds of caveats you have in mind are to restrict this principle to situations in which a discussion of cause and effect might be reasonable in the first place?

Laplace: Absolutely. I don't want to get involved in discussions of whether X causes $2X$ or whether the monthly changes in height of my elder son are causing the monthly changes in height of my younger son.

Instead, let's consider a real, practical, and indeed, sometimes lifesaving kind of causal inference—the kind of inference we make in scientific medicine. From that perspective, a discussion of cause and effect starts from the assumption that there is a population of units (say, patients in a clinical trial) and a set of treatments (say, drug vs. placebo). For each potential assignment of a treatment to a unit, there is a well-defined outcome that we could, in principle, discover by assigning that treatment to that unit. If we could simply systematically give all the units each kind of treatment and observe the outcomes, we could discover which treatments caused particular outcomes. Causal inference is difficult because we can usually only find out what would happen to a particular unit under one treatment. We can't observe the counterfactual—what would have happened if we'd chosen another treatment. We can't observe whether for example, a particular patient would also have recovered if he had taken the placebo rather than the drug.

Narrator: [See J. Neyman, Sur les applications de la thar des probabilities aux experiences Agaricales: Essay des principle, 1923, as excerpted in English in Dabrowska and Speed, 1990; Rubin, 1974.]

Meno: Why do you say "usually"? Isn't it logically impossible to see the same unit under two treatments?

Laplace: Well, in some situations it may be reasonable to assume that the effect of applying the treatment to the unit is sufficiently short-lived that we can later apply another treatment to the same unit and then compare the outcomes. The effect of applying the second treatment would be assumed to be the same as if it had been applied first.

One would typically do this with a set of units and randomize the order of treatments. For instance, if you wanted to see if a particular drug had short-term side effects, you might use a within-subjects design—give each patient the drug and

then, after a pause, give the patient the placebo (and vice versa).

On other occasions, we might think that distinct units were sufficiently similar in all respects that their outcomes under the same treatment might be assumed to be identical for practical purposes. We assume, for instance, that a new patient is similar enough to the patients in our sample so that the drug will affect the patient in the same way.

Meno: But, how can you make that assumption without a population of identical twins? Surely, any such assumption will be untestable; you can't escape the fundamental problem of causal inference so easily.

Laplace: Yes, of course. . . . If you like to drink your skepticism neat, then we might ask how we know that the future will conform to the past and, failing any kind of satisfactory answer, abandon the whole epistemological roadshow.

I mention these within-subjects or crossover experimental designs because I think they may be relevant to what our toddlers are doing.

Meno: Let's come back to that, but first I want to follow up on the weak causal Markov condition. How precisely do you see it as justifying causal inference in your medical example?

Laplace: If there is dependence between the treatment assignment and the outcome of the experiment, then according to the weak causal Markov condition, (a) treatment is causing outcome, (b) outcome is causing treatment, or there is a common cause of outcome and treatment . . . (or some combination thereof) (Figure 13-1).

Meno: I see, and if treatment were randomized, then that means that (b) and (c) are ruled out because the treatment a patient receives is determined by

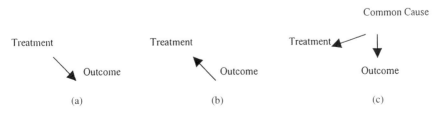

FIGURE 13-1 (a) Treatment causes outcome; (b) outcome causes treatment; (c) treatment and outcome have a common cause.

the randomizer (e.g. the flip of a coin) rather than the patient's (potential) response to the drug or any common cause (e.g., the doctor's beliefs about the patient).

Laplace: Yes—in fact, if there is a time order (i.e., outcome does not exist) prior to the treatment being assigned, then we might rule out (b) a priori, but randomization is required to eliminate (c) as a possibility.

Meno: When we say *dependence*, what do we mean? Presumably we don't mean that the outcome is always entirely determined by the treatment?

Laplace: The case in which outcome is determined by treatment is an important special case, and we return to it in a minute, but in describing the weak causal Markov condition we have in mind probabilistic dependence: The distribution of outcomes in the treatment group and in the control group are different. Naturally, this only makes sense if we have some population or hypothetical population of units.

Meno: I see, so this condition is only supposed to apply to causation between variables, not between individual events.

So we agree that, subject to certain caveats, dependence, whether probabilistic or deterministic, implies the presence of a causal connection. What about the reverse? Suppose that we do not observe any dependence between two variables, what may we then conclude? Is it reasonable to conclude that treatment does not cause the outcome?

Laplace: That assumption is an instance of the assumption known as the causal faithfulness condition. But, here the way is less straightforward. For instance, suppose that we give a group of patients a treatment to reduce the amount of insulin in the body (e.g., by changing it into some other form), but that the body responds by generating additional insulin, exactly matching the amount removed by the drug.

Meno: I see. In the situation you describe insulin level remains unchanged regardless of whether the patient has taken the drug or the placebo, so we might think that the drug had no causal effect. However, if we were able to prevent the body from generating additional insulin, then the drug would have an effect?

Laplace: Yes. For instance, it would have an effect in a population of diabetics. This is an instance of the point made about causal effects defined relative to a comparison of two (counterfactual) outcomes corresponding to different treatments. The fact that an intervention does not change any individual outcome does not mean that in the context of a second intervention (e.g., destroying the body's capability to produce insulin) the intervention will not change any outcomes.

Meno: But, is this a real problem? Within the population of nondiabetic patient treatments, the drug would, in fact, have no effect on the outcome for any individual, so for practical purposes, it is just as if it had no causal influence at all.

Laplace: Agreed. However, such cases may present problems if we want accurate representations of causal systems. These representations are useful because they allow us to say not only what has happened or even what will happen, but also what would happen if we made new interventions. For instance, suppose we want to represent a causal system with a directed graph. If the presence of a directed path is taken to indicate that there is an effect, and the graph is intended to represent the effects of simultaneous interventions on more than one variable, then one is faced with a choice between a graph that disobeys the faithfulness condition (e.g., by including an edge from the drug to the insulin level in the body) and a graph that is faithful (e.g., by omitting an edge from the drug to insulin level) but does not correctly predict the results of multiple interventions.

There are other situations for which the distribution of outcomes may not change under different treatments, so that there is no dependence that may be observed in a randomized experiment, but at the same time each person's pair of counterfactual outcomes are different under the different treatments. For instance, imagine a treatment that switches a person's gender. If the treatment and control groups initially have equal numbers of men and women, then the proportion of females in the treatment and control groups will be the same at the end of the experiment.

Meno: But the treatment would have had a noticeable effect on the individuals in the treatment group.

Laplace: That is if you are willing to assume that the people in the treatment group would not also have spontaneously switched gender had they been in the control group. (Isn't that the kind of assumption you warned me about?) Also, note that the effect would only be "evident" if you knew the gender the individual would have had if untreated. For instance, suppose there is a treatment that has this effect in the first few days after conception, before it is possible to determine the child's gender. In this case, you would not be able to observe any change; hence, there would be no way to observe the effect directly.

Meno: I see; so, every individual's outcome would be different under treatment and control, yet there would be no way to discover this from looking at the distribution of outcomes in treatment and control.

Narrator: For a human population, the ratio of males to female births is not equal; hence, given a large enough sample size, one would still be able to detect the effect.

Meno: These scenarios still seem slightly outlandish. They appear to me to be like causal illusions: Like a masterful *trompe l'oeil*, our initial impressions of the situation are incorrect, but on further inspection we can see what is really going on. Might we not agree that, absent other information, we might adopt as a working hypothesis that the absence of dependence implies the absence of a causal relationship?

Laplace: I'm fairly comfortable with that. There are technical arguments that may be advanced for such a principle: If there is independence between treatment and outcome, although treatment causes outcome, then several causal pathways must "cancel out," and this is unlikely to happen by chance. However, there is one situation that may often arise in which faithfulness routinely fails. Faithfulness often fails if the causal relationships are deterministic.

Meno: Let me see if I understand the distinction that you have in mind. In general, if a variable X has a causal effect on a variable Y, then knowing the value of X may inform us about the distribution of possible values of Y, but it will not tell us which specific value Y will take on. However, if the relation between X and Y is deterministic, then knowing X, we know the value taken on by Y.

Laplace: Exactly. Consider, for example, a room with an energy-saving lightbulb connected to a light sensor. The bulb only goes on when the room grows dark. Now, consider the "treatment" of opening versus closing the blinds in the room, the outcome being whether there is light in the room. It is easy to see that if the causal relationships are deterministic (i.e., the light sensor and lightbulb never fail), then pulling down the blind has no effect on the outcome variable. So, using the principle that absence of dependence indicates absence of causation, we should conclude that opening the blind has no causal effect on the light in the room.

Narrator: It is important here that the outcome, whether the light is on or off, is binary. If we had a continuous measure of the quality of light in the room, then the relationships would not be deterministic (clouds, streetlights, etc.).

Meno: Isn't this simply the scenario of the insulin-lowering drug mentioned?

Laplace: Yes and no. It is insofar as we have two mechanisms canceling one another. There is a difference, however, in that because our outcomes are determined, there is less room for detecting change by slightly perturbing the scenario. By contrast, if we allowed the relationships to be probabilistic, so that the light sensor and bulb sometimes failed, then it would be easy to detect an effect: Simply count the proportion of time there is light when the blinds are open versus the proportion of the time there is light when the blinds are closed. If the sensor or bulb ever fail, then the latter proportion must be smaller.

Narrator: This tacitly assumes that the probability of failure is unrelated to whether the blinds are open or closed.

Meno: It is unless you happen to do the experiment in an environment with permanent sunshine or darkness, such as the poles or anywhere on Mercury. I see you are arguing that causal relationships that are not deterministic are more likely to obey the causal faithfulness condition. Ironically, the "noise" in a probabilistic system may help us understand more about how the system works than we can understand in the apparently simpler deterministic case.

Laplace: Absolutely. In fact, this point becomes even clearer and more pressing if we consider contexts with more variables. So far, we have only been considering a single candidate cause (the treatment) and a single effect (the outcome). But, of course, causal structures may be a lot more complicated than this (Figure 13-2).

Meno: For those contexts, don't we have to assume the strong causal Markov condition?

Laplace: Yes. Let us review this condition. We need a few more concepts first. If X causes Y, let us say that X is a (causal) *parent* of Y, and Y is a (causal) *child* of X. Similarly, let us say U is a (causal) *ancestor* of V if there is a sequence of variables starting with U and ending with V such that each variable in the chain is the parent of the next. If U is a causal ancestor of V, then we will say that V is a (causal) *descendant* of U. Finally, say that a set of variables is *causally sufficient* if any common causal ancestor of two or more variables is included in the set.

Meno: So, in these terms, the strong causal Markov condition states that, in a causally sufficient set of variables, if we know the values taken by the parents of a given variable X, then learning the values taken by other variables that are not descendants of X tells us nothing about (the distribution of) X itself.

Laplace: Yes, that is exactly right. In fact, for systems in which all causal relationships between parents

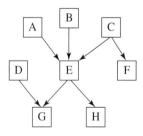

FIGURE 13-2 A, B, and C are parents of E; G and H are children of E; A, B, C, D, and E are ancestors of G; E, G, and H are descendants of B. The set {A, B, E, G} is causally sufficient; the sets {E, F} and {F, H} and {F, G} are not causally sufficient. According to the strong causal Markov condition, G is independent of A, B, C, F, and H given E and D.

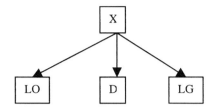

FIGURE 13-3 A simple garage door opener: X is the opener; LO is a light on the opener; D is the door opening; LG is a light in the garage.

and children are linear, the weak causal Markov condition implies the strong condition.

Meno: In this context, the causal faithfulness condition now asserts that every independence relation is a consequence of the strong causal Markov condition applied to the true causal graph. Only independence relations that follow from the causal Markov condition will appear in the data. If some other independence relation appears, then the causal faithfulness assumption has been violated.

Laplace: Again, exactly right. With these concepts in hand, we are now in a position to discuss the problems brought about by deterministic relations. Consider a simple situation with a common cause: Pressing the garage door opener X leads to a light blinking on the opener LO, the door opening D, and a light going on in the garage LG (Figure 13-3).

Meno: So, the Markov condition tells us that if we know whether the opener X was pushed, then D, LO, and LG are irrelevant to one another. In technical parlance, D, LO, and LG are mutually independent conditional on X.

Laplace: Correct, but here is the problem: Suppose that the relationship between the door opener being pressed and the light on the opener LO is deterministic, so that this light goes on when and only when the opener is pressed. It is now easy to see that if I see the opener light, then I immediately know that the opener has been pressed even if I have not observed this directly. But, it then follows that the door opening D and the garage light LG are independent given only knowledge of the light on the opener LO. This independence does not follow from the causal Markov condition: If the relationship between X and LG were not deterministic, then this extra independence would not hold, yet the causal graph would be the same.

Meno: So far, I follow. Suppose I were to try to make inferences about causal structure from conditional independence, assuming the causal Markov condition and, contrary to fact, the causal faithfulness condition held? All such procedures use the fact that under these conditions, if X is a causal parent of Y, then X and Y will always be dependent regardless which other variables we know (or condition on). I do not see that causing immediate problems here because this extra independence of D and LG given LO simply tells us that there can be no edge between D and LG, which is correct.

Laplace: Yes, but there are more unfaithful independence relations here. We already know that LO and LG are independent once we know X. But, if X and LO are logically equivalent, then LG and X are also independent once we know LO because we know LO if and only if we know X. Likewise, D and X are independent once we know LO.

Meno: I see; so, in fact we will end up with no edges except the one between X and LO.

Laplace: I'm afraid so.

Meno: I see now why those proposing the causal faithfulness condition as an inferential principle for learning causal structure explicitly exclude deterministic contexts. In those contexts, the faithfulness assumption will often (in fact, usually) be false.

Narrator: For example, Spirtes, Glymour, and Scheines (1993) state: "We will not consider algorithms for constructing causal graphs when such deterministic relations obtain, nor will we consider tests for deciding whether a set of variables X determines a variable Y" (p. 57).

Determinism in Children's Causal Inferences

Meno: Can we return to children's learning?

Laplace: By all means.

Meno: Inspired by my discussion with Socrates about geometry, I also have concluded that empirical developmental psychology is the best way to answer epistemological questions. So, I have been reading the developmental literature and find that several authors have put forward the suggestion that children learn causal structure by "implementing" inference algorithms that rely on the Markov and faithfulness assumptions.

Laplace: I think I have heard of this. Can you give me an example?

Meno: In one set of experiments, children were shown a device that was called a *blicket detector*, a box with the capability of emitting a sound when blickets were placed on it.

In these experiments, objects of two different types, let us say A and B, were placed on the detector. The children observed the detector making a noise in certain configurations and were then asked various questions.

Laplace: I think I follow.

Meno: In one experiment, 3- and 4-year-old children were divided into two groups. One group, in the one-cause condition, were shown the following sequence of events:

A on detector with noise

B on detector without noise

A and B on detector with noise (repeated twice)

The second group, in the two-cause condition, were shown the following:

A on detector with noise (repeated three times)

B on detector without noise (once)

B on detector with noise (repeated twice)

In each case, the children were then asked if each object was a blicket. In the one-cause condition, children said that Object A was a blicket more than twice as often (96% vs. 41%). In the two-cause condition, they were roughly equally likely to say that A and B were blickets (97% and 81.5%, respectively). In another version of the experiment, children were asked which of the two objects was a blicket. The results were similar.

Narrator: [See Gopnik, Sobel, Schulz, and Glymour, 2001, Experiment 1.]

Laplace: I think I follow the logic that the children might have used, but I do not see the connection to Markov and faithfulness.

Meno: Isn't it obvious? The children took the frequencies observed in the data and observed that in the one-cause condition

$$0 = P(\text{Noise} \mid \text{not A and B}), P(\text{Noise} \mid \text{A and not B}) = P(\text{Noise} \mid \text{A and B}) = 1$$

Hence, the presence of A makes Noise more likely, and Noise and B are independent given A. If the children also believe that the detector does not make a noise without a trigger, so $P(\text{Noise} \mid \text{not A and not B}) = 0$, then Noise and B are also independent given not A. Hence, by the faithfulness condition we may conclude that B is not a cause of Noise. Because A and Noise are dependent, by the Markov condition they are causally connected: It could be that the fact that A is on the detector causes the noise, that the noise causes A to be on the block, or that there is some common cause of both events. However, both the description of the blicket detector and the fact that A is placed by an investigator suggest that the placement of A is an external intervention (i.e., it is *exogenous*), hence we may conclude that A is a cause of noise.

Laplace: I see; if the placement of the block near the detector were not performed by a human (e.g., it was a consequence of some larger mechanism), then we might conclude that there was some common cause at work.

Meno: Exactly. You still look skeptical.

Laplace: I have several concerns with this argument. Broadly, I am not convinced that the formalism of probability theory needs to be invoked to explain the logic that is used here. After all, the relationships between the detector and the blocks are deterministic, aren't they, at least in the one-cause task? Every time a blicket is placed on the detector, it goes off. Further, I think that if probability theory were used in the way that is suggested, then we would be less good at learning causal relationships than in fact we are. Third, I am skeptical about invoking the faithfulness assumption in this context because as an inferential principle I believe that it is incompatible with

a belief that one is observing a simple deterministic system.

Meno: Please go on. What do you see as problematic about the use of probability theory.

Laplace: Were I a child, I would be hesitant about regarding the observed (relative) frequencies seen in such a small number of cases as representative of the probability that any of these events would happen in these conditions.

Meno: Why shouldn't one do so?

Laplace: Well, suppose that I first showed the following four outcomes:

Nothing on detector without noise

A on detector with noise

A on detector without noise

Nothing on detector with noise

Meno: So, from faithfulness I would conclude that A is not a cause of the noise because the probability of noise is independent of A: $P(\text{Noise} \mid \text{A}) = P(\text{Noise} \mid \text{not A}) = 1/2$.

Laplace: But, here is the problem. If you continue to apply the same logic, and I now tell you that I am going to place A on the detector, then before you see the outcome, you can conclude that you will believe that there is a causal relationship between A and the noise.

Meno: That seems like an absurd outcome. How does it follow?

Laplace: Well, if we place A on the detector and it makes a noise, then with that additional observation, according to the observed frequencies, $P(\text{Noise} \mid \text{A}) = 2/3$, while $P(\text{Noise} \mid \text{not A}) = 1/2$, so noise and A are dependent. Conversely, if we place A on the detector and it fails to make a noise, then $P(\text{Noise} \mid \text{A}) = 1/3$; $P(\text{Noise} \mid \text{not A}) = 1/2$, so again A and the detector are dependent. In fact, even before I show you any data, if you know how many trials you plan under each condition, you may be able to conclude that, if the observed frequencies are assumed to be representative, then there will have to be a causal connection. For example, if we plan an odd number of trials in some condition and assume that the observed frequencies in those trials are representative, then it will simply have to follow that the frequencies will indicate dependence.

Narrator: This assumes that the outcome is binary.

Meno: I see the problem. But, it is important to remember that we are merely observing the reasoning patterns employed by young children; there is no reason to assume that their inferences should abide by normative principles.

Laplace: Indeed. Psychologists have often documented our "irrational" belief in the "law" of small numbers.

Narrator: Tversky and Kahneman (1982, p. 7) describe the law of small numbers as the belief "according to which even small samples are highly representative of the populations from which they are drawn."

Laplace: But, I think it is equally important to bear in mind that there may be more than one explanation for the observed behavior. Furthermore, the inferences made in the one- and two-cause condition experiment you described seem eminently reasonable—one would not expect an adult, even one attuned to statistical inference, to reason any differently. Surely you would agree that if we can explain children's behavior in these experiments without suggesting that they are systematically irrational, then that would be a preferable outcome?

Meno: Agreed. On reflection, I realize that when inferences about causal structure are made by machine learning algorithms employing faithfulness and Markov conditions, then these are based on databases containing hundreds, if not thousands, of cases.

Laplace: Yes—without further assumptions, any reasonable statistical procedure would be agnostic about the presence or absence of dependence from samples as small as those used by the children in the experiment you described.

Meno: Is it not possible that the children think it is safe to conclude that these small samples are representative because they are presented by a trusted adult figure in the person of the experimenter?

Laplace: One might think this, but I see two problems. First, if one really believed that one was observing a blicket detector that was not deterministic, then surely one must believe that it is outside the control of the experimenter to make it produce or fail to produce a noise on any particular occasion? In which case, there is no way for the experimenter to ensure that the data are representative: Although they might choose when to place or not to place the blocks, whether a noise is produced would not be entirely within the experimenter's control, so "representativeness" could not be guaranteed.

Hence, when the detector appears to behave indeterministically, the child would have to believe that the experimenter in fact controlled all aspects of the device and was creating the illusion of probabilistic data to (beneficently) reveal the true probabilistic properties of the device (that would pertain in the absence of the experimenter?). Although, of course, this is in fact how these experiments are conducted, I believe it would be an unusual 3-year-old who would adopt this as their working hypothesis.

Narrator: In principle, even with an indeterministic device, an experimenter might control the observed proportions by choosing to stop at an "appropriate" point. However, it would again be rather surprising if feelings of trust with respect to the experimenter were parlayed in such an elaborate manner: The sensitivity of frequentist statistical inferences to the choice of stopping rule was something that only became widely understood within the last 50 years.

Meno: I agree.

Laplace: Second, if it could be demonstrated that the children had such deep trust in the experimenter that they would consider this a plausible scenario, then one might seriously question the ecological validity of any inferences made about causal learning that took place in such a scenario.

Meno: Suppose I accept, as you appear to be arguing, that such small samples cannot be regarded as data on which one may reliably base conclusions about probabilities. You mentioned that you thought that the causal inferences made might be explained as normative without reference to probability theory. Can you expand on that?

Laplace: You read me correctly: From a statistical perspective, very little can be obtained from such small samples, other than the fact that certain combinations of events are possible (have nonzero probability). When I say *statistical perspective*, I mean if one starts out with the hypothesis that there are probabilistic causal relationships between the variables.

If this is the viewpoint with which we typically viewed the world, then it is somewhat surprising, perhaps even inexplicable, that most people would agree on the correct answer to the blicket question, at least in the one-cause scenario.

Meno: Some psychologists have made many of the same arguments and argue that therefore children's inferences must be constrained by a great deal of prior knowledge in a Bayesian way.

Narrator: [*See Tennenbaum and Griffiths, chapter 10, this volume.*]

Laplace: If we are successful in providing a normatively rational explanation for children's inferences, then it will not be surprising if similar conclusions would be drawn by a hypothetical Bayesian agent. Some might even regard this as necessary.

However, I do not believe that this is the only explanation for such inferences, and indeed, I think that such an account leaves unresolved as many questions as it addresses.

Meno: Can you be more specific? Doesn't the Bayesian approach, in principle, provide a complete description of how to update one's beliefs?

Laplace: That it does. However, I would argue that a psychological theory should explain why people agree on the "correct" answer in the one-cause blicket experiment. The Bayesian approach does not prescribe any specific set of prior beliefs; in fact, one might expect different agents with different life experiences to have different beliefs. For example, Calvinist children might think that Divine intervention was responsible for the blicket detector making a noise at precisely the moment when the block was placed on it; Jungians might think it was just another instance of synchronicity at work.

Without an explanation regarding why we all have similar prior beliefs pertaining to such situations, the Bayesian account does not explain why we have the beliefs that we have.

Meno: I see. You contend that for any particular set of (posterior) beliefs we have after making some observations, a proponent of Bayesian inference might always concoct a hypothetical set of prior beliefs for us, which had we had them and had we been Bayesian would have resulted in the beliefs we have. But, because this could have been done for any set of posterior beliefs, the existence of such a set of prior beliefs in any given case does not constitute evidence that we arrived at our beliefs by Bayesian means.

Laplace: Indeed. Further, I believe that there is a computational issue that arises.

Meno: How so?

Laplace: It is a simple consequence of Bayes' rule that any hypothesis that is initially assigned probability 0 will continue to be assigned probability 0 regardless of the evidence that is observed.

Meno: I'm familiar with that, but how is it relevant here?

Laplace: The upshot is that if we do not wish to be unable to learn the true causal structure eventually, then we must ensure that we do not assign it probability 0 initially. Because the number of candidate causal structures increases quickly with the number of variables, an ideal Bayesian reasoner is faced with the prospect of keeping track of personal beliefs concerning hundreds, if not millions, of candidate hypotheses.

Meno: This is required if we are to be "ideal" Bayesians, but couldn't we be flawed Bayesians? For example, just entertaining seriously a few hypotheses, while regarding the remainder as having some small probability that we don't bother to update?

Laplace: We might, but again, as with the specification of prior beliefs, I believe that the "meat" of any such account lies in the details of how and why such an approximation scheme works in practice.

Narrator: J. Tennenbaum (personal communication, 30 January 2005) has proposed that a causal learner might approximate a (Metropolis-Hastings) Markov chain Monte Carlo scheme for sampling from a posterior distribution. For example, a learner could keep in mind a single model but be continually switching from one model to another even in the absence of any new data (but with the probability of switching determined by the data observed so far). At any given moment, the learner would have "in mind" only one model but would continually be changing this model, so that over an extended period the proportion of the time that the model is in mind would approximate the posterior probability. This is an intriguing idea, but it still requires that the learner have "access" to prior probabilities assigned to all possible models. (The issue of explaining/specifying priors also remains.)

Meno: I also see that most of us would consider it possible for us eventually to learn about a system with a structure that has features unlike anything we have ever seen, whereas an ideal Bayesian would need to have initially considered such a system at the outset. This reminds me of a discussion I once had with Socrates concerning the apparent problem of coming to learn anything new.

Narrator: [*See Plato*, Meno 80 D.]

Laplace: Although I would not wish to rule out a Bayesian inferential approach per se, I believe that there is another, perhaps simpler, way forward: The apparent conflict between strong human agreement concerning the correct answer in the (one-cause) blicket and statistical agnosticism from small amounts of data suggests to me that most people do not adopt a statistical perspective on these problems, Bayesian or otherwise. Instead, they assume that they may simply be observing a deterministic system.

Meno: I can certainly see how that might simplify matters in the one-cause situation: The detector makes a noise if and only if Block A is placed on it; Block B is irrelevant.

Laplace: This is exactly what I had in mind, but nothing comes for free. In arriving at this conclusion, we have used the (weak) causal Markov assumption: The observation that the machine makes a noise after Block A is placed on it is interpreted as an intervention (or treatment), namely, placement of Block A then leading to an effect (or outcome), namely, the noise. The weak causal Markov condition invites us to conclude that there is a causal connection underlying the observed association. Under the hypothesis that placement of Block A is

an (exogenous) intervention, this implies that A is the cause of the noise.

Meno: That tells us that A is a cause of the noise. But, how do we eliminate the possibility that B is also a cause? In the analysis, we described the investigators assumed faithfulness and assumed that the failure of B was representative, that is, that in general there was no dependence between B and the noise. How can we draw this conclusion without those assumptions?

Laplace: Rather than employ faithfulness, we simply employ another parsimony principle: Because no other causal relationships are required to explain the observed events, we assume that none are present.

Meno: Of course. Faithfulness may also be viewed as a parsimony principle in the sense that, as employed in some learning, it leads us to choose stochastic causal structures with fewer parameters. Here, in the one-cause condition we presume that there is no relationship between Block B and the noise, not because we have observed them to be statistically independent, but simply because we can explain all of the observed noises without assuming that B will lead the detector to make a noise.

Laplace: Absolutely right. From my point of view, we have not nearly enough data to say anything about the statistical independence of B and the detector.

Meno: But, wouldn't this sort of deterministic inference just collapse to good old-fashioned deductive logic? A is a blicket if and only if, if A was placed on the detector then the detector activates.

Laplace: Not exactly. Standard propositional logic does not include methods for dealing with causal interventions.

Meno: Let me see if I understand. When we have a set of propositions such as

Socrates is a man implies Socrates is mortal.

Socrates is mortal implies life insurance will not be free.

these implications are supposed to hold true always, whereas we wish to consider situations in which, via external intervention, some propositions are no longer true.

Laplace: Precisely. If there is a medical breakthrough, some (rich?) people's lives might be extended indefinitely. In such a case, the first proposition might no longer hold true—we might intervene to make Socrates immortal—but the second will no doubt continue to hold true. The propositions in a causal model are thus "modular" in the sense that an ideal intervention can override some propositions while leaving others intact.

Narrator: [*See Appendix*; *Pearl, 2000, Chapter 7*; *Schulz et al., chapter 5, this volume.*]

Laplace: Thus, this "causal logic" has features that make it different from classical deductive logic. In particular, the difference between interventions and contingencies is inferentially crucial, but there is no such distinction in classical logic. Both children and adults seem to be appropriately sensitive to that distinction.

Narrator: [*See, for instance, Gopnik et al., 2004; Steyvers, Tenenbaum, Wagenmakers, and Blum, 2003; Lagnado et al., chapter 10, this volume.*]

Meno: I can see that assuming that things are deterministic and applying a causal logic simplifies matters, but surely such an assumption is too stringent to be of much use in real life, when evidence is almost never deterministic. For that matter, the data presented in the two-cause condition are incompatible with a deterministic functional relationship. Remember that in the experiment children see A set off the detector 3/3 times, and B set it off 2/3 times. They conclude that both blocks are blickets. But, here on one occasion we have block B alone and a noise, and on another occasion we have block B alone and no noise. The same is true of other developmental experiments. In one of the puppet machine experiments, for example (Gopnik et al., 2004), one puppet almost always, but not always, makes the other puppet go.

Laplace: It is true that the two-cause condition is incompatible with a belief that whether a noise is produced is determined entirely by which blocks are present. However, by hypothesizing an additional unobserved variable, for example, a loose connection between the battery and the buzzer or the amount of pressure the experimenter applied when placing the object, one could easily construct a deterministic model that was compatible with the observed data. Then, you could make

inferences about this deterministic model in the way I described.

Meno: But, is there any evidence to suggest that agents are willing to postulate the existence of such unobserved causes to "save" their belief in determinism. I seem to recall reading something.

Laplace: Indeed, there is. Consider the following experiment:

Children are initially told that the experimenter likes to trick her confederate. The children then see a light, which is activated by a switch. There is also a ring on the light, which must be in place for the light to work.

Children are divided into two groups. In the first group (stochastic causation condition), the confederate makes eight attempts to turn the light on by pushing the switch but is successful only on two occasions. In the second group (deterministic causation condition), the confederate is successful on all eight attempts. After seeing these eight trials, the experimenter then reveals a small key chain flashlight to the children, which has not been seen previously. Both groups of children are then asked to make it so that the switch does not work. Most of the children (15 of 16) in the stochastic causation group then reach for the flashlight even though they have never seen it do anything (one child chose the ring). By contrast, in the deterministic causation group almost all of the children (14 of 16) choose to remove the ring (two choose the flashlight).

Narrator: [*Schulz, Sommerville, and Gopnik, in press, Experiment 1.*]

Meno: Interesting. So, this indicates that the children in the stochastic causation group do not believe that "things just happen." They think that if the light is not working, there must be a (deterministic) explanation, and they are sufficiently invested in finding such an explanation that they are willing to hypothesize that an entirely new object has such powers.

But isn't it problematic that children are willing to attribute such hidden variables so easily? With enough hidden variables, we can represent any input-output function by an infinite variety of different graphs. Having too many causal answers is just as bad as having too few, and accurate causal inference will be just as difficult in these cases.

The children will be like Freudians or astrologers who can explain everything and therefore cannot really explain anything.

Laplace: But, the experiment points to more than that: Notice that most of the children in the deterministic causation group did not attribute causal powers to the flashlight. This suggests that the children do not hypothesize hidden variables in a promiscuous fashion. Rather, they do so parsimoniously and systematically. The events observed in the deterministic causation condition do not require any additional variables to be fully explained.

Meno: Still, it seems to me that there is a problem here. Let me return to your garage door example and consider the situation in which I do not directly observe whether you pressed the opener X, although we do observe the other three variables D, LO, and LG. There are then no deterministic relationships among the observed variables, yet I will still fall into error if I make inferences based on faithfulness. For example, LG and D are independent given LO; hence, I will suppose that they are not causally connected, when in fact they are.

Laplace: Absolutely right.

Meno: Well, then, here is what I do not understand. If deterministic relations, even between observed and unobserved variables, are incompatible with using faithfulness, and yet any indeterministic system may be viewed as a deterministic system with hidden variables, then how does it ever make sense to assume faithfulness? Because you seem comfortable with using faithfulness in some indeterministic contexts, doesn't your argument prove too much?

Laplace: An excellent observation. Is there no room left in this world for faithfulness? Here is the solution to your dichotomy. Suppose for a moment that we are omniscient demons, knowing the entire causal nexus.

Meno: "Laplacian" demons?

Laplace: If you insist. Given any set of observed variables, we will add variables to the set until, for any two variables in the set, if they have a common cause, then that variable is included in our set. Such a set of variables may be called *causally sufficient*. If there are no deterministic relationships

among this larger set of (observed and unobserved) variables, then we may proceed to use faithfulness in our analysis of the original variables that we observed.

Meno: Of course, if we were the demon, we would not need to use faithfulness to infer the structure.

Laplace: Agreed. This is obviously a thought experiment. The point is that there is a well-defined set of variables among which we require there to be no deterministic relationships to safely base inferences on faithfulness.

Meno: I see. The scenario with the garage door opener obviously fails the test.

Laplace: Indeed. A simple way in which this condition can be satisfied is if each variable in the system is subject to at least one independent cause.

Meno: I see; so, deterministic relationships are not problematic in a system in which each variable has many causal parents.

Laplace: This is provided that we do not observe all of them, and that is usually the case in complex systems.

Meno: But this is highly problematic in deterministic systems in which variables have only a few parents.

Laplace: Whenever we make causal inferences, we are not considering all the possible variables, observed or hidden, that exist in the universe, but only a small subset of those variables.

Narrator: [*See also Glymour, chapter 18, this volume.*]

Laplace: Metaphysically, we may have a hard time imagining genuinely indeterministic causal relations. But, even if we are metaphysical determinists, in complex settings we often simply ignore the unobserved variables we think are responsible for indeterministic appearances, especially in complex cases—we brush them off as "noise" that is irrelevant for causal inference. From a formal perspective, this epistemological brush-off has just the same consequences as believing in metaphysical indeterminism.

Meno: From what you say, simple deterministic systems are problematic for causal inference from conditional independence relations. Yet, many mechanical devices one can think of behave in exactly this way. After all, the blicket detector is just such a system and so are the other "machines," like the puppet or the gear-toy machine that developmentalists have used to test children's causal inferences. This brings us back to the original question of how children manage to learn such systems with so little data? If they do not use faithfulness to infer complex noisy causal systems, then how else could they manage to learn so much so quickly and accurately?

Laplace: Now, you ask me to enter the realm of conjecture. I can only guess, but I believe there are a number of factors that work to children's advantage.

Let us turn to faithfulness first. As we described, it serves to identify when variables are not causally related. This is important because, in the right context, it allows these algorithms to establish that a particular variable is unconfounded or exogenous—it is not itself affected by other variables in the system.

Meno: I see. Once we have established that variable X is exogenous, then we only require the causal Markov condition to conclude that anything dependent on X is caused by X. If X is exogenous, then we have ruled out the possibility of common causes and ruled out the possibility that anything else is causing X. But, if we cannot use faithfulness, then how else could we establish exogeneity?

Laplace: Children might establish exogeneity in other ways. For one thing, children, unlike data-mining programs, can actively intervene on the causal systems they are learning about. In fact, in their spontaneous play they perform such interventions all the time. It is what parents call "getting into everything." Children might have a background theory that allows them to attribute the property of exogeneity to actions they undertake. In particular, like adults, children might assume that their own intentional actions are the result of free will and so are intrinsically exogenous.

Meno: But in the blicket detector experiments, children do not get to intervene on the system; they just watch other people's interventions.

Laplace: This raises an interesting point. If children also assume that the actions of others are analogous to their own actions—particularly that they are also the result of free will and so are exogenous—then they could make similar inferences by just watching other people manipulate objects.

Meno: I see. In fact, interestingly, several experiments have shown that children will distinguish between actions performed by agents assumed to be like the children themselves and those performed by nonagents.

Narrator: [See Meltzoff, Somerville, chapters 2 and 3 this volume. Also see Schulz, Sommerville, et al., 2005, Experiment 4.]

Meno: Children do not simply observe patterns of association but see goal-directed agents around them performing actions. Thus, a child might be more like a first-year graduate student in a lab or a historian of science, who may be fairly sure that if these otherwise well-adjusted adults spend a lot of time manipulating something, then it is probably causally efficacious in some way.

In fact, some developmentalists, as well as grown-up psychologists, have already argued for the significance of interventions in human causal inference.

Narrator: [See Schulz et al., chapter 5, this volume; Lagnado et al., chapter 8, this volume; Hagemeyer et al., chapter 6, this volume.]

Meno: In this respect, human inference is different from the perspective of a data-mining program, which cannot exclude the possibility that the variables are completely unrelated to one another (or completely confounded by unobserved variables). Other experiments have shown that children can use interventions on deterministic systems to make complicated inferences about the causal structure of those systems—distinguishing common causes, common effects, and causal chains.

Narrator: [See Schulz et al. chapter 5, this volume; Schulz et al., in press.]

Meno: But, what you say suggests that interventions will be especially important, in fact, indispensable, if we want to understand deterministic systems.

By the way, earlier you mentioned crossover or within-individual experiments as playing a role. Can you expand on that point?

Laplace: As mentioned in our discussion, the "fundamental problem of causal inference" is that we typically do not get to view the outcomes for the same subject under two different treatments. Randomization serves to construct groups of subjects whose distributions of outcomes under the same treatment may be considered to be similar.

However, a child typically does not do experiments on a large group of blicket detectors. The child typically only has one detector, but it is often reasonable to assume that different interventions leave the device unchanged.

Meno: Yes—although it is possible to imagine that Block A is somehow "imprinted" on the blicket detector, like tweed trousers on a newly hatched Lorenzian duckling, causing it to squawk when (and only when) its first love is again placed on it—this is certainly not the first hypothesis that springs to mind. Indeed, the word *detector* seems to rule this out.

Laplace: Precisely. It would be an unusual (although perhaps not irrational) child who would say, "Block A is the blicket—it was blicketized by being the first object placed on the detector!"

Some interventions have permanent irreversible effects on objects, such as dropping the glass on the tile floor or pouring ink on the Persian rug, but the fact of irreversibility is usually plain to see. Interventions that lead to undetectable, but permanent, irreversible effects are less common. Hence, children live in a world amenable to within-subject crossover designs.

Meno: Indeed, you could think of children's repetitive spontaneous play with objects as just such an experimental strategy. Grown-up psychologists often treat children's perseveration as a sign of stupidity or at least lack of executive control. But, it also might be an excellent way to get within-subject information, in particular to check that there have been no irreversible changes, so that the same intervention continues to produce the same effect.

In this way, the fundamental problem is avoided, and individual causal effects can be inferred.

Laplace: Yes, in fact, when combined with the assumption of determinism, it also makes feasible inferences about the existence of unobserved hidden causes of a single variable and the causal effect of such hidden causes (i.e., whether they are inhibitory or generative).

Narrator: [*See Schulz, Sommerville, et al., in press, Experiments 2 and 3.*]

Laplace: The Markov and faithfulness conditions sometimes make it possible to infer the existence of an unobserved common cause of two variables in indeterministic systems, and there is some evidence that adults and children make such inferences. But, inferences about the existence of single unobserved causes cannot be made purely on the basis of conditional independence and dependence. (Clustering of imputed "disturbance" terms would be one way to proceed.) Yet, children also seem to make such inferences.

Narrator: [*See Gopnik et al., 2004; Kushnir, Gopnik, Schulz, & Danks. 2003; Schulz et al., chapter 5, this volume.*]

Meno: This may also solve another problem: One concern that I have had with the standard approach to causal inference based on directed acyclic graphs (also called Bayesian networks) is that all causal relationships are asymmetric: If X is a cause of Y, then Y is not a cause of X. In particular, under the standard account of interventions, if we were to intervene on Y, then we would produce no change in X—cyclic systems are explicitly ruled out. Yet, there are simple systems in which causal relationships appear to be reversible. For instance, I can pull the engine of a toy train, and the tender will be pulled along, but if I choose to push the tender forward, then the engine will also be moved. And, in some experiments children seem to infer such cyclic relationships. In the gear-toy experiments, for example, children hypothesized that Gear A might sometimes move Gear B while at the same time Gear B might sometimes move Gear A.

Narrator: [*See Schulz et al., chapter 5, this volume; Schulz et al., in press.*]

Laplace: Reversibility of the type you describe is simple to include in an account of intervention in which two variables are related deterministically and the relationship is one to one, so that each value of X corresponds to a unique value of Y and vice versa. This is a model of intervention corresponding to reversing edges rather than breaking edges. For example, if prior to intervention we have $A \rightarrow B \rightarrow C$ and we then intervene on C, then this will lead to $C \rightarrow B \rightarrow A$.

Narrator: This intervention model may be generalized to having p input variables and p output variables, provided that each possible vector of values for the outputs corresponds to a unique vector of values for the inputs.

Meno: Like any working hypothesis, assuming determinism or near determinism (i.e., a few unobserved variables) will work well if true but may be highly misleading when false.

Laplace: But, again, we do not learn causal relationships purely out of intellectual curiosity. Considerations of utility also play a role. Deterministic causal systems are, by definition, more reliable, and thus more useful, once we have learned them. If our goal is to manipulate the world around us, then learning the subtleties of an unreliable system may not be worth the effort.

In If a system is complex and indeterministic, then we have no hope of learning how to manipulate it, absent large amounts of data; hence, unless we really can gather a lot of data, from a pragmatic point of view we are losing little by ruling out such systems at the beginning.

Remaining Problems

Meno: You've convinced me that a near-deterministic experimental causal logic may serve children as well as the full apparatus of probabilistic Bayes net causal learning algorithms. But, do you see no role for indeterminism in children's learning?

Laplace: That may be going too far. I almost always would qualify anything I say. Empirically, children do seem to use observed frequency as a way of estimating causal strength, much as adults do. For instance, it has been shown that children think a block that sets off the detector 2/3 times has "more special stuff inside" than one that only sets it off 1 of 3 times. Of course, these judgments don't involve causal structure—the sort of judgments captured by causal graphs, but only the parameterization of those graphs.

Narrator: [See Kushnir and Gopnik, 2005.]

Meno: Don't these experiments necessitate the use of indeterministic models as cognitive constructs?

Laplace: An indeterministic model provides one explanation, but observe that it is also possible to see these experiments concerning the amount of special stuff as revealing that children are capable of using different levels of description of frequency rather than using indeterministic models per se.

Meno: How so?

Laplace: If we view the three responses resulting from placing the block on the detector three times in succession as a single response that takes four values 0, 1, 2, 3 (rings of 3), then we can build a deterministic model for the system. Certain blocks lead to a response of 1 of 3; others lead to a response of 2 of 3. For example, it might be the case that every time we place a given block on the detector a constant (deterministic) amount of special stuff is transferred to the detector. The detector accumulates special stuff until a threshold is reached, at which point the detector makes a noise, and its special stuff reservoir is depleted by some (fixed) amount. Although a given block always transfers the same amount, different blocks transfer different amounts.

Meno: I see. If we may set aside your metaphysical theory of special stuff for a moment, there appears to be a more general point here. Your reasoning seems to suggest that another route to incorporating seemingly indeterministic data into a deterministic world view is simply to provide a level of description for our variables that avoids recording the outcome in any specific case but rather just describes ensembles of outcomes. Thus, Y is a deterministic function of X, but Y takes values such as never, rarely, often, always, which refer to collections of individual observations.

Narrator: Note that in a deterministic system a given set of inputs either always or never produces a certain output.

Laplace: Indeed. This is an instance of the following idea, which is familiar from regression: Knowing someone's height does not allow us to predict their weight, but the average weight in a given subpopulation of people who are all of exactly the same height may be a simple deterministic function of that height. If the variable Y takes on values such as never or rarely, then it is basically recording the average (rate) of occurrence of an event under some condition. Thus, we may describe deterministically the way in which X (special stuff) influences the average response (frequency of the detector ringing).

Meno: This also raises a question regarding what it means to "use" an indeterministic model. Regression can be thought of as a statistical procedure derived from a probability model, or it can simply be thought of as line fitting. I could use the regression line for making predictions without explicitly assuming a probability model. In this case, am I or am I not using an indeterministic model?

Laplace: I agree that this is not so clear.

Meno: To my mind, psychological causation seems in some sense far more indeterministic than physical causation, and yet we know that children infer the structure of psychological systems as quickly and easily as they make physical inferences.

Narrator: [*See Schulz and Gopnik, 2004.*]

Laplace: Yes. Other agents are often quite unpredictable in the way in which they respond to us. Our daily interactions certainly provide plenty of time to gather data about those who are closest to us. On the other hand, such indeterministic systems may not have a fixed causal mechanism. Agents around us are changing even as we are learning about them: One of the ways in which they change is that while we learn about them they also are learning about us. This makes the learning task a bit more complicated because data are not generated by a fixed underlying distribution. You may be smiling at me because you like me, because you think that I like you, or more deviously, because you think you have made me think that you like me and so on.

Meno: Virologists and pathologists sometimes have to study systems that are constantly evolving and that change the way they function in response to interventions.

Laplace: Indeed, but viruses that evolve quickly are much harder to combat than those that do not.

Another difference is that in such circumstances the simple fact of gathering data—observing your expressions—is itself an intervention in the system. As every parent of a toddler soon finds

out, often the best way to ensure that a tantrum continues is to try to find out what is wrong. So, it is puzzling that children make these inferences as easily as they do. On the other hand, the fact that children often manipulate their parents and vice versa suggests that perhaps humans are less hard to predict than we might like to believe.

Meno: Making the analogy between the way in which scientists and statisticians analyze their data and the way in which children learn from observations around them seems to me to leave two important parts of the process unexplained: hypothesis generation and concept formation. Do you agree?

Laplace: Absolutely. Statistical analysis of causation often gives no account regarding how particular variables are chosen as candidate causes or effects. Heuristics based on observing other agents may be of assistance to children in this regard. For example, Mommy seems to spend a lot of time fiddling with that little black box, so let me investigate it; someone or something turns the TV off, so let me see if I can find out what it is.

Machine learning algorithms often have a well-defined hypothesis space through which they perform some sort of search. However, children face a much less well-defined, hence larger, search space and arguably do not carry a giant list of all possible causal hypotheses. (This also causes problems for Bayesian accounts.) Choosing good candidate hypotheses in such circumstances seems like a hard problem, but one that they do well. Experiments such as those in which hidden causes (the flashlight) were hypothesized give a tantalizing glimpse of this process in action.

Meno: Finally, Laplace, as I say my association with Socrates has taught me the importance of empirical developmental findings. How could we test your ideas about determinism empirically?

Laplace: I regard the experiments relating to the key chain flashlight described as empirical evidence that children are willing to postulate the existence of hidden variables merely from observations that appear to be indeterministic in a manner not compatible with a conditional independence-based approach because such approaches only postulate common causes. Naturally, this does not rule out the use of probabilistic models in other settings.

More generally, I speculate that if we give children the same problem in a deterministic or near-deterministic way and in a way that genuinely requires them to compute conditional probabilities, then I predict that they will solve it in the deterministic case and not the probabilistic one. All the published studies have been deterministic or nearly so. I have a feeling that some unsuccessful probabilistic experiments might be lurking in wastebaskets and desk drawers.

Meno: Maybe so, but the experimental problem is harder than you might think. As you said, it may be that we use indeterministic information just when we assume that there are many uncontrolled variables, lots of noise in the system. But, a developmental psychologist's first task is to make sure that the problem is clearly posed, and there are no extra factors that might be distracting the child. You may be able to persuade undergraduates that they should only pay attention to the information about probabilities on the sheet directly in front of them. But, it will be much harder to persuade young children to do so (and even with undergraduates, the individual differences among participants suggest that they also may be considering other factors).

Narrator: [See Lagnado et al., chapter 10, this volume; Hagmeyer et al., chapter 10, this volume.]

Meno: How can we be sure that children only pay attention to the variables we control while at the same time leaving them the impression that there are many other uncontrolled variables lurking in the background, and therefore that indeterminism might be appropriate?

Laplace : Perhaps we might exploit the indeterminism of psychological relations.

Meno: I see; suppose we show the child that Bunny the fussy eater will eat plain peanuts one of three times you offer them but will eat them three of four times when you add salt, although he never eats salt alone. The salt influences the probability distribution of Bunny's preferences. Will children infer that the salt has a causal effect on Bunny's actions in this indeterministic case?

Laplace: I think it would be interesting to see how children would respond. However, I believe that, as with the special stuff experiments, it would be possible for someone to describe the result of the experiment deterministically, without reference to probabilities, by saying that, "Bunny frequently eats peanuts with salt, but rarely eats them without."

As with our discussion concerning the pros and cons of a Bayesian explanation of human reasoning, I believe that although many observations may be compatible with a child entertaining an indeterministic model, I think it is unlikely to be necessary. Probability is a relatively recent addition to the set of descriptive methods used by scientists. It was also one that was fiercely resisted at first. Probability may seem to be an integral part of the metaphysical landscape in the 21st century, but it certainly was not always thus.

Meno: Oh, dear. We appear to have raised as many interesting issues as we have resolved. At least we have established the importance and primacy of experimental evidence in informing our theorizing.

As my dear friend Lavoisier says:

In the practice of the sciences imagination, which is ever wandering beyond the bounds of truth, joined to self-love and that self-confidence we are so apt to indulge, prompt us to draw conclusions which are not immediately derived from facts; so that we become in some measure interested in deceiving ourselves.

[In contrast] . . . when we begin the study of any science, we are in a situation, respecting that science, similar to that of children; and the course by which we have to advance is precisely the same which Nature follows in the formation of their ideas. . . . We ought to form no idea but what is a necessary consequence, and immediate effect, of an experiment or observation. (p. 4)

References

Eberhardt, F., Glymour, C., & Scheines, R. (2005). On the number of experiments sufficient and in the worst case necessary to identify all causal relations among N variables. *Proceedings of the 21st Conference on Uncertainty and Artificial Intelligence*, Fahien Bacchus and Tommi Jaakola (eds.), AUAI Press, Corvallis Oregon, pp. 178–184.

Gopnik, A., Glymour, C., Sobel, D., Schulz, L., Kushnir, T., & Danks, D. (2004). A theory of causal learning in children: Causal maps and Bayes nets. *Psychological Review, 111*, 1–31.

Gopnik, A., Sobel, D., Schulz, L., & Glymour, C. (2001). Causal learning mechanisms in very young children: 2-, 3-, and 4-year-olds infer causal relations from patterns of variation and covariation. *Developmental Psychology, 37*, 620–629.

Kushnir, T., & Gopnik, A. (2005). Young children infer causal strength from probabilities and interventions. *Psychological Science, 16*, 678–683.

Kushnir, T., Gopnik, A., Schulz, L., & Danks, D. (2003). Inferring hidden causes. In R. Alterman & D. Kirsch (Eds.). *Proceedings of the 24th Annual Meeting of the Cognitive Science Society*. Boston: Cognitive Science Society.

Lavoisier, A. L. (1994). *Elements of Chemistry* (R. Kerr, Trans.). Chicago: Encyclopedia Britannica. (Original work published 1789)

Mackie, J. L. (1965). Causes and conditions. *American Philosophical Quarterly, 2/4*, 261–264.

Neyman, J. (1923). Sur les applications de la thar des probabilities aux experiences Agaricales: Essay des principle. Roczniki Nauk Rolniczych (Annals of Agricultural Sciences X, 151. Excerpts reprinted (1990) in English (D. Dabrowska and T. Speed, Trans.) in *Statistical Science* 5: 463–472.

Pearl, J. (2000). *Causality*. New York: Oxford University Press.

Rubin, D. B. (1974). Estimating causal effects of treatments in randomized and non-randomized studies. *Journal of Educational Psychology, 66*, 688–701.

Schulz, L., & Gopnik, A. (2004). Causal learning across domains. *Developmental Psychology, 40*, 162–176.

Schulz, L. E., Gopnik, A., & Glymour, C. (in press). Preschool children learn about causal structure from conditional interventions. *Developmental Science*.

Schulz, L. E., & Sommerville, J. (in press). God does not play dice: Causal determinism and preschoolers' causal inferences. *Child Development 11(2)*: 427–442.

Spirtes, P., Glymour, C., & Scheines, R. (1993). *Causation, prediction and search* (Springer Lecture Notes in Statistics No. 81). New York: Springer-Verlag.

Steyvers, M., Tenenbaum, J., Wagenmakers, E. J., & Blum, B. (2003). Inferring causal networks from observations and interventions. *Cognitive Science, 27*, 453–489.

Tversky, A., & Kahneman, D. (1982). *Judgement under uncertainty: Heuristics and biases*. Chapter 1 in D. Kahneman, P. Slovic, and A. Tversky (eds.), Judgment under Uncertainty: Heuristics and Biases, UK: Cambridge University Press.

Appendix

This appendix outlines simple methods for learning cause-effect relationships from small numbers of interventions in a causal system in which all nodes are binary, and all endogenous variables (i.e., with parents) are a (deterministic) disjunction of conjunctions of their parents. We present an algorithm that lays out a simple experimental procedure that enables the learner to learn first indirect and then direct causes. In contrast to other machine learning algorithms, this procedure does not say anything about what should be inferred from passive observations. This is in keeping with the contention (of Laplace) that interventions allow learners to avoid the complexities of probabilistic inference. Further, the algorithm focuses on what causes a specific outcome variable. Again, this reflects the view (again stated by Laplace) that learners are often attempting to (re)produce a particular outcome (e.g., make it go, make Mommy smile, etc.).

The method outlined here is relevant to the blicket experiments (and others like them) only insofar as a participant might view the actions of the person putting the blocks on the detector as (partially) carrying out the sequence of interventions sketched in this method.

Basic Notions and Definitions

Consider a deterministic causal model in which all variables are Boolean, taking values true or false. We also refer to these states as on and off, respectively. We suppose an underlying directed causal graph in which every vertex with parents is a logical function of its parents taking the specific form of a disjunction of conjuncts:

$$x = (p_{11} \wedge p_{12} \cdots \wedge p_{1k1}) \vee (p_{21} \wedge \cdots \wedge p_{2k2}) \vee \cdots \vee (p_{t1} \wedge \cdots \wedge p_{tkt}). \qquad (*)$$

Here, the $\{p_{ij}\}$ are all in the set pa(v) of parents of v in the causal graph, which we will require to be acyclic (i.e., containing no directed cycles).

Intuitively, v is true if all of the p_{ij}'s inside at least one of the parentheses are true. This also includes as special cases a network in which each vertex with parents is either a conjunct or a disjunct of its parents.

This is a strong restriction that rules out many possible relationships between causes and effects (see discussion here). However, it is general enough to cover most (all?) experiments considered in the developmental literature while still being simple enough to allow a relatively direct inferential method. At a crude level, it captures the idea present in many experiments that "something" (a given conjunction) makes "it" (*v*) "go" (be true). There is also a close connection to Mackie's (1965) INUS (Insufficient but Necessary part of a condition which is itself Unnecessary but Sufficient for the effect) model.

Let **E** be the set of exogenous variables and **V** be the set of endogenous variables. We will define an *instance* of the system to consist of an assignment of truth values to all of the exogenous variables (i.e., those without parents), which we will denote by **E** = **e**. Because there is an equation of the form (*) for each of the endogenous variables, an assignment of values to the exogenous variables automatically assigns truth values to all of the endogenous variables.

Let $\Phi_X(\mathbf{e})$ be the value assigned to the endogenous variable X when the exogenous variables are assigned **e**. Similarly, we define the set of true or on variables associated with an assignment as follows:

$$\Phi^T(\mathbf{e}) = \{v \mid v \in \mathbf{V}, \Phi_X(\mathbf{e}) = T\}$$

and likewise

$$\Phi^F(\mathbf{e}) = \{v \mid v \in \mathbf{V}, \Phi_X(\mathbf{e}) = F\}.$$

Note that we have not (and will not) put any distribution over the exogenous variables.

The following are some examples described in this format.

Example 1: One-cause blicket detector

> *Exogenous variables:* Block 1 present? (B1); Block 2 present? (B2).
>
> *Endogenous variable:* Detector making a noise? (D).
>
> *Graph:* B1 → D B2
>
> *Functional relationship:* D = B1

This is the trivial case of (*) where $t = 1$, and $k_1 = 1$. We have, for instance, $\Phi^T(B1 = T, B2 = F) = \{D\}$; $\Phi^T(B1 = F, B2 = T) = \{\ \}$. (Here $\{\ \}$ indicates the empty set.)

Notational convention To simplify notation, we often simply describe an assignment via the subset of exogenous variables taking on value *T*, it being

implicit that the remaining variables take the value *F*. Thus, for example, we may reexpress the statements above as follows:

$$\Phi^T(\{B1\}) = \{D\}; \Phi^T(\{B2\}) = \{\ \}$$

This convention simplifies expressions, but it is also based on the intuition that the default state for exogenous variables is false or off. Thus, if we were to physically implement a particular assignment, we would only need to pay attention to those exogenous variables assigned the value true as the remaining exogenous variables would already be in the false state.

Example 2: Two-cause blicket detector

Endogenous and exogenous variables are the same as in Example 1.

> *Graph:* B1 → D ← B2
>
> *Functional relationship:* D = B1 ∨ B2

Here, $t = 2$, $k_1 = k_2 = 1$.

Example 3: Twin piston engine

See Glymour, chapter 14, this volume.

> *Exogenous:* Key present? (K)
>
> *Endogenous:* Fuel Intake 1 open? (F1); Spark? (S); Fuel Intake 2 (F2)? Piston 1 moves? (P1); Piston 2

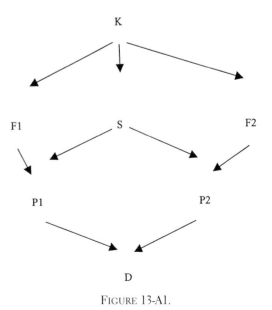

FIGURE 13-A1.

moves? (P2); Drive Shaft moves? (D) (see Figure 13-A1).

Functional relations:

$$F1 = K; S = K; F2 = K; P1 = F1 \wedge K;$$
$$P2 = F2 \wedge K; D = P1 \wedge P2.$$

The following is an important consequence of our restriction on the functional forms of the parent-child relationships:

Lemma 1: If **e1** and **e2** are two assignments to **E** such that

$$\{X \mid X \in \mathbf{E}; X \text{ assigned } T \text{ by } \mathbf{e1}\} \subseteq \{X \mid X \in \mathbf{E};$$
$$X \text{ assigned } T \text{ by } \mathbf{e2}\}$$

then $\Phi^T(\mathbf{e1}) \subseteq \Phi^T(\mathbf{e2})$.

In words, if Assignment **e2** turns on every exogenous variable turned on by **e1**, then at least as many endogenous variables are turned on by **e2** as by **e1**.

Interventions

So far, we have not described operations for intervening in the system. An intervention turns an endogenous variable into an exogenous variable, forcing it to take a given value, and striking out the equation previously governing it. All other equations remain in place. We will simply denote this via expanding our assignment to include the intervened variables Z. By a natural extension of the previous notation, we will let $\Phi_X(E = e, Z = Z)$ be the value assigned to the endogenous variable X under this assignment and intervention. Likewise, the set of (remaining) endogenous variables taking the value T under this intervention is then represented via $\Phi^T(E = e, Z = Z)$.
For example, in the piston engine example, we have

$$\Phi^T(K = F) = \{\ \},$$
$$\text{but } \Phi^T(K = F,\ P1 = T,\quad P2 = T) = \{D\}$$

expressing the fact that if the key is absent, then nothing happens, but if the key is absent and we force both pistons to move, then the drive shaft turns.

In the schemes described next, we will only ever consider interventions that force variables to take the true state. Thus, as before we can simplify notation by recording only the set of exogenous variables taking the value T and the set of endogenous variables forced to take the value T. For example, the above statements can be expressed as $\Phi^T(\{\ \}) = \{\ \}$, but $\Phi^T(\{P1, P2\}) = \{D\}$.

More generally, under an assignment and intervention represented by the set $\mathbf{W} = \mathbf{E}^* \cup \mathbf{A}$, where $\mathbf{E}^*$ is a subset of the exogenous variables $\mathbf{E}$, and $\mathbf{A}$ is a subset of the endogenous variables $\mathbf{V}$, we mean the following:

(i)   Assignment of true to the variables in $\mathbf{E}^*$,

(ii) Assignment of false to the variables in $\mathbf{E} \backslash \mathbf{E}^*$ (i.e., those not in $\mathbf{E}$), and

(iii) An intervention forcing the variables in $\mathbf{A}$ to take the value true.

This notation is not fully general in the sense that we cannot express interventions forcing endogenous variables to take the value false or off. However, for our purposes this is not a problem: As stated, the learning methods we describe next only ever require us to perform interventions forcing endogenous variables to take the value true.

We will sometimes refer to such an assignment and intervention as an intervention on $\mathbf{W}$ ($= \mathbf{E}^* \cup \mathbf{A}$). This is a slight abuse of terminology because in fact we are assigning to $\mathbf{E}$ ($= \mathbf{E}^* \cup (\mathbf{E} \backslash \mathbf{E}^*)$) and intervening on $\mathbf{A}$. However, because interventions simply make endogenous variables exogenous, assignments to exogenous variables may be viewed as trivial interventions.

Similarly, we will refer to the state that a given variable X (endogenous or exogenous) takes under $\mathbf{E}^* \cup \mathbf{A}$: If X is in $\mathbf{E}$ or in $\mathbf{A}$, then this is specified directly by the intervention; if not, then X's value is given by $\Phi_X(\mathbf{W})$. If X takes the value true under $\mathbf{W}$, then we will say that X is turned on by $\mathbf{W}$. The set of variables turned on under $\mathbf{W}$ consists of $\mathbf{W} \cup \Phi^T(\mathbf{W})$.
Finally, we note the following properties

Lemma 2: $\Phi^T(\mathbf{W}) \subseteq \text{de}(\mathbf{W})$, where $\text{de}(\mathbf{W})$ is the set of descendants of $\mathbf{W}$.

In words, the set of endogenous variables taking the value true under $\mathbf{W}$ is a subset of the descendants of $\mathbf{W}$.

Lemma 3: For any set $\mathbf{A} \subseteq \mathbf{V} \cup \mathbf{E}$ and any variable $X \notin \mathbf{A}$,

$$\Phi_X(\mathbf{A}) = \Phi_X(\mathbf{A} \cap \text{an}(X)) = \Phi_X((\mathbf{A} \cap \text{an}(X)) \cup \mathbf{W})$$

where $\mathbf{W}$ is an arbitrary subset of $(\mathbf{V} \cup \mathbf{E}) \backslash (\text{an}(X) \cup \{X\})$.

In words, the truth value taken by an (endogenous) variable X only depends on the values assigned to variables (either exogenous or intervened on) that are ancestors of X.

Learning Indirect Causes From Interventions: How Can I Make It Go?

We can now describe a simple method for answering the following question: For a specific variable X in a causal model, how do I get it to "go" with the least effort?

We are not necessarily trying to find the direct causes of X, we merely require a nonredundant set of minimal sufficient causes. We formalize this question as follows: For a given variable X, find a set $\mathbf{A}$ such that $\mathbf{A}$ does not contain X, turning on all the variables in $\mathbf{A}$ makes X take the value T, and no proper subset of $\mathbf{A}$ makes X take the value T.

Such a set $\mathbf{A}$ may be found in a simple manner: First, try turning on each variable in turn (if necessary by intervention) other than X itself. If successful, stop; otherwise, try sets of size two, and so on.

More formally, we have the following algorithm.

Input: A target variable X

Output: A set $\mathbf{A}$ such that $X \in \Phi^T(\mathbf{A})$, but for any proper subset $\mathbf{A}^* \subset \mathbf{A}$, $X \notin \Phi^T(\mathbf{A})$,

or failure if no such set exists.

How algorithm

For $k = 1$ to $|(\mathbf{V} \cup \mathbf{E}) \backslash \{X\}|$

For each subset $\mathbf{A} \subseteq (\mathbf{V} \cup \mathbf{E}) \backslash \{X\}$, such that $|\mathbf{A}| = k$

If $X \in \Phi^T(\mathbf{A})$, return $\mathbf{A}$

Until all subsets of size k from $(\mathbf{V} \cup \mathbf{E}) \backslash \{X\}$ have been tried.

$k = k + 1$

If $k > |(\mathbf{V} \cup \mathbf{E}) \backslash \{X\}|$, then report failure and return.

Failure will only occur if the target variable is in fact exogenous or if (contrary to the assumptions of the algorithm) we are not able to intervene on all variables in the system.

Example piston engine   If we attempt to get the drive shaft to turn ($D = T$), then the algorithm will terminate with $k = 1$, with the set $\mathbf{A} = \{K\}$ because this is

the only set of size 1 making the engine turn over. Note that K is an ancestor but not a parent of D. This will be true in general:

> Lemma 4: The set $\mathbf{A}$ resulting from the how algorithm consists of ancestors of the target variable X.

Sketch of proof: Suppose for a contradiction that $\mathbf{A}$ contained a variable that was not an ancestor of X. Consider the set $\mathbf{A}^* = \mathbf{A} \cap \text{an}(X)$. By Lemma 3, $\Phi_X(\mathbf{A}) = \Phi_X(\mathbf{A} \cap \text{an}(X)) = \Phi_X(\mathbf{A}^*)$. So, in particular, if $X \in \Phi^T(\mathbf{A})$, then $X \in \Phi^T(\mathbf{A}^*)$. But, by hypothesis because $\mathbf{A}$ contains a vertex that is not an ancestor of $\mathbf{A}$, $|\mathbf{A}^*| < |\mathbf{A}|$, so the set $\mathbf{A}^*$ would have been considered first by the algorithm, which is a contradiction.

The number of interventions required to find the set $\mathbf{A} = \{K\}$ in the piston example depends on the ordering of the variables. Under the worst ordering, we would need to perform six sets of interventions, each forcing a single variable to take the value true. In the best case, only one intervention is required.

Note that, in a system containing no conjunctions, it will only be necessary to consider sets of size 1 in the how algorithm; hence, the outer loop is unnecessary. This corresponds to the simple scheme of getting into everything by which a child simply pushes each button in turn (literally or figuratively) until the desired effect is obtained.

Because various child-proofing schemes involve conjunctions, we conjecture that such systems may be harder to learn. For example, on some dishwashers, when the child lock is activated, pressing any button causes two buttons to flash, which must then be pressed simultaneously to proceed. Similarly, some stair gates require a button to be pushed and a pedal to be pressed simultaneously.

Learning Direct Causes From Interventions: Why Does That Make It Go?

The how algorithm succeeds in finding an intervention that makes a given variable X go, that is, take the value true, but as we saw in the piston example, it does not necessarily identify the direct causes or, equivalently, the parents of X in the graph. Thus, a causal learner might ask this as a follow-up: Given that $\mathbf{A}$ makes X go, why does $\mathbf{A}$ make X go?

We reformulate this question as follows: Can we identify parents of X that are turned on by $\mathbf{A}$ and consequently turn on X? We emphasize that this is clearly a limited answer to the question, Why does **A** make X go? In particular, if **A** is a set of parents of X, then we will simply return the answer that, **A** makes X go because **A** makes X go, which, though true, is not very illuminating.

The idea behind the algorithm is that if a set **A** turns on X but does not consist solely of parents of X, then if instead we were to turn on only the parents of X that are turned on by **A**, it will lead to a reduction in the number of variables turned on overall. Put more formally: For a given variable X and set **A** that turns on X, can we find a set **P** such that

(a) $X \notin \mathbf{P}$, but $X \in \Phi^T(\mathbf{P})$, that is, **P** turns on X;
(b) $\mathbf{P} \subseteq \mathbf{A} \cup \Phi^T(\mathbf{A})$, that is, every variable in **P** is turned on by **A**;
(c) There is no proper subset $\mathbf{P}^*$ of the variables turned on by **P**, that is, $\mathbf{P}^* \subset \mathbf{P} \cup \Phi^T(\mathbf{P})$, such that $X \notin \mathbf{P}^*$, but $X \in \Phi^T(\mathbf{P}^*)$.

Condition (c) states that there is no proper subset of the variables that take the value true under **P**, which does not contain X, and which will make X take the value true. Note that it also follows from this that no proper subset of **P** will make X take the value true.

> Lemma 5: A set **P** satisfying conditions (a), (b), and (c) will consist of parents of X that are either descendants of **A** or are themselves in **A**.

Proof: First suppose that **P** is not a subset of pa(X). Consider the set $\mathbf{P}^* = (\mathbf{P} \cup \Phi^T(\mathbf{P})) \cap$ pa(X). Because $X \in \Phi^T(\mathbf{P})$, and by construction, the variables in pa(X) are assigned the same values under $\mathbf{P}^*$ as they take under **P**, it follows that $X \in \Phi^T(\mathbf{P}^*)$. However, $X \notin \mathbf{P}^*$. Now, $\mathbf{P}^* \subseteq$ pa(X), but by hypothesis **P** is not a subset of pa(X). Thus, $\mathbf{P}^*$ is a strict subset of $\mathbf{P} \cup \Phi^T(\mathbf{P})$; hence, **P** does not satisfy Condition (c), which is a contradiction.

That the variables in **P** are descendants of **A** follows from $\mathbf{P} \subseteq \mathbf{A} \cup \Phi^T(\mathbf{A})$ and Lemma 2.

We now outline the algorithm for finding the set **P**:

Why algorithm

Input: A set **A** and vertex X such that $X \in \Phi^T(\mathbf{A})$;

Output: A set **P** satisfying Conditions (i), (ii), and (iii);

0. Let $\mathbf{P} = \mathbf{A}$;

1. For each vertex $P \in \mathbf{P}$

For $k = 1$ to $| (\mathbf{P} \cup \Phi^T(\mathbf{P})) \backslash \{P, X\} |$

For each subset $\mathbf{P}^* \subseteq (\mathbf{P} \cup \Phi^T(\mathbf{P})) \backslash$ $\{P, X\}$ such that $| \mathbf{P}^* | = k$

If $X \in \Phi^T(\mathbf{P}^*)$, then let $\mathbf{P} =$ $\mathbf{P}^*$ and return to Step 1.

Until all subsets of size k from $(\mathbf{P} \cup$ $\Phi^T(\mathbf{P})) \backslash \{P, X\}$ have been tried.

$k = k + 1$

If $k > | (\mathbf{P} \cup \Phi^T(\mathbf{P})) \backslash \{P, X\} |$, output **P**.

Step 1 attempts to remove each vertex in turn from the set **P** but at the same time intervene on additional variables that were turned on by **P**. If we are successful in removing a given vertex from **P**, then we replace **P** with $\mathbf{P}^*$ and start the search all over again.

We finish by illustrating the algorithm on the piston engine example.

> After running the how algorithm, we obtained the set $\mathbf{A} = \{K\}$, which made the target variable D take the value true.
>
> Initially, $\mathbf{P} = \{K\}$, and there is only vertex P to remove.
>
> The smallest subset of $\Phi^T(\{K\}) \backslash \{D\} = \{F1, F2, S, P1, P2\}$, which turns on D, is
>
> $\mathbf{P}^* = \{P1, P2\}$; thus, we set $\mathbf{P} = \mathbf{P}^* = \{P1, P2\}$ and go back to Step 1.
>
> Because **P** is now the set of parents of D, we are unable to remove any vertices from the set, and the algorithm terminates.

Exactly how many interventions are required depends on the ordering of the variables. Under the worst ordering, we would have to perform five sets of interventions on sets of size 1 and then 10 interventions on sets of size 2 before we found {P1,P2}, giving 15 sets of interventions in total. Under the best ordering, we would only need 6. Because there are no vertices in $\Phi^T(\{P1,P2\}) \backslash \{D\}$, there are no new experiments required to confirm that this set satisfies Conditions (a), (b), and (c).

Note that we have only uncovered some of the causal structure. In this example, we found all of the parents of X. In general, we would only find a subset of the parents corresponding to one of the conjuncts in the equation (*).

To find the whole structure of the piston engine would require us to choose each endogenous variable as the target (X) and then to run the how and why algorithms in turn. Although perhaps laborious, it is worth noting that in this way the simple interventionist procedure would allow us to recover the whole structure. In contrast, a procedure based on passive observation leaves a large set of possible structures (see Glymour, chapter 14, this volume).

In the worst-case these algorithms perform exponentially many experiments. See Eberhardt et al. (2005) for related work on causal Bayes nets.

Relaxing the Assumption on Functional Relationships

Two questions arise from this analysis. Could the algorithms be extended to cover the case in which the relations between the variables are not restricted to disjunctions of conjunctions, for example, in which negations of variables are permitted? Conversely, are there many causal structures that we encounter in our daily existence in which the functional relationships are not of this form?

Consider a staircase with a light and a light switch at the top and bottom of the stairs. In the usual manner in which such switches are configured, flipping one switch while leaving the other unchanged always changes the state of the light (from on to off or vice versa). A little thought reveals that such a system implements an XOR gate, for example, things might be wired so that if both switches are up or both are down, then the light is off; otherwise, it is on. This is the simplest structure that cannot be handled in the framework considered. However, it is worth noticing that we are almost never in a position to operate both switches at once. As long as we only operate one switch and regard the other as fixed in its state, then the subsystem consisting of the single switch confronting us and a lightbulb falls within our framework.

As this example illustrates, an analysis of such structures is harder because there is less clear correspondence between interventions and outcomes.

14

Learning the Structure of Deterministic Systems

Clark Glymour

Whether our everyday world of middle-size dry goods and wet liquids appears deterministic or indeterministic seems to depend on how closely and finely we resolve circumstances and variables and which systems we consider. Sometimes, when I turn the key to my old truck, the door unlocks and sometimes not. If one examined how the key teeth fit the lock spindle in any particular case, then I suppose it would seem deterministic. How my teen-aged daughter, Madelyn Rose, responds when I call her down from her room seems completely indeterministic—hard to predict whether the result will be silence, the appearance of a grumpy daughter, or the appearance of a cheerful daughter. The more human action is involved, the more indeterministic things seem.

Whether and how people learn causal relations in deterministic systems seems remarkably little studied. Here are some obvious questions:

1. Suppose subjects can manipulate A, and A determines B, B determines C, but C does not determine B. B and C, if they both occur, occur simultaneously. A, B, and C may each have two or multiple values. Can subjects discover that C does not cause B? Do they realize that they cannot tell whether A influences C by a route other than through B (e.g., after experimenting for a while, if they are then given the power to control B, will they predict that varying A will vary C when B is fixed, or not, or say they can't tell?)?
2. Can subjects determine the structure of a simple cascade of effects when they have no time cues. For example, when they can manipulate the exogenous variables X, Y, Z, and X, Y cause W, and Y, Z cause R, and W and R cause Q?
3. Given experience manipulating inputs to a relatively simple system and observing resultant states and given full information regarding its causal structure, if the structure is then disrupted (e.g., a link removed or a variable fixed at a value, as in stuck-at-zero faults in logic circuits), can subjects identify the fault?

I do not know the answer to these questions, but I have something to say about Question 2. The psychological perspective and the computational

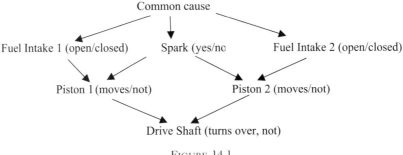

FIGURE 14-1

algorithms concerning how causal structure may be learned that inspired some of the chapters in this book were developed for indeterministic systems. A similar inspiration for deterministic systems would be nice to have. There are significant engineering issues as well. Fault diagnosis in deterministic systems is essentially about learning the structure of a deterministic causal system with some background knowledge and with data on the behavior of the system under a limited range of interventions. This chapter is about the issues that arise in modifying the search procedures that are correct for indeterministic systems so that they are correct and informative for deterministic systems.

I have a simple example that illustrates many of the issues. The example is sufficiently elementary that a procedure that could not provide correct information about it would not be of much interest. Consider a simple two-piston engine of the kind one used to see sometimes on motor scooters but with some modifications. It works like this: Fuel is squirted into Intake 1, and fuel is squirted into Intake 2. A spark fires, which pushes down the pistons, which turns the drive shaft. At this level of description, the system looks like that in Figure 14-1.

Of course, much finer descriptions are true of the system, but this one will do. Suppose one does not know how any of this works, but (a) experiments can

be done randomizing the sparks and fuel intakes independently, and (b) the piston motions and the drive shaft motions can be observed in each case. With such experiments, we break the common cause that synchronizes the fuel intakes and sparking, and we are really investigating the system of Figure 14-2.

To avoid issues about time series, I assume something unrealistic: The Drive Shaft turns when and only when both pistons move—it would make only minor differences to the discussion if instead the drive shaft moved when either piston moved. So, because this is a deterministic system, the states of the system can be given by a kind of truth table, as in Table 14-1.

It is important to observe what determines what in the example. The values of Fuel Intake 1, Spark, and Fuel Intake 2 together determine the values of the three remaining variables. The values of Piston 1 and Piston 2 together determine the value of Drive Shaft. Additional deterministic relations hold for particular values of variables. For example, when Piston 1 = Moves, then always Fuel Intake 1 = Open and Spark = Yes. And, when Piston 1 = Not, then always Drive Shaft = Not. These facts have interesting consequences.

Now, suppose we experiment by simultaneously and independently randomizing Fuel Intake 1, Spark, and Fuel Intake 2, and in each case note the results for the other variables. The probability of each value

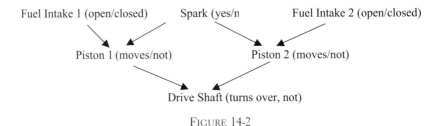

FIGURE 14-2

TABLE 14-1

Fuel Intake 1	Spark	Fuel Intake 2	Piston 1	Piston 2	Drive Shaft
Open	Yes	Open	Moves	Moves	Turns over
Open	Yes	Closed	Moves	Not	Not
Open	No	Open	Not	Not	Not
Closed	Yes	Open	Not	Moves	Not
Open	No	Closed	Not	Not	Not
Closed	Yes	Closed	Not	Not	Not
Closed	No	Open	Not	Not	Not
Closed	No	Closed	Not	Not	Not

of the other variables is given by their respective conditional probabilities on the values of their direct causes. Noting that the probability of any value of a two-valued variable must be (1 – the probability of the other value), the joint probability distribution of all values of the system in Table 14-1 can be described as in Table 14-2.

The question is this: How could we discover the causal structure in Figure 14-1 from the joint probability distribution described in Table 14-2? (One way, of course, to find the structure in Figure 14-1 would be to do further experiments, but that does not answer the question posed.)

If the system were not quite deterministic, then we would know how to discover the structure. Suppose, for example, small unmeasured factors might independently influence the pistons and the drive shaft, so

that the probability distribution looks something like Table 14-3 instead of Table 14-2.

Then, we could discover the structure (from appropriate samples) in Figure 14-1 by using any of several algorithms, the PC algorithm, for example. PC is a computational and statistically more efficient version of the following idea:

1. In a system of variables with no unobserved common causes, X directly influences Y, or Y directly influences X, if and only if for every subset **S** of the remaining variables there are values for variables in **S** such that X and Y are not independent given those values.
2. If X is independent of Z conditional on **S** and each of X, Z directly influences or is directly influenced by Y, and Y is not in **S**, then X, Z both directly influence Y.

TABLE 14-2

Probability (Fuel intake 1=Open)=p1;
Probability (Spark=Yes)=p2;
Probability (Fuel intake 2=Open)=p3
Probability(Piston 1=Moves | Fuel Intake 1=Open and Spark=Yes)=1
Probability(Piston 1=Moves | Fuel Intake 1=Open and Spark=No)=0
Probability(Piston 1=Moves | Fuel Intake 1=Closed and Spark=Yes)=0
Probability(Piston 1=Moves | Fuel Intake 1=Closed and Spark=No)=0
Probability(Piston 2=Moves | Fuel Intake 2=Open and Spark=Yes)=1
Probability(Piston 1=Moves | Fuel Intake 2=Open and Spark=No)=0
Probability(Piston 1=Moves | Fuel Intake 2=Closed and Spark=Yes)=0
Probability(Piston 1=Moves | Fuel Intake 2=Closed and Spark=No)=0
Probability(Drive Shaft=Turns | Piston 1=moves, Piston 2=moves)=1
Probability(Drive Shaft=Turns | Piston 1=Moves, Piston 2=Not)=0
Probability(Drive Shaft=Turns | Piston 1=Not, Piston 2=Moves)=0
Probability(Drive Shaft=Turns | Piston 1=Not, Piston 2=Not)=0

TABLE 14-3

Probability (Fuel Intake 1=Open)=p1;
Probability (Spark=Yes)=p2;
Probability (Fuel Intake 2=Open)=p3
Probability(Piston 1=Moves | Fuel Intake 1=Open and Spark=Yes)=1− ε
Probability(Piston 1=Moves | Fuel Intake 1=Open and Spark=No)=ε/3
Probability(Piston 1=Moves | Fuel Intake 1=Closed and Spark=Yes)=ε/3
Probability(Piston 1=Moves | Fuel Intake 1=Closed and Spark=No)=ε/3
Probability(Piston 2=Moves | Fuel Intake 2=Open and Spark=Yes)=1− δ
Probability(Piston 1=Moves | Fuel Intake 2=Open and Spark=No)=δ/3
Probability(Piston 1=Moves | Fuel Intake 2=Closed and Spark=Yes)=δ/3
Probability(Piston 1=Moves | Fuel Intake 2=Closed and Spark=No)=δ/3
Probability(Drive Shaft=Turns | Piston 1=Moves, Piston 2=Moves)=1−γ
Probability(Drive Shaft=Turns | Piston 1=Moves, Piston 2=Not)=γ/3
Probability(Drive Shaft=Turns | Piston 1=Not, Piston 2=Moves)=γ/3
Probability(Drive Shaft=Turns | Piston 1=Not, Piston 2=Not)=γ/3

The PC algorithm applies these ideas this way: First, make an undirected graph with nodes that are all of the variables (Figure 14-3).

Now, for each pair of variables, remove the edge between them if they are independent in probability. Because we assumed that Fuel Intake 1, Fuel Intake 2, and Spark were randomized independently, they will be independent, and we can remove the edges among them (Figure 14-4).

We record that we did not have to condition on any variables in removing these edges. Now look back at Figure 14-2. There is no pathway or common source of influence connecting Fuel Intake 1 with Piston 2 or

Fuel Intake 2 with Piston 1. Fuel Intake 1 behavior does not influence Piston 2 behavior or vice versa, and nothing influences them both; it is similar for Fuel Intake 2 and Piston 1. Now, look at Table 14-3. The probability distribution for Piston 2 depends on Fuel Intake 2 and Spark, and the probability of neither of these variables depends on Fuel Intake 1. So, we expect that, on examining the data, we would find that Fuel Intake 1 is independent of Piston 2, and Fuel Intake 2 is independent of Piston 1. Removing the edges and noting that we relied on an unconditional independence relation in doing so, we have what is shown in Figure 14-5.

Now, considering the distribution in Table 14-3 once more, note that the probability distribution for Drive Shaft is completely specified, in every case, by the values of the two piston variables, which means Drive Shaft is independent of Fuel Intake 1, Spark, and Fuel Intake 2, conditional on any assignment of values to Piston 1 and Piston 2. Because of these conditional independence relations, remove the edges between Drive Shaft and these variables, noting which variables were conditioned on in each case, to obtain Figure 14-6.

In Figure 14-2, the piston variables do not influence one another, and Spark is their only common cause. In Table 14-3, the distribution of Piston 1 and the distribution of Piston 2 are given by conditional probabilities. The only variable conditioned on in both cases is Spark, and all of the variables conditioned on are

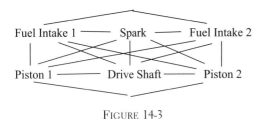

FIGURE 14-3

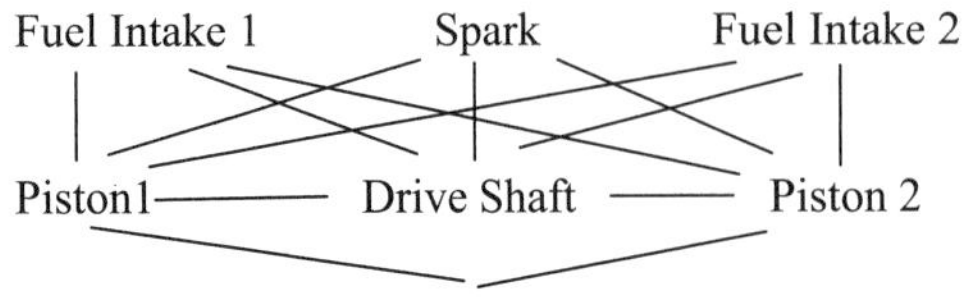

Fuel Intake 1   Spark   Fuel Intake 2

Piston1   Drive Shaft   Piston 2

FIGURE 14-4

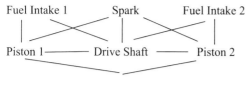

FIGURE 14-5

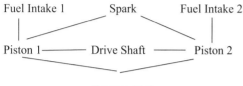

FIGURE 14-6

independent of one another. So, we should find that Piston 1 and Piston 2 are independent conditional on any value of Spark. We remove the edge between the piston variables, and note that we conditioned on Spark in doing so, to obtain Figure 14-7.

We have arrived at the undirected skeleton of Figure 14-2 simply by using the independence and conditional independence properties of the distribution in Table 14-3. Further, we can direct all of the edges. Fuel Intake – Piston 1 – Spark is directed as Fuel Intake → Piston 1 ← Spark because we did not have to condition on Piston 1 to remove the edge between Fuel Intake 1 and Spark; if the influences had not both been directed into Piston 1, then Fuel Intake 1 would have been unconditionally associated with Spark via one of three mechanisms (Fuel Intake 1 → Piston 1 → Spark, or Fuel intake 1 ← Piston 1 ← Spark, or Fuel intake 1 ← Piston 1 → Spark), and we would have had to condition on Piston 1 to make Fuel Intake 1 and Spark independent.

By similar reasoning, because each edge in Figure 14-7 occurs in some triple of the form X-Y-Z with no edges between X and Z, and because of the variables we did not have to condition on to remove edges between the two end variables of each such triple, we find all of the orientations and recover Figure 14-2 exactly.

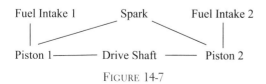

FIGURE 14-7

Why does this work? Because our example satisfies two principles:

The causal Markov assumption (CMA): In a causally sufficient system **V** of variables (i.e., no common causes of variables in **V** are left out of **V**), if Y is not an effect of X, then Y is independent of X conditional on each assignment of values to all of the direct causes of X.

The faithfulness assumption: All of the conditional independence relations in the distribution are consequences of the CMA applied to the directed graph of causal relations.

In the example, all of the direct influences and their directions were unambiguously identified by the algorithm. That is not true of every example, of course, because often if two causal graphs imply the same independence and conditional independence relations when the CMA is applied, then no algorithms can distinguish them without extra information. Two such graphs are said to be Markov equivalent. The PC algorithm, for example, in general returns a description of a Markov equivalence class. It happens that, in the example of Figure 14-2, the Markov equivalence class has but one member.

The faithfulness assumption is essential to avoid incorrectly eliminating true influences because of independence or conditional independence relations. For example, if the probability distribution were not as in Table 14-2, but instead somehow specified that Piston 2 is independent of Drive Shaft conditional on Piston 1, the PC algorithm would have removed the connection between Piston 2 and Drive Shaft.

So, why does something like this not work with the deterministic case, with the distribution in Table 14-2? The answer is because the distribution in Table 14-2 is not faithful to the graph of Figure 14-2. Determinism produces extra conditional independence relations. If, conditional on a set of values for some variables, another variable X is constant—has its value uniquely determined—then conditional on those values X is independent of every variable. Because in the deterministic system values of Fuel Intake 1, Fuel Intake 2, and Spark determine the values of every other variable, conditional on values of these three, Piston 1 and Piston 2 are independent of Drive Shaft.

One way to think about the deterministic case is to assume that PC *would* give correct results were it not for deterministic conditional relations and consider

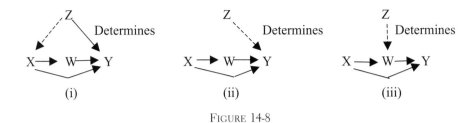

FIGURE 14-8

what adjacency and directional relations could then be inferred from nondeterministic relations within the deterministic system.

A determining variable Z (or set of such variables) can produce a conditional independence between X and Y in one of the following ways (Figure 14-8):

(i)   By, for each value of Z, fixing a value of X,
(ii) Or by, for each value of Z, fixing a value of Y,
(iii) Or by, for each value of Z and for each trek between X, Y (i.e., a direct path from X to Y or from Y to X or pair of paths to X and Y from a common source Z) fixing the value of some variable on that trek.

In Case (i), X is independent of W and of Y conditional on Z; in Case (ii), X is independent of W and of Y conditional on Z as well. In Case (iii), however, X is not independent of Y conditional on Z. If there were no X → Y edge, then in each case removing an X-Y connection because of the independence of X, Y conditional on Z would not have led to an error. But, if there is, in reality, an X-Y direct connection, as shown, then in Cases 1 and 2, but not Case 3, X, Y would be independent conditional on Z, and the X-Y direct connection would be erroneously removed. The moral is that we cannot reliably remove edges between two variables, say X, Y, when they are independent conditional on a variable or set of variables with values that determine unique values for X or unique values for Y. All we can do is note that such edges are indeterminate: Unless the edge is removed because of conditioning on some other variable (W for instance) that does not determine X and does not determine Y, we do not know whether these edges are really present.

So, the upshot is that when dealing with deterministic systems we should modify the PC algorithm so that we only remove an undirected edge between two variables, X, Y when X and Y are independent conditional on some set of variables with values that do not uniquely determine X or uniquely determine Y, and when an edge is not thus removed but X and Y are independent conditional on some variable or set of variables that determines X or determines Y, we should mark the edge as uncertain. In the example of Figure 14-2, this means we would not, for example, remove the edge between Spark and Drive Shaft because those variables are independent conditional on the values of the two piston variables because the values of the two piston variables determine the value of Drive Shaft.

That is not enough. Look at Table 14-2 again and notice the relation between Spark, Drive Shaft, and Piston 1. When Piston 1 = Moves, in every case Spark = Yes. Hence, Spark and Drive Shaft are independent conditional on Piston 1 = Moves. But, when Piston 1 = Not, in every case, Drive Shaft = Not. Hence, Spark and Drive Shaft are independent conditional on Piston 1 = Not. Thus, in every case Spark and Drive Shaft are independent conditional on the value of Piston 1. So, if we used the PC procedure, then we would remove an edge between Spark and Drive Shaft. In our example, this gives the correct result—but suppose Spark *did* cause Drive Shaft directly as well as indirectly through the pistons (never mind how, just imagine). Then, we would be wrong to remove the edge. In fact, in a deterministic system, we cannot reliably decide whether such an edge is present, and we should modify the search further to mark such edges as uncertain unless they are removed by some other, nondeterministic, conditional independence. Let us see what this does for our example. Start again with the fully connected graph (Figure 14-9) and use Tables 14-1 and 14-2.

As before, we can remove the independencies among variables that do not determine one another, to obtain Figure 14-10.

Piston 1 and Piston 2 are indeterministically independent conditional on Spark, so we derive Figure 14-11.

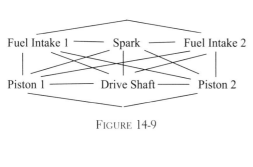

FIGURE 14-9

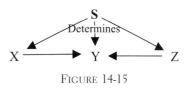

FIGURE 14-15

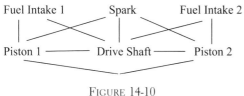

FIGURE 14-10

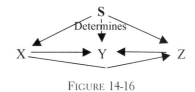

FIGURE 14-16

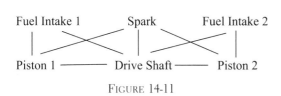

FIGURE 14-11

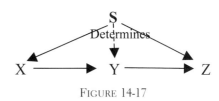

FIGURE 14-17

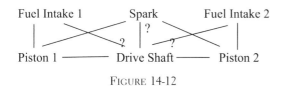

FIGURE 14-12

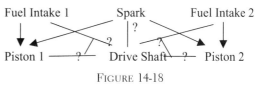

FIGURE 14-18

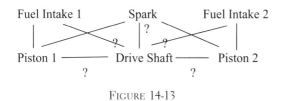

FIGURE 14-13

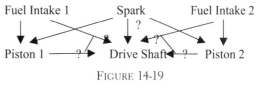

FIGURE 14-19

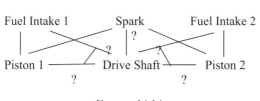

FIGURE 14-14

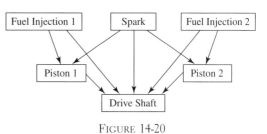

FIGURE 14-20

Fuel Intake 1 is independent of Drive Shaft conditional on Piston 1 and Spark, but the independence is deterministic because when Spark and Piston 1 are 0, Drive Shaft must be 0, and when Spark is 1 and Piston 1 is 0, fuel intake must be 0, and when Spark and Piston 1 are 1, fuel intake must be 1. The same two variables are also independent conditional on Piston 1 and Piston 2, but the values of these variables determine the value of Drive Shaft. So, the edge between Fuel Intake 1 and Fuel Intake 2 must be marked with a question mark. The same is true for Fuel Intake 2 and Drive Shaft, and as we have seen, also for Spark and Drive Shaft. So, we have the diagram of Figure 14-12.

Notice that Piston 1 and Drive Shaft are deterministically independent conditional on Fuel Intake 1, Spark, and Fuel Intake 2 and similarly for the relation between Piston 2 and Drive Shaft. In a deterministic system, all "endogenous" variable pairs will be deterministically independent conditional on some set of other variables. Hence any edge between endogenous variables must be marked with a question mark (Figure 14-13).

At this point, the relevant reasoning becomes different from the indeterministic case. The data tell us the following: Piston 1 and Drive Shaft are not independent. So, there must be some mechanism connecting them. Hence, either Piston 1-Drive Shaft is real or at least one of Fuel Intake 1 and Spark is directly connected to Drive Shaft. But, if Piston 1-Drive Shaft is not real and Fuel Intake 1-Drive Shaft is not real, then Fuel Intake 1 would be independent of Drive Shaft, contrary to the data. Hence, the Fuel Intake 1-Drive Shaft edge is real, the Piston 1-Drive Shaft edge is real, or both. Similar reasoning holds for Drive Shaft, Piston 2, and Fuel Intake 2. And, of course, if neither Piston 1 nor Piston 2 direct connections with Drive Shaft exist, then the direct Spark-Drive Shaft connection must exist. The nonmonotonic, disjunctive relations quickly become complicated. Connect pairs of edges, at least one of which must exist by an arc (Figure 14-14).

There are further problems in determining which variables are directly connected. Consider Figures 14-15 and 14-16. In Figure 14-15, S determines Y, but not X or Z. Because S is the source of a trek connecting X and Z, X and Z will be independent unless S is conditioned on. But conditioning on any value of S fixes a value of Y, and Y is a collider; conditioning on a value of Y creates an association between X and Z. So, no matter which variables are conditioned on nondeterministically, X and Z remain associated, and we cannot determine whether Figure 14-15 or Figure 14-16 is the case. This problem does not arise in the example of Figure 14-2, but it can

in other cases. Whenever there is a set of variables S that determines a set of variables on undirected paths between X and Z and X and Z are not nondeterministically independent conditional on any set of variables, the undirected edge between X and Z must be marked as questionable.

In the indeterministic case, we could direct all of the edges in our example without any prior information about the orientation of any of the edges. The principle was that if X-Y-Z is found such that X and Z do not share an edge, then X and Z are independent conditional on some set of variables, and Y must either be in no such sets or in all of them, accordingly as X → Y → Z or not. So, if we found a set making X, Z independent and not containing Y, then both edges must be directed into Y; in other terms, Y is a collider on the path from X to Z. That is not generally true in deterministic cases. Consider Figure 14-17.

Notice that we do not need to condition on Y to make X and Z independent. Conditioning on S alone will fix a value of Y and make X and Z independent. If we applied the rule we use for indeterministic cases, then, because we do not need to condition on Y to make X and Z independent, we would wrongly conclude that there is a collider at Y on a path from X to Z. The rule for indeterministic systems will accommodate such cases if we apply it only when the conditioning set that removes the X-Z connection does not determine Y. Hence, continuing with our example we immediately find Figure 14-18. We can also order the uncertain edges, using the same principle (Figure 14-19).

We did not need to make use of the information that Fuel Intake 1, Fuel Intake 2, and Spark are not caused by the other variables, although we could have used this as prior knowledge.

A modification of the PC algorithm that uses all of these points, except for marking edges as questionable, is presented next.

PCD_Discrete

Arguments: Data set D with variables $V = \{V1,...,Vn\}$, percentage of determination p.
Returns: Mixed graph G over V.
Lets Sepset ($\{V1, V2\}$) be a map (to be constructed) from size-2 sets of variables to sets of variables.

Step A

Form the complete undirected G over $V1,...,Vn$.

Step B (Determine Fast Adjacency Search)

For each depth d = 0,1,..., until no more edges can be removed:

For for each variable X:

"next_y":

For each adjacent variable Y to X:

Let adjX=adj(X) − Y

Let adjY=adj(Y) − X

For each subset Sx of adjX up to size d: If there is no combination C of values of Sx for which some category x of X exists such that p% of data points satisfying C have category x or some category y of Y exists such that p% of data points satisfying C have category y,

If $X \perp Y \,|\, Sx$,

remove X−Y from G.

Set Sepset({X, Y}) to Sx.

Continue "next_y".

For each subset Sy of adjY up to size d: If ther is no combination C of values of Sy for which some category x of X exists such that p% of data points satisfying C have category x or some category y of Y exists such that p% of data points satisfying C have category y,

If $X \perp Y \,|\, Sy$,

remove X−Y from G.

Set Sepset({X, Y}) to Sy.

Continue "next_y."

Step C

Orient colliders in G, as follows:

For each variable X:

For each pair of variables Y, Z adjacent to X:

If Y and Z are not adjacent,

If X is not in Sepset({Y,Z});

If there is no combination C of values of Sepset({Y,Z}) for which some category x of X exists such that p% of data points satisfying C have category x,

Orient $Y \rightarrow X \leftarrow Z$.

Step D

Apply orientation rules until no more orientations are possible. Rules to use: away from collider, away from

cycle, kite1, kite2. (These ae Meek's rules R1, R2, R3, and R4.)

Away from collider:

For each variable A:

For each B, C in adj(A):

If $B \rightarrow A−C$:

Orient $B \rightarrow Z \rightarrow C$.

Else if $C \rightarrow A−B$:

Orient $C \rightarrow A \rightarrow B$.

Away from cycle:

For each variable A:

For B, C in adj(A):

If $A \rightarrow B \rightarrow C$ and $A−C$:

Orient $A \rightarrow C$.

Else if $C \rightarrow B \rightarrow A$ and $C−A$:

Orient $C \rightarrow A$.

Kite 1:

For each variable A:

For each nodes B, C, D in adj(A) such that $A−B, A−C, A−D$, and!$(C−D)$:

If $C \rightarrow B$ and $D \rightarrow B$:

Orient $A \rightarrow B$.

Kite 2:

For each variable A:

For each nodes B, C, D *in adj*(A) *such that* A−B, A−D, B *is not adjacent to* D, *either* A−C, A → C, *or* C → A,

If $B \rightarrow C$ and $C \rightarrow D$:

Orient $A \rightarrow D$.

Else if $D \rightarrow C$ and $C \rightarrow B$:

Orient $A \rightarrow B$.

For data generated from the structure in Figure 14-2 with the probability distribution in Table 14-3, the implementation of PCD in the TETRAD IV program gives just what we should expect.

Figure 14-20 is typically produced at sample size 100 and significance level .05, and at sample size 50 and significance level .05 with prior knowledge of time order; at sample size 20 at significance level .1 and prior knowledge of time order, an average of two edge differences (added or omitted) from Figure 14-20 occur.

This at least suggests that information about the structure of some small deterministic systems can be obtained at small sample sizes given knowledge of time order. Larger samples give similar information with more complex systems. But, in all cases what is learned is what causes what and what does not. Otherwise, the mediating mechanisms are ambiguous.

The difficult thing is to say in which general circumstances PCD or some other algorithm for deterministic cases is correct and maximally informative. We cannot usefully assume that the answer is for faithful cases. We could consider conditions of limited faithfulness, like this: If in Graph G, X and Y are independent conditional on all values of Z and some value of Z determines neither X nor Y, then the Markov assumption applied to G implies that X is independent of Y conditional on Z (equivalently, X, Y are d-separated with respect to Z).

I believe, but have not proved, that PCD discrete is sound if the Markov assumption is supplemented with this assumption. It is evidently not complete, as the disjunctive reasoning in the example shows.

Part III

CAUSATION, THEORIES, AND MECHANISMS

Introduction to Part III:
Causation, Theories, and Mechanisms

From: mherskovits@psych.ucarcadia.arcadia.edu
To: brook_russell@turing.carnegietech.edu

Brook,

I have to admit that I'm having second thoughts. It's true that it's all exciting still. But I worry that the gaps—the differences in background assumptions and interests and concerns—are just going to be too great to overcome.

In some ways the normative computational project seems like just the opposite of the psychological project. The computationalists, after all, are most interested in designing systems that can do just the things that human beings can't, like extracting causal structure from masses of correlational data all at one time. People, and children especially, seem to do things differently. As Thomas Richardson (chapter 3) pointed out, like scientists themselves, children can do experiments, and they can do them repeatedly. And, they make inferences from small samples instead of the enormous databases that the computer systems operate on. But, ironically, we do not seem to have good computational accounts of precisely how this sort of experimentation leads to accurate causal conclusions.

And there's another thing that's bothering me. Remember the whole point of this in the first place was to explain the nature and development of our intuitive theories? But, I think I'm losing the connection between this sort of general causal learning and theory-formation. For instance, one of the main functions of intuitive theories is to provide explanations—I know Henry Wellman has tons of terrific data about that. But there doesn't seem to be anything in the formalisms that corresponds to explanation. Theories also seem to constrain the kind of causal inferences we can make. When we have a theory, the theoretical laws we formulate and the assumptions we make influence the way we interpret the evidence. Again, there doesn't really seem to be a good place for that kind of top-down effect of prior knowledge in the formalism.

There's one more thing. I can't seem to get rid of this nagging sense that all those intuitions about mechanisms must come from somewhere—they must play some role or other. But, it's not at all clear just what that role is or how ideas about mechanism fit with causal Bayes nets. Maybe "mechanisms" are just more and more little arrows connecting the variables. I think there must be more to it than that.

Anyway, maybe this is just a temporary let-down. I thought I should let you know and see what you think about it.

All the best,

Morgan

From: brook_russell@turing.carnegietech.edu
To: mherskovits@psych.ucarcadia.arcadia.edu

Dear Morgan,

I have to confess I've been having some of the same doubts myself. But, you know I was looking at the papers for this last workshop, and I do think that there may be some answers there. Woo-Kyung Ahn and Michael Strevens are both going to talk about how we can integrate ideas about mechanism and causal structure and intervention. And, Clark Glymour gives an example of how you could adjust your assumptions about causality to apply these ideas to the particular domain of social relations. Then Josh Tenenbaum, Tom Griffiths, and Sourab Niyogi are going to discuss ideas about representing theories and showing how the prior knowledge encoded in those theories can shape inferences (chapters 19 & 20).

Anyway, surely the measure of any relationship isn't just the initial excitement but the potential for long-term productivity. If this one works, it won't be because all the problems are solved but because we have a succession of ideas, thoughts, experiments, and discoveries, each unfolding from the one before. And, we can gain strength from both the similarities and the differences if we change and evolve together. So, let's see how it goes at the workshop, be patient, think hard, and hope for the best, which would, after all, be very good indeed.

Brook

15

Why Represent Causal Relations?

Michael Strevens

The Question

Why should the mind represent causal relations? Because they are there, goes the simplest answer. But, this is not good enough: There is much that is there in the external world, but that is not represented—though it could be—because it is not important enough to merit a place in the limited space inside the skull.

Thus, the next simplest answer: We represent causal information because knowledge of causation is important for getting around the world safely and extracting from it what we need and desire. This is true enough, but again not entirely satisfactory. Much of the knowledge that enables us to navigate the world for fun and profit can be represented in noncausal form, for example, as information about correlations.

This observation suggests a strategy for answering the question. Compare and contrast information about causal relations with information about correlations and show that causal information is somehow better, at least sometimes, for getting what we want. What follows is an attempt to implement this strategy.

There are, broadly speaking, two different advantages that causal information might have over statistical information. (In what follows, I use *statistical* more or less interchangeably with *noncausal*.) First, it might be that there are some aspects of the world that can be captured using causal representations but not mere statistical representations, and that knowledge of these properties of our surroundings has some practical use for us. Second, it might be that everything worth knowing for practical purposes can in principle be expressed using statistical representations, but that the causal representation of certain kinds of facts is especially efficient given our particular means and ends.

I call these two explanations of our use of causal representations, respectively, the external and the internal explanations because, whereas the external explanation points to aspects of the outside world that can be represented only using causal representations, the internal explanation points to elements of the system of causal representation itself—the system existing inside our heads—that are especially user friendly.

Which explanation is correct? It is certainly too soon to answer such a categorical question. This chapter, however, declares an interest, focusing on explanations of the internal variety, for the following reason:

Decades, even centuries, of work on the metaphysics of causation by philosophers holds out no great hope for the external approach. It is not that philosophers are agreed that causal claims say nothing that cannot be said by statistical claims—far from it. Debate is as lively as ever regarding whether there are sui generis causal relations in the world that it is the privilege of causal language alone to represent, with the realists about causation arguing for and the empiricists against (Sosa & Tooley, 1993). It is rather that, even on realist theories that posit such sui generis facts, what is implied by the facts over and above a certain pattern of correlations is not, on the face of it, information that is in itself useful in day-to-day life. In other words, even on realist theories of causation, the practical use of a causal fact lies entirely in the correlations it entails. There is thus a working philosophical consensus that correlations are good enough for everyday life—a consensus that, if correct, implies that an attempt to give an external explanation for our use of causal representations must fail. This consensus has been challenged, recently and vigorously by Woodward (2003) in particular (discussed in the section on asymmetry and control), but as things currently stand, there is good (if not conclusive) reason to focus on the internal approach to explaining the existence of causal cognition.

A good discipline for an internalist explainer is to assume, for tactical reasons, empiricism about causal language, that is, to assume that there is nothing said by causal claims—more generally, nothing captured by causal representations—that cannot be said by statistical claims. The advantage of the causal way of speaking and thinking must then of necessity be found, not in what is said, but in how it is said. In what follows, I adopt this discipline.

Note that the statistical claims—the claims about correlations and so on—that exhaust the content of a causal claim will be quite complex. Empiricist theories of causation long ago abandoned simple analyses of causal language on which, for example, to say c is a cause of e is just to say c is correlated with e. It is this complexity that opens the way to an internal explanation of causal representation because, if a causal scheme organizes the facts about correlation rather differently from, and apparently more simply than, a statistical scheme, then there may be real advantages to choosing one organization over the other. The challenge is to show that the causal scheme picks out especially important parts of the statistical information and arranges them conveniently for later use.

Imagine, then, a world, perhaps our own, at any rate in many ways not too different from our own, in which every fact can be captured by statistical claims—the kind of world imagined by the metaphysical empiricists. Show that, in such a world, creatures like us would gain some real practical advantage from causal cognition. Show, in other words, that if causation did not exist, then it would be necessary, or at least highly desirable, to invent it.

Two Features of Causal Representation

The first question to ask is as follows: What are the features that distinguish a causal scheme of representation from a statistical scheme? Perhaps that is too large and unwieldy a way to begin, however. I ask instead, What are the organizational or logical features that distinguish the causal claim "c is a cause of e" from the statistical claim "c is correlated with e"?

I organize this chapter around two such features: asymmetry and the supposition of an underlying mechanism. Each in its own way points to an interesting explanation, or explanations, of the utility of the causal scheme of representation. Let me characterize, loosely, the relation between causation, asymmetry, and underlying mechanism.

First, consider asymmetry. Correlation is a symmetric relation in the sense that "c is correlated with e" means exactly the same thing as "e is correlated with c". Causation is not: "c is a cause of e" means something different from "e is a cause of c" (although in some cases both may be true).

As promised at the end of the preceding section, I assume for the sake of the argument that the asymmetric information represented by the causal claim can also be represented by some set of statistical claims. (Certainly, although correlation itself is a symmetric relation, there is normally no shortage of asymmetry in the complete statistics of the associations between two event types c and e.) The question I ask in the following section is what advantage there might be in tracking an asymmetric relation between event types rather than a symmetric relation such as correlation. The various answers take the discussion far beyond the advantages of asymmetry itself.

Second, consider underlying mechanism. Unlike the statistical claim "c is correlated with e", the causal claim "*c* is a cause of *e*" implies the existence, or so I will suppose, of a mechanism connecting *c* and *e* and in virtue of which *c* causes *e*. You should not think that facts about mechanism are supposed to exist entirely at the metaphysical level as ineffable necessary connections, hidden strings, or causal oomphs. On the contrary, the nature of a causal connection's underlying mechanism is normally amenable to regular empirical investigation: The conditions required for, and the various intermediate steps that constitute, its operation can be inferred or even directly observed.

In any case, for the tactical reasons given, I assume that the information contained in claims about the workings of a causal connection's underlying mechanism is ultimately statistical information. But, a causal claim makes room for this information in its own characteristic way; the question, then, is whether representing the relevant facts as information about an "underlying mechanism" has practical advantages for the user.

Of what follows, the discussion of asymmetry is drawn for the most part from previous work on the philosophy and psychology of causation by Reichenbach (1956), Pearl (2000), Glymour (2001), Woodward (2003), and others; for this reason, I keep the presentation relatively short and simple, directing your attention if appropriate to the primary sources. In the discussion of the inferential role of information about underlying mechanism, I strike out on my own, developing ideas from my earlier work on the psychology of causal reasoning (Strevens, 2000).

There is a final clarification, a terminological note, and a hint to the reader: Some claims of the form "*c* is a cause of *e*" are what philosophers call *singular* causal claims, concerning particular events or occurrences, and some are causal generalizations, concerning types of event. For example, "my eating eggplant last night prevented me from sleeping" is a singular claim, whereas "eating vegetables causes insomnia" is a causal generalization. Both kinds of causal claims play an essential role in causal cognition, singular claims because the end product of causal reasoning is so often the prediction and control of individual facts and happenings, generalizations because reasoning about singular events is invariably guided by information about the causal tendencies of the event types to which they belong.

Some of the literature on causal generalizations, including much work on Bayesian networks, talks about variables rather than event types. The differences

between these two notions are not important for the purposes of the discussion in this chapter.

The sections on asymmetry and prediction, asymmetry and control, and underlying mechanism are self-contained and so may be read independently of the others. If you have time for nothing else, read the section on underlying mechanism.

Asymmetry

Which asymmetric aspects of the world's statistical web might be especially usefully represented by a causal schema? Usefully, you might ask, with respect to what end? The three cardinal aims of science are said to be explanation, prediction, and control. I organize the discussion of asymmetry around the more practical goals of prediction and control.

Asymmetry and Prediction

Hans Reichenbach suggested in *The Direction of Time* (1956) that the roots of causal thinking could be found in certain pervasive asymmetrical statistical patterns in our world. I focus on one such pattern, which I call the *Reichenbach asymmetry* (invidiously because Reichenbach investigated several such patterns and synecdochically because there is more to the pattern than its lack of symmetry).[1] Reichenbach's view that causal representations always go along with certain statistical asymmetries has been put to work in various ways by philosophers and other students of causality. Preeminent for my purposes is the asymmetries' use to give an internal account of the purpose of causal cognition that invokes the utility of causal representation as either an explanatory or a predictive tool.

Reichenbach emphasized the explanatory importance of causal representation (see, in particular, 1956, p. 152). I focus rather on prediction—not much of a departure because, for logical empiricists such as Reichenbach, explanation and prediction have much in common. What follows does not capture anything like the full range and subtlety of Reichenbach's attempt to understand causality and causal thinking in terms of statistical relations; indeed, the particular position I lay out cannot be ascribed to Reichenbach at all; it is a deliberately simplified version of section 22 of *The Direction of Time*.[2]

Let me begin by characterizing the statistical pattern that I am calling the *Reichenbach asymmetry*. The fundamental notion employed in the characterization is a statistical relation captured by a construction that I call a *Reichenbach dyad*. A Reichenbach dyad consists of two entities: a single event that I call the *focal event* and a set of events that I call the *parent events*. The term *parent* hints at the causal interpretation that is to come, but you should bear in mind that the definition of a Reichenbach dyad is purely statistical—it makes no reference to causal relations.

A focal event and a set of parent events form a Reichenbach dyad just in case:

1. The parent events occur before the focal event,[3] and
2. Conditional on the parent events, the occurrence of the focal event is statistically independent of the occurrence of any previous event, that is, any event occurring before the focal event. In other words, once the parent events are taken into account, the occurrence of any other event preceding the focal event can be ignored in determining the focal event's probability.

This is only a rough version of Condition 2; the precise condition is specified below.

There are three remarks regarding dyads. First, the definition of a Reichenbach dyad should remind you of the causal Markov condition from the Bayesian network literature discussed elsewhere in this volume; however, unlike that condition, it makes no reference to causal relations. (In this respect, it is closer to the original acausal Markov condition used to represent purely statistical information in acausal Bayes nets.)

Second, in Reichenbach's view, the probabilities attaching to events are simply the probabilities attaching to the corresponding event types. The statistical clause of the definition of a Reichenbach dyad, then, is satisfied in virtue of probabilistic facts about event types, whereas the temporal clause is satisfied in virtue of facts about the temporal ordering of the particular events in the dyad.[4] For a philosopher with a frequency-based notion of probability—such as Reichenbach—the probability distributions attached to event types will be determined in turn by the statistics of singular events, so the asymmetry as a whole will be a matter of the patterning of singular events.

Third, the definition needs the following refinement: The independence relation must hold not only conditional on the occurrence of all of the parent events, but also conditional on any combination of the parent events' occurrence and nonoccurrence. If there are two parent events, for example, then the

relation must hold conditional on the occurrence of both, on the nonoccurrence of both, on the occurrence of the first and the nonoccurrence of the second, and on the nonoccurrence of the first and the occurrence of the second.

Reichenbach notes that the world we live in is statistically patterned in a certain way: It is full of Reichenbach dyads. More exactly, for almost every event, there is a Reichenbach dyad for which it is the focal event, and—this is what gives the claim bite—these dyads have relatively small sets of parent events.[5]

This pattern is the Reichenbach asymmetry. That it is indeed an asymmetry is because of the temporal asymmetry in the definition of a dyad. (It was in virtue of this asymmetry, or something close to it, that Reichenbach suggested that the time order of events can be determined from information about conditional independences; unlike Reichenbach, I of course am taking a time ordering of events as given.)

In a Reichenbach-asymmetric world, Reichenbach held, there is a close relationship between the dyads and the causal structure of the world. To simplify somewhat,[6] there is a Reichenbach dyad in the actual world just in case there is a causal structure in which the parent events of the dyad are the direct causes of the focal event, that is, just in case there is a causal structure of the form shown in Figure 15-1.

The co-occurrence—note, not necessarily an equivalence—of causal and statistical structure is the linchpin of everything that follows. It can be exploited in various ways, all suggested by Reichenbach in some form.

First, it can be used to construct a metaphysics of cause or, as Reichenbach would say, a semantics for causal language: Define *cause* so that for one event to be a cause of another simply is for certain

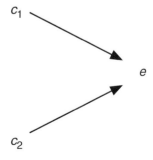

FIGURE 15-1 The causal structure for a Reichenbach dyad with c_1 and c_2 as parent events and e as the focal event. Arrows run from cause to effect.

Reichenbach dyads to exist. On the most straight-forward definition, one event is a (direct) cause of another just in case the one belongs to the parents in a dyad for which the other is focal.

Second, an epistemologist may use the statistical structure to discover causal structure, inferring the existence of the sort of structure shown in Figure 15-1 whenever the right Reichenbach dyads exist. Spirtes, Glymour, and Scheines's (2000) system for inferring causal structure is, in effect, a sophisticated version of this proposal (although it employs statistical subtleties that I have not even hinted at here).

Third, the coincidence of causal and statistical structure underwrites an alternative representational scheme for statistical facts, a scheme that represents the fact that a set of events constitutes a Reichenbach dyad using the sort of graph structure shown in Figure 15-1 rather than a set of probability statements. It is of course this third use that interests me, suggesting as it does the beginnings of an internal explanation for causal cognition.

The sort of internal explanation I have in mind hinges on three posits:

1. That the world is Reichenbach asymmetric,
2. That a causal network diagram—a *directed acyclic graph* or DAG in the Bayesian networks parlance—is an especially compact way of representing Reichenbach dyads in a Reichenbach-asymmetric world, and
3. That representing the Reichenbach dyads has great practical utility in a Reichenbach-asymmetric world given the asymmetries in our own epistemic situation.

These three premises imply if not that a causal schema is indispensable for certain kinds of reasoning about the world, then at least that it is highly advantageous. (As a caveat, I do not have much to say about the relationship between DAGs and causal representation; I simply assume that they tend to go together, leaving the hard work to the neo-Reichenbachians.)

In what follows, I assume the existence of the Reichenbach asymmetry for the sake of the argument. What of the other two premises? The advantage of a causal network diagram, or DAG, as a representation of the facts about Reichenbach dyads and other more complex conditional facts about independence of the same sort is as follows: A many-noded DAG—a graph that represents the causal structure in which a number of events are embedded—identifies a Reichenbach

dyad for every event that has its parents represented. To record this information as a set of statements about probability would require every such event to be mentioned a number of times, once as a focal event and then many times as parent. By contrast, the DAG "mentions" every event just once. The DAG thus provides a compact (and computationally convenient) representation of the dyadic relations. The compactness of the DAG is due in considerable part to that aspect of the world's Reichenbach asymmetry that guarantees that almost every parent in a dyad is the focal event of some other dyad.

To the last premise, then. Why is tracking the Reichenbach dyads so useful, and useful in particular in a world pervaded by Reichenbach asymmetry? As I said, I focus on predictive utility, that is, the usefulness of dyadic information in trying to ascertain whether some event will occur in the future given what you know now.

Consider how predictions are made using purely statistical information. You wish to predict whether some event e will occur. What you want to calculate is the probability of e; if it is high, then you predict that e will occur and act accordingly; if low, then you predict that it will not occur. In calculating the probability, you want to take into account all of your background knowledge as this will result in the most accurate predictions (the *principle of total evidence*). Thus, you want to calculate the probability of e conditional on everything you know, which is an onerous task. You must not only keep track of every event that has occurred, but also must make use of a probability distribution so fantastically detailed that it is well defined over all of these events.

Your task is much simpler, however, if you know that a very small subset of your background knowledge screens off the rest from the event e that you are trying to predict—if you know that, once you conditionalize on the small subset, conditionalizing on the rest will make no difference to the probability of e. Then, you may, with a serene heart and a clear epistemological conscience, track only the events in this subset and invoke a probability distribution defined over only these events (and of course over e).

It is precisely this predictive advantage that a Reichenbach dyad supplies to organisms like us who have direct knowledge of past but not of future events. In the simplest case, the event e that you want to predict is the focal event of a Reichenbach dyad in which all of the parent events are known to have occurred, and no events occurring at the same time or after the focal event are known to occur. The probability of *e* conditional on the parent events is then the best predictor of *e* available to you. Thus, only *e*'s parents need to be taken into account, enormously simplifying your predictive task.

The more complex case in which you have knowledge about only some of the parent events cannot be handled so easily, but again, information about the conditional independences is extremely helpful.

In either case, note, the *asymmetry* of the Reichenbach asymmetry comes into its own: It is because the temporal asymmetry of the dyad reflects the temporal asymmetry in our knowledge of the world—we have far more knowledge of the past than of the future—that the dyads are so useful, despite the temporally qualified nature of the independence relations they represent.[7]

Here, then, is the skeleton of an internal explanation of the role of causal cognition. A would-be predictor has great need of information about conditional independences. In a Reichenbach-asymmetric world, the class of such information most useful to asymmetric knowers like us can be stored compactly using a causal network representation. The role of causal representations in our psychology is to exploit this efficiency. (For a fuller discussion of the psychological utility of DAGs, see Glymour, 2001.)

I have two nonpsychological remarks. Observe that a world containing the Reichenbach asymmetry will be symmetric overall if it also contains the pattern you might call the reverse Reichenbach asymmetry: For (almost) every event *e*, there is a set of "child" events that (a) occur after *e* and (b) create a conditional independence between *e* and any other event occurring after *e*. In a deterministic world, you ought to expect precisely such a pattern. As writers on causation and statistical mechanics beginning with Reichenbach have noted, however, although a deterministic world may have the reverse asymmetry at the microlevel, if it conforms to the second law of thermodynamics, then it will not have the asymmetry nearly so extensively at the macrolevel, that is, relative to a coarse graining of events (because any candidate set of children will have to be specified finely for the independence relation to hold and so will be lost in a coarse graining). Such a world will have both the forward- and backward-looking asymmetries, then, but the forward-looking asymmetry may be far more apparent to macroscopic beings like us. (Some writers would argue that the second law also explains the asymmetry of our epistemic situation in virtue of which, as argued, the forward-looking asymmetry is far more *useful* to macroscopic beings.)

As noted at the beginning of this section, I have discussed just one asymmetric pattern used in Reichenbach's investigation of the causal and statistical order of the world. There are other such patterns. (*The Direction of Time* [1956] itself discusses two more: the conjunctive fork and the mark asymmetry that inspires Salmon's 1984 account of causation.) The work described in this section should, then, be regarded as part of a wider research program, which is perhaps still in its early stages.

Asymmetry and Control

To have control over an event is to be able to manipulate nature in such a way that the event occurs. Woodward (2003) argued that the most important function of causal representation is to encode manipulability relations. Because the relation between causality and manipulability is discussed at length elsewhere in this volume (in chapters 1 and 4), I confine myself in this section to the briefest sketch of the way in which manipulability might provide an internal explanation of causal cognition.

A simple example demonstrates the difference between manipulability and prediction. Consider the relationship between a switch and light. There is a strong correlation between the switch's being in the on position and the light's shining. As a result, you can use your knowledge of the switch's position to predict whether the light is shining, or just as surely, you can use your knowledge regarding whether the light is shining to predict the switch's position. But, this predictive symmetry breaks down when it comes to control: You can change whether the light is shining by changing the state of the switch, but you cannot change the position of the switch by changing the state of the light, for example, by removing the bulb or breaking the main circuit. When we say that toggling the switch causes the light to go on but deny that changing the state of the light causes the switch to be toggled, according to Woodward we are asserting something like this asymmetry.

The purpose of the asymmetric language of causation, then, is to capture the asymmetric facts about manipulability. (As an exercise, how are the facts about manipulability related to Reichenbach's [1956] concerns in *The Direction of Time*: the statistical asymmetries, the second law of thermodynamics, and the direction of time itself? Horwich's work [1987] is a useful resource on such questions and contains a brief discussion of the manipulationist approach to causation.)

Woodward (2003) suggests that causal language can capture facts about manipulability that are beyond the reach of any mere statistical claim, in the sense that facts about manipulability are not reducible to statistical facts (p. 28). Perhaps, then, he would endorse an external explanation of causal cognition: We think causally because causal representations capture facts about manipulability that are both of great practical utility and beyond the expressive range of statistical language.

I think, however, that this cannot be correct. Even if Woodward is right in holding that the facts about manipulability are not purely statistical facts, a simple and familiar argument shows that the practical aspect of manipulability facts—that is, the consequences of manipulability facts that are relevant to our practical decision making—can be captured statistically.

Briefly, the argument is as follows:

1. Anything that makes a practical difference makes a publicly observable difference. You and I can both see, for example, that my flicking the switch changes the state of the light, but that my removing the bulb does not change the state of the switch.
2. Any observable pattern can be represented by a statistical claim.
3. Therefore, everything contained in a manipulability claim that is of practical use to us could be stated using purely statistical language.

In short, all we need to know about manipulability in our world can be represented statistically. The fact that flicking a switch turns on a light is stated as a correlation not between the on state of the switch and the light's shining, but between the fact of flicking and the subsequent change of the light's state. The fact that breaking the light bulb does not toggle the switch is stated as a lack of correlation between the breaking and a subsequent change of the switch's state. (For a way of making the same point from within the Bayes nets framework, see Spirtes et al., 2000, section 3.72.)

There is no external explanation of causal cognition to be found in the insights of Woodward and others about the relation between causality and manipula-

bility, then. There may well be an internal explanation, however.

Consider what I am calling the practical content of our knowledge about manipulability. This content can, I have argued, be given a statistical representation; it could be encoded in a list of correlations. But, might it not be more economical to encode it in a causal DAG?

A good case can be made that the causal representation is more efficient. But, it is a complicated issue because even the causal representation is rather more complex than you might think: To provide useful information about manipulability, a DAG must represent not only the various features of the world that are to be manipulated, but also the manipulating actions themselves, in particular, the various actions that can be taken by the manipulator—pushings, pullings, switchings, and so on. There are a great number of these, and there is no shortcut to the causal representation of this information or, at least, no shortcut that is not also a shortcut for the probabilistic representation of the same information.

Thus, having given the barest sketch of the explanation, I leave the hard work to the modern-day proponents of the view that the impetus for our causal thinking is the need to represent relations of manipulability.

Underlying Mechanism

Assume that for every type of causal relation, that is, every fact of the form *c* causes *e*, we causal cognizers suppose that there is an underlying mechanism in virtue of which occurrences of *c* bring about occurrences of *e*. Perhaps this is not always true—perhaps causal relations considered fundamental are not thought to have an underlying mechanism—but ignore these exceptions for the sake of the discussion.

On the face of it, imagining the existence of underlying mechanisms might seem to be a species of metaphysical daydreaming. You may think that there is a mechanism or you may not, but it will not make a difference to the serious business of everyday causal inference; in particular, it will not make a difference to your use of causal knowledge to predict and control the aspects of the world that matter to you.

My first goal in this section is to refute such a view. Everyday causal inference of the most mundane and utilitarian sort, I show, makes use of information about underlying mechanisms on a regular basis. Any account of practical causal reasoning must be in part an account of the inferential role of information about mechanisms.

In the course of the demonstration, I employ a notion of underlying mechanism on which there is more to a mechanism than "hidden strings" attaching cause to effect. In my sense, the operation of a mechanism may be in large part entirely observable in the form of various intermediate steps in a causal process. In accordance with my overall strategy in this chapter, I go even further and assume that information about underlying mechanisms—certainly, the useful part of information about underlying mechanisms—can be captured completely by noncausal, probabilistic representations. But, although it can be organized as a body of statistical claims, conceiving of and organizing this information instead as though it concerns an underlying mechanism is, I argue, more productive in a number of ways.

The Inferential Role of Information About Mechanisms

What is the inferential role of our knowledge of a causal relation's underlying mechanism? I answer this question by discussing an example that I have written about elsewhere, the causal relations that underwrite the characteristic appearances of a biological species member,[8] for example, a lemon's yellow color or a tiger's ferocity.

An emerging consensus in the psychological literature on natural kind concepts, and on species concepts in particular, holds that there is a natural human tendency to conceive of the relation between a species and its characteristic properties as causal. This is an assumption common to the psychological essentialists (Gelman, 2003; Medin & Ortony, 1989) and to my work on this topic (Strevens, 2000). If it is allowed that wherever we humans posit a causal relation, we also tend to posit a mechanism, then both the essentialists and I hold that, for every species and known characteristic property, humans typically believe in the existence of a mechanism, common to all members of the species, that causes the property. For example, all humans who know that tigers are ferocious posit the existence of a single mechanism, common to all tigers, that causes ferocity. In what follows, I assume this without argument.

When children first learn that, say, lemons are yellow, they normally know little or nothing of the mechanism by which lemons acquire their characteristic color. Their commitment to the existence of a mechanism, then, is solely that: a commitment but nothing more. As they develop, they learn something about the workings of the mechanism. Immature lemons are green, but they develop their characteristic color over time, with their skin gradually colored by some internal process as they mature. This knowledge is slight and superficial, but it can have considerable influence on ordinary causal reasoning, as I now show.

The causal relation between membership of a species k and a given characteristic observable property p will be represented by a causal generalization roughly of the following form: An organism's being a member of species k causes it to have property p.[9] For example, the connection between lemonhood and yellowness is represented as the mental equivalent of the following sentence: A fruit's being a lemon causes it to be yellow. The connection between tigerhood and ferocity is represented as follows: An animal's being a tiger causes it to be ferocious.

A causal claim of this form is good for two things: inferring from an organism's species that it has certain observable properties and inferring from an organism's observable properties that it is a member of a certain species.

You perform the first sort of inference, which may be called *projection*, when you stay well away from tigers on the assumption that they are ferocious or avoid eating lemons on the assumption that they are sour. You perform the second sort of inference, which is always called *categorization*, when you classify something with all the characteristic observable properties of a lemon—something that is yellow, football shaped, sour, and so on—as a lemon.

A projection takes you from the antecedent to the consequent of the represented causal relation, inferring from the presence of a cause, namely, species membership, the presence of a characteristic effect. A categorization, by contrast, takes you from the consequent to the antecedent of the causal representation, inferring from the presence of a cluster of characteristic effects the presence of something that typically causes those effects. (For some other ways to integrate causal thinking into the process of categorization, see chapters 11 and 12, this volume.)

The significance of knowledge of an underlying mechanism lies in its ability to modify both kinds of inference, most often, although not always, in its ability to defeat them—to give you reason not to infer the presence of the effect from the presence of the cause or vice versa. In illustrating this inference-mediating power, I discuss projection and categorization separately.

First, regarding projection, the basic form of a projective inference is as follows:

1. Organism x belongs to species k,
2. An organism's being a member of species k causes it to have observable property p, therefore
3. x will have p.

By following this inferential pattern whenever you can—by inferring, of any member of k, that it has p—you will not do too badly in this world. But, you could do better. The reason is that, even when the premises of the inference hold true, the conclusion may not. Some members of a species will lack the characteristic properties of that species.

For example, lemons are characteristically yellow, but immature lemons are green. Skunks are characteristically four-legged, but injured skunks may be three-legged. Tigers are characteristically ferocious, but sedated tigers are not. Uncharacteristic specimens of a species, you see from these examples, far from rare.

What makes an uncharacteristic specimen possible is that the existence of an underlying mechanism connecting species membership with the appearance of a characteristic property does not guarantee the presence of the property. Broadly, there are three reasons that the property might not be present. First, the conditions required for the mechanism to operate properly may not have been present. This is true for immature lemons, for example, for which the yellowing mechanism has not had the time it needs to do its work. Second, something may have interfered with the mechanism, preventing it from operating properly. This is true for the sedated tiger, with the sedatives temporarily disabling the behavioral or other mechanisms responsible for ferocity. Third, the mechanism may have operated properly, so that the characteristic property was present at one time, but some outside force may have since undone the mechanism's work. This is true for the injured skunk: It originally had four legs, but one has been lost.

The more you know about underlying mechanisms, the better you are able to predict the breakdown of the relation between species membership and observable properties and so to know when not to make a projection on the grounds of species membership: You avoid the error of projecting the yellowness of immature lemons or the ferocity of tigers that are sedated, or ill, or have been tamed.

The utility of mechanism knowledge is general: The mechanism underlying any causal generalization "c is a cause of e" can break down or have its effects undone, so that some instances of c are not accompanied by instances of e. The more you know about the workings of the mechanism, the better you will be able to recognize the circumstances in which a breakdown or a reversal is likely and so the better you will be at recognizing cases in which the presence of an e should not be inferred from the presence of a c.

Your projective prowess as a mechanistic reasoner about a given causal connection, then, will increase in proportion first to your knowledge of the connection's underlying mechanism and second to the frequency and systematicity of the connection's exceptions.

Let me now discuss categorization. The basic form of a categorical inference is as follows:

1. Organism x has observable properties p.
2. An organism's being a member of species k causes it to have observable properties p,
3. There is no other likely cause of x's having p, therefore
4. Organism x belongs to species k.

(Note that, in most categorizations, p is a complex of observable properties—although categorization is sometimes possible on the basis of a single characteristic property, as when you recognize a fruit by its taste.)

In virtue of Premise 3, a categorical inference is more complex than a projective inference. The need for this premise is an entirely general feature of inferring from effects to causes as opposed to inferring from causes to effects. To see this, suppose that c causes e. If you know that a c has occurred, then the presence of other potential causes of e makes your inference that an e occurs no less secure. But, if you know that an e has occurred, the presence of other potential causes of e should most definitely deter you from inferring the presence of a c unless you have further information.

The further information is often, if not always, information about or pertinent to underlying mechanisms. If you have some knowledge of how this particular *e* was caused, then you may be able to rule out potential causes of *e* other than *c*, or alternatively, you may be able to rule out *c* itself as a cause of the *e*.

Let me illustrate this claim by returning to causal connections between species and their observable properties. Suppose you observe some green, lemon-shaped fruit on a tree. Are they lemons or limes? You cannot taste them, so you have only the usual visual information to go on, namely, their color and shape. They have the characteristic color and shape of limes, so a diagnosis of limehood would seem apt. But suppose you know that it is early in the growing season. Then, if you know something about the mechanism underlying color in lemons, that color takes some time to develop, you know that you cannot use the inference schema to categorize the fruit as limes because Premise 3 does not hold: There is a possible cause of the fruit's greenness other than limehood. If, by contrast, you know nothing about the underlying color mechanism but simply think of lemons as yellow, then you will not gasp the precariousness of the inference to limehood.

A natural reaction to this description of the lemon/lime inference is to question whether an elaborate causal framework is necessary to encode the information. Why not simply record a correlation between lemonhood, immaturity, and greenness? Then, the fruit in question will resemble two different prototypes (using the term *prototype* loosely), the prototypes for lime and immature lemon, and the inferrer will exhibit the appropriate level of uncertainty regarding the fruit's category.

As I have said several times, if you want an internalist explanation of causal cognition, then it is unhelpful to contrast causal with statistical information as though each were sui generis; it is better to contrast a causal representation of statistical information with other schemas for representing the same sort of information. The question then becomes one of organization rather than extent: What is the most flexible and efficient way of storing statistical information about, say, lemons, their color, and their maturity?

This question is properly the subject of the next section, but I lay some of the groundwork here. Let me begin by making a case for the great flexibility of the causal schema, in particular the flexibility of the part of the schema inhabited by underlying mechanisms, as a means for representing inferentially relevant information by considering some other ways that information about mechanism affects categorization.

In the example, information about mechanism rightly inhibited categorization, but in other cases, it opens the way to categorizations that would otherwise fail to be made. I have in mind categorization tasks involving uncharacteristic specimens: members of a species that lack some characteristic property of the species.

Consider, for example, the three-legged skunk. Knowing that the mechanism underlying skunks' four-leggedness, although it causes skunks to grow four legs, does not maintain the legs once grown—so that a severed leg will not grow back—provides the foundation for understanding that a skunk or other quadruped may easily lose a leg despite being characteristically four-legged and so allows us to categorize an otherwise skunklike three-legged animal as a skunk. (Somewhat deeper knowledge of the mechanism shows that there are other ways, such as congenital defects, in which the mechanism may fail to ensure four-leggedness.)

There are a thousand ways that a specimen might turn out to be uncharacteristic. Although it is possible, in principle, to store a statistical profile for every one of these possibilities, so that examples of each will be correctly classified (or at least classified as intelligently as background information allows) should they be encountered, it is far more efficient—especially given that most varieties of uncharacteristic specimens will be rather rare—to store a great deal of information about characteristic specimens. This information gives you your best chance of recognizing that a particular observable but uncharacteristic property was not produced naturally, that is, not produced in accordance with the kind of causal law specified in Premise 2 of the categorization schema. Once you know that a property is not naturally produced, you know that it is not a clue to species membership. You are free—in fact, you are obliged—to ignore it and to use whatever other information you have to make a categorization. In this way, information about the normal operation of mechanisms is used to classify abnormal specimens correctly. I return to the question of the efficiency of the causal schema in the next section.

An extreme case of an uncharacteristic specimen is the sort of organism described in Frank Keil's (1989) "transformation" experiments. In these experiments, a raccoon is supposedly subjected to a cosmetic makeover so comprehensive that it is visually (and olfactorily) indistinguishable from a skunk. Such an animal has all the characteristic properties of a skunk, but knowing that it came to have these properties unnaturally—that is, not in accordance with the mechanism by which real skunks come to have them—you resist the inference from skunk appearance to skunkhood. Such a case is too bizarre to play a part in explaining the practical function of causal cognition, but it does a good job of exposing the causal underpinnings of our reasoning about uncharacteristic properties. I made the case that this reasoning is driven by knowledge about the underlying mechanism in Strevens (2000).

Let me summarize some of the ways in which knowledge of underlying mechanism can have an impact on everyday projection and categorization. Take as a paradigm the causal connection between lemonhood and yellowness. The more I know about the mechanism underlying this connection, the better I am able:

1. Given a lemon, to see when the mechanism will fail to operate and so to see that I should resist the projection from lemonhood to yellowness, as when I know that the lemon has not had time to develop its characteristic color.
2. Given a lemon, to see when the successful operation of the mechanism may have been later permanently undone and so to see that I should resist the projection from lemonhood to yellowness, as when I know that the lemon has been daubed with a nonyellow dye (because I know that a lemon cannot "grow its color back").
3. Given a yellow fruit, to see when the lemonhood/yellowness mechanism was not responsible for the yellowness and so to see that I should resist the categorization from yellowness to lemonhood, as when I know that the fruit has been daubed with a yellow dye.
4. Given a nonyellow fruit, to see that the color of the fruit is not produced in accordance with a fruit/color mechanism and so to proceed (on other grounds) to categorize the fruit as a lemon despite its color, as when I know that an otherwise lemony fruit owes its nonyellow color to being daubed with a dye.

In the first three cases, knowledge of mechanism gives you reason to refrain from making inferences that

would otherwise seem reasonable; in the fourth case, knowledge of mechanism gives you reason to make an inference that would otherwise seem questionable.

Note that the last, inference-enabling function requires general knowledge of the mechanisms by which fruits acquire their colors; such knowledge may in fact play a role in any of the cases described. Note also that knowledge of mechanism is even more useful in categorization than in projection; this reflects the greater in-principle complexity of categorical inferences.

Virtues of the Mechanism Schema: Efficiency

The information that we conceive of as concerning a causal connection's underlying mechanism is relevant, I have shown, to the task of everyday inference. By my working assumption, this information could in principle be represented in statistical form. Why, then, represent it causally?

I give two quite different, though complementary, answers to this question. The first answer, presented in this section, continues the strategy I have pursued so far: It makes a case that the causal scheme does an excellent job of representing practically significant information in an efficient way. The next section presents the second answer: The causal character of a representation might encourage certain especially good search strategies for the information that is to be represented.

First, let me discuss the explanation from efficiency. Because information about underlying mechanism can be used in so many ways, a case for the overall efficiency of the causal representation of such information would be complex. Let me focus instead on a single application, discussed above: the use of mechanism information to recognize that an organism is an uncharacteristic, although genuine, member of a species and, more particularly, to recognize that the uncharacteristic appearance of the specimen is no barrier to the categorization. When you conclude that an immature, green lemon is a lemon, that a three-legged skunk is a skunk, or that a raccoon transformed to look exactly like a skunk is a raccoon, you use mechanism information in this way.

Consider three ways of dealing with uncharacteristic specimens:

1. Ignore them. Simply represent the characteristic observable properties of each species and use these as the basis for categorization. This is how

uncharacteristic specimens are dealt with by, for example, the prototype theory of concepts (Rosch, 1978). Using this strategy, an uncharacteristic specimen may still be classified correctly if it resembles the characteristic specimens of the correct category more than those of any other category.

2. Catalogue the exceptions. Store a separate prototype, for example, for immature lemons and three-legged skunks.

3. Think causally: Represent the mechanisms by which a species' characteristic properties are caused and ignore, for the purposes of categorization, properties that are not caused in these ways.

Of the three, I suggest that the third, causal strategy gives you the best ratio of accurate categorizations to cognitive effort. The second strategy, maintaining a complete list of exceptions, is extremely resource intensive. The first strategy involves a rather modest commitment of cognitive resources—although not that much more modest than the causal strategy—but offers a much less sophisticated handling of uncharacteristic specimens. The sources of the uncharacteristic properties are entirely ignored, and a crude resemblance heuristic is used to classify nonparadigmatic specimens. Such a strategy may be good enough much of the time, but the causal strategy offers far more inferential control for little additional investment.

The causal, or mechanism-based, strategy, then, offers a promising middle point between the prototype and the exception list strategies. Like the prototype strategy, it requires relatively few resources because it stores information only about normal specimens, not about abnormal specimens. Unlike the prototype strategy, it stores information not only about the observable properties of normal specimens, but also about the process that leads to the appearance of the normal properties. Because the appearance of uncharacteristic properties is necessarily caused either by some kind of irregularity or abnormality in this process or by an overriding or reversal of the process, the causal strategy is able to reliably distinguish unusual category members from category nonmembers.

To appreciate the efficiency of the causal strategy, it is important to understand that a small amount of knowledge about mechanisms can go a long way. (This is just as well because humans tend not to know much about mechanisms; Wilson & Keil, 2000.) No deep insight into developmental biology is needed to see that a normally four-legged creature can lose a leg or that a dyed lemon does not receive its color naturally. Much sophistication can be added to your causal inferences, then, at a very low price. Observe also that there is never an obligation to learn about mechanisms. If a certain causal connection is unimportant to you, then you need not seek out and retain any information about its underlying mechanism.

In a somewhat different vein, note that there is nothing mysterious about mechanism information, by which I mean that it is not hard to see how the same information, or at least its practically useful component, might be stated in statistical form. That lost legs are not regrown or that the natural color of a lemon is achieved without outside influence are observable phenomena, although less easily observed, of course, than the number of legs or the color themselves. What is recorded, in a representation of an underlying mechanism, is not in the first instance something essentially metaphysical, but rather the stages and symptoms of the sequence of events that leads to the appearance of the relevant characteristic observable property. These are the clues—the observable clues because if they were unobservable they would be useless—that distinguish the normal from the abnormal production of the property.

What distinguishes the representation of the mechanism, then, is first an attention to the details of a process and second a concern with representing what is normal rather than what is exceptional about the process. My corresponding claims are first that attending to some of the details of production can have a real practical payoff, and second that by recording the details of normal or paradigmatic production processes only, these benefits come at relatively little cost in cognitive resources.

Let me bolster this discussion of the uses of the mechanism-based strategy in biological reasoning with a few words on physical reasoning, drawing on the investigations of Shultz (1982) (see also Ahn, Kalish, Medin, & Gelman, 1995). Shultz showed children of various ages between 3 and 10 years scenarios in which three events occurred, two of which were candidate causes for the third. The subjects had to decide which of the events was the actual cause, the aim of the experiment being to pit against one another two different rules for causal attribution. What Shultz called the *Humean rule* picks out as the cause of an effect another event that is spatiotemporally contiguous with the effect and that is of a type that covaries with events of the same type as the effect. The *generative transmission* rule, by contrast, picks out as the cause the event that is connected to the effect by way of the appropriate mechanism. The signs of mechanical connection in Shultz's experiments are all observable and take the form of certain conditions' holding. For example, for a tuning fork to cause a hollow container to resonate, the fork had to be vibrating and situated in front of the open end of the container, and the space between them had to be unobstructed.

Shultz's (1982) older subjects tended overwhelmingly to favor the generative transmission rule: When the conditions for the operation of the mechanism obtained for one putative cause and not the other, the event for which they obtained was named the actual cause, even though, thanks to the clever design of the experimental scenarios, the Humean rule pointed to the other event.[10] The children were using information about mechanism in causal reasoning about Shultz's physical scenarios, then, in much the same way that they are using information about mechanism in the biological scenario considered above.

Shultz's (1982) experiments, I must point out, take information about causes as an inferential end in itself. Thus, these are not cases for which thinking causally is a means to a noncausal inferential end; they do not directly support my conclusion that thinking in terms of mechanisms would be valuable, given the event patterns in our world, even if everything worth knowing could be cast as a statistical fact. What they do show is that mechanisms play a similar role in reasoning about physical correlations as they do in reasoning about biological correlations; what remains to be demonstrated is how great an advantage in efficiency such reasoning might, on the whole, provide by comparison with noncausal styles of statistical reasoning. What I have laid out here is the beginning, not the end, of a mechanism-based explanation of the efficiency of causal cognition.

Virtues of the Mechanism Schema: Search Strategies

Humans believe that, for every causal connection, there is an underlying mechanism, or so I have assumed, and will continue to assume, in this discussion. The belief in an underlying mechanism can manifest itself in three ways. First, as information pertinent to the nature of the mechanism arrives, you retain it and file it in the appropriate place. Second, when making inferences to which mechanism information is relevant, you retrieve the information and put it to work. Third, and more proactively, you may go looking for further information to apply in this way; that is, you may search for more information about mechanisms.

So far, I have focused on the first two aspects of the commitment to mechanism, arguing that the information we regard as concerning an underlying mechanism is particularly useful in our practical causal inferences. This postulate about the practical utility of the information can equally well be used to explain the third aspect of causal thinking: If the information is good to have, then there is every reason to seek it out.

In what follows, I focus on the way that we search for information about mechanism, describing a further element of causal cognition that influences not only the way that the information is put to use in later inference, but also the way in which we go about acquiring the information in the first place. As you will expect, I want to suggest that there is something about the causal way of thinking that makes for an especially efficient search strategy, that is, a search strategy that turns up a great deal of information for relatively little investment.

I propose that our conceiving of mechanism information as causal motivates us, when looking for such information, to adopt what I call the *constraint from below*. The content of this constraint is roughly that any postulated mechanism ought to be "implementable," and indeed implemented, by mechanisms at the appropriate *basic level*. For example, any physical mechanism must be at root constructed from basic physical mechanisms, any biological mechanism from basic biological mechanisms, any psychological mechanism from basic psychological mechanisms, and so on.

Clearly, the content of the constraint greatly depends on what is meant by *appropriate basic level*. I have three important remarks on this notion: First, as suggested by my examples, there may be different basic levels for different kinds of phenomena. The basic level for mental phenomena, for example, may be distinct from the basic level for physical phenomena.

Second, that a level is basic does not entail that it is metaphysically fundamental. That the basic level for mental phenomena, for example, is different from the basic level for physical phenomena allows—although it certainly does not require—that basic level mental processes are themselves physically implemented. There may be a hierarchy of implementation, then, among the basic levels themselves. I do not explore the inferential role of such a hierarchy here, although belief in a hierarchy would clearly affect the cognitive significance of the constraint from below.

Third, the identity of the basic levels is not built into the constraint from below and, indeed, is never known apodictically. Your beliefs regarding the number, nature, and extent of the basic levels are always under revision, sometimes radically so.[11]

What is useful about the constraint from below? There are two separate questions to address. The first concerns the validity of the constraint. The second asks how, even if correct, a doctrine that sounds more like a metaphysical thesis than a piece of helpful advice could play a role in improving our everyday inference.

I want to focus on the second question, so let me assume without any argument that, with the basic levels properly identified, the assumption about universal implementability explicit in the constraint from below is more or less true. (The more radical antireductionists among philosophers of science will demur.) How is this fact practically relevant?

The wrong way to apply the constraint is to insist that no mechanism be postulated—perhaps even no causal connection posited—until an underlying implementation is found, that is, until the operation of the mechanism is completely understood in terms of the appropriate basic level. Pursuers of this policy will indeed be lost in thought (insofar as teaching responsibilities and administrative duties allow).

The aim of the constraint is not to place impediments on the path to finding an underlying mechanism but, on the contrary, to clear the path and to speed the search. Given a few beliefs about the applicable basic level, the constraint from below will point to certain areas, and away from certain others, as sources of information about underlying mechanism. To learn the truth about the mechanism underlying the yellowness of lemons, look inside, not outside, the lemon. Look for characteristically biological processes, not mental processes. Ignore the possibility that lemons get their yellowness the same way that

gold gets its yellowness, but take seriously the possibility that lemons get their yellowness in the same way as grapefruit, and so on.

Even if you are wrong in many of your beliefs about the basic levels, the influence of the constraint from below will tend to be largely or wholly positive. On almost any view that anyone has ever had about the workings of biological mechanisms, the last paragraph's sage counsel regarding where to look for the lemon/yellowness mechanism holds. The constraint from below, for all its appearance of heavy-duty metaphysicking, is a fount of good, practical advice in the search for causal information. Ironically, the constraint is liable to cause trouble only when you know—or think you know—much more about the workings of the world than a modest, amateur causal inquirer. But, that is a story for another time.

In short, then, the assumption, which I take to be built into our system of causal reasoning, that every causal connection has an underlying mechanism, together with the meat added to the notion of *underlying* by the constraint from below and some rudimentary knowledge about the basic level, prompts a search strategy for mechanistic information that is better than most.

Virtues of the Mechanism Schema: Overview

Let me now step back to summarize the various ways in which thinking about causal connections as having underlying mechanisms improves day-to-day causal inference, even if the mechanistic information is nothing but a certain kind of statistical information in another guise.

1. The mechanism schema provides a compact representation of certain information about normal or characteristic specimens that can be used to decide whether to proceed with various projections and categorizations in an intelligent way.
2. The mechanism schema invites us to make mechanism-based inferences using the information that it encodes, by representing it in a form that makes its relevance to simple causal inference—inference from cause to effect or effect to cause—immediate.
3. This relevance made clear, the mechanism schema invites us not only to make mechanism-based inferences but also to search out the

information we need to do so—to find the mechanical reality underlying a causal connection.

4. Because the mechanical information is subject to the constraint from below, the search for information about mechanism is guided in part by wider beliefs about the workings of the appropriate basic level.

It has been my working assumption in this chapter that all of the information mentioned—the information contained in a simple causal claim, the information about the mechanism that underlies the causal connection asserted by the claim, and the information contained in beliefs about the appropriate basic level brought to bear by way of the constraint from below—can be represented in statistical form.[12]

What, then, is the origin of the peculiar phenomenological character of causal beliefs? It cannot be in their content (at least, not in their content extensionally conceived, for example, not in their truth conditions). This leads naturally to the suggestion that the causal phenomenology is due to the particular inferential role played by causal information in the human mind, that is, the role characterized immediately above.

I am not sure that this suggestion can account for the sense of causal oomph we experience when one billiard ball strikes another. Perhaps the oomph ought to be explained in some completely different way, for example, as an aspect of our sensory phenomenology, as suggested by Leslie (1994). I do think that the inferential role investigated in this section is at least a part of the explanation for the sense of hidden connectedness in the world as we experience it causally, the sense that behind the scenes—or below the scenes—something is going on, something on which everything we see depends.

Conclusion

I have surveyed a number of quite different approaches to explaining the prevalence of causal cognition. They are all internal explanations: They focus on the organizing power, rather than the expressive power, of causal representation schemas.

Each of these explanations assumes that, even if the world is Humean, in the sense that every fact can be captured by some purely statistical claim or other,

it is a very particular Humean world: Its pattern of correlations is a very particular pattern, with very particular properties. It has the Reichenbach asymmetry, it exhibits certain asymmetric patterns of manipulability, or it is the sort of pattern that is amenable to characterization in terms of the language of underlying mechanism, consistent with the constraint from below.

It is this special, perhaps unusual, property of the worlds' correlations that makes causal cognition so useful. The practical value of causal thinking lies, then, not in its ability to capture facts in principle out of the reach of statistical vocabulary, but in its ability to organize statistical facts—given certain unusual patterns in those facts—in an especially effective way and perhaps also to organize the search for those facts just as efficiently.

It is quite striking how much can be said in favor of each of the proposed internal explanations of causal cognition's practical value and how many opportunities there are for still more proposals. The complete explanation of the form of causal cognition looks to be rich and complex indeed.

That the existence and structure of causal cognition is best explained internally allows, but does not imply, that the world is Humean. A modern causal realist, or opponent of Humeanism, will aim to explain the particular pattern of correlations we see around us—the pattern that is so amenable to causal encoding—as a consequence of something bigger than statistics at work in the external world. It is only because of a metaphysics that posits more than can be said in Humean or statistical terms that the world contains these special kinds of correlations, or so the causal realist argues; they are our best clue that there is something else out there. Our system of causal inference has developed to exploit the unusual correlations for practical purposes only; yet, despite its purely instrumental rationale, it points past mere patterns of fact and gestures, however vaguely, at a causal world beyond.

ACKNOWLEDGMENT Thanks to David Danks and Clark Glymour for comments, advice, and Bayesian networks lore.

References

Ahn, W., C. W. Kalish, D. L. Medin, & S. A. Gelman. (1995). The role of covariation versus mechanism information in causal attribution. *Cognition, 54,* 299–352.

Gelman, S. A. (2003). *The essential child: Origins of essentialism in everyday thought.* New York: Oxford University Press.

Glymour, C. (2001). *The mind's arrows: Bayes nets and graphical causal models in psychology.* Cambridge, MA: MIT Press.

Horwich, P. (1987). *Asymmetries in time.* Cambridge, MA: MIT Press.

Keil, F. C. (1989). *Concepts, kinds and conceptual development.* Cambridge, MA: MIT Press.

Leslie, A. M. (1994). ToMM, ToBy, and agency: Core architecture and domain specificity. In L. Hirschfeld and S. A. Gelman (Eds.), *Mapping the mind* (pp. 119–148). Cambridge, England: Cambridge University Press.

Medin, D., & A. Ortony. (1989). Psychological essentialism. In S. Vosniadou and A. Ortony (Eds.), *Similarity and analogical reasoning* (pp. 179–195). Cambridge, England: Cambridge University Press.

Medin, D. L., & S. Atran (Eds.). (1999). *Folkbiology.* Cambridge, MA: MIT Press.

Pearl, J. (2000). *Causality: Models, reasoning, and inference.* Cambridge, England: Cambridge University Press.

Reichenbach, H. (1956). *The direction of time.* Berkeley, CA: University of California Press.

Rosch, E. (1978). Principles of categorization. In E. Rosch and B. Lloyd (Eds.), *Cognition and categorization* (pp. 27–48). Hillsdale, NJ: Erlbaum.

Salmon, W. (1984). *Explanation and the causal structure of the world.* Princeton, NJ: Princeton University Press.

Shultz, T. R. (1982). *Rules of causal attribution,* Vol. 47:1, *Monographs of the Society for Research in Child Development.* Chicago: Chicago University Press.

Sosa, E., & Tooley, M. (1993). *Causation.* New York: Oxford University Press.

Spirtes, P., Glymour, C., & Scheines, R. (2000). *Causation, prediction, and search* (2nd ed.). Cambridge, MA: MIT Press.

Strevens, M. (2000). The essentialist aspect of naive theories. *Cognition,* 74,149–175.

Wilson, R. A., & Keil, F. C. (2000). The shadows and shallows of explanation. In F. C. Keil and R. A. Wilson (Eds.), *Explanation and cognition* (pp. 87–114). Cambridge, MA: MIT Press.

Woodward, J. (2003). *Making things happen: A theory of causal explanation.* New York: Oxford University Press.

16

Causal Reasoning as Informed by the Early Development of Explanations

Henry M. Wellman & David Liu

This volume focuses on the relation between causal understanding and theory formation. We address this relation by concentrating primarily on one everyday theory—theory of mind—and on causal understandings as embodied in causal explanations. This volume also aims, at least in part, to foster dialogue between developmental scientists and the scholars in philosophy and computer sciences who have developed causal Bayes net accounts of causal knowledge and learning. We contribute to this dialogue by highlighting an apparent conundrum: On the one hand, explanations are particularly characteristic of everyday causal understanding and particularly important in the development of everyday conceptions. On the other hand, on the surface at least, causal Bayes nets seem silent on how to characterize explanations and on what role explanations might play in causal learning. Our hope is to spark more explicit inclusion of explanation in such causal theorizing. This would importantly expand the implications of such theories for development and the implications of development for such theories.

Background

Certain features of our approach to theory of mind and to causal development provide the context for our primary claims and analyses.

Theory of Mind

Theory of mind refers to our everyday or folk psychology. The key idea is that our everyday understanding of persons is mentalistic—we construe people in terms of their inner psychological states, such as their hopes, ideas, plans, feelings and doubts.

Philosophers and psychologists often characterize this everyday system of reasoning about mind, world, and behavior as a belief-desire psychology (D'Andrade, 1987; Fodor, 1987; Stitch, 1983; Wellman, 1990). In short, crucial to our understanding of persons' actions, lives, and minds is what the person thinks, knows, and expects coupled with what he or she wants, intends, and hopes for. Why did Bill go to the drawer? He *wanted* his chocolate and *thought* it was in the drawer.

Everyday psychological reasoning also includes reasoning about the origins of mental states (Bill wants candy because he is hungry), so belief-desire psychology incorporates a variety of related constructs, such as drives and preferences that ground one's desires and perceptual-historical experiences that ground one's beliefs. It also includes emotional reactions that result from these desires, beliefs, preferences, and perceptions: Bill will be disappointed because the chocolate is not in the drawer.

Considerable research has demonstrated children's mental-state understandings generally and their belief-desire reasoning specifically. One of the earliest and most frequent demonstrations focused on children's understanding of beliefs, particularly false beliefs. In a typical false belief task, a character, say Bill, puts some chocolate in a drawer but then while he is away (and cannot see), someone moves the chocolate to a cupboard instead. On Bill's return, children are asked, "Where will Bill look for his chocolate?" or "Where does Bill think his chocolate is?"

Even children as young as 3.5 and 4 years accurately predict that Bill will mistakenly look for the chocolate in the original location (Avis & Harris, 1991; Moses & Flavell, 1990; Wimmer & Perner, 1983). Such responses show, potentially, an understanding of how mind causes action yet differs from reality, because Bill's action is predicted on the basis of his thoughts about the world rather than the world itself.

More generally, numerous studies now document that, during early childhood, children increasingly, insistently view people as mental beings: beings that intend, desire, think, know, remember, and feel emotions (see Wellman, 2002, for review). Why do children come to understand people in such mentalistic fashions? Why do we adults do so? Arguably, a primary reason is that these mentalistic construals allow us to make sense of, to explain, people's actions and lives.

Indeed, according to one theoretical perspective, our everyday folk psychology is an everyday *theory* about people and minds—hence the phrase *theory of mind*. Theories explain phenomena; an everyday theory of mind, therefore, is driven by explanation. This *theory theory* account (see Gopnik & Wellman, 1994; Wellman, 1990; Wellman & Gelman, 1998) is only one account among several that have been proposed for characterizing naïve psychological reasoning, as we will discuss later. But a theory theory perspective gives reason to think of explanations as central and important for theory of mind.

Development of Causal Knowledge

Arguably, how causal reasoning develops gives us particular insight into its structure and character—what is basic and what is less so. Traditionally, back to Piaget (e.g., 1929), psychologists thought causal reasoning was late developing and preschool children were "precausal." That Piagetian account has been thoroughly replaced, however, by awareness that even young children are sensitive to causal relations and structures.

One reason for this shift in conclusions is a shift in methods. Traditional investigations, such as Piaget's, depended on asking for and analyzing children's explanations. Thus, Piaget asked children questions like, "Why does the sun come up in the morning?" or "How does a bicycle go?" A number of authors have noted that this reliance on explanations probably falsely characterized children's understanding (e.g., Bullock, Gelman, & Baillargeon, 1982). Consequently, most contemporary research has focused instead on simpler judgment tasks that assess causal predictions. As Bullock et al. (1982) report in their results (which focus on children's understanding of physical causality):

> Children's explanations for events did not seem to reflect the same level of causal reasoning as did their judgments or predictions. ... The results are, of course not a surprise to anyone working with preschool-age children. Children are more likely to demonstrate their reasoning in actions and simple choices than explanations. (p. 246)

It makes some sense, not only empirically but also conceptually, that causal predictions could be easier than (and developmentally precede) sensible causal explanations. Arguably, causal predictions can be based on detecting specific causal regularities (the relation between X and Y), but causal explanations typically require referring specific events to some larger, more general framework, principles, constructs. That is, predictions involve inferring how initial events lead to or produce certain later ones (and thus could be achieved just on the basis of statistical regularities between specific events). But, causal explanations involve understanding how some later outcome was brought about by earlier events, as understood in terms of some more general system or framework of causal forces, factors, and processes. It is in line with many developmental accounts to assume that, developmentally, understanding specifics precedes understanding generalities. On this view, more abstract generalities are developed from specific details (as general categories are abstracted from specific instances), so explanations would be developed from specific causal inferences or predictions.

In addition, consider Gopnik et al.'s (2004) insightful article linking together children's causal reasoning and a causal Bayes net perspective:

> Causal knowledge is important for several reasons. Knowing about causal structure permits us to make wide-ranging predictions about future events. Even more important, knowing about causal structure allows us to intervene in the world to bring about new events—often events that are far removed from the interventions themselves (p. 3).

If prediction and intervention manifest the everyday importance of causal knowledge, then developmentally they may be most fundamental and so earliest to appear.

In contrast to the view that prediction has developmental precedence over explanations, however, we want to advance the exact opposite view. In development and in everyday causal reasoning, explanation often (perhaps typically) has precedence over prediction. Beyond prediction and intervention, explanation is fundamental to, and not just peripheral to or a by-product of, human causal reasoning. Further, we want to propose that explanation does important work in the process of causal learning and development. This does not mean that we believe that traditional investigations, such as Piaget's, accurately portray young children's abilities. The phenomena Piaget presented for explanation were often difficult and unfamiliar, the wording of his questions was often ambiguous and confusing, and his coding of children's answers was problematic (see, e.g., Estes, Wellman, & Woolley, 1989). But, we do claim that young children often find simple explanations easier than simple predictions and judgments.

Here is how we proceed. First, we argue briefly for the idea that explanations often may be easier than predictions. Then, we provide some data, mostly from our research, that underwrite the importance of explanations to even young preschool children. Then, we provide evidence that explanations are central to the processes that produce knowledge acquisition and change within human development. What about the beginning of causal understandings in infancy?

We argue that explanations may precede predictions even in infancy. We conclude with proposals on how emphasizing the role of explanations might reshape our understanding of the nature of causal knowledge and learning in general.

Explanations May be Easier Than Predictions

In several situations, it seems plausible to argue that explanations could be generally easier than predictions. Compare two scenarios. In a *prediction* scenario, a person, Jill, wants to find her dog. Her dog might be in the doghouse or at the park (or under the stairs, etc.). Causal prediction essentially involves answering such questions as, Where will Jill go to look for her dog?

In a parallel *explanation* scenario, Jill also wants to find her dog. Again, her dog might be in the doghouse, or at the park, or under the stairs, and so on. Jill goes to the park to look for her dog. Causal explanation essentially involves answering questions such as, Why did Jill go there?

For prediction, the problem-space seems large. Jill might go anywhere, any action outcome might be plausible depending on what information Jill has about her dog (what kind of places her dog likes best) and about various locales (which is closer, further) and depending on how strongly motivated Jill is, her other interests, her ability to do the required acts, and so on. For explanation, the problem-space seems more restricted because we already know where Jill went, and we only need to explain, to postdict, *that*.

Similarly, compare these two scenarios. In a prediction scenario, we have a sidewalk (in Michigan) and the fact that the temperature is dropping. The prediction question is, What's going to happen to the sidewalk? ("Hmm?")

In the parallel explanation scenario, we again have a sidewalk, the fact that the temperature is dropping, *and* an outcome; for example, there is ice on the sidewalk. The explanation question is, Why is there ice on the sidewalk? ("It got so cold that water froze on the sidewalk.")

As captured in these paired comparisons, to provide a convincing explanation often seems decidedly easier than to make a compelling prediction. Explanation is not necessarily easy, because there are multiple possibly relevant causes and frameworks to consider and the causes must be understood.

But, it seems easier than prediction because in the case of explanation there is (at least) one additional enlightening fact: what, in fact, actually did take place—the outcome of the causal chain. Explanation is a form of postdiction, and postdiction seems easier than prediction because postdiction includes at least one more piece of relevant information: The actual outcome that was caused constrains what the reasoner need consider.

Relatedly, in philosophy of science, it is an axiom that more credit accrues to scientific theories that can make accurate predictions of as-yet unobserved phenomena and not merely explain observed phenomena after the fact. In the practice of science, therefore, it is commonly accepted that being able to provide post hoc explanations is relatively easy and certainly is not as rigorous a test of a theory as being able to provide predictions. Explanations are easier for scientific theories because there has already been a peek at the results. Similarly, explanations are easier for naïve theories because there has already been a peek at the outcomes.

Or, consider this phenomenon. Unexpected, surprising things often occur, and they are especially powerful prods to causal reasoning. When something unusual happens, we want to know how and why. Think about some such unexpected event (e.g., your cousin Phil, who seemed so focused on his career as a surgeon, moves to Hawaii to work as a bartender on the beach). If it is surprising and unexpected, then it may be difficult to explain, but often it is possible to do so at least in part ("Oh, Phil always did seem so stressed with work, and he really enjoyed the one time he vacationed in Hawaii"). Note, however, in the focal case in which the event is indeed surprising and unexpected, then that same event (admittedly difficult to explain) was, in fact extremely difficult (even impossible) to predict ("Many people are stressed with work and enjoy vacationing in Hawaii. Who would have guessed that Phil would actually quit his job and move to Hawaii?"). If it was predictable, then we would not have been surprised, and it would not have been unexpected.

So, in multiple cases explanation seems easier than prediction. It is possible to be somewhat more precise about when and how this occurs. Our concern here is everyday cases of thinking about the causal relation between some cause or causes C and some effect or effects E. In some situations, prediction and explanation would be equally easy or hard; this is most obvious if we are dealing with a case in which a single cause necessarily produces a single effect. In that case, reasoning from cause to effect (prediction) or effect to cause (explanation) seems equally feasible, easy, or difficult. In everyday life, however, we are rarely in the situation of considering a single cause that necessarily produces a single effect.

More often, multiple causes produce an effect; multiple effects are produced by a cause; causes require multiple enabling conditions to be effective; and so on. In such cases, prediction will sometimes be easier than explanation. For example, when a single effect is necessarily caused by multiple causes, being aware of the role of *any* of these causes could allow prediction of the effect, whereas knowledge of the effect still leaves many possible candidate causes. So, in that case explanation seems more difficult.

Often, however, explanation will be easier than prediction. For example, when a single cause can possibly produce multiple effects, other enabling conditions are almost always necessary for the cause to produce a particular effect. A drop in temperature might cause ice to form on the sidewalk, but there had to be water on the sidewalk and an absence of salt or deicer for this process to occur. Knowing that Bill wanted his chocolate and thought it was in the drawer still does not translate into perfect prediction of Bill's behavior—other enabling conditions (such as that Bill is at home where the drawer is) are necessary. In all these cases, for the task of explaining that the effect occurred, one already knows that the enabling conditions must have been in place. They must have been in place because the event did occur, so those factors can be ignored.

More generally, as in the scenarios outlined, explanation often presents the reasoner with at least one additional piece of relevant information: the actual occurrence of a specific effect E. That additional information often prunes away several causal factors or paths from consideration. In fact, knowing the outcome provides a particularly important piece of information because outcome information significantly reduces the problem space in the same way that reverse engineering does. It is far easier to engineer a radically new sort of clock if one has a working clock (from a competitor, say) to disassemble, to analyze, and to work from. Similar to taking apart a clock to see how it works, reverse engineering also occurs in explanation in taking apart a causal chain to see how it works. Instead of having to work out the forward causal chain, with its large number of possible outcomes, working out the reverse causal chain narrows the possibilities.

Consideration of childhood development also offers at least one additional, empirical reason that it is plausible that explanations might be easier than predictions, at least for young children. This reason follows from the fact that explanations proceed in a backward (postdiction) direction, from E to C. Predictions require looking forward to the future, from C to the future occurrence of E. Numerous studies show that early in life preschool children are better at thinking and talking about the past than the future (e.g., Sachs, 1983). A developmental precedence for explanations over predictions would align sensibly with this well-demonstrated childhood precedence of thinking about the past over thinking about the future. Indeed, it may be that thinking about the past is easier for young children than thinking about the future because, just as in the scenarios given, the past has in fact occurred and in that sense is more constrained than the future.

With these plausibility arguments as background, we want to reconsider what children's explanations can tell us about their causal understanding. To reiterate, for the most part we consider explanations in the realm of theory of mind—psychological explanations. To foreshow our claims, we believe data show that children's causal explanations are often early achieved, cogent, revealing of the nature of causal reasoning, and crucial for the development of that reasoning. We believe that because children's conceptual development is theory-like, and thus motivated by explanation, and because explanation is easier than prediction, that explanation constitutes a cornerstone for building causal knowledge.

Empirical Importance and Frequency of Explanations in Childhood

As demonstrated in research, young children prove to be interested in explanation. Specifically, they frequently seek and provide explanations, including especially psychological explanations of the sort implied by theory of mind.

Consider, first, data regarding children's seeking of explanations from those around them. Callanan and Oakes (1992) had mothers of preschoolers keep 2-week-long diary records of children's causal questions (e.g., "Why?" "How come?") during everyday activities, such as mealtime. Results showed that children asked numerous causal questions about a variety of events, including mechanical phenomena ("How does that wheelchair work?") and natural phenomena ("Why do stars twinkle?"). Importantly, however, the largest number of children's questions focused on the causes of human activity—requesting explanations for people's motivations and behaviors (e.g., "Why did he do that?").

Of course, diary records can be more a reflection of parents' concerns than their children's. Therefore, Hickling and Wellman (2001) examined extended transcripts of everyday conversation for children's naturally occurring causal questions and explanations, using explicit causal terms such as *why*, *because*, *how*, and *so*. The analyses encompassed more than 120,000 child utterances from the CHILDES (Child Language Data Exchange System) database (MacWhinney & Snow, 1985, 1990) for several children, recorded in everyday parent-child conversation, week by week or month by month, as these children grew from 2 to 5 years of age. On average, causal questions appeared as early as there were recorded transcripts, with *why*-questions some of the earliest causal utterances that children produced. Indeed, causal questions appeared earlier than causal statements (mean age at earliest appearance 2 years 5 months vs. 2 years 8 months) and thus were produced more frequently than causal statements at age 2.5 years (65% questions vs. 35% statements). These conversational data thus provide systematic, empirical support for the commonplace, anecdotal observation that there is an early period during which young children engage in intense explanation seeking, especially through use of *why*-questions. Thus, the data confirm an early childhood interest in having things explained.

What are the topics of children's everyday requests for explanation? Consistent with the findings of Callanan and Oaks (1992), the children in Hickling and Wellman's (2001) study requested explanations of human activities—why a person did something—in approximately 70% of their causal questions as 2-, 3-, and 4-year-olds. Explanations for physical-object events (20%), for events focusing on animals (5%), or for a variety of other entities such as plants or natural phenomena like clouds (5%) were also requested, although less frequently. These findings show that young children are concerned with explanation and actively seek it out. Central to this early explanatory fascination is a curiosity about how to explain the activities of human beings.

Explaining Actions

Young children not only seek explanations, but also provide them. When children provide explanations, they, like adults, include two parts: the topic or entity to be explained and the explanation itself. Regarding topic, in the Hickling and Wellman (2001) research, 81% of children's explanations in their everyday conversations explained the actions, movements, and states of themselves and others. That is, just as in their requests for explanation, the focal entity for children's own explanations were largely people. This explanatory emphasis on persons is confirmed in other research as well (Dunn & Brown, 1993; Hood & Bloom, 1979). For example, Dunn and Brown recorded 2-hour samples of conversations from fifty 3-year-olds and their parents and found that explanations for human action and states constituted the majority of children's explanations.

How do children explain the various entities of their conversations? Hickling and Wellman (2001) coded the explanations children provided into several explanation modes. These included psychological explanations ("I'm going to get the door *because I want to*"); social-conventional explanations (explanations citing rules and conventions, such as "I have to stop now *because it's lunch time*"); physical explanations ("The nail broke *because it got bent*"); and biological explanations ("She got sick *because of germs*"). Hickling and Wellman also included a category of behavioral

explanations ("I got my hands dirty *because I ate blueberries*"). Here, the child's reasoning cited certain behavioral connections or regularities but did not explicitly mention any underlying cause or mechanism (e.g., no mention of biological aspects of eating or psychologically wanting blueberries). Such instances were considered behavioral (or "associational") and separated from the other categories to avoid overinterpretation of children's psychological reasoning. We concentrate on Hickling and Wellman's findings regarding psychological versus physical explanations, the two predominant and earliest-developing forms. Figure 16-1 shows some of those data.

As is clear in Figure 16-1, when young children provided explanations for human entities, they most often provided psychological explanations, more than 35% of the time, followed closely by social-conventional explanations, more than 25% of the time. In total, therefore, about 65% of children's explanations were psychosocial explanations. Critically, children appropriately restricted these psychosocial explanations in domain-specific ways: Even children as young as 2 years rarely provided psychological explanations for physical objects. Rather, the movements and properties of inanimate physical entities were almost always explained via physical explanations (e.g., "The curtain moved because the wind blew it").

Conversational data like these are complemented by experimental studies designed to elicit children's explanations (e.g., Inagaki & Hatano, 1993, 2002; Lagattuta & Wellman, 2001; Schult & Wellman, 1997). For example, Schult and Wellman solicited explanations

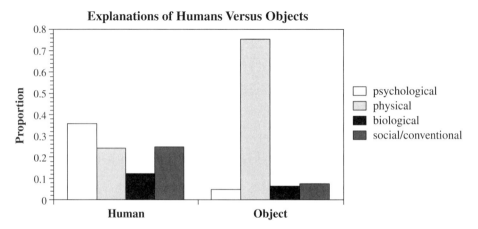

FIGURE 16-1 Explanations of humans versus objects from Hickling and Wellman (2001).

from 3- and 4-year-olds for a variety of human actions and movements: *intended actions* (a person wants to do something and does what he or she wants); *mistaken actions* (a person wants to do something but mistakenly does something else); *physically caused actions* (a person's movement is caused by the wind, gravity, or some other physical force); and *biologically caused actions* (a person's movement is caused by a biological mechanism, such as fever, fatigue). Children's responses were coded for psychological explanations as well as for physical and biological explanations.

Concentrating again on psychological versus physical phenomena and explanations, young children often provided psychological explanations. Nearly 100% of children's explanations for intended actions, even those of 3-year-olds, were psychological explanations. Moreover, 88% of 3-year-olds' explanations (and 93% of 4-year-olds' explanations) for mistaken actions were also psychological explanations (e.g., "He didn't know . . ."). In contrast, preschoolers provided physical explanations almost exclusively for physically caused human movements. Note that both for mistakes and for physically caused acts, the target character wanted something but in fact did something else instead (as we have briefly outlined). Yet, children's explanations differentiated between those two occurrences. For mistakes, their explanations referred to psychological constructs such as beliefs, desires, and so on. For physically caused actions, their explanations referred to physical constructs such as contact, solidity, gravity, and so on. Inagaki and Hatano (1993, 2002) also showed that preschool children provide psychological explanations for voluntary, but not involuntary, behavior.

Explaining Mental States

The phenomena and events to be explained by folk psychology include much more than action. For example, we appeal to beliefs and desires to explain a person's other mental states, such as their emotions: "Why is he so sad?" because "He wanted a pet but didn't get one."

As outlined, explanations not only attempt to identify the cause of some event that has occurred, but also attempt to make that occurrence sensible by reference to a larger framework. We have found that young children's explanations of persons' emotional states provide especially revealing evidence of how

they refer to and depend on a larger framework of connected, coherent understanding of minds and lives.

Lagattuta and Wellman (2001) provided initial data of this sort by having young children provide explanations to scenarios such as the following:

One day Anne goes to the circus with her favorite baby doll. When Anne is talking to Bozo the clown, Bozo accidentally steps on the doll and breaks it. Anne feels sad. Well, many days later Anne is at her friend, Jane's, birthday party. It is time for the party show. Anne sees Bozo the clown dance into the room. She starts to feel sad. Why does Anne start to feel sad right now?

Across multiple studies, young children revealed impressive competence in explaining such emotions in relation to historical (past experience) and mental (thinking) causes. The majority of 3-year-olds and nearly all 4- through 6-year-olds explained the person's emotions as caused by thinking about the past (e.g., "Anne's sad because she's thinking about her doll breaking"), at least at times. Between 3 and 6 years, preschoolers became increasingly consistent in producing such historical-mental explanations. Often, children provided still more precise explanations that we called *cognitive cuing explanations* (e.g., "Anne's sad because the clown makes her think about her broken doll"). Note that these explanations not only refer to thinking about the past, but also explain further that the thoughts about the past had been caused by a reminder in the present scene. By 5 years, the majority of explanations were cognitive cuing ones.

In several ways, these explanations reveal that, in reasoning backward from effects to causes, young children's explanations also appeal to larger coherent systems of constructs and causes. First, young children connected together several different kinds of mental states and experiences into a single explanation (e.g., thoughts about a past experience triggered by seeing a visual reminder cause a current experience of feeling sad). Moreover, these explanations revealed a crucial understanding that a person's mental states and experiences cohere in an individual-specific, life-historical way. That is, young children summed together episodes and mental states, over the focal person's experiences, to create an explanation for that individual's reactions. In contrast, children consistently predicted that Anne's friend Jane, who had not had the prior negative experience, would feel happy instead of sad at the birthday party.

Using scenarios parallel to the one about Anne, Lagattuta and Wellman (2001) also varied such things as the valence of the emotion to be explained (if the target character was sad or happy), the match between the character's emotion and the current situation (if the character's emotion was typical or unusual for the current situation), and the match between two people's emotions in the same current situation (identical vs. different emotions). Through these manipulations, it became clear, developmentally, that young children at first only consistently provide historical, mentalistic explanations for scenarios just like the one for Anne: when they are asked to explain why someone was currently feeling negatively in a conventionally positive situation (e.g., Anne feels sad at the party). These experimental tasks, then, not only reveal coherent explanatory understandings, they suggest that young children's explanations of negative emotions provokes and encourages them to think about people in relation to their thoughts and to their past experiences.

Lagattuta and Wellman (2002) confirmed this possibility by examining, longitudinally, how parents and preschoolers emphasize, ask questions about, and explain emotions during everyday conversations between the ages of 2 and 5 years. In brief, those analyses showed that everyday conversations about negative emotions are indeed rich in the topics and features that seem critical for explanations of people in terms of their minds and individual life histories. Specifically, children and their parents provided more than twice as many explanations for emotion during discussions about negative versus positive emotions ($M = 37\%$ vs. 13% for children and 45% vs. 14% for adults). Not only did children and parents provide more explanations about negative emotions, but also they were more likely to seek explanations for negative emotions. In addition, children's conversations about negative emotions, but not positive emotions, revealed frequent discussions about connections between emotions and other mental states—again revealing children's appeal to coherent systems of explanation.

Explanations Lead Development

Beyond evidence of early fascination with explanation and production of sensible explanations that appeal to larger causal frameworks, there is also evidence that explanations may lead predictions in children's development of causal reasoning. Such evidence is available for children's reasoning about false belief. Recall the false belief task about Bill: Without his seeing it, his chocolate is moved from drawer to cupboard. Bill returns wanting his chocolate. The child is asked, "Where will Bill look for his chocolate?"

That "standard" task of course is a prediction task: The child predicts where Bill will look or what he thinks. False belief tasks can be converted to parallel explanation tasks, however. For example, Bill's chocolate is moved without his seeing. Bill returns wanting his chocolate *and* goes to look for it in the drawer. The child is asked, "Why did Bill go there?" In these contrasting tasks, a false belief prediction requires saying that Bill would go to the drawer, and a false belief explanation requires saying that Bill went to the drawer because "That's where he thought it was," "He doesn't know it was moved," or similar explanations.

Bartsch and Wellman (1989) were the first to compare these tasks of prediction versus explanation, and they found something intriguing. Young children were better at making false belief explanations than false belief predictions. Young children who were unable to predict Bill's mistaken action (based on his false belief) could provide a false belief explanation (e.g., "He thought it was there") when they saw Bill mistakenly searching in the wrong place.

Perner (1991) advanced a critique of the Bartsch and Wellman data by claiming that it was possible the task demands might have been easier for explanations than predictions (see also Wimmer & Mayringer, 1998). It is not clear that this critique is correct, however. First, note that to be correct on prediction the child need only choose one of two options (drawer/cupboard). To be correct on explanation, however, the child needs to talk appropriately about beliefs or knowledge when there are numerous other things the child could talk about (appropriately or inappropriately). So, the probabilities of being correct by chance alone seem to favor the prediction task rather than the reverse. Moreover, versions of the explanation task have been designed to overcome Perner's objections. These revised tasks also show explanation to be easier than prediction (Bartsch & Campbell, 2003; Robinson & Mitchell, 1995). Indeed, Tardif, Wellman, and Cheung (2004) showed that false belief explanations were easier than false belief predictions even for Chinese children. This provides a strong test of the relation between explanation and prediction because Chinese preschool children are asked many fewer explanation questions in everyday conversation than young children in the United States (Miao, 1986).

Data like these suggest that, beyond a vehicle for revealing emerging childhood insights, children's psychological explanations may lead their predictions. If so, then explanations may well be part of the mechanism for the development of children's understanding about false belief, narrowly, and about people and minds more generally. Regarding this point, research investigating individual differences in children's theories of mind provides relevant evidence.

Individual Differences

Children rarely talk about people when alone but do so with others. Although most families talk about people's actions and emotions during their everyday interactions, these discussions vary from family to family. Family conversations differ in the frequency with which children and parents make references to their own and others' emotions and cognitive mental states (Dunn, Brown, & Beardsall, 1991; Hughes & Dunn, 1998; Ruffman, Slade, & Crowe, 2002); the amount of information (including talk about mental states) that is encouraged and provided when describing past experiences (Fivush, 1991; Reese, Haden, & Fivush, 1993); and critically, how often children and parents talk about the causes and consequences of psychological and physical phenomena, that is, engage in causal explanatory conversations (e.g., Dunn & Brown, 1993; Hickling & Wellman, 2001).

This early variability in how parents and children talk about the social world does indeed predict the development of children's later performance on sociocognitive tasks. Importantly, several studies have shown that children's affective perspective taking skills and false belief understanding at 4 and 5 years can be predicted by differences in how often children talked about emotions and other mental states with their mothers (Bartsch & Wellman, 1995; Dunn et al., 1991; Ruffman, et al., 2002); their siblings (Brown, Donelan-McCall, & Dunn, 1996); and even their close friends (Hughes & Dunn, 1998) when they were 2 and 3 years old.

Aside from talk about mental states generally, variability in the frequency of explanation during everyday conversations is a critical predictor of individual differences in children's psychological understanding. For example, Peterson and Slaughter (2003) used a careful self-report instrument to assess mothers' style of conversation with their preschool children. After controlling for chronological and mental age, mothers' frequency of providing explanations for mental states (by elaborating on the causes or consequences of everyday mental occurrences—such as pretending, forgetting, knowing, or not knowing) correlated significantly with their children's performance on a battery of false belief tasks. In contrast, mothers' frequency of simply mentioning mental states did not correlate with their children's theory-of-mind performance.

Longitudinal, naturalistic data provide still more compelling information. For example, in an often-cited longitudinal study, Dunn and her colleagues (1991) collected speech samples of everyday conversations of 50 mother-child pairs when the children were 33 months old and then later assessed children's false belief understanding and affective perspective taking using laboratory tasks at 40 months. Results showed that the frequency at which children provided explanations about the causes and consequences of everyday events at 33 months predicted their affective perspective taking and their false belief knowledge 7 months later. In a later report, Dunn and Brown (1993) more precisely differentiated children's talk about causal phenomena at 33 months into such categories as talk about physical reality, talk about behavior, talk about social rules, and talk about internal states (feelings, desires, thoughts, and beliefs). Children's causal talk about internal states was the only category consistently related to their performance on later sociocognitive tasks.

Ruffman et al. (2002) also report that causal talk about persons in earlier time periods (at 3 years) predicts performance on theory-of-mind tasks at later time periods (at 3.5 and 4 years). Bartsch and Wellman (1995) report some complementary analyses focusing solely on children's conversations. They correlated the age at which children first talked about beliefs (by making genuine references to persons thoughts, beliefs, and knowledge) to aspects of their own and their parents' talk about mental states at earlier ages. By far the strongest correlation was the correlation between earlier psychological explanations and later references to beliefs, $r = .84$. Those children who as 2.5-year-olds engaged in the most frequent conversations about the psychological explanations for persons' behavior (by citing the actor's desires) were the ones who first made reference to persons' beliefs and knowledge as 3- and 4-year-olds.

Microgenetic Research

Of course, correlations between the frequency and content of children's or parents' explanations during everyday conversations and children's later knowledge about minds cannot prove direct causal relationships. Evidence for such causal relationships are more persuasively confirmed through experimental studies.

For this reason, among others, Amsterlaw and Wellman (2006) conducted an initial, microgenetic study of theory of mind (focused on children's acquisition of an understanding of false belief). A microgenetic study is a special type of longitudinal study in which behavior is sampled frequently—two or three times a week—to get a fine-grained picture of developmental change. Siegler (1995a), among others, argues that not only does cross-sectional research make the analysis of change impossible, even typical longitudinal methods are problematic because data collection is so widely spaced. Within research on theory of mind, for example, the longitudinal study with the most frequent sampling tested children on false belief tasks three times at half-yearly intervals, at age 3 years 11 months, 4 years 6 months, and then 5 years 0 months (Hughes & Dunn, 1998). Microgenetic methods address these concerns. In one sort of microgenetic design, to capture change, researchers "choose a task representative of the cognition in question, hypothesize the types of everyday experiences that lead to change, and then provide a higher concentration of these experiences than ordinary" (p. 413). False belief is a representative theory of mind task; seeking and providing explanations may well be an everyday experience leading to change.

Amsterlaw and Wellman (2006) began with younger 3-year-olds for whom a pretest showed that they systematically failed numerous false belief tasks as well as several other classic theory-of-mind tasks. In the course of everyday development, it would take such young children about 1 year to go from consistently making false belief errors to consistent correct performance (Wellman, Cross, & Watson, 2001). Amsterlaw and Wellman confirmed, with a control group, that if such young "failers" engaged in their typical, everyday experiences, then 10 or so weeks later they had made virtually no progress in false belief understanding or in their performance on other

theory-of-mind tasks (see also Flynn, O'Malley, & Wood, 2004). Indeed, Amsterlaw and Wellman also took a similar young group of failers and required them to make false belief judgments (in standard prediction tasks) again and again over many weeks and multiple sessions. Children were given implicit feedback on their false belief predictions by showing them endings to the stories or vignettes, endings in which the actors acted appropriately, that is, acted mistakenly but in accord with the false beliefs specified by the events (e.g., unseen changes of location). This was Amsterlaw and Wellman's comparison group. For this group (in spite of many weeks experience of seeing their false belief predictions fail), there also was little change in children's false belief understanding or more general theory of mind knowledge.

Focally, however, Amsterlaw and Wellman (2006) took a third group of failers, hypothesized that explanation is key, and so presented those children false belief situations and asked them to explain the characters' actions (much as in the illustrative explanation task we described earlier). This third group was the focal microgenetic group. For them (and them alone), there was significant improvement from initially making consistent false belief errors (being incorrect 88% of the time) to later being consistently correct (performing correctly 79% of the time). Moreover, these microgenetic children also improved on several other theory-of-mind tasks. For example, microgenetic children as a whole improved on the explanations they gave when asked to do so during their day-by-day sessions. Differences in children's explanations, as elicited by their experiences in the different groups, accounted for their pre- to post-test improvement or lack of improvement. Specifically, regression analyses showed that explanations during the microgenetic sessions were significantly related to degree of improvement on false belief judgments during the microgenetic sessions, controlling for a host of other factors ($R^2 = .53$). Moreover, children's explanations were also related to post-test gains, again controlling for other factors ($R^2 = .64$).

These microgenetic data are complemented by some short-term training studies (e.g., Appleton & Reddy, 1996; Lohman & Tomasello, 2003), but the Amsterlaw and Wellman (2006) study is unique in providing extended microgenetic analyses of change, approximating the protracted development of everyday life. To reiterate, from a perspective that views naïve psychology as undergoing theory change (in contrast to several other perspectives), explanation should constitute a core mechanism for development (see Box 1). Regardless of differing theoretical emphases, the data suggest explanations are revealing and important.

Infants

The claim that explanations are often easier than predictions, and might lead causal reasoning, might seem to

meet its doom when we consider infants. Infants do not explain things, at least not so we can hear them. Earliest conventional explanations, apparent in Hickling and Wellman (2001), are at about age 2 years.

However, even infants understand causality; they give causal judgments of a sort. In the realm of physical causality, for example, by the last half of the first year, infants understand that physical barriers cause physical movement to stop. In keeping with our focus on social cognition more than physical cognition,

---

Box 1: Explanations Foster Knowledge Acquisition in Other Domains

Researchers who have studied students' comprehension of texts have frequently demonstrated that readers who ask themselves questions while they read comprehend better (Trabasso & Suh, 1993). Indeed, requiring students to answer questions about the text as they go along—to answer inserted or adjunct questions—enhances comprehension and learning (e.g., Hamilton, 1985). Questions that ask for explanations of what has been read are often particularly effective (e.g., Andre, Mueller, Womack, Smid, & Tuttle, 1980). More specifically, studies of science learning have demonstrated that adults who more actively explain to themselves textbook passages show better comprehension of scientific principles (e.g., Chi, Bassock, Lewis, Reimanm, & Glaser, 1989). Thus, when students learn physics from book examples, better learners more often spontaneously explain to themselves the authors' underlying reasoning (Chi et al., 1989). And, when students are trained to provide such explanations for themselves, they learn more (Chi, de Leeuw, Chiu, & LaVancher, 1994).

Siegler and his colleagues conducted several microgenetic training studies that addressed directly the role of explanation in younger children's understanding of number and physical amounts. Siegler (1995b) focused on children's learning of conservation of number in Piagetian conservation tasks. In that study, three groups of 5-year-olds, all of whom initially failed conservation-of-number tasks, received training on multiple conservation-of-number tasks over four successive training sessions. Children in a feedback-only group were given corrective feedback on their conservation judgments by an experimenter (e.g., were told "No, actually

the two rows have the same number"). Children in an explain-own-reasoning group were asked to explain their own predictions (e.g., "How did you know that?"). Children in an explain-experimenter's reasoning group were given corrective feedback by an experimenter, then asked to explain the experimenter's reasoning (e.g., "Actually the two rows are the same. How do you think I knew that?"). Across several different measures of performance and learning, children in the explain-experimenter's reasoning group outperformed the other groups. By their final session, children in that group were essentially 70% correct on conservation tasks, whereas children in the other two groups were 40% correct or less. Note that children in both the explain-experimenter's-reasoning and the feedback-only groups received information about what could be considered to be the true outcome of certain events (after counting or after moving the items, the numbers are in fact the same). However, only children in the explain-experimenter's-reasoning group had to explain those outcomes.

Pine and Siegler (2003) present two further studies, this time targeted to 5- to 7-year-old children's developing understanding of a balance beam (for which children made predictions about whether various combinations of weight would make the beam balance and could see if their predictions were correct). Their second study provides an important contrast. In that study, they compared producing explanations for the balance beam events versus simply seeing the events and being asked to think about them further. There was a significant advantage for children who had to provide explanations over just generally engaging in equal amounts of extended thinking about the problems.

In short, providing explanations significantly influences children's causal reasoning and causal learning.

we describe one representative infant study in the realm of social cognition.

In attempting to track infant understandings that might lead to later theory of mind, a key question concerns intentionality—when do infants understand that a person's goals, their desires, cause and shape their behaviors. Infants might understand intentional human action as intentionally caused—as directed to and shaped by the actor's goals—or instead they might see such actions as mere physical movements.

Consider the study of Phillips and Wellman (2005); infants saw a person reach over a barrier and grasp an object, as shown in Figure 16-2. Once the infants were habituated, the barrier was removed, and they were shown two test events. One test event showed a direct reach for the object; the other showed an indirect reach. These test events contrast two different construals of the person's actions, one in terms of goal directedness and one in terms of physical motions of the arm. If in habituation the infant interprets the actor's action as goal directed (as the actor going as directly as possible to get the target object), then when the barrier is removed, the direct reach is the expected action, and the indirect reach would be more attention worthy. In the indirect reach test event, although the actor's arm movement remains the same as during habituation, the actor is no longer going directly to get the object.

In fact, during the test 12-month-olds look longer at the indirect reach. They dishabituated to the indirect reach (even though it is showing the exact arm movement as in habituation) and did not dishabituate to the direct reach (even though it actually shows a different physical arm movement). This pattern is consistent with the hypothesis that infants construe the reach as goal directed. (See Gergely, Nadasdy, Csibra, & Biro, 1995, and Sodian, Schoepper, & Metz, 2004, for similar data.)

Several control conditions indicate the infants actually construe human action in terms of goal directedness. The most critical condition, we believe, appears in our research and involves showing the infant the same actions as in Figure 16-2 but with no goal object. In part, this controls for the possibility that infants might just prefer to look at a curving arm motion. But, more crucially, if infants see the actions in Figure 16-2 as goal directed, then they should react differently if there is no goal object. So, for infants in the control condition, habituation and test were identical to those for infants in the experimental condition except that no object was ever present. In this case, because there was no object, there was no presentation of a goal-directed action in habituation. And, in this case, appropriately, 12-month-old infants did not prefer the indirect reach test event. So, the experimental data do not just show a preference for looking at the curved arm motion. Infants do not prefer that in the control condition. They show appropriate differentiation between actions with and without goal objects. In sum, infant looking is sensitive to the goal directedness of the action. Nine-month-olds (but not the 6-month-olds) evidenced the same pattern of findings (Csibra, Gergely, Biro, & Brockbank, 1999; Wellman & Lalonde, 2004).

These sort of habituation methods are often thought to measure infants' expectations, their predictions. But, in fact, we believe these methods more clearly assess postdiction than prediction. In the study depicted in Figure 16-2 (and habituation or preferential-looking studies more generally), the infant's understanding can (and most likely does) proceed backward. From seeing the actor's action successfully achieve an object (grasp a ball), the infant could then understand it as an action directed toward that goal (the ball). The infant, at this stage, is not necessarily predicting at the outset where the action will go but only recognizing its goal

  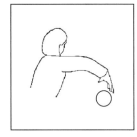

Habituation   **Direct reach test event**   **Indirect reach test event**

FIGURE 16-2 A depiction of the reaching events presented to infants in the study of Phillips and Wellman (2002).

attainment after the fact (see Gergley & Cisbra, 2003, for a similar analysis). The infant, after the outcome has been observed, could recognize how it came about, that is, postdict the event. Indeed, note in our control condition that if there was no target object (so the action does not result in a clear object outcome), then infants did poorly.

This sort of analysis applies to all the earliest demonstrations of infant understanding of causality. They all involve test event recognition of the causal regularities that have already occurred—not expectations in advance (prediction), but appropriate recognition after the actions have been completed (postdiction) (see Box 2).

Box 2: Infant Versus Toddler Findings

Analyzing infant looking-time findings as revealing explanations or postdictions, rather than predictions, helps explain a puzzling discrepancy in children's performances from infancy to toddlerhood. This discrepancy has been increasingly commented on and demonstrated in research, causing some researchers to wonder what infant looking-time methods show us at all.

To illustrate, Spelke et al. (1992) showed that even 2-month-old infants react appropriately to the displays in Figure 16-3. Infants were first habituated to a ball rolling behind a screen and the screen being raised to show the ball had come to rest behind it. Then, they were shown two test events in which a barrier (partly visible above the screen) was placed behind the screen before the ball rolled. Infants looked longer at the inconsistent test event (shown in Figure 16-3), showing that they expected the rolling ball to stop on contact with the solid wall, and found it attention worthy when it did not. Such data suggest that even young infants understand that solid objects cannot pass through solid barriers.

However, Clifton and colleagues (Berthier, DeBlois, Poirier, Novak, & Clifton, 2000) then presented 2-year-olds with events of the sort shown in Figure 16-4. In these displays, the ball rolls behind the screen while the child watches. Then, the child is asked to find the ball. The 2-year-olds performed considerably below chance searching for the ball; that is, they searched for it on either side of the solid barrier. Thus, 2-year-olds acted as if they did not understand that solid objects cannot pass through solid obstacles. Hood, Cole-Davies, and Dias (2003) present similar findings in which toddlers seemed not to know something that infants appear to know, given infant looking-time data.

From our current perspective, one factor that differentiates these studies of infants versus toddlers is that the infant studies require only postdiction.

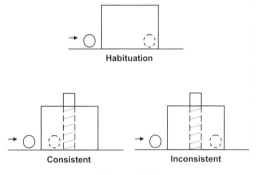

FIGURE 16-3

After the outcome is shown, then (and only then) the infant recognizes what should (and should not) have happened. The toddler paradigm, however, requires prediction. To search appropriately, in advance of seeing any outcome, the toddler must predict where the ball should be. So, by this analysis, the habituation method assesses postdiction—explanation— whereas the toddler method assesses prediction. If explanation, or at least postdiction, precedes (is easier than) prediction—as we argue—then looking-time competence would precede later predictive competence.

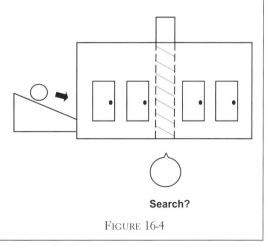

Search?

FIGURE 16-4

Implications for Theory Development and for Causal Learning

Explanation plays a central role in children's causal learning, we contend—whether it is learning about people and minds or, beyond the social and mental world, learning about physical phenomena. This has implications for how to characterize the nature and development of theory of mind and how to characterize human causal learning.

As mentioned at the beginning of this chapter, we favor a theory theory account of theory of mind—our everyday folk psychology is an everyday theory about people and minds. Theories explain phenomena, and explanations are central to theories; thus, a theory theory account places explanations at the center of everyday conceptual understanding and development (see Bartsch & Wellman, 1989; Gopnik, 2000; Gopnik & Wellman, 1994; Wellman, 1990). One reason we prefer this account is because it is the only one that gives a central role to explanations.

One alternative account (e.g., Baron-Cohen, 1995; Leslie, 1994) argues for the existence of an innate theory-of-mind module. Such a module "spontaneously and post-perceptually processes behaviors that are attended, and computes the mental states which contributed to them" (Scholl & Leslie, 2001, p. 697). Modular accounts do not emphasize explanations, but rather they emphasize the modularized computations that lead to mental state attributions. In fact, current evolutionary accounts of modular cognition focus exclusively on how specialized information processors increase the organism's ability to solve adaptive problems by making accurate predictions of the environment and responding accordingly. In this account, understanding and providing explanations are unnecessary for solving adaptive problems. In these adaptiveness accounts, for example, one needs to predict whether a conspecific will cheat in a cooperative relationship, but one does not need to explain why a conspecific cheated (Cosmides & Tooby, 1994). Any sort of conscious understanding and explanatory insights are mere epiphenomena of solving adaptive problems. As another example, syntactic modules parse linguistic inputs quickly without people having or needing any explanatory insights into the structure of language. According to modular accounts, theory of mind works similarly.

A different alternative to theory theory proposes that children and adults understand mental states not through theoretical constructs like belief and desire but rather through a simulation process in which they assess their own possible experience in a situation and attribute similar states to others (e.g., Harris, 1992, 2000). Explanations play no crucial role in simulation accounts either, which concentrate instead on children's developing abilities to engage in attribution by simulation. As with modular accounts, the central focus of simulation accounts is simply solving the problem of attribution. Development follows the child's increased ability to simulate.

In short, of the different accounts of theory-of-mind development, only in theory theory do explanations play a central role. Only theory theory predicts a fundamental and motivating role for explanations in development, predicts that explanations lead development, and insists that explanations provide part of the mechanism underlying development. As we argue in this chapter, such an account more accurately matches the empirical data: Explanations provide a motivating role in children's thinking about people, they lead predictions in development, and they influence how development proceeds.

How does this emphasis on explanations relate to or inform causal Bayes net approaches to causal learning? Let us use the work of Gopnik et al. (2004) as a springboard. In that article, the authors use the construct of causal maps to help consider how causal learning and reasoning proceeds. Causal maps are to be understood on analogy to spatial cognitive maps. Spatial cognitive maps "allow animals to represent geometric relations among objects in space nonegocentrically, generating new information and relations not previously directly experienced, and then to generate new spatial inferences" (p. 5). An animal that maps the spatial layout of a maze from limited exposure to it "can use that information to make new inferences about locations in the maze" (p. 5). On analogy to spatial maps, causal maps assemble specific experiences into a larger system that we use to infer new causally rich information/knowledge as evident in future predictions and interventions.

The philosopher of science Toulmin (1953/1967) goes further to suggest a general analogy from theories to maps.

We have seen how natural it is to speak of ourselves "finding our way around" a range of phenomena with the help of a law of nature, or "recognizing where on the map" a particular object of study belongs. In doing so, we are employing a cartographical analogy which is worth following up: for . . . the analogy between physical theories and maps extends for quite a long way and can be used to illuminate some dark and dusty corners in the philosophy of science. (chapter 4, "Theories and Maps") (p. 94)

Using this notion of causal maps helps us articulate our conclusions.

Causal maps can be thought of as capturing larger explanatory frameworks and knowledge. A map captures not only one or two local regularities, but also provides a larger structured framework in which numerous specific observations are placed and ordered. In the case of causal maps, the idea is that numerous causal regularities are assembled into a larger coherent framework. Once assembled, such causal maps certainly allow prediction and intervention, but assembling a causal map in the first place seems to us to be more like an act of postdiction than prediction. And, once assembled, beyond prediction and intervention, causal maps provide explanations. That is, some single regularity is made sense of (i.e., is explained) by its place within the larger map—the larger system of causal forces of which it is a part (as represented in the causal map).

To elaborate on this briefly, consider again spatial maps. A spatial map can be importantly distinguished from a set of directions. Directions (such as how to get from the airport to home by turning left, then right, etc.) provide spatial predictions and interventions— following the directions gets you home. A spatial map is more than a list of directions, however (and may or may not be precisely useful for getting home). A map shows that home is north of the airport, that there are multiple routes home, and that in going from airport to home the bay is on the left and the mountains are on the right. In short, a spatial map organizes spatial information into a larger informative network. The same applies, we believe, to a properly rich notion of causal maps. Causal maps not only spell out predictions and interventions, but also organize causal information into a larger, coherent explanatory network of understandings.

What about causal learning? In their article, Gopnik et al. (2004) devote much of their attention to the question of how causal knowledge might be learned and acquired. They answer in terms of Bayes net modeling. In general, their answer points to learning algorithms that use causal Bayes nets and that adjust the nets when they generate failed predictions rather than accurate ones. Crudely, the model of learning they emphasize proceeds as follows: On the basis of observation the learner assembles an initial causal understanding, then using that understanding makes a causal prediction (or predicts the outcome of a causal intervention), then observes the outcome that occurs, and when there is a difference (the initial prediction mismatches the observed outcome) the learner revises the initial causal understanding. Thus the emphasis for learning is on failed predictions and the learning currency is predictive accuracy.

We argue, however, that for everyday causal learning in the service of theory development, the emphasis actually is on unsatisfying explanations, and the learning currency is explanatory adequacy. That is, the learner does more than tally failed and successful predictions. Effective learning depends on providing explanations, not just predictions, then assessing and reassessing one's satisfying and unsatisfying explanations. That is, we propose (yet again) that the engine of naïve theory change in children and adults is similar to that of scientific theory change. In science, new theories are constructed to explain existing data (so explanations figure prominently in theory creation). Failed predictions are useful in deciding between competing scientific theories, but failed predictions cannot create new theories. That is the role of explanations.

In support of this perspective, recall that in the Amsterlaw and Wellman (2006) microgenetic study, children in the comparison group made predictions and observed those predictions were wrong. But, this yielded no change in their understandings. Children in the focal microgenetic group explained (or attempted to explain) their predictions. This process of attempting to explain predictions did yield significant changes in children's understandings. Thus, attempting to explain new information (e.g., explain what happened instead of what was mistakenly predicted) seems most important for causal learning.

Our demonstrations of the power and precedence of explanations in learning and development raise an important question. What accounts for the power of explanations? What is the special learning leverage they provide? The answers to these questions are not clear yet, but we see several (probably interrelated) possibilities. First, being motivated or provoked to provide an explanation requires at the least more extended processing of an event, outcome, or occurrence. However, we do not think that extended processing is the most important part of the story (see Box 1). So, second attempting to provide an explanation requires the learner to construe the phenomena in question in additional, "larger" terms, in terms of constructs, concepts, frameworks recruited to explain and make sense of the phenomena.

For learning, therefore, explanations recruit the power (the computational leverage) of employing two levels of analysis, not just one—in this case, the phenomena themselves and the additional interpretative constructs, causal maps, or frameworks that explain the phenomena. That is, from our perspective, children's causal understandings include several levels of analysis—at the least a level concerned with certain surface phenomena and regularities (e.g., X precedes Y with some sort of regularity) and another level that frames, interprets, and provides a causal analysis of the surface phenomena. Call this the interplay between evidence and theory. At the level of evidence, children see states of the world and patterns of behavior, but at the level of theory, they also analyze or construe these in terms of desires, beliefs, and intentions. Children also distinguish between appearances and the mental states that might produce appearances (e.g., the emotion that might cause a facial display of sadness) and between appearances and representations (e.g., the conditions that might cause someone to misrepresent—to believe falsely—some apparent object or identity). Thus, construing actions in terms of underlying mental states embodies (at least) two levels of analysis. Such alternative analyses fuel attempts to compare, share, merge, and create new conceptions, including especially new causal conceptions.

Indeed, if one construes everyday theory of mind as embodying framework theories as well as specific theories (Wellman, 1990) along with evidential phenomena (observable behavior, appearances, and states of the world), then explanations recruit and require resources at multiple (not just dual) levels of analysis. As Tenenbaum & Griffiths (this volume) argue, these multiple levels are particularly fertile ground for learning the causal structure of the world.

Last, we hark back to our plausibility arguments about explanation being easier than prediction in dealing with causality. In explanation, an additional piece of information, the outcome of the causal chain, is considered. This additional piece of information constrains the problem space of the causal problem and reduces concern about enabling conditions. Being easier, explanation provides the initial steps to learning about a particular domain's causal framework. That is, explanation provides a smaller problem space for working out the initial hypotheses that build into a causal theory. Just as reverse engineering provides a smaller problem space for working out a device's design, over time children discover reliable patterns in their reverse-engineered explanations and from those form and strengthen connections in causal maps that allow for predictions.

The confluence of people's motivation to explain along with explanation's leading role in theory development make explanation fundamental in any models of causal reasoning development. In this chapter, we took theory of mind as a case study for demonstrating the precedence of explanation in learning and development. However, we believe that the central role of explanation extends to many domains of conceptual development.

ACKNOWLEDGMENTS   Support for the preparation of this chapter was provided by the National Institutes of Health (grant HD-22149 to H. M. W.) and funds from the McDonnell Foundation.

References

Amsterlaw, J., & Wellman, H. M. (2006). Theories of mind in transition: A microgenetic study of the development of false belief understanding. *Journal of Cognition and Development, 7,* 139–172.

Andre, T., Mueller, C., Womack, S., Smid, K., & Tuttle, M. (1980). Adjunct questions facilitate later application, or do they? *Journal of Educational Psychology, 72,* 533–543.

Appleton, M., & Reddy, V. (1996). Teaching 3-year-olds to pass false belief tests: A conversational approach. *Social Development, 5,* 275–291.

Avis, J., & Harris, P. L. (1991). Belief-desire reasoning among Baka children. *Child Development, 62,* 460–467.

Bartsch, K., & Campbell. (2003). *The acquisition of belief understanding: Repeated questioning and emotion cues facilitate belief explanations by young children.* Paper presented at the biennial meeting of the Society for Research in Child Development, Tampa, FL, April 2003.

Baron-Cohen, S. (1995). *Mind blindness*. Cambridge, MA: MIT Press.

Bartsch, K., & Wellman, H. M. (1989). Young children's attribution of action to beliefs and desires. *Child Development*, 60, 946–964.

Bartsch, K., & Wellman, H. M. (1995). *Children talk about the mind*. New York: Oxford University Press.

Berthier, N. E., DeBlois, S., Poirier, C. R., Novak, M. A., & Clifton, R. K. (2000). Where's the ball? Two- and 3-year-olds reason about unseen events. *Developmental Psychology*, 36, 394–401.

Brown, J. R., Donelan-McCall, N., & Dunn, J. (1996). Why talk about mental states? The significance of children's conversations with friends, siblings, and mothers. *Child Development*, 67, 836–849.

Bullock, M., Gelman, R., & Baillargeon, R. (1982). The development of causal reasoning. In W. J. Friedman (Ed.), *The developmental psychology of time* (pp. 209–254). New York: Academic Press.

Callanan, M. A., & Oakes, L. M. (1992). Preschoolers' questions and parents' explanations: Causal thinking in everyday activity. *Cognitive Development, 7*, 213–233.

Chi, M. T. H., Bassock, M., Lewis, M. W., Reimanm, P., & Glaser, R. (1989). Self explanations: How students study and use examples in learning to solve problems. *Cognitive Science*, 13, 145–182.

Chi, M. T. H., de Leeuw, N., Chiu, M., & LaVancher, L. (1994). Eliciting self-explanations improves understanding. *Cognitive Science*, 18, 439–477.

Cosmides, L. & Tooby, J. (1994). Origins of domain specificity: The evolution of functional organization. In L. Hirschfeld & S. Gelman (Eds.) *Mapping the mind* (pp. 85–116). NY: Cambridge University Press.

Csibra, G., Gergely, G., Biro, S., & Brockbank, M. (1999). Goal attribution without agency cues: The perception of "pure reason" in infancy. *Cognition*, 72, 237–267.

D'Andrade, R. (1987). A folk model of the mind. In D. Holland & N. Quinn (Eds.), *Cultural models in language and thought* (pp. 112–148). Cambridge, England: Cambridge University Press.

Dunn, J., & Brown, J. (1993). Early conversations about causality: Content, pragmatics and developmental change. *British Journal of Developmental Psychology*, 11, 107–123.

Dunn, J., Brown, J., & Beardsall, L. (1991). Family talk about feeling states and children's later understanding of others' emotions. *Child Development*, 27, 448–455.

Estes, D., Wellman, H. M., & Woolley, J. (1989). Children's understanding of mental phenomena. In H. Reese (Ed.) Advances in child development and behavior, Vol. 21 (pp. 41–89). Orlando, FL: Academic Press.

Fivush, R. (1991). Gender and emotion in mother-child conversations about the past. *Journal of Narrative and Life History*, 1, 325–341.

Flynn, E., O'Malley, C. O., & Wood, D. (2004). A longitudinal, microgenetic study of emergence of false belief understanding and inhibition skills. *Developmental Science*, 7, 103–115.

Fodor, J. A. (1987). *Psychosemantics: The problem of meaning in the philosophy of mind*. Cambridge, MA: Radford Books/MIT Press.

Gergely, G., & Cisbra, G. (2003). Teleological reasoning in infancy. The naïve theory of rational action. *Trends in Cognitive Sciences, 7*, 287–292.

Gergely, G., Nadasdy, Z., Csibra, G., & Biro. (1995). Taking the intentional stance at 12 months of age. *Cognition*, 56, 165–193.

Gopnik, A. (2000). Explanations as orgasm and the drive for causal understanding. In F. Keil & R. Wilson (Eds.), *Cognition and explanation*. Cambridge, MA: MIT Press.

Gopnik, A., Glymour, C., Sobel, D. M., Schulz, L. E., Kushnir, T., & Danks, D. (2004). A theory of causal leaning in children: Causal maps and Bayes nets. *Psychological Review, 111*, 3 –32.

Gopnik, A., & Wellman, H. M. (1994). The theory theory. In L. Hirschfeld & S. Gelman (Eds.), *Domain specificity in cognition and culture* (pp. 257–293). New York: Cambridge University Press.

Hamilton, R. J. (1985). A framework for the evaluation of the effectiveness of adjunct questions and objectives. *Review of Educational Research*, 55, 47–85.

Harris, P. L. (1992). From simulation to folk psychology: The case for development. *Mind & Language*, 7, 120–144.

Harris, P. L. (2000). *The work of the imagination*. Oxford, England: Blackwell.

Hickling, A. K., & Wellman, H. M. (2001). The emergence of children's causal explanations and theories: Evidence from everyday conversation. *Developmental Psychology*, 37, 668–683.

Hood, L., & Bloom, L. (1979). What, when, and how about why: A longitudinal study of early expressions of causality. *Monographs of the Society for Research in Child Development* (Serial No. 181).

Hood, B., Cole-Davies, V., & Dias, M. (2003). Looking and search measures of object knowledge in preschool children. *Developmental Psychology*, 39, 61–70.

Hughes, C., & Dunn, J. (1998). Understanding and emotion: Longitudinal associations with mental-state talk between young friends. *Developmental Psychology*, 34, 1026–1037.

Inagaki, K., & Hatano, G. (1993). Young children's understanding of the mind-body distinction. *Child Development*, 64, 1534–1549.

Inagaki, K., & Hatano, G. (2002). *Young children's naive thinking about the biological world*. New York: Psychology Press.

Lagattuta, K., & Wellman, H. M. (2001). Thinking about the past: Early knowledge about links between prior experience, thinking, and emotion. *Child Development, 72*, 82–102.

Lagattuta, K. H., & Wellman, H. M. (2002). Differences in early parent-child conversations about negative versus positive emotions: Implications for the development of psychological understanding. *Developmental Psychology, 38*, 564–580.

Leslie, A. M. (1994). ToMM, ToBy, and agency: Core architecture and domain specificity in cognition and culture. In L. Hirschfeld & S. Gelman (Eds.), *Mapping the mind: Domain specificity in cognition and culture* (pp. 119–148). New York: Cambridge University Press.

Lohman, H., & Tomasello, M. (2003). The role of language in the development of false belief understanding: A training study. *Child Development, 74*, 1130–1144.

MacWhinney, B., & Snow, C. (1985). The child language data exchange system. *Journal of Child Language, 12*, 271–296.

MacWhinney, B., & Snow, C. (1990). The child language data exchange system: An update. *Journal of Child Language, 17*, 457–472.

Miao, X. (1986). *Youer dui yuwenci de lijie–youer huida teshu yiwenju de fazhan tedian* [Preschooler's understanding of question words–Developmental characteristics of preschoolers' answers to questions]. In M. S. Zhu (Ed.), *Ertong yuyan fazhan yanjiu* [Research in children's language development] (pp. 126–134). Shanghai, China: East China Normal University Press.

Moses, L., & Flavell, J. (1990). Inferring false beliefs from actions and reactions. *Child Development, 61*, 929–945.

Perner, J. (1991). *Understanding the representational mind*. Cambridge, MA: MIT Press.

Peterson, C. C., & Slaughter, V. (2002). Opening windows into the mind: Mother's preferences for mental state explanations and children's theory of mind. *Cognitive Development, 18*, 399–429.

Phillips, A. T., & Wellman, H. M. (2005). Infants' understanding of object-directed action. *Cognition, 98*, 137–155.

Piaget, J. (1929). *The child's conception of the world*. London: Routledge & Kegan Paul.

Pine, K. J., & Siegler, R. S. (2003). *The role of explanatory activity in increasing the generality of thinking*. Paper presented at the biennial meeting of the Society for Research in Child Development, Tampa, FL, April.

Reese, E., Haden, C. A., & Fivush, R. (1993). Mother-child conversations about the past. *Cognitive Development, 8*, 403–430.

Robinson, E. J., & Mitchell, P. (1995). Making children's early understanding of the representational mind: Backwards explanation versus prediction. *Child Development, 66*, 1022–1039.

Ruffman, T., Slade, L., & Crowe, E. (2002). The relation between children's and mothers' mental state language and theory-of-mind understanding. *Child Development, 73*, 734–751.

Sachs, J. (1983). Talking about there and then: The emergence of displaced reference in parent-child discourse. In K. E. Nelson (Ed.), *Children's language* (Vol. 4, pp. 1–28). Hillsdale, NJ: Erlbaum.

Scholl, B. J., & Leslie, A. M. (2001). Minds, modules, and meta-analysis. *Child Development, 72*, 696–701.

Schult, C. A., & Wellman, H. M. (1997). Explaining human movements and actions: Children's understanding of the limits of psychological explanation. *Cognition, 62*, 291–324.

Siegler, R. S. (1995a). Children's thinking: How does change occur? In W. Schneidu & F. Weinert (Eds.), *Memory performance and competencies* (pp. 405–430). Hillsdale, NJ: Erlbaum.

Siegler, R. S. (1995b). How does change occur: A microgenetic study of number conservation. *Cognitive Development, 28*, 225–273.

Sodian, B., Schoepper, B., & Metz, U. (2004). Do infants apply the principle of rational action to human agents? *Infant Behavior & Development, 27*, 31–41.

Stich, S. (1983). *From folk psychology to cognitive science*. Cambridge, MA: Bradford Books.

Tardif, T., Wellman, H. M., & Cheung, K.-M. (2004). False belief understanding in Cantonese-speaking children. *Journal of Child Language, 31*, 779–800.

Toulmin, S. (1953/1967). *The philosophy of science*. London: Hutchinson.

Trabbaso, T. & Suh, S. (1993). Understanding text: Achieving explanatory coherence through on-line inferences and mental operations in working memory. *Discourse Processes, 16*, 3–34.

Wellman, H. M. (1990). *The child's theory of mind*. Cambridge, MA: Bradford/MIT Press.

Wellman, H. M. (2002). Understanding the psychological world: Developing a theory of mind. In U. Goswami (Ed.), *Handbook of childhood cognitive development* (pp. 167–187). Oxford, England: Blackwell.

Wellman, H. M., Cross, D., & Watson, J. (2001). Meta-analysis of theory of mind development: The truth about false belief. *Child Development, 72*, 655–684.

Wellman, H. M., & Gelman, S. A. (1998). Knowledge acquisition in foundational domains. In D. Kuhn & R. Siegler (Eds.), *Cognition, perception and language. Vol. 2: Handbook of child psychology* (5th ed., pp. 523–573). New York: Wiley.

Wellman, H. M., & LaLonde, N. (2004). *Understanding of goal-directed action in 9-month-olds*, Unpublished manuscript, University of Michigan, Ann Arbor.

Wimmer, H., & Mayringer, H. (1998). False belief understanding in young children: Explanations do not develop before predictions. *International Journal of Behavioral Development*, 22, 403–422.

Wimmer, H., & Perner, J. (1983). Beliefs about beliefs: Representation and constraining function of wrong beliefs in young children's understanding of deception. *Cognition*, 13, 103–128.

17

Dynamic Interpretations of Covariation Data

Woo-kyoung Ahn, Jessecae K. Marsh, & Christian C. Luhmann

In discovering causes of events, people evidently use various types of evidence or cues (e.g., Einhorn & Hogarth, 1986). Virtually all models of causal learning (e.g., Cheng, 1997; Rescorla & Wagner, 1972) have focused on how causal relations are learned based on covariation information—namely, information about whether the presence or absence of one event (C or ~C) co-occurs with the presence or absence of another event (E or ~E). Thus, in all of these models, relevant input data are classified as CE, ~CE, C~E, or ~C ~E, as summarized in Figure 17-1. Existing models of causal learning have stipulated different ways in which these four types of covariation evidence would or should be combined to evaluate the causal relationship among events. Yet, these models in their current forms share an underlying assumption that all events of a given type (e.g., CE) play an identical role in assessing causal strength.

One model of causal induction combines covariation information into a contingency measure called

ΔP (e.g., Jenkins & Ward, 1965). The value of ΔP is calculated as follow:

$$\Delta P = \left(\frac{(CE)}{(CE)+(C \sim E)} \right) - \left(\frac{(\sim CE)}{(\sim C \sim E)+(\sim CE)} \right)$$

(17-1)

According to Equation 17-1, the different types of covariation information play a static role in assessing contingency. For example, all events of type CE play a role in increasing ΔP regardless of the context.

		Effect	
		Present	Absent
Cause	Present	CE	C~E
	Absent	~CE	~C~E

FIGURE 17-1 A traditional two-by-two contingency table used in models of causal learning.

It cannot be the case that some CE increases ΔP and some CE decreases ΔP.

Another causal induction model computes a measure called causal power from covariation information (Cheng, 1997; Novick & Cheng, 2004). For instance, the simple causal power for a generative cause is computed as follows:

$$\text{Power} = \frac{\Delta P}{\left(1 - \left(\frac{(\sim CE)}{(\sim C \sim E) + (\sim CE)}\right)\right)} \quad (17\text{-}2)$$

Again, it should not be difficult to see that, as in ΔP, the types of covariation information play static roles in computing an estimate of causal strength in the PowerPC theory.

Another dominant class of models is associative learning models, such as the Rescorla-Wagner (RW) model (Rescorla & Wagner, 1972). In this model, the associative strength V on the nth trial for each cue is updated according to the following calculation:

$$\Delta V_n = \alpha\beta(\lambda - \Sigma V_{n-1}) \quad (17\text{-}3)$$

In this equation, λ is 1 when the outcome is present and 0 when the outcome is absent. The parenthetical quantity is the amount of error on the nth trial; the difference between the outcome (λ) and the summed associative strength of the present cues (ΣV_{n-1}). The saliency of the cue and the outcome are represented by the positive quantities α and the β parameters, respectively.

Like other models of causal learning, the RW model treats all observations of a given type uniformly (see Wasserman, Kao, Van Hamme, Katagiri, & Young, 1996, for details). For instance, when encountering a CE event, the change in association strength of C is as follows:

$$\Delta V_{\text{Cause}} = \alpha\beta(\lambda_{\text{Outcome}} - \Sigma V_{\text{Cause+Context}}) \quad (17\text{-}4)$$

Given normal values for the necessary parameters, this quantity will be positive and increase the perceived strength of the relationship between the cause and effect. Similarly, for all C~E events, the change in association is as follows:

$$\Delta V_{\text{Cause}} = \alpha\beta(\lambda_{\text{NoOutcome}} - \Sigma V_{\text{Cause+Context}}) \quad (17\text{-}5)$$

This quantity will be negative, leading to a decrease in the perceived strength of the relationship between cause and effect.[1]

Unlike the assumption shared by the discussed models, we believe that each type of evidence in Figure 17-1 is open to multiple causal interpretations. For instance, when C is present and E is absent, then it may be because there is a negative relationship between C and E, because there is no relationship between the two, or because C is indeed a cause of E but some necessary precondition was not satisfied. Similar interpretations can be made for each type of contingency information (see Table 17-1).

The decision about which interpretation to use is presumably influenced by multiple factors. One plausible influence is the reasoner's belief about the causal relationship at the time the observation is encountered. Of course, such beliefs should in turn depend on previously encountered observations. For example, if prior observations lead a reasoner to believe in a positive relationship between two variables, the reasoner may be more likely to interpret subsequent events according to the positive interpretation column in Table 17-1. If someone else believes that there is a negative relationship between events, that person may make interpretations more like those in the negative interpretation column.

In this chapter, we review three sets of studies, demonstrating that people spontaneously treat the same type of evidence differently because of beliefs developed during prior causal induction. In particular, our major thesis throughout these studies is that people develop hypotheses about causal relations early during causal learning and interpret subsequent data in light of these hypotheses. As a result, the reasoner's working hypothesis can then lead to identical data playing different roles. Such dynamic interpretations of data result in the primacy effect in causal learning, inferences about unobserved, alternative causes, and interpretations of ambiguous stimuli.

Primacy Versus Recency Effects in Causal Induction

The use of an existing hypothesis in the interpretation of contingency information has great implications for the evaluation of sequential information. If a reasoner is given a set of evidence that suggests that C causes E, subsequent negative information may be reinterpreted in one of the ways shown in Table 17-1. For example, a piece of C ~E evidence may be interpreted as an

TABLE 17-1 Possible Interpretations for Each Type of Evidence

Evidence	Positive Interpretation	No Relation Interpretation	Negative Interpretation
CE	C caused E, so E occurred when C occurred	C has nothing to do with E, and C and E just happened to occur together	C suppresses E, but something went wrong, so C and E occurred together
~C~E	C causes E, and E did not occur because C did not occur	C has nothing to do with E, and it just happened that E did not occur when C did not occur	C suppresses E, and E did not change because its true cause did not occur
C~E	C causes E, but E did not occur because something went wrong	C has nothing to do with E	C spppresses E, so E did not occur because C occurred
~CE	C causes E, but E was caused by something else in this case	C has nothing to do with E	C suppresses E, so E occurred because C did not occur

example of the failure to satisfy a precondition, and a piece of ~CE evidence may be seen as the presence of an alternative cause. Conversely, on first encountering a majority of negative evidence at the beginning of an information set, people would interpret CE as a spurious correlation and ~C~E as an absence of any relationship.

Dennis and Ahn (2001) tested the prediction that the order in which people encounter evidence would influence causal strength estimates because people initially develop different hypotheses, which result in different interpretations of subsequent covariation information. Participants observed a sequence of trials, each describing the presence or absence of two events, and then judged the causal strength between the two events at the end of the sequence. Participants in the positive-first condition observed the bulk of the positive evidence, followed by the bulk of the negative evidence without any explicit marking for when the second set began. In the negative-first condition, participants observed the bulk of the negative evidence followed by the bulk of the positive evidence. Although the order was different, all participants observed ΔP of 0.

The PowerPC theory (Cheng, 1997) does not predict an order effect. Contingency-based models calculate the causal strength of an event over all available trials at once when enough observations are accumulated. Order of information does not change the probabilities used in Equation 17-2. Therefore, the ordering of information in Dennis and Ahn (2001) should have no effect on estimates of causal strength according to these models.

In the RW model, the strength of association between cue and outcome is updated at each trial, making the model sensitive to the sequence in which a series of learning trials is presented. In our simulation of the Dennis and Ahn (2001) experiments, the RW model yielded clear recency effects for almost every logical combination of parameters. The RW model predicts the recency effect because the degree to which an outcome is surprising determines associative learning. Evidence suggesting a positive relationship would be more surprising after a bulk of negative evidence (negative-first condition) than in the absence of such negative evidence (positive-first condition). Similarly, negative evidence is more surprising after presentation of positive evidence (positive-first condition) than in the absence of such evidence (negative-first condition). Consequently, in both conditions, the later information is more surprising and hence has a larger impact on associative strength, resulting in the recency effect.

Unlike the predictions of these two models, Dennis and Ahn (2001) found a primacy effect: Participants in the positive-first condition gave much higher estimates than those in the negative-first condition. Given that the primacy effect can pose a critical problem for all existing models of causal induction and that some research has found the opposite order effect of recency (Collins & Shanks, 2002; López, Shanks, Almaraz, & Fernández, 1998), it is crucial to understand the conditions under which the primacy effect occurs. Dennis (2004) and Marsh and Ahn (2005b) examined two possible reasons for obtaining the recency effect in causal induction.

One possible methodological difference between studies finding recency and those finding primacy is the frequency with which estimates of causal relations were made by participants. López et al. (1998) asked participants to estimate causal strengths multiple times during learning (step-by-step estimates), whereas Dennis and Ahn (2001) asked for the estimate only at the end of learning (end-of-sequence estimates). Hogarth and Einhorn's (1992) analysis of tasks used in the impression formation literature found that end-of-sequence estimates induced primacy, whereas step-by-step estimates tend to induce recency. Hogarth and Einhorn explain that impression formation involves belief updating, and the first piece of evidence (or an amalgamation of the first few pieces) serves as the anchor in end-of-sequence tasks. The anchor then serves as the guide by which all other information is updated, resulting in a force toward primacy. On the other hand, in step-by-step tasks, people are forced to revise their hypotheses whenever they generate a new estimate, and thus the first piece of evidence no longer serves as an anchor after an estimate is made. According to Hogarth and Einhorn's belief-updating model, the weight of each new piece of evidence is adjusted based on a mechanism similar to the RW model: The more new information differs from the current position, the more weight it receives. Therefore, as in the RW model, the recency effect is predicted for step-by-step estimation.

Collins and Shanks (2002) presented a more direct investigation of the effects of estimate frequency on causal induction judgments. Using the same paradigm as in Dennis and Ahn (2001), they found that an end-of-sequence estimation procedure created a primacy finding, whereas more frequent estimation (every 10 trials) produced recency. Careful examination of Collins and Shanks's procedure produces reasons to suspect that the recency effect might have been induced by demand characteristics of the frequent estimate condition. Asking for an estimate only at the end of a sequence may implicitly cue participants to integrate over all information they have seen to make an estimate (e.g., "Because I have not been asked to make an estimate yet, then they must want me to use all of the information I have seen"). However, when some type of judgment is asked for every 10 trials, participants can interpret this as a cue that only the current information should be used (e.g., "Because I am repeatedly asked to make an estimate, there must have been some change in the data

that warrants only using the most recent information"). Collins and Shanks failed to take cautionary measures to prevent this type of misinterpretation, as has been done in other studies (e.g., Catena, Maldonado, & Candido, 1998). Collins and Shanks compounded this problem by instructing participants that they will improve over the course of the experiment ("Although initially you will have to guess, by the end you will be an expert!" p. 1147).

Dennis (2004) replicated the work of Collins and Shanks (2002) with two critical modifications. Participants were asked to make causal strength estimates at every trial. This frequency was the strongest possible manipulation for the frequency of estimation argument, but at the same time, it reduces the demand characteristics in that there is no incremental set of data that participants might think as more important. Second, at each judgment, participants were asked to consider all data they had seen so far. Adding these instructions favors neither the recency nor the primacy effect, but eliminates the potential demand characteristics. With these two measures taken to eliminate the demand characteristics, Dennis found a strong primacy effect despite the fact that participants had to make step-by-step judgments.

A second possible explanation of recency effects is task complexity. López et al.'s (1998) learning materials were much more complex than those of Dennis and Ahn (2001). López et al.'s participants received information about a disease X and three possible symptoms. In one half of the learning sequence (the contingent block), one of these symptoms (A) was always paired with another (B). When the compound symptoms AB were presented, the patient usually had the disease, but when symptom B occurred alone, the disease was usually not present. This pairing suggests B was a worse predictor of the disease than was A. In the other half of the sequence (the noncontingent block), Symptom A was paired with a new cue (C). In this block, however, the disease occurred as often with C alone as with Compound AC, suggesting that Symptom C was a better predictor than A. Comparing the two blocks, higher ratings of the relationship between Symptom A and the disease should be given for the contingent than the noncontingent block. The order of these two blocks was manipulated to create different conditions in which either the contingent block was presented first or the noncontingent block was first. López et al. found that ratings of the relationship between Symptom A and the disease were higher in conditions in which the contingent block was last (hence a recency effect).

López et al.'s (1998) design becomes complicated in that they simultaneously presented another set of stimuli with the same structure during the same learning phase (e.g., two contingent blocks each instantiated in its own disease). Furthermore, participants were simultaneously presented with two more sets of materials for the opposite order condition, thereby leading to symptom information for four diseases presented simultaneously. As a way to approximately illustrate complexity of the task given in this experiment (albeit in a somewhat arbitrary way), we can say that across all four sets of materials, participants had up to 20 hypotheses (3 single cues and 2 configural cues in each set times 4 sets) to keep track of by the time they got to the end of the experiment. Under this situation, the recency effect is more likely because participants would lose track of the hypotheses that they were testing and base their judgments on the most recent evidence. Participants could also fail to develop any hypotheses until later trials. In contrast, Dennis and Ahn's (2001) participants kept track of only one hypothesis. Marsh and Ahn (2005b) propose that the recency effect found in López et al. (1998) is an artifact of an overly complex procedure. Using the identical stimuli and procedure as López et al. but reducing the number of hypotheses to be tested to 5, we found a strong primacy effect (Marsh & Ahn, 2005b, Experiment 1).

In another experiment, Marsh and Ahn (2005b) doubled the cognitive load during learning by using two sets of stimulus materials, such that the number of causal relations to be considered would be 10. (This still would be half the amount López et al. found in 1998.) Given this increase, neither a recency nor a primacy effect was found. In this study, participants' spatial and verbal working memory capacity was also measured. We believe that the primacy effect did not occur in López et al.'s study because there were too many hypotheses to be examined early. If a subject has a large working memory capacity, then that subject would be more likely to be able to handle keeping track of so many hypotheses and be more likely to show the primacy effect. Indeed, Marsh and Ahn (2005b) found that participants' verbal working memory capacity positively correlated with the amount of primacy effect.

To summarize, work on order effects suggests that basic covariation information can be interpreted differently over the course of learning. As was indicated by results from Dennis and Ahn (2001), Dennis (2004), and Marsh and Ahn (2005b), information early in a learning sequence can greatly color the interpretation of later information. It is proposed that this early information serves as a basis by which hypotheses about causal relationships are formed. Later information is then differentially interpreted in overall estimates of causal strength. Such malleable interpretations are in contrast with the standard view of covariation data as uniform, static information.

Unobserved Alternative Causes

Models such as ΔP (Cheng & Novick, 1992), PowerPC (Cheng, 1997), and RW (Rescorla & Wagner, 1972) use information about whether an event occurred (such as in Figure 17-1) to evaluate the causal strength of variables. There are situations, however, in which such information is not available. Imagine a situation in which a doctor is treating a new disease. The doctor believes that there are two potential causes of the disease. The first is exposure to high levels of mercury, which can be measured using a blood test. The second is thought to be a genetic anomaly that is currently undetectable. In this case, one of the ostensible causes (the genetic anomaly) is unobservable. With respect to this cause, patients may be grouped as either having the disease or not, but they cannot be further broken down into the categories shown in Figure 17-1 (e.g., CE vs. ~CE and C~E vs. ~C~E). Such situations thus pose a problem for models that rely on contingency information as their input; these models cannot render judgments about the unobserved cause because the necessary input is not available.

Luhmann and Ahn (2003, 2006) demonstrated that, unlike the difficulties manifest in current models, people spontaneously make causal judgments about unobserved causes. The experimental situation used in these studies mirrors the example given in the preceding section. In each case, there were two causes and one effect. One of the causes was fully observable (similar to the mercury levels), and one was unobserved (similar to the genetic anomaly). The effect was always observable. In their Experiment 1, Luhmann and Ahn (2003) found that although they were allowed to withhold their judgments, participants were willing to make estimates on causal strength of unobserved causes. Because unobserved causes do not yield covariation information, these findings imply that people used a different source of knowledge to make judgments about the unobserved causes.

A critical finding of Luhmann and Ahn (2003) was that observations of what the authors refer to as *unexplained effects* led to differential causal judgments of the unobserved cause. Unexplained effects are occasions on which the effect occurs in the absence of any observed cause. In the above example, unexplained effects would be an instance in which a person contracts the disease but tests negative for mercury. Luhmann and Ahn (2003) found that people judged the unobserved cause to be stronger when such instances of unexplained effects occurred than when they did not occur.

Unexplained effects imply the existence and operation of an unobserved alternative cause on those occasions, and this belief triggers the creation of a hypothesis about the unobserved cause. Because unexplained effects indicate that the unobserved cause was responsible for the effect on that occasion, the hypothesis about the unobserved cause should initially posit a positive (i.e., generative) relationship of nonzero strength between the unobserved cause and the effect. This hypothesis is assumed subsequently to operate as described in the preceding section; that is, the hypothesis about the unobserved cause will color the interpretation of subsequent experience.

Specifically, our prediction was that if people maintain a hypothesis about the unobserved cause, then observations should be interpreted as confirming this belief (Lord, Ross, & Lepper, 1979). Thus, in conditions with unexplained effects, participants should believe the unobserved cause to be responsible for the target effect and thus interpret observations to conform to this belief. For instance, in the subsequent CE trials (i.e., joint presence of the observed cause and the effect), participants would believe that the unobserved cause is likely to be present as well, whereas in the subsequent ~C~E trials, they would believe that the unobserved cause is unlikely to be present. Next, we describe two experiments testing this prediction.

The first study sought to evaluate people's explicit beliefs about the presence or absence of the unobserved cause. To do so, we provided participants with a causal learning task like that used by Luhmann and Ahn (2003). To reiterate, one of the causes and the effect were fully observable, and the other cause was unobservable. In addition, after each trial, we explicitly asked participants to judge how likely it was that the unobserved cause was present on that occasion. Twenty-four participants viewed each of the four contingencies shown in Table 17-2 and made their likelihood judgments using an 11-point scale (0, definitely not pressed; 10, definitely pressed).

Table 17-3 shows mean ratings broken down by the four conditions and four trial types. The first finding to note is that the unobserved cause is most likely to be present during unexplained effects (~CE) trials, as expected. In the next analyses, we examined whether participants interpreted trials in light of their beliefs about the unobserved cause. If participants are interpreting observations as consistent with their beliefs about the unobserved cause, then they should believe that the unobserved cause covaries with the effect more in the two conditions with unexplained effects than in the two conditions without unexplained effects.

To test this, we compared CE trials and ~C ~E trials, the only trial types shared among the four conditions. If participants believed the unobserved cause covaried with the effect (which we predicted to be the case in the conditions containing ~CE), then participants should believe the unobserved cause to be more likely present on CE trials and more likely absent on ~C~E trials; the unobserved cause should covary with the effect. Participants who do not believe the unobserved cause covaried with the effect (which we predicted to be the case in the conditions without ~CE) may believe that the likelihood of the unobserved cause being present is more similar on these two trial types; the unobserved cause should not covary with the effect.

For each participant, their average rating for ~C ~E trials was subtracted from their average rating for CE trials. This composite score serves as an index of the degree to which participants believed the unobserved cause to vary with the effect. A 2 (C ~E present/absent)×2 (~CE present/absent) repeated measures analysis of variance was performed on this composite. This analysis revealed a significant main effect of unexplained effects (~CE trials), $F(1, 23)=8.77$, mean square error=84.52, $p < .01$, because the composite was higher in conditions that included ~CE (Mean [M]=3.60) than on conditions that did not include ~CE ($M = 1.72$). This analysis suggests that unexplained effects not only lead to the perception of a stronger unobserved cause (as demonstrated by Luhmann & Ahn, 2003), but also led participants to

TABLE 17-2 Contingencies Used in Each of the Four Conditions

Condition	~CE Present, C~E Absent		~CE Present, C~E Present		~CE Absent, C~E Absent		~CE Absent C~E Present	
	E	~E	E	~E	E	~E	E	~E
Contigency structure	C 10	0	C 10	10	C 10	0	C 10	10
	~C 10	10	~C 10	10	~C 0	10	~C 0	10

Each condition contains CE and ~C~E observations. Only the presentation of ~CE and C~E observations differs.

believe that the unobserved cause covaries with the effect. Participants interpreted the unobserved cause differently on identical trials depending on whether they had observed unexplained effects.

Thus, we have demonstrated that unexplained effects result in the belief that the unobserved cause covaries with the effect and the belief that the relationship between the unobserved cause and the effect is strong. An obvious question is whether these beliefs are related. It seems plausible that people are able to make causal judgments about unobserved causes (and were confident in these judgments; see Luhmann & Ahn, 2003) because they have information about how the unobserved cause covaries with the effect. This information is not present in the input as current theories of causal learning assume but rather is imposed on the input by the reasoner. To explore whether people's trial-by-trial beliefs influence their subsequent causal judgments, a second experiment was conducted using a paradigm similar to that of Dennis and Ahn (2001) as described in the preceding section.

Fifty participants viewed each of two causal situations. The two situations used the set of trials represented in Figure 17-2. This set of trials was divided into two blocks, although there was nothing to indicate this to participants. One block contained unexplained effects, and the other did not. These two

blocks could be ordered in one of two ways; the block containing unexplained effects could be presented either first or second. After viewing all trials, participants were asked to judge the causal strength of both the observed and unobserved cause. Note that, because the only manipulation was the order of the two blocks, participants always saw the same set of covariation data by the end of the sequence. Thus, any differences between conditions cannot be a result of the number or type of trials observed.

We predicted an order effect for the following reasons: When participants observed unexplained effects early, considerably more evidence was available to interpret as consistent with, and thus reinforce, the hypothesis about the unobserved cause. This additional reinforcement would lead participants to perceive the unobserved cause as a strong causal influence. When participants observed unexplained effects late in experience, a significant number of the observations had already occurred and thus were not interpreted in light of the newly formed hypothesis. This would lead participants to perceive the unobserved cause as a weaker influence.

As summarized in Figure 17-3, participants gave a significantly higher rating for the unobserved cause in the early unexplained effects condition ($M=73.50$, standard deviation [SD]=25.90) than in the late-unexplained-effects condition ($M=61.66$, $SD=27.79$),

TABLE 17-3 Average Trial-by-Trial Likelihood Ratings for the Various Trial Types in Each Condition Plus Marginal Averages

Condition	~CE Present, C~E Absent			~CE Present, C~E Present			~CE Absent, C~E Absent			~CE Absent, C~E Present		
	E	~E		E	~E		E	~E		E	~E	
Likelihood (U)	C 5.80		5.80	C 5.38	3.41	4.40	C 4.10		4.10	C 5.26	3.76	4.51
	~C 7.51	2.15	4.83	~C 7.84	1.82	4.83	~C	3.16	3.16	~C	2.7	2.70

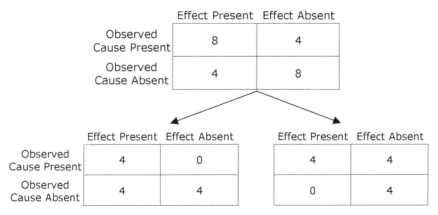

	Effect Present	Effect Absent
Observed Cause Present	8	4
Observed Cause Absent	4	8

	Effect Present	Effect Absent
Observed Cause Present	4	0
Observed Cause Absent	4	4

	Effect Present	Effect Absent
Observed Cause Present	4	4
Observed Cause Absent	0	4

FIGURE 17-2 A summary of the observations presented to participants. The contingency table summarizes the covariation of the observed cause and the effect. The set of observations was divided into two blocks. One block contained unexplained effects; the other did not. The order of these blocks was manipulated.

$t(49)=2.89$, $p<.01$. These results support the idea that observations obtained after creating an unobserved cause hypothesis act to reinforce the hypothesis.

Note that this is not the only possible outcome. Theoretically, when participants in the late unexplained effects condition first observed an unexplained effect, they could create an unobserved cause hypothesis and reevaluate all previously obtained observations. Such retrospective reevaluation would likely require significant cognitive resources and thus may not be a generally economical strategy.

Consistent with the work of Dennis and Ahn (2001), these studies indicate that identical observations can be interpreted differently depending on the beliefs held by the observer. The two studies reported in this section demonstrate that such dynamic interpretations occur when evaluating unobserved causes just as they do with observed causes. Moreover, this differential interpretation influenced both explicit likelihood ratings and causal strength ratings. These findings suggest that unobserved causes are sometimes treated very much like observed causes. The observer can establish beliefs about an unobserved cause, interpret observations to overcome the absence of covariation information, and subsequently compute causal strength.

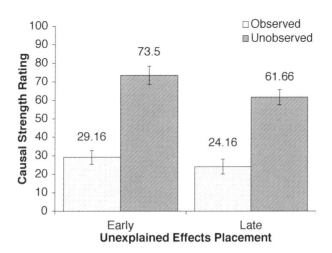

FIGURE 17-3 Participants' mean causal strength judgments. Error bars indicate standard error.

Dynamic Interpretations of Ambiguous Stimuli

As discussed, the major models of causal reasoning (e.g., Cheng, 1997; Cheng & Novick, 1990; Rescorla & Wagner, 1972) deal with information that is uniformly presorted into the standard contingency table (see Figure 17-1). What occurs if information pertaining to a possible causal relationship is not so clearly defined regarding which of the four evidence types it represents? For example, consider trying to assess whether high stress causes insomnia. There are some events that are obviously instances of the presence of high stress (e.g., taking medical school entrance exams) and some events that are easily classified as the absence of high stress (e.g., sunbathing on a tropical island). However, there exists a wide spectrum of events between these two extremes that are not so clearly classified as the absence or presence of stress (e.g., waiting in a crowd, writing an e-mail, celebrating a milestone birthday). How would a reasoner assess a hypothesis such as "High stress causes insomnia" when the great amount of ambiguously identified evidence has no clear place in the classic representations of causal information?

Similar to how an existing hypothesis can affect the interpretation of sequential information and influence beliefs about an unobservable cause's operation, a governing hypothesis can be used to assess ambiguous causal information. For example, imagine that a reasoner keeps experiencing events in which high stress preceded a night of insomnia, whereas insomnia never followed a stress-free day. The reasoner then is asked to assess whether a friend was experiencing high stress given the observation that after a day spent reading the person did not sleep. The reasoner would use the belief that high stress causes insomnia to interpret the observation as an instance of a high-stress day. Even though a day of reading in itself might not be stressful (e.g., reading the latest romance novel) or could be stressful (e.g., searching job postings in the classifieds), the given instance of reading would be classified as stressful because such an interpretation matches the reasoner's existing theory of the relation between events. In this way, information not inherent to the standard representation of covariation information would influence causal estimation.

To test the hypothesis that a governing causal hypothesis can cause an ambiguous event to be reinterpreted as a specific instance outlined in Figure 17-1, Marsh and Ahn (2005a) introduced ambiguous causal candidates into a traditional causal induction paradigm.

Participants were presented with trial-by-trial evidence that indicated a strong covariation between two easily distinguishable, well-defined causal candidates and an outcome (see Figure 17-4 for actual trial frequencies). In one such sequence, for example, participants saw evidence that depicted bacteria that were of long length (the candidate cause) as predominantly paired with the presence of nitrogen in soil samples (the effect event), whereas bacteria that were short were paired with the absence of nitrogen. To this basic paradigm, trials were added throughout the trial sequence depicting a candidate cause that was ambiguous regarding its membership in the cause-present or cause-absent class. In the previous example, these ambiguous trials would take the form of bacteria of intermediate length paired with the presence of nitrogen. The question of interest was whether participants would be willing to include this information in their assessments of causal information.

To address specifically if and how ambiguous information may be incorporated into evidence about causal relationships, Marsh and Ahn (2005a) in their Experiment 1 had participants report how many pieces of evidence they had observed by asking four questions that corresponded to the types of information found in Figure 17-1 (e.g., "On how many cases were the bacteria long and the nitrogen was present?" represented the CE cell). It was hypothesized that participants would use their current belief about the causal relationship between events to incorporate the ambiguous information into the traditional types of covariation evidence. For instance, if a participant believed that long bacteria (C) were generally associated with the presence of nitrogen in soil samples (E), then evidence depicting an ambiguous causal candidate (A) paired with the presence of nitrogen (i.e., a piece of AE evidence) would be interpreted as a piece of CE evidence. Under the same hypothesis, information that depicted the ambiguous cause in the absence of the effect (A~E) would be interpreted as evidence of type ~C~E. Therefore, ambiguous evidence of type AE should only be reflected in the CE estimate and likewise for ambiguous evidence of type A~E and the ~C~E estimate. Estimates of the two types of negative evidence should not be affected by ambiguous information because the negative evidence does not correspond to a way in which a hypothesis could be used to interpret ambiguous information. These predictions are depicted in Figure 17-4.

Participants in Marsh and Ahn's study (2005a) spontaneously assimilated ambiguous information into estimates of causal information. (See Figure 17-4 for mean

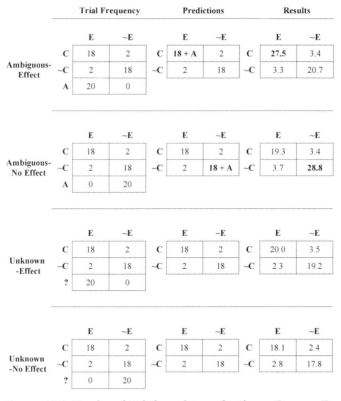

FIGURE 17-4 Number of trials for each type of evidence. C, cause; E, effect; A, ambiguous candidate cause; ?, unknown value of candidate cause.

estimates of the four types of evidence.) Specifically, if the ambiguous causal candidate was always paired with the presence of the target effect (ambiguous-effect), significantly more information was reported of type CE ($M=27.5$) than of type $\sim$C$\sim$E ($M=20.7$), $t(19)=2.7$, $p<.02$. If the ambiguous causal candidate was always paired with the absence of the effect (ambiguous-no effect), more information was reported of type $\sim$C$\sim$E ($M=28.8$) compared to type CE ($M=19.3$), $t(19)=3.3$, $p<.01$. In both of these conditions, there was no difference in the amount of information reported between the C$\sim$E and $\sim$CE cells, $p>.20$. These findings are as predicted if participants were using an existing belief about the relationship between well-defined events to interpret ambiguous information.

The described results could have been found because participants felt forced by the constraints of the task to report ambiguous information instead of excluding this information or classifying it as a separate type of evidence from Figure 17-1. To guard against these possibilities, participants were not told ahead how many or what frequency estimates they would make. In this way, participants could have represented ambiguous information as a separate class of information during the experiment with the expectation that they would be able to report it as such in final estimates. As a further precaution along these lines, the actual questions for estimation were presented one at a time in a random order. Ignorance of the complete spectrum of questions to be asked would have allowed participants to categorize ambiguous evidence as an additional category of information not represented in Figure 17-1. However, participants still incorporated ambiguous evidence.[2]

Another interesting finding is that the assimilation of ambiguous information was not complete, as can be noticed in Figure 17-4. If all of the trials illustrating the ambiguous candidate cause were assimilated by the governing causal hypothesis, then the key cells in Figure 17-4 should be closer to a total of 38 trials. It appears that only about half of the ambiguous trials that could have been incorporated into estimates were assimilated as such. These results seem sensible: For ambiguous information to be assimilated by an existing hypothesis, said hypothesis must first be created. In the beginning of the experimental sequence, participants have yet to form a theory of how the possible causal candidates are associated with the effect. At that point, participants would not be able to informatively classify the ambiguous evidence. After observing information, the relationship between candidate cause and effect would have become clearer, allowing the formation of a causal hypothesis and subsequent interpretation of ambiguous evidence. Because pieces of evidence depicting ambiguous causes were sprinkled throughout the trial sequence, the early ambiguous evidence was experienced without the benefit of a governing hypothesis and therefore would not have been included in frequency estimates. As discussed with respect to unobserved causes, the cognitive load involved may be too great for the retrospective incorporation of ambiguous information. Therefore, only ambiguous information presented after the formation of a hypothesis could have been interpreted through the lens of the hypothesis and thereby included in frequency estimates.

In another study (Marsh & Ahn, 2006a), we further examined if the strength of the hypothesized causal relation would moderate the amount of ambiguous information that is assimilated into causal judgments, such that the stronger the causal relation is believed to be, the more assimilation should occur. For example, if a person believes that high stress is always followed by insomnia, then any day with an ambiguous level of stress that was followed by insomnia should be counted as an example of high stress occurring with insomnia. However, belief in a weak relationship implies that every time high stress is present, insomnia does not necessarily follow. If a person believes that high stress is not necessarily followed by insomnia, then there is no principled reason to believe that every ambiguous stress day would occur with insomnia. This person should therefore be willing not to incorporate all ambiguous stress/insomnia days as examples of high stress and insomnia. In this way, the incorporation of ambiguous information would be mediated by the strength of the governing hypothesis so that less ambiguous information should be incorporated at weaker contingencies.

To test the effect of believed strength in causal relations, Experiment 2 of Marsh and Ahn (2006a) compared the treatment of ambiguous information in causal relationships of differing strengths. Four conditions were presented, each portraying a different strength relationship between the well-defined trials

and the presence of the effect: a perfect relationship condition ($\Delta P=1.0$), a strong relationship condition ($\Delta P=0.6$), a weak relationship condition ($\Delta P=0.3$), and a no relationship condition ($\Delta P=0$). The exact trial frequencies used in this experiment can be seen in Figure 17-5. In all of the conditions, the ambiguous causal candidate always appeared with the presence of the effect, and there were 20 such ambiguous trials. We predicted that for the no relationship condition no preferential sorting of ambiguous evidence should occur because no hypothesis regarding the relationship between events could be formed. In contrast, for the three conditions for which a relationship existed between well-defined events (i.e., the perfect, strong, and weak conditions), the ambiguous evidence would be incorporated into the frequency estimate that matched the governing hypothesis, specifically the CE cell. Furthermore, the amount of assimilation would be a function of the strength of the relationship between the well-defined events.

Figure 17-5 depicts the results for the described experiment (Marsh & Ahn, 2006a). For the three conditions in which a relationship existed between the well-defined events, ambiguous evidence was incorporated into the CE frequency estimates as predicted. This finding is evidenced by significantly greater information reported in the CE cell than the ~C ~E cell for all three conditions, all t's>2.82, all p's$<.009$. Also as predicted, this difference was not significant in the no relationship condition, $p>.18$.

The results of this experiment also show that different amounts of assimilation were reported depending on the strength of the existing covariation relationship. By subtracting the ~C ~E estimate from the CE estimate for each condition, the amount of information that was preferentially sorted into the CE cell was calculated. These difference scores were then compared across conditions to see if more information was being sorted into the CE cell at different causal relational strengths. Figure 17-6 shows a graph of the mean difference scores for the four conditions. As the graph shows, the stronger the covariation between well-defined events, the more information was preferentially sorted into the CE estimate. Significantly more information was preferentially sorted in the CE estimate than the ~C ~E estimate in the perfect relationship condition ($M=7.8$) compared to the weak relationship condition ($M=3.4$). More information was also sorted preferentially in the perfect condition compared to the no relationship condition ($M=1.6$) and into the strong condition ($M=6.7$) compared to the no relationship

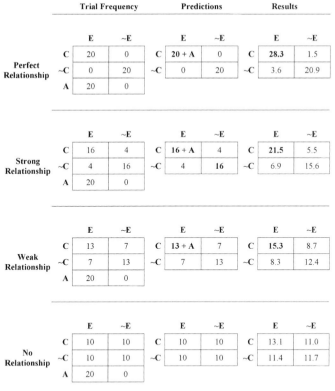

FIGURE 17-5 Number of trials for each type of evidence for multiple
relationship strengths. C, cause; E, effect; A, ambiguous candidate
cause.

condition, all t's>2.37, all p's<.03. In short, the
strength of the believed causal relations greatly affects
the amount of ambiguous information that is incorporated into estimates of causal information.

Having demonstrated the influence of the governing hypothesis on interpretations of ambiguous stimuli,
an interesting question is whether people would assimilate *any* unknown information. That is, how robust is
this phenomenon? To examine this issue, we created
(Marsh & Ahn, 2006a) a condition in which the
ambiguous causal candidate was replaced with an
unknown candidate cause. More specifically, the
unknown candidate was marked with a question mark
and the word *unknown* appeared instead of a picture of
the bacteria. In the instructions, participants were told
that there was no information known about the candidate cause for these trials. Going back to our previous
example of the relationship between high stress and
insomnia, the unknown trials would be similar to a situation in which a reasoner has no information about
the stress of the target person's day (or any information
that can be used to infer the level of stress that day) and
only learned that the person suffered from insomnia.

Note that, just like our ambiguous stimuli, an
unknown candidate cause does not inform whether a
given observation is positive or negative evidence
toward a hypothesis. Thus, participants could also
assimilate these trials in a way similar to how they
assimilated ambiguous stimuli. For instance, if participants initially believed that the target effect is caused
by a target cause, then participants could infer that an
unknown cause paired with the presence of the effect
must have been a case where the candidate cause was
present, and when the unknown cause was paired
with the absence of the effect, then the causal candidate must have been absent. This would be the most
sensible inference to make if a person is forced to
guess about the state of the unknown causal candidate. For instance, if high stress correlates with insomnia, on encountering a person who suffers from
insomnia, it would be reasonable to guess that the person experiences a lot of high stress. Therefore, it is
possible and even plausible in our experiments that
people would spontaneously make inferences about
unknown causal candidates as they did for ambiguous
causal candidates.

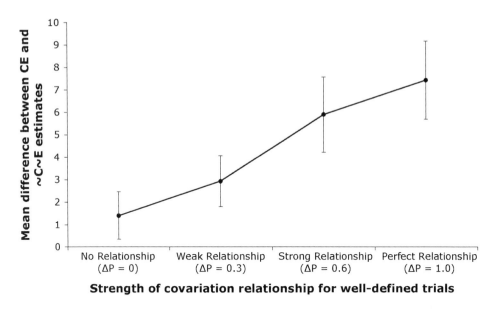

FIGURE 17-6 Mean difference between CE and ~C~E scores. Error bars indicate standard error.

In contrast, the mere presence of uncertainty might not be sufficient to provoke assimilation. Instead, ambiguous stimuli might need to be present for assimilation to spontaneously take place. The presence of ambiguous stimuli might trigger a need to classify the stimuli one way or another, which in turn results in assimilation. For instance, on encountering a bacterium with medium height, one might be enticed to determine whether it is long rather than simply leaving it as an undeterminable state and ignoring it.

To test the boundaries of which types of causal candidates would be incorporated into estimates of causal information, participants in Experiment 1 of Marsh and Ahn (2005a) were also given two additional conditions that contained unknown candidate causes. The representation of an unknown candidate cause was paired with the presence of the effect in one condition (unknown-effect) and the absence of the effect in the other (unknown-no effect). Because unknown information is lacking any type of structure on which a hypothesis can operate, it should not be incorporated into estimates of causal information. This prediction was validated in that estimates in the ambiguous conditions differed from the unknown conditions only in the cells predicted if ambiguous information was being incorporated via a governing hypothesis. That is, in the ambiguous-effect condition the CE cell mean estimate was greater than in the unknown-effect condition, and the ~C~E cell was

greater in the ambiguous-no effect condition than the unknown-no effect condition. Furthermore, estimates for the four cells of the unknown conditions did not significantly differ from the number of well-defined trials presented (see Figure 17-4), demonstrating that participants can choose to exclude covariation information and are not bound to include it by the demands of the task.

We have demonstrated that people will incorporate information depicting an ambiguous causal candidate into their reports of relevant causal information. This was found despite the fact that participants had no advance knowledge of trial frequencies they would be asked to estimate. Participants could have excluded the ambiguous information in favor of waiting to classify it as a type of evidence not found in the classic representation of covariation information. Instead, participants spontaneously classified ambiguous causal candidates as the presence or absence of the candidate cause according to their governing hypothesis of the causal relationship.

Conclusion

As posited in the beginning of this chapter, we believe that covariation information can be dynamically interpreted during the process of causal learning. We have shown that such hypotheses can result in the discounting of later information in an information sequence, resulting in a primacy effect. We have also shown that causal hypotheses can alter the interpretation of covariation information into supporting an alternative, unobserved cause. In the last section, we likewise showed that an existing hypothesis could cause information that does not fit the normal representation of covariation information to be included into judgments of causal relationships. In particular, evidence that was ambiguous and normally has no place in the models of causal reasoning was reinterpreted by existing hypotheses and rendered usable.

The covariation-based models of causal induction have often been described as models of how people learn completely novel causal relations based on raw, untainted covariation data (see Tenenbaum, Griffiths, & Niyogi, chapter 19, this volume, for a more elaborated approach). We would argue that even when learning novel causal relations, people are driven to interpret covariation data in light of their own governing hypothesis. Such dynamic interpretations of covariation data are beyond the scope of existing covariation-based models.

References

Catena, A., Maldonado, A., & Candido, A. (1998). The effect of frequency of judgement and the type of trials on covariation learning. *Journal of Experimental Psychology: Human Perception and Performance, 24*, 481–495.

Cheng, P. W. (1997). From covariation to causation: A causal power theory. *Psychological Review, 104*, 367–405.

Cheng, P. W., & Novick, L. R. (1990). A probabilistic contrast model of causal induction. *Journal of Personality and Social Psychology, 58*, 545–567.

Cheng, P. W., & Novick, L. (1992). Covariation in natural causal induction. *Psychological Review, 99*, 365–382.

Collins, D. J., & Shanks, D. R. (2002). Momentary and integrative response strategies in causal judgment. *Memory & Cognition, 30*, 1138–1147.

Dennis, M. J. (2004). *Primacy in causal strength judgments: The effect of initial evidence for generative versus inhibitory relationships.* Unpublished doctoral dissertation, Yale University, New Haven, CT.

Dennis, M. J., & Ahn, W. (2001). Primacy in causal strength judgments: The effect of initial evidence for generative versus inhibitory relationships. *Memory & Cognition, 29*, 152–164.

Einhorn, H. J., & Hogarth, R. M. (1986). Judging probable cause. *Psychological Bulletin, 99*, 3–19.

Hogarth, R. M., & Einhorn, H. J. (1992). Order effects in belief updating: The belief-adjustment model. *Cognitive Psychology, 24*, 1–55.

Jenkins, H. M., & Ward, W. C. (1965). Judgment of contingency between responses and outcomes. *Psychological Monographs: General and Applied, 79*, 1–17.

López, F. J., Shanks, D. R., Almaraz, J., & Fernández, P. (1998). Effects of trial order on contingency judgments: A comparison of associative and probabilistic contrast accounts. *Journal of Experimental Psychology: Learning, Memory, and Cognition, 24*, 672–694.

Lord, C. G., Ross, L., & Lepper, M. R. (1979). Biased assimilation and attitude polarization: The effects of prior theories on subsequently considered evidence. *Journal of Personality & Social Psychology, 37*, 2098–2109.

Luhmann, C. C., & Ahn, W. (2003). Evaluating the causal role of unobserved variables. In R. Alterman & D. Kirsh (Eds.), *Proceedings of the 25th Annual Conference of the Cognitive Science Society* (pp. 734–739). Mahwah, NJ: Erlbaum.

Luhmann, C. C., & Ahn, W. (2006). BUCKLE: *A model of unobserved cause learning.* Unpublished manuscript, Yale University, New Haven, CT.

Marsh, J. K. & Ahn, W. (2003). Interpretation of ambiguous information in causal induction. In R. Alterman & D. Kirsh (Eds.), *Proceedings of the 25th Annual Conference of the Cognitive Science Society* (pp. 775–780). Mahwah, NJ: Erlbaum.

Marsh, J. K. & Ahn, W. (2006a). *Ambiguity in causal learning.* Unpublished manuscript, Yale University, New Haven, CT.

Marsh, J. K., & Ahn, W. (2006b). Order effects in contingency learning: The role of task complexity. *Memory & Cognition, 34*, 568–576.

Novick, L. R., & Cheng, P. W. (2004). Assessing interactive causal influence. *Psychological Review, 111*, 455–485.

Rescorla, R. A., & Wagner, A. R. (1972). A theory of Pavlovian conditioning: Variations in the effectiveness of reinforcement and nonreinforcement. In A. H. Black & W. F. Prokasy (Eds.), *Classical conditioning II: Current theory and research* (pp. 64–99). New York: Appleton-Century-Crofts.

van Hamme, L. J., & Wasserman, E. A. (1994). Cue competition in causality judgments: The role of nonpresentation of compound stimulus elements. *Learning and Motivation, 25*, 127–151.

Wasserman, E. A., Kao, S.F., Van Hamme, L. J., Katagiri, M., & Young, M. E. (1996). Causation and association. In D. R. Shanks, K. J. Holyoak, & D. L. Medin (Eds.), *Causal learning: The psychology of learning and motivation* (Vol. 34, pp. 208–264). San Diego, CA: Academic Press.

18

Statistical Jokes and Social Effects

Intervention and Invariance in Causal Relations

Clark Glymour

One core of the idea of causation is that interventions from outside a system would change things inside, whatever the boundary may be. Another, according to a long philosophical tradition, is that causal relations are stable, regular, and invariant. On one side, I want to emphasize that psychological theories that do not distinguish intervention from association are non-starters. On the other, I want to emphasize that, when we turn to many kinds of causal relations, the connection between interventions and causation is broken, and various kinds of invariance do not hold.

> Did you hear the one about the statistician who always carried a bomb with him whenever he flew on an airplane?
>
> No, why?
>
> Because he calculated it would be very improbable that there would be two bombs on the same airplane.

You drive your car to the auto repair shop for a tune-up. Gas mileage has been slipping a bit. You are assigned a mechanic named Pearson, who disconnects the spark plug wires and then hooks up a battery tester. "Why are you testing the battery?" you ask. "Well," he says, "because I disconnected the spark plug wires, the battery may have died." "What!" you exclaim, "The battery was charged when I drove in here. How could unplugging the spark plug wires discharge the battery?" "Well," says Pearson, unfazed, "disconnecting the spark plug wires means the engine won't start, you agree?" You agree, and he continues, "And a car not starting is positively correlated with a dead battery, right?" "Yeah," you say, "but . . ." "So I have to check whether the battery is dead."

A paper by Sloman and Lagnado (2005) confirms that when people are given verbal descriptions of simple causal systems and of interventions that change the state of downstream features, most of them do not make such stupid inferences. Of itself, this is an utterly unremarkable result, and the reason some subjects give contrary responses is, I expect, because the problems are presented only verbally or deal with unfamiliar cover stories rather than with simple, familiar physical systems. What *is* remarkable, as Sloman and Lagnado explain, is that various psychological and normative accounts of the content of causal claims say that the stupid inferences should be made, say nothing about whether they should be made, or have considerable difficulty explaining why they should not be made, and that only one available normative theory, the theory of causal Bayes nets, straightforwardly agrees with normal, intelligent reasoning in such problems and gives a systematic, computational account of such inferences. The criticisms Sloman and Lagnado advance turn on logical points that have been made on many occasions by philosophers (Dowe & Nordhoff, 2004; Lewis, 1999; Mackie, 1974; Reichenbach, 1954), but they are made more vivid by the experiments. Just as computer scientists require a program for every point about reasoning, psychologists require an experiment, which is, of course, why philosophy is so much more economical a subject.

Karl Pearson (1911) claimed that causation is nothing but correlation, and influential contemporary psychologists seem to agree, as do some influential philosophers (Jeffrey, 2004). The general version of that idea is that inference using causal beliefs is no different from inference with conditional probabilities—the probability of one event given another. Taken literally, the statistical jokes result. But, the view that probabilities on interventions reduce to conditional probabilities is consistent with the causal Bayes net framework, and with Sloman and Lagnado's (2005) experimental findings, if interventions are represented as exogenous variables that can affect the variable we think of as manipulated, and if a joint probability distribution is assumed on all variables, including the intervention variables. With that representation and an appropriate probability distribution, the probability of an event conditional on an intervention can be calculated as a probability conditional on a value of the intervention variable (Spirtes et al., 1993/2000, chapter 3). In general, but not always, the probability of a value x of a variable X on an intervention I_y that forces a value y on a variable Y, is different than the probability that x=X conditional on Y=y. The error of the counterfactual reasoning-is-just-conditional-probability-reasoning viewpoint is in omitting the causal features—intervention variables that directly influence one or more substantive variables but are not influenced by substantive variables—that distinguish the proper variables to condition on, and their relations to other variables, thus mistaking the relevant conditional probabilities (Meek & Glymour, 1994).

Another alternative hypothesis is that people understand causal claims as logical conditionals "A causes B" means: "A and B, or B and not A, or not A and not B," which is equivalent to "not both A and not B." The 19th century mathematical philosophers Boole and Frege suggested such a view, and it is reasserted in contemporary mental model theory by Goldvarg and Johnson-Laird (2001). No contemporary philosopher I know of subscribes to the view because of a century of reflection on the logica of causal claims. For example, taken literally, the account implies that any fact, actual event, or state of affairs is a cause of any other. That hurricane Ivan struck Pensacola is a cause of the election of a German pope. Material conditionals are monotonic in the antecedent—if "if A then B" is true, then "if A and C, then B" is also true—but causal conditionals are nonmonotonic. Sloman and Lagnado (2005) point out that their experimental results are inconsistent with the supposition that subject understanding of A causes B is that A materially implies B because on that construal subjects should infer that A is not the case given the information that B is not the case, no matter how the absence of B comes about.

Sloman and Lagnado (2005) propose that Goldvarg and Johnson-Laird (2001) could reply that subjects are assuming another causal factor, call it C, so that their mental model for A causes B is as follows: A and not C and B, or not A and not C and B, or not A and not C and not B, or A and C and not B. On this hypothesis, not A does not follow from not B, so the majority of subjects are giving normative responses, according to the mental model theory, in Sloman and Lagnado's experiments. No distinction between observation and intervention is required.

This does not work. If subjects use nothing but deductive inference once they have formed causal beliefs, which I believe is Johnson-Laird's view (private communication), then they should have no opinion about the value of A given the value of B—there is no deductive connection. Suppose instead they make probabilistic inferences. The mental model model for Sloman and Lagnado's (2005) experiments is that A causes B, and C prevents B. We then have the following table of possibilities and probabilities:

A	C	B	Probability
T	T	F	$p1$
T	F	T	$p2$
F	T	F	$p3$
F	F	T	$p4$
F	F	F	$p5$

where the sum of the pi values is 1. The probability that A is true is $p1+p2$. Given the fact that B is false, the probability that A is true is $p1/(p1+p3+p5)$. The two values are different; therefore, subjects following this model should think the information that B does not occur changes the probability of A, which agrees with Sloman and Lagnado if the value of B is observed, not forced from outside. But, the probability that A is true given that B is false and that C is true is $p1(p1+p3)$, again not equal to the probability of A. If C=T represents an intervention, then on this model the intervention should change the probability of A, contrary to the experimental result.

What is needed to make the mental model framework generate Sloman and Lagnado's (2005) result (i.e., that the probability that A is true is the same as the probability of A conditional on the truth of C and the falsity of B) is, in addition, that C and A are independent in probability. For if $Pr(A=T)=p1+p2=p1/(p1+p3)=Pr(A=T | C=T \text{ and } B=F)$, then $Pr(A=T \text{ and } C=T)=p1=(p1+p2)(p1+p3)=Pr(A=T)Pr(C=T)$. This is formally equivalent to postulating a causal Bayes net in which A and C partially determine B.

The upshot is that if psychologists want their account of the content of causal judgement to agree with banal facts, then they need the essentials of the causal Bayes net framework, however those essentials may be disguised. But, conundrums remain.

Social Effects, Interventions, and Invariance

When psychologists design experiments about causal judgment, the usual idea is that particular kinds of objects have the power to bring about particular kinds of events in kinds of specifiable circumstances. Blickets, when placed on blicket detectors, have the power to set off lights and sounds; liquids of a special type have the power to make plants grow taller; chemicals of a certain

type have the power to prevent germs from living; and so on. Although psychologists differ in the aspect of causal power that interests them—conditions for its exhibition versus measures of its strength, for example—they seem to agree with philosophers that causal powers must have some stability or "invariance" properties. All of this makes a reasonable package to account for what goes on in the development of children's understanding of the world: Children focus on objects, including persons; attribute properties, observed or not, to objects; and sort objects by their attributed properties, including causal powers. Children could not learn the causal powers of an object if those powers were not stable, and there would be no predictive or other value to sorting objects according to an attribute that is not stable over a range of cases.

I wonder whether a class of events of a type that are familiar and important in everyday life have causes of this sort. The events I have in mind can occur in physical contexts, but they are preeminently social: events that constitute an outcome of cooperative or competitive actions. Children discover early on the value of adult help, perhaps somewhat later the value of cooperation. They are engaged in competitions the moment they are mobile and in the company of other mobile children. I do not know how and when a causal understanding of such phenomena emerges. My question here is what that understanding could be. Consider some adult examples:

My favoritie racehorse, Sunday Brunch, seldom won races, but occasionally he did. He had, as they say, a track record. Sunday Brunch had lots of abilities, notably the ability to run pretty fast for a mile or so, abilities he had because of his bloodline, good care, and fair training. On the record, we should say that Sunday Brunch had the capacity to win some thoroughbred races. Here are my questions: Did Sunday Brunch have a power, a causal power, to win races? If so, how should that power be measured?

I own an old pickup truck, which is not so light; I can only lift the front end with the help of two fairly strong men. Do I have a causal power to lift my pickup truck?

I vote for president. My candidates usually lose, but the candidates I have favored have never won by exactly one vote. Do I have a causal power to elect the president?

It seems to me that in such cases our views of mechanism and causation begin to come apart.

To win, Sunday Brunch must run, and the mechanism by which he does is particular to him, an attribute of him. The same is true for every other horse. But, Sunday Brunch wins only if an unstable relational property obtains—his competitors do not run the track as fast as he does. The relation is unstable in part because it is not a property of any particular set of individuals, but of a collection with varying members and because it does not reduce to any simpler, less-relational property. Outcomes produced by cooperation tend to have the same logical feature. Voting is a combination of cooperation and competition. If the candidate I vote for wins by more than a single vote, then the mechanism by which that victory came about was nothing other than the vote of each individual, including my own, but individual votes had no causal power to bring about the victory: The result would have been the same if I had not voted or had voted differently. This is why, in the considerable philosophical literature on attributing a causal role to individual events, voting is never mentioned.

Cooperation and competition should therefore be expected to present problems for formal models of our understanding of causation, and I think they do. Consider the examples discussed next.

In the considerable literature on the psychology of causal judgment, one theory—sometimes referred to as unconditional ΔP—holds the following: Given information that A and B, both binary variables, are potential, independent causes of binary E, people take the causal power or efficacy of A to be

$$\Delta P_A = \Pr(E \mid A) - \Pr(E \mid \sim A) \text{ and analogously for B.} \quad (18\text{-}1)$$

Another theory, Cheng's (1997), holds that in the same circumstances, people take the causal power of A to be

$$p_A = \Pr(E \mid A) - \Pr(E \mid \sim A)/[1 - \Pr(E \mid \sim A)]. \quad (18\text{-}2)$$

A, B, and E are to be understood to take either 0 or 1 as values—the values may code for absent or present. Where context should make it unambiguous, as in Equations 18-1 and 18-2, I let, for example, A abbreviate A=1 and ~A abbreviate A=0.

The ΔP relation accords with a linear representation in which

$$\Pr(E) = aA + bB \quad (18\text{-}3)$$

with a and b real constants with a sum that is between 0 and 1. The constants a and b represent the causal power of A and B, respectively, to produce E (Griffiths & Tenenbaum, 2000). Cheng derives her formula for causal power (assuming generative causes) from

$$P(E) = \Pr(A)p_A + \Pr(B)p_B - \Pr(A)\Pr(B)p_A p_B \quad (18\text{-}4)$$

where p_A, p_B are real constants between 0 and 1.

Equation 18-4 results (Glymour, 2003) from taking probabilities on both sides of the Boolean equation:

$$E = (A \cdot q_A) \oplus (B \cdot q_B) \quad (18\text{-}5)$$

where A, B, q_A, q_B are jointly independent Boolean (binary) variables; p_A is the probability that $q_A = 1$, and so on; $\oplus$ is Boolean addition (i.e., ordinary addition except that $1+1=1$); and $\cdot$ is Boolean multiplication (i.e., ordinary multiplication).

The difference in the two theories seems simply to be whether E is regarded as a real additive function of A and B or a Boolean additive function of A and B. There is, however, this question: Are the parameters representing causal power in the ΔP model Equation 18-3, and in Cheng's 1997 model Equation 18-4 and Equation 18-5 invariant to the addition of further independent causes?

The parameters representing causal power in Equation 18-3 are not in general invariant. The reason is obvious: If a further cause C is added to Equation 18-3, with a real constant c, a+b+c must now be less than 1. Either big causes (a+b close to 1) must prevent supplementation of the system with a new big cause or else the values of a and b must shrink with the addition of a new big cause.

Consider a pan balance with a fixed weight W in the left pan and two weights A and B that can be put in the right pan, and let E=1 if the weights in the right pan lower it below the left pan. Let the fulcrum of the pan balance be stochastic and the probability of the left pan rising be dependent on the total weight in the right pan. We have $\Pr(E)=aA+bB$, where A now indicates that A is on the pan, B indicates that B is on the pan, and a/b=Weight (A)/Weight (B), with a+b~1.

Assuming independent identically distributed trials, ΔP_A can be estimated as follows: Take a large number of trials in which A occurs with probability $\Pr(A)$ and B with independent probability P(B).

Estimate $\Pr(E \mid A)$ by the frequency of E when A occurs. Estimate $\Pr(E \mid \sim A)$ by the frequency of E when A does not occur. The difference is ΔP_A, which gives a maximum likelihood estimate of a and is similar for ΔP_B and for b. If a third substantial weight C now is available for the right pan, then we have $\Pr(E)=a'A+b'B+cC$. If $a+b+c>1$, then a' and b' cannot be equal to a and b, respectively. The causal power of A and of B to lower the right pan, as measured by ΔP, depends on the presence or absence of C, although in any intuitive sense the causes A, B, and C do not interact.

In Cheng's theory (1997), $\Pr(E)=\Pr(A)p_A+\Pr(B)p_B-\Pr(A)\Pr(B)p_Ap_B$ when only weights A and B are considered, and when C is added, still assuming independence,

$$\begin{aligned}\Pr(E)=&\Pr(A)p'_A+\Pr(B)p'_B+\Pr(C)p_c\\&-\Pr(A)\Pr(B)p'_Ap'_B-\Pr(A)\Pr(C)p'_Ap_C\\&-\Pr(B)\Pr(C)p_Bp_C\\&+\Pr(A)\Pr(B)\Pr(C)p_{A'}p_Bp_C.\end{aligned} \quad (18\text{-}6)$$

The question is whether $p'_A=p_A$ and so on, assuming that all probabilities for A, B, and E conditional on any values of A, B are unaltered given that $C=0$. But, it follows from that assumption, and from the fact that (6) implies that p'_A can be estimated from cases in which $C=0$, that

$$\begin{aligned}p'_A=&\Pr'(E \mid A, C=0)-\Pr'(E \mid \sim A, C=0)\\&/\Pr'(E \mid \sim A, C=0)\\=&\Pr(E \mid A, C=0)-\Pr(E \mid \sim A, C=0)\\&/\Pr(E \mid \sim A, C=0)=p_A\end{aligned} \quad (18\text{-}7)$$

Cheng's causal powers are invariant under expansion of the set of independent potential causes.

The invariance is in a way an artifact of the assumption that the occurrence of the causes, weights A, B and C, are independent, and the balance pan is stochastic, not deterministic. With a deterministic balance, each weight, or combination of weights, would have a causal power of 1 or of 0. Voting is something like this and is problematic for that very reason. I have no causal power to determine the outcome of an election unless all other votes are tied, but in that case I do have the power to decide the election and so, in analogy, do all other voters. So, one cannot say that any individual voter could never be a cause of the outcome, but the causal power of any individual to determine the outcome is 0 or 1,

depending on how all others voters vote. Invariance fails. The individual causal power cannot be measured in Cheng's way (1997) or in any other I can think of. Causal Bayes nets do not help here at all. The result is a bewilderment in ethics, law, and political philosophy whenever causality is taken to imply counterfactual circumstances on interventions, and responsibility is thought to require causality, and degree of responsibility must be rationally measured. If a change in a single vote for George Bush *l'enfant* would have changed neither the outcome nor the probability of the outcome, then the vote is not, on the principles we have been examining, a cause of his presidency, but that cannot relieve such voters of responsibility for it lest a supermajority in any conspiracy guarantee the innocence of all conspirators.

I do not know what human subjects would say if asked about causal power or efficacy in an experiment of the kind the stochastic pan balance suggests. I recommend the experiment. There remains the normative question regarding whether a quantity should be called a causal power if it does not show the kind of invariance to additional causes that Cheng's (1997) theory provides. Cheng says not, and Woodward (2003), I think, should agree, although this is not a sort of invariance he discusses. I guess I think it is a complicated question about how we sort out the metaphysics of causation. It is easy to imagine cases that might prompt one to doubt that invariance of this kind is essential to causal relations. Zero sum competitions—examples of what is called late preemption in the philosophical literature (Dowe & Nordhoff, 2004)—illustrate one kind of problem.

Consider the poor spermatozoon, trying to fertilize an ovum, in competition with other spermatozoa. Each has a certain probability of success, but that probability changes with the number of competitors. The success of any one defeats the success of any other. I see no obvious way to represent the causal power of a sperm cell so that it is invariant under expansion of independent potential causes, that is, competition from other sperm cells.

Consider the simplest modification of Cheng's framework, in which causal powers constrain one another. In Cheng's representation, $p_A=p(q_A=1)$ is the probability that A causes E given that A occurs, and $q_A=1$ asserts that if A occurs, then A causes E. So, to account for zero sum competition, we could specify that at least one of A, B, q_A, q_B must be zero:

$$E=(q_A \cdot A) \oplus (q_B \cdot B); \qquad (18\text{-}8a)$$

$$A \cdot B \cdot q_A \cdot q_B = 0 \qquad (18\text{-}8b)$$

I understand the invariance of the causal power of A to mean that $Pr(q_A=1)=p_A$ is insensitive to the values of A, B, and q_B. The causal power of A will be invariant only if

$$\begin{aligned}
&Pr(q_A=1 \mid A=1, B=1, q_B=1)\\
&\quad =Pr(q_A=1 \mid A=1, B=0, q_B=1)\\
&\quad =Pr(q_A=1 \mid A=1, B=1, q_B=0)\\
&\quad =Pr(q_A=1 \mid A=1, B=0, q_B=0). \qquad (18.9)
\end{aligned}$$

But, it is immediate from (8b) that $Pr(q_A=1 \mid A=1,$ $B=1,$ $q_B=1)=0$. Hence, the causal power of A (respectively, of B) is invariant only if it is 0. The same point can be made another way. For q_A to be independent in probability of A, B, and q_B, and symmetrically for q_B, we must then have:

$$Pr(A \cdot B \cdot q_A \cdot q_B)=Pr(A)Pr(B)\,Pr(q_A)\,Pr(q_B) \quad (18.10)$$

for all values of the arguments. But, for $A=B=q_B=1$, from (8b) it follows that $Pr(q_A=1 \mid A=B=q_B=1)=0$. Hence, if the probability that $q_A=1$ is other than 0 conditional on any values of A, B, q_B, then it follows that p_A is not invariant.

Cheng's (1997) theory has resources. We might represent the zero-sum competition as a case in which each potential cause of E is also a preventive cause of other potential causes of E, as with:

$$E=[q_A \cdot A \cdot (1-q_{BA}B)] \oplus [q_B \cdot B \cdot (1-q_{AB}A)] \quad (18\text{-}11)$$

where $q_{BA}=1$ if B occurs and B prevents A from causing E and so on, But, this also does not produce invariance of $p_A=Pr(q_A=1)$. To ensure that A and B do not *both* cause E, we must require that $A \cdot B \cdot q_A \cdot$ $q_B \cdot (1-q_{BA}) \cdot (1-q_{AB})=0$. Hence, $p_A=Pr(q_A=1)$ cannot be invariant under all variations of the values of A, B, q_B, q_{BA}, and q_{AB}. To beat the point, if $A \cdot B \cdot q_B^*$ $(1-q_{BA}) \cdot (1-q_{AB})=1$, then p_A must be 0. Similar difficulties arise if we try to deal with the case by supplementing (8a) with an interaction term as did Novick and Cheng (2004).

One could try to represent the zero-sum case as an interaction with a hidden cause of E, but that does not seem to work naturally with causal powers. A zero-sum competition of A, B, for example, could be represented as:

$$E=(q_A \cdot A \cdot C) \oplus (q_B \cdot B \cdot (1-C)) \qquad (18.12)$$

where C is a hidden variable. But, then we have the oddity that $qa=qb=1$. In that case, we may as well dispense with causal powers and assume that total causes determine effects, as Thomas Richardson has suggested children do, and as Luhmann and Ahn (in a rather preposterous essay; in press) have claimed everyone does. One solution, I suppose, is to argue that experiments show that adults make judgments as if they hold causal powers to be less than 1 in many contexts, but treat causal powers as equal to 1 in zero sum competitions. But, if that is so, then in experiments with zero-sum competitions, elicited values of efficacy or causal power should be close to 1. I doubt they would be because I think with independent variables elicited values are likely to approximate the frequency with which a variable causes the effect.

The zero-sum case above is like a race, but more extreme. In observing a race, data are presented regarding who will win—whoever is in the lead just before the finish line. The zero-sum formulas here apply when there are no such data: One and only one will win—cause the effect—but which one does win is either random or determined by unseen values of an unseen variable or variables. A question more interesting to psychology than to metaphysics is whether people do ever interpret sequences as zero-sum competitions of this kind or whether they can be brought to do so by data. After all, "effects" in a zero-sum competition might be interpreted as not causal at all, but as a random occurrence. Consider the following experiment then: Show repeated trials in which three balls of different colors move in parallel toward a black ball, which changes color to match the color of one of the approaching balls, with equal probabilities for each color. Now, for each pair of colored balls, show repeated trials in which the two balls approach the black ball, which changes color at random to match the color of one of the colored balls that is present. I suppose it would be of some interest to know whether, given such evidence and given a new trial in which a ball of a single color is present and approaches the black ball, people now predict that the black ball will change color to match. No matter how that turns out, given the outcomes of such single-color ball trials for balls of each color, I see little choice but to interpret the trials with multiple balls as zero-sum competitions.

Cheng (private communication), has suggested that the statistical and causal structure of a race might be represented by the right-hand side of her equation multiplied by a number that represents the probability of winning the race. The proposal represents a sensible intuition: Individuals have no invariant causal power for winning the race, only a probability of winning. More or less invariant causal powers are attributable only to the component activities that go into running, well or poorly. This brings us back to Sunday Brunch, the horse I rode in on.

Sex, Race, and Bicycles

Finally, consider whether sex and race can be causes. We cannot intervene to change someone's race; we cannot intervene to change someone's sex; yet, we think both features may influence a person's circumstances and the events that befall that person. There are standard remarks that try to evade the proposition, for example, that it is the perception by others of someone's race or sex that are causes, say, of employment or favors or education, not race or sex itself. That will not wash. Perception is the perception of something, and that something, race or sex, seems a cause of resulting treatment. Perception is merely an intermediate in the mechanism by which the effect comes about.

It is the same with many properties. Mountain bikes are stolen more often than touring bikes. If a bicycle is stolen, then it may be *because* it was a mountain bike, but no intervention on *that* bicycle could have made *that* bicycle a touring bike. The counterfactuals may remain in some vague sense true if we understand them as claims about counterpart objects or persons in other possible worlds—she would have got the job if she had been a man; the bike would not have been stolen if it had been a touring bike—but there are no corresponding interventions. Yet, it can be true that the property of being a mountain bike did cause the bicycle to be stolen, and her sex did prevent her from getting the job. Causality is still more subtle than our theories.

ACKNOWLEDGMENTS   I am grateful to Patricia Cheng and to James Woodward, Dave Lagnado, Steve Sloman, and Maddie Glymour for helpful discussions. Research for this chapter was supported in part by a Human Systems Technology grant from the Office of Naval Research to the Florida Institute for Human and Machine Cognition.

References

Cheng, P. (1997). From covariation to causation: A causal power theory. *Psychological Review, 104,* 367–405.

Dowe, P., & Noordhof, P. (Eds.) (2004). *Cause and chance: Causation in an indeterministic world.* Routledge.

Glymour, C. (2003). *The mind's arrows.* Cambridge, MA: MIT Press.

Goldvarg, E., & Johnson-Laird, P. N. (2001). Naïve causality: A mental model theory of causal meaning and reasoning. *Cognitive Science, 25,* 565–610.

Griffiths, T., & Tenenbaum, J. (2000). Structure and strength in causal judgement. *Proceedings of the 2000 Conference on Neural Information Processing.*

Jeffrey, R. (2004). *Subjective probability (the real thing).* Cambridge, England: Cambridge University Press,

Lewis, D. (1999). *Papers in metaphysics and epistemology.* Cambridge, England: Cambridge University Press.

Luhmann, C., & Ahn, B. (in press). The meaning and interpretation of causal power: A critique of Cheng (1997) and of Novick and Cheng (2004). *Psychological Review.*

Mackie, J. (1974). *The cement of the universe.* Oxford, England: Clarendon Press.

Meek, C., & Glymour, C. (1994). Conditioning and intervening. *British Journal for Philosophy of Science, 45,* 1001–1021.

Novick, L., & Cheng, P. (2004). Assessing interactive causal influence. *Psychological Review, 111,* 455–485.

Pearl, J. (2000). *Causality.* New York: Oxford University Press.

Pearson, K. (1911). *The grammar of science.* London: Black.

Reichenbach, H. (1954). *Nomological statements and admissible operations.* Amsterdam: North Holland.

Sloman, S., & Lagnado, D. (2005). Do we "do"? *Cognitive Science 29,* 5–39.

Spirtes, P., Glymour, C. & Scheines, R. (2000). *Causation, prediction and search* (Springer Lecture Notes in Statistics) (2nd ed.). Cambridge, MA: MIT Press. (Original work published 1993).

Woodward, J. (2003). *Making things happen.* New York: Oxford University Press.

19

Intuitive Theories as Grammars for Causal Inference

Joshua B. Tenenbaum, Thomas L. Griffiths, & Sourabh Niyogi

Introduction

This chapter considers a set of questions at the interface of the study of intuitive theories, causal knowledge, and problems of inductive inference. By an intuitive theory, we mean a cognitive structure that in some important ways is analogous to a scientific theory. It is becoming broadly recognized that intuitive theories play essential roles in organizing our most basic knowledge of the world, particularly for causal structures in physical, biological, psychological, or social domains (Atran, 1995; Carey, 1985a; Kelley, 1973; McCloskey, 1983; Murphy & Medin, 1985; Nichols & Stich, 2003). A principal function of intuitive theories in these domains is to support the learning of new causal knowledge: generating and constraining people's hypotheses about possible causal relations; highlighting variables, actions, and observations likely to be informative about those hypotheses: and guiding people's interpretation of the data they observe (Ahn & Kalish, 2000; Pazzani, 1987; Pazzani, Dyer, & Flowers, 1986; Waldmann, 1996). Leading accounts of cognitive development argue for the importance of intuitive theories in children's mental lives and frame the major transitions of cognitive development as instances of theory change (Carey, 1985a; Gopnik & Meltzoff, 1997; Inagaki & Hatano, 2002; Wellman & Gelman, 1992).

Here, we attempt to lay out some prospects for understanding the structure, function, and acquisition of intuitive theories from a rational computational perspective. From this viewpoint, theory-like representations are not just a convenient way of summarizing certain aspects of human knowledge. They provide crucial foundations for successful learning and reasoning, and we want to understand how they do so. With this goal in mind, we focus on three interrelated questions (Table 19-1). First, what is the content of intuitive theories? What kinds of knowledge are represented and in what formats? Second, how do intuitive theories guide the acquisition of new knowledge? Theories subserve multiple cognitive functions, but their role in guiding learning is surely one of the most fundamental. Third, how are intuitive theories acquired? What, if anything, do mechanisms for theory-guided learning have in common with mechanisms for learning at this more abstract level—for

TABLE 19-1 Three Questions About Intuitive Theories

1. What is the content and representational structure of intuitive theories?
2. How do intuitive theories guide the acquisition of new causal knowledge?
3. How are intuitive theories themselves acquired?

acquiring or revising a theory itself? It goes without saying that these questions are profound and difficult ones. Our inquiry is at an early stage, and any answers we can give here are at best preliminary.

We adopt a "reverse-engineering" approach to these questions, aiming to explain what intuitive theories bring to human cognition in terms that would be valuable in designing an artificial computational system faced with the same learning and reasoning challenges (Anderson, 1990; Chater, 1999; Marr, 1982; Oaksford & Shepard, 1987). This approach proceeds in two stages. First, we identify a core set of computational problems that intuitive theories help to solve, focusing on the role of theories in learning and reasoning about causal systems. Second, we propose a formal framework, based upon the principles of Bayesian inference, for understanding how these computational problems may be solved—and thus for understanding how intuitive theories may fulfill some of their crucial functions.

There are many places one could start in characterizing the functional roles that intuitive theories play in cognition. From a reverse-engineering viewpoint, it makes sense to start with causal learning and reasoning—behaviors that have dramatic consequences for people's success and survival in the world and for which intuitive theories seem to play a critical role. Everyday causal inference operates under severe conditions, far more challenging than the scientist's preferred setting of a controlled laboratory experiment. A medic arriving at a trauma scene may need to make a snap judgment about what is wrong with the victim after seeing just a few suspicious symptoms; there is no time for exhaustive tests. A child may discover a new causal relation given only a few observations of a novel system, even in the presence of hidden variables or complex dynamics. Successful causal inferences in the presence of sparse data require strong expectations about what types of causal hypotheses are possible, plausible, or likely a priori. To learn and reason about novel causal systems, these expectations must go far beyond mere records of previous experience. Intuitive theories provide the

necessary glue between the inferential past and present. They specify general causal principles, abstracted from prior experience, that allow us quickly and reliably to generate appropriate spaces of hypotheses for causal inference and to apprehend an infinite range of new causal systems.

Because causal inference can unfold on multiple levels of abstraction, intuitive theories must also be defined on multiple levels. To reason about the causes behind a specific observed event, we need intuitive theories that generate hypotheses for alternative configurations of causes for that event. To learn the structure of causal relations between variables in a system, we need intuitive theories that generate hypotheses about alternative causal structures for that system. To learn such a theory itself, we need higher-order intuitive theories that generate hypotheses about theories at the next level down. The need to characterize theories at more than one level of abstraction is familiar from debates in the philosophy of science (Carnap, 1956; Kuhn, 1970; Lakatos, 1970; Laudan, 1977; Quine, 1951; see Godfrey-Smith, 2003, for a review) and has also been introduced into research on cognitive development through Wellman's distinction between specific theories and framework theories (Wellman, 1990; Wellman & Gelman, 1992). Such a hierarchy of theory representations provides a unifying approach to inferring the causes of individual events, identifying the structure of causal relations between variables in a system, and learning about the abstract structure of higher-order theories—all from finite and often sparse data.

Consideration of the role of theories in causal inference places constraints on the formalisms that can be used to represent intuitive theories. In particular, we argue that one widely used framework for representing causal relationships, known as causal graphical models or causal Bayesian networks (Glymour, 2001; Pearl, 2000), is not sufficiently expressive to represent intuitive theories in their full generality and power. While Bayesian networks may be able to represent the lowest level of causal theories in our hierarchy, they cannot express the kind of abstract principles that are a key part of higher-level theories. In making this argument, we draw an analogy to generative grammar in linguistics: a Bayesian network that describes the causal structure of a particular causal system is like a parse tree that describes the syntactic structure of a particular sentence. Of deeper and more general significance in linguistics is the set of abstract principles—the grammar—that generates all possible parse trees for the infinite but constrained set of grammatical sentences in a given language. So, too, in the study of causal inference should our focus be on theories at this more abstract level: causal grammars that generate hypothesis spaces of possible causal networks in a given domain of reasoning.

Construing intuitive theories as causal grammars helps to clarify the computational problems that a formal account of theories must address, as each of these problems has a direct analogue in linguistics. The analogy also suggests how such problems can be solved. The second stage of our reverse engineering of intuitive theories consists of formalizing the inferences involved in learning and reasoning about causal systems in a Bayesian framework. Any Bayesian inference requires a space of candidate hypotheses and a prior probability distribution over that hypothesis space. We cast intuitive theories *as hypothesis space generators*, systems of knowledge that generate the hypothesis spaces that make Bayesian causal inference possible. Drawing on the idea that theories are defined at multiple levels, we adopt a hierarchical Bayesian framework in which intuitive theories defined at each level of the hierarchy generate hypothesis spaces for the more specific level below. This hierarchical Bayesian proposal specifies precise functional roles for intuitive theories in causal learning and offers an approach to answering our second and third questions from Table 19-1: how theories guide the acquisition of new causal knowledge and how theories themselves can be learned.

Approaching the computational problems posed by intuitive theories from the perspective of Bayesian inference ultimately provides us with the opportunity to assess answers to our first question—what is the knowledge content of intuitive causal theories?—in terms of how well they function in this formal framework. Many possible representational structures for causal knowledge could be interpreted as theories in our hierarchical Bayesian framework, and they may coexist at different levels of the hierarchy. In this chapter, we have little to say about the precise nature of these representations, beyond the argument

that causal Bayesian networks are too limited to capture the content of higher-level intuitive theories. A detailed discussion of two more promising approaches for representing higher-level theories, or causal grammars, is the subject of a companion chapter (Griffiths & Tenenbaum, chapter 20 this volume).

Intuitive Theories as Causal Networks

Although computational accounts of intuitive theories have not been readily forthcoming, significant progress has been made recently in the related area of causal network modeling. By a causal network, we mean a set of causal relations that holds among variables representing states of affairs in the world, which may or may not be observable. The tools of causal graphical models, causal Bayesian networks, and functional causal models (Heckerman, 1998; Pearl, 2000; Spirtes, Glymour, & Scheines, 1993; see also this volume), provide formal frameworks for representing, reasoning about, and learning causal relationships. These approaches explicate the connection between causality and statistical dependence. They distinguish causality from mere correlation or association, and they show how and under which-circumstances causal relations can be induced from observations of the statistical dependencies between variables.

Causal networks have already received some attention in the cognitive science literature as rational accounts of adult and child behavior in causal learning experiments (Glymour, 2001; Gopnik & Glymour, 2002; Gopnik et al., 2004; Gopnik & Schulz, 2004; Griffiths, Baraff, & Tenenbaum, 2004; Griffiths & Tenenbaum, in press; Lagnado & Sloman, 2004; Sloman, Lagnado, and Waldmann, this volume; Sobel, Tenenbaum, & Gopnik, 2004; Steyvers, Tenenbaum, Wagenmakers, & Blum, 2003; Tenenbaum, Sobel, Griffiths, & Gopnik, submitted; Tenenbaum & Griffiths, 2001, 2003; Waldmann, 1996). These applications have been fairly small scale. Subjects typically learn about one or a few causal relations from a small number of observations. The successful application of causal networks in these cases raises the question of whether some of the same computational tools could be applicable to larger-scale problems of cognitive development, in particular to elucidating the structure and origins of our intuitive causal theories.

The most direct line of attack is simply to identify intuitive theories with causal networks. This is how we read the proposal of Gopnik and colleagues (Gopnik & Glymour, 2002; Gopnik & Schulz, 2004), and it is related to Rehder's proposal for modeling "theory-based" categorization, or categorization based on "theoretical knowledge," using causal networks (Rehder, 2003, chapter this volume). An appealing feature of this proposal is that it suggests a set of ready answers to our three guiding questions about the structure and function of intuitive theories (Table 19-1). What are intuitive theories? They are (something like) causal graphical models. How are theories formed? Using (something like) the existing learning algorithms in the graphical models literature (Pearl, 2000; Spirtes et al., 1993). How are theories used to guide learning of new causal relations? By providing constraints for causal model learning algorithms based on the structure of previously learned causal relations.[1] In short, the proposal to model intuitive theories as causal networks promises to fill in the missing foundations of a computational account of cognitive development by drawing on already established and well-understood formal tools.

This proposition is tempting; there is clearly something "theory-like" about causal graphical models. Yet, these models are also fundamentally limited in ways that intuitive theories are not. Most accounts of intuitive theories in cognitive development emphasize the importance of abstract concepts and causal laws, in terms of which people can construct causal explanations for the phenomena in some domain (Carey, 1985b; Wellman, 1990). Causal graphical models may often be useful for representing the causal explanations that an intuitive theory generates, but they do not and cannot represent the abstract concepts and causal laws that are the core of the theory and that set the terms in which those causal explanations are constructed.

To illustrate the strengths and weaknesses of viewing theories as causal graphical models, consider Graph 1, shown in Figure 19-1. This network might represent some aspects of a person's knowledge about several common diseases, their effects (symptoms), and causes (risky behaviors). It can support probabilistic causal inferences (as a Bayesian network) if we assign to each variable a probability distribution conditioned on its parents (direct causes) in the network (Pearl, 1988, 2000). Such a representation is theory-like in several ways. Most fundamentally, it permits causal inferences to be made from sparse data. Given one or more

observed symptoms in a sick individual, the network suggests a constrained set of causal explanations: the presence of one or more diseases causally linked to those symptoms. The network also assigns relative probabilities to those hypotheses. If some of the patient's relevant behaviors are observed as well, then those probabilities over the hidden disease variables will change to reflect the most probable routes from observed behaviors to observed symptoms. For instance, if a person is coughing, then that suggests they might suffer from bronchitis or flu but provides no indication of heart disease. Observing that they also suffer from a headache would increase the probability of flu; observing that they habitually smoke would increase the probability of bronchitis.

What this network description misses is theoretical knowledge of a more abstract kind: knowledge about classes of causal variables and laws governing the causal relations between those classes. For instance, there appears to be a common domain theory underlying Graphs 1–4 but not Graph 5 or Graph 6. Graphs 2–4 differ from Graph 1 in the precise causal links they posit: Graph 2 posits that smoking causes flu but not lung cancer; Graph 3 represents only a subset of the conditions that Graph 1 does but includes all the same causal links defined on that subset; Graph 4 posits a novel unnamed disease linking working in a factory with chest pain. Yet, Graphs 1–4 all express the same abstract regularities, which could be characterized in terms of two principles:

> **P1**: There exist three classes of variables: *Symptoms*, *Diseases*, and *Behaviors*. These classes are open and of unspecified size, allowing the possibility that a new variable may be introduced, such as the new disease in Graph 4.

> **P2**: Causal relations between variables are constrained with respect to these classes: direct links arise only from behaviors to diseases and from diseases to symptoms. These links may be overlapping (e.g., diseases tend to have multiple effects, and symptoms tend to have multiple causes).

Principles P1 and P2 are not explicitly represented in Graphs 1–4, although they are instantiated in those networks. No single causal network defined over particular behaviors, diseases, and symptoms (e.g., *Smoking*, *Bronchitis*, *Coughing*) could capture these principles. Rather, P1 and P2 specify a large

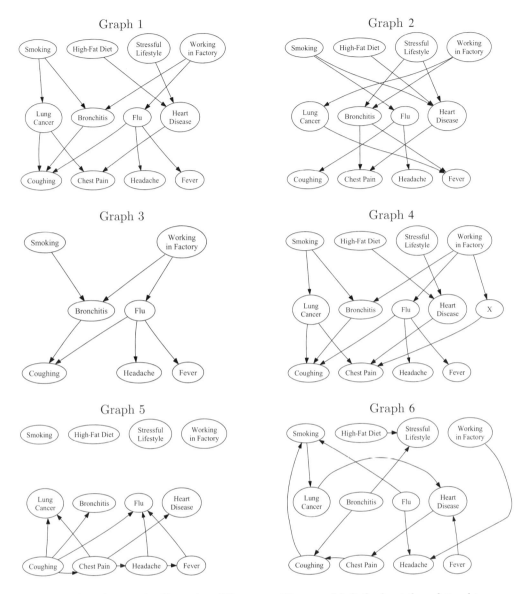

FIGURE 19-1 Causal networks illustrating different possible sets of beliefs about the relationships among behaviors, diseases, and symptoms.

(potentially infinite) but constrained class of causal networks, which includes Graphs 1–4 but excludes Graphs 5 and 6. We view this more abstract level of knowledge as a core component of intuitive domain theories. Although knowledge of a causal network structure like Graph 1 may support reasoning from effects to causes in specific situations, it is knowledge of abstract principles like P1 and P2—transcending any specific network—that allows people to formulate appropriate hypotheses for new causal structures in a given domain and thereby to learn and reason

about novel causal relations or causal systems so effectively.

Framework Theories and Specific Theories

Although not the focus of contemporary research on causal learning and reasoning, abstract causal knowledge at the level of principles P1 and P2 has traditionally been recognized as critical in both scientific and intuitive theories. Twentieth century philosophers of science often distinguished the day-to-day level of theorizing from a more abstract framework level of theoretical knowledge—principles, concepts, or terms that shape the possible specific theories a scientist can construct (Godfrey-Smith, 2003). Such an abstract level of knowledge appears in Carnap's (1956) "linguistic frameworks," Kuhn's (1970) "paradigms," Lakatos's (1970) "research programs," and Laudan's (1977) "research traditions."

Inspired by this line of thinking, Wellman and Gelman (1992) formulated a distinction between specific and framework theories that they argued would be useful for understanding children's intuitive theories of the world:

> Specific theories are detailed scientific formulations about a delimited set of phenomena.... Framework theories outline the ontology and the basic causal devices for their specific theories, thereby defining a coherent form of reasoning about a particular set of phenomena. (p. 341)

Although she does not explicitly distinguish these two levels of theory structure, Carey (1985b) clearly seems to have framework-level knowledge in mind when she characterizes a child's theory as follows:

> A theory consists of three interrelated components: a set of phenomena that are in its domain, the causal laws and other explanatory mechanisms in terms of which the phenomena are accounted for, and the concepts in terms of which the phenomena and explanatory apparatus are expressed. (p. 394)

Traditionally, both philosophers of science and cognitive developmentalists have considered framework-level theories to be in some sense deeper and more fundamental than specific theories. A framework expresses the abstract causal principles that hold across all systems in a broad domain, providing a language for constructing specific theories of those systems. Specific theories, though they carry much of the burden for everyday prediction, explanation, and planning, thus cannot be acquired or even formulated without the machinery of framework theories. The most dramatic instances of theory change are thought to take place at the level of frameworks, as in Kuhn's paradigm shifts, or the conceptual revolutions of childhood studied by Carey (1985a), Wellman (1990), and others. At the same time, the role of specific theories and their interaction with framework-level knowledge cannot be ignored. Framework theories typically come into contact with the raw data of experience only through the specific theories that they generate. A framework is only as good as the specific theories it supports.

In sum, if our ultimate goal is a computational understanding of intuitive theories and their place in causal inference, we need to develop formal tools for representing both framework and specific theories and formal tools for inference and learning that account for how specific theories support predictions and explanations about specific events, how framework theories support the construction and acquisition of specific theories in their domain, and how framework theories themselves may be acquired. Clearly, our current state of understanding is far from meeting these requirements. We are in a position, however, to make progress on a more constrained version of this program: developing formal tools that allow us to represent abstract causal knowledge like principles P1 and P2, to understand the role of this knowledge in learning and reasoning about specific causal networks like Graph 1, and to explain how such knowledge itself could be acquired. This is our goal for the remainder of this chapter and chapter 20.

The relationship between principles P1 and P2 and causal graphical models is analogous to the relationship between framework and specific theories in several ways. Like a specific theory, Graph 1 spells out the causal relationships that hold among a delimited set of variables. The network does not explicitly represent any framework-level knowledge—anything that resembles an ontology or causal laws defined over the entities identified within that ontology. The network also does not define "a coherent form of reasoning" for the disease domain, which would extend beyond the particular variables already specified in the network to learning about novel diseases, symptoms, or behaviors.

Relative to a specific causal network like Graph 1, the abstract principles P1 and P2 provide something more like framework-level knowledge. These principles specify an ontology of kinds of causally relevant variables (P1) and the basic causal laws (P2) that can be used to construct causal networks like Graphs 1–4. Just as framework theories provide the explanatory principles from which specific theories in a domain are built, the principles P1 and P2 identify the relationships from which causal networks can be built in the disease domain. If someone tells you about a new disease Y, then P1 and P2 lead you to expect that Y will have some symptoms and some behavioral causes, and that these causes and effects may overlap with one or more familiar diseases. If you observe a novel combination of familiar symptoms in a sick individual, then P1 and P2 suggest that a possible explanation is the existence of a new hidden variable—a new disease causally linked to those symptoms—rather than a web of new connections between the symptoms themselves.

A change in an individual's framework theory may fundamentally alter the specific theories they can construct (e.g., Wellman, 1990) or even the concepts they can be said to possess (Carey, 1985a; Gopnik & Meltzoff, 1997). Likewise, a change in the principles P1 and P2 would lead a learner to construct qualitatively different types of causal network structures and to reason about diseases in fundamentally different ways—perhaps even to the point at which we would no longer say they had the same concept *Disease*. Graph 5 appears to derive from the same ontology as Graph 1 (i.e., P1), but instead of P2 follows a set of causal laws that we might call P2′: symptoms cause diseases rather than the other way around, symptoms also cause other symptoms, and there are no links between behaviors and the other conditions. P1 and P2′ may reflect a logically possible alternative (if nonveridical) theoretical framework, with a coherent but different mode of reasoning from that of P1 and P2. In contrast, someone whose beliefs correspond to Graph 6 appears to lack a coherent mode of reasoning in this domain. Graph 6 is inconsistent with both P1 and P2 or seemingly with any ontology and causal laws that would give some regularity to its structure of causal links. Somebody whose beliefs are represented by Graph 6 not only has different beliefs about how particular diseases work than someone whose beliefs correspond to Graph 1 but seems not to possess the same ontological concepts of *Disease*, *Symptom*, or *Behavior*—at least not in the causally relevant sense; they do not know how diseases in general work.

To clarify, we do not mean to suggest that P1 and P2 should necessarily be seen as a framework theory in Wellman and Gelman's sense, or that Graph 1 should be seen as a specific theory, but only that the relation between these two levels of causal knowledge is analogous to the relation between frameworks and specific theories. When cognitive developmentalists speak of a child's framework theory, they are typically referring to much more abstract knowledge than P1 and P2, with much broader scope sufficient to encompass a full domain of intuitive biology or intuitive psychology. Yet, we see value in treating the concepts of framework theory and specific theory as relative notions, with more abstract frameworks providing constraints on more specific models across multiple levels of abstraction and scope. Relative to knowledge about a specific causal network such as Graph 1, principles such as P1 and P2 do appear to play a framework-like role. If we can develop formal tools for understanding how theoretical knowledge operates at both of these levels and how they interact in learning and inference, then we expect to have made real progress toward the larger program of a computational understanding of intuitive theories.

Intuitive Theories as Causal Grammars

The proposal to identify intuitive theories with causal networks appeared promising in large part because the formal tools of causal graphical models offered ready answers to the questions we raised in the introduction (Table 19-1): What is the representational content of theories, how do theories support new inferences, and how are theories themselves learned? But, as we have just argued, this view of intuitive theories does not address the structure, function, or acquisition of more abstract framework-like causal knowledge, such as principles P1 and P2 or the relation between these abstract principles and learning and reasoning with specific causal networks. The remainder of this chapter and chapter 20 describe some initial attempts to approach these questions formally.

Our work on intuitive theories has been guided by an analogy to the linguist's project of working out generative grammars for natural languages and accounting for the use and learnability of those grammars (Chomsky, 1965, 1986). This causal grammar analogy (Tenenbaum & Niyogi, 2003) has been so fruitful for us that it is worth discussing in some detail here, both to motivate the specific proposals we offer and to provide more general suggestions for how future work on intuitive theories might proceed.

There is a long history of analogies between linguistic grammars and scientific theories, dating back at least to Chomsky's early work on generative grammar in language (Chomsky, 1956, 1962). Chomsky characterized a native speaker's knowledge of grammar as "an implicit theory of that language that he has mastered, a theory that predicts the grammatical structure of each of an infinite class of potential physical events" (Chomsky, 1962, p. 528). Chomsky (1956) explicitly speaks of an analogy between theories and grammars:

> Any scientific theory is based on a certain finite set of observations and, by establishing general laws stated in terms of certain hypothetical constructs, it attempts to account for these observations, to show how they are interrelated, and to predict an indefinite number of new phenomena.... Similarly, a grammar is based on a finite number of observed sentences . . . and it "projects" this set to an infinite set of grammatical sentences by establishing general "laws"... [framed in terms of] phonemes, words, phrases, and so on.... (p. 113)

It is striking—if not necessarily surprising—how closely Chomsky's characterization of grammatical knowledge here resembles the characterization of framework-level intuitive theories in cognitive development, as exemplified by the quotations from Carey and Wellman and Gelman in the preceding section. Central to the Chomskyan program has always been an analogy between the descriptive goals of the linguist and the goals of the child learning language. Both are engaged in a form of theory building, seeking to identify the general laws and grammatical categories that govern a language's structure, based on observations of primary linguistic data and guided by some (metatheoretic or innate) constraints on the space of candidate grammars.

Chomsky's grammars-as-theories analogy was intended to motivate hypotheses about the content and function of linguistic grammars, but here we use the analogy in the opposite direction, to inspire models for intuitive theories based on the development of generative grammar in linguistics. Arguably, this is now the more profitable direction in which to run the analogy. The last 50 years have seen significant progress in formal and computational models for language—but not so much progress in understanding causal theories, either intuitive or scientific.[2] We first review some relevant ideas from generative grammar in language and then discuss their implications for theories of causal grammar.

A Bird's-Eye View of Generative Grammar

Figure 19-2 introduces the grammar analogy through several intuitive (if perhaps overly simplistic) examples.

Like the sample causal networks for different disease theories shown in Figure 19-1, Figure 19-2 shows samples of hypothetical utterances and syntactic (phrase structure) analyses for several simplified languages. These examples clearly do not begin to approach the richness of natural language, any more than the examples shown in Figure 19-1 approach the richness of our intuitive knowledge about diseases (or biology more generally). The aim is merely to illustrate how knowledge of syntactic structure in language, as with intuitive theories in causal domains, can be usefully characterized in terms of multiple interacting levels of abstraction and to suggest parallels between the sorts of representations that could be useful in linguistic grammars and causal theories.

Figure 19-2a shows utterances from a simplified English-like language. Informally, each sentence consists of a subject noun followed by a verb phrase, and each verb phrase consists of a verb followed by a noun (the direct object). This phrase structure is depicted with the skeleton of a parse tree above each utterance in the figure. It is a canonical form for many simple sentences in English or other languages with SVO (subject-verb-object) word ordering.

Figure 19-2b shows different utterances apparently in the same language, obeying the same syntactic principles. Hearing a speaker utter these sentences, we would not doubt that the individual speaks English (or a simplified version thereof), even though we might be suspicious of the particular beliefs they appear to hold. The situation is analogous to Graph 2 in Figure 19-1, representing the beliefs of an individual who has the standard framework-level understanding of what behaviors, diseases, and symptoms are and how they are causally related, but who has different beliefs about the specific causal links that exist between particular behaviors, diseases, and symptoms.

Figure 19-2c shows a case analogous to Graph 5 in Figure 19-1: an individual who appears to follow a consistent grammar defined over the same syntactic categories and the same lexical items as the speakers represented in Figures 19-2a and 19-2b, but with different rules prescribing how these categories can be combined to form possible syntactic structures. In particular, the utterances in Figure 19-2c appear to obey SOV (subject-object-verb) ordering, as is characteristic of Korean, Japanese, Turkish, and many other languages, rather than the SVO ordering characteristic of English.

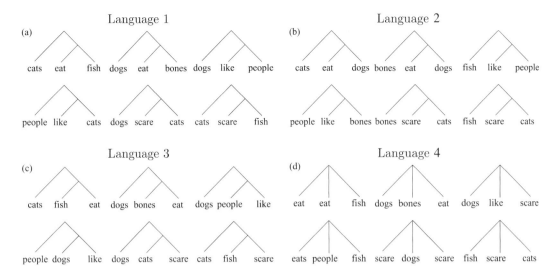

FIGURE 19-2 Example sentences and syntactic structures for several simplified languages.

Finally, Figure 19-2d shows a case analogous to Graph 6 in Figure 19-1: an individual who appears to follow no consistent grammar or at least no grammar that constrains the set of possible utterances based on syntactic rules or categories that are at all like those in English.

More formally, theories of generative grammar posit at least four levels of structure to knowledge of language, which may serve as a guide for how to think about corresponding levels of abstraction in intuitive theories. These levels of representation are quite distinct in their forms but are functionally interdependent: each higher level of abstraction *generates* the structures at the level below, and thus constrains the possible lower-level structures that could be encountered. Language comprehension and language acquisition—the main computations for which the language faculty is responsible—are processes of inductive inference that can be defined in terms of this representational hierarchy. In both comprehension and acquisition, the challenge is to infer some unobservable structure at an intermediate level of abstraction by integrating observed data from a lower level generated by that structure and constraints on possible forms for that structure generated by higher levels of the abstraction hierarchy.

These four levels of structure in language can be loosely characterized as shown in Figure 19-3a The lowest, most concrete level are utterances: sequences of words, spoken or written. One level up

in abstraction are syntactic structures: parse trees or other hierarchical representations of phrase structure over which the meanings of utterances are defined. Language comprehension—or, more precisely, syntactic comprehension or parsing—is the process of inferring the syntactic structure that gave rise to an observed utterance. This inference problem presents an inductive challenge because the set of possible syntactic structures that can be inferred for any language is, in principle, infinite in extent and complexity, and the data almost always underdetermine the true underlying structure.

To explain how people can recover an infinite set of syntactic structures from appropriate linguistic utterances, linguists posit a third level of knowledge more abstract than any syntactic structure. The grammar—or, more precisely, the syntax—of the language generates a strongly constrained (but still infinite) space of candidate syntactic structures that could be hypothesized to explain utterances in that language. Although there is no universal consensus on the content or architecture of syntax, most theories are based on some set of abstract categories and rules for how those elements in those categories can be composed to generate allowable syntactic structures. Figure 19-3a labels this level of knowledge "syntactic categories and rules," but for shorthand we may refer to it simply as the "syntax" or the "grammar" of the language.

To give a concrete example, in the case of the simplified language in Figure 19-2a the syntax could be specified by means of a *context-free grammar*, with the categories N, V, VP, and S, and the following rewrite rules:

$$S \to N\ VP$$
$$VP \to V\ N$$
$$N \to \{dogs \mid cats \mid fish \mid people \mid bones \mid \ldots\}$$
$$V \to \{eat \mid like \mid scare \mid \ldots\}. \tag{19-1}$$

A speaker who grasps these abstract rules of syntax, and who recognizes that the syntactic categories of nouns and verbs are open classes (capable of adding new words), can effectively produce and understand an infinite set of grammatical utterances—not just the limited sample depicted in Figure 19-2a. On hearing the novel utterance "Dogs like blickets," these principles would allow a competent listener to infer that "blickets" is in the N (noun) category, and hence that "people like blickets" and "blickets eat bones" are also grammatical (if not necessarily true) utterances.

This grammar is sufficiently simple that there are no parsing ambiguities for the utterances in Figure 19-2a. Each utterance can be generated by the grammar in exactly one way. But in natural language use, syntactic ambiguity is common, which has led to the development of probabilistic grammars. Probabilistic grammars (see Charniak, 1993; Jurafsky & Martin, 2000; Manning & Schütze, 1999) augment the deterministic rules of traditional grammars with probabilities, so that each grammar now specifies a probability distribution over the possible syntactic structures in a language (and, typically, over possible utterances as well). Identifying the syntactic structure most likely to have given rise to a particular observed sentence then becomes a well-posed problem of statistical inference: selecting from among all syntactic structures that represent consistent parses of the sentence the structure that has highest probability under the probabilistic grammar.

Besides the problem of parsing, the other great inductive challenge in language is the problem of grammar acquisition: inferring the correct categories and rules of syntax from primary linguistic data. Like parsing, grammar acquisition also requires would-be language users to infer unobservable structures from highly underconstrained data. In principle, there is no limit to the number of grammars that could be posited to explain a given corpus of utterances. For instance, the utterances in Figure 19-2a could have been produced from the following grammar:

$$S \to A\ A\ A$$
$$N \to \{dogs \mid cats \mid fish \mid people \mid bones \mid \quad (19\text{-}2)$$
$$eat \mid like \mid scare \mid \ldots\},$$

in which there are no distinguished syntactic categories and no meaningful constraints on allowable word combinations.

To explain how children acquire the grammar of their native language, linguists have proposed a solution that is parallel to the standard account of parsing but is elevated in abstraction. Hence the highest level of structure shown in Figure 19-3, *Universal Grammar* or UG. UG comprises the innate knowledge that every child brings to the task of language acquisition. Just as the grammar of a language generates a constrained space of syntactic structures that could serve as hypotheses for parsing in that language, the principles of UG could be said to generate a highly constrained space of possible grammars for all human languages, thereby enabling grammar acquisition to occur in the face of what would otherwise be severely inadequate data (Nowak, Komarova, & Niyogi, 2003). For instance, it may be reasonable to posit that UG rules out grammars such as (19-2) and allows grammars such as (19-1).

As in the comprehension of syntactic structure, deterministic constraints on possible hypotheses are not sufficient to remove all ambiguities in acquisition and ensure that the correct grammar can simply be deduced from the observed data. Again, some type of probabilistic inference is required. To illustrate why, consider the following grammar:

$$S \to N\ VP$$
$$VP \to V\ N$$
$$N \to \{dogs \mid cats \mid fish \mid people \mid bones \mid \ldots\}$$
$$V \to \{eat \mid like \mid scare \mid fish \mid people \mid \ldots\}. \tag{19-3}$$

This grammar is just like (19-1) except that fish and people are now categorized as verbs (V) in addition to nouns (N). It is surely not in violation of the principles of UG for words to be categorized as both nouns and verbs. Indeed, many words in English bear such dual identities (including the words "fish" and "people"). Or, consider another grammar,

$$S \to N\ VP$$
$$VP \to V$$
$$VP \to V\ N \tag{19-4}$$
$$N \to \{dogs \mid cats \mid fish \mid people \mid bones \mid \ldots\}$$
$$V \to \{eat \mid like \mid scare \mid \ldots\},$$

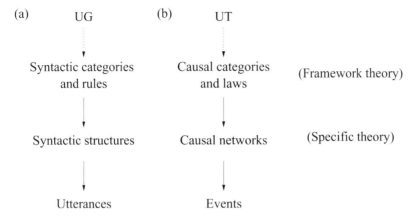

FIGURE 19-3 An analogy between multiple levels of structure in (a) knowledge of language and (b) causal knowledge. Each level generates structures at the level below, thereby establishing necessary constraints on the hypothesis space for inductive inference. UG, universal grammar; UT, universal theory.

which allows verbs to appear in intransitive forms, such as "cats eat," in addition to the transitive forms (e.g., "cats eat fish") shown in Figure 19-2a and generated by grammars (19-1) or (19-3). Again, UG should clearly allow grammars of this sort.

How could language learners infer which of these grammars is the true generative system for their language? In particular, how are they to know that certain rules should be included in the grammar, and others that seem equally plausible by the standards of UG (and that would in fact be correct in other languages) should be excluded? Probabilistic inference again provides a principled framework for answering these questions (e.g., Charniak, 1993). Probabilistic methods can identify the correct grammar underlying a corpus of utterances because the correct grammar should assign the observed utterances higher probabilities than will incorrect grammars. Under the hierarchical scheme of Figure 19-3, a grammar assigns probabilities to possible utterances through a two-stage process, by generating syntactic structures with various probabilities, which in turn give rise to concrete utterances with various probabilities. The correct grammar will generate all and only the syntactic structures necessary to give rise to the observed utterances. Alternative grammar hypothesis will be hurt by *undergenerating*—failing to generate syntactic structures necessary to produce a class of observed utterances—or by *overgenerating*—generating syntactic structures that are not part of the language and that would give rise to a class of utterances not in fact observed. Either under- or overgeneration in a

grammar hypothesis would lead to less accurate probabilistic expectations about the observed utterance data and hence weaker inductive support for the grammar.

One final inference problem in language is worth noting for the sake of the causal analogy: inferences at the lowest level of Figure 19-3a, about partially observed utterances. Because the speech signal is inherently noisy, any individual word in isolation may be mistaken for a similar-sounding word, and listeners would be well served if they could interpolate potentially misheard words from the context of more clearly perceived surrounding words. Because language must be processed online in real time, listeners would also be well served if they could predict later words in an utterance from the context of earlier words. These inferences at the utterance level may be given the same treatment as inferences at higher levels of Figure 19-3a. Just as UG generates a constrained hypothesis space of possible grammars for a language, and just as a grammar generates a constrained hypothesis space of possible syntactic structures for an utterance, a syntactic structure generates a constrained hypothesis space of possible complete utterances that can be used to guide interpolations or predictions about missing words. For instance, if a speaker of the language in Figure 19-2a hears "dogs scare . . ." it is a better bet that ". . ." should be filled in by "cats," "people," or "fish" than by "like" or "eat" (or by nothing) because the most likely syntactic structure underlying "dogs scare . . ." suggests that ". . ." should be a noun rather than a verb or silence. This sort of inference is a central component of state-of-the-art speech-recognition systems based on probabilistic grammars (Jurafsky & Martin, 2000) and is probably important in human language processing as well.

In sum, human language users draw inductive inferences about unobserved structure at each level of the hierarchy in Figure 19-3a, based on data from lower levels and constraints from higher levels. Each level of structure can be viewed as a generator of hypothesis spaces for candidate structures at the next level down and, indirectly, for all levels below it. Because every level above the utterance is unobserved (and typically even the utterance level is only partially observed), it is critical that inferences at all levels be able to proceed in parallel, based on only partial input from levels above and below. The child learning language will typically be uncertain not only about the grammar of that language, but also about the syntactic structure of many utterances heard, as well as some of the words in each utterance. Yet, somehow, after only a few years of experience, every normal child becomes an expert on all these levels. The inferential machinery underlying language learning and use must thus support a hierarchy of interlocking probabilistic inferences, operating over multiple levels of increasingly abstract representations.

Toward Causal Grammars

We have invested some energy here in reviewing elements of generative grammar because all of these elements—and the whole picture of language they support—have valuable parallels in the realm of intuitive causal theories. These parallels include:

- The decomposition of knowledge representation into at least four levels of increasingly abstract structure.
- The kinds of representational ingredients required at each level.
- The nature of the inductive problems to be solved at each level and the factors that make these problems challenging.
- The manner in which levels interact, with each level generating a hypothesis space of candidate structures for the level below.
- The importance of probabilistic generative processes, which support hierarchical probabilistic inferences upward from observed data at the lowest level to multiple higher levels of abstraction.

Of course, there are other important disanalogies between the fields, and flaws even in the parallels we focus, on but still the analogy as a whole offers important lessons for how to develop formal treatments of intuitive causal theories.

Figure 19-3b shows a four-level decomposition of representation in causal theories—analogous to the four-level picture of linguistic knowledge in 19-3a. The data at the lowest, most concrete level consist of events, or instances in which the variables in a causal system take on particular values. In causal inference, these events are interpreted as having been generated from a structure one level up, a network of cause-effect relations, such as Graph 1 in the disease domain. Just as a particular linguistic utterance may be derived from an abstract syntactic structure by choosing specific words to fill the abstract categories in the structure, a particular event configuration may be generated by choosing values for each variable in a causal network conditioned on its direct causes. The formal tools of causal graphical models can be used to describe these two levels of structure and their interaction. In particular, the standard problem of inference in causal graphical models is just the problem of inferring unobserved causes or predicting future effects based on a hypothesized causal network structure—analogous to the lowest-level linguistic inferences of interpolating or predicting an incomplete utterance based on a hypothesized syntactic structure.

As we have already argued, networks of cause-effect relations such as Graph 1 are only the lowest level of structural description in a hierarchy of abstraction. Just as the specific phrase structures in a particular language are generated by a more abstract level of knowledge—the grammar or syntax of that language—so are the specific causal networks in a particular domain generated by more abstract knowledge, which we can think of as a kind of causal grammar or causal syntax for that domain. Loosely speaking, in the terminology of the preceding section, a causal grammar corresponds to an intuitive domain theory at the framework level, while the causal networks generated by the grammar correspond to specific theories developed within the overarching framework theory for that domain. The real payoff of the linguistic analogy comes in its suggestions for how causal theories at this more abstract framework level may be represented, as well as how they function to guide new inferences about causal structure and how they may themselves be acquired.

Just as theories of linguistic syntax are typically framed in terms of abstract syntactic categories and rules for composing phrase structures that are defined over those categories, so can we start to formalize the syntax of a causal domain theory in terms of abstract causal categories of entities, properties, and states and rules for composing causal network structures defined over those categories. Principles P1 and P2 are a first attempt in this direction for a fragment of the disease domain: P1 specifies three categories of variables, and P2 specifies the rules by which variables in those categories can be connected into networks of cause-effect relations to generate causal networks like Graph 1, but not those like Graph 5 or 6. In the following chapter, we present two more formal schemes for representing the grammars of causal framework theories and principles such as P1 and P2. These two formalisms work differently, but they share the basic notion of a generative syntax, with rules for constructing causal networks that are defined over abstract causal categories.

The primary functional role of a grammar for causal inference is essentially the same as the role played by grammar in language comprehension: to provide the constraints that make possible successful inductive inferences of structure at the level below. As in linguistic parsing, inferences about the causal network structure that gave rise to a set of observed events are highly underconstrained. Many logically possible causal networks will be able to explain the sparse event data that a learner typically observes. The causal grammar reduces this problem by generating only a constrained set of causal network hypotheses that the learner need consider. The causal grammar may also be probabilistic, generating some network structures with higher probability than others, which will further help to resolve ambiguities present in the learner's data.

Some of the causal grammar's constraints on network hypotheses may be domain-general, but others will vary substantially across domains, in keeping with the crucial role of abstract theories as the frameworks on which people's distinctive understandings of different domains are built. For instance, causal grammars in many domains might assign higher probabilities to structures with fewer causal links or fewer hidden (intrinsically unobservable) causes, a la Ockham's razor. But in any one domain, a particular hypothesis that posits strictly more unobservable structure may be more likely under the causal grammar if it accords better with the specific causal laws

of that domain. For instance, consider a learner for whom Graph 1 describes that learner's current theory of specific diseases and P1 and P2 comprise a framework-level theory. The learner now observes a previously unseen correlation between a known behavior B (e.g., *Working in Factory*) and a known symptom S (e.g., *Chest Pain*) in a number of individuals. Guided by P1 and P2, the learner may infer that a causal chain is likely to go from B to S through some particular but undetermined disease node Y. Because no such path exists in Graph 0, the learner infers that most likely one of the following new structures is needed: either a new causal link from B to a known cause of S (e.g., *Heart Disease*) or a new causal link to S from a known effect of B (e.g., *Bronchitis*). If no new link to or from an existing disease node can be added without conflicting with other knowledge, P1 and P2 suggest that a new, previously unobserved disease node Y may exist, and that Y is causally linked to both B and S (as shown in Graph 4). Other logically simpler hypotheses, such as inserting a single causal link directly from B to S or from S to B, are ruled out by the ontology of P1 and the causal laws of P2.

Note that this approach to learning causal network structures from data is different from how that problem has traditionally been approached, either in machine learning (Spirtes et al., 1993; Pearl, 2000) or cognitive psychology (Cheng, 1997; Gopnik et al., 2004; Shanks, 1995), as a primarily bottom-up process of fitting or constructing a causal model that best accounts for the observed patterns of correlation among events. The causal grammar view treats causal learning as more of a parsing operation, integrating top-down as well as bottom-up constraints in a search for the best causal model among just those candidates consistent with the learner's domain understanding. This view seems to offer more promise for explaining how people can successfully infer causal structures from so little data—sometimes just one or a few observed events, or much less than would be needed even to compute reliable correlations among events.

Finally, we turn to the problem of acquiring framework-level causal theories. Just as probabilistic grammars for languages may be learnable from a finite observed corpus of utterances, causal grammars could also be learnable via statistical methods from observations of a finite observed sample of systems in a given domain. Two aspects of this analogy are particularly worth noting. First, as with the grammar of a language, crucial constraints on causal domain theories may come from knowledge at higher levels of abstraction. Some aspects of a causal grammar may be conditioned by a truly basic (and innate) foundation, a *Universal Theory* 'UT' by analogy to UG in linguistics. But other constraints are likely to come from levels of framework-like knowledge in between the innate foundation and the frontiers of domain theories in which learning typically occurs. For instance, principle P2 in the disease domain grammar only specifes which kinds of causal links may be present; it does not require that any particular causal link necessarily exist. That may be a general quality of causal grammars in biological or social domains, in which there appears (at least to most novices) to be a fair amount of arbitrariness in the causal relations that exist. In contrast, causal relations in physical domains may be more highly structured and lawful. For example, every sample of a certain type of element or particle necessarily interacts with other elements or particles in the same way.

As with linguistic grammars, the empirical adequacy of hypotheses about causal theories at the framework level are evaluated only indirectly, on the success or failure of the causal networks they generate. To the extent that a causal-grammar hypothesis tends to generate causal networks that in turn generate the kinds of events a learner frequently observes, that grammar will receive inductive support. As in linguistics, a grammar may fail to predict optimally either by undergenerating or overgenerating. The peril of undergeneration should be clear: if a causal grammar generates only a small subset of the causal networks that the true grammar does, then typically there will be many systems in the domain for which that hypothetical grammar offers no reasonable description. As an example of overgeneration, consider a grammar in the disease domain that is equivalent to principles P1 and P2 except that it combines disease and symptom variables into a single class ("disymptoms") and allows causal links between any two variables in that class. This "disymptom" grammar is strictly more general than principles P1 and P2. Now, suppose that we observe data produced according to Graph 1. Although both grammars are capable of generating the correct generating network, the data will provide more inductive support for principles P1 and P2 than for the "disymptom" grammar because the overly general variant generates many more competing causal-network hypotheses that are far from the truth (and under which the observed data would be highly unlikely).

Summary

Viewing intuitive theories in terms of a hierarchy of increasingly abstract knowledge representations has led us to formulate problems of causal inference on three interlocking levels:

1. *Inferring causes and predicting effects.* Infer the hidden causes of an observed event, or predict its unobserved effects, given a theory at the most specific level: a network structure relating causes and effects in the relevant system.

2. *Inferring causal networks.* Infer the structure of a theory at the most specific level — a network of causal relations — that governs a system of observed variables given more general framework-like knowledge: the principles constraining candidate causal structures in the relevant domain.

3. *Inferring causal principles.* Infer the principles that organize a set of observed causal systems, given higher-level theoretical frameworks: knowledge about a larger domain that encompasses those systems, or domain-general assumptions.

Everyday causal inference unfolds at all of these levels simultaneously, although novel inferences at higher levels may be relatively rare for adults (Gopnik & Meltzoff, 1997). This formulation of causal induction raises a significant computational challenge: explaining how all of these inference problems can be solved in concert.

In the remainder of this chapter, we propose a response to this computational challenge that exploits the common form of all three problems: knowledge at a more abstract level generates a constrained space of candidate hypotheses to be evaluated based on data from lower levels of abstraction. The tools of Bayesian inference can be used to formulate any one of these inferences in rational statistical terms. We propose a hierarchical Bayesian framework in which hypotheses are defined at multiple levels of abstraction and coupled together based on the constraints that each hypothesized structure imposes on hypotheses at lower levels. This hierarchical framework unifies all three levels of inference and shows how a learner may in principle tackle them all simultaneously.

The next section introduces the technical machinery of our hierarchical Bayesian framework. If this appears to be a big step up in mathematical rigor without a clear immediate payoff, then we suggest viewing it as a long-term investment. Analogous hierarchical probabilistic models have been proposed in computational linguistics for integrating language acquisition, syntactic parsing, and speech recognition (Charniak, 1993; Jurafsky & Martin, 2000; Manning & Schütze, 1999): candidate probabilistic grammars are evaluated based on how much probability they assign to the most likely parses of an observed corpus of utterances; individual word outputs from a probabilistic speech recognizer are constrained or reevaluated based on how well they fit with the most likely parses of the surrounding utterance. Although many important aspects of representation and computation remain to be worked out, it is fair to say that the introduction of sophisticated probabilistic models with multiple levels of knowledge representation has revolutionized and reinvigorated the field of computational linguistics over the last decade. We have similarly high hopes for the future of research on intuitive causal theories.

A Hierarchical Bayesian Framework for Causal Inference

We begin with a brief review of the basics of Bayesian inference and then show how to extend these ideas to multiple levels of inference in a hierarchy of intuitive theories, where each level functions as a hypothesis space generator for the level below.

Basic Bayes

Bayesian inference provides a general framework for how rational agents should approach problems of induction. We assume an agent who observes some data $\mathcal{D}$ and considers a space of hypotheses $\mathcal{H}$ about the processes by which that data could have been generated. The agent's a priori beliefs about the plausibility of each $h \in \mathcal{H}$, before seeing $\mathcal{D}$ but drawing on background knowledge $\mathcal{K}$, are expressed in a *prior probability* distribution $P(h|\mathcal{K})$. The principles of Bayesian inference indicate how the agent should modify his or her beliefs in light of the data $\mathcal{D}$, computing a *posterior probability* distribution $P(h|\mathcal{D},\mathcal{K})$.

The key engine for updating beliefs in light of data is *Bayes' rule*,

$$P(h\,|\,\mathcal{D},\mathcal{K}) = \frac{P(\mathcal{D}\,|\,h,\mathcal{K})P(h\,|\,\mathcal{K})}{P(\mathcal{D}\,|\,\mathcal{K})}. \quad (19\text{-}5)$$

The likelihood $P(\mathcal{D}|h,\mathcal{K})$ encodes the predictions of each hypothesis h—the probability of observing $\mathcal{D}$ if h were true. The denominator $P(\mathcal{D}|\mathcal{K})$ is an average of the predictions of all hypotheses in the hypothesis space, weighted by their prior probabilities:

$$P(\mathcal{D}\,|\,\mathcal{K}) = \sum_{h' \in \mathcal{H}} P(\mathcal{D}\,|\,h',\mathcal{K})P(h'\,|\,\mathcal{K}). \quad (19\text{-}6)$$

This denominator serves to normalize the terms that appear in the numerator, ensuring that the posterior $P(h|\mathcal{D}, \mathcal{K})$ can be interpreted as a proper probability distribution over hypotheses.

The content of Bayes' rule can be understood intuitively by thinking about what factors make for strong arguments from observed data to hypothesized explanations in science. To say that some observed data $\mathcal{D}$ provide provide good reason to believe in hypothesis h, at least two conditions must hold. First, the hypothesis must predict the data. The stronger the predictions that h makes about $\mathcal{D}$, the more support h should receive from the observation of $\mathcal{D}$. Second, independent of the data, the hypothesis must be plausible given everything else we know. One can always construct some post hoc hypothesis that is consistent with a particular experimental finding, but such a hypothesis would not be considered a good explanation for the data unless it was a well-motivated and principled consequence of our background knowledge. The combined influence of these two factors is captured in the numerator of Bayes' rule: the posterior probability assigned to some hypothesis h on seeing $\mathcal{D}$ is proportional to the product of the prior probability $P(h|\mathcal{K})$, reflecting the a priori plausibility of h, and the likelihood $P(\mathcal{D}|h,\mathcal{K})$, reflecting the extent to which $\mathcal{D}$ is predicted by h. The denominator reflects a third factor that also influences belief dynamics in science, although its rational status is not always appreciated. Data $\mathcal{D}$ provide better support for hypothesis h to the extent that the data are surprising. That is, either the data are unlikely given our background knowledge, or they would not be predicted under most plausible alternative hypotheses. The former condition is just equivalent to saying that $P(\mathcal{D}|\mathcal{K})$ is low, and the lower this term, the higher the posterior probability in Equation 19-5. The latter condition is just a different framing of the same situation, as expressed in Equation 19-6: $P(\mathcal{D}|\mathcal{K})$ will be low when $P(\mathcal{D}|h'\mathcal{K})$ is low for plausible alternative hypotheses (those for which $P(h'|\mathcal{K})$ is high).

In short, Bayesian inference provides a rigorous mathematical representation of a basic principle of scientific common sense: to the extent that a given hypothesis is well motivated and strongly predictive of the observed data and to the extent that the predicted data are surprising or otherwise unexpected, the hypothesis is more likely to be true. Our contention here is that this approach to inductive inference also offers useful insights into commonsense reasoning and learning with intuitive theories.

Bayes' rule can be applied to any problem requiring an inference about the process that produced some observed data. Different types of inductive problems will involve different types of hypothesis spaces and different types of data, with appropriately modified priors and likelihoods. In the next section, we formalize the three problems of causal inference identified above in Bayesian terms, identifying the hypothesis space and data used in each case and explaining how the priors and likelihoods are determined.

A Hierarchical Bayesian Framework

Expressing causal inference problems in Bayesian terms emphasizes the importance of constraints on which hypotheses are possible or likely a priori. Expressing multiple inference problems at different levels of abstraction in a hierarchical Bayesian framework emphasizes the coupling of these constraints across levels of inference.

In presenting our hierarchical framework, we adopt the following terms and notation. A *system* is a set of causally related variables within a *domain*. For a system of N variables $\mathbf{X}=\{X_1, \ldots, X_N\}$, an *instance* is an assignment of values to these variables, $\mathbf{x}=\{x_1, \ldots x_N\}$. We use uppercase letters to indicate variables, lowercase to indicate their values, and boldface to indicate a set of variables or their values. For any instance $\mathbf{x}$, a subset of variables $\mathbf{x}_{obs}$ are *observed* (i.e., the values of those variables in that instance are known), and the remainder $\mathbf{x}_{unobs}$ are *unobserved* (i.e., take on unknown values). A *data set d* consists of the observed portions of M instances of some system, $d=\{\mathbf{x}_{obs}^{(1)}, \ldots, \mathbf{x}_{obs}^{(M)}\}$. Depending on the level of causal inference, the data $\mathcal{D}$ available to the learner may consist of a single observed instance of a system, a data set d of multiple instances of the same system, or multiple data sets, each from a different system in the same domain.

The three inference problems from the preceding section—inferring causes from effects, inferring causal networks from cause-effect observations, and inferring the principles underlying causal network

structures in a domain—unfold at different levels of abstraction. To cast all these problems in a unified Bayesian inference framework, we define a hierarchy of increasingly abstract theories $T_0, T_1, \ldots, T_U$ as the basis for a hierarchical generative model of the data. The subscript indicates the level of theory, with U the highest level (Figure 19-4). Theories at each level of the hierarchy generate hypothesis spaces and prior probability distributions for Bayesian inference at the level below. The lowest-level theory T_0 is a causal network defined on the variables of a particular system, generating hypotheses about the values of those variables and defining a distribution $P(\mathbf{X}|T_0)$. The next level T_1 is a set of principles that generates a hypothesis space of causal networks T_0, defining a prior distribution $P(T_0|T_1)$. This suggests a more precise definition of a domain as the set of systems that can be generated by a theory T_i for $i>0$. Higher-level theories are defined recursively: for any $i>0$, a theory T_i generates a hypothesis space of theories T_{i-1} with an associated prior distribution $P(T_{i-1}|T_i)$, giving rise to a hierarchy of increasingly general theories, each with a corresponding (increasingly general) domain.

Inferring Causes and Predicting Effects

Inferring hidden causes or predicting future effects can both be formulated as problems of inferring the values of the unobserved variables in an instance $\mathbf{x}$. In many cases where only a subset of variables are observed, $\mathbf{x}_{obs}$ are effects, and $\mathbf{x}_{unobs}$ are their causes, but the problem remains the same if $\mathbf{x}_{obs}$ correspond to causes or a mixture of causes and effects. In Bayesian terms, we seek to compute the posterior distribution over $\mathbf{x}_{unobs}$ given $\mathbf{x}_{obs}$. Such an inference requires knowledge of a hypothesis space of possible values that $\mathbf{x}_{unobs}$ could take on, the prior probabilities of those values, and the probability of observing the data $\mathbf{x}_{obs}$ conditioned on those values. A causal network T_0 can be used to generate values of $\mathbf{x}$ and consequently supplies all of these ingredients.

Taking T_0 as our background knowledge $\mathcal{K}$, we can compute the posterior distribution on $\mathbf{x}_{unobs}$ by applying Bayes' rule (Equation 19-5), letting $\mathbf{x}_{obs}$ play the role of the data $\mathcal{D}$ and $\mathbf{x}_{unobs}$ the role of the hypothesis h. T_0 specifies the hypothesis space $\mathcal{H} = \mathcal{H}_0$, the prior probability $P(\mathbf{x}_{unobs}|T_0)$, and the likelihood $P(\mathbf{x}_{obs}|\mathbf{x}_{unobs},T_0)$. We thus have

$$P(\mathbf{x}_{unobs} \mid \mathbf{x}_{obs}, T_0) = \frac{P(\mathbf{x}_{obs} \mid \mathbf{x}_{unobs}, T_0)P(\mathbf{x}_{unobs} \mid T_0)}{P(\mathbf{x}_{obs} \mid T_0)} \quad (19\text{-}7)$$

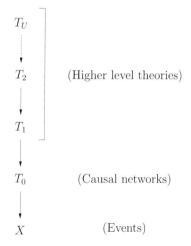

T_U (Higher level theories)

T_2

T_1

T_0 (Causal networks)

X (Events)

FIGURE 19-4 A hierarchical probabilistic model corresponding to the hierarchy of abstraction in causal theories shown in Figure 19-3. Theories at each level of abstraction define a prior probability distribution over candidate theories at the next level down, bottoming out in the observed data X. Bayesian inferences about theories at each level combine information from the observed data, propagated upward by successful lower-level theories, with top-down constraints from higher-level theories (and ultimately perhaps some universal conceptual skeleton for all theories T_U).

where the denominator can be computed by summing over all values $\mathbf{x}_{\text{unobs}}$ allowed by T_0:

$$P(\mathbf{x}_{\text{obs}} \mid T_0) = \sum_{\mathbf{x}_{\text{unobs}} \in \mathcal{H}_0} P(\mathbf{x}_{\text{obs}} \mid \mathbf{x}_{\text{unobs}}, T_0) P(\mathbf{x}_{\text{unobs}} \mid T_0) \quad (19\text{-}8)$$

Evaluating Equation 19-7 is just the standard process of inference in a Bayesian network. The network not only sets up the hypothesis space for these computations, but also allows the computation to be carried out efficiently. It provides a structured representation of the joint probability distribution over all variables that enables Equations 19-7 and 19-8 to be computed by simple local computations (Pearl, 1988; Russell & Norvig, 2002).

Inferring Causal Networks

The problem of inferring causal network structures from cause-effect observations can be formalized as identifying the T_0-level theory that best explains a data

set d of M partially observed instances of a system. Standard "data-mining" algorithms for learning causal networks (e.g., Spirtes et al., 1993; Pearl, 2000; Heckerman, 1998) offer one approach to this problem, but for several reasons they are not promising as rational accounts of human causal learning. These algorithms require large samples to identify correlations among variables, yet human learners are willing to infer causal relationships from only a few observations, for which correlations cannot be identified reliably (Gopnik et al., 2004; Gopnik & Schulz, et al., 2004; Griffiths et al., 2004; Griffiths & Tenenbaum, 2005; Schulz et al., 2004; Steyvers et al., 2003, submitted).

Human learners are able to learn causal structure from such limited data because they draw on strong prior knowledge that generic data-mining algorithms for learning causal networks are not designed to exploit. Rather than treating all variables of a causal system as equal a priori, as those algorithms do, people will typically conceive of the variables in terms of properties and relations on objects. Domain-specific theories at a more abstract level—knowledge about classes of objects and predicates and causal laws relating these classes—will set up strong expectations about the kinds of causal network structures and functional dependencies between variables that are likely to be encountered. This is the function of principles P1 and P2 in the disease domain. The scenario in the preceding section, in which a learner infers a novel hidden disease variable to explain a newly observed behavior-symptom correlation, is one example of how such domain theories may guide human learning of causal structure. People also have domain-specific knowledge about how kinds of causal mechanisms work. This knowledge may be quite skeletal (Keil, 2003), but it is often sufficient to generate useful constraints on the nature of the functional dependency between causes and their effects. By specifying whether a hypothetical causal link—if it exists—is likely to be deterministic or probabilistic, generative or inhibitory, strong or weak, independent of other links or interacting with them, skeletal mechanism knowledge may allow learners to infer, from much less data than would be required without those expectations, which causal relations do in fact exist.

This knowledge-driven approach to causal structure learning fits naturally into our hierarchical Bayesian framework. We want to compute a posterior distribution over causal networks T_0 given a data set d

and relevant background knowledge $\mathcal{K}$. The background knowledge $\mathcal{K}$ takes the form of a more abstract theory T_1, which generates a hypothesis space $\mathcal{H}_1$ of causal networks T_0 and a prior on that hypothesis space $P(T_0|T_1)$. The probability of the data set d under each network T_0 can be computed as follows: T_0 specifies a joint distribution over the system's variables $\mathbf{X} = \{X_1, \ldots, X_N\}$, which determines the probability $P(\mathbf{x}_{obs}^{(i)}|T_0)$ of the ith partially observed instance (Equation 19-8). Assuming each instance in d is sampled independently, the total probability of the data set is

$$P(d\,|\,T_0) = \prod_{i=1}^{M} P(\mathbf{x}_{obs}^{(i)}\,|\,T_0). \qquad (19\text{-}9)$$

We can now apply Bayes' rule (Equation 19-5) to compute the posterior probability of a particular causal network T_0 given a data set d and a higher-level theory T_1:

$$P(T_0\,|\,d, T_1) = \frac{P(d\,|\,T_0)P(T_0\,|\,T_1)}{P(d\,|\,T_1)}, \qquad (19\text{-}10)$$

where the denominator is

$$P(d\,|\,T_1) = \sum_{T_0 \in \mathcal{H}_1} P(d\,|\,T_0)P(T_0\,|\,T_1). \qquad (19\text{-}11)$$

The sum over all possible networks in Equation 19-11 may be computed exactly for very small systems but in general requires some kind of stochastic sampling-based approximation scheme (e.g., Friedman & Koller, 2000).

Several cognitive scientists have proposed that human causal learning is best thought of as a knowledge-based, theory-based, or top-down process (e.g., Waldmann, 1996; Lagnado & Sloman, 2004; Lagnado, Hagmayer, Sloman, and Waldmann, this volume). However, these proposals have been relatively qualitative and informal. There has not been a widespread effort to propose and test principled domain-general frameworks for modeling theory-based induction of causal structure, as there has been for more bottom-up associative accounts (Rescorla & Wagner, 1972; Cheng & Novick, 1990; Cheng, 1997; Lober & Shanks, 2000; Danks, 2003). Our analysis aims to formalize the knowledge that guides causal structure learning, and to provide a rational account of how it does so. The roles of both top-down constraints from prior knowledge and bottom-up influences from observed data are reflected in the two terms in the numerator of Equation 10: the higher-order theory T_1 defines the prior probability $P(T_0|T_1)$ and delimits the set of causal networks under consideration, while the data favors some networks within this set via the likelihood $P(d|T_0)$. In a series of papers (Griffiths et al., 2004; Griffiths & Tenenbaum, 2005; Tenenbaum & Griffiths, 2001, 2003; Steyvers et al., 2003), we have shown how this theory-based Bayesian framework can be used to build rational and quantitatively accurate models of people's inferences about causal structure from limited data.

Inferring Causal Principles

The machinery for theory-based inference of causal network structures T_0 can be extended up the hierarchy of theories, making it possible, in principle, to learn a theory at any level. For instance, given data $\mathcal{D}$ drawn from one or more causal systems in a domain, we can make inferences about the T_1-level principles that govern those systems (e.g., abstract classes of variables and causal laws such as principles P1 and P2 in the disease domain). We compute a posterior distribution over T_1 theories by applying Bayes' rule (Equation 19-5) to a hypothesis space $\mathcal{H}_2$ generated by a higher-order theory T_2.

$$P(T_1\,|\,\mathcal{D}, T_2) = \frac{P(\mathcal{D}\,|\,T_1)P(T_1\,|\,T_2)}{P(\mathcal{D}\,|\,T_2)}. \qquad (19\text{-}12)$$

Assuming that $\mathcal{D}$ consists of L independent data sets $\{d_1, \ldots, d_L\}$, we can compute the likelihood $P(\mathcal{D}|T_1)$ as

$$P(\mathcal{D}\,|\,T_1) = \prod_{i=1}^{L} P(d_i\,|\,T_1). \qquad (19\text{-}13)$$

Each term $P(d_i|T_1)$ corresponds to the denominator in Bayes' rule applied at the next level down (Equation 19-11), obtained by summing over all causal networks T_0 generated by T_1 for each of the systems represented in $\mathcal{D}$. $P(T_1|T_2)$ is the distribution over theories at level T_1 defined by the higher-level theory T_2. $P(\mathcal{D}|T_2)$ is computed in the same way as $P(d|T_1)$, except that it requires summing over all theories T_1 in $\mathcal{H}_2$, as well as all causal networks T_0 in the hypothesis space $\mathcal{H}_1$ associated with T_1. $P(\mathcal{D}|T_2)$ can be used to make inferences about T_2 given $\mathcal{D}$ and so on up the hierarchy.

This analysis shows that an ideal learner should be able to acquire higher-level causal theories from data given an appropriate hypothesis space of candidate theories. In practice, as each new level of theory adds a whole hypothesis space of hypothesis spaces that the learner must sum over, carrying out all the required computations quickly becomes intractable. Bayesian statisticians often approximate exact inference in hierarchical models by replacing a sum over all hypotheses with a search for the most probable hypothesis or with a sum over a sample of hypotheses generated by Markov chain Monte Carlo techniques (e.g., Gilks, Richardson, & Spiegelhalter, 1996). An interesting open question is how the cognitive processes involved in theory change and acquisition might correspond to some of these methods for approximating Bayesian inference with complex, hierarchically structured hypothesis spaces.

There may also be processes involved in the acquisition of higher-order theories that are not so clearly evidential in nature, or that draw on types of evidence that are different from direct observations of systems in the world. For instance, when a child hears an adult talking about the causal structure of a complex domain such as intuitive biology or psychology (e.g., Carey, 1985a; Gopnik & Meltzoff, 1997), invoking various hidden causes and abstract concepts, the child might receive useful evidence about the relative value of alternative hypotheses for higher-order, framework-level theories in these domains. It is far from clear how to capture the inferences a child might make from such data in terms of our hierarchical Bayesian framework, but this remains another important open question for the research program to address.

Summary

We began this chapter with three guiding questions (Table 19-1): What is the knowledge content and representational form of intuitive theories? How do intuitive theories guide the acquisition of new casual knowledge? How are intuitive theories themselves acquired? Rather than stipulating arbitrarily the properties that intuitive theories should have or trying to give a fully general account of theories, we have presented a rational analysis of causal induction and restricted ourselves to accounting for those aspects of intuitive theories necessary to explain how people perform these tasks.

The key challenge of causal induction we identified was the need to make inferences about unobservable causal relations from sparse observed data. We argued that these inferences are made possible by strong constraints from more abstract levels of causal knowledge. These constraints often arise from domain-specific principles that run counter to simplicity or other general-purpose inductive biases, such as when a novel association between a risky behavior and a known medical symptom is attributed to an indirect link via an unknown disease rather than to a direct causal link between the behavior and symptom.

Inspired by proposals from developmental psychology and philosophy of science, we suggested that both networks of causal relations and the more abstract causal principles that constrain them may be thought of as intuitive domain theories, but at different levels of abstraction. These levels of abstraction correspond roughly to the notions of specific theories and framework theories introduced by Wellman and Gelman (1992), but we expect there will typically be multiple levels of increasingly abstract, broad-coverage, framework-like causal knowledge. Each level in this hierarchy of theories provides constraints on candidate theories at the next level down and is itself constrained by knowledge at higher levels, perhaps ultimately grounding out in a "universal theory" of conceptual primitives underlying all intuitive domains.

Viewed from this hierarchical perspective, our initial questions about the structure, function, and acquisition of intuitive causal theories now come down to these two: How do we represent knowledge of causal structure at multiple levels of theoretical abstraction, and what processes of inference connect those knowledge levels to support learning and reasoning across the hierarchy? Existing computational formalisms based on causal Bayesian networks may be appropriate for characterizing causal theories at the most specific level, but they do not extend to the higher levels of abstraction for which this hierarchical picture calls out.

As a first step toward answering these questions, we proposed the causal grammar analogy: a framework for thinking about representation and inference in a hierarchy of causal theories based on parallels with some classic representational structures and inferential mechanisms that have been posited to explain language comprehension and acquisition. Just as the grammar of a natural language generates a constrained hypothesis space of syntactic structures considered in sentence comprehension, so does the set of abstract causal principles (or the framework theory) for a domain generate a constrained hypothesis space of causal network structures (or specific theories) considered in causal induction. Just as linguistic grammars can be expressed in terms of a set of abstract syntactic categories and rules for composing instances of those categories into viable syntactic tree structures, so can higher-order causal theories—or causal grammars—be expressed in terms of a set of abstract categories of causal variables and rules for how variables in those classes can or must be related to form plausible causal network structures. Both linguistic grammars and causal grammars must also be reliably learnable, based on a combination of the primary data available to people and the constraints on possible grammars provided by more abstract, possibly innate conceptual primitives. Hypotheses about linguistic grammars or causal grammars can only be evaluated indirectly, based on how well the specific syntactic tree structures or causal network structures that they generate explain the observed primary data.

Finally, we outlined a more formal approach to learning and reasoning in a hierarchy of theories based on the tools of hierarchical Bayesian models. This analysis provides a principled and unified approach to solving causal induction problems at all levels of our hierarchy of abstraction. At its heart is the idea that intuitive theories at each level of abstraction generate hypothesis spaces for Bayesian inference about theories at lower levels and are themselves learned via Bayesian inference over hypothesis spaces generated by higher-level theories. Thus, the inductive mechanisms operating at each level of abstraction are essentially the same, and they can proceed in parallel to support coupled inferences at all levels.

This Bayesian framework provides a rational analysis of how inference and learning can operate in a hierarchy of intuitive causal theories, but it does not directly address the question of how to represent the structure and content of those theories. In terms of Table 19-1, we have presented a formal answer to the second and third questions, but only an incomplete answer to the first question: theories at the lowest, most specific level might be represented as causal Bayesian networks; higher-level theories will require more expressive representations, somewhat like generative grammars. The companion to this chapter (Griffiths & Tenenbaum, chapter 20, this volume)

examines in detail two possible representational frameworks for theories at higher levels of abstraction, based on graph schemas and predicate logic. We show precisely how each of these two representational frameworks can fulfill the functional role of T_1-level theories in our hierarchical Bayesian picture, how they support inferences about specific cause-effect relations from sparse data, and how they may themselves be learned or adjusted based on the data observed. We identify complementary strengths and weaknesses of each representation, ultimately arguing that neither of these formalisms provides a fully adequate account of the structure and function of abstract causal theories. Still, a consideration of these alternatives lays out the challenges for future work and offers some possibilities for what the answers may look like.

ACKNOWLEDGMENTS   We thank Elizabeth Baraff, Charles Kemp, Tania Lombrozo, Rebecca Saxe, and Marty Tenenbaum for helpful conversations about the material in this chapter. JBT was supported by the Paul E. Newton Career Development Chair and a grant from the NTT Communication Sciences Laboratory. TLG was supported by a Stanford Graduate Fellowship.

References

Ahn, W., & Kalish, C. (2000). The role of mechanism beliefs in causal reasoning. In R. Wilson & F. Keil (Eds.), *Cognition and explanation* (pp. 199–225). Cambridge, MA: MIT Press.

Anderson, J. R. (1990). *The adaptive character of thought* Hillsdale, NJ: Erlbaum.

Atran, S. (1995). Classifying nature across cultures. In E. E. Smith & D. N. Osherson (Eds.), *Thinking: An invitation to cognitive science* (Vol. 3, pp. 131–174). Cambridge, MA: MIT Press.

Carey, S. (1985a). *Conceptual change in childhood* Cambridge, MA: MIT Press.

Carey, S. (1985b). Constraints on semantic development. In J. Mehler (Ed.), *Neonate cognition* (pp. 381–398). Hillsdale, NJ: Erlbaum.

Carnap, R. (1956). Empiricism, semantics, and ontology. In (2nd ed). Chicago: University of Chicago Press.

Charniak, E. (1993). *Statistical language learning* Cambridge, MA: MIT Press.

Cheng, P. (1997). From covariation to causation: A causal power theory. *Psychological Review, 104,* 367–405.

Cheng, P. W., & Novick, L. R. (1990). A probabilistic contrast model of causal induction.*Journal of Personality and Social Psychology*, 58, 545–567.

Chomsky, N. (1956). Three models for the description of language. *IRE Transactions on Information Theory*, 2, 113–124.

Chomsky, N. (1962). Explanatory models in linguistics. In E. Nagel, P. Suppes, & A. Tarski (Eds.), *Logic, methodology, and philosophy of science* (pp. 528–550). Stanford, CA: Stanford University Press.

Chomsky, N. (1965). *Aspects of the theory of syntax* Cambridge, MA: MIT Press.

Chomsky, N. (1986). *Language and problems of knowledge: The Managua lectures* Cambridge, MA: MIT Press.

Danks, D. (2003). Equilibria of the Rescorla-Wagner model. *Journal of Mathematical Psychology*, 47, 109–121.

Friedman, N., & Koller, D. (2000). Being Bayesian about network structure. In *Proceedings of the 16th Annual Conference on Uncertainty in AI* (pp. 201–210). Stanford, CA.

Gilks, W., Richardson, S. & Spiegelhalter, D. J. (Eds). (1996). *Markov chain Monte Carlo in practice.* Suffolk: Chapman and Hall. Boca Raton, FL.

Glymour, C. (2001). *The mind's arrows: Bayes nets and graphical causal models in psychology.* Cambridge, MA: MIT Press.

Godfrey-Smith, P. (2003). *Theory and reality.* Chicago: University of Chicago Press.

Gopnik, A. Glymour, C. (2002). Causal maps and Bayes nets: A cognitive and computational account of theory-formation. In P. Carruthers, S. P. Stitch, & M. Siegal (Eds.), *The cognitive basis of science.* Cambridge, England: Cambridge University Press.

Gopnik, A., Glymour, C., Sobel, D., Schulz, L., Kushnir, T., & Danks, D. (2004). A theory of causal learning in children: Causal maps and Bayes nets. *Psychological Review*, 111, 1–31.

Gopnik, A., & Meltzoff, A. N. (1997). *Words, thoughts, and theories.* Cambridge, MA: MIT Press.

Gopnik, A., & Schulz, L. (2004). Mechanisms of theory formation in young children. *Trends in Cognitive Science*, 8, 371–377.

Griffiths, T. L., Baraff, E. R., & Tenenbaum, J. B. (2004). Using physical theories to infer hidden causal structure. In *Proceedings of the 26th Annual Meeting of the Cognitive Science Society.*

Griffiths, T. L., & Tenenbaum, J. B. (2005). Structure and strength in causal induction. *Cognitive Psychology*, 51(4), 285–386.

Heckerman, D. (1998). A tutorial on learning with Bayesian networks. In M. I. Jordan (Ed.), *Learning in graphical models* (pp. 301–354). Cambridge, MA: MIT Press.

Inagaki, K., & Hatano, G. (2002). *Young children's thinking about biological world.* New York: Psychology Press.

Jurafsky, D., & Martin, J. H. (2000). *Speech and language processing.* Upper Saddle River, NJ: Prentice Hall.

Keil, F. C. (2003). Folkscience: Coarse interpretations of a complex reality. *Trends in Cognitive Science*, 7, 368–373.

Kelley, H. H. (1973). The processes of causal attribution. *American Psychologist*, 28, 107–128.

Kuhn, T. S. (1970). *The structure of scientific revolutions* (2nd ed). Chicago: University of Chicago Press.

Lagnado, D., & Sloman, S. A. (2004). The advantage of timely intervention. *Journal of Experimental Psychology: Learning, Memory, and Cognition*, 30, 856–876.

Lakatos, I. (1970). Falsification and the methodology of scientific research programmes. In I. Lakatos & A. Musgrave (Eds.), *Criticism and the growth of knowledge.* Cambridge: Cambridge University Press.

Laudan, L. (1977). *Progress and its problems.* Berkeley, CA: University of California Press.

Lober, K., & Shanks, D. (2000). Is causal induction based on causal power? Critique of Cheng (1997). *Psychological Review*, 107, 195–212.

Manning, C., & Schütze, H. (1999). *Foundations of statistical natural language processing.* Cambridge, MA: MIT Press.

Marr, D. (1982). *Vision.* San Francisco, CA: Freeman.

McCloskey, M. (1983). Intuitive physics. *Scientific American*, 284, 114–123.

Murphy, G. L., & Medin, D. L. (1985). The role of theories in conceptual coherence. *Psychological Review*, 92, 289–316.

Nichols, S., & Stich, S.(2003). *Mindreading: An integrated account of pretense, self-awareness and understanding other minds.* Oxford, England: Oxford University Press.

Nowak, M. A., Komarova, N. L. & Niyogi, P. (2003). Computational and evolutionary aspects of language. *Nature*, 417, 611–617.

Oaksford, M., & Chater, N. (1999). Ten years of the rational analysis of cognition. *Trends in Cognitive Science*, 3, 57–65.

Pazzani, M. (1987). Inducing causal and social theories: A prerequisite for explanation-based learning. In *Proceedings of the Fourth International Workshop on Machine Learning* (pp. 230–241). Irvine, CA: Morgan Kaufmann.

Pazzani, M., Dyer, M., & Flowers, M. (1986). The role of prior causal theries in generalization. In *Proceedings of the Fifth National Conference on Artificial Intelligence* (pp. 545–550). Philadelphia, PA: Morgan Kaufmann.

Pearl, J. (1988). *Probabilistic reasoning in intelligent systems*. San Francisco, CA: Morgan Kaufmann.

Pearl, J. (2000). *Causality: Models, reasoning and inference*. Cambridge, England: Cambridge University Press.

Quine, W. O. (1951). Two dogmas of empiricism. *Philosophical Review, 60*, 20–43.

Rehder, B. (2003). A causal-model theory of conceptual representation and categorization. *Journal of Experimental Psychology: Learning, Memory, and Cognition, 29*, 1141–1159.

Rescorla, R. A., & Wagner, A. R. (1972). A theory of Pavlovian conditioning: Variations on the effectiveness of reinforcement and non-reinforcement. In A. H. Black & W. F. Prokasy (Eds.), *Classical conditioning II: Current research and theory* (pp. 64–99). New York: Appleton-Century-Crofts.

Russell, S. J., & Norvig, P. (2002). *Artificial intelligence: A modern approach* (2nd ed). Englewood Cliffs, NJ: Prentice Hall.

Shanks, D. R. (1995). *The psychology of associative learning*. Cambridge, England: Cambridge University Press.

Shepard, R. N. (1987). Towards a universal law of generalization for psychological science. *Science, 237*, 1317–1323.

Sobel, D. M., Tenenbaum, J. B., & Gopnik, A. (2004). Children's causal inferences from indirect evidence: Backwards blocking and Bayesian reasoning in preschoolers. *Cognitive Science, 28*, 303–333.

Spirtes, P., Glymour, C., & Schienes, R. (1993). *Causation prediction and search*. New York: Springer-Verlag.

Steyvers, M., Tenenbaum, J. B., Wagenmakers, E. J., & Blum, B. (2003). Inferring causal networks from observations and interventions. *Cognitive Science, 27*, 453–489.

Tenenbaum, J. B., & Griffiths, T. L. (2001). Structure learning in human causal induction. In T. Leen, T. Dietterich, & V. Tresp (Eds.), *Advances in neural information processing systems 13* (pp. 59–65). Cambridge, MA: MIT Press.

Tenenbaum, J. B., & Griffiths, T. L. (2003). Theory-based causal inference. In S. Becker, S. Thrun, & K. Obermayer (Eds.), *Advances in neural information processing systems 15* (pp. 35–42). Cambridge, MA: MIT Press.

Tenenbaum, J. B., & Niyogi, S. (2003). Learning causal laws. In *Proceedings of the 25th Annual Meeting of the Cognitive Science Society*. Hillside, NJ: Erlbaum.

Tenenbaum, J. B., Sobel, D. M., Griffiths, T. L., & Gopnik, A. (submitted). *Bayesian inference in causal learning from ambiguous data: Evidence from adults and children*.

Waldmann, M. R. (1996). Knowledge-based causal induction. In D. L. Medin, D. R. Shanks, & K. J. Holyonk (Eds.), *The psychology of learning and motivation* (Vol 34, pp. 47–88). San Diego, CA: Academic Press.

Wellman, H. M. (1990). *The child's theory of mind*. Cambridge, MA: MIT Press.

Wellman, H. M., & Gelman, S. A. (1992). *Cognitive development: Foundational theories of core domains*. Annual Review of Psychology, 43, 337–375.

20

Two Proposals for Causal Grammars

Thomas L. Griffiths & Joshua B. Tenenbaum

Introduction

In chapter 19 we introduced a framework for thinking about the structure, function, and acquisition of intuitive theories inspired by an analogy to the research program of generative grammar in linguistics. We argued that a principal function for intuitive theories, just as for grammars for natural languages, is to generate a constrained space of hypotheses that people consider in carrying out a class of cognitively central and otherwise severely underconstrained inductive inference tasks. *Linguistic grammars* generate a hypothesis space of syntactic structures considered in sentence comprehension; *intuitive theories* generate a hypothesis space of causal network structures considered in causal induction. Both linguistic grammars and intuitive causal theories must also be reliably learnable from primary data available to people. In our view, these functional characteristics of intuitive theories should strongly constrain the content and form of the knowledge they represent, leading to representations somewhat like those used in generative grammars for language. However, until now we have not presented any specific proposals for formalizing the knowledge content or representational form of causal grammars. That is our goal here.

Just as linguistic grammars encode the principles that implicitly underlie all grammatical utterances in a language, so do causal grammars express knowledge more abstract than any one causal network in a domain. Consequently, existing approaches for representing causal knowledge based on Bayesian networks defined over observable events, properties, or variables are not sufficient to characterize causal grammars. Causal grammars are in some sense analogous to the "framework theories" for core domains that have been studied in cognitive development (Wellman & Gelman, 1992): the domain-specific concepts and principles, that allow learners to construct appropriate causal networks for reasoning about systems in a given domain and the expectations about which causal relations are more or less likely a priori, which enable causal learning to proceed from the sparse data typically encountered.

Chapter 19 describes a hierarchical Bayesian framework that more precisely formalizes the relationship between causal grammars and causal Bayesian networks. A learner's observations of the world are interpreted in terms of a hierarchy of increasingly abstract and general theories, with each level generating a hypothesis space and prior probability distribution for theories at the level below, thereby allowing those lower-level theories to be learned in a top-down fashion based on only sparse bottom-up input. The most specific level of intuitive theories concerns cause-effect relationships between observable events, properties, or variables, which can be formalized as causal Bayesian networks. Higher levels of abstraction require something like the representational powers of generative grammars, specifying categories of variables and rules for how composing those categories to construct the constrained space of causal networks that are possible in a given domain. For instance, to recall an example from chapter 19, a learner's beliefs about possible causal network structures in a simplified medical domain might be characterized by these two principles:

P1 There exist three classes of variables: symptoms, diseases, and behaviors. These classes are open and of unspecified size, allowing the possibility that a new variable may be introduced.

P2 Causal relations between variables are constrained with respect to these classes: Direct links arise only from behaviors to diseases and from diseases to symptoms. These links may be overlapping (e.g., diseases tend to have multiple effects, and symptoms tend to have multiple causes).

Figure 20-1 shows several causal networks (Graphs 1–4) that are consistent with these principles, as well as two networks (Graphs 5 and 6) that would be impossible or "ungrammatical" under this theory.

In this chapter, we examine in detail two proposals for formalizing causal grammars, the first based on a type of graph grammar that we call a *graph schema* and the second based on a typed predicate logic. We present applications of each approach to characterizing several small-scale intuitive theories and show how these approaches support quantitative modeling of behavioral studies on causal learning and theory acquisition with both child and adult subjects. Both proposals are defined in a probabilistic setting so that we can show precisely how they support causal learning and how they themselves can be learned using the

hierarchical Bayesian framework of chapter 19. For neither approach will we be able to give fully satisfying accounts of learning at both of these levels because of an inherent tradeoff in the representational power and learnability of any grammar: To the extent that a causal grammar generates rich and subtle constraints on possible causal networks, it will be harder to acquire that grammar from observed data. Presenting two different proposals for causal grammars allows us to explore this tradeoff and lay the groundwork for future attempts to give a full account of the use and origins of abstract causal knowledge.

Causal Grammars in a Hierarchical Bayesian Framework

Before turning to our two proposals, we briefly recap the necessary formal machinery for hierarchical Bayesian learning from chapter 19. Causal Bayesian networks are identified with theories at the lowest, most concrete level of the abstraction hierarchy, level T_0. We typically identify causal grammars with the T_1-level theories that define hypothesis spaces of T_0-level structures and assign prior probabilities to those hypotheses, thereby guiding inferences about the causal network structure T_0 most likely to have given rise to some observed data set d. A Bayesian learner evaluates a causal network hypothesis T_0 based on its posterior probability,

$$P(T_0 \mid d, T_1) = \frac{P(d \mid T_0)P(T_0 \mid T_1)}{P(d \mid T_1)}, \quad (20\text{-}1)$$

where the denominator is

$$P(d \mid T_1) = \sum_{T_0 \in \mathcal{H}_1} P(d \mid T_0)P(T_0 \mid T_1). \quad (20\text{-}2)$$

The causal grammar T_1 specifies a probabilistic process for generating causal network hypotheses. The total set of networks generated by the grammar comprises the hypothesis space $\mathcal{H}_1$. The probability with which the grammar generates any particular network T_0 yields its prior probability $P(T_0|T_1)$.

Our hierarchical Bayesian analysis also provides a framework for understanding how T_1-level theories may be inferred from data. Given a higher-level theory T_2 that specifies a prior over causal grammars $P(T_1|T_2)$ and a collection of data sets $\mathcal{D}$ from one or

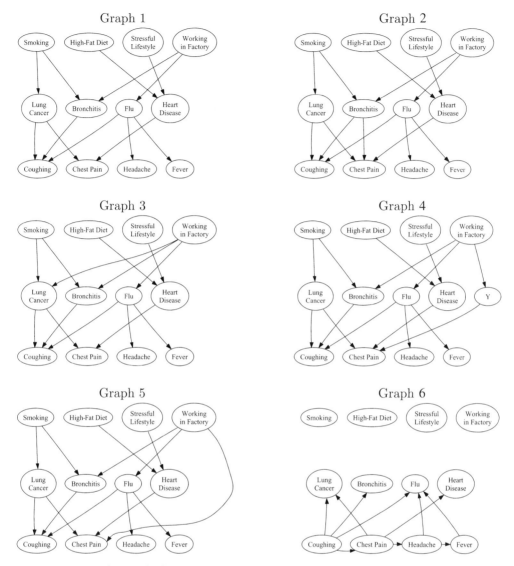

FIGURE 20-1 Causal networks illustrating different possible sets of beliefs about the relationships among behaviors, diseases, and symptoms. The same underlying causal grammar generates Graphs 1–4 but not Graphs 5 or 6.

more systems in the domain, the posterior probability distribution over causal grammars is

$$P(T_1 \mid \mathcal{D}, T_2) = \frac{P(\mathcal{D} \mid T_1)P(T_1 \mid T_2)}{P(\mathcal{D} \mid T_2)}. \quad (20\text{-}3)$$

The denominator $P(D|T_2)$ is computed in a similar fashion to Equation 20-2 but sums over theories at levels T_0 and T_1. In discussing our two proposals for causal grammars, one of the critical questions that arises is how such representations could be learned.

Equation 20-3 provides a theoretical answer to this question, but actual application of these methods to rich structures such as our causal grammars can pose significant computational challenges.

Theories as Graph Grammars

One approach to formalizing causal grammars—or higher-level causal theories—is in terms of a probabilistic graph grammar. In concrete terms, the grammar can be thought of as a machine that outputs samples from an infinite subset of labeled directed graphs drawn from some probability distribution. Each of these graphs represents the causal structure underlying a causal Bayesian network, but the graphs are not themselves equivalent to Bayesian networks: they must be supplemented with a semantic interpretation of the variable that each node represents, and a specification of how each variable depends functionally or probabilistically on its parents in the graph. Putting these complexities aside for now, a grammar for causal graphs is still a useful starting point for formalizing some aspects of abstract causal theories.

This section focuses on one elementary family of graph grammars sufficient to represent coarse probabilistic constraints on candidate causal network structures. We call these models *graph schemas*. They generalize an earlier proposal of Tenenbaum and Niyogi (2003). Graph schemas are clearly not adequate to express all theorylike knowledge at levels T_1 or above, but they provide a simple example of how we can begin to formalize abstract causal theories at a level beyond specific causal networks, how those theories could guide Bayesian learning of causal network structure, and how the theories may themselves be learned.

Graph Schemas

A graph schema G is a probabilistic generative model for labeled directed graphs. The key components of the schema are a set of *node classes* and the *class graph*, a directed graph defined over the node classes. (In the context of causal structure learning, each node corresponds to a variable in a causal graphical model, so we use the terms *node* and *variable* interchangeably.) Generating a graph from a graph schema involves two stages: (a) creating some number of graph nodes and assigning them to node classes; (b) creating connections between nodes in accordance with the class graph, which specifies whether a causal connection may (or must) exist from a particular variable i to a particular variable j as a function of their classes $C(i)$ and $C(j)$. A probabilistic (or deterministic) process must be defined for each of these stages, the details of which may vary from domain to domain. But, the basic structures of the set of node classes and the class graph are often sufficient to characterize some important features of a domain theory.

Figure 20-2 shows a graph schema that we refer to as G_{Dis}, which is intended to capture the constraints expressed by the principles P1 and P2 in our simplified disease domain. Consistent with P1, there are three node classes, labeled B, D, and S. Corresponding lowercase letters (b, d, s) are used to denote specific nodes in each class. All classes are *open*, meaning that the number of nodes in each class is potentially unbounded. Consistent with P1, the two arcs in the class graph specify allowed causal connections: $D \rightarrow S$ specifies that variables in Class D may connect causally to variables in Class S, and $B \rightarrow D$ specifies that variables in Class D may connect causally *to* variables in Class S. Both arcs are dashed to indicate that they represent laws about *possible* causal relations: links that may exist but need not. That is, any individual variable d∈D may be a cause of any individual node s∈S, but need not be. A solid arc n the class graph indicates a *necessary* causal relation, in which every node in one class is causally linked to every node in the other class.

Like a generative grammar for a language, G_{Dis} specifies abstract classes of entities (variables, instead of words) and rules about the relations (causal relations, instead of syntactic relations) that may exist between entities of various types. By analogy with linguistic grammars, we say that a graph schema G *generates* Graph i if there exists some way to partition (parse) the nodes in Graph i into the node classes of G such that all the edges in Graph i are consistent with the possible or necessary connections specified in the class graph of G. As with a grammar for language, a graph grammar can be augmented with probabilities to enable learning and inference. A probabilistic model can be defined over a graph schema by specifying (a) a distribution over the number of nodes in the graph and the number of nodes in each open class and (b) distributions over which specific causal links exist between nodes in classes connected in the class graph. For G_{Dis}, one way of defining these probabilities is shown in Figure 20-2. The number of nodes in each class follows a power law distribution $P(N) \propto 1/N^\alpha$, with a class-specific exponent α. After sampling an appropriate number of nodes in each class, a causal link is generated independently at random between each pair of nodes in classes connected in the class graph, with some probability β characteristic of the parent and child classes.

The graph schema G assigns a probability $P(\text{Graph } i|G)$ to any causal network Graph i over a set of N labeled nodes in its domain. $P(\text{Graph } i|G)$ is nonzero if and only if G generates Graph i. The sizes of the graphs generated by a schema are not bounded but must be finite. The probabilities $P(\text{Graph } i|G)$ are

Node classes:

Class	Symbol	Status
Behavior	B	open
Disease	D	open
Symptom	S	open

Class graph:

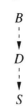

Generative model:

1. *Generate nodes in each class.*

$$N_B \sim \text{PowerLaw}(\alpha_B)$$
$$N_D \sim \text{PowerLaw}(\alpha_D)$$
$$N_S \sim \text{PowerLaw}(\alpha_S)$$

2. *Generate causal relations between pairs of nodes.*

Condition	Relation	Probability
$b \in B, d \in D$	$b \to d$	β_{BD}
$d \in D, s \in S$	$d \to s$	β_{DS}

FIGURE 20-2 A graph schema G_{Dis} for networks of diseases, their causes, and their effects.

normalized to sum to one over all labeled directed graphs with any finite number of nodes. If Graph i represents the structure of a particular causal network (T_0), then G can be thought of as those aspects of the T_1-level theory that generate a hypothesis space and prior over such structures: $P(T_0|T_1)$. Figure 20-3 shows two graphs sampled from $P(\text{Graph } i|G_{dis})$, each with $\alpha_B = \alpha_D = \alpha_S = 2$ and $\beta_{BD} = \beta_{DS} = 1/2$.

Examples of graph schemas in different domains

Figures 20-4 through 20-6 show schema-based graph grammars for several other domains. None of these grammars comes close to capturing all of people's abstract causal knowledge in the corresponding domain, and important details are oversimplified. The point is merely to illustrate some of the variations in abstract causal knowledge that can arise across domains and how these variations can be represented with different graph schemas. Only the qualitative structure of the graph schemas are shown, specifying the node classes and the possible and necessary causal links between classes.

The essentialist theory G_{Ess} (Figure 20-4a) generates causal networks corresponding to simple essentialist concepts for natural kinds (inspired in part by Rehder, chapter 12, this volume; Rehder and Burnett, in press). Different networks (e.g., Figure 20-4b) generated by this schema could describe different biological species, with different features or different causal relationships between features. They could also describe the same species as a learner acquires more or different beliefs about its characteristic properties and their causal connections. All of these networks place a single essence node in the same abstract causal role. The grammar captures this shared essentialist framework that underlies, supports, and constrains the infinite space of possible species concepts (Gelman, 2003). Under G_{Ess}, every species has a single essence, a single label, and one or more features. In our terminology, the essence class E and label class L are closed, but the feature class F is open. Causal relations may exist between any pair of features (represented by the dashed $F \to F$ edge in Figure 20-4a). The essence is also necessarily a cause of every feature (represented by the solid $E \to F$ edge); even for superficial features not directly a consequence of the essence, the causal relations that give rise to those features depend on the functioning of mechanisms that are themselves generated by the

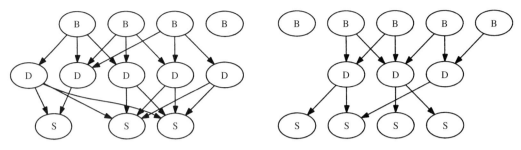

FIGURE 20-3 Causal networks sampled from G_{Dis}.

concept's essence. Finally, a causal link necessarily runs from the single essence variable to the single label variable, reflecting the lexical assumption that each concept has a single name.

The *magnetism* theory G_{Mag}, (Figure 20-5a) generates networks appropriate for reasoning about physical causal relationships between the positions of a system of magnets (Class M), magnetic objects (Class T), and nonmagnetic objects (Class U). (Magnetic objects, such as a ball bearing, are magnetizable but not sources of magnetic force.) Different systems may have different numbers of objects in these classes (e.g., Figure 20-5b), but in every system, the position of every magnet causally influences the position of every magnet and every magnetic object. The schema G_{Mag} captures these abstractions by positing three open node classes and necessary causal connections from Class M to itself and from M to T.[1]

The rational agent theory G_{Agent} (Figure 20-6), generates causal networks appropriate for a simple version of intuitive psychological reasoning. Different networks generated by this grammar could be appropriate for reasoning about different agents or different types of agents, with different specific beliefs, desires, and actions available to them. The graph schema is meant to capture the causal mental architecture that is in common across all these systems of rational agency. An agent has some set of actions A that can be produced, as well as two classes of mental states, beliefs B and desires D. Which action is chosen at a particular time depends on the agent's beliefs and desires. Variables in Class W describe relevant aspects of the state of the world. Actions may affect world states, and world states in turn affect the agent's beliefs. The agent's desires are not directly affected by the world but may be affected by the agent's beliefs about the world.[2] As with the graph schema G_{Dis} for the disease domain, all edges in the class graph for G_{Agent} are dashed, indicating only possible rather than necessary causal relations.

An intriguing difference between causal theories in different kinds of domains is suggested by the different patterns of necessary and possible causal relations in these graph schemas. Physical theories may be more

(a)

Node classes:

Class	Symbol	Status
Essence	E	closed: $|E| = 1$
Label	L	closed: $|L| = 1$
Feature	F	open

Class graph:

(b)

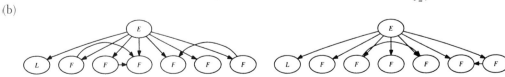

FIGURE 20-4 (a) A graph schema G_{Ess} for essentialist categories of natural kinds (cf. Rehder, chapter 12, this volume). (b) Causal networks sampled from the grammar.

(a)

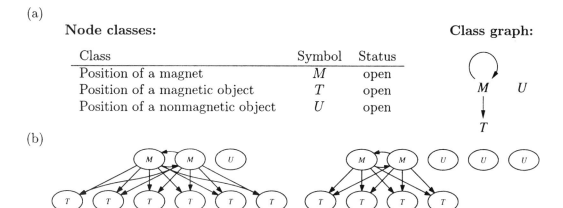

Node classes:

Class	Symbol	Status
Position of a magnet	M	open
Position of a magnetic object	T	open
Position of a nonmagnetic object	U	open

Class graph:

(b)

FIGURE 20-5 (a) A graph schema G_{Mag} describing the effects of magnets on other objects. (b) Causal networks sampled from the grammar.

likely to specify necessary causal links, as in G_{Mag}, in which every variable of a certain class possesses the same causal power (or lack thereof) with respect to every variable of another class. Psychological or biological theories may be more likely to specify possible causal links, as in G_{Dis}, G_{Agent}, or G_{Ess}, in which a variable's ontological class may constrain its possible cause-and-effect relations but does not determine them necessarily. The necessary relations that characterize the essence of a natural kind concept in G_{Ess} may be an exception that proves this rule: Essentialist intuitions give rise to some of the few inviolable and all-or-none judgments about otherwise graded conceptions of natural species (Gelman, 2003). Admittedly, this particular generalization is speculative, but some such generalizations about broad classes of domains could form the content of more abstract causal theories at higher levels of the theory hierarchy—well above the T_1 level that is our focus here.

The Role of Graph Schemas in Learning Causal Structure

As a model for T_1-level theories in our hierarchical Bayesian framework, probabilistic graph schemas should support the learning of causal network structures (T_0-level theories) and should themselves be learnable given a suitable hypothesis space of graph schemas (a T_2-level theory). To illustrate how graph schemas guide the learning of causal structure, consider how the schema G_{Dis} explains an inference discussed in chapter 19: positing the existence of a new disease to explain the observation of a previously unseen correlation between a symptom (e.g., chest pain) and a behavior (e.g., working in factory).

We first need to define more precisely the probabilistic model implied by each causal network of behaviors, diseases, and symptoms. In particular, we need to specify how the probability that an effect

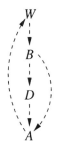

Node classes:

Class	Symbol	Status
World states	W	open
Beliefs	B	open
Desires	D	open
Actions	A	open

Class graph:

FIGURE 20-6 A graph schema G_{Agent} corresponding to a simple theory of mind for intentional agents.

occurs depends on the presence or absence of its causes. We assume a noisy-OR functional form for these cause-effect relationships (Pearl, 1988). This function is a probabilistic generalization of a logical OR gate, allowing each cause an independent opportunity to bring about the effect. If an effect E is caused by $C_1, \ldots, C_N$, then the noisy-OR states that

$$P(E=1 \mid c_1, \ldots, c_N) = 1 - (1-w_0) \prod_{i=1}^{N} (1-w_i)^{c_i} \quad (20\text{-}4)$$

where $E = 1$ indicates that the effect occurs, and c_i takes on the value 1 if the cause occurs and 0 otherwise. Here, w_i is the *causal power* of cause i (cf. Cheng, 1997), the probability that cause i will produce the effect. The parameter w_0 represents the probability that the effect will occur in the absence of any causes. For the purpose of this demonstration, we assume that the probability that a patient exhibits each behavior is 0.1; that behaviors cause diseases with power $w_i = 0.1$, and diseases occur spontaneously with $w_0 = 0.001$; that diseases cause symptoms with power $w_i = 0.8$, while symptoms occur spontaneously with $w_0 = 0.001$. We also assume that $\alpha_D = 2$.

Figure 20-7 shows how the graph schema G_{Dis} predicts that the posterior probabilities of five structures should change as evidence for a new correlation accumulates. For simplicity, we assume that only the first five structures shown in Figure 20-1 are under consideration.[3] Graph 1 is the *null hypothesis*, asserting a set of relationships among behaviors, diseases, and symptoms that is consistent with our medical intuitions. Graph 2 adds an additional link from bronchitis to chest pain. Graph 3 adds an additional link from working in factory to lung cancer. Graph 4 introduces a new disease Y, which connects working in factory to chest pain. Graph 5 adds an additional link from working in factory to chest pain; this link has causal power $w_i = 0.8 \times 0.15 \ 0.08$ for consistency with the assumptions of the other graphs. The data set d consists of 1,000 samples from Graph 1 together with some number of "anomalous" instances in which patients' only relevant behavior is working in a factory, and their only symptom is chest pain. For each patient, only the patient's relevant behaviors and symptoms are observed, not the diseases.

Figure 20-7a shows the log-likelihood log $P(d \mid \text{Graph } i)$ as a function of the number of anomalous instances observed. This quantity embodies the bottom-up influence of the data on evaluating these causal structure hypotheses independent of the domain constraints embodied in the graph grammar. With no anomalous instances, these data are most likely under Graph 1, consistent with the fact that they were generated from this structure. As the number of anomalous instances increases, the data become more likely under structures that allow for a correlation between working in factory and chest pain. The network with a direct link between working in factory and chest pain and the network that postulates a new disease linking these conditions (Graph 5) give the highest probability to these data. The network that postulates a link from working in factory to lung cancer (Graph 3) starts off equal to those hypotheses but declines in probability as more anomalous cases are observed (without any appearance of coughing, the other symptom associated with lung cancer).

We can compute the posterior probability of each of these graph structures by applying Bayes' rule, as in Equation 20-1. We want to compute $P(T_0 \mid d, T_1)$, where T_0 refers to one of the five graphs described above, and T_1 is the graph schema G_{Dis}. The prior $P(T_0 \mid T_1)$ has both qualitative and quantitative implications for these posterior probabilities. Graph 5 is not generated by G_{Dis} and consequently has a prior probability of 0. The remaining structures are all generated by the grammar, but with different probabilities. Graphs 1–3 are all approximately equally probable. Graph 4 is far less probable for two reasons. First, it is less likely that a structure with five disease nodes will be generated than a structure with four disease nodes because the probability of the number of nodes is proportional to $1/|D|^2$. Second, there are many more structures with five disease nodes than four, and consequently the average probability of any one of those structures is lower than the average probability of any one structure with four disease nodes.

Figure 20-7b shows the posterior probabilities of the different causal networks. Despite receiving maximal likelihood (along with Graph 4) given three or more anomalies, Graph 5 has zero posterior probability because of its inconsistency with G_{Dis}. As the number of anomalous instances increases, there are three discrete stages in the evolution of the posterior probabilities of the other networks. At first, Graph 1 remains favored by both the prior and the likelihood, and the apparent correlation is dismissed as just a coincidence. In the second stage, it becomes clear that the correlation between working in a factory and experiencing

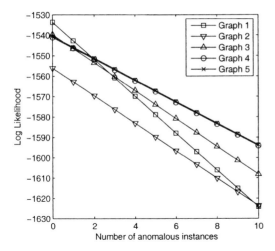 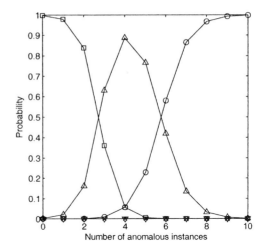

FIGURE 20-7 Learning from a correlation between working in factory and chest pain. (a) Likelihood functions for different structures as a function of the number of new instances in which working in factory and chest pain co-occur. (b) Posterior probabilities resulting from combining these likelihoods with the prior specified by G_{Dis}.

chest pain is genuine, and the likelihood favors the other structures. However, the prior is strongly against a new disease, so it seems most plausible that working in a factory is actually a cause of lung cancer, and it is just a coincidence that these patients do not also have the symptom of coughing associated with lung cancer. Finally, the likelihood overwhelms the prior's bias, and it becomes apparent that this pattern of data is evidence for an entirely new disease.

Learning Graph Schemas

To the extent that the skeletal structure of intuitive theories can be captured by graph schemas for causal networks, the development of intuitive theories may be characterized in terms of changes in those graph schemas. A theory may develop via changes in the causal relations that are necessary or possible, as well as in more radical ways—akin to what Carey (1985) calls "radical conceptual change": Node classes may be added or deleted, split or merged. Often, the explanatory power of a theory is deepened by adding a new class of hidden causes. For instance, the construction of the disease class of unobservable intervening causes between behaviors and symptoms might have been an important development in medical reasoning. Similarly, Rehder (chapter 12, this volume) posits that essentialist concepts of natural kinds are a relatively late development. Initially, the graph schema for natural kind concepts might look more like a prototype

theory, G_{Pro} (Figure 20-8). There is no underlying essence node and no explicit representation of causal links between features. Concepts are simply a bundle of one or more features, each linked directly and independently to the concept label.

There are probably many ways by which knowledge at the level of graph schemas can change or grow. One mechanism could be inductive learning from known causal networks or observed patterns of cause-and-effect co-occurence. Kemp, Griffiths, and Tenenbaum (2004) have developed a computational framework for discovering class structures in relational data that can be used to learn a version of probabilistic graph schemas. The learning algorithm takes as input one or more causal networks T_0 and automatically discovers the classes that are needed to capture the causal relationships among nodes and the probability of a relationship existing between nodes in each pair of classes. This framework does not explicitly distinguish laws for necessary or possible causal links but treats them as special cases of a more general probabilistic model. The learning algorithm makes no a priori assumption about the number of node classes but adopts a prior on node-class assignments that prefers to cluster most nodes into a few large classes. The learner can thus automatically discover the most parsimonious grammar, with the smallest number of classes, capable of generating the observed causal network structures.

The model defined by Kemp, Griffiths, and Tenenbaum (2004) effectively computes $P(T_1|T_0,T_2)$,

Node classes: **Class graph:**

Class	Symbol	Status
Label	L	closed: $|L| = 1$
Feature	F	open

F

$\downarrow$

L

FIGURE 20-8 A graph schema G_{Pro} for a prototype theory of natural-kind concepts.

the probability of a graph schema given an observed causal network generated from that grammar and some T_2-Level background knowledge. It does so by defining the distributions $P(T_0|T_1)$ in Equation 20-2 and $P(T_1|T_2)$ in Equation 20-3. To learn a graph schema directly from observations of the variables in a causal system—that is, to compute $P(T_1|\mathcal{D},T_2)$—this model can be combined with the Bayesian framework for learning the causal network structure described, which specifies $P(\mathcal{D}|T_0)$.

There has been relatively little empirical work looking at how people learn abstract theories at the level of a graph schema. Tenenbaum and Niyogi (2003) found that people were able to discover a set of classes and causal laws that determined the novel causal relationships among a set of objects in a virtual world. The objects in their experiments consisted of blocks that could be moved around and brought into contact with other blocks. When two blocks came into contact, one or both (or neither) could light up, depending on their class memberships and the causal laws operative in the virtual world. The experiments conducted by Tenenbaum and Niyogi (2003) examined how well people learned theories corresponding to the graph schemas shown in Figure 20-9a. Participants found it easiest to learn laws specifying necessary causal links, such as "Every object belongs to either Class A or B, and every object lights up objects in the other class but not those in the same class." The graph schemas G_1 and G_2 have such a structure. Laws specifying possible but not necessary causal relations, such as G_3 and G_4, were more difficult to learn but still learnable when the node classes played asymmetric roles, such as, "Every object belongs to either Class A or B, and objects in Class A may or may not light up objects in Class B." When the node classes played symmetric roles in a law specifying possible causal links—such as, "Every object belongs to either Class A or B, and any object may light up one or more objects in the other class but not any in the same class"—the theory was most difficult

(indeed, practically impossible) for participants to learn.

Kemp et al. (2004) applied their Bayesian algorithm for learning graph schemas to the same tasks and showed that it accounts for the relative difficulty that participants had in learning these different grammars. Figure 20-9b shows for all four graph schemas how the evidence for the correct theory accumulates as more objects are encountered (see Kemp et al., 2004, for details). Evidence is computed as the logarithm of the ratio of the probability of the data under two T_2-level theories: one in which the causal relations between the objects are generated by a graph schema (with an unknown number of classes) and another in which each object belongs to its own class (and thus no nontrivial graph schema is appropriate). The evidence for the correct grammar-based theory increases in all cases as more objects and relations are observed, but the rate of increase varies across the four theories in accordance with their relative ease of learning. Intuitively, graph schemas that make more constrained predictions about possible causal networks should be easier to learn because they assign higher probability to the causal networks they do generate. The empirical difficulty of learning was in accord with this principle. For instance, graph schemas specifying necessary causal relations were the easiest to learn, and they were the most constraining because an assignment of objects to classes uniquely specifies a single causal network that must be observed.

Extensions and Limitations

The notion of a graph schema can be extended in many ways to capture richer domain structures. One extension is to allow objects to belong to multiple classes. These classes might form a hierarchy, with each object in a set of nested classes, or a factorial structure, with each object belonging to one class from each of a number of groups. Furthermore, the grammar might depend on the attributes of the objects

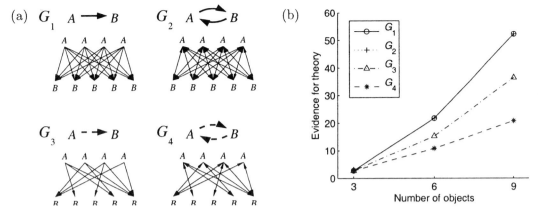

FIGURE 20-9 (a) Class graphs and sample networks representing the four graph schemas explored in the experiments of Tenenbaum and Niyogi (2003). (b) The evidence for a theory based on a graph schema increases as learners encounter more objects exhibiting causal relations consistent with that schema but at a different rate for different graph schemas. Human learners demonstrate the same ordering in the difficulty of learning these graph schemas.

in addition to their class. Another possibility is to allow some type of generative intermediate representations in the grammar, analogous to the nonterminals in context-free grammars for language, which could correspond to mechanisms of transmission linking causes and effects (e.g., Shultz, 1982).

Although graph schemas provide a simple way to capture some of the abstract knowledge in T_1-level theories, they leave out other knowledge that is fundamental to intuitive theories and essential for generating hypothesis spaces of causal structures. Foremost is their lack of a sufficiently expressive ontology. They take the nodes or variables of a causal network as primitive entities without explaining how those variables—or the classes of variables represented in a graph schema—derive from knowledge about types of entities and their properties. Their representations of causal relations and the laws that generate those relations are also fundamentally limited. The class graph of a graph schema specifies which causal relationships are possible or necessary but not which functional form those relationships take on if they exist. This knowledge of how effects depend on their causes should form a crucial part of both T_0- and T_1-level knowledge. At the T_0 level, it is necessary to compute the probability of an observed data set given a causal network structure or to make predictions about how novel interventions will affect a causal system. At the T_1 level, it provides valuable constraints on possible

causal network models and thus plays a critical role in explaining how T_0-level theories can be inferred from limited data.

Theories as Logical Grammars

Just as there are many different formalisms that one can adopt for representing linguistic grammars, varying greatly in complexity and coverage, so are there different approaches to formalizing causal grammars. Some of the shortcomings of graph grammars as accounts of T_1-level theories can be addressed by adopting a richer representational language based on a probabilistic version of predicate logic. Logical grammars can specify more complex and realistic ontologies in which the types of entities and predicates defined over those entities determine the space of causal Bayesian networks generated by the grammar. Unlike the graph grammars presented in the previous section, which generate only the labeled directed graph skeletons of causal networks, these logical grammars generate full T_0-level theories, each comprising a set of semantically grounded variables, a network of cause-effect relations, and the functional dependencies between causes and effects. By defining a probabilistic model over these logical grammars, analogous to the introduction of probabilities in graph grammars, we can specify a complete probabilistic generative model for T_0-level theories with a well-defined prior distribution $P(T_0|T_1)$. Probabilistic models defined over logical knowledge representations are a promising area of contemporary artificial intelligence research (e.g., Friedman, Getoor, Koller, & Pfeffer, 1999; Pasula & Russell, 2001). Our approach is closest in spirit to the Bayesian logic framework of Milch, Marthi, and Russell (2004).

The theories we consider in this section are defined using a probabilistic typed (or many-sorted) form of predicate logic. In predicate logic, a set of abstract entities are named with constants, and the properties of those entities are stated using predicates that apply to constants.[4] When referring to logical notions, we will write constants as lowercase letters or words and predicates as capitalized words. For example, in defining a theory of diseases, we could use ChestPain(p) to indicate that a particular person, represented by the constant p, had the property of having chest pain. In some cases, we might want to talk about a predicate without committing to a particular entity, which can be done by introducing a logical variable, which we write as a capital letter. Quantification over logical variables can be used to define the set of entities for whom a predicate holds. For example, if we had a world containing three entities, indicated by constants p_1, p_2, and p_3, we could indicate that they all suffered chest pain using the expression $\forall$ P ChestPain(P), where P is a logical variable that can take on values corresponding to each of the three entities, and $\forall$ is the universal quantifier, indicating the truth of the proposition it concerns for all values of the variable over which it quantifies. A typed logic divides entities into types and places constraints on the types of entities to which predicates can apply. We use the same notation used for predicates to refer to types, because types are naturally translated into predicates (e.g., Enderton, 1972). In the case of diseases, we might want to distinguish two types of entities—People and Objects—and assert that ChestPain is a predicate that can only apply to entities of type People.

This discussion of the properties of logic already reveals one of the ways in which logical representations of theories can go beyond graph grammars: They support rich ontologies, defined in terms of types of entities and the predicates that apply to them. We will illustrate some of their other properties and show how such theories may constrain people's causal inferences via an in-depth discussion of the blicket detector experimental paradigm (Gopnik, 2001; Gopnik & Sobel, 2000; Sobel, Tenenbaum, & Gopnik, 2004; Tenenbaum, Sobel, Griffiths, & Gopnik, submitted). This paradigm

showcases people's ability to make causal inferences about novel physical systems from limited data—just one or a few observations—when guided by appropriate prior knowledge. Traditional bottom-up approaches to learning causal relationships based on rational assessments of correlation, partial correlation, or other statistical measures (e.g., Cheng, 1997; Glymour, 2001; Gopnik et al., 2004; Shanks, 1995) are not readily applicable here because people do not observe sufficient data to compute these statistics. Our framework provides a rational account of both adults' and children's causal inferences in this paradigm, as well as strong quantitative predictions with a minimum of free numerical parameters.

Relative to the graph grammar formalisms of the preceding section, the added power of logical grammars comes at a price. Their richer ontologies introduce more details and greater complexity, making it harder to define satisfying theories that go beyond the simplest systems. It is also much less clear how these logical theories could be learned in full generality, although we can give analyses of several special cases in the blicket detector paradigm. We discuss extensions to our logical framework and prospects for explaining learning at the end of this section.

The Blicket Detector

Gopnik and Sobel (2000) introduced a novel paradigm for investigating causal inference in children; participants are shown a number of blocks along with a machine—the blicket detector. The blicket detector activates—lights up and makes noise—whenever a blicket is placed on it. Some of the blocks are blickets, others are not their outward appearance is no guide. Participants observe a series of trials; on each, one or more blocks is placed on the detector, and the detector activates or not. Participants are then asked which blocks have the power to activate the machine.

Gopnik and Sobel demonstrated various conditions under which children successfully infer the causal status of blocks from just one or a few observations (Gopnik et al., 2001; Sobel et al., 2004). Two experiments of this kind are summarized in Table 20-1. In these experiments, children saw two blocks, a and b, placed on the detector either together or separately across a series of trials. On each trial, the blicket detector either became active or remained silent. Table 20-1 gives the proportion of 4-year-olds who identified a and

TABLE 20-1 Probability of Identification as Blickets for 4-year-old Children and Deterministic and Probabilistic Theories

Condition	Stimuli	Children		Deterministic		Probabilistic	
		a	b	a	b	a	b
One cause	$e^+\|a^+b^-$ $e^-\|a^-b^+$ $2e^+\|a^+b^+$	.91	.16	**1.00**	**.00**	.99	.07
Two cause	$3e^+\|a^+b^-$ $2e^+\|a^-b^+$ $e^-\|a^-b^-$	.97	.78	?	?	**1.00**	**.81**
Indirect screening-off	$2e^+\|a^+b^+$ $e^2\|a^+b^-$	.00	1.00	.00	**1.00**	.13	.90
Backward blocking	$2e^+\|a^+b^+$ $e^+\|a^+b^-$	1.00	.34	**1.00**	**β**	.93	.41
Association	$e^+\|a^+b^-$ $2e^+\|a^-b^+$	.94	1.00	**1.00**	**1.00**	.82	.98
Backward blocking (rare)	$2e^+\|a^+b^+$ $e^+\|a^+b^-$	1.00	.25	**1.00**	.17	.91	.26
Backward blocking (common)	$2e^+\|a^+b^+$ $e^+\|a^+b^-$	1.00	.81	**1.00**	.83	.98	.86

Note: The one cause and two cause conditions are from Gopnik, Sobel, Schulz, and Glymour (2001, Experiment 1). The indirect screening-off, backward blocking, association, backward blocking (rare), and backward blocking (common) conditions are from Sobel, Tenenbaum, and Gopnik (2004, Experiments 2 and 3). **Boldface** indicates the predictions of the model favored by the theory selection procedure outlined in the section on learning logical theories.

b as blickets after several different sequences of trials, encoding contact between the blocks and the detector with the variables A and B and the detector response of the detector with the variable E. Tenenbaum, Sobel, Griffiths, & Gopnik (submitted) tested adults with a similar paradigm, obtaining quantitative judgments that could be used to evaluate the precise predictions of competing computational models. They also used stimuli that were intended to provide ambiguous evidence regarding whether blocks were blickets. These data are not presented in Table 20-1 but are discussed in the Comparison With Alternative Accounts section.

We explain the blicket-detector inferences that children and adults draw with reference to a T_1-level theory, expressed using probabilistic logic. This account elaborates on our earlier theory-based model of blicket-detector inferences (Tenenbaum & Griffiths, 2003) by making the theory used in that analysis explicit. The theory should embody people's expectations about how machines (and detectors) work, informed by the specific instructions and familiarization experience provided to experimental participants. For the experiments described in Table 20-1, the blicket detector was introduced to children as a blicket machine, and children were told "blickets make the machine go." In a familiarization phase prior to the critical experimental trials, children saw blocks that activated the machine identified as blickets and blocks that did not activate the machine identified as not blickets. A theory expressing the relevant background knowledge is sketched in Figure 20-10.

This theory has three parts, specifying an ontology, prescriptions regarding causal structure, and expectations about the functional form of causal relations.[5] The constraints on causal structures and functional form together constitute the causal laws expressed in the theory. As a generative grammar for causal Bayesian networks, the three components of the theory respectively generate the nodes of the network, the causal links between nodes, and the local conditional probability distribution for each node as a function of its causes. We describe this generative model but first we explain the content of the theory in more detail.

The *ontology* identifies the types of entities in the domain and predicates defined on those types. The types are organized hierarchically, with the first cut into Object, Power, and Trial. The Object type further divides into Block and Machine. The predicates are divided into structural and causal predicates. The *causal* predicates specify the kinds of variables that will appear as nodes in causal networks (T_0-level theories) describing systems in the domain. The *structural* predicates concern the basic properties of the entities in the domain and determine which causal relationships can or must hold among causal predicates applied to those entities—that is, the constraints on candidate causal networks defined over grounded causal predicates.

In this case, there are two types of causal predicates, variables that can participate in causal relationships: Contact(O, O', T) is true if objects O and O' are in contact on trial T; Active(M, T) is true if machine M is active on trial T. These predicates each apply to a particular Trial, representing discrete temporal intervals of the experiment. There are two structural predicates: Has(P, O) is true if object O has power P (e.g., if an object is a blicket), and Activates(P, M) is true if power P activates machine M, (e.g., if a machine is a blicket detector). Under this construal, being a blicket or a blicket detector is like being an acid or a base. It is to belong to a class of causal agents or causal patients, defined by the roles that they play in certain laws of causal interaction (White, 1995).

So far, we focused on the logical structure of the ontology. The probabilistic aspect of the ontology defines a distribution for the number of entities of each type and specifies the probability with which structural predicates hold. In Figure 20-10, the numbers of blocks, machines, powers, and trials are assumed to follow power law distributions with parameters α_B, α_M, α_P, and α_T, respectively. These distributions are not of consequence in the experiments we analyze; all blocks and machines are assumed to be observed, and there is just one relevant power concept, blicket, that is introduced verbally at the beginning of each experiment. The probability with which

each object has a particular power (e.g., is a blicket) β is an important variable . Because there is only one power, blicket, and one machine, d, and d is explicitly called a blicket detector, the prior probability γ that Activates(blicket, d) is true can be assumed to be 1.

The causal laws of a theory specify which causal relations between variables may, must, or are likely to exist and what form they take. We divide causal laws into the aspects relevant to causal structure and those that concern functional form. The structural prescriptions of the theory determine the probability that particular causal relationships exist. Each rule consists of a set of conditions stated in terms of structural predicates, under which a causal relationship between two causal predicates holds with some probability. The causal law in Figure 20.10 asserts that contact between an object and a machine on a given trial will cause the machine to be active on that trial if the object has some power (e.g., is a blicket) and the machine is activated by that power.

The structural component of the causal laws concerns only the presence or absence of causal links between variables. The strength of those links (e.g., the probability that on any one trial, the presence of the cause will indeed lead to the presence of the effect) are determined by the functional form component of the theory, which specifies the probability distribution associated with each causal predicate. This theory posits a noisy-OR form for the conditional probability distribution of any machine activating given contact with objects that can activate it. For simplicity, we reduce these noisy-OR functions to just a single parameter ϵ, representing the *error rate* of a detector, the probability of a miss or false alarm. To begin, we assume a deterministic detector with $\epsilon = 0$. This has two important implications. First, the detector cannot activate unless a blicket is in contact with it ($\omega_0 = 0$). Second, placing a blicket on the detector will always activate the detector ($\omega_i = 1$). These two assumptions are equivalent to the "activation law" of Sobel et al. (2004): A blicket detector will be active if and only if one or more blickets is in contact with it. Because people always observe which objects are in contact on each trial, the prior probabilities for contact relations are irrelevant.

The deterministic detector theory generates a hypothesis space $\mathcal{H}_1$ of causal networks defined for any set of trials involving any number of blocks and detectors. The generative process defines a prior probability distribution over that space, indicating which causal structures are more or less likely a priori.

Ontology:

Types	Number
Object	
Block	$N_B \sim \text{PowerLaw}(\alpha_B)$
Machine	$N_M \sim \text{PowerLaw}(\alpha_M)$
Power	$N_P \sim \text{PowerLaw}(\alpha_P)$
Trial	$N_T \sim \text{PowerLaw}(\alpha_T)$

Structural predicates	
Has(Power,Object)	$\sim \text{Bernoulli}(\beta)$
Activates(Power,Machine)	$\sim \text{Bernoulli}(\gamma)$

Causal predicates
Contact(Object,Object,Trial)
Active(Machine,Trial)

Causal laws:

Structure:

Condition	Relation	Probability
Has(P,O) $\wedge$ Activates(P,M)	$\forall$T Contact(O,M,T) $\rightarrow$ Active(M,T)	1

Functional form:

Contact(O,O',T) $\sim$ Bernoulli($\cdot$)
Active(M,T) $\sim$ Bernoulli(ν) for ν given by a noisy-OR function

Cause	Strength
(Background)	$w_0 = \epsilon$
Contact(O,M,T)	$w_1 = 1 - \epsilon$

FIGURE 20-10 Sketch of a probabilistic logical theory for causal induction with blicket detectors.

The process by which a causal network is generated from the theory is as follows:

1. *Generate nodes.* Sample a set of entities of each type from the distribution specified in the **Ontology**. Sample the structural predicates for these entities using the appropriate probabilities. Generate the set of grounded causal predicates. Each of these grounded predicates can be thought of as a binary variable that is true or false. These variables comprise the nodes of the causal network.
2. *Generate links.* Conditioned on the values of the structural predicates, sample causal links between nodes from the distribution stated in the **Structure** component of the theory's **Causal laws**.
3. *Generate local conditional probabilities.* For each node, define a local conditional probability as specified in the **Functional form** component of the theory's **Causal laws** and set the appropriate parameters (or sample them from some prior distribution).

The set of grounded causal predicates is obtained by applying each causal predicate to all entities that can act

as its arguments. Assuming that we have two blocks a and b, a single detector d, a single power blicket, and the knowledge that d is activated by this power, the set of grounded predicates is as follows: Contact(a, d, T), Contact(b, d, T), and Active(d, T) for each trial T. These grounded predicates are the variables on which the possible causal networks (or T_0-level theories) are defined.

Because causal relationships are constant over all trials T, we can express these causal networks in terms of four graph structures as shown in Figure 20-11a. For shorthand, we use the variables A and B to represent Contact(a, d, T) and Contact (b, d, T), respectively, and E to represent Active(d, T). The prior probabilities of these networks $P(\text{Graph } i|T_1)$ are determined by the parameter β in the T_1 theory—that is, the prior probabilities that Has(blicket, a) and Has(blicket, b) are true—because a causal relationship between a block and a detector exists if and only if that block has the power that activates the detector.

The posterior probability distribution over the set of causal networks generated by the theory can be evaluated for each set of trials shown in Table 20-1, identifying the observed events as the data set d and

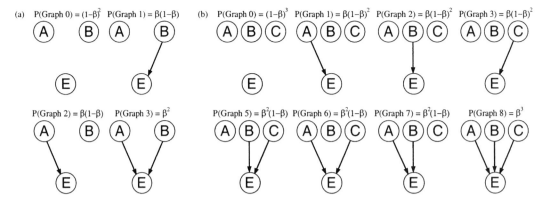

FIGURE 20-11 Graph structures generated by the causal theory for the blicket detector. (a) The hypothesis space for two blocks, a and b; (b) the hypothesis space with three blocks, a, b, and c. A, B, and C denote Contact (a, d, T), Contact (b, d, T), and Contact (c, d, T), respectively; E indicates Active (d, T). These causal networks are implicitly quantified over all trials T.

applying Bayes' rule as in Equation 20-1. In the blicket detector experiments, learners are typically asked to judge whether a block (such as a) is a blicket. This question asks whether Has(blicket, a) is true. Because Has(blicket, a) is logically equivalent to the existence of a causal link between Contact(a, d, T) and Active(d, T), this question can be reduced to a Bayesian inference over causal network structures: Given some observed trials with a blicket detector d, the probability that a block is a blicket is the probability that the causal link Contact(b, d, T) → Active(d, T) exists in the causal network describing the observed system. This can be evaluated by summing the posterior probability of the models in which such a causal relationship exists. For instance, to evaluate the probability that a is a blicket, we compute

$$P(A \rightarrow E \mid d, T_1) = \sum_{T_0 \in \mathcal{H}_1} P(A \rightarrow E \mid T_0) P(T_0 \mid d, T_1)$$

$$(20\text{-}5)$$

For the simple hypothesis space shown in Figure 20-11a, this is just $P(\text{Graph } 2 \mid d, T_1) + P(\text{Graph } 3 \mid d, T_1)$.

The predictions of the deterministic detector theory are given in Table 20-1. The theory's predictions correspond qualitatively with children's judgments but cannot explain all of the inferences observed. In particular, they cannot explain the two cause condition in Experiment 1 of Gopnik et al. (2004), which served as an associative control for the one cause condition. In the two cause condition, children saw the detector activate when block a was placed on it (alone) on three of three trials and saw the detector activate when block

b was placed on it (alone), but only on two of three trials. These data are not compatible with any causal network generated by the deterministic detector theory, and thus the theory's predictions are undefined (indicated by the question marks in Table 20-1).

The two cause data set can be explained by relaxing one of the assumptions of the deterministic detector theory to allow blickets to activate detectors only some of the time. We can make this change by allowing ϵ to take on some value greater than 0. This *probabilistic detector* theory not only gives the same predictions as the deterministic detector theory in the limit as $\epsilon \rightarrow 0$, but also predicts that both a and b are blickets with probability 1 in the two-cause condition. Different values of ϵ give different predictions. The predictions of this theory with $\epsilon = 0.1$ and $\alpha = 1/3$ are shown in Table 20.1. This model captures some of the finer details of children's judgments that are not captured by the deterministic detector, such as the fact that b is judged less likely to be a blicket than a in the two-cause condition.

Comparison With Alternative Accounts

Besides our theory-based Bayesian account, at least two other accounts have been proposed for how children or adults might infer causal structure in the blicket detector paradigm: (a) using a domain-general algorithm for learning causal structure based on statistical dependencies; (b) using domain-general deductive reasoning augmented with domain-specific assumptions about the relevant class of causal mechanisms (e.g., detectors). Each approach is simpler in some way than our theory-based Bayesian framework, but each is also unable to explain the full range of people's inferences in this paradigm.

Gopnik et al. (2004) advocate the first alternative, proposing that children's causal inferences can be explained by standard bottom-up algorithms for learning causal graphical models (e.g., Pearl, 2000, Spirtes, Glymour, & Schienes, 1993). In particular, they argue that these algorithms will infer the same causal structure (which objects are blickets) that children do in the blicket detector experiments, given observations of the variables A, B, and E across trials. However, the Spirtes et al. and Pearl algorithms require as input the probabilistic dependence and independence relations among a set of variables, and these relations cannot be inferred with any reliability from the small number of trials presented to human learners in the experiments. At least an order of magnitude more data—or some domain-specific assumptions about the causal mechanisms at work—would be necessary for one of these algorithms to work as a rational account of human causal learning. Gopnik et al. (2004) finesse this issue by proposing that learners assume the observed data frequencies can be safely multiplied by some large number, but this assumption is clearly unjustified in many cases. Effectively, it serves to introduce crucial aspects of the deterministic detector theory without making them explicit because it is justified only in those domains in which causal systems are deterministic and fully observable (Tenenbaum et al., submitted).

There is a clearer rational basis for accounts of children's reasoning in logical terms. An assumption that the blicket detector activates if and only if there is a blicket in contact with it, plus elementary deductive reasoning capacities, is sufficient to explain all of children's inferences discussed so far (except in the two-cause condition). However, neither this deductive model nor the Spirtes et al. (1993) or Pearl (2000) bottom-up structure learning algorithms can address another core aspect of human causal inference. Under all these alternative approaches, learners evaluate candidate causal structures in a binary fashion: each structure is either consistent or inconsistent with the data. There is no provision for representing graded degrees of belief about the existence of a causal relation, either a priori, based on expectations about which network structures are more or less plausible, or a posteriori, after observing data that are more or less compatible with multiple structures.

In contrast, our theory-based account naturally explains these gradations, through the probabilistic form of the theory and the probabilistic character of the causal inference process. For instance, after all trials have been observed in the backward blocking condition, the posterior probability that block is a blicket reduces to β, the prior probability that any block is a blicket (assuming the deterministic theory). This reduction to the prior occurs because, having observed that block a unambiguously activates the detector (and hence is definitely a blicket), the data now provide no evidence either way about b. More generally, even if the data do not provide unambiguous evidence about the status of any one block, they can suggest that some blocks are more likely to be blickets than others, while the prior probability β modulates the overall probability that any block is a blicket. Sobel et al. (2004) and Tenenbaum et al. (submitted) have shown that adults and children reason in accord with these graded predictions.

Tenenbaum et al. (submitted, Experiment 1) studied an analog of the backward blocking condition of Sobel et al. (2004, Experiment 1) and attempted to manipulate the β parameter—the prior probability of encountering objects with the causal power to activate the detector. The experiment was performed with adults to measure more precise graded judgments. They used a superpencil detector—rather than a blicket detector—that determined whether apparently normal pencils contained a special kind of lead called superlead. Participants were randomly assigned to two groups, varying in how they were introduced to the notion of superlead. Both groups of participants were initially shown 12 pencils placed on the detector one at a time. In what we refer to as the rare condition, only 2 of these pencils caused the detector to activate. In the common condition, the detector activated for 10 of the 12 pencils. It was hypothesized that learners would set the β parameter in their theories to something like the base rate of causally efficacious objects: 1/6 in the rare condition and 5/6 in the common condition.

The judgment phase had three stages. In stage 1, the baseline, participants were simply shown 2 new pencils, a and b. In stage 2, participants saw a and b placed on the detector together, and the detector activated. In Stage 3 just a was placed on the detector, and the detector activated. After each stage, participants were asked to rate the probability that a and b were superpencils. Mean ratings after the first (baseline) stage in each condition were used to set β in our model. Then, the same values of β were used to predict judgments in the remaining stages. Mean ratings in the rare and common conditions are shown in Figure 20-12(a) and 12(b), respectively, along with our model's predictions.

Manipulating the base rate of superpencils during familiarization had the expected effect on people's baseline judgments: β was estimated at 0.19 in the rare condition and 0.78 in the common condition. It also affected subsequent judgments as predicted by our Bayesian model under the deterministic detector theory (or the probabilistic detector theory with $\omega = 1 - \epsilon$ as $\epsilon \to 0$). The probability of a and b being superpencils increases after the first trial; then, the second trial provides unequivocal evidence that a is a superpencil, and the probability that b is a superpencil returns to the prior β. Sobel et al. (2004, Experiment 3) replicated this study with 4-year-old children using the blicket detector but collecting only binary judgments (blicket, not a blicket) and without the first two stages of judgment. Table 20-1 shows the percentage of children who labeled the a and b objects as blickets in each condition. These results showed the same effect of varying prior probabilities seen in the model predictions and adult judgments.

These results are consistent with our theory-based Bayesian account of causal inference, but they do not provide the strongest possible test of whether people's inferences are truly Bayesian. A deductive reasoning account that simply defaults to the observed base rates of causal powers when the data are ambiguous could predict people's judgments just as well. Tenenbaum et al. (submitted, Experiment 2) also asked whether people could make more subtle graded inferences from ambiguous evidence in a fashion consistent with the theory-based Bayesian account. This experiment was equivalent to the superpencil backwards blocking (rare) condition, except in the judgment phase. Now that phase began by introducing three new pencils, a, b, and c, and asking for baseline ratings of the probability that each pencil was a superpencil. Participants then saw a and b placed on the detector together, causing the detector to activate, and gave new ratings. Finally, they saw a and c placed on the detector together, causing the detector to activate, and were asked to rate the probability that each of the three pencils was a superpencil. The mean ratings are shown in Figure 20-12c.

Model predictions are also shown in Figure 20-12c, with β calibrated to the mean probability rating on the first (baseline) judgment. Figure 20-11b shows the hypothesis space $\mathcal{H}_1$ of causal network structures generated by the T_1 theory. With three blocks, there are now eight possible networks. As in Equation 20-5, the probability that any given block is a blicket is calculated by summing the probability of all network hypotheses in which that block's position is a cause of the detector's activation.

In this experiment, people received no unambiguous clues that a particular pencil was a superpencil: There were no trials on which a single pencil caused the detector to activate. Nonetheless, after the final trial, people were able to infer that a was likely to be a superpencil, while b and c were less likely to be superpencils, with higher judged probability than at the start of the judgment phase but lower than the peak judgment after the first trial. These judgments are strongly in accord with our theory-based Bayesian account. Figure 20-12c shows that the Bayesian model yields four qualitatively distinct levels of belief over the course of the judgment phase, which are all matched by statistically significant differences in the corresponding ratings of participants. Qualitatively similar inferences were made by 4-year-old children in an analogous experiment with the blicket detector: After the final trial, children were most likely to say that a, but not b, or c was a blicket (Tenenbaum et al., submitted, Experiment 3).

In sum, our theory-based Bayesian framework can explain how people make successful causal inferences about novel physical systems from just one or a few observations, as well as the gradations of judgment and the effects of prior knowledge that arise. These phenomena are not easily explained by other existing approaches to rational causal inference based on deductive reasoning or bottom-up detection of probabilistic dependencies. Our framework also provides a strong quantitative predictive model with essentially no free numerical parameters. Qualitative assumptions were needed about the form of people's intuitive theories for how machines (or detectors) work, but we would argue that these assumptions are necessary in some form for any account that seeks to give a rational explanation of people's judgments in these scenarios.

Although our discussion here focused on the blicket detector, the same approach of Bayesian inference over logical theories provides a useful framework for understanding causal induction in a variety of settings. In Griffiths (2005) and Griffiths and Tenenbaum (in preparation), we show how this approach can explain people's judgments in identifying causal structure from

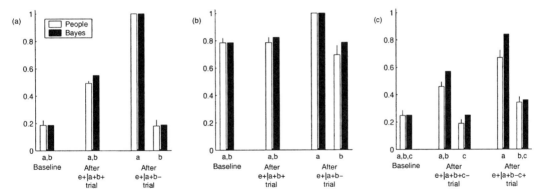

FIGURE 20-12 Adult judgments with superpencils, an analog of the blicket detector task, from Tenenbaum, Sobel, and Gopnik (submitted). Parts (a) and (b) show inferences from the same set of trials, but with different prior probabilities for superpencils, being rare and common respectively. (c) Inferences from ambiguous evidence.

contingency data (Griffiths & Tenenbaum, in press), reasoning about mechanical systems (Gopnik et al., 2004), identifying causal relations and hidden causes with dynamic events (Griffiths, Baraff, Tenenbaum 2004), and evaluating evidence for causal relations between variables in different domains (Schulz & Gopnik, in press). The integration of Bayesian inference mechanisms with a logical theory for generating causal network hypotheses accounts for the effects of several important dimensions along which these learning scenarios vary: the number of independent data points observed (ranging from just 1 or 2 samples to 60–100 samples); the availability of active interventional data in addition to purely passive observational data; the possibility of and strength of evidence for hidden causes; the availability of dynamic real-time observations rather than merely discrete trials; and the a priori plausibility of a mechanism linking candidate causes and effects.

Learning Logical Theories

The logical theories outlined in this section are a proposal for a T_1-level representation, specifying one level of our hierarchy of theories. As with graph grammars, statistical inference can in principle be used to learn these T_1-level theories, but the greater representational expressiveness of predicate logic leads to a vastly larger hypothesis space of candidate theories—and thus a much more challenging learning problem in general.

A constrained but quite tractable form of theory learning is parameter estimation: inferring the values of numerical parameters in the theory such as those controlling the number of entities of some type (e.g., the γ parameters in Figure 20-10), the frequency with which some structural predicate holds (e.g., the β or γ parameters), or the strength of probabilistic causes (e.g., the ϵ parameter). The rare-common manipulation in the backward-blocking experiments shows adults and children can rationally adjust their beliefs about one parameter in the theory's ontology (β) to reflect the apparent abundance of a causal power (being a blicket).

More formally, in these experiments people act as if they are inferring the theory with maximum likelihood out of all candidates in a one-dimensional hypothesis space of possible theories parameterized by β. This sort of learning is certainly less general than discovering a full theory with new classes and causal laws, as in the experiments of Tenenbaum and Niyogi 2003), but it is also more general than just learning the parameters or structure of a single causal network (learning at the T_0 level). The knowledge acquired about β exists at the T_1 level, specifying a prior distribution over possible causal networks that can be defined for any number of new entities in this domain.

In the remainder of the section, we show how similar parametric learning can take place concerning the functional form of a theory's causal laws. The blicket-detector theory in Figure 20-10 specifies the error rate of a detector in terms of a parameter ϵ. We have outlined two different versions of the theory, for deterministic detectors and probabilistic detectors which take $\epsilon = 0$ and $\epsilon > 0$, respectively. In some cases, such as the one cause and two-causes experimental conditions, the probabilistic-detector theory seems to better characterize children's inferences. However, the instructions the children received suggested that the deterministic theory might be more appropriate. This raises an interesting learning question: How might a learner choose between these different theories as descriptions of a causal system? Our hierarchical Bayesian framework provides an answer. In this simple case, we have just two candidate T_1 theories that differ only in the functional form of their causal laws: the deterministic theory and the probabilistic theory. We can use Bayes' rule to compute a posterior distribution over these theories, $P(T_1| \mathcal{D}, T_2)$, as shown in Equation 20-3.

Figure 20-13 shows how this process of inferring the T_1-level theory with an appropriate functional form can operate concurrently with identifying which blocks are blickets—an inference about causal networks at the T_0-level. The figure shows how the posterior distribution over the two theories—deterministic and probabilistic—evolves as the data $\mathcal{D}$ grow with each additional trial in the two-cause condition. The bottom row shows the corresponding changes in the judged probabilities that blocks a and b are blickets, an average of the predictions of each T_1 theory weighted by their posterior probabilities $P(T_1|\mathcal{D}, T_2)$. The prior $P(T_1|T_2)$ assigns a probability of .99 to the deterministic theory and .01 to the probabilistic theory, consistent with both task instructions and an intuitive bias toward determinism in mechanical systems. The base rate of blickets β is set to 1/3, and the noise level ϵ for the probabilistic theory is set to 1/10.

In the two-cause condition, the first three trials are all $e^+|a^+b^-$: events in which block a is placed on the detector and the detector activates. This is sufficient to identify a as a blicket under either theory. The fourth trial is $e^-|a^- b^+$: b is placed on the detector, and the detector does not activate. Under the deterministic theory, b would definitely not be a blicket. Under the probabilistic theory, there remains a small chance that b is a blicket, and because the probabilistic theory is still viable, the probability that b is a blicket is nonzero but extremely low. On the fifth trial, $e^+|a^-b^+$, the detector activates when b is placed on it. The fourth and fifth trials are mutually contradictory under the deterministic theory—together they have a probability of 0—so the posterior over theories now switches

suddenly to favor the probabilistic theory with probability 1. Under that theory, the data so far are uninformative about whether b is a blicket because we assumed equal probabilities of the two types of error in the detector. It is just as likely that b is a blicket and the fourth trial was bad luck, or that b is not a blicket and the fifth trial was a fluke, so the probability reverts to the prior β. The sixth trial provides further evidence that b is actually a blicket, $e^+|a^-b^+$. The final prediction is that a is very likely to be a blicket, and b is slightly less likely, matching the judgments of the children in the work of Gopnik et al. (2001).

Ultimately, parametric learning of T_1-level theories is far from a complete solution to the problem of how people acquire rich representations of abstract causal knowledge. It is an open question how (and even whether) people learn T_1 theories in their full generality, not to mention theories at levels T_2 and above. Techniques of inductive logic programming (Muggleton, in press) may provide one computational approach to these problems, but it is not at all clear that these techniques can scale up to humanlike knowledge, or that they bear any similarity to human learning mechanisms. Formal computational frameworks for inductive learning will likely need to be extended to incorporate other cognitive capacities, such as analogy and natural language, that can provide crucial scaffolding for building appropriate hypothesis spaces of candidate theories.

Conclusion

This chapter explored two proposals based on graph schemas and typed predicate logic for formalizing the content and representational form of abstract causal theories. Each of these formalisms was cast as a probabilistic generative grammar for causal networks, inspired by an analogy between the computational problems of causal inference and natural language processing. We discussed each approach in terms of how it could account for the functional roles that abstract theories must play in a hierarchical Bayesian framework for causal inference and learning (Tenenbaum, Griffiths & Niyogi, chapter 19, this volume), chiefly, how the theory supports learning of causal network structures (or lower-level theories) and how the theory could itself be learned or tuned based on observations.

We hope that readers find each of these frameworks for causal grammar intriguing but hardly satisfying. We see them as proposals for what a causal grammar might look like rather than fully developed accounts. We close this chapter with three lessons that we have learned in the course of trying to formalize intuitive theories as causal grammars.

First, to approach human-level competence in models of intuitive theories, as in natural language grammars, it will be necessary to integrate two schools of thought that have often been treated as incommensurate or in opposition: probability and statistics on the one hand and logical and symbolic representations on the other hand. Although this view is not yet fully accepted by researchers in generative linguistics, many computational linguists have recognized that probabilistic models defined over rule-based grammatical representations, such as stochastic finite-state grammars or context-free grammars, offer significant advantages over purely statistical or purely symbolic models while preserving the best features of both (Charniak, 1993; Jurafsky & Martin, 2000; Manning & Schütze, 1999). Logical or rule systems provide representational richness and the capacity for abstraction; probabilistic models provide the capacity for inductive inference from observed data. These same considerations motivate our proposals for expressing intuitive theories as probabilistic generative models defined over graph grammars or typed logical systems. We believe that some such integration of probability and structured rule systems will be necessary to explain how abstract causal knowledge guides the learning of new causal relations and can itself be learned from experience.

Second, in formal models of intuitive theories, as with formal models of grammar in linguistics, there will often be a tradeoff between representational capacity and learnability. For instance, hidden Markov models are much more limited than stochastic context-free grammars in terms of the syntactic regularities they can represent, but their structure can be induced from data much more readily by statistical methods. Likewise, the graph schemas we presented in the section third are much more limited as accounts of intuitive theories than are the typed logics we presented in the section fourth, but we can give a principled and tractable algorithm for learning graph schemas (Kemp et al., 2004), but we cannot yet do that for logical theories. At this early stage, it is valuable to pursue multiple approaches to formalizing theories with the hope of ultimately converging on a framework that is both sufficiently and learnable.

Finally, definitive accounts of people's intuitive theories are likely to be elusive, just as they are with natural language grammars. It is not easy to work backward, from observations of people's judgments about linguistic utterances or cause-effect relations to formal accounts of the unobservable abstract knowledge that they bring to bear in making those judgments. In this chapter, we have not attempted to claim that any particular formal model necessarily corresponds in detail to people's intuitive theory in some domain. We have merely proposed some possible models of intuitive theories that could account for aspects of people's causal inference capacities and argued for the importance of certain general

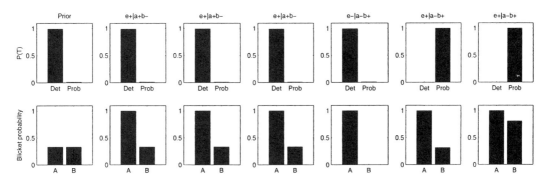

FIGURE 20-13 Learning functional form. The bar graphs along the top of the figure show the probabilities of two theories, with Det indicating the deterministic detector theory and Prob indicating the probabilistic detector theory. The bar graphs along the bottom show the probabilities that the blocks A and B are blickets. The probabilities after successive trials are shown from left to right.

characteristics of these models. Progress on a formal account of intuitive causal theories is likely to be slow and painstaking for some time, and initially we may be able to give precise accounts only for rather small-scale domains such as the blicket detector paradigm. But, if indeed there is an analogy between our project and the career of linguistics, from the early days of generative grammar through the contemporary computational era, then we can look forward to a most interesting journey.

ACKNOWLEDGMENTS   We thank Elizabeth Baraff, Tania Lombrozo, Rebecca Saxe, and Marty Tenenbaum for helpful conversations about this work. Many of the ideas in this chapter emerged from discussions and collaborations with Sourabh Niyogi and Charles Kemp. TLG was supported by a Stanford Graduate Fellowship. JBT was supported by the Paul E. Newton Career Development Chair and a grant from NTT Communication Sciences Laboratory.

References

Carey, S. (1985). *Conceptual change in childhood.* Cambridge, MA: MIT Press.

Charniak, E. (1993). *Statistical language learning.* Cambridge, MA: MIT Press.

Cheng, P. (1997). From covariation to causation: A causal power theory. *Psychological Review, 104,* 367–405.

Enderton, H. B. (1972). *A mathematical introduction to logic.* New York: Academic Press.

Friedman, N., Getoor, L., Koller, D., & Pfeffer, A. (1999). Learning probabilistic relational models. In T. Dean (Ed.), *Proceedings of the 16th international joint conference on artificial intelligence (IJCAI)* (pp. 1300–1309). San Francisco, CA: Morgan Kaufmann.

Gelman, S. A. (2003). *The essential child: Origins of essentialism in everyday thought.* New York: Oxford University Press.

Glymour, C. (2001). *The mind's arrows: Bayes nets and graphical causal models in psychology.* Cambridge, MA: MIT Press.

Gopnik, A., Glymour, C., Sobel, D., Schulz, L., Kushnir, T., & Danks, D. (2004). A theory of causal learning in children: Causal maps and Bayes nets. *Psychological Review, 111,* 1–31.

Gopnik, A., & Sobel, D. (2000). Detecting blickets: How young children use information about novel causal powers in categorization and induction. *Child Development, 71,* 1205–1222.

Gopnik, A., Sobel, D. M., Shulz, L. E., & Glymour, C. (2001). Causal learning mechanisms in very young children: 2, 3, and 4-year-olds infer causal relations from patterns of variation and covariation. *Developmental Psychology, 37,* 620–629.

Griffiths, T. L. (2005). *Causes, coincidences, and theories.* Unpublished doctoral dissertation, Stanford University, Stanford, CA.

Griffiths, T. L., Baraff, E. R., & Tenenbaum, J. B. (2004). Using physical theories to infer hidden causal structure. In K. Forbus, D. Gentner, & T. Regier (Eds.), *Proceedings of the 26th annual meeting of the cognitive science society* (pp. 446–451). Mahwah, NJ: Erlbaum.

Griffiths, T. L., & Tenenbaum, J. B. (in preparation). *Theory-based causal induction.*

Griffiths, T. L., & Tenenbaum, J. B. (2005). Structure and strength in causal induction. *Cognitive Psychology, 51,* 354–384.

Jurafsky, D., & Martin, J. H. (2000). *Speech and language processing.* Upper Saddle River, NJ: Prentice Hall.

Kemp, C., Griffiths, T. L., & Tenenbaum, J. B. (2004). *Discovering latent classes in relational data* (Tech. Rep. No. AI Memo 2004–019). Cambridge, MA: Massachusetts Institute of Technology.

Manning, C., & Schütze, H. (1999). *Foundations of statistical natural language processing.* Cambridge, MA: MIT Press.

Milch, B., Marthi, B., & Russell, S. (2004). BLOG: Relational modeling with unknown objects. In T. Dietterich, L. Getoor, & K. Murphy (Eds.), *ICML 2004 workshop on statistical relational learning and its connections to other fields* (pp. 67–73). Banff, Canada.

Muggleton, S. H. (in press). Statistical aspects of logic-based machine learning. *ACM Transactions on Computational Logic.*

Pasula, H., & Russell, S. (2001). Approximate inference for first-order probabilistic languages. In B. Nebel (Ed.), *Proceedings of the 17th international joint conference in artificial intelligence (IJCAI)* (pp. 741–748). San Francisco, CA: Morgan Kaufmann.

Pearl, J. (1988). *Probabilistic reasoning in intelligent systems.* San Francisco: Morgan Kaufmann.

Pearl, J. (2000). *Causality: Models, reasoning and inference.* Cambridge, England: Cambridge University Press.

Schulz, L., & Gopnik, A. (2004). Causal learning across domains. *Developmental Psychology, 40,* 162–176.

Shanks, D. R. (1995). *The psychology of associative learning*. Cambridge, England: Cambridge University Press.

Shultz, T. R. (1982). Rules of causal attribution. *Monographs of the Society for Research in Child Development, 47* (Serial No. 194).

Sobel, D. M., Tenenbaum, J. B., & Gopnik, A. (2004). Children's causal inferences from indirect evidence: Backwards blocking and Bayesian reasoning in preschoolers. *Cognitive Science, 28,* 303–333.

Spirtes, P., Glymour, C., & Schienes, R. (1993). *Causation prediction and search*. New York: Springer-Verlag.

Tenenbaum, J. B., & Griffiths, T. L. (2003). Theory-based causal induction. In S. Becker, S. Thrun, & K. Obermayer (Eds.), *Advances in Neural Information Processing Systems 15* (pp. 35–42). Cambridge, MA: MIT Press.

Tenenbaum, J. B., & Niyogi, S. (2003). Learning causal laws. In R. Alterman & D. Kirsh (Eds.), *Proceedings of the 25th annual meeting of the cognitive science society*. Hillsdale, NJ: Erlbaum.

Tenenbaum, J. B., Sobel, D. M., Griffiths, T. L., Gopnik, A. (submitted). *Bayesian inference in causal learning from ambiguous data: Evidence from adults and children*.

Wellman, H. M., & Gelman, S. A. (1992). Cognitive development: Foundational theories of core domains. *Annual Review of Psychology, 43,* 337–375.

White, P. A. (1995). *The understanding of causation and the production of action: From infancy to adulthood*. Hillsdale, NJ: Erlbaum.

Notes

Chapter 1

1. See Hitchcock, 2001, and Woodward, 2003.
2. As Woodward, 2003, chapter 3, observes, the arrow-breaking aspect of interventions reproduces a number of other features of Lewis's theory, including what look like "miracles."
3. For details, see Woodward, 2003, chapter 5.
4. Although I lack the space for detailed discussion, it is worth observing that examples of this sort have implications for the claim, common among both philosophers and psychologists, that interventionist counterfactuals hold only "in virtue" of facts about the existence of connecting causal processes and mechanisms, with these capturing what is really fundamental to causation. On its most straightforward reading, this claim is simply false: From the fact that there is a connecting causal process, transmission of energy and the like from the motion of the cue stick to trajectory of the eight ball, we can deduce almost nothing about which interventionist counterfactuals associated with this process are true. Any explanation of why these interventionist counterfactuals hold will need to appeal to generalizations that are far more specific (e.g., the laws of conservation of energy and momentum), and it is plausible that these will also have a counterfactual element built into them.
5. It is thus a mistake to think of a plausible account of mechanisms and an interventionist account of causation (or Bayes net approaches) as in opposition to one another. See Glymour, 1998, for a similar view.
6. In the interests of moving the discussion along, I am riding roughshod over a number of complications and possibilities. Of course, it is possible to hold that there is no straightforward correspondence between what causation is and how we think about it; this was Hume's view on one natural interpretation. My view is that positions of this sort are not interesting when advanced as mere logical possibilities; instead, the way in which people think and learn about causation (and how these fail to correspond to what causation is) needs to be spelled out, and it needs to be shown how these explain known experimental results. Unlike Hume, contemporary philosophers rarely do this.
7. As Gopnik has noted, the obvious analogue here is with vision. People do not just have visual experiences and make visual judgments; in addition, these are often veridical. An adequate theory should explain how this happens.
8. In contrast, there is evidence (Schottmann & Shanks, 1992) that causal perception of collision phenomena is *not* sensitive to such contingency information, although judgment of causal efficacy is. In other words, process theories fit better with causal perception than causal judgment tasks. One may thus conjecture that causal perception phenomena explain some of the intuitions that underlie causal process theories.
9. To guard against possible misunderstanding, let me say explicitly that I do not regard it as a *necessary* condition for subjects to possess and to be guided by an interventionist conception of causation that they be able to reason explicitly with counterfactuals; subjects also can possess an implicit understanding of aspects of counterfactual reasoning, as revealed, for example, in nonverbalized planning. The argument is simply that explicit use of counterfactual reasoning and explicit recognition of its connection to causal claims is sufficient to establish that subjects are operating with a broadly counterfactual conception of causation.

A similar point holds for subjects' explicit recognition of the connection between causal claims and interventions.

10. Exactly why this is true is a matter of ongoing discussion; see Sommerville, chapter 3, this volume, and Lagnado and Sloman, 2004, for some alternative suggestions.

11. For some suggestions among broadly similar lines, see Glymour, in press.

12. See Wegner, 2002. Of course, as Wegner documents, there are illusions of agency, but their existence does not show (and Wegner does not claim) that the feeling of agency is generally an unreliable clue to voluntariness.

13. An example is as follows: Shortly after inserting the key to unlock my car door, a car alarm goes off in a neighboring car, leaving me with the very strong impression that my action has caused the alarm to go off.

14. Whether this is correct is of course an empirical matter. I do not claim that it is obvious, merely that it is a conjecture worth exploring.

15. Thanks to Daniel Povinelli for a helpful conversation that corrected a serious misunderstanding of his views in a previous draft.

16. Indeed, it might be argued, uncharitably, that the apes behave pretty much as though they *are* guided by this heuristic, and that this simply shows what a gap there is between use of the heuristic and full-fledged causal understanding. In this connection, it is also worth noting that if the human possession of the concept of *force* is closely linked to the abilities displayed in launching experiments, as both Povinelli and Tomasello and Call suggest, and if apes fail to possess such a concept, it would seem to follow that they will behave quite differently from human children in, for example, looking time experiments involving launching phenomena. My prediction is that there will be no dramatic difference, again illustrating that, when linked to launching phenomena in the way described, possession of the concept of force is not sufficient for the kind of causal understanding displayed by humans.

17. As the passage quoted above makes clear, the experiments it describes have not actually been performed. It would be worthwhile to do them.

18. David Danks, personal communication; Alison Gopnik, personal communication. Needless to say, it would be worthwhile to explore this issue in the context of primate causal understanding by means of more systematic experiments.

19. Note also that there is nothing unobservable about this intermediate variable; that is, if the apes fail at the task under discussion, then it is not because they fail to postulate unobservable intermediate variables

but rather because they fail to recognize the relevance of an observable intermediate variable.

20. The systematic interrelationships between causal understanding and the ability to discern one's intentions and goals as well as those of others are also one of the main themes of Sommerville's chapter 3 in this volume.

21. See Gopnik and Schulz, 2004, for a similar line of thought.

Chapter 5

1. Throughout, we assume some familiarity with the causal Bayes nets formalism (that is, we assume that readers have already read the introduction to this book). Thus, we use terms like causal graphs, the causal Markov assumption, and conditional independence and dependence without definition.

2. We kept the example deliberately simple. Of course, if the state of the grass were measured as a continuous variable (how wet is it?) rather than as a binary one (is it wet or dry?), then you might observe that the front yard was *wetter* when it had rained than when it had not. In that case, the intervention to set the sprinkler would not break the arrow between the weather and the grass and knowing something about the front yard would still tell you something about the back. The arrow would be similarly preserved if you invested in an expensive sprinkler that only turned on when it had not rained, which might be a better choice for your lawn but (because the state of the sprinkler is no longer exogenous to the graph) a bad example of an intervention.

Chapter 6

1. The implications of interventions cannot always be derived from observations (see Pearl, 2000, chapter 3, for a specification of the conditions).

Chapter 7

1. For further discussion of some of the details of Reichenbach's theory, see the asymmetry and prediction section of Michael Strevens's chapter 15, this volume.

2. For a somewhat different take on this problem, see Strevens's chapter 15, this volume.

3. Woodward makes the same point at the end of the interventionism section of his chapter 1, this volume.

4. See, for example, Mellor (1995, chapter 12). Lewis (2000) offers an account of "Causation as Influence," in effect denying the distinction. Collins (2000) argues, against Lewis, for maintaining this distinction.

5. The chemical agents are not quite the same because those found in birth control pills are synthetic hormones that differ slightly from the hormones naturally produced by the body. Moreover, the level of hormones introduced into the body through oral contraceptives is substantially less than the level created by pregnancy. The first difference is not really essential to the structure of the example, but the second is because it is this difference in hormone levels that is responsible for the difference in causal strength between pregnancy and birth control pill use.

6. In general, however, it is not invariant under the addition or subtraction of variables elsewhere in the model; see Hitchcock (2001b) for details.

7. The original version of Newcomb's problem is presented in Nozick (1969), but this version of the problem contains a distraction that hides the underlying moral.

8. Another interpretation is that moving the joystick is a common cause of camouflage of the appearance of the plane. On this interpretation, the camouflage is not causally related to safe passage of the minefield at all. But, if just some subjects interpreted the results in the way described in the text and just some of those interpreted "efficacy" in terms of net effect or component effect, then we might expect the average efficacy to be distinguishable from zero or at least to be slightly positive if not statistically significant. In fact, the average efficacy rating was slightly negative.

Chapter 8

1. See Glymour and Cooper (1999); Pearl (2000); and Spirtes, Glymour, and Scheines (2000).

2. See, for example, recent proceedings of Uncertainty and Artificial Intelligence conferences, available at http://www.sis.pitt.edu/~dsl/UAI/.

3. See, for example, www.phil.cmu.edu/projects/csr.

4. The computing tool R^4 is available at www.r-project.org/.

5. The computing tool TETRAD is available at www.phil.cmu.edu/projects/tetrad.

6. See Eberhardt, Glymour, and Scheines (2005); Murphy (2001); and Tong and Koller (2001).

7. See, for example, Glymour and Cooper (1999); Pearl (2000); and Spirtes, Glymour, and Scheines (2000).

8. Ideal interventions are only one type of manipulation of a causal system. We can straightforwardly use the CBN framework to model interventions that affect multiple variables (so-called fat-hand interventions), as well as those that influence, but do not determine, the values of the target variables (i.e., that do not "break" all of the incoming edges). Of course, causal learning is significantly harder in those situations.

9. Strictly, this is the CBN with parameters set to the maximum likelihood estimates.

10. This team included Richard Scheines, Joel Smith, Clark Glymour, David Danks, Mara Harrell, Sandra Mitchell, Willie Wheeler, Joe Ramsey, and more recently, Matt Easterday.

11. The Causality Lab is available free at www.phil.cmu.edu/projects/causality-lab.

12. This is if the instructor writing the exercise allows the student to "see" the population.

13. This is assuming, of course, that the statistical inferences are correct.

14. The d-separation enables us to compute the independence relations entailed by a causal graph.

15. For a detailed but accessible primer, read the chapter on score-based versus constraint-based methods in Glymour and Cooper (1999).

Chapter 10

1. See Tenenbaum and Griffiths (this volume) for a general computational-level approach that aims to incorporate such prior knowledge.

Chapter 11

1. Many-valued features can be modeled as multiple binary features as in the SUSTAIN (Supervised and Unsupervised STratified Adaptive Incremental Network) model (e.g., Love, Medin, & Gureckis, 2004), although at some computational cost. Note that a feature is binary or continuous based on values that it might plausibly take and not the actually observed values. For example, height is continuously valued even though, in real life, we only see finitely many values for height in a population.

2. We thus collapse together, for example, Erickson & Kruschke's (1998) ATRIUM (Attention To Rules and Instances on a Unified Model), Kruschke's (1992) ALCOVE (Attention Learing COVEring map) model, Lamberts's (1998, 2000) EGCM (Extended Generalized Context Model), and Nosofsky and Palmeri's (1997) EBRW (Exemplar-Based Random Walk), which are all equivalent to Nosofsky's (1986) generalized context model for static problems. An interesting open question is whether the equivalencies described here can be used to understand the theoretic relationships among the response time models.

3. The GCM is equivalently (and more typically) expressed as the exponential of a sum of distances

rather than as the product of exponentials used here. The GCM also allows for other distance measures (e.g., Euclidean); the equivalencies described in the next section continue to hold for other distance measures (although with different auxiliary conditions).

4. Early prototype models assumed that the similarity ratings were the *sum* of the distance on each dimension rather than the product. Subsequent work has shown these additive models to be worse than multiplicative ones (see, e.g., Minda & Smith, 2001).

5. More precisely, there must be a Bayes net in which the graph is a perfect map for (i.e., is Markov and faithful to) the probability distribution.

6. It does not actually matter whether the graphical structure is treated as a Bayes net or a Markov random field (where every directed edge is converted to an undirected edge). The set of probability distributions is the same.

7. There is an apparent tension here between the condition of a regularity constraint on the $P(F_i \mid E)$ terms (suggesting that the GCM cannot model all probability distributions) and Ashby and Alfonso-Reese's (1995) proof that the GCM can, in the limit of infinitely many exemplars, model any probability distribution. Given that the notion of infinitely many exemplars is psychologically unrealistic, the equivalencies described here require the category to have only as many exemplars as E (the unobserved variable) has values. That restriction results in the need for the regularity constraint.

8. Using the Lauritzen-Wermuth-Frydenberg chain graph Markov property, this graph implies $F_1 \perp F_4$; $F_1 \perp F_3 \mid \{F_2, F_4\}$; and $F_2 \perp F_4 \mid \{F_1, F_3\}$.

9. Proof: Using the equivalencies in the Luce choice rule yields $P(\text{respond "}A\text{"} \mid X) = P(X \mid A)/\Sigma P(X \mid M)$. Multiply the top and bottom by $P(A)$ and use $P(A) = P(M)$ for all M to reduce to $P(X \mid A) \times P(A)/P(X)$, which is just $P(A \mid X)$.

10. This type of theory is frequently called Bayesian, particularly by computer scientists and statisticians. I avoid using that term here because for many philosophers and psychologists Bayesian includes a much larger set of commitments than this theory requires.

11. The following discussion is qualitative, but the proposed framework has a precise mathematical description.

Chapter 12

1. Strevens (chapter 15, this volume) enumerates a number of reasons why, in a particular case, the causal laws associated with a category may fail to generate a typical property: the conditions required for the causal

mechanisms to operate may be absent and something may interfere with those mechanisms. The current appeal to probabilistic causal mechanisms can subsume both of these cases. Strevens also notes that some outside force may operate to remove a property after it is generated.

2. The hedge "all else being equal," which appears twice in this paragraph, refers to the fact that strength of the evidence that S_i provides for the disease D will of course also depend on the evidence that it provides for some other disease (and the prior probability of D and those other diseases). This issue is discussed further in Experiment 2. The purpose of the discussion to this point is simply to establish how the likelihood of D given a symptom $P(D \mid S_i)$ is going to vary as a function of the probability that D generates that symptom $P(S_i \mid D)$.

3. Of course, many real-world cases of classification are likely to involve both diagnostic and prospective reasoning. From symptoms (e.g., those of lymphoma), one might hypothesize the presence of a particular disease (HIV). One might then look for the presence of potential causes of that disease (e.g., a blood transfusion) to corroborate the hypothesis.

4. For example, in terms of causal model theory, each feature i in Figure 12-11A would have a b_i parameter representing the probability that it occurs in category members. The probability that a given object was generated by that category, $P(O|C)$, would then be

$$p(O|C) = [\Pi_{i \in P} b_i][\Pi_{i \in A}(1 - b_i)]$$

where P is the set of C's features present in O, and A is the set of C's feature absent in O. Alternatively, category membership could be based on O's similarity to the category's prototype. Note that these two alternatives would be equivalent if a multiplicative similarity rules was used (Hampton, 1998; Nosofsky, 1992; J. D. Smith & Minda, 2000) because they would both involve multiplying rather than summing evidence. Of course, in Figure 12-11 we are again considering only the evidence of an object O's category membership with respect to a single category. The extent to which a feature provides evidence for category membership will also depend on the likelihood that that feature is associated with *other* categories. See Experiment 2 for discussion.

5. Strevens (2000, chapter 15, this volume) also considers categorization a kind of causal inference but argues that the causal laws relate observable properties and the kind itself, rather than a defining or essential feature. However, this approach provides no principled explanation for why children younger than 2 or 3 years old

are "phenomenalists" on transformation tasks like those of Rips, concluding that an animal is what it looks like (Keil, 1989). The current proposal explains the developmental shift in terms a specific developmental sequence in which unobserved causes are first postulated and then become defining (or near-defining) of category membership.

Chapter 15

1. Reichenbach connected the asymmetry of his statistical patterns to the statistical mechanical roots of the second law of thermodynamics and ultimately to the direction of time, but this aspect of his work is passed over here.

2. I might add, though, that the ideas about causality presented in *The Direction of Time* (1956), a work left unfinished at the time of Reichenbach's death, are not easily understood as a unified whole. Like another well-known philosopher of causality, he could be accused of having given several incompatible definitions of cause. I suppose that Reichenbach would have replied, in the logical empiricist spirit, that each of his definitions has its advantages and disadvantages, and that it would be a philosophical error to insist that any one definition must be uniquely correct.

3. It might be better to say before or at the same time as the focal event, but it is simpler to leave things as they are in the main text.

4. The probabilistic facts about event types, note, will themselves often refer to the temporal order of the probabilified events. For example, the probability of hearing a loud bang after the trigger is pulled is much higher than the probability of hearing a bang before the trigger is pulled, and so on.

5. Without the additional claim, nothing has been said because there is a trivial dyad for any focal event in which the set of parent events contains every other event.

6. What follows posits a relationship that is closer than anything Reichenbach would have endorsed; as I remarked, I am simplifying his view considerably. Specifically, what I identify as a necessary and sufficient condition for one event to be the cause of another is for Reichenbach only a necessary condition. See *The Direction of Time* (1956), section 22 for the details.

7. An exception to this rule, the kind of case in which you have some direct knowledge of events caused by the focal event—a case of retrodiction, presumably—can contribute to the internal explanation on the introduction of statistical relations more complex than those represented by Reichenbach dyads. These

relations are also very efficiently represented by a DAG.

8. By *species*, here I mean what might be better called a folk genus or a generic-specieme (Medin & Atran, 1999).

9. Psychological essentialists maintain in addition that the causation is represented as going by way of an essence, but the truth or otherwise of this posit will make no difference to what I have to say here.

10. Only the 3-year-olds failed to show a definite preference for the generative transmission rule and then only in some scenarios.

11. A philosopher would say that everything that is known about the basic levels is known a posteriori rather than a priori, but in a psychological context, the use of the term *a priori* tends to run together the question of innateness and the question of immunity to empirical refutation. My claim is that all beliefs about the basic levels are considered subject to revision in the light of the empirical evidence.

12. How might the information contained in the constraint from below be reduced to statistical language? Relative to a set of basic levels and some information about their workings, the answer might go, roughly, as follows: The constraint contains information about where certain kinds of correlations—the correlations that make up information about mechanism—are found. The constraint identifies clues, then, and says: Look for your correlations where you find these clues. You might say that it asserts a kind of meta-correlation, a correlation between the clues and other correlations.

Chapter 17

1. When the cause is absent (the bottom row in Figure 17-1), the strength of the relationship is predicted not to change (cf. van Hamme & Wasserman, 1994).

2. In an earlier version of this task (Marsh & Ahn, 2003), participants were likewise not given information ahead of time about which estimates would be requested. However, all four questions were presented simultaneously on the same screen. Participants incorporated ambiguous information into their estimates with this design as well.

Chapter 18

1. The observation that the additive ΔP model is not invariant under addition of independent causes, while Cheng's model is, I owe entirely to conversation with Patricia Cheng.

Chapter 19

1. For example, suppose that a correlation is observed between A and B, and it is known that no direct causal connection exists between A and B. If a third variable V is known to be a cause of A, then this knowledge suggests two simple hypotheses for interpreting the correlation between A and B: V may be a cause of B or B may be a cause of V.
2. Readers familiar with linguistics literature will recognize the questions in Table 19-1 as based on an analogy to Chomsky's standard questions about knowledge of language (e.g., Chomsky, 1986). It is no accident where we started given where we figured to end up.

Chapter 20

1. This graph schema may look implausible as a template for generating causal graphical models because it generates graphs with directed cycles. However, the problem is easily remedied by imposing a simple discrete dynamics on the variables. Each variable in each node class is indexed by time step, and causal connections between nodes x and y in fact connect $x^{(t)}$, the state of variable x

at time t, to $y^{(t+1)}$, the state of variable y at time $t + 1$. By default, each state variable should also depend on its value at the previous time step.
2. Like G_{Mag}, this graph schema oversimplifies by leaving out the dynamic nature of these state variables. But, those dynamics can be included here just as we outlined for G_{Mag} in Note 1 by indexing each variable by a time step and unfolding all causal connections between each time step and the next.
3. Graph 6 provides such a poor fit to the observed data that its likelihood would not show up on Figure 20-7.
4. The abstract entities referred to in a logical theory need not correspond to any kind of physical object. Logical approaches to number theory consider entities that correspond to numbers, and we consider entities that correspond to intervals of time.
5. The particular versions of those components shown in Figure 20-10 represent just one of many possible choices that could work here. We assume this particular theory because it is simple and fairly intuitive, not because we think it corresponds precisely to people's theories in these experiments. However, we argue that something like the key principles expressed in this theory are critical to explain people's inferences in blicket detector tasks.

Index